Franchising

An Entrepreneur's Guide

Fourth Edition

Richard J. Judd | Robert T. Justis

Australia • Brazil • Japan • Korea • Mexico • Singapore • Spain • United Kingdom • United States

Franchising: An Entrepreneur's Guide
Fourth Edition

Richard J. Judd | Robert T. Justis

Executive Editors:
Michele Baird

Maureen Staudt

Michael Stranz

Project Development Manager:
Linda deStefano

Senior Marketing Coordinators:
Sara Mercurio

Lindsay Shapiro

Senior Production / Manufacturing Manager:
Donna M. Brown

PreMedia Services Supervisor:
Rebecca A. Walker

Rights & Permissions Specialist:
Kalina Hintz

Cover Image:
Getty Images*

* Unless otherwise noted, all cover images used by Custom Solutions, a part of Cengage Learning, have been supplied courtesy of Getty Images with the exception of the Earthview cover image, which has been supplied by the National Aeronautics and Space Administration (NASA).

For product information and technology assistance, contact us at
Cengage Learning Customer & Sales Support, 1-800-354-9706

For permission to use material from this text or product, submit all requests online at **cengage.com/permissions**
Further permissions questions can be emailed to
permissionrequest@cengage.com

ISBN-13: 978-0-759-36705-0

ISBN-10: 0-759-36705-1

Cengage Learning
5191 Natorp Boulevard
Mason, Ohio 45040
USA

Cengage Learning is a leading provider of customized learning solutions with office locations around the globe, including Singapore, the United Kingdom, Australia, Mexico, Brazil, and Japan. Locate your local office at:
international.cengage.com/region

Cengage Learning products are represented in Canada by Nelson Education, Ltd.

For your lifelong learning solutions, visit **custom.cengage.com**

Visit our corporate website at **cengage.com**

Printed in the United States of America

The authors dedicate this work to their families:

Sue, Jill, and Jeri Justis; and Andrea, Laura, Francine, Richard, and Rachel Judd.

CONTENTS IN BRIEF

CONTENTS

Chapter 10   **Accounting and Financial Statements: Presentation and Uses 265**

PREFACE

Buying a piece of a tested idea is the central attraction of franchising. This unique approach to business has spread throughout the world, and its success far overshadows its youth as a method of doing business. Franchising is the fastest growing method of doing business in the world today.

This book is written for students of franchising as well as franchisors, franchisees, or prospective franchisees. A three-part perspective is developed throughout the book concerning the franchisor–franchisee relationship: First, a franchisor and franchisee are independent businesspeople who must manage their separate business affairs; second, the franchisor and franchisee are dependent upon each other in order to be successful in business; and third, the franchisor–franchisee relationship brings with it an interdependent contractual obligation that is legally binding upon both parties.

Many readers have a particularly keen interest in learning about franchising because they see themselves as prospective franchisees. Research, interviews, and observations consistently show that such persons should (1) learn about the nature of franchising, and (2) understand the role of franchisor before, (3) determining if they have what it takes to be successful franchisees. This book is intended to help people develop a clear picture of franchising and franchisors and to provide some insights that will assist them in making their own personal decisions about entering the field. The information in the text is presented in a format designed to answer major franchising questions.

The seven stages of a franchised business life cycle formulate the seven major sections of the text.

1. *Nature of Franchising*. Prior to starting a franchised business as either a franchisor or a franchisee, it is important to understand the nature of the franchising method of business. A franchised business has unique features not typically found in a business run by an independent owner-operator. Also, there are definitely pros and cons of becoming involved in franchising. Chapters 1 and 2 address these considerations.

2. *Getting into Franchising*. One of the most exciting decisions anyone will ever make is to get into franchising either as a franchisee or franchisor. Regardless of the approach, it is essential that the individual understand and work through the necessary steps to successfully enter franchising. The successful franchisee or franchisor needs to develop the appropriate business plan and understand the suitable marketing, management, sales, and operations necessary to achieve to desired success. Chapters 3 through 8 are devoted to developing this knowledge.

3. *Franchisor Operations*. This section is designed to explain the location, site selection, accounting, financial management, and information systems important to franchising. Chapters 9

through 12 explain the basic operations of franchising systems. These areas are crucial to correctly developing and expanding the franchise system.

4. *Franchising and the Law*. What is a franchise disclosure document (UFOC)? What are the documents that define a franchise? Why are trademarks often considered the heart of the franchise? Why would the franchisee be entrusted with trade secrets? What legal activities help or hinder franchising? What is intellectual property and why is it so important in franchising? The law as it relates to franchising is broad and diverse, covering topics such as contractual requirements, torts, franchisor–franchisee rights, trademarks, registration requirements, antitrust, territorial rights, price fixing, and tying agreements. These areas are covered in Chapters 13 and 14.

5. *The Franchisee*. This section, comprising Chapters 15 through 18, focuses on franchisees and what qualifications a franchisor seeks in a prospective franchisee. Franchise opportunities, royalties, advertising, training, marketing, management, and other factors of interest to the franchisee are described and methods of financing are discussed. Management and marketing skills a franchisee may be expected to have or be willing to develop are also discussed. The section also delves into franchisees' legal rights and what a franchisee can expect to encounter in the normal course of operating the business.

6. *The Franchisor–Franchisee Relationship*. One of the most important aspects of continuing a successful franchising program is to develop a strong franchisor–franchisee relationship. Chapters 19 and 20 explore the multifaceted relationships between franchisees and franchisors, examining these relationships from a business perspective as well as from a legal perspective. Different ways of developing and handling franchise relationship programs are discussed. Fairness, communication, and growth are key watchwords when working with the franchisor–franchisee relationship.

7. *Current Issues in Franchising*. There are many areas of vital importance to franchising. The international market has grown to become the major source of profits for many U.S. franchise systems. State rules and regulations are continuing to be important in franchise growth and development. Franchising continues to grow throughout the world, as discussed in Chapters 21 and 22.

Throughout the book, success stories are included to add practical knowledge and provide special insight into franchising. Biographical sketches show what individual and franchise organizations are doing in relation to the topic of the chapter and how their activities further the development of this burgeoning field. Case studies are provided at the close of chapters to help the reader analyze franchise situations and develop sound judgment in handling issues and problems that can arise in a franchised business. The appendices present additional information about franchising and the Internet, public traded franchises, and franchise trade organizations.

This book has been a work of love, sweat, and tears. The major push for writing this text has come from franchisors and franchisees interested in seeing the field of franchising explored in depth. Special thanks are extended to writers assisting in the writing, development, and presentation of chapters in this book, including Andy Caffey, YeSho Chen, Joyce Young, and Audhesh K. Paswan. Additional thanks go to Tony Martinez and Brian Osborne who helped edit, rewrite, and diagram a large portion of this book. Special appreciation is given to Erin Hebert, Miles Farr, Brenda Gatlin, and Susan Sartwell for typing and coordinating different parts of the book. In addition, Richard Judd acknowledges Dean Ron McNeil, Dyanne Ferk, Mark Puclik, and Ardeshir Lohrasbi at the University of Illinois-Springfield and Dr. Joe Bohlen.

ACKNOWLEDGMENTS

This book has been a work of love, sweat, and tears. The major push for writing this text has come from franchisors and franchisees interested in seeing the field of franchising explored in depth. Special thanks are extended to writers assisting in the writing, development, and presentation of chapters in this book, including Andy Caffey, YeSho Chen, Joyce Young, and Audhesh K. Paswan. Additional thanks go to Tony Martinez and Brian Osborne who helped edit, rewrite, and diagram a large portion of this book. Special appreciation is given to Erin Hebert, Miles Farr, Brenda Gatlin, and Susan Sartwell for typing and coordinating different parts of the book. In addition, Richard Judd acknowledges Dean Ron McNeil, Dyanne Ferk, Mark Puclik, and Ardeshir Lohrasbi at the University of Illinois-Springfield and Dr. Joe Bohlen. In addition, Rich gratefully acknowledges the guidance, skill and support provided by Greg Albert, Acquisitions Editor.

FRANCHISING: HISTORY AND OVERVIEW

In studying this chapter, you will:

- Learn about the historical development of franchising.
- Learn an operational definition of franchising.
- Become able to distinguish between various types of franchises.
- Learn what are the "top ten" franchises by various categories.
- Develop an understanding of how the franchising concept has been applied in various retail businesses.

INCIDENT

During her college years Francine worked both part time and full time at several restaurants. She learned enough from her first waitressing experience to be selective. She learned the importance of good management, clean surroundings, efficient operations, and a general working environment that encourages good customer service as well as opportunity for employee growth and advancement. Her most enjoyable and profitable work arrangement has been at a successful franchised restaurant where she had been promoted to shift manager.

As a college graduate with a major in the arts, Francine sees that her culinary interest and study of the arts blend nicely into restauranting by providing careful menu planning, appropriate decor, table ambience, and quality of service. She learns fast. Francine wants to begin a career as an independent franchisee, perhaps with the same franchise system where she has been most recently employed. From experience she realizes it is the success of this franchise system that is the foremost reason for her career decision.

Francine sees franchising as the leading edge of U.S. business and wants to be part of it with a first-rate company. Francine believes she would be a successful restaurateur and franchisee. She wants to be independent but realizes she needs further development in business practices and help in all aspects of this highly competitive food service industry. She has some knowledge about how a franchisee should operate but believes she needs additional knowledge, training, and experience. Although Francine does not know what is expected of a franchisee by the franchisor, she believes she will succeed through her strong desire to learn and her commitment to hard work.

Francine dreams of taking an extended vacation, perhaps to Europe, Asia, or South America. She knows that dream is several years away. First she wants to learn how she can become successful as a restaurant franchisee.

1-1   INTRODUCTION

Franchising has a track record as a way to speed growth through expansion of business. Recent estimates anticipate franchise unit growth to become turbocharged, in the 12 to 14 percent range in the new millennium.

Since the 1950s, franchising has been the leading edge of business by showing impressive growth rates in overall sales and market share. At points of economic downturn, franchising has shown its resilience by *squeezing margins*—decreasing operating costs while increasing unit sales, and then taking a leading position in economic recovery. The general economy has been strong. Economic forecasters, government officials, and business leaders note that the increase in persons waiting to become franchisees will expand the franchise industry itself. Franchising should be on the forefront of even further improvements in the economy, enhancing the overall strength and vitality of U.S. business at home and abroad.

William Cherkasky, president of the Educational Foundation of the International Franchise Association, considers franchising as the key to business success. Over 800,000 franchised business establishments in the United States, and about 150,000 more scattered around the world, carry the logo of a U.S. franchise system. According to Cherkasky:

> The key is that the franchisee typically has invested body, soul, available hours and the family savings, and borrowing power in that business. That franchisee has bet the ranch on the franchisor delivering his end of the deal in a concept that works, the management services that open and keep the business going (including advertising, public relations, personnel and purchasing decisions), and his own ability to work hard and intelligently to make the business successful.[1]

Those 800,000 business establishments in the United States represent over $1 trillion in annual sales, which is over 40 percent of all retail sales and 17 percent of gross domestic product (GDP). Sound big? You bet. Franchising is the biggest chunk of economic activity that uses a particular business system.

Franchising is often considered a single industry, but actually it is not. Do not think that McDonald's, Burger King, Dunkin' Donuts, and Wendy's is all there is to franchising. Franchising is found in sixty-five different kinds of industries, from fast food, to health care, hotels, automobiles, home cleaning, education, leisure time services, home improvement, travel, pet care, funeral services, printing, accounting, e-business, and so forth. Nearly any kind of legitimate business that you can imagine—*if it is successful*—is involved in franchising.

Franchising has been such a success for some firms that they have become giants within their respective industries; companies such as Ford, General Motors, Anheuser-Busch, Coca-Cola, Holiday Inns, Pepsi Cola, and Hertz have become distinct leaders, comparable in scope of operation and sales volume to some traditional giants of U.S. business and industry such as Union Carbide, IBM, General Foods, Alcoa Aluminum, and U.S. Steel.

A franchisor uses the franchise's community goodwill, financial equity, business location, and personal drive and motivation to expand the franchise system. The franchisee uses the franchisor's brand or trademark, proven methods of operation, marketing resources, and technical advice to enter, develop, and maintain consumer demand, and ultimately to succeed as a small business owner-operator within the community. The franchisee is often given an opportunity to be part of a turnkey operation (which involves the site, building, architecture, equipment, work flow, and customer service plans completely determined and installed by the franchisor), with limited capital and prior experience, while having a good chance of success.

1-1a   Franchising Defined

Franchising may be defined as a business opportunity by which the owner (producer or distributor) of a service or a trademarked product grants exclusive rights to an individual for the local distribution and/or sale of the service or product, and in return receives a payment or royalty and conformance to quality standards. The individual or business granting the business rights is called the **franchisor**, and the individual or business granted the right to operate in accordance with the chosen method to produce or sell the product or service is called the **franchisee**.

The U.S. Department of Commerce provides a broader definition: "Franchising is a method of doing business by which a franchisee is granted the right to engage in offering, selling, or distributing goods or services under a marketing format which is designed by the franchisor. The franchisor permits the franchisee to use the franchisor's trademark, name, and advertising."[2]

Franchising, then, can be approached from the perspective of both the franchisor and the franchisee. For a franchisor, franchising allows the expansion of a proven concept and method of operation from a single unit to a large operation with multiple locations and multiple product or service offerings. The franchisee has the opportunity to utilize proven methods of operation, large-scale, high-impact advertising, recognized brands or trademarks, and continuing management and technical assistance. These advantages are not typically given to the independent small business owner who may be selling a similar product or service.

From either of these two perspectives, franchising can be quite appealing. For a franchisor, the franchise approach to business allows growth through an expanding distribution system. Similarly, franchising can be attractive to an individual desiring to be an independent business owner. The franchising concept provides an opportunity for the franchisee to succeed as a small business owner because of the knowledge, methods, competitive experience, and advertising clout of the franchisor. The franchising method helps franchisor *and* franchisee by providing an agreement that allows both to bring their particular strengths to the business arrangement.

This business arrangement, otherwise called a franchise opportunity, has three major components: (1) a trademark or logo, (2) the use of a product or service following a marketing plan, and (3) a payment or royalty fee. These components constitute the essence of what is generally referred to as a franchise, whether the arrangement happens to be in auto and truck sales, convenience food stores, restaurants, cleaning services, or gasoline retailing.

Ways of describing franchising are summarized in Table 1-1. Each description can serve as an operating definition to allow the reader at least an understanding about the nature of franchising. The authors prefer the first definition: a business opportunity in which the owner (producer or distributor) of a service or trademarked product grants rights to an individual for local distribution and/or sale of the service or products, and in return receives a payment or royalty and conformance to quality standards. This definition encompasses more than the others and also specifies the activities of the primary parties—franchisor and franchisee. It is this definition which we will use throughout the text.

1-1b   Types of Franchising

In the United States, **product and trade name franchising** has evolved from the time when suppliers made sales contracts with dealers to buy or sell certain products or product lines. In this relationship, the dealer acquires the trade name, trademark, and/or product from the supplier. The dealer (franchisee) identifies with the supplier (franchisor) through the product line. Historically, this approach to franchising has consisted of distribution from a single supplier (or manufacturer) to a large number of dealers either directly or through regional supply centers (see Figure 1-1). An objective of the supplier is to have a dealer (or dealership) in each community or area, to provide the product to all potential customers within a geographic area, region, or the whole country. This

TABLE 1-1	WAYS OF DESCRIBING FRANCHISING
Business Opportunity	An owner (producer or distributor) of a service or trademarked product grants rights to an individual for local distribution and/or sale of goods or services, and, in return, receives a payment or royalty and conformance to quality standards.
Pattern or Method of Doing Business	A franchisee is granted a right to offer, sell, or distribute goods or services under a marketing format as designated by the franchisor.
Franchise Opportunity	Three components—a trademark and/or logo, the use of a product or service following a marketing plan, and the payment of a royalty fee—constitute the essence of a franchised business.
Licensing Relationship	A franchisor of a product, service, or business method grants distribution rights to affiliated dealers (the franchisees); these rights often include exclusive access to a defined geographic area.
Continuing Relationship	A franchisor provides a licensed privilege to do business and provides management and technical assistance and training in return for a consideration from the franchisee.

franchising approach has been used in the auto and truck, soft drink, tire, and gasoline service industries.

It is estimated that product and trade name franchising accounted for approximately $420 billion in sales in 2000, or about 50 percent of all domestic franchise sales. Of that total, soft drink bottlers had sales of approximately $41.5 billion, gasoline service stations $184.4 billion, and auto and truck dealers $192.8 billion.[3]

Because of demographic shifts, competition, and slowing of the U.S. population growth, soft drink bottlers believe consumption is likely to rise 2 to 2.7 percent, which is a slower rise in consumption compared to the 1980s. Changing lifestyles and demographic shifts toward older consumers has reduced the industry's growth potential from the 1990s into the beginning of the twenty-first century. As a result, this condition has beverage bottlers moving to introduce more beverages such as teas, waters, and juice drinks into the market in complementary niches to their wine, beer, or soda brands. This trend will likely continue for at least the next five-to-ten years.

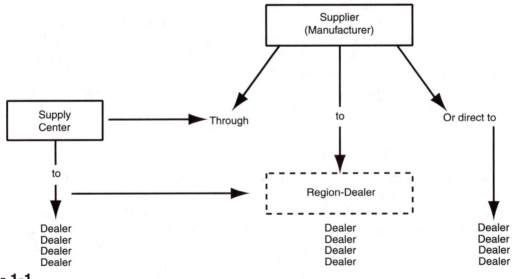

FIGURE **1-1**

Typical Product and Trade Name Franchising

By 1990, there were 24,000 dealerships, owned by 14,850 dealer principles and representing about 50,000 franchises. The average number of vehicles sold per franchise has increased substantially. In 1986, about 20 percent of the dealers accounted for 80 percent of automobile retail sales. Economy of scale, coupled with attrition in rural dealerships and population clusters, have influenced the shift in dealership concentration to the metropolitan areas.[4] In the mid-1990s, nearly 90 percent of auto and truck dealers had more than one franchise. This multifranchise trend has been influenced by dealers' attempts to achieve a balance in their business risk by representing numerous franchised brands, which allows a dealer to service various market segments simultaneously and enables the franchisee to become less dependent on one franchisor for their livelihood.

Business-format franchising concerns the primary elements of the **business-opportunity approach** to franchising, described in Table 1-1. This franchising involves the **format** or approach to be used by a franchisee in providing the franchisor's product or service line to the customer. Business-format franchising has been responsible for the tremendous growth in franchising since the 1950s. This approach to franchising has fostered rapid expansion in the restaurant, food service, hotel-motel, printing, retailing, and real estate sectors of the U.S. economy.

Most new franchising agreements that are reached today are of the business-format type. Business-format franchising has enjoyed long-term growth over the past thirty-five years. In 1972, there were 189,640 franchised establishments with gross sales of $28.7 billion. Fifteen years later, in 1987, the number of franchised establishments had increased by almost 163,000 units (86 percent), while sales increased to $170.8 billion (nearly a 600 percent increase). In 1997, the 380,000 franchised units in the United States accounted for $410 billion in gross sales. There were more than 100,000 franchised units of U.S. franchise systems operating in other parts of the world.[5]

The origins of franchising can be traced back through mercantile codes and common law to the Middle Ages. At that time, it was accepted practice for local governments to offer important persons, who might also be high church officials, a license granting them the right to maintain civil order, determine and collect tax revenues, and make other special tax assessments. The licensee (or franchisee) paid the licensor (franchisor) a specified sum from the tax revenues collected or assessments made in order to receive military or other forms of protection. In this way, a monarchy could control the lands within its sphere of influence by providing protection while extracting tax revenues.

During the early nineteenth century in England, tavern and pub owners were experiencing financial hardship, and many did not have enough money to maintain their establishments as required under English law. As a result, many pub and tavern owners turned to the brewing companies for financial assistance. In return for financial assistance, the tavern and pub owners were required to buy all their beer from a particular brewer. However, the owners were not regulated or restricted in any other way by the brewers. They were free to conduct their business as they saw fit. This arrangement assured brewers outlets for distributing their product. Over time, many pubs were bought by brewers who then rented the establishments to tenants who managed the business.

1-1c Early Franchising in the United States

Probably the earliest example of franchising in the United States is the McCormick Harvesting Machine Company, which in 1850 commissioned "exclusive local agents"[6] to sell and service its machinery. A typical agent for McCormick was an independent businessperson who usually had other interests besides selling McCormick Harvesters. McCormick later instituted company-owned stores to distribute and sell its products. The first example of a consumer goods firm to use a franchise-oriented system of distribution was the Singer Sewing Machine Company. During the 1850s, Singer experienced difficulty in marketing its new product. Because the sewing machine was an innovative product, Singer first needed to educate the potential consumer about the benefits of using a "machine" for sewing. Since the sewing machine industry was in its infant stage of development, Singer did not have the capital to hire a large sales staff or open numerous company branch offices. Agents working on commission were a natural choice to demonstrate, sell, and repair the Singer line of sewing machines. Once the sewing machine caught on with the general public, however, Singer changed its marketing approach to sell and service its machines exclusively through company-owned offices during the 1860s.

The industrial revolution of the late 1800s was a significant event precipitating changes in distribution methods. Certain industries began to concentrate in specific geographic areas—automobile manufacturers in Michigan, tire makers in Ohio, and oil refineries in Pennsylvania, New York, and New Jersey, for example. The automobile industry provides the earliest lasting example of franchising in our economy. Around the turn of the century, an auto manufacturer was typically an assembler of component parts produced by other manufacturers. Until 1910, almost all automobiles were sold directly to the customers from assembly plants. Shortly thereafter, new selling methods arose: Direct mail campaigns began, agencies were established on a consignment basis, traveling salespeople canvassed rural America, and large department stores often became outlets for certain manufacturers. Only one of these approaches seemed to meet with much success—the use of agents on a consignment basis. This success led to the development of franchise networks for the various automobile manufacturers. Thereafter, the concept spread to other product and service industries. A brief chronology of these developments is presented in sections 1-1d through 1-1g.

1-1d   Automotive Industry

In 1898, William E. Metzger of Detroit became the first franchisee of the General Motors Corporation. He sold steam automobiles. From that simple beginning, other franchising relationships were established by manufacturers and enterprising individuals for the distribution of electric and steam automobiles.

Henry Ford envisioned mass production and mass sales of his Model T. Making the assembly-line production profitable required an efficient mechanism for the distribution of the product. Because Ford lacked the ready capital to establish multiple retail outlets in a short time, however, he focused on establishing dealers in as many communities as possible. The number of dealers was limited only by the anticipated production levels of Ford cars from the assembly plant.

Other auto manufacturers soon followed suit. As a result, the auto industry emerged as the first industry to use the franchise approach to distribution. Even today, the automobile industry accounts for about 50 percent of all franchise sales.

The huge success of the franchise approach in the auto industry was the result of the establishment of exclusive geographic territories. These territories eliminated intrabrand competition. As demand for automobiles grew, the automobile companies became financially stronger and began to franchise with independent dealers on a large scale. By allocating territorial rights and limiting the number of franchisees in specified locales, the manufacturers were able to convince the franchisees to sell only those automobiles manufactured by the parent company.

1-1e   Other Business Sectors

The methods of franchising that proved so successful in the auto and petroleum industries had application in other business sectors as well. Critical to franchise development was the opportunity for a franchisor to expand by utilizing the capital and motivation of local owner-operators (franchisees). For the franchisee, offering a standardized product or service with brand recognition to the consumer would provide strong appeal to the consumer to purchase the product or service from the local (franchised) business.

Rexall drugstores began with a gathering of about forty druggists called together by Louis Ligget in 1902. Ligget's idea was to set up a company to manufacture private-label drugs to be distributed and sold exclusively by these druggists. The important goal of the venture was to increase profit as a result of reducing manufacturing and sales costs as well as eliminating middlemen. After some time, Rexall began to open store-owned locations, becoming a corporate chain while still maintaining franchises.

Western Auto, an auto parts company based in Kansas City, began in 1909 by establishing an associate dealership program which enabled persons to open their own stores if they had the money and ambition, even if they had no prior retail experience. Western Auto assists dealers in finding an appropriate site, selecting merchandise, advertising, arranging credit, designing store layout, planning grand openings, and training employees. However, Western Auto has a distinct characteristic that separates it from other franchise systems: It requires no fee or royalty from its franchisees. Instead, it believes it receives sufficient compensation from its markup on Western Auto products sold to its dealers.

In 1925, Howard Johnson offered three flavors of "superior" blend ice cream in his Wollaston, Massachusetts, drugstore. Through franchising, his ice cream business expanded to a group of restaurants on the East Coast. In 1940, the first Howard Johnson Restaurant appeared on a turnpike, and in 1954 the first motor lodge opened.

The franchise concept was ushered into retail sales when two tailors joined forces and developed a franchise firm called Mode O'Day, which became known as the "biggest little store in the world." The 1930s also saw the advent of the Avon Cosmetics, Fuller Brush, and Culligan franchise systems. Fifty years later, Ronald McDonald is known as an image to kids and adults far and wide because of the success of the McDonald's franchise network throughout the world.

1-1f Franchising from 1950 to 1990

It was not until the early 1950s that the boom in franchising took place. Many companies that today are known to virtually every American household got their start during this period. In 1955, Ray Kroc started McDonald's, stressing "quality, service, cleanliness, and value." That same year, Harlan Sanders found a niche in the food industry with Kentucky Fried Chicken. In 1959, the International House of Pancakes opened its doors and has since sold breakfast to countless millions.

In the 1960s, many types of businesses entered the franchising field for the first time. Products and services being offered through franchise relationships now included clothing, business services, groceries, convenience stores, laundries, lawn services, printing, security systems, and vending. In 1968, the franchise industry recorded sales of over $100 billion—more than 10 percent of the gross national product and over 25 percent of the sales of the entire retail industry.[7] With this dramatic development, fast-buck operators and other unethical businesspeople began using the franchising concept for illegal personal gain. The Small Business Committees of the U.S. Senate and House of Representatives held hearings concerning fraudulent franchising practices. Based on these hearings and with the support of the franchising industry, in the early 1970s several states adopted disclosure and registration requirements for franchised businesses. In 1979, the Federal Trade Commission (FTC) passed Rule 436.1, the Franchise Disclosure Act. This act identifies the twenty-three sections that a franchise disclosure document (or prospectus) must have. The disclosure document is prepared by the franchisor and given to a prospective franchisee prior to the establishment of a franchise agreement, or contract, between the parties.

During the 1970s, franchising continued to grow. In 1979, total sales of all franchised businesses was approximately $116 billion through 396,000 business outlets. In 1980, these sales had jumped to over $334 billion generated through over 442,000 establishments. Over the decade, sales had increased over 255 percent, while the number of franchised business units had increased 5 percent.[8]

The 1980s was a period of continued emphasis on franchising in the U.S. economy. Many people saw the opportunity, through franchising, to invest their funds and energy in the development of business opportunities. Franchising opportunities had rapid growth in the service industries such as restaurant, computer, electronics, and convenience food store businesses.

The main reason for the continued interest and the growth in the number of franchised outlets was the success rate of franchises compared with that of independently owned businesses. Approximately 50 percent of new independent business ventures fail within one year, with 65 percent failing by the end of five years. Failures are often due to lack of management skills and insufficient capital for the line of business pursued. In contrast, in 1984, only 3.3 percent of the number of franchised outlets were discontinued—for any reason.[9] One reason for the low rate of failure—or discontinuance in franchising—is the franchising agreement itself, which in most franchising relationships has a renewal clause.

1-1g   The 1990s and into the Millennium

Franchising is an integral part of the structural makeup of U.S. and world business. The franchising boom is a result of two major trends in the American way of life. The first trend is the surge in entrepreneurial spirit, the desire "to start a business of my own." Franchising offers an opportunity to budding entrepreneurs to achieve personal and professional goals more quickly and with less risk than they would incur by "going it alone" as independent small business owners. The second trend is the change in lifestyles in the United States and Western Europe which has put growing emphasis on service and convenience.

Each of these trends is particularly conducive to the business-format approach to franchising. For example, the dramatic growth of two-income households has brought with it increased sales of fast food, home cleaning, specialty services, child care centers and health care facilities, and banking services offering no-appointment-needed service and extended hours. Higher incomes have also contributed to the surge in recreational activities, as well as to an increase in the number of motels, hotels, auto rental companies, and other franchised firms catering to travelers.

There has also been a trend toward **conversion franchising**, whereby an owner of an existing business becomes a franchise to acquire some benefit from association with the franchisor, such as a nationally recognized brand or trademark or a customer referral network. Conversion franchising has had particular success in real estate and restaurants and is becoming apparent in construction, electronics, nonfood retailing, home repair, and various types of business services. Century 21 and RE/MAX real estate firms are perhaps the best known franchise systems that follow a conversion business-format approach.

Statistics bear out the phenomenal growth of U.S. franchising in international markets, particularly in business-format franchising. The appeal of franchising transcends economics. Foreign governments in many parts of the world are encouraging franchising in their countries because business ownership is a proven source of social and political stability. For companies seeking an effective way to master the trade barriers and cultural differences, franchising offers a viable method to create new opportunities.

Franchised businesses (corporate and franchisee owned) operate over 800,000 establishments in the United States in 2007, provide over 10 million jobs, have a payroll in excess of $250 billion, and produce over $650 billion in output. Thus, franchised businesses account for approximately 7.5 percent of all private sector jobs, 5 percent of all private sector payroll, and 4 percent of all private sector output. In other words, franchised businesses employ about the same number of people as do all manufacturers of durable goods such as cars, trucks, planes, computers, communications equipment, primary metals, wood products, and instruments. The top five states for franchised businesses and jobs are (in descending order) California, Florida, Illinois, Georgia, and Michigan.

States with the least number of franchises and associated jobs include (in descending order) Alaska, Delaware, Maine, and Hawaii.

1-2 WHAT'S HOT RIGHT NOW?

Various lists and rankings of franchised systems are presented in this section to help the prospective franchisee or budding franchisor to identify a variety of opportunities, market trends, and growth areas in the overall franchise industry. Numerous factors are considered in the rankings developed by the periodical *Entrepreneur,* including financial strength, system stability, growth rate, size of system, years in business, length of time franchising, start-up costs for prospective franchisees, and other factors to develop a comprehensive view of the franchise industry. Specific information regarding any of the following franchise systems can be acquired by subscribing to *Entrepreneur* or by going to http://www.entrepreneur.com/franchises/toptenlists/index.html.

TOP TEN FRANCHISES IN 2007

Subway

Dunkin' Donuts

Jackson Hewitt Tax Service

7-Eleven, Inc.

The UPS Store and Mail Boxes Etc.

Domino's Pizza, LLC

Jiffy Lube Int'l. Inc.

Sonic America's Drive-In

McDonald's

Papa John's Pizza

Six of the top ten franchise systems for 2007 are in retail fast food. One is an auto service center (Jiffy Lube); one is a convenience outlet (7-Eleven); one is a business and retail service firm (The UPS Store and Mail Boxes Etc.); and one is a business and customer tax service (Jackson Hewitt). Each is a strong, vibrant franchise system that represents top franchise opportunities. Subway tops the list of franchises for the third year in a row.

TOP HOME-BASED FRANCHISE OPPORTUNITIES IN 2007

Jani-King

Matco Tools

Servpro Industries Inc.

Chem-Dry Carpet and Upholstery Cleaning

Budget Blinds Inc.

Bonus Building Care

Jazzercise Inc.

CleanNet USA Inc.

The top new franchise systems represent a wide variety of customer services that do not require storefront operations. The particular industry highlighted in 2007 for franchise system development and new franchisee business formations is the retail/domestic and commercial cleaning, maintenance, and upkeep services. Home-based franchises can be found in a broad array of retail, business, and consumer services.

TOP TEN FRANCHISES WITH START-UP COSTS LESS THAN $50,000 IN 2007

Jackson Hewitt Tax Service

RE/MAX Int'l. Inc.

Jani-King

Curves for Women

Liberty Tax Service

Merle Norman Cosmetics

Kumon Math & Reading Centers

Jan-Pro Franchising Int'l. Inc.

Chem-Dry Carpet & Upholstery Cleaning

Bonus Building Care

The fast-track, lower cost franchise systems for 2007 cluster in the residential and commercial cleaning industry, personal and business services, women's products and services, and real estate sales and service. This list for 2007 demonstrates the rapidly increasing demand for commercial and domestic services, women's products, and supplemental education.

TOP NEW FRANCHISES FROM FRANCHISE 500 IN 2007

iSold It

United Shipping Solutions

Massage Envy

Super Suppers

Dream Dinners Inc.

WineStyles, Inc.

System4

N-Hance

Bonus Building Care

Identification of franchise systems on the top ten new franchises list is based on the potential reach of the respective franchise systems, their appeal in various markets, and breadth of application across location possibilities. Once again, service leads the list of top new franchises: personal, domestic, and business.

**FASTEST GROWING FRANCHISES FROM THE FRANCHISE
500 IN 2007**

Subway

Jan-Pro Franchising Int'l. Inc.

Dunkin' Donuts

Coverall Cleaning Concepts

Jazzercise Inc.

Jackson Hewitt Tax Service

RE/MAX Int'l. Inc.

CleanNet USA Inc.

Bonus Building Care

Jani-King

**TOP TEN U.S. FRANCHISORS SEEKING FRANCHISEES OUTSIDE
THE UNITED STATES IN 2007**

Subway

Dunkin' Donuts

Domino's Pizza, LLC

McDonald's

The UPS Store and Mail Boxes Etc.

RE/MAX Int'l. Inc.

Curves

Sonic America's Drive-In

InterContinental Hotels Group

Century 21 Real Estate LLC

Clearly, the downturn in the economy in the late 1990s and early 2000s is not a hindrance to franchising. Firms that are represented on the Franchise 500 by *Entrepreneur* increased 10.2 percent in 2002 over the previous year and have retained strong growth into 2007. Companies represented on the top tlstingss in this section are both new and old, spanning a variety of industries. Careful examination of the Franchise 500 indicates that fresh-Mex fast-casual dining, senior care, child care, information technology consulting, specialized personal fitness, and home improvement and home care businesses are making a lot of "noise" in the franchised arena.

Mexican food has grown rapidly in popularity nationwide. The Hispanic and Latino population increased 58 percent during the decade of the 1990s and now represents over 9 percent of the U.S. population. Fresh-Mex franchise systems have spawned and grown rapidly to meet the new demand for fast and casual fresh-Mex foods. However, McDonald's and other major fast-food franchise systems have not been left behind, having added Mexican items such as tacos, burritos, and salads to allow customers more variety in tastes and experiences.

Senior and child service providers have increased dramatically in the last ten years to give the boomers a hand by providing care at each end of life's spectrum—the young and the aged. In-home services for seniors is a rapidly growing business niche. Child enrichment programs through supplemental education programs and one-on-one tutoring assist in ensuring that "no child is left behind."

Information technology services have exploded during the decade of the 1990s and into the twenty-first century. Though the industry remains highly fragmented today, franchise systems in IT consulting are moving quickly to create recognizable name brands that business and home-based customers could rely upon to solve their IT issues, needs, or problems.

Further, fitness clubs have come into the forefront, such as the women-only fitness center—Curves for Women—to help women develop the interest and then the habit of fitness. A variety of other niche businesses have developed in areas such as home improvement and repair, window fashions, software, and health conscious "lean" fast foods. These quick-response business developments in franchising are tapping into today's changing demographics and technologies.

1-2a   Retail Franchising

Retailing is the prime area of growth for the business-format approach to franchising. Much of this growth has taken place since the 1950s and several examples have already been mentioned. Due to the extremely competitive nature of most markets, it is difficult to ascertain exact information about number of business units and gross sales by retail business sector.

A study was authorized by the International Franchise Association (IFA) Foundation to develop a profile of the U.S. franchise industry. The profile contains a statistical abstract of U.S. franchise systems based on Uniform Franchise Offering Circular (UFOC) data.[10] In addition, composite findings of a study conducted by Price Waterhouse Coopers in 2004 provide data about the economic impact of franchised businesses in the United States.[11]

- Four food industries (bakery, fast food, restaurants, and retail food) comprise 34 percent of the franchise population.

- The two largest categories (fast food and retail) together constitute 29 percent of the franchise population.

- The fast-food industry has the highest percentage of systems—18 percent of the total franchise population, with over 220 franchise system concepts.

- Of franchise systems that have 501 or more domestic franchised units, 27 percent of those systems are in fast food.

- Fast food and retail combine to account for about 41 percent of all franchise systems with 501 or more domestic franchised locations.

- About 75 percent of the franchise population have ten or fewer company-owned units.

- Fast-food systems account for 43 percent of all systems with more than 501 domestic company-owned units.

- The franchise population (total number of domestic franchise systems) is about evenly divided between those systems with more than fifty total units and those with fifty or fewer total units.

- Sixty-two percent of franchisors in the franchise population have been in business for twelve years or more.

- The printing and lodging industries have both had 83 percent of their systems in business for more than twelve years, while the travel industry has 64 percent of their systems offering franchises for twelve years or more.

- The vast majority (88 percent) of franchises charge an initial franchise fee of $40,000 or less.

- All (100 percent) of the business-related, education, personnel, printing, and travel franchise industries provide opportunity to renew after the initial term.

- The restaurant industry offers the lowest percentage (11 percent) of systems with franchisor-sponsored financial assistance programs.

BUSINESS-FORMAT FRANCHISING COMPOSITE DATA IN 2004

- QUICK SERVICE RESTAURANTS

  Franchisor owned: 1.2 million jobs; $12.2 billion payroll; sales of $46.4 billion through 61,500 establishments

  Franchisee owned: 1.5 million jobs; $15.6 billion payroll; sales of $60.3 billion through 82,800 establishments

- LODGING

  Franchisor owned: 34,400 jobs; $0.6 billion payroll; sales of $2.3 billion through 1,600 establishments

  Franchisee owned: 399,200 jobs; $7.4 billion payroll; sales of $26.7 billion through 18,800 establishments

- TABLE/FULL SERVICE RESTAURANTS

  Franchisor owned: 461,200 jobs; $5.6 billion payroll; sales of $18 billion through 17,700 establishments

  Franchisee owned: 493,500 jobs; $5.7 billion payroll; sales of $19.2 billion through 21,300 establishments

- RETAIL FOOD

  Franchisor owned: 81,800 jobs; $1.3 billion payroll; sales of $3.3 billion through 6,300 establishments

  Franchisee owned: 515,500 jobs; $8.5 billion payroll; sales of $20.6 billion through 39,300 establishments

- AUTOMOTIVE

  Franchisor owned: 21,250 jobs; $0.6 billion payroll; sales of $1.9 billion through 4,100 establishments

  Franchisee owned: 127,300 jobs; $3.4 billion payroll; sales of $11.2 billion through 24,700 establishments

- BUSINESS SERVICES

  Franchisor owned: 25,300 jobs; $8.7 billion payroll; sales of $19.3 billion through 25,750 establishments

  Franchisee owned: 1,123,300 jobs; $45.2 billion payroll; sales of $100.6 billion through 134,350 establishments

- REAL ESTATE

  Franchisor owned: 6,150 jobs; $0.2 billion payroll; sales of $1.2 billion through 1,200 establishments

  Franchisee owned: 142,600 jobs; $4.5 billion payroll sales of $28 billion through 28,150 establishments

- RETAIL PRODUCTS AND SERVICES

  Franchisor owned: 134,100 jobs; $2.7 billion payroll; sales of $6.4 billion through 19,000 establishments

Franchisee owned: 297,600 jobs; $6 billion payroll; sales of $14.3 billion through 42,174 establishments

- PERSONAL SERVICES

  Franchisor owned: 134,500 jobs; $4.7 billion payroll; sales of $11.2 billion through 9,800 establishments

  Franchisee owned: 619,300 jobs; $21.6 billion payroll; sales of $51.3 billion through 45,050 establishments

- COMMERCIAL AND RESIDENTIAL SERVICES

  Franchisor owned: 7,000 jobs; $0.2 billion payroll; sales of $0.5 billion through 1,100 establishments

  Franchisee owned: 237,200 jobs; $8.1 billion payroll; sales of $17.3 billion through 37,600 establishments

ALL BUSINESS-FORMAT FRANCHISES

  Franchisor owned: 2,285,800 jobs; $38.8 billion payroll; sales of $110.4 billion through 148,000 units

  Franchisee owned: 5,502,600 jobs; $126.1 billion payroll; sales of $349.6 billion through 474,300 units

---

PRODUCT AND TRADE NAME FRANCHISING COMPOSITE DATA IN 2004

- AUTOMOTIVE AND TRUCK DEALERS

  Franchised: 1,460,900 jobs; $57.6 billion payroll; sales of $115.2 billion through 60,300 establishments

  % of line of business: 88.1%; 88.1%; N/A 31.9% establishments

- GASOLINE SERVICE STATIONS

  Franchised: 528,700 jobs; $7.9 billion payroll; sales of $41.7 billion through 82,350 establishments

  % of line of business: 56.4% 58.0% N/A 64% establishments

- BEVERAGE BOTTLING

  Franchised: 22,100 jobs; $0.7 billion payroll; sales of $7.7 billion through 2,600 establishments

  % of line of business: 6.9% 7.4% N/A 5.9% establishments

From the data just identified about the franchise population by industry categories, a general picture of franchising emerges. Franchised food systems comprise a large portion of business-format franchising in terms of number of units in operation, size of the food industry relative to other franchised industry categories, the large variety among franchise systems offering food products and services, and the relative large size of individual franchised systems. Clearly, the franchising of food systems has been a great success within the overall franchise industry. The growth and size of the franchised food industry is second only to the auto and beverage industries, which are product and trade name franchise systems. In addition, there is relative stability across all categories of franchise systems, with average age of franchise systems within the United States being twelve years or more.

The growth of franchise sales, as a percent of total retail sales, has continued along a steady growth trend. In 1975, franchising accounted for approximately 28 percent of total retail sales. The percentage increased to 34 percent of total retail sales in 1990, 38 percent in 2000, and is estimated to approximate 43 percent of total retail sales by 2010.

Retailing Nonfood

The retail environment is characterized by fierce competition for market share. Recently, an increasing number of nonfood retailers have turned to franchising. The franchising formula has been known to be a better way to compete by having centralized purchasing, established management techniques, brand and firm name recognition, and proven market strategies.

Most of the major trends that occur in retailing affect franchised retailers. In like manner, retail approaches and market strategies of franchised dealers influence the trends in retailing. Strong franchise chains such as Deck the Walls, Silk Plants Plus, Pot Pourri, Pearle Vision Centers, Benetton, and Batteries Plus establish strong market presence and seek to keep up with changing consumer habits. Recently, there is a noticeable shift among franchised and other nonfood retailers positioning themselves as specialty shops and "boutiques" to keep with consumer tastes, habits, and desire for convenience.

Restaurants: All Types

The restaurant industry is one of the most dynamic segments of franchising. Restaurant companies that started operations prior to 1975 waited over six years before starting to franchise. That time frame has dramatically shortened to less that one year for restaurant chains developed after 1986.

The restaurant franchisors approved over 92 percent of the proposed franchise transfers in 1998 and nearly 47 percent of these franchise systems have been in business twelve or more years.

For all franchised restaurant systems, about 80 percent of the units are franchisee owned and 20 percent are company owned. All restaurants require a royalty fee, and over 80 percent require an advertising fee. The median price for a single-unit franchise fee is about $30,000. About 10 percent of restaurant franchisors offered financial assistance to franchisees.

Franchised Restauranting as a Food Distribution System

In 1998, franchise restaurant chains with three or more units accounted for 46 percent of all restaurants in the United States. Franchisee units grew by 4.2 percent between 1997 and 1998, while franchisors added 1.4 percent to their existing corporate-owned units. This is the first time in memory that independent (franchisee-owned) units grew faster than corporate-owned (franchisor) units. In 2007, this trend continues.

The majority of restaurants can be classified into one of three categories: fast food, casual dining, or midscale. Midscale chains typically do not fit as either casual dining or fast food and tend to be so-called family-oriented restaurants such as Denny's or Perkins. Casual dining chains can be illustrated by Pizzeria Uno or various grill buffet chains such as Shakey's, Sizzler, or Golden Corral. Obviously, McDonald's, Burger King, Wendy's, Long John Silver's, and the like are notable as fast-food chains.[12]

In 1999, there were over 213,000 chain restaurants in the United States, of which 55 percent, or about 117,400, were within the biggest restaurant chains. Franchised retail food sales account for over $24 billion is sales and have payrolls of almost $10 billion. Restaurant chains with numerous corporate and franchisee units have become potent food distribution systems with distinct competitive advantages over small chains and independent small operators.[13]

The fast-food sector accounted for 70 percent of all restaurant sales. Casual dining restaurants and sandwich segments, such as Applebee's, Panera Bread, Chili's, and T.G.I. Friday's, constitute 6 percent of the restaurants and 15 percent of sales. It is likely that value-oriented pricing will become the norm as casual dining continues through to the mature stage of its growth cycle.

The midscale sector, comprised of such firms as Big Boy, Denny's, Shoney's, and Ponderosa accounted for 14 percent of sales and 9 percent of units in the top one hundred chains. Share of sales and number of units in this category have experienced some decline over the past few years.[14]

Franchise systems have seen double-digit growth in a number of establishments during much of the 1990s. Almost 45 percent of franchisors require their franchisees to be owner-operators, but 93 percent do not require their franchisees to have prior experience in the food industry. Typically, the franchisors do not own the real estate for their franchisees. Sixty-three percent of the franchisors require franchise payments on a monthly basis, with the remaining 37 percent requiring payments on a weekly basis. Ninety-seven percent of the franchisors charge a recurring royalty fee and 89 percent charge an advertising fee as well. Nearly 25 percent of the franchisors offer financial assistance to franchisees and only about 10 percent make earnings claims in their disclosure documents.

Hotels, Motels, and Campgrounds

Consistent with the sizable capital investment required in the hotels, motels, and campground category of retail franchising, 60 percent of franchisees have a twenty-year term for their franchise agreements and 73 percent of the franchise agreements contain a renewal option. Of significance to note, 36 percent of the franchisors require that the franchisee be owner-operator of the franchise; 36 percent of the franchisors also require that the franchisee have prior industry experience to become a franchisee. Other than real estate services, no other category has a greater requirement, which is understandable due to complexity and sophistication of the knowledge base and systems required to operate these franchises.

The lodging industry is changing rapidly as independent hotel and motel owners are declining in presence. Over one-half of all U.S. hotel rooms belong to recognized franchised chains—when seasonal boarding rooms, inns, and hotels with twenty-five rooms or less are eliminated from the count. Family and business travel have been on the rise. In light of these trends, both economy-priced and mid-to-upper-scale motels and hotels have experienced growth. Competition is keen in the economy-priced sector increasing the need for efficiency of operations and cleanliness of the physical settings for motel and hotel owner-operators. Business travel still accounts for 60 percent of hotel and motel business, which suggests why there has been growth in the mid-to-upper-scale motel-hotel accommodations.

Over time, lodging franchisors have modified their marketing strategies and tactics. For example, several major hotel chains have adopted the "hub and spoke" concept from the airline industry. This concept is based on the notion that a single customer will purchase variations of a product or service depending on conditions and circumstances. It has been demonstrated that a certain facility within a city will be chosen when the travel purpose is business, whereas a different hotel or motel in the same city would be chosen if the trip is family based or personal. This idea has led to tiered approaches by franchised lodging chains—such as Quality Inns, Holiday Inns, and Marriott Hotels—which operate luxury, midpriced, and economy lodging facilities. This approach to market segmentation is likely to continue well into the twenty-first century. Clearly, the segmented approach and careful market positioning of hotel-motel accommodations give the guest a definitive choice in price, convenience, ambience, and amenities.

Recreation, Entertainment, and Travel

Growth of the recreation, entertainment, and travel franchise business category has been strong and is projected to continue well into the twenty-first century. Over 58 percent of franchisors have franchise agreements with a term of ten years, with almost 17 percent having perpetual franchise agreements. More than 63 percent of the franchisors do not require that the franchisee be the owner-operator, and only 14 percent require prior experience in the appropriate recreation, entertainment, or travel industry.

Nearly all (99 percent) of existing franchising units in this category are franchisee owned. The recreation, entertainment, and travel category is one of the fastest growing sectors in franchising. Included in this group are travel agencies, miniature golf courses, movie theaters, and dance studios.

Automotive Products and Services

About 48 percent of auto products and services franchisors require that advertising and royalty fees be paid to the franchisor on a weekly basis, whereas the remaining 52 percent require such fees be paid monthly. This franchise business category has the highest percentage of franchisors that insist on being on the prime or headlease for franchisees (30 percent) that lease their real estate. Ninety-seven percent of these franchisors require a royalty fee and 75 percent require an advertising fee.

Revenue growth for franchised automotive aftermarket products and services has averaged about an 8 percent increase yearly since the mid-1980s. The consumer force behind this growth is the graying of the U.S. car population. Not only has the number of cars that are on the road increased, but also the percentage of cars more than eight years old has increased in the total car market during the 1990s.

The do-it-yourself (DIY automotive products market increased from 10 percent of the total aftermarket business in 1983 to 45 percent of the aftermarket by 1995 and has continued to grow into the twenty-first century.[15] Franchised service chains are in a good position to counter the DIY threat. Franchise firms specializing in muffler replacements, lube jobs, oil changes, and transmission repair have been able to provide good and efficient services while charging less than independent dealers. Plus, having regional or national name recognition has given them an advantage over "back-alley mechanics." Specialty franchises such as Tidy Car, Speedy Lube, Midas, Precision Tune, Econo Lube 'n Tune, Car-X Muffler and Brake, Batteries Plus, and Aamco Transmissions illustrate the offering of auto products and services.

Business Aids and Services

The business aids and services sector of franchising includes accounting and financial planning firms, businesses and services, consulting and brokerages, education and training, gifts, and fundraising specialists. Nearly one-half of the franchisors in this category execute franchise agreements for ten-year terms. About one in three franchise systems offer some form of financial assistance to franchisees. The growth of business aids and services franchises coincides with the overall shift in the U.S. economy from manufacturing to information and services. An increasingly complex tax system has heightened the demand for accounting, financial planning, tax preparation, and legal services for individual and small businesses.

Printing, Copying, and Sign Products and Services

The printing, copying, and sign products and services category of franchisors has the highest ratio of franchisors who make earnings claims (44 percent, which is almost 2.5 times greater than the average for all franchisor respondents). Nearly all franchisors require a royalty fee and over 80 percent require an advertising fee. American Sign, Fastsigns, Signs on Site, American Speedy, Lazerquick, PIP Printing, and Sir Speedy are example franchise chains in this business category.

Employment and Personnel Services

The employment and personnel services category has the highest ratio of franchisors (85 percent) that require the franchisee be an owner-operator of the business. (See Table 1-2) This ratio is over 1.5 times the average of all franchise systems. All franchisors require a royalty fee, and in addition, almost 65 percent require an advertising fee. About 30 percent of the franchise systems in this business category offer financing for franchises, and 20 percent make an earnings claim in their disclosure document.

| TABLE 1-2 | PERCENTAGE OF COMPANIES THAT REQUIRE FRANCHISEES TO BE OWNER-OPERATORS OR HAVE PRIOR INDUSTRY EXPERIENCE |

All Respondents

Percentage of Companies that Require Franchisees to be Owner/Operators, or have Prior Industry Experience

	Owner/Operator		Prior Experience	
Category	YES	NO	YES	NO
All Respondents	51.0%	49.0%	10.6%	89.4%
Restaurants (All Types)	42.4%	57.6%	10.3%	89.7%
Hotels, Motels & Campgrounds	36.4%	63.6%	36.4%	63.6%
Recreation, Entertainment & Travel	35.7%	64.3%	14.3%	85.7%
Automotive Products and Services	51.5%	48.5%	3.1%	96.9%
Business Aids and Services	50.0%	50.0%	14.8%	85.2%
Printing, Copying, & Sign Prdcts. & Svcs.	55.6%	44.4%	0.0%	100.0%
Employment Services	85.0%	15.0%	10.0%	90.0%
Maintenance & Cleaning Services	47.6%	52.4%	14.3%	85.7%
Construction, Home Improvement	62.5%	37.5%	15.6%	84.4%
Convenience Stores	75.0%	25.0%	0.0%	100.0%
Laundry & Dry Cleaning	40.0%	60.0%	0.0%	100.0%
Educational Products & Services	50.0%	50.0%	33.3%	66.7%
Rental Services: Auto & Truck	20.0%	80.0%	0.0%	100.0%
Rental Services: Equipment & Retail	40.0%	60.0%	0.0%	100.0%
Retailing: Non-Food	57.1%	42.9%	9.5%	90.5%
Retailing: Food (non-convenience)	44.8%	55.2%	6.9%	93.1%
Health and Beauty Aids	45.0%	55.0%	15.0%	85.0%
Real Estate Services	60.0%	40.0%	40.0%	60.0%
Miscellaneous Services	55.6%	44.4%	0.0%	100.0%

New information technologies—office automation in particular—have created strong demand for temporary workers with specialized skills in computer applications and IT. In addition, light industrial, health care, and finance and accounting specialists are required more frequently that in years past. Often, employers cite the use of temporary workers as a means of managing workload peaks and valleys by hiring temporaries on a project-by-project basis. Example firms in this business category include Express Personnel Services, ACT Health Care Services, Dunhill Staffing Systems Inc., and Labor Finders International Inc.

Maintenance and Cleaning Services

Company-owned units have revenues significantly greater than franchisee units. Sixty percent of franchisors require monthly fee payments; 30 percent require weekly fee payments. Almost 95 percent charge a royalty fee and 42 percent require an advertising fee. Only 10 percent of the franchisors make earnings claims and 57 percent offer financing to franchisees. Examples of franchised opportunities in this category are Merry Maids, Chem-Dry Superior Carpet & Upholstery Cleaning, Bonus Building Care, Molly Maid, Blue Magic Pool Service, and American Restoration Services.

Construction and Home Improvement

About 50 percent of the construction and home improvement franchisors have term agreements for ten years. This business category has the second highest ratio (over 60 percent) of franchisors who require the franchisee to be an owner-operator. Only 6 percent of the franchise systems in this category are operated by a parent (franchisor) company with the remaining ones operated by franchisees. Almost 70 percent of franchisors require franchise payments to be made on a monthly basis. Nearly 97 percent of franchisors require royalty fees while 58 percent also require an advertising fee. About 34 percent of franchisors offer financing for the franchisee, and 16 percent make earnings claims in their disclosure documents. Sample franchised construction and home improvement chains include BathCrest Inc., Certa ProPainters, The Closet Factory, Crack Team USA, and Contractor Online.

Convenience Stores

Franchise agreements for convenience stores are typically written for ten-year terms and a large majority (75 percent) require that the franchisee be the owner-operator. It is interesting to note, franchisors typically do not require prior experience. Franchisors require payment of royalty and advertising fees. About 25 percent of franchisors provide financing assistance to franchisees.

Convenience stores are in a highly competitive environment. The franchised convenience store chains have moved to the forefront with additional conveniences to the consuming public (i.e., extended hours, Sunday hours, takeout foods, coffee bars, ATM services, and authorized gaming lotteries). Some have joined with gas service pumps to enhance overall convenience for the general consumer. Recently, co-branding between complementary franchise systems has allowed aggressive moves in the convenience store marketplace, providing nationally branded hot fast foods and specialty services such as dry cleaning, along with the traditional convenience store items. Sample firms in this category include Mobile Oil, along with Taco Bell, 7-Eleven Inc., Dairy Mart Convenience Stores, Express Mart, Stage Mart, and White Hen Pantry.

Laundry and Dry Cleaning

About 80 percent of the laundry and dry cleaning franchisors have a ten-year term for their franchise agreement. About 40 percent require that the franchisee be an owner-operator, but few if any require prior experience on the part of the franchisee. Sixty percent require monthly payments from franchisees with the remainder requiring weekly payments. About 60 percent of the franchisors offer financing for franchisees. Sample firms include Martinizing, Dryclean USA, and Comet Cleaners.

Health and Beauty Aids

The health and beauty aids business category has sustained single- to double-digit growth during the 1990s. Franchisees own about 75 percent of the total number of establishments. Nearly all franchisors (95 percent) require a royalty fee and 84 percent require an advertising fee. Almost 37 percent of franchisors offer some form of financial assistance to franchisees and 26 percent of the franchisors indicate they make earnings claims in their disclosure document. Franchise systems that illustrate this business category include Cost Cutters Family Hair Care, Merle Norman, The Lemon Tree, Snip n' Clip, Fit America, Great Earth Vitamin Stores, Slimmer Image, Medicap Pharmacy, and Visiting Angels Living Assistance Services.

Real Estate Services

About one-half of the real estate franchisors have a ten-year term on their franchise agreement and one-half have a five-year term. All franchisors have renewal options. Sixty percent of the franchisors require the franchise to be an owner-operator and 40 percent require prior industry experience. Real estate services have experienced explosive growth through franchising, particularly through converting existing real estate agencies and brokerages into franchised businesses linked nationally and internationally with one another. Current examples include Assist-2-Sell, Homevestors, National Tenant Network, RE/MAX, Remerica Real Estate, and United Capital Mortgage Assistance.

Recent Trends in Franchising

The decade of the 1990s and the beginning of the twenty-first century have demonstrated phenomenal growth in many new service areas that have been appropriate for franchise systems. The shifts in the economy that provided new opportunities in the business-format franchise area have been the result of several factors. First, demographic shifts bring the baby boomers to maturity and retirement within the next ten to twenty years. Baby boomer preferences have been shifting from raising families to having kids in college, looking toward retirement with substantial investments, multiple minivacations within a year, and upscale amenities for the person and the home. Second, we have transitioned from a manufacturing-based economy to a service- and technology-based economy, the double-income household, consumer desire for increased convenience, and the increased involvement of women, minorities, and the handicapped in the production of goods and services within the business world. Third, through the rapid advance of information technology and travel efficiencies, the world has rapidly become a global marketplace. E-commerce, business-to-business (B2B) networks, Web pages, and online shopping have brought fundamental changes to the ways of doing business.

The implications of these trends are far reaching. Convenience, flexibility, and quality have long been the buzzwords in business-format franchising. Note also the importance placed on training for franchisees and their employees by franchise systems. Table 1-3 shows that initial training is provided by franchisors in all nineteen categories of franchised businesses. Clearly, the great majority of franchise systems recognize the importance of initial training for incoming franchisees.

Table 1-4 shows the percentages by franchise business category where franchise contracts were terminated and percentages where franchised units were required by the respective franchise system. The highest contract termination rates were shown in employment services, construction and home improvement, nonfood retailing, and rental services: auto and truck. Generally, notice how low the percentage rates are for reacquisition by franchisors across all of the business categories. The percentages suggest that when franchise businesses are in trouble (which may be from 1 to 24 percent, depending on the business category), the percent of contracts terminated are quite small, averaging only 6.7 percent across all business categories. This small percentage contrasts sharply with start-up firms and those surviving up to at least the fifth year of existence, where percentage of failure ranges between 20 and 70 percent.

With the increased emphasis on convenience—particularly due to the rapid increase of women in the workforce—franchise systems are intent to increase the speed of service without diluting quality. Today, most adult women work outside the home, surrendering home-time hours into employment-based hours. This trend has irrevocably altered traditional family life and consumer behavior. As a result, convenience is a top priority for most working men and women. Ten-minute oil changes, hit-and-run convenience store purchasing, and Kwik-Kopy are business names and concepts that illustrate this change in consumer desire for speed and efficiency. Franchised systems that can develop and maintain high quality in the products and services and meet the convenience priorities of the purchasing public have not only become successful businesses, but also have become leaders in their respective fields. Franchising has proven that it can offer a high level of standardized quality, brand image, favorable reputation, and convenience that many people today find important for guiding their consumer decision processes.

In addition, the recognizable increase in demand for high-quality goods and services has spurred entry into specialty products and services delivery by franchise systems. This increased demand is particularly noticeable in the fields of clothing, home furnishings, decorating, health care, food, security systems, travel services, and telecommunication products and services.

TABLE 1-3   FRANCHISE COMPANY CHARACTERISTICS: TRAINING

All Respondents

Category	Percent Offering Initial Training (%)
All Respondents	98.3
Restaurants (All Types)	98.3
Hotels, Motels, and Campgrounds	100
Recreation, Entertainment, and Travel	92.9
Automotive Products and Services	97
Business Aids and Services	100
Printing, Copying, and Sign Products and Services	100
Employment Services	95
Maintenance and Cleaning Services	100
Construction and Home Improvement	100
Convenience Stores	75
Laundry and Dry Cleaning	100
Educational Products and Services	100
Rental Services: Auto and Truck	100
Rental Services: Equipment and Retail	100
Retailing: Nonfood	100
Retailing: Food (nonconvenience)	100
Health and Beauty Aids	100
Real Estate Services	100
Miscellaneous Services	96.3

Results of a gender study by the Office of Advocacy of the U.S. Small Business Administration indicate that two industry categories have a significantly higher than average percentage of women as sole franchise owners: children's products and services (48.03 percent) and travel (31.5 percent). Seven other industries report female-owned franchised units at 10 percent or more (see Table 1-5)[16].

In the same study, the highest percentage of minority ownership of franchises is indicated to be in cleaning products and services (19.2 percent), carpet, drapery, and upholstery cleaning (18.8 percent), laundry and dry cleaning services (14.6 percent), printing and copying services (13.5 percent), motels, hotels, and campgrounds (12.6 percent), food: ice cream and yogurt (10.4 percent), and food: restaurant and quick services (10.3 percent). See Table 1-6.

An increased number of women and minorities have become owner-operators in franchised systems. Major fast-food franchise systems have made great strides in recruiting and developing women- and minority-owned franchised businesses. Franchise systems are following suit in other franchised business areas as well. This trend should continue in the twenty-first century.

The emergence of the two-career family and twenty-four-hour communications capabilities at home and at work will force many businesses to alter their hours of operations. As businesses extend their hours and days of operations, "blue laws" have gradually reduced across the United States. Longer hours of operation and flexible work schedules likely will create more jobs, particularly part-time employment for persons with little or no prior work experience. The challenge to

TABLE 1-4   FRANCHISE STABILITY RATE

All Respondents of Franchisee-Owned Units Opened in Last 5 Years		
Category	Percent Contract Terminated	Percent Reacquired by Franchisor
All Respondents	**6.7%**	**0.0%**
Restaurants (All Types)	5.9%	0.0%
Hotels, Motels & Campgrounds	4.6%	N/A
Recreation, Entertainment & Travel	8.1%	N/A
Automotive Products and Services	6.1%	0.0%
Business Aids and Services	6.5%	1.1%
Printing, Copying, & Sign Prdcts. & Svcs.	6.5%	0.0%
Employment Services	15.9%	0.1%
Maintenance & Cleaning Services	5.9%	0.0%
Construction, Home Improvement	11.7%	0.3%
Convenience StoresN/A	N/A	
Laundry & Dry Cleaning	N/A	N/A
Educational Products & Services	N/A	N/A
Rental Services: Auto and Truck	19.1%	N/A
Rental Services: Equipment & Retail	N/A	N/A
Retailing: Non-Food	10.7%	N/A
Retailing: Food (non-convenience)	5.0%	3.8%
Health and Beauty Aids	1.7%	0.0%
Real Estate Services	N/A	N/A
Miscellaneous Services	7.9%	4.1%

franchise systems will be to provide high-quality training and attractive salary and benefit packages for employees who work full and part time, and evenings or weekends only.

International Franchising

U.S. franchise systems enter foreign markets using a variety of methods, including franchising directly to individuals and operating company-owned units, or through joint ventures. Selling a master franchise has been shown to be the most popular technique and the fastest approach for market entry and capturing market share. Entering foreign markets can be difficult and time consuming. The success (or failure) of franchising in international markets depends on several factors, including the franchisor's success in domestic competitive position and market penetration, its ability to expand based on its knowledge and expertise, and its ability to adapt to countries that have cultural and language differences.[17]

The franchise companies that have entered into the international marketplace for expansion have tended to first enter countries where the cultural and language differences are minor or of almost no significance; and then, enter countries where the markets are large and a history of satisfactory import-export trade practices have been in existence over time. Historically, the two countries that have experienced the most importation of U.S. franchising are the United Kingdom and Canada; next are Japan, Mexico, Germany, Austria, and France. There is little evidence of

<table>
<tr><td colspan="2">TABLE 1-5</td><td colspan="4">FEMALE FRANCHISE OWNERSHIP BY INDUSTRY</td></tr>
</table>

		Highest Percentage			
Industry/Average Cost	Total	Female	Female/Male	Male	Unknown
Children's Products and Services	1,066	512	305	193	56
$59,571	100%	48%	28.6%	18.1%	5.3%
Travel	1,381	435	42	640	264
$57,000	100%	31.5%	3%	46.3%	19.1%
Accounting and Tax Services	1,651	326	112	604	609
$19,433	100%	19.8%	6.8%	36.6%	36.9%
Health Aids and Services	1,890	299	185	1,342	64
$75,029	100%	15.8%	9.8%	71%	3.4%
Business Products and Services	1,653	245	286	835	287
$65,188	100%	14.8%	17.3%	50.5%	17.4%
Cleaning Products and Services	1,931	237	776	692	226
$29,586	100%	12.3%	40.2%	35.8%	11.7%
Hairstyling and Cosmetics	2,593	295	570	765	963
$60,749	100%	11.4%	22%	29.5%	37.2%
Schools and Teaching	1,161	124	240	512	285
$110,033	100%	10.7%	20.7%	44.1%	24.6%
Employment and Personnel	1,222	122	260	556	284
$63,911	100%	10%	21.3%	45.5%	23.2%

Source: S. Crawford, *Women and Minorities in Franchising and Financing Practices* (Washington, DC: U.S. Small Business Administration, Office of Advocacy, May 1999), 8, 14.

cultural or language difficulties posing problems too large to resolve in these and an expanding list of other countries.

The appeal of franchising appears to transcend economic, cultural, and even political differences as well. Note the expansion over the past decade of companies such as McDonald's, KFC, Pepsi Cola, Coca-Cola, and other franchise systems into Russia, Rumania, Singapore, Hong Kong, Africa, India, Israel, China, Indonesia, and Malaysia. A number of foreign governments have opened their borders, encouraging franchising because business ownership is a proven source of social and political stability. Some political scientists and government economists suggest that franchising can play an important role in bringing stability and economic reform to the Middle East and other countries beset by turmoil.

1-2b   A Microview of Franchisors and Franchisees

Franchisors

In 1994, Robert Robicheaux of the University of Alabama at Tusculoosa conducted a study of 155 franchise systems to determine franchise executive compensation for that same year.[18] Demographic traits of the CEO indicate an average age of 48.8 years. The majority (94.2 percent) of the CEOs were men; 5.8 percent were women. Eighty-six percent of the CEOs responding indicated having an equity position within the franchise company. The CEO was the founder of the firm 47.7

TABLE 1-6   INDUSTRIES BY PERCENTAGE OF MINORITY-OWNED UNITS

Industry/Average Investment	Highest Percentage		
	Total	Minority Units	% Minority Units
Cleaning Products and Services $22,744	5,644	1,080	19.2
Hairstyling and Cosmetics $8,500	133	25	18.8
Laundry and Dry Cleaning Services $87,167	636	93	14.6
Miscellaneous $52,825	2,608	374	14.3
Printing and Copying Services $174,000	1,323	179	13.5
Motel, Hotels, and Campgrounds $1,594,375	438	55	12.6
Food: Ice Cream and Yogurt $146,800	96	10	10.4
Food: Restaurant and Quick Services $291,356	23,917	2,468	10.3

Source: S. Crawford, *Women and Minorities in Franchising and Financing Practices* (Washington, DC: U.S. Small Business Administration, Office of Advocacy, May 1999), 8, 14.

percent of the time. The mean average years the CEO had been with the franchise company was 10.4 years and had held the CEO position for a mean of 8.1 years.

The CEOs were asked to provide an overall assessment of the economic condition of their particular franchise business category. Seventy-three percent of the CEOs indicated that the economic condition of their industry was "somewhat" to "very good," whereas 16 percent indicated it was "about average" and 11 percent indicated it was "somewhat poor." Further, 79 percent of these CEOs believed the economic conditions for their particular franchise industry would be "somewhat good" to "very good," whereas 16 percent indicated it would be "somewhat poor."

The survey indicated that the net profit before tax for the responding franchise companies had a mean average of 12.4 percent of net sales revenues with the median being 10 percent of net sales revenues. These figures suggest that responding firms see their market performance as solid and that they are generally confident in their ability to enhance sales and increase profitability while continuing to expand the size of their business through company and franchisee-owned units.

The Franchisee

In 1996, *Franchise Times* surveyed more than a thousand franchisees. The survey was completed by the survey research firm of Erdos and Morgan and reported in *Franchise Times*.[19] The survey results reflect attitudes and performance of franchisees in a variety of industries ranging from fast food, restauranting, and catering (30 percent) to business services and computers (14 percent) to printing, photography, signs, and retail (6 percent each). On balance, the franchisee community is satisfied with being in a franchise system, and would recommend it to others. Three of four franchisees believe their franchise operations are lucrative enough for them, and franchising meets their needs for independence, opportunity, and job security.

SUMMARY

The franchising concept as we know it was not a major factor in U.S. business until automobile, petroleum, and other product and trade name manufacturers and processors sought to expand by penetrating new markets through franchise dealerships. Most of the early U.S. manufacturers did not have sufficient capital available to expand as rapidly as they would have liked while still maintaining absolute control over each outlet.

Franchising of commission agents, dealers, and licenses was of great advantage to these industries during their infancy. The manufacturers could focus their attention, knowledge, and capital on the products themselves, and mass market advertising. This left customer relations, point-of-sale business practices, and the responsibility for service after the sale with the dealer or local business owner. The concept served both the manufacturers (franchisors) and their dealers (franchisees) well. The automobile, auto parts, and soft beverage industries grew to meet the demand of their customers.

Business-format franchising has been found to be a practical tool for franchisors and franchisees in the areas of service, entertainment, and consumer nondurable retail sales. Stories of phenomenal sales, sales growth, and long-term success of various franchise systems illustrate the durability, practicality, and profitability of business-format franchising in restaurants, business services, hotels and motels, auto services, and many other retail business sectors. Each of the nineteen business categories where franchising is found in the retail arena is discussed in broad descriptive terms directly associated to franchising.

Specific data about franchising by business category is highlighted in table format for ease of identification and comparative analysis of one business category with another. Information about the CEOs and other senior management by salary level based on survey fundings is provided. Intentions concerning growth and further development of their franchise systems through expansion of company units and/or franchisee units is presented along with other demographic data about the CEOs, gross revenues of the franchise systems, and the CEO's general assessment of the economic condition of their particular franchise industry.

Demographic data as well as average sales, number of employees, average earnings, profitability, and factors that contribute to franchisee satisfaction and dissatisfaction are highlighted. This information gives a microview on the life of an online franchisee in the U.S. marketplace.

Franchising by its very nature tends to create new business. It allows the small or midsize business to compete with giant corporations through the use of the franchisor's trademark, know-how, and product-service quality standards. Because of the assistance offered by the franchisor, even those with limited experience and capital may become successful in the world of franchising.

KEY TERMS

Business-format franchising: involves a specific FORMAT or approach required by the franchisor of the franchisee to following when providing the products and/or services to the customer.

Business-opportunity approach: an informal generic description about the franchisor-franchisee relationship, wherein an owner of a product or service grants rights to an individual for local distribution and/or sales of the goods or services who, in return, provides a fee or royalty back to the owner.

Format: the approach to be used by a franchisee in providing the franchisor's product or service line to the customer.

Franchisee: the individual or business granted the right by the franchisor to operate in accordance with the chosen method to produce or sell the product or service.

Franchising: a business opportunity by which the owner (producer or distributor) of a service or a trademarked product grants exclusive rights to an individual for the local distribution and/or sale of the service or product, and in return receives a payment or royalty and conformance to quality standards.

Franchisor: the individual or business granting the business rights to a franchisee.

Product and trade name franchising: a franchising relationship in which the dealer acquires the trade name, trademark, and/or product from the franchisor/supplier.

McDonald's

Hello, Mr. Kroc

Ray Kroc was fifty-two years old—an age when many people begin thinking about retirement—when he founded the company that has become the McDonald's of today. Kroc, who dropped out of high school at age fifteen to drive a Red Cross ambulance in World War I, was a constant dreamer, a salesman who never stopped looking for the ultimate product to peddle. He began by selling paper cups to sidewalk vendors in Chicago, took a fling at Florida real estate, and had ultimately built a good business as the exclusive distributor for Multimixer milkshake machines.

It was the sale of Multimixers which first drew him to the McDonald brothers' hamburger stand in San Bernardino, California. After all, if he could discover the secret of how they sold 20,000 shakes each month, how many more milkshake machines could he sell? But when Kroc showed up at McDonald's one morning in 1954 and saw the rapidly moving line of customers buying bags of burgers and fries, he had but one thought: "This will go anyplace. Anyplace!"

After the McDonald brothers explained that they didn't have the personal desire to oversee the expansion of their concept across the nation, Ray Kroc became their exclusive franchising agent for the entire country. A great salesman had discovered his ultimate product. Kroc formed the new franchising company on March 2, 1955, under the name of McDonald's System, Inc.

On April 15, 1955, his prototype McDonald's restaurant began business in Des Plaines, Illinois,

opened with the help of Art Bender, who thus had served the first McDonald brothers' hamburger and the first Ray Kroc McDonald's hamburger. Bender went on to open the first of Kroc's McDonald's franchises in Fresno, California, and ultimately retired owning seven restaurants.

Rather than tinker with a successful format, Kroc retained the McDonald's formula of a limited menu, quality food, an assembly-line production system, and fast, friendly service—adding to that his own demanding standards for cleanliness. Indeed, the operating principle of quality, service, cleanliness, and value (OSC&V) continues at McDonald's today.

It was in the area of franchising, however, where Kroc uniquely applied the lessons of his sales background to create a successful organization. In many ways, it was a matter of necessity.

Kroc's agreement with the McDonald brothers was to limit the franchise fee to $950 per restaurant and charge a service fee of only 1.9 percent of restaurant sales—with 0.5 percent of that going back to the McDonald brothers. In addition, Kroc decided early on that the McDonald's system would not be in the business of selling franchise owners their equipment, supplies, or food. The company did, however, purchase or lease much of the real estate where the restaurants were located, a program that soon produced a valuable competitive asset in its own right.

So it was in Kroc's best interest to do everything possible to ensure that his franchise owners could build their sales. If they failed, he would fail with them, and vice versa. *Kroc used his persuasive salesman's skills to convince his first franchisees to sign on, to line up prospective suppliers, to inspire the first team of company managers, and to convince lenders to finance his young company. Kroc so firmly believed in his dream that he didn't take a dollar in salary from the company until 1961. The formula worked.*

At the end of 1956, McDonald's fourteen restaurants reported sales of $1.2 million and had served some 50 million hamburgers. In just four years, there were 228 restaurants reporting $37.6 million in sales, and the company had sold its 400 millionth hamburger midway through 1960.

To enjoy further growth, however, Kroc knew he had to buy out the McDonald brothers in order to loosen the restrictive agreement under which he had been operating. For all the restaurants' success, Kroc's company had netted a meager $77,000 profit in 1960 and was carrying $5.7 million in long-term debt.

The brothers asked for a flat $2.7 million in cash—$700,000 of which they would pay in taxes, leaving $1 million for each of them. A fair price at that time, thought the McDonald's, for inventing the fast-food industry.

Kroc managed to obtain a loan in 1961—based on the company's real estate values—and though it ultimately cost him $14 million to repay it, he bought the ability to control his growing system.

That same year, he opened Hamburger University in the basement of a restaurant in Elk Grove Village, Illinois—a training facility for new franchisees and store managers which has grown to be a worldwide institution utilizing sophisticated training techniques and high-level management courses.

THE STAGE WAS SET FOR McDONALD'S PHENOMENAL GROWTH

Today, McDonald's is the largest and best-known global food service retailer, with more than 29,000 restaurants in 120 countries. Still, our global market potential is enormous. On any day, even as the market leader, McDonald's serves less than 1 percent of the world's population. Efforts to increase market share profitability and customer satisfaction have produced high returns to shareholders—a compound average of 17 percent over the past ten years. McDonald's 2006 year-end systemwide sales were over $41.6 billion from more than 31,000 restaurants.

REVIEW QUESTIONS

1. What reasons can be given for the dramatic development of franchising in the United States?

2. What is meant by product and trade name franchising?

3. What is meant by business-format franchising?

4. Why does a franchisee often have a higher probability of success than a typical owner-operator of a small business?

5. Why does franchising, by its very nature, tend to create new business?

6. What are the primary demographic traits of franchisees? Of franchisors?

FRANCHISING QUIZ: FACT OR FICTION?

1. T   F   Frozen Fusion is the first franchise company owned by an American Indian tribe.

2. T   F   The majority of Popeye's Chicken locations in Korea seat about 160 people and are two stories tall compared to domestic locations that seat about 30 people and are one story.

3. T   F   Roto-Rooter provides drain cleaning services to areas that include 90 percent of the U.S. population.

4. T   F   Franchisors on average must qualify about 200 prospects before finding an appropriate franchise candidate.

5. T   F   Over 55 million customers visit Taco Bell restaurants each week.

6. T   F   Since its first bakery opened in 1985, nearly 32 million people have sampled Cinnabon's cinnamon rolls.

7. T   F   According to Radio Shack, 94 percent of all Americans live or work within a five-minute drive of a Radio Shack store.

8. T   F   U.S. Department of Agriculture statistics identify the annual per capita pizza consumption is 24 pounds and Saturday night is the favorite pizza night.

9. T   F   Pizza Hut opens a new store about every forty-three hours and Subway opens a new store about every twenty-four hours.

10. T   F   According to the Small Business Administration, an average franchisee owns 3.5 units and maintains or creates, on average, 32.6 jobs annually.

Source: U.S. Government and individual corporate reports.

(If you answered "True" to all the questions above, you are correct.)

REFERENCES

Arthur Anderson & Co., *Franchising in the Economy, 1989–1992* (Washington, DC: International Franchise Association, Education Foundation, Inc., 1992), 115.

Cherkasky, William B., "Franchising: a Key to Business Success," *Franchising Research* 1(3) (1996):5.

Church, Nancy Suway,*Future Opportunities in Franchising: A Realistic Appraisal* (New York: Pilot Industries, Inc., 1979), 11.

Crawford, Samuel,*Women and Minorities in Franchising and Financing Practices* (Washington, DC: U.S. Small Business Administration, Office of Advocacy, May 1999).

"Franchise Times 1996 Franchisee Survey," *Franchise Times* (August 1996): 27–29.

Franchise Yearbook 1988 (Los Angeles: Entrepreneurial Group, Inc., 1988).

Kostecka, Andy and U.S. Department of Commerce, *Franchising in the Economy, 1985–1987* (Washington, DC: U.S. Government Printing Office, 1987), 52.

Kostecka, Andy, U.S. Department of Commerce, and Bureau of Industrial Economics and Minority Business Development Agency, *Franchise Opportunities Handbook* (Washington, DC: U.S. Government Printing Office, 1983), 27.

PriceWaterhouseCoopers, "Economic Impact of Franchised Businesses," a report for the International Franchise Association Education Foundation, Washington: DC, 2004.

Robicheaux, Robert, *Franchise Executive Compensation Survey, 1994* (Tuscaloosa: University of Alabama). Also in *Franchise Update* (1995).

The Business Failure Record (New York: Dun & Bradstreet, 1988, 1992, 1996).

The Naisbitt Group, *The Future of Franchising: Looking 25 Years Ahead to the Year 2010* Washington, D.C., (1986).

"Top Franchises for 2007," *Entrepreneur Magazine,*(April 2007).

Shubart, Ellen, "Franchising's Just Fine, Thanks: Poll," *Franchise Times* (August 1996) 27–29.

Whittemore, Meg, "The Great Franchise Boom," *Nation's Business* (September 1984) 20–24.

NOTES

1. W. B. Cherkasky, "Franchising: A Key to Business Success" *Franchising Research* 1(3) (1996): 5.
2. A. Kostecka and U.S. Department of Commerce, *Franchising in the Economy, 1985–1987* (Washington, DC: U.S. Government Printing Office, 1987), 2.
3. Ibid.
4. Ibid.
5. Cherkasky, "Franchising," 5–6.
6. N. Suway Church, *Future Opportunities in Franchising: A Realistic Appraisal* (New York: Pilot Industries, Inc., 1979), 11.
7. A. Kostecka, U.S. Department of Commerce, and International Trade Association, *Franchising in the Economy, 1983–1985* (Washington, DC: U.S. Government Printing Office, 1985), 28–31.
8. Ibid.
9. Ibid.
10. Information highlights adapted from *The Profile of Franchising*, vol. 3 of *A Statistical Abstract of 1998 UFOC Data*, prepared by FRANDATA Corporation (Washington, DC: IFA Educational Foundation, Inc. February 2000).
11. PriceWaterhouseCoopers, "Economic Impact of Franchised Businesses," a report for the International Franchise Association Education Foundation (Washington, DC, 2004).
12. Adapted from "Franchising in the Economy: Fast Food's Big Role," in *The Franchise Handbook* (Fall 2000), 22.
13. Ibid.
14. Ibid.
15. The Naisbitt Group, *The Future of Franchising: Looking 25 Years Ahead to the Year 2010* (1986), 10–12.
16. S. Crawford, *Women and Minorities in Franchising and Financing Practices* (Washington, DC: U.S. Small Business Administration, Office of Advocacy, May 1999), 8, 14.
17. Arthur Anderson & Co., *Franchising in the Economy, 1989–1992* (Washington, DC: International Franchise Association Education Foundation, Inc., 1992), 108–110.
18. R. Robicheaux, *Franchise Executive Compensation Survey, 1994* (Tuscaloosa: University of Alabama). Also in *Franchise Update* (1995).
19. "Franchise Times 1996 Franchisee Survey," *Franchise Times* (August 1996: 27–29.) Results of the survey showed that franchisees average over $1.4 million in gross sales annually; the average franchisee owns 3.5 units; about one-third of existing franchisees are considering the addition of more franchised units; and three of four franchisees (75 percent) described themselves as either "very" or "somewhat" satisfied with their franchised business. The primary reasons for franchisee satisfaction because of franchising offers are as follows: independence (78.2 percent), a growth opportunity (58 percent), high earnings (35.1 percent), and job security (29.3 percent). The 25 percent who would not recommend franchising cite the franchise purchased is not lucrative enough, the franchisee receives insufficient support from the franchisor, or for long hours required. Two-thirds of those who would not recommend franchising say there is insufficient franchisor support. Only 13 percent of the unsatisfied franchisees cite not enough decision-making authority as their source of dissatisfaction.
A franchisee employs, on average, 32.6 employees; almost ninety (89.4) percent employ fewer than 49 workers.
Ninety-two percent of franchisee respondents participate in only one franchise system, an overwhelming majority, which is a sign of loyalty to their respective franchise system.

Source: Adapted from Shubart, "Franchising's Just Fine, Thanks: Poll," *Franchise Times* (August 1996): 27–29.

RECOGNIZING FRANCHISING OPPORTUNITIES

In studying this chapter, you will:

- Understand why the franchising concept has become so successful in America as well as international business.

- Learn the advantages of franchising for both the franchisor and the franchisee.

- Learn the potential disadvantages of franchising to the franchisor and the franchisee.

- Learn the seven steps for franchise protection before investing in a franchise.

- Be able to identify the typical elements included in a franchising agreement.

INCIDENT

Tom is considering going into business for himself. He is twenty-eight years old and recently completed an MBA degree with a concentration in finance. He spent six years working part to full time in an accounting practice while putting himself through school. He recently married his college sweetheart and works full time for the accounting firm as an analyst doing financial and performance audits for the firm's clients. He works on a team with two other people. Tom believes that with another year or two of experience he can become a senior analyst with the firm. However, Tom sees the next five to ten years will require a significant amount of time being on the road, perhaps three to four days a week for eight to ten months in a year. Tom and his wife, Carrie, look toward beginning a family, and though Tom does not mind being on the road, he knows he will want to devote as much time as possible to his family.

Tom is beginning to consider a career move. He and Carrie have had serious talks about a possible change. He would like to open his own consulting business. He is confident of his technical skills in finance and accounting, but is worried about his lack of knowledge and experience about owning and operating a business himself. For this reason, he wants to learn more about business opportunities in franchised accounting and financial services. He believes a franchising approach could provide for him a specific format for operating a business and provide training and skill in how to find and develop a client base.

Is Tom a likely candidate for becoming a franchisee? Is Tom the type of person that a franchise system would encourage to become a franchisee?

2-1   INTRODUCTION

Franchising provides the means for a person to own and operate a small business using a workable business format. Franchising is a joint effort between the franchisor and the franchisee with mutually approved activities which may include site selection, interior and exterior decoration, product preparation, advertising, selling skills, buying, and employee training.

2-2   JOINT BUSINESS RELATIONSHIP

Franchising is an exciting opportunity for franchisor and franchisee. Both have an opportunity to use their capital resources and desire to succeed in a cooperative business relationship in order to generate fair and equitable profits that will reward their individual commitments and efforts. As a method of distribution of products and services, franchising provides opportunities for growth and long-term success for both parties. Before committing to a franchising relationship, however, it is important to evaluate the situation of the franchisor and the franchisee and the critical factors of the business opportunity being considered.

In franchising, often the factors critical to success are rooted within the franchisor–franchisee relationship. A franchisor operates one business—the franchise system. Also, the franchisor *influences* other business operators—the franchisees—as they run their own businesses as parts of an integrated *franchise system*. Because the franchisor and franchisee have different roles to play in achieving success for the franchise system, they need to understand the importance of cooperation and mutual trust in developing and maintaining successful franchised businesses. With this understanding, the franchisor and franchisee can reach their own personal goals while contributing to the achievement and success of each other.

2-3   FRANCHISING BASICS

Franchising is a successful means of operating a business for two primary reasons: (1) the preparation a franchisee undertakes before opening a licensed franchise outlet, and (2) the degree of personal involvement brought to the business activities by both franchisee and franchisor. The greatest difference between starting a franchised business venture and opening an independent business lies in the training and preparation provided to the franchisee prior to opening the franchised outlet. Typically, a franchisee is taught how to initiate, run, and control all ownership and operating functions of the business.

A franchisor will generally grant the franchisee limited use of the trademark or trade name and the system (business format) in return for a royalty fee. The franchisee is trained in the proper use of trade secrets, operating procedures, product and service promotion, and employee training, if necessary, to develop and maintain a profitable franchised business.

For example, Orange Julius allows its franchisees to use the name, trademark, and logo, and sell the special drink products in return for a royalty fee of 5 percent on gross sales, plus an additional advertising fee of 1 percent of gross sales. In addition, most of the outlet locations are owned or leased by Orange Julius and then leased or subleased to franchisees at a small profit.

Another example is First Interstate Bancorp of California. This bank holding company consists of formerly independent banks now in the First Interstate Bancorp network. Local ownership and equity is maintained through the local corporation and its board of directors, but the name and logo of First Interstate Bancorp, plus the basic financial products offered to the public, are controlled by the franchisor. The local bank pays First Interstate Bancorp a fee based on interest income. It is important to note, the use of the trade name and the financial service systems constitute the *value added* by the franchisor to the franchisee.

In the automotive industry, the car or truck is the trademarked product provided by the franchisor (e.g., General Motors Pontiac Division) to the franchisee—the local Pontiac dealership. In contrast to the auto/truck example are gasoline stations. In this example, often the most important *value added* by the franchisor is the amount and regularity of advertising allocated by the franchisor to a specific market area. Advertising and name recognition are often the most important *value added* by the franchisor in the fast-food industry.

2-4   FRANCHISING ADVANTAGES AND DISADVANTAGES

The many success stories in franchising include McDonald's, Singer Sewing Machine Company, General Motors, Coca-Cola, Kentucky Fried Chicken, Midas, Century 21, Wendy's, and Holiday Inns. These provide visible examples of large, successful franchised systems. Today, other types of businesses are seeking growth through franchising. Doctors, lawyers, dentists, accountants, and opticians have developed franchise systems, some of which have multistate markets. Home services such as maid services, heating and air conditioning, remodeling, babysitting, carpeting, decorating, and eldercare franchises have developed and are achieving success.

Most recently, home-based franchised business opportunities have had explosive growth. Why? A carefully designed and operating franchise system will target markets of two-income families with more disposable income and less disposable time. Comprehensive training, large exclusive territory, and ongoing franchisor support minimize risk for the franchisee and franchisor. In essence, the benefits to be gained from a successful franchising chain are enormous.

2-4a   Advantages to the Franchisee

The franchisee gains certain potential advantages from being involved in a franchise relationship. The five main advantages are discussed in this section.

Established Product or Service

Often, consumers are already aware of the name and reputation of the product or service the franchise system offers, a significant advantage to the prospective franchisee. Each year most mainline franchise systems spend millions of advertising dollars to keep the public aware of their gasoline, soft drink, food, or service. Such franchisors generally spend a large portion of the advertising budget on national campaigns through television or radio commercials and full-page advertisements in popular magazines and newspapers. If a franchise system deals with a specialty product such as Snap-on Tools, the most effective advertising may be through trade publications and truck advertising targeted at specific market segments such as home repair buffs and auto mechanics.

In contrast to national franchise systems, small franchisors tend to use local print, electronic media, and point-of-purchase promotions to attract customers within a region or more localized area. In either case, the franchisor commonly shares advertising costs with the local franchisee. Typically, the franchisor will charge the franchisee an advertising fee based on the gross revenues generated by each of the franchised units in the region or area.

Technical and Managerial Assistance

A second major advantage to the franchisee is the technical and managerial assistance provided by the franchisor. One can become a franchisee without prior experience in a certain line of business because the franchisor will provide the instruction necessary to operate a franchised unit, including onsite training in a pilot store. Once operating his or her own franchised unit, the franchisee receives ongoing support and assistance in managing day-to-day operations and advice for dealing with any crisis situations which arise in the operation of the business.

Most business consultants would warn a potential entrepreneur not to attempt a business venture in an unfamiliar field. Franchising provides an opportunity to do exactly that—and be successful. In fact, some franchise systems *prefer* franchisees that have no prior experience in their particular business field. The franchisor can train the new franchisee in the methods and procedures of the franchise company. There will be little or nothing to be unlearned, no bad habits to break. In effect, many franchisors look not for people who know the industry but for people who are motivated to achieve success and are willing to learn and follow franchisor guidance and instruction.

The new franchisee will receive technical assistance which often includes location and site selection, store layout and design, store remodeling (if the franchisee is converting an existing site), inventory purchase and control methods, equipment and fixture purchasing or leasing, and assistance with the grand opening of the new franchised business. Although many franchise systems provide a broad array of specific services as identified in this section, some franchisors provide only selected types of assistance. The types of technical assistance provided are usually what the franchisor has found to be *absolutely essential* for helping the franchisee to become successful. Prospective franchisees should realize that a full range of technical assistance is not always offered by every franchise system to its franchisees.

Quality Control Standards

A third major advantage to the franchisee concerns the quality control standards imposed by the franchisor upon the franchisee. Properly administered and controlled, such standards help the franchise to achieve constructive, positive results by ensuring product or service uniformity throughout the franchise system. By setting and maintaining high standards, a franchisor does the franchisee a genuine service. The franchisee will learn what operations and performance are necessary to be a success. Further, standards of quality are vital in presenting a consistent patronage image, ensuring return business, maintaining employee morale and pride in work, and instilling in employees the value of teamwork.

But, why would a franchisee want to continually have to meet standards imposed by someone else? As long as the quality standards are assessed and maintained, the standards serve both franchisor and franchisee. For example, if restaurant franchisees courteously and efficiently serve an appealing meal in an attractive and comfortable setting, then they have a better chance to attract and maintain a large, loyal clientele, which clearly benefits the franchisor as well.

Less Operating Capital

The fourth major advantage often cited is that an entrepreneur can open a franchised business with less cash than if he or she were to open a business independently. Why? First, a franchisee can start up with considerably less operating capital because the business may not require as much inventory as a comparable nonfranchised business. Second, the knowledge and experience of the franchisor available to the franchisee concerning how much stock is needed and when to reorder can dramatically reduce the potential for aging of stock, waste or spoilage of perishables, and unprofitable storage of low demand items. Third, a new franchisee may be able to receive some financial assistance in the form of credit, as cash or as inventory consigned from the franchisor or from the franchisor's financial resources. Also, other factors associated with a new venture, such as having access to existing architectural drawings for the store and knowing how best to utilize floor space for the product or service, can save the franchisee countless hours and dollars, especially considering the number of seat-of-the-pants judgments that must be made three to six months prior to opening a new business.

Other advantages can be realized once the business is in operation. For example, the franchisee may share collateral benefits, such as business insurance and health insurance, which because of the group buying power of the parent company are often less expensive than the same coverage sought independently. A franchisee also may have a higher profit margin than a comparable independent business owner because of group purchasing power, proven operation and quality standards, potentially lower inventory costs, and product or service improvements made through research and development by the franchisor that will become available to the franchisee. Such advantages enable the franchisee to keep the product or service competitive.

Opportunities for Growth

A fifth potential advantage concerns growth opportunities for operating a territorial franchise. A **territorial franchise** guarantees no competition from the same franchisor within a specified geographic boundary. It may later be in a position to subfranchise or license other persons to operate stores belonging to the territorial franchisee. If a new franchised company is enjoying successful growth, its franchisees could have more opportunity for financial gain as territorial franchisees. In an **operating franchise**, an owner-operator runs the business usually within an exclusive territory and receives assistance from the franchisor (parent company) or from both a territorial franchisee *and* the parent company. The main distinction, then, is that the operating franchisee typically does not have the legal right to establish subfranchisees or licensees; the territorial franchisee does. However, there is no real standard within the franchise field to clearly distinguish a territorial franchise from an operating franchise for all franchised companies. There are even a fair number of operator franchisees who, after careful reinvestment of profits into new locations for the franchised company, have developed their own chain of outlets within the franchise chain. Examples of this can be found in Orange Julius, A&W Root Beer, and Mister Donut. Therefore, opportunity for growth as a franchisee exists whether one has territorial rights or is in business simply as an operating franchisee.

The common thread through these five advantages concerns the *advice and assistance available from the franchisor to help the franchisee become successful,* which the franchisor could not have offered without having gained a thorough understanding of the business by spending considerable time in the specific business field. Therefore, the opportunity to benefit from another's experience—to learn from someone else's mistakes—is the primary advantage of entering a franchising relationship.

These five advantages have to be tempered with a disclaimer, however, because what is suggested as distinct advantages to the franchisee may not be so for *every* franchisee. What may be a decided advantage to one could be inconsequential to another. Therefore, the merits and demerits, advantages and disadvantages, for an individual should be considered in relation to the conditions surrounding a particular franchising opportunity.

2-4b   Disadvantages to the Franchisee

Most franchising agreements work well for both the franchisor and the franchisee. The franchising agreement is meant to develop a strong relationship between these two mutually bound profit seekers. The franchising approach helps both parties realize profits and develop a healthy and prosperous business life. Potential disadvantages to the franchisee, however, are discussed in this section.

Failed Expectations

The franchisor's business expertise, experience, selling methods, trademark, and advertising typify what a franchisee seeks to acquire. Because of such assistance, the franchisee sees value in the franchisee–franchisor relationship. Without such assistance, there would be little reason for a prospective business owner to enter a franchising agreement. But if a franchisor's sales practices mislead a potential franchisee about what he or she will receive from the franchisor, the franchisee's expectations will of course not be met. Misleading or fraudulent sales practices can actually victimize some potential franchisees.

Franchises are promoted through newspapers, magazines, trade conventions, telegrams, the Internet, and even phone calls from franchised companies. Some prospective franchisees fail to carefully read the fine print or consult an attorney and as a result lack understanding of the legal and practical implications of the agreement.

What the franchisor will provide is written in the franchising agreement, not necessarily in the sales literature associated with the agreement. Because these agreements can be rather lengthy and are often in small print, some prospective franchisees may not understand what they are about to agree to legally. If a prospective franchisee seeks a modification in the contract, the franchisor may be unwilling to approve any such modification, especially if it represents a substantial deviation from the standard contract.

Franchisors often contend they can serve franchisees best when franchisees conform to quality standards. In drafting the franchising agreement, franchisors particularly focus on the factors believed to be most important to ensure this conformance. It is implicitly important to the franchisor that a prospective franchisee recognize the psychologically superior position the franchisor likes to maintain.

Service Costs

Another consideration that can be an enduring disadvantage to a franchisee is that services provided by a franchisor have costs which must be borne by the franchisee. These services are expense items to the franchisee. In some instances, they may be of dubious value. It may be difficult for the franchisor to maintain the services promised and initially rendered as stipulated in the written franchising agreement. The franchisee could find the franchise fees or royalties excessive, especially after being in business for several months and realizing the effect that the royalties and fees are having on the franchisee's anticipated return on investment. Franchisees may even find it psychologically difficult to share profits earned from their own business by remitting a required percentage back to the franchisor.

Overdependence

The third potential disadvantage to the franchisee concerns the franchisor–franchisee relationship. The relationship may prove to be detrimental if a franchisee develops a problem of overdependence on the franchisor. A franchisee can become too dependent on the advice of the franchisor to address operations, crises, changing market conditions, pricing strategy, or promotions and so may fail to apply commonsense and knowledge of local customers and market conditions.

Recent discussion with a franchisor of auto parts illustrated this disadvantage. This franchisor has a policy of no price discounting, *if possible*, to maintain a uniform pricing structure across the franchised organization's outlets. A franchisee in a large city in the Southwest failed to take note of the phrase "if possible" and so lost an opportunity to substantially increase volume by attracting the regular business of an auto repair and service center with seventeen locations. The franchisee could have obtained a contract with the repair center if he had been willing to adjust the bid downward only 0.2 percent. In this case, the franchisor rightfully scolded the franchisee for not using commonsense. A fairly knowledgeable businessperson knows that the guarantee of a large volume of business is a solid reason for price discounting.

Restrictions of Freedom of Ownership

The franchising contract may contain restrictions or requirements that an independent businessperson would not have to satisfy. For example, territorial restrictions imposed by the franchisor may limit the number of potential customer contacts a franchisee might see; or, territories may overlap or be inequitably determined by a franchisor. The franchisee may be required to offer a particular product or service that he or she would not otherwise choose to offer. Further, a franchisee may find that some of the franchisor's advertising or promotions are impractical given local market conditions, or that a promotion or advertisement is offensive or unwisely encourages the sale of relatively unprofitable product or service lines offered by the franchise.

Termination of Agreement

The next major disadvantage concerns a franchisee's decision to terminate the franchising relationship as a result of perceived or real differences with the franchisor. Lack of cooperation from the franchisor can make it difficult to sell the business to a prospective buyer or to simply dissolve the business entirely. Virtually every franchising agreement contains provisions concerning the franchisee's transfer rights, termination and renewal of the agreement, or a covenant not to compete. Any one or all three of these provisions could be invoked by the franchisor if the franchisee fails to heed all the provisions of the franchising agreement.

Performance of Other Franchisees

Perhaps the least-considered potential disadvantage to the franchisee is the effect that lackluster performance by other franchisees can have on one's own business. If the franchisor becomes lax in managing the franchise system or does not enforce the quality standards imposed throughout the network, poor performance by some in the franchise network can affect the sales of others. Usually, a customer of a multiunit franchised company will tend to blame the entire franchise and not the single operating unit for poor service or low quality. As the franchising adage goes, a stale cup of coffee at one location will lose customers for other locations.

The common theme in these disadvantages involves the dependence the franchisee has on the franchisor. The greatest disadvantage is the tendency by franchisees to be overly dependent on the franchisor and franchise system. Franchisees can depend too much on advice from the parent company, rely too heavily on its advertising and promotion efforts, or follow too closely the operating manual suggestions while neglecting their own commonsense and intuitive understanding of the local market and conditions.

In summary, the franchisee must determine whether the advantages of the franchisor's training, operation manuals, blueprints, and products and services outweigh the disadvantages always present in working with a parent company. The franchisee should carefully weigh the possible advantages against the disadvantages, while at the same time analyzing the potential profitability of the business, to determine his or her willingness to enter this business activity with the conditions imposed by the franchisor. A franchisee should realize that even though he or she owns the business, certain standards and performance quotas will be established and demanded by the franchisor to ensure that the franchise system will be profitable and successful in the competitive business environment.

2-4c   Advantages to the Franchisor

Considering possible channels of distribution for General Motors cars, Alfred P. Sloan saw the two primary options to be "manufacturer-owned, manager-operated dealerships, or the selling of cars by anyone and everyone, as cigarettes are sold—with the manufacturer maintaining a system of service agencies." Sloan concluded that the "franchise system, which has long prevailed in the automobile industry, is the best one for manufacturers, dealers, and consumers."[1] The success of franchising in the auto industry is well documented, but the franchising approach has not worked as well in the selling of furniture, for instance. One the other hand, franchising has become quite successful in appliance sales, oil distribution, restauranting, convenience stores, and many service-oriented business fields.

Expansion

Most businesses grow through expansion of their distribution system. Yet the average business owner wishing to broaden distribution of a product or service may not have the same options to consider as Sloan. In fact, franchising may be the only viable option for growth, unless that owner would choose to become part of a larger existing company as a captive producer or a franchisee, or choose to expand at a slow pace by saving profits earned from the principal business. Whereas a business with sizable funds can choose from several alternatives to expand distribution, a business with limited capital and experience may find franchising to be the only viable method of expansion. Expansion efforts are costly and franchising provides an opportunity to share this burden on the road to success.

WHITE HEN PANTRY STORES

White Hen Pantry stores will soon begin to disappear from the Chicago area as 7-Eleven assimilates the locally owned convenience chain. The acquisition is to make the Chicago area one of 7-Eleven's giant top five markets. White Hen franchise owners have the option to operate under the current name until the original franchise agreement runs out, but some area owners are already switching over.

Adapted from "White Hens Here in Slow Rebranding to 7-Eleven Name," Business Ledger (12 February 2007), www.thebusinessledger.com/articles.artId=1443.

Perhaps the single greatest reason for an entrepreneur to create a franchising chain is to allow a business to expand with limited capital, risk, and equity investment. A franchisor does not have to inject large sums of money or incur major debt to expand the business into new locations. Franchisors can authorize and then locate franchised operations in selected areas gradually or they can choose to develop rapidly by licensing business locations throughout a region or country.

A franchised company requires few management personnel and therefore has a lower staff payroll and fewer staff problems. This suggests a greater likelihood of effective monitoring and control of company operations. Also, a franchisor may find potential investors willing to buy into the franchised company if the company is seen to promise growth and continuing profitability. Similarly, persons with little or no experience in the franchisor's business field may be willing to buy a franchise as a potentially profitable investment. Thus, franchising can attract capital through direct investment in the parent company or through the sale of franchises to be used for expansion of the franchise system.

The franchising approach provides an opportunity for the parent company to expand into geographic areas that otherwise might not be likely locations for expansion. When a franchised company acquires a franchisee within a particular community, the franchisee may be able to acquire a commercial site that the parent company would be unable to acquire because of the fear of potential influence patterns and other vagaries that can be associated with zoning ordinances, business regulations, and licensing restrictions in the local community.

Another reason to expand through franchising is that this type of growth can simplify the management structure and reporting requirements associated with expansion, especially compared with the expansion of a corporate chain. For a corporate chain, a strategy that looks for more rapid growth than the corporation has previously experienced usually requires the formation of a sizable management structure to develop, implement, monitor, and control the enhanced level of operations. Unless a corporation carefully manages its growth phase, growth can be as much a problem as an opportunity. The capacity of central management to control the business activity may not be able to keep pace with the growth of the corporation itself. When this happens, inconsistency in operations, breakdowns in communications, coordination problems, and even cash flow and liquidity problems can virtually negate the advantages of the expansion. In contrast, rapid expansion through a franchising network enables the franchisor to devote more time to operational planning, market analysis and assessment, quality control, and strategies for improving the franchise system itself.

Motivation

Another advantage to the franchisor is that the franchisee is usually more motivated than the company-employed manager. When a franchised unit is operated by an owner as opposed to a company-employed manager, that unit will usually benefit from the owner's motivation, self-direction, and personal interest in the success of that operation. In addition, the franchisee is often a respected and influential member of the local community, and so will have community support which will be of assistance in developing a franchised outlet.

DID YOU KNOW?

Of workers in large firms, 28 percent are satisfied with their jobs.
Of workers at small businesses, 41 percent are satisfied with their jobs.
Adapted from Entrepreneur (December 2006): 32, www.entrepreneur.com/expandbeyond.

Operation of Nonunion Business

In the decision whether to franchise, a business owner should also give consideration to the area of employee and labor relations. There is greater likelihood that company-owned units would be more attractive to union organizers than franchised units, largely because a single franchised operating unit is less likely to be unionized and to develop labor relations appropriate to the local supply-and-demand conditions of the labor pool. The advantage to the franchisor in this regard is the savings in the amount of wages and benefits to be paid to the employees. To put it in plain terms, often it costs less to operate a nonunion business.

Bulk Purchasing

An advantage exists for franchisors in businesses that require inventory of parts, completed units for sale, and supplies or packaging associated with the production or sale of the product. Economy of scale in purchasing (i.e., purchasing power) can be achieved more rapidly by a company choosing franchising compared with a company that expands through company-owned units.

Other Advantages

Another advantage is that a franchisor is free to use part of the company's capital for purposes other than expansion, because the franchisee has also invested capital in the new operating unit. In addition, cooperative advertising (with franchisor and franchisee sharing costs of advertising) tends to achieve much more than individual advertising. Because the franchisee is usually a member of the local community where the franchised unit is opened, the franchisor also is less likely to stir up hostility than he or she would by opening a "foreign" or non locally owned corporate chain store. Finally, because the franchisee is a local citizen, not just someone moving into a community to manage a chain store, the franchisee would tend to have a perspective different from that of the corporate manager and would try to ensure community acceptance, sales growth, and profitability over a longer term.

2-4d   Disadvantages to the Franchisor

Franchising is not a miraculous or problem-free solution to a distribution problem. The idea of using money belonging to other individuals to finance the major part of a business expansion is no doubt exciting, but the application of that idea can be fraught with difficulty. The foremost challenge is how to maintain control of the expanding franchise system and oversee the general operation of each business. Also, a franchisee may in time reevaluate the franchising relationship and come to the conclusion that success would come, even without the franchisor. Two perspectives are used to describe potential disadvantages. First, advantages of company-owned units will be discussed alongside disadvantages of franchised units; second, difficulties associated with the franchisor–franchisee relationship will be listed.

Company-Owned versus Franchised Units

Expanding operations by establishing company-owned units has several clear advantages over expanding by franchising. A parent company has more control over units the company owns; can institute changes in policy and procedures more readily; can change company mission and market strategy more quickly and perhaps more effectively; and can test out new products or processes with less time and paperwork. Also, because the company controls the outlets by virtue of ownership, the system of reporting—the monitoring and control of the operating units—should be more efficient and effective because of the hierarchy of managerial authority. The ownership not only establishes company strategies and operating policies but is also assured of the implementation of these strategies by virtue of its maintaining ownership of the company through to the retail distribution outlets. Those responsible for carrying out the operations of a company-owned retail outlet are employees of the company, not independent business owners. And, regardless if the ownership chooses to expand through company-owned outlets or through franchising, it will need to offer basically the same services from the home office—sales promotion, marketing research, accounting and information systems, and a field sales department or unit.

Two other significant points tend to favor the company-owned approach over the franchising approach to expansion. First, a franchisee might typically expect to recover the initial investment in perhaps two to three years—a 33.3 to 50 percent return on investment to the franchisee. This means that the franchisor has effectively lost out on making this remarkable profit single handedly. The franchisor could probably get the money necessary for expansion more cheaply by dealing directly with equity investors or obtaining loans from financial institutions. Second, there can be some legal advantages to a company-owned, fully integrated operation. Integrated chains of stores such as Federated Department Stores—which owns Macy's, Bloomingdales, and recently acquired the May Company names such as Famous-Barr, L. S. Ayers, Foley's, Marshall Fields, and Lord and Taylor—or WalMart Stores, Inc. have become successful without franchising. According to author Charles Vaughn, "Integrated chains do not so often come under antitrust fire, class action suits, and other legal attacks."[2] Litigation can drag on for so long and become so costly that a business owner considering franchising could be scared off for the legal reason alone.

Potential Problems

Within the franchisor–franchisee relationship are three categories of potential disadvantage for the franchisor: problems of recruitment, communication, and freedom.

Recruitment.

The recruitment problem concerns the difficulty of finding promising franchisees. Although many seek franchising as a means to enter business, most prospective franchisee candidates lack the experience, motivation, or the proper capital backing needed to become successful franchisees. Also, prospective franchisees may not fully realize the amount of time, work, and responsibility required to own and operate an ongoing franchised business.

Communication.

As in any business relationship, communication problems can arise. In franchising, a franchisee may develop a sense of independence and no longer feel a need to rely on the franchisor for the successful operation of the business; he or she may conclude that the business would run just as smoothly without the franchisor's advice and seek to discontinue the relationship. This feeling can stem from the franchisee's having to pay fees and royalties established by the franchising agreement. Most franchisees pay fees to the franchisor on the basis of the franchised unit's gross income. Some franchisees may have a difference of opinion as to what constitutes "gross income" or develop a reluctance to disclose gross income figures to the franchisor. For this reason it is important that the formula for determining any fees or royalties be clearly stated in the written franchising agreement and understood by both franchisor and franchisee. When such understandings exist, the likelihood of resentments based on unclear language or personal intent can be minimized. Also, communication problems can arise between the field office staff and the individual franchisees. The franchisor's staff is available to assist as well as monitor performance of franchisees. Both parties play an important part in the successful delivery of the product or service through the franchised company network. In any organizational arrangement, however, misunderstandings, personality differences, and political maneuverings can blunt the effectiveness of the franchising system to deliver the product or service. Each party to the franchising agreement should operate within the proper boundaries of the agreement, the laws governing business transactions, and professional codes of ethics. When those involved in continuing business transactions deal with one another honestly and professionally, communication problems will not typically occur.

Loss of Freedom

The third potential disadvantage concerns the franchisor's loss of freedom as new franchisees become part of the franchise system. Independent business persons can easily make decisions and change policies within their organizations; but once a franchise system is developed, the franchisor or parent company must get permission (often negotiated individually) from franchisees to introduce new products, to add or eliminate services, or to change operating policies. Thus, the franchisor stands to lose a substantial amount of control as a franchise system increases its size. It can become difficult for the franchisor to modify product or process in order to meet the ever-changing needs of customers, particularly if the franchise system is spread across a large geographic area containing varied consumer markets. For example, in 1997, McDonald's introduced a fifty-five-cent "meal deal" to increase overall sales value. It was resisted by franchisees for cost and profitability concerns. The company then limited the offer for only the breakfast hours, only to drop it later.

Careful examination of the franchising-only approach in contrast to the company-owned-only approach to business growth has brought many successful companies to the following conclusion: The use of a combination of company-owned and franchisee-owned operating units appears to be superior to the use of either approach exclusively.[3] Thus, the two approaches do not have to be considered mutually exclusive; they can supplement each other, stimulating growth for the company and strengthening the firm's ability to meet the challenges and opportunities of the marketplace.

2-5 FRANCHISING YOUR BUSINESS

With the success that has come to many firms that became franchise systems over the past forty to fifty years, many small business owners have asked themselves the question: "Can I turn this into a franchise system?" Various thoughts can come into a business owner's mind about growth, recognition, opportunity for significant increase in income, and so forth, but serious consideration should not be given to the idea of becoming a franchisor until the business owner has done considerable homework. Before the business owner gives any thought to the legal issues determined and franchise documents developed, a host of business issues should first be addressed.

The first step for a business owner to assess whether to become a franchisor is to carefully evaluate the present business on several criteria. Being the only one to offer a particular product or service in your market area is not all that important. Being the first business to franchise in a product or service category is not that important either.

Consider the experience of Dave Thomas, founder and CEO of Wendy's International. When Thomas started Wendy's in 1972, conventional wisdom strongly suggested that the existing hamburger or fast-food chains had already saturated the market. The same belief was said about pizza chains. Entering the pizza restaurant business in 1983, John Schnatter, founder of Papa John's

Pizza, was given little chance for success. The market was "nearly saturated" by the existing chains such as Pizza Hut (1959), Pizza Inn (1963), and Domino's (1967), as well as other lesser known chains that Papa John's Wendy's would have as competitors.[4]

The dot.com craze that began in the early 1990s, and saw a meltdown in 2000 to 2001, serves as another example. Conventional wisdom in the 1990s was to bring out a new Internet concept or application, whether it be for business to business (B2B) or business to consumer (B2C). Venture capital flowed into Internet start-ups based on the rising promise of Internet marketing. Little credence was being given to the idea that a business must provide value in order to survive. The meltdown of NASDAQ (nearly a 62 percent decline in value between March 2000 and March 2001) demonstrates that "conventional wisdom" may be a craze, nothing more than fuzzy-headed thinking. Both NASDAQ and the NYSE have rebounded completely and have reached new highs in both market exchanges in 2007, reflecting the strong growth and resilience of the U.S. economy.

Regardless of what the so-called experts say, the market will accept great products and services that meet consumer needs—what the consumer wants and in the way the consumer wants it. As consumer attitudes, interests, and tastes change, large firms in the marketplace often feel secure. Without a constant eye on the changing interests, attitudes, and habits of the consumer large firms, their market share can be vulnerable to small innovative providers of competitive products and services. At some point, the big firm may find it is no longer the guerilla on the block. Large firm inertia has given rise to creation and rapid development of firms such as Starbucks, Kinkos, Home Depot, UPS, Yahoo, and Amazon.com.

2-5a Consider the Criteria for a Good Franchise

What should one look for to assess the feasibility if a business is franchisable? If it can, will my franchised system be successful? The following questions can help a prospective franchisor determine whether to take the steps to develop a franchise system.

Do I have the entrepreneurial spirit for being a business owner/franchisor

The prospective franchisor/business owner is willing to influence change. Often found among successful franchise entrepreneurs are traits such as willingness and interest to scan for opportunities, taking initiative and action, and then persevering to reach closure on the opportunity.[5] This type of person, as founder of a franchise system, incorporates such traits into the firm's strategy, continually searching the marketplace for new opportunities to expand the franchise system.

Do I have a prototype store or unit

If you are not currently in business and being successful at it, stop. If you have an existing store or operating unit ask yourself several questions. Do I continue to have trouble training employees to understand the process of how I do business? Do I think that I can be more operationally efficient but cannot seem to get there? Is my profit margin smaller than what I think it can be? Can I make a profit and meet the price competition I face in the market? Do I see more first-time customers than returning customers? Do I know what my firm is distinctly competent in providing to the customer? Am I trying to be "all things to all people," expanding my product and service line to meet any competitive contingency? If three or more of these questions are on target, stop. You are not ready to enter the competition as a franchisor.

Once a small business owner is confident that the operating unit or store is operating efficiently, making reasonable profits, has regular repeat customers, and has operating methods that you have taught to employees successfully, *then* open another store, and perhaps a third store. If your confidence has remained high and you know from your experience as a successful multiunit small business that the questions raised here are not central to what you do everyday, then you are ready to consider becoming a franchisor.

It is not absolutely essential for a small business to have two or more locations before assessing franchising, but it is helpful. Issues such as managerial coordination, ordering, inventory, scheduling, accounting, equipment, location, multisite advertising, and vendor issues can arise for a business with two or more locations that are not readily identifiable within a single location business. Such issues as these are often encountered by multiunit operators and must be overcome to become a successful franchise system.

Can I replicate my prototype unit(s)

Is the operating system, operating so smoothly at the prototype location, transferable to other locations—which will not be owned and operated by me—so that every customer is delivered precisely the same product or service, the same way, every time? Can I document the knowledge and experience of being a business owner-operator of my business into methods and procedures that will work every time for someone else? Can I do so in any location?

Can I teach my system for operating this business to others—prospective franchisees and their staffs

A franchisor must provide not only the methods of preparing and delivering the products or services, but also the methods or skills needed to operate a business. Do I have the patience and skill to teach adult learners my process so they can duplicate it successfully? Can the operating requirements—for both product and service preparing and delivery as well as the "business" side of the business—be learned in a few days to a few weeks? Or, will it take two or more years to learn how to successfully run this business?

In a critical and dispassionate view, are the products or services I have any good?

Step away from your own biases about the products or services you provide to a customer. Do you know what the customer really thinks about your product or service? How do your customers view your product or service? In comparing your products or services with the best of the competition, how do your offerings compare? Is any product or service you offer superior to the competition? If not, why? If so, in what way? How have you determined price? Is price based primarily on costs, or on competitive pressure? Is price based on characteristics or the desired image of the product or service? Is service after sale part of the offering price? Do you have a warranty program? How often is it sold and how is it priced with regard to the original product or service offered? Precisely what is the feature that makes your product or service superior to the competition? Is this just your opinion? Do you have any primary market data to support your opinion? If not, why?

Can your product or service meet the test of distance

Will your product or service sell in the next town up the road? Will it sell in Peoria? San Jose? New York? Los Angeles? and Dodge City? How about Waterloo, Iowa? Even if you have the best products or services offered in a particular business category in your town, are you sure anyone outside your neighborhood or town will want them? Often, the only true test is to open a location in another town and operate the business using the same standards and practices as you do in your prototype or original store unit.

Does your product or service provide you with a differential advantage over the competition

Have you carefully assessed your products or services against your competition's products or services? Have you sampled your customers to learn why they buy from you? On what was your criteria based: Convenience? Price? Quality of product or service? Is the feature that distinguishes your product or service from the competition sustainable? Is it easy to imitate? Is your differential advantage based on newness of equipment that can be purchased by the competition at any time?

What have you done to make sure consumers will want your product or service tomorrow

Customer purchasing patterns will change. How might a change affect the popularity of or desire for your product or service? Are alternatives or substitutes to your product or service being discussed within the trade? Have any alternatives or substitutes been introduced? Are consumers beginning to choose an alternative product to yours? If so, do you have a strategy to adapt to changes in consumer preferences or market conditions? For example, overall annual sales figures for soft drink beverages have become fairly stable recently. Has the soft drink market finally reached maturity in the United States? Coca-Cola is not waiting to find it. Coca-Cola Company has recently acquired fruit drinks, teas, and natural beverages to move with the changing tastes of today's consumer for nonalcoholic, healthful beverages.

Do you know who is your competition

If you sell hamburgers and fries, are your competitors other hamburger and fries businesses? People choose alternative food options such as pizza or chicken instead of hamburgers and fries. Perhaps even the frozen dinners and singles in the freezer case at the grocery store compete with you for that consumer's dollars. As a franchisor, you will need to understand your competitive strengths. Are they product quality? Price? Speed of delivery? Unique application? Low cost? What is it that makes you not only different but also better than your competition? Can you upgrade your products or services? If so, how? Can you adapt with changing technology? As a franchisor you will have to be sure that you have both market strength and adaptability internal to your franchise system to survive and grow in the long term.

Are your growth plans realistic or a fantasy

If you only want two or three locations, perhaps you should not consider franchising. Develop your small chain of company-owned operations and go about your business. However, if you plan to open twenty locations in the first year of franchising and thirty the following two years and fifty locations for each of the next four years, and so forth, then franchising may be the right choice for your growth plans.

Although a host of stories abound about rapid growth in franchising, for most new franchisors, growth does not come as fast as they expected. Depending on the particular industry or business classification and the investment range required for expansion, a typical franchisor may open from five to ten units in the first year and five to fifteen units in the second year. Please consider, five to ten locations in a year is pretty impressive growth for a business entering its first stage of chain development.

Before charging off to sign up the charter group of franchisees, a franchisor should answer several questions. Are my expansion goals realistic? The answer often reduces down to "how financially capable is the new franchise system to support the growth goals?" Also, as you develop new franchise locations, how will you maintain quality and consistency at your home base, the prototype unit that you have so carefully developed? Can someone else run it as well as you? As you consider the growth of the franchise system, is what you have to offer the type of franchise people would want to own?

Further, the budding franchisor should ask: Who can afford my franchise as I plan to price it? Are there sufficient numbers of prospective franchisees available to achieve my growth goals? How do I plan to reach them? How far away do I go beyond my prototype location to attract and sign up franchisees and meet the first-year growth goal?

What skills will be needed by a franchisee to run my kind of business effectively

Are the necessary skills so specialized that finding and then effectively training prospective franchisees will prove to be difficult? How many employees will need to be hired by new franchisees to have the unit run efficiently? Do I train these people or should I rely on the franchisee to train them? What about job descriptions and human resources policies? Have I developed a personnel manual for the franchisees?

To begin strong, the franchise system will need a realistic pool of potential franchisees who are capable of buying the franchise and also can operate their new business to your standards. They will need to recruit and hire staff after the first round of assistance you provide. They will need to provide much of the needed training after the initial training is accomplished with each new franchisee. Given the nature of your specific franchise system and its operational needs, is there a sufficient pool of labor available to support your franchise system's growth and continued development?

What type and how much support can I provide to my franchisees

Good franchise systems will provide all the needed ingredients for franchisees to operate efficiently and succeed as a business. The central need for the franchisee is that the franchisor continue to deliver a program of sustainable competitive advantage for the franchise system. This means the franchisor provides the appropriate products, services, training, advertising program, operational procedures, reporting methods, research and development, field support, and other factors that allow for continual efficient and effective operation of the franchise system.

Asking oneself these questions can provide a good assessment of what a potential franchisor's comparative advantage may be, and lead to security that the product and service feature will provide advantage in the marketplace and appraise oneself of the minimum requirements for developing a chain through franchising.

Remember, consumers are fickle and more sophisticated than ever before. Entering franchising, prospective franchisors must know their product and service offerings well and know how the unique or distinguishing feature of the product and service offered will sustain a comparative advantage for the firm as it competes in the marketplace. The franchisor must also know the operations process well and be able to communicate that process through training and provision of an understandable operations manual.

2-6   IS MY FIRM READY TO FRANCHISE?

A franchisor guides and assists a network of independently owned and operated businesses that produce the products or services authorized in the franchise agreement. The principle work of the franchisor is the effective operation and growth of a franchise system. Three other issues crucial to the development and maintenance of the franchise system are trademarks, sufficiency of capital for the franchisor, and amount to charge for the franchise license. Each issue is addressed in this section.

Does my franchise business have a protectable trademark?

A trademark is a symbol of a product or service and the level of quality provided by the owner of the mark (franchisor) and its licensee (franchisee). The trademark identifies the franchisor as responsible to control the quality of the licensees' (franchisees') products and services offered to the public. Licensed trademarks constitute the identity of the franchise system. The three kinds of trademarks are coined, suggestive, and descriptive trademarks.

> *Coined trademarks* can be a recognizable word or set of letters unrelated to the products or services it identifies, for example, Mobil, Midas, Visa, Kodak, Exxon, and Xerox.

> *Suggestive trademarks* identify a characteristic or feature of the franchisor's goods or services, for example, 7-Eleven (food store chain), Cyclone (wire fencing), *Business Week* (magazine), Tie Rak (ties and accessories), Snap-on (mechanics tools), Quik-N-EZ (convenience and gas store), and Mustang (car).

Descriptive trademarks are considered to be the weakest type of legal trademark and can be difficult to protect. A descriptive mark describes the product or service that is sold. Also, surnames or geographic locations are considered appropriate descriptive trademarking. The difference between a suggestive mark and descriptive mark is imprecise and may be no more than a judgment call. Examples of descriptive trademarks are Holiday Inn (motel chain), Vision Center (eyeglass and optical clinic), Outback Steakhouse (restaurant chain), and Milwaukee's Best (beer).

A franchisor should be careful to select a trouble-free trademark that can be registered. A trademark search should be made to determine the rights of any others that hold the same or similar trademark. When the mark is cleared, it should be registered on the Principal Trademark Register which constitutes notice of use and a nationwide claim on the mark.

Do I have enough capital to develop and implement the franchise program

A business entering into franchising will incur substantial expenses before the first franchisee is signed up. In addition to the questions raised and information developed in the previous section, if trade identity (i.e., a trademark) is needed, then consulting, legal, and accounting or reporting services are likely to be incurred. The franchisor will need to hire and train management and field personnel, develop a marketing program for the franchise system and a sales promotion program for the franchisees' products and services, meet compliance regulations with regard to franchise sales, and guide and assist the newly minted franchisees along their way toward success as franchised business owners.

If a franchisor sets the initial franchise fee or royalty rate on franchisee product and service sales too low, then the franchise headquarters may be unable to acquire sufficient financial resources to effectively monitor and support the franchise system. This situation raises the final question for the prospective franchisor.

What amount should I charge for my franchise

For a business to be franchised successfully, it must be profitable. Once the franchisor starts collecting fees, royalties, advertising fees, and maybe other fees such as specific training needs and site development, the franchisor may earn enough income to offset the costs of developing and maintaining a franchise system. However, the franchisor must also look at the bottom line for the franchisee. With the added costs created by the franchise system on each franchisee, will the franchisee still be profitable? Also, will the franchisee be able to receive an acceptable return on the investment made?

In addition, financial and operational questions that have direct impact on franchisees should be taken seriously by a budding franchisor. The questions are within the scope of responsibility of the franchisor. They should be addressed tactfully with an eye toward fairness to both parties—franchisee and franchisor. See Table 2-1.

The budding franchisor should have a clear understanding of the assumptions being used, the pattern of growth sought, and all facts possible applied to the myriad questions raised here to determine the amount of the initial investment. The amount should be both appropriate for the franchisee and sufficient for the franchisor to run the businesses independent but cooperatively.

2-6b   Corporate Chain, Franchise Chain, or Both?

Why would a franchise system want to have corporate stores? In the first instance, it is usually easier to raise capital with corporate stores. Generally, investors would believe that a company should own corporate locations or stores because such ownership shows that the franchise system believes that their franchise concept does in fact work! The underlying rationale is that, if the economics of a franchised unit operates profitably, why would the franchise system not own any

TABLE 2-1	TO DETERMINE WHAT TO CHARGE FOR A FRANCHISE

- How much initial investment should be required upfront?
- How much of the initial investment must be in cash?
- Could a franchisee be allowed to finance a portion of the initial investment? If so, how much?
- How much inventory will need to be carried?
- How often will inventory turn over in a week/month/year?
- Is spoilage a factor? If so, what is the rate of spoilage?
- Does the franchisee need a storefront?
- Does the franchisee need to build a building to franchisor specifications?
- Should the franchisor have the right of refusal on site selection?
- Does the franchisor want to own the land and/or building of the franchised business?
- Do the advantages outweigh the costs?
- How long should it take a new franchised location to break even?
- Should the franchise system consider using master franchising or co-branding licensing?

units itself? Thus, if a franchise system owns no units, potential investors could reasonably question if the franchise concept can be economically profitable.

Second, by owning corporate locations, the franchisor is likely to be acutely aware of not only revenues but also the profitability and investment quality of the business itself. The economic reasoning would be that the franchisor would have vested interest to lower costs through operations and system developments, product quality improvements, and continual improvements in supply agreements. Without corporate stores, a franchisor may have more incentive to improve revenues than to improve unit capital requirements or profitability.

Third, by having corporate locations, a franchisor remains close to the final customer, the end user of the franchise system's product or service. One crucial weakness for franchise systems that do not have corporate locations is that the franchisor may see the franchisee as its customer, which can be trouble if the franchisor fails to keep up with changing market conditions and customer needs and wants.

Fourth, by owning some corporate locations, a franchisor is in the position to take over a troubled or failing franchised unit, if deemed necessary; and finally, many franchisors believe that one should be able to successfully operate one or more units in order to effectively support franchisees.

Then why have any franchised units at all? There are several good reasons. First, some markets may be too small to economically justify corporate locations. Second, franchising provides the opportunity for much faster market penetration and development than just opening corporate locations. Third, it has been shown over and over again that franchisees will most always outperform corporate managers when considering both efficiency and effectiveness criteria. Finally, some people do not want to be employees of a corporation. They would rather apply their skill and drive running their own business, as a franchisee.

Perhaps then, should one consider not having any corporate locations at all? There are two significant reasons why a business should not become a pure franchised system. First, if a system only has franchisees, the system itself will likely lack sufficient capital to expand. A franchisor following the "pure" franchising model, seeking to acquire sufficient capital for expansion and growth, could focus attention upon franchise sales at the expense of providing support to existing franchisees. Second, by not having any corporate locations, the franchisor avoids potential conflicts with franchisees that may rise based on markets and site locations.

TABLE 2-2	BEST SITUATIONS IN WHICH TO FRANCHISE YOUR BUSINESS

- Most restaurant concepts can be franchised, but those that need chefs rather than cooks or have an intricate menu are more difficult.

- Firms that have broad product and/or service appeal and consumer acceptance are a natural for franchising as long as the market trends support long-term viability and growth.

- Firms whose operating margins allow for franchise fees to be charged and still leave an adequate ROI for both the franchisor and franchisee are generally suitable for franchising.

- Firms in *fragmented industries* (where most of the businesses are small and/or independent) that would benefit from brand consolidation are candidates for franchising. Consider the hair care industry of thirty years ago. It was mostly stand-alone barber shops and beauty salons. Now you have large franchise chains such as Supercuts and Great Clips with strong-to-dominant positions. However, it is still a fragmented market—even thirty years later. So, the opportunity for growth is still good.

- Firms in a stable or growing industry, where the industry itself is unburdened by significant regulation, are franchisable.

- Firms that have internal systems that are simple to execute, that can draw from a large labor pool of qualified candidates, or that can train franchisees to use the technology in a reasonable time are franchisable as well.

2-7 WHAT KINDS OF BUSINESSES SEEM TO BE APPROPRIATE TO BECOME FRANCHISED?

Dave Thomas, founder and CEO of Wendy's International, has great insight on many franchise topics. In general terms, most any business can lend itself to business-format franchising, but historically firms that sell their products or services at retail have had wider appeal than others. Thomas's advice[6] to a prospective franchisor trying to decide whether a company can be successfully franchised is provided in Table 2-2.

NEW BRANDS ARE FRANCHISING AT A BREAK-NECK SPEED

In the marketplace of 2007, what's driving business concepts into the franchise industry is the speed of the market. For example, the public's reliance on the restaurant industry is seeing exponential growth each year, which increases the opportunity for emerging and even start-up restaurant ideas to go immediately to franchising as a growth model.

There were ninety-nine new overall franchise concepts identified during the fourth quarter, making it the most robust quarter of 2006 according to FRANDATA.

That brings the annual total to 306 new franchise systems beginning for 2007

Adapted from L. Tutor, "Out of the Gate," QSR Magazine (27 April 2007), www.qsrmagazine.com/articles/features/101/new_brands-1.phtml.

2-8 INVESTING IN A FRANCHISE

Every business investment involves risk. For a potential franchisee, investing in a franchise is somewhat different from buying stocks or bonds or investing in bank certificates. Investing in a franchise generally requires both time and money. For most franchisees, time will be the greatest contribution made to the business venture: Sixty-five to eighty hours of work every week is common during the start-up of a franchised outlet.

The cost of investing in a franchise also varies according to the success of that particular franchised company. Coca-Cola bottlers, General Motors dealerships, and McDonald's restaurants are often known as *blue-chip franchises* because of their successful track records. In other, newer fields such as electronics and computing, franchised companies are newer and so investments in them are perceived as being more risky or speculative, even though these companies may be wildly successful in the future.

When investigating a franchise, one is relying not only on the performance record of the company, but also on one's personal experience, business skills, and attitude for franchise ownership. It is important that a prospective franchisee have a good understanding of his or her current business strengths and weaknesses in the fields being considered, as well as the management skills necessary to run any business.

MEXICAN QSR FRANCHISES

Mexican quick serve restaurant (QSR) franchises are experiencing double-digit growth which may be due, in part, to an overburgered marketplace. For example, a southern California chain called Baja Fresh Mexican Grill was recently purchased by Wendy's, which may be responsible for part of the current burrito mania that is spreading across the Southwest and making inroads in other parts of the country.

FranchiseHelp OnLine recently interviewed Martin Sprock, CEO and founder of Moe's Southwest Grill, a hot new player in the Mexican quick serve market. Even the name Moe's is unusual. It is an acronym for "Movie stars, Outlaws, and Entertainers." The artwork at the store sites is representative of these three groups. Instead of Southwest stucco, tile, and natural woods, what one gets is an atmosphere punctuated with the tunes from the Grateful Dead or Jimmy Hendrix.

Moe's is fanatical about being fresh. Like others in this rapidly growing food category, fresh is the recurring theme. The ingredients are prepared in the morning just before lunch, and in the afternoon for the dinner customers. All ingredients are prepared from scratch. To illustrate, Moe's doesn't even have a freezer. The chicken and steak portions are marinated and grilled without the use of lard or animal fat. Each menu item is cooked in front of the customer with menu item names from comedy movies or TV shows such as *Friends, Seinfeld, Fletch,* and *Airplane.*

The Moe's chain, founded in 2001, opened forty units in 2002 and projections called for 125 units by 2003. Moe's substantial growth has not slowing. New units are opening at a rate of two per week which will soon accelerate to three. Choosing the right locations has been instrumental in successfully launching Moe's. Sprock's multiunit franchise owners intend to extend out of the Southwest with planned openings in cities such as Miami, Raleigh, and Charleston.

Adapted from FranchiseHelp OnLine.com 4(3, part 1) (March 2003 and March 2007).

2-8a   If A Franchise System Is Struggling

Most all franchisors believe that their franchise system has potential for long-term success. However, if there has been a series of bad decisions, mismanagement, and a significant loss of customer base, what should the franchisor do? Where should the franchisor begin when problem solving? What should be the franchisor's main focus?

Step One

Listen to and learn from the existing franchisees. Without them, there is no company. Use group meetings, conference calls, one-on-one visits, e-mail, and telephone calls to communicate with each franchisee. Actively listen to find out what is important to the franchisee and the reasons why they believe the franchise system is failing them. Being able to air their concerns is the first step for franchisees to eliminate feelings of motivation, distrust, and tension felt between them and their franchisor. The outcome is clear: Learn what needs to change and take action to make those changes. It may require implementing strong national and local marketing programs, or bringing out new products and services. It may be that new training programs are needed for each franchisee and the respective employees. It may require strategy to improve profitability at the franchisee level.

Step Two

Once the factors are determined—based on franchisee input—take the steps to create the changes necessary. Involve the franchisees in each project needed, to alleviate tension, lack of motivation, and mistrust. Franchisees will know they are not only a part of the changes agreed upon but also that they have responsibilities to constructively create and implement the changes needed. Without the franchisees' buy-in, the proposed changes are likely to fail.

Step Three

In conjunction with the work that is to be done at an operational level of the franchise system, the corporate office must examine the business model it has followed that brought on the declines. It is likely that part of the problem that created the decline of the franchise company is the weakness in the franchisor's corporate model or the franchisee's business model, which lead to poor profitability, distrust, and low motivation. Franchisors should work with successful franchisees to develop new core metrics of the franchisee business model, to create the new or revised business model. This needs to be developed in a fashion that can be broken down into step-by-step how-tos, which every franchisee can implement.

Step Four

Create a culture of urgency within the corporate staff that emanates strong desire to provide valuable support to franchisees and to keep commitments. The focus is continual success of the franchisee.

Step Five

Reexamine the franchise system from top to bottom. In doing so, one may find that the franchise system is no longer the right size. The corporate level may be overstaffed and providing poor service and support. Sound leadership can develop the steps necessary to turn the franchise around for greater success in the future.

The prospective franchisee should consider additional aspects before investing in a franchise. The *Franchise Opportunities Handbook,* developed and distributed by the U.S. Department of Commerce, suggests seven areas of protection to consider before investing in a franchise (see Table 2-3).

There is a risk associated with any form of investment, and some franchises present a greater degree of risk than others. If a person decides to leave a good job to purchase and operate a franchise, he or she will probably have a lot more to lose than if that person were to choose a less risky form of investment. After all, there is always a chance that the franchise will not succeed.

Often one asks, "Which franchise system should I invest in?" No one else is you. All that anyone else can do is provide you with factual information and advice which may steer you away from a dead end or a bad decision. Do the research necessary to make a wise franchise investment decision. You must put in the time, collect secondary and primary information, assess it, examine your motives and goals, and then make an informed decision. Without a careful analysis of adequate information, a person can make the most costly decision of their lifetime.

TABLE 2-3	SEVEN STEPS FOR FRANCHISE PROTECTION

1. Protect yourself by self-evaluation.
2. Protect yourself by investigating the franchise.
3. Protect yourself by studying the disclosure document.
4. Protect yourself by checking out the disclosures.
5. Protect yourself by questioning earnings claims.
6. Protect yourself by obtaining professional advice.
7. Protect yourself by knowing your legal rights.

Source: U.S. Department of Commerce, *Franchise Opportunities Handbook* (1984), xxx–xxxii.

There are many ways to get good information about franchising. Seek out good publications in print, gather firsthand information at franchise trade shows, and search the newest vehicle to become informed about franchising—the Internet. Perhaps the most important place to look is at current franchisees. They know what works and does not work in their franchise system. Examine all sources of information available, because it is the only way you will be able to get a complete picture of the franchise industry and the particular franchise system you may join.

2-8b   Investigation

It is wise to investigate the franchise being considered by comparison shopping of other franchises in the same line of business, just as it is a good idea to look at more than one car, major appliance, or house before deciding which to buy. A *disclosure document* (sometimes called an offering circular or prospectus) will help in making the comparison in risks involved, expectations of the franchisor, franchising fees, any continuing payments required after the franchise is open, restrictions on the product or service offered, assistance and training available, statistical information about the franchise, financial statement of the franchisor, and any claims of earnings.

Carefully examine the disclosure document. Check the accuracy of the information therein by talking with more than one franchisee of that company, because no single opinion can accurately paint a composite picture of the company. If the franchise is worth considering, talk with franchisees who have been in business at least one year, as well as with a new franchisee and a well-established franchisee who has a proven track record. Across this range of franchisees, one should be able to get good advice about what to expect in the first year as well as in the future.

It is also important to examine any claims made by the franchisor or the franchised company's representative concerning sales, income, or profits expected from the franchise. Earnings claims are only *estimates*; there is no assurance that every franchisee will do as well. We will address earnings claims in another chapter as well as discuss the disclosure document in some detail.

Before deciding to come onboard with a certain franchisor, obtain independent professional assistance in reviewing and evaluating the franchise. Such assistance and advice is of particular importance in reviewing the financial statement provided and the franchising agreement to be signed. The assumption should not be made that a disclosure document reveals all that needs to be known about the rights, responsibilities, and consequences of signing a franchising agreement with a company. The disclosure document is not designed to serve that purpose. Prospective franchisees should learn precisely what they will be legally bound to do or restricted from doing, any requirements of state or local laws as they apply in the particular business field, and answers to any personal liability or taxation questions that should be considered before signing a binding contract and entering business. There is no way of stating everything that should be considered before signing, but at least one should be certain that every important promise made by the franchisor or parent company is in writing, clearly stated in the contract.

2-8c Financial Requirements

To promote an understanding of the financial requirements placed on a potential franchisee, we examine in this section those which franchisors and franchisees must consider.

Franchisor

As discussed earlier, a franchisor must consider capital requirements prior to the development of a franchise system and on a continuing basis as the system is maintained and further developed. The four capital requirement areas a franchisor must address are as follows:

1. Capital requirements for industrial research, prototype development, marketing research, and blueprint development

2. Capital requirements for the franchise package including all disclosure statements, franchisee recruitment, promotions, product and service development costs, and operations development costs

3. Working capital requirement involving the initial advertising and franchisee recruitment expenditures

4. Reserve and legal capital requirements, including money for registering the firm to do business within a state and for meeting the state's licensing or disclosure requirements (In many states, a certain amount of capital is required to be maintained—as a reserve—in order to do business in that state.)

In addition to these considerations, there can be hidden costs which must be borne, including unexpected legal, accounting, and research costs. The franchisor should consider each category of expenditure both from a chronological perspective and in terms of the total financial commitment. A chronological perspective means that capital must be available as each phase of the franchise development plan is entered. (More will be said about the phased development of a franchise system in Chapter 3.) Also, it is important that capital in all requirement categories be available when payment for these expenditures comes due. This places a formidable burden on the franchisor during development of a franchise system.

The capital requirements for a franchise operation can vary, although certain key capital requirements seem to be associated with any franchise organization (see Table 2-4). Typically, a

TABLE 2-4 CAPITAL REQUIREMENTS

	Minimum Requirements	Maximum Requirements
Research and blueprints	$ 5,000	$ 50,000
Franchise development	25,000	100,000
Working capital	50,000	500,000
Reserve legal capital	30,000	300,000
Total capital required	$110,000	$950,000
(Excluding prototype development)		

franchisor's initial capital requirements may fall somewhere between $110,000 and $950,000, plus those expenses necessary to build and furnish a company-owned prototype store or outlet. For example, a prototype outlet may be the original restaurant, used as the "design store" for all those that follow. Often a prototype is also used as the showcase or training facility for prospective franchisees. The prototype expenditures will involve the costs of land, building, fixtures, and equipment. The fixed costs of the prototype can run anywhere from $5,000 for leasing space, to over $1 million for a restaurant and as much as $7 to $15 million for a hotel or motel.

Franchisee

Like the franchisor, the franchisee will also have financial requirements to consider prior to becoming part of a franchise system. Specifically, the capital requirements or concerns of a franchise can be enumerated in the following six categories.

1. Franchising fee

2. Real estate or rental costs, including building costs

3. Personal living and travel costs

4. Equipment costs

5. Start-up expenses and inventory

6. Working capital

The start-up expenses include all legal costs associated with opening any business, such as the review of the franchising agreement plus any leases or contracts to be signed by the franchisee. In addition, an initial inventory would need to be purchased and financial commitments made before the business opens. Inventory selection may be guided by the terms of the franchising contract. For example, a drive-up and walk-in restaurant would likely have napkins, cups, plates, food packaging, place mats, and other items carrying the franchise trademark or logo. Auto parts stores and auto repair shops may have a specified inventory that comes from the parent company. Each type of franchise may vary considerably as to how much trademarked product or packaging is required for any initial inventory level in a start-up franchised business.

Other costs can become substantial and must be planned for carefully. For example, to be considered seriously as a franchisee for several of the nationally known hamburger systems, one should have about $700,000 in credit and $150,000 in liquid assets with which to lease or buy the land, building, and equipment; purchase supplies; and hire employees to operate the restaurant. If, on the other hand, the franchised system arranges for the restaurant site and to have the restaurant built, the additional cost to the franchisee may be $20,000. Added to the franchising fee of $20,000, this means a new franchisee would need $40,000. These figures are not out of the ordinary, but at the same time, not all franchising fees or start-up expenses and required credit lines are in the same range as these. Some are higher, such as in hotel or motel franchises, and many are lower. For example, a franchisee may be able to open a carpet cleaning franchise with as little as $10,000 total capital commitment.

As observed, initial costs can be substantial and working capital requirements to maintain adequate cash flow and keep the business afloat can be heavy. A franchisee should not discount personal living costs either. If an owner of a franchised business puts in sixty or more hours per week, he or she should be compensated for that time, not just in business profits but also in salary. A salary is an expense item of the business, whereas the profit made from the business is a residual.

With the financial resources required, personal time and energy committed, and risks associated with entering any business venture, franchising is not really a get-rich-quick opportunity for most franchisors and franchisees. Certainly there are some who have "made it quick," but many franchisors consider their businesses to be long-term investments and will shun prospective franchisees interested only in a fast buck. "If you are going to do that, we don't want you," says David Thomas, founder of Wendy's International.[7] Many other respected franchise organizations share Thomas's view. In effect, franchisees are not advised to get in the game unless they are planning to remain for the long haul.

The primary consideration for the franchisee is that the capital required will likely be the same or more for starting a franchise business than it will be for starting an independent business in the same field. Almost all basic business expenses (real estate, equipment, inventories, personal expenses, and start-up costs) remain the same regardless if the business is independent or a franchise. There are additional costs for a franchise including franchising fees, royalties, travel costs to and from the training facility, and training fees. It is not possible to state absolutely that the costs of becoming a franchisee will be higher than the costs of opening an independent business in the same field, but it is likely they will be higher because many people would not enter business with the amount of new equipment, the same-size building, the amount budgeted for advertising, and the costs incurred for training as they would in many franchised businesses.

2-8d   Sample Financials for Selected Lines of Franchised Businesses

Tables 2-5, 2-6, and 2-7 review business analysis information for four broadly defined categories within franchising. Included in the business services category are franchise systems such as personnel services, printing, and travel. Franchised building and construction, and a broad array of janitorial, cleaning, and supply services constitute the maintenance services category. Included in the franchised retail category are automotive, pet services, photographic services, retail food and child-related franchised systems. Education franchised service is a category unto itself. Note the number of firms reported in each category constitute a sample of providers for each category. The information shown has been provided voluntarily by franchised systems. These data are not intended to indicate precise representation of business or financial analysis for these franchise categories. Instead, the data are illustrative of franchised firms operating within the respective categories. The study was conducted by Profit Planning Group for the International Franchise Association (IFA). Data shown reflect business and financial performance reported for 2000 and subsequently published by the IFA in 2001.[8] More current data are not yet available.

Typical elements included in a franchising agreement are listed in Table 2-8. The list is not meant to contain specific elements included in *all* franchise agreements; rather, this list indicates what is *typically* included in a franchise agreement. Each franchise system is unique, having particular requirements or conditions that may not be found in the agreements of other franchise systems. Yet, the listed elements are common, and so should be understood and planned for in considering a franchised business.

Further discussions of financial topics such as cash flow, financial statements, and financial ratios are presented in Chapters 10, 11, and 16.

The income statement summarized the flow of incoming and outgoing funds for the entire year, 2000. It reflects the ability of franchise management/ownership to make sales, control expenses, and thereby earn profit. The income statement serves as a report card of management's performance over the year.

2-8e   Franchisor–Franchisee Relationship

Franchisors and franchisees have a relationship somewhat different from relationships in other cooperating business ventures. Being a franchisee is more than just managing an outlet of a company-run distribution system, or carrying a product for retail sale that has been purchased

TABLE 2-5   ANALYSIS BY LINE OF BUSINESS: OPERATING RATIOS

	Business Services	Education Related	Maintenance Services	Retail
Number of Firms Reporting	7	4	19	7
Typical Franchising Revenue	$10,387,000	$3,403,285	$3,114,292	$3,487,098
Employee Productivity Ratios				
Franchising Operations Employees	19	N/A	4	8
Franchising Revenue per Employee	$249,378	N/A	$381,769	$102,282
Gross Margin per Employee	$247,621	N/A	$293,522	$102,223
Payroll per Employee	$79,758	N/A	$116,749	$39,260
Salary per Employee	$66,503	N/A	$104,580	$38,404
Number of Franchise Locations	400	123	138	185
Locations Opened (% of total locations)	5.7	18.4	15.8	7.9
Locations Closed (% of total locations)	3.6	6	4.6	0.9
Locations Relocated (% of total locations)	0.3	0	0	0
Licenses Transferred/Resold (% of locations)	3.5	0.4	2.8	4
Franchise Revenue per Location	$26,988	$26,593	$24,848	$12,935
Locations per Franchise Employee	13	N/A	18	11
Initial Franchise Fee				
Low	$25,000	N/A	$15,450	$19,500
High	$40,000	N/A	$40,000	$20,000
Royalty Fee (% of franchisee sales/revenue)				
Low	3.5	N/A	3.5	4.9
High	6.3	N/A	6	6
National Advertising Fee				
Low	1	N/A	1	1
High	1.5	N/A	2	1
Total National Advertising Fees Collected	$1,333,470	N/A	$310,567	$0

and inventoried from a variety of wholesales, distributors, or manufacturers. Being a franchisor requires planning, monitoring, and an involvement with the franchisee that differs from the sort of interaction between the head of a company and the managers of the company-owned outlets or retailers willing to carry the product line.

Kentucky Fried Chicken franchisee in Lincoln, Nebraska, expressed the relationship rather clearly. Jim Gaylord's description of the franchisor–franchisee relationships is as follows:

> What is the relationship like? We really have three types of relationships. There is the legal agreement between the franchisor and franchisee—which requires certain activities and responsibilities from each party. Then, there is the business relationship which ties the two firms together in day-to-day activities of providing service to customers. The legal relationship is static, while the business relationship is dynamic—moving and flowing with the changing conditions of being in business. It is this business relationship that really bonds the franchisor and franchisee together. I call this relationship the "marriage." The basic understanding exists to meet the public's needs while relying on one another to provide the best products and services to the

TABLE 2-6   ANALYSIS BY LINE OF BUSINESS: INCOME STATEMENT

	Business Services	Education Related	Maintenance Services	Retail
FRANCHISE OPERATIONS INCOME STATEMENT				
Revenue				
Franchise Fees	94.9%	89.5%	86.9%	87.3%
Compliance Fees (reinstatement and late fees)	0.0	0.0	0.0	0.0
Product and Services (equipment. mdse., etc.)	3.0	10.2	11.3	11.1
Miscellaneous Income	2.1	0.3	1.8	1.6
Total Revenue	100.0	100.0	100.0	100.0
Cost of Sales (Product and Services)	3.2	9.7	11.5	18.1
Gross Profit	96.8	90.3	88.5	81.9
OPERATING EXPENSES				
Employee Expenses				
Employee Salaries, Wages, and Bonuses	26.1	17.1	30.2	35.0
Payroll Taxes	2.5	0.9	2.6	3.4
Group Insurance (medical, hospitalization)	1.4	1.1	1.1	1.5
Employee Benefits (pension, profit sharing)	1.3	0.0	0.4	1.1
Employee Training	0.1	0.2	0.3	0.4
Total Employee Expenses	**31.3**	**19.3**	**34.6**	**41.3**
Facilities Expenses				
Lease/Rent or Ownership in Real Estate	5.1	2.9	2.5	3.2
Repairs and Maintenance	0.2	0.0	0.6	0.7
Utilities (heat, light, power, water)	0.4	0.0	0.2	0.5
Property Taxes	0.1	0.0	0.0	0.1
Depreciation	1.5	0.9	1.0	2.4
Total Facilities Expenses	**7.3**	**3.8**	**4.3**	**6.9**
General and Administrative Expenses				
Telephone/Communication	1.1	0.5	1.6	1.1
Travel and Entertainment	1.9	5.8	2.8	2.9
Bad Debt Losses	1.9	0.9	3.4	0.5
Store Closing Expenses	0.0	0.0	0.0	0.0
Miscellaneous G&A Expenses	14.6	20.7	5.3	6.1
Total G&A Expenses	**19.5**	**27.9**	**13.1**	**10.6**
Franchise Development				
Franchise Sales Advertising and Promotion	4.9	11.7	6.0	6.4
Prospect Evaluation	0.4	3.9	1.1	0.1
Miscellaneous Franchise Development	0.7	1.8	1.2	0.6
Total Franchise Development Expenses	**6.0**	**17.4**	**8.2**	**7.1**
Other Franchise Operations Expenses				
Franchisee Communication and Incentives	2.3	1.6	4.2	0.2
Compliance (mystery shopping, audit rsch., etc.)	2.7	6.2	3.4	0.5
Consumer (customer relations, complaints, etc.)	0.0	0.0	0.0	0.0

TABLE 2-6 (CONTINUED)

	Business Services	Education Related	Maintenance Services	Retail
All Other Franchise Operations Expenses	3.2	1.2	5.3	5.5
Total Other Franchise Opns. Exp.	8.3	9.0	12.8	6.2
TOTAL OPERATING EXPENSES	**72.4**	**77.4**	**73.0**	**72.1**
Operating Profit	**24.4**	**12.9**	**15.5**	**9.8**
Other Income	0.0	0.0	0.2	0.2
Interest Expense (exclude mortgage interest)	1.5	0.0	1.2	0.2
Other Nonoperating Expenses	2.4	0.0	0.0	0.0
Profit before Taxes	**20.5%**	**12.9%**	**14.5%**	**9.8%**

customer as possible. The third relationship is hard to describe. There are two independent business people, a franchisor and a franchisee, each acting individually for their own best interest. After all, each is a separate business. They don't have a joint tax return.[9]

The authors' discussion with other franchisees and several franchisor operating businesses in auto parts, lodging, carpet cleaning, and phone book covers reaffirms the same concept, even though different words were used and different examples given. In effect, the franchisor–franchisee relationship has three distinct elements or parts: the legal agreement or contract, the business relationship to deliver the agreed-upon product or services to the customer, and the independent stature of each party as franchisor or franchisee (see Figure 2-1).

Awareness of this three-part relationship is essential to understanding the franchising approach to business. Whether one is interested in learning about franchising or in becoming a franchisee or a franchisor, it is very important to understand the relationship and the perspectives and approaches of both parties in the relationship. This triad is also useful for describing the reasons franchising has become so successful as an approach to business in our economy: Because a franchisee is generally more motivated and personally involved than a salaried manager of a business and so would work harder, a franchisor would need fewer employees to maintain the same number of operating stores; also, the quality controls established by the franchisor, when properly developed and reasonably enforced, will help maintain standards of excellence throughout the franchise system and so help to ensure the profitability of the business.

The legal agreement and the operations manual associated with it typically describe the role in the franchise system that franchisor and franchisee play. The supporting descriptions and guidelines in these documents provide direction for the operating policies and procedures contained in the operations manual. Within such an agreement usually a percentage of gross sales is stipulated to be allocated for national and local advertising programs. In addition, franchisees may join together to buy supplies. As stated, franchisees may buy larger quantities when placing group orders and receive discounts because of the size of their orders.

Also, franchising allows greater market penetration because the development of several market locations can occur simultaneously. Franchisees do the development in their particular market areas as independent business owners. The franchisor serves as the strategist or controller, and the franchisee serves as the developer. The franchisee is an independent businessperson, motivated to succeed. The franchisee is not an employee; the franchisee is self-employed while being involved in a joint venture with the franchisor.

TABLE 2-7   ANALYSIS BY PROFITABILITY LEVEL: INCOME STATEMENT

	Typical IFA Member	High Profit IFA	Negative Profit IFA
FRANCHISE OPERATIONS INCOME STATEMENT			
Revenue			
Franchise Fees	87.8%	97.2%	95.8
Compliance Fees (reinstatement and late fees)	0.0	0.0	0.0
Product and Services (equipment, mdse., etc.)	10.8	1.7	1.9
Miscellaneous Income	1.4	1.1	2.3
Total Revenue	**100.0**	**100.0**	**100.0**
Cost of Sales (Product and Services)	11.2	4.5	8.4
Gross Profit	**88.8**	**95.5**	**91.6**
OPERATING EXPENSES			
Employee Expenses			
Employee Salaries, Wages, and Bonuses	30.9	25.1	35.4
Payroll Taxes	2.6	2.2	3.5
Group Insurance (medical, hospitalization)	1.2	1.3	1.0
Employee Benefits (pension, profit sharing)	0.6	0.3	0.1
Employee Training	0.2	0.2	0.1
Total Employee Expenses	**35.5**	**29.2**	**40.1**
Facilities Expenses			
Lease/Rent or Ownership in Real Estate	3.4	2.8	4.1
Repairs and Maintenance	0.6	0.1	0.7
Utilities (heat, light, power, water)	0.3	0.3	0.0
Property Taxes	0.1	0.0	0.1
Depreciation	1.4	1.2	1.8
Total Facilities Expenses	**5.9**	**4.3**	**6.7**
General and Administrative Expenses			
Telephone/Communication	1.6	1.1	2.8
Travel and Entertainment	3.9	3.0	9.4
Bad Debt Losses	3.2	2.7	11.5
Store Closing Expenses	0.0	0.0	0.0
Miscellaneous G&A Expenses	7.6	4.3	15.1
Total G&A Expenses	**16.2**	**11.1**	**38.9**
Franchise Development			
Franchise Sales Advertising and Promotion	6.9	4.0	8.5
Prospect Evaluation	0.7	1.0	2.3
Miscellaneous Franchise Development	0.5	1.8	0.3
Total Franchise Development Expenses	**8.1**	**6.8**	**11.1**
Other Franchise Operations Expenses			
Franchisee Communication and Incentives	2.4	2.7	0.5
Compliance (mystery shopping, audit rsch., etc.)	2.6	1.4	7.6

TABLE 2-7   (CONTINUED)

	Typical IFA Member	High Profit IFA	Negative Profit IFA
Consumer customer relations, complaints, etc.)	0.0	0.0	0.0
All Other Franchise Operations Expenses	3.4	5.3	5.5
Total Other Franchise Operations Expenses	**8.3**	**9.4**	**13.6**
TOTAL OPERATING EXPENSES	**74.0**	**60.8**	**110.4**
Operating Profit	**14.8**	**34.7**	**-18.8**
Other Income	0.0	0.6	0.0
Interest Expense (exclude mortgage interest)	0.8	0.0	2.5
Other Nonoperating Expenses	0.0	0.0	0.0
Profit before Tax	**13.9%**	**35.3%**	**−21.3%**

TABLE 2-8   TYPICAL ELEMENTS COVERED IN A FRANCHISING AGREEMENT

Franchising	Bookkeeping
Fee	Equipment
Signs	Supplies
Quality control	Location requirements
Business hours	Personnel (appearance and training)
Advertising	Facilities
Decor	Franchisor–franchisee relationships
Products and/or services available	Maintenance
Reporting	Others
Royalties	

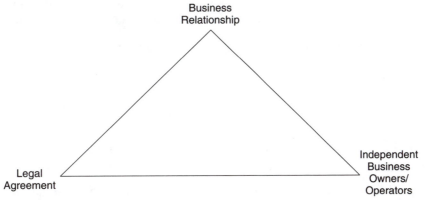

FIGURE **2-1**

The Franchisor-Franchisee Relationship

2-8f   An Overview and Summary of the Main Question: Is It Franchisable?

Assessing the franchising option to determine if a business concept is franchisable will require an analysis of economic conditions, markets, industry characteristics, business models, and target customers. The iFranchise Group suggests that the following points, among others, be assessed to determine if a company is ready for franchising as well as its likelihood for success as a franchise system.[10]

- Credibility. To sell franchisees, a firm must be credible in the eyes and mind of potential franchisees. Factors such as firm size, number of franchised units, years of operation, efficiency and effective operation of the prototype unit, strength of management, and brand awareness to name are important criteria.

- Transferability of knowledge. Can the system's approach be learned and implemented efficiently and effectively, particularly by persons with no prior experience in the industry?

- Differentiation. Is the system's products and services sufficiently differentiated from those of the primary competition? This may be through the product and services offered, a reduced investment cost, or a unique marketing strategy proven effective in the target markets.

- Successful prototype operations. A refined prototype is needed to demonstrate that the system of product and service delivery is workable and profitable. The prototype should also serve as the testing location for new product, marketing tactics, merchandising, and operational efficiencies.

- Documented systems. The systems for operation of a franchise must be available in a manner that communicates effectively to franchisees. The franchisor needs policies, procedures, forms, and business practices that are comprehensive and user friendly.

- Affordability. Can prospective franchisees afford the franchise in question?

- Return on investment. A franchise must be profitable, after royalty payments, for the franchisee to earn an adequate return on the investment of both time and money invested.

- Capital. Franchising is a low-cost method of expanding a business for the franchisor. The scope of the expansion plan must be realistic given the market conditions, cost of capital, resources required to achieve the anticipated expansion plan, and market conditions and trained franchisees to implement the expansion.

- Commitment to solid successful relationships. Successful franchisors focus on building solid relationships with their franchisees that are mutually cooperative and rewarding.

- Strength of management team. This is the most important aspect contributing to the success of any franchise system's program.

KEY TERMS

Operating franchise: an owner-operator run franchise business usually with an exclusive territory who usually does not have the right to establish sub-franchisees or licensees.

Territorial franchise: a franchisee is guaranteed by the franchisor that no competition will come from the same franchisor within a specified geographic boundary. The frqancvhi8see may have opportunity for establishing additional franchised units within the stated territorial boundary.

Dave Thomas

Wendy's Founder and Senior Chairman of the Board

Dave Thomas was born on July 2, 1932, in Atlantic City, New Jersey. He never knew his birth parents, but a couple from Kalamazoo, Michigan, Rex and Auleva Thomas, adopted him when he was six weeks old. Auleva died when Dave was five and his early years included numerous moves from state to state as his adoptive father sought work. These frequent moves proved challenging for Dave, who found himself without roots or a sense of belonging. Always the new kid on the block, Dave sought refuge in work. One of the things he enjoyed most during his childhood was going to restaurants to eat. There he'd see families eating together and enjoying the friendly atmosphere. He decided at an early age that he was going to have his own restaurant with great tasting food where families would visit again and again.

The Early Years

Dave started working at age twelve, delivering groceries in Knoxville, but was fired after a misunderstanding with his boss about his vacation. His second job was as a soda jerk at Walgreen's, but he was fired again when his boss found out Dave was not sixteen.

While applying for his next job, twelve-year-old Dave landed a job at the counter at the Regas Restaurant in Knoxville. He worked hard during his twelve-hour shifts, afraid he'd lose yet another job. The Regas brothers treated Dave like one of the family, providing him with encouragement and a caring mentorship that had a positive and lasting effect on him.

By the time Dave was fifteen, he had moved again and was working full time at the Hobby House Restaurant in Fort Wayne. As his father and stepfamily prepared for another move, Dave decided to stay in town and took a room at the local YMCA. Shortly thereafter, he made the biggest mistake in his life: He dropped out of high school to work full time. He thought he could learn more about the restaurant business with a hands-on education than he could learn in school.

When he was eighteen, Dave joined the army, eventually becoming one of the youngest soldiers to manage an enlisted men's club. After the service he returned to the Hobby House, where he met his future wife, Lorraine, a waitress, whom he married in 1954.

Dave Meets the Colonel

In 1956, Dave and his boss Phil Clauss opened a barbecue restaurant called The Ranch House. There, Dave met the man who became one of the greatest influences in his life—Colonel Harland Sanders, founder of Kentucky Fried Chicken. Clauss bought a KFC franchise from Colonel and Dave was in the chicken business.

In 1962, Clauss offered Dave a chance to turn around four failing KFC carry-outs Clauss owned in Columbus, Ohio. If Dave could turn the carry-outs around and pay off a big debt, Clauss would give him 45 percent of the business.

Although daunting, this was the kind of challenge Dave liked. He realized the restaurants were failing because they lacked focus. He cut the hundred-item menu to a handful of choices, focusing on chicken and side items. To increase public awareness, Dave added the famous bucket of chicken logo, and implemented some effective marketing campaigns that included trading buckets of chicken for radio air time. The restaurants began to prosper and he added four more restaurants. In 1968, his boss sold the restaurants back to KFC for $1.5 million, making Dave a millionaire at age 35. He then joined the parent company as regional operations director.

The Call of Hamburgers

While working for KFC, Thomas remained drawn to hamburgers. Although experts said America did not need another hamburger restaurant, Dave opened the first Wendy's Old Fashioned Hamburgers restaurant on November 15, 1969, in Columbus. He named the restaurant after his eight-year-old daughter Melinda Lou, nicknamed "Wendy" by her older brother and sisters.

The first Wendy's menu included fresh, made-to-order hamburgers, chili, fries, soft drinks, and a Frosty Dairy Dessert. The decor was homey, with bentwood chairs and tiffany-style lamps. Thomas planned to open several restaurants around Columbus, giving his children a place to work during the summers.

Competitors scoffed at this young entrepreneur, but Wendy's grew and prospered. In 1973, Dave began franchising the Wendy's concept, pioneering the idea of selling franchises for entire cities and parts of states, rather than single units.

Wendy's grew rapidly, with more than a thousand restaurants opening in its first one hundred months. That rapid growth continues. Wendy's and its franchisees now operate more than six thousand restaurants in the United States and around the world.

The TV Spokesman

In early 1989, Dave agreed to appear in "a few" Wendy's commercials as the company spokesman. In April, the Dave Thomas campaign began, and the homey style of the advertising has made Dave one of the nation's most recognizable spokesmen. In May 1999, Dave celebrated the tenth anniversary of the campaign.

In September 1996, the Dave Thomas campaign reached a special milestone when Dave filmed his landmark 500th commercial, making this the longest running advertising campaign featuring a company founder as spokesperson.

While advertising a variety of Wendy's products, Dave has appeared with several famous celebrities in his commercials, including soap opera star Susan Lucci, blues great B. B. King, and Olympic gold medalist Kristi Yamaguchi. Dave has emerged from Wendy's advertising campaign as an American folk hero. His honesty and old-fashioned values shine through and have solidified his popularity.

Dave as a Canadian Mountie?

In 1995, Wendy's merged with Tim Horton's, the second largest quick service restaurant chain in Canada, which features coffee and fresh baked goods. Tim Horton's has operated as a Wendy's subsidiary. This partnership enabled Dave to realize another dream: This merger enhances Wendy's growth and strength as a worldwide company while encouraging the development opportunities of both chains. Dave believes the merger is a marriage of two strong companies that were founded on the concept of quality and service. Though profitable, Horton's was sold by Wendy's in 2006.

The Importance of Giving Back

Dave strongly believes in giving back to the communities that support his business. He is a longtime supporter of a variety of charities, such as St. Jude Children's Research Hospital in Memphis; Children's Hospital in Columbus; Children's Home Society of Florida; and The Ohio State University Cancer Research Institute.

A cause closest to his heart is adoption. In 1990, he became a national spokesman for the White House Initiative on adoption, called "Adoption Works...For Everyone." Since then, Dave has been a national adoption advocate, working to raise awareness for the tens of thousands of children who need permanent homes and loving families.

In 1992, Dave established the Dave Thomas Foundation for Adoption, a not-for-profit foundation focused on raising public awareness about adoption, helping reduce the red tape from the process, and making adoption more affordable. Dave donates all of his profits from sales of his autobiography Dave's Way, published in 1991, and his second book, Well Done, published in 1994, to the foundation.

Personal Accomplishments

Although dropping out of school was Dave's biggest mistake, it led to one of his greatest accomplishments. In 1993, forty-five years after leaving school, Dave earned his GED certificate and received his high school diploma from Coconut

Creek High School in Fort Lauderdale. He was voted most likely to succeed by the graduating class, and attended the prom with his wife Lorraine, where they were named prom king and queen.

From his early days as a soda jerk and short order cook, to becoming an entrepreneur and TV spokesman, Dave has been recognized for his work in the restaurant industry and for children. He's a Horatio Alger Award recipient, holds honorary degrees from Duke, Baylor, and Clemson universities, among many others, and is a 33 degree Mason.

Dave has received every major restaurant industry honor and countless entrepreneur and man of the year awards. The adoption community has honored him with a variety of awards, and Dave has attended special receptions at the White House in recognition for his work for adoption. He has also testified before Congress in support of tax credits for adoptive parents.

On the rare occasions when he's not in the studio making commercials or traveling the country for interviews or speeches, you might find Dave on the golf course, perfecting his game. A golf lover, Dave has played in dozens of charity golf tournaments, including Wendy's Three-Tour Challenge to benefit adoption.

Dave's commitment to Wendy's and to America's children is what motivated him to continue working when others might have retired. He accomplished a great deal in his life, but he considered his family—his loving wife of more than forty years, five children, and fourteen grandchildren his greatest accomplishment.

REVIEW QUESTIONS

1. What are the principal reasons franchising can be a positive experience for both the franchisor and the franchisee?

2. Which of these reasons are common to both franchisor and franchisee?

3. Which of these reasons are different for the franchisor and the franchisee?

4. Who—the franchisor or the franchisee—has a greater potential or advantage through the franchising concept? Explain your reasons.

5. What questions should a business owner address before trying to enter franchising?

6. What capital requirements are associated with any franchised business?

7. Can you identify other areas where financial concerns or commitments may have to be addressed if the business considered involves retailing a product? Retailing a service? Wholesaling a product?

8. What are the typical elements covered in a franchising agreement between a franchisor and a franchisee?

CASE STUDY

Thought it Was Safer Than Starting His Own Business

After nearly thirty years of employment which ended as a senior executive in the automotive parts industry, Fred wanted to make a change in his life pattern. To quote: "I was tired of moving at such a fast pace and sick of traveling ten to twelve days a month." He wanted to go back to his hometown of Indianapolis to pursue semiretirement and stay the rest of his years there running a business.

When his former employer, a midsize firm in the automotive supply industry, was acquired three years ago, Fred took the buyout funds and bought a car repair franchise in a close-in suburb to Indianapolis. He expanded over the next seven years and now has five franchised locations in the greater Indianapolis market. The last two businesses he financed primarily by revenues generated from his first two car repair locations.

The transition from being a senior executive to a jack-of-all-trades franchised business owner has been bumpy. Even with twenty-seven full-time employees (not counting himself and his wife), Fred is putting in long hours and feels stressed on a daily basis. Though his businesses are making money, Fred frequently works ten-hour days and spends evenings submerged in paperwork. Fred sighs, "I'm supposed to be semiretired, but am working as hard if not harder than ever before."

Fred's plight is not uncommon in the franchise world. Buying a franchise can ensnare would-be entrepreneurs that have a dream of independence and self-fulfillment by creating financial exposure, headaches, and the stresses of business ownership—while someone else collects royalties on every dime that comes through the door, not to mention advertising and other fees; and all the while the franchisor dictates most every detail of what Fred can (and cannot) do, including the types of signage to put up, how to price services and parts, how much overtime to pay employees, and who will be his suppliers. As Fred states, "Violate the agreement, even in some small way, and the franchisor can take the franchise back. Then, where would I be? I'm stuck. I feel captured. I'm unhappy."

Fred believed that running a franchise business would mean being his own boss and running his own company, which he now believes is a misconception. Fred believes that, in reality, his business venture of five service centers is more like leasing a trademark and the real boss is the franchise system that sold him the privilege.

Case Questions

Is Fred ill-suited to be a franchisee, or, perhaps, did he just not understand what he was getting into at the contract signing?

Could Fred's misconceptions be common among franchised business owners?

What could Fred have done prior to signing the contractual agreement to better inform himself about the business relationship?

What should Fred do now, if anything?

References

The Franchise Handbook (Milwaukee: Publisher Fall 2000).

iFranchise Group. "12 Criteria of Franchisability," 28 August 2006, www.ifranchise.net//Index.cfm?Container_Id=287.

Justis, Robert T., "Franchisors: Have You Hugged Your Franchisee Today?" *Nation's Business* (February 1985): 46–49.

Kichul, Jill and Lisa Gundry, "Prospecting for Strategic Advantage: The Proactive Entrepreneurial Personality and Small Firm Innovation," *Journal of Small Business Management* 40(12) (2002): 85.

Leroux, Charles, "Franchising America: One Man's Sad View of Our Roadsides," *Chicago Tribune* (31 March 1985): 1, 3.

McGuire, E. Patrick, *Franchised Distribution*, a Research Report from the Conference Board.

"Mexican QSR Franchises," *Franchise HelpOnline.com* 4(3, part 1) (March 2003).

Monson, Catherine, "Turning around a Struggling Franchise Company," *Franchising World* (January 2007), www.franchise.org/Franchise-Industry-News-Details.aspx?id=32044.

Piper Marbury Rudnick & Wolfe Franchising Law Group, "Development of a Franchise Program," in Resource Center of Franchise Association, March 2001.

Profit Planning Group (Boulder, Colorado), *2001 Benchmarking Report* (Washington, DC: International Franchise Association), 5.2001.

Seltz, David D., *How to Get Started in Your Own Franchised Business* (Rockville Center, NY: Farnsworth Publishing Company, Inc., 1980).

Sloan, Alfred P., Jr., *My Years with General Motors* (Garden City, NY: Doubleday & Company, 1964).

"Statistics Show Graphically," *Entrepreneur* (December 2006): 32, www.entrepreneur.com/expandbeyond.

Thomas, David and Michael Seid, *Franchising for Dummies* (New York: IDG Books, 1999).

Tutor, Laura. "Out of the Gate: Why New Brands Are Franchising at a Break-neck Speed," *QSR Magazine* (27 April 2007), www.qsrmagazine.com/articles/features/101/new_brands-1.phtml.

U.S. Department of Commerce, *The Franchise Opportunities Handbook* (Washington, DC: U.S. Government Printing Office, 1984).

Vaughn, Charles L., *Franchising*, 2nd ed. (Lexington, MA: Lexington Books, D. C. Heath Company, 1979).

"Where's the Beef in Franchising?" *Money* (March 1985): 149–152.

"White Hens Here in Slow Rebrand to 7-Eleven Name," *Business Ledger* (12 February 2007), www.thebusinessledger.com/Articles.asp?artId=1443&isuID=86.

NOTES

1. A. P. Sloan, Jr., *My Years with General Motors (Garden City, NY: Doubleday & Company, 1964), 301.*
2. C. L. Vaughn, *Franchising, 2nd ed. (Lexington, MA: Lexington Books, D. C. Heath Company, 1979), 65.*
3. Ibid.
4. D. Thomas and M. Seid, *Franchising for Dummies (New York: IDG Books), 275.*
5. J. Kichul and L. Gundry, "Prospecting for Strategic Advantage: The Proactive Entrepreneurial Personality and Small Firm Innovation," *Journal of Small Business Management 40(12) (2002): 85.*
6. Adapted from Thomas et al., *Franchising for Dummies, 288.*
7. "Where's the Beef in Franchising?" *Money (March 1985): 152.*
8. Profit Planning Group (Boulder, Colorado), *2001 Benchmarking Report (Washington, DC: International Franchise Association), 5.2001.*
9. Interview with E. James Gayford in *KFC Franchisee (September 1998). Adapted from original interview in September 1985.*
10. iFranchise Group, a consulting organization into the franchise industry has these points considered as "criteria of franchisability." The points provided are adapted from their list criteria as available from http://www.ifranchise.net/Index.cfm?Container_Id=287. Any organization that is considering the option to become a franchise company should make careful examination of these points before implementing a franchising strategy.

THE FRANCHISOR BUSINESS PLAN

In studying this chapter, you will:

- **Understand what is meant by a business plan.**
- **Identify and understand the elements of a franchisee recruitment package.**
- **Learn about the elements essential for a franchisee operations package.**
- **Learn why it is important to do a feasibility study of the franchise concept, resources to be utilized, and market sought.**
- **Learn how to do a franchisor business plan feasibility study.**

INCIDENT

Jon is excited about an idea he has for starting a new ice cream franchise in town. He wants to go into business for himself, set his own hours, and create his own profit.

Jon has talked to several franchisors that have franchised outlets in different towns. Also, he has talked with several ice cream franchisees. They were all helpful in giving him their own personal experiences in the franchise business. Everyone he has talked with shares his enthusiasm. With several estimates of possible start-up costs from other franchisees and a brief franchise description pamphlet from a prospective franchisor, Jon went to see his banker.

The banker asked him how many other ice cream stores are currently operating in town; Jon responded that there are two; however, he neglected to include the five soft-serve ice cream stores in town. He also neglected to mention the frozen yogurt store that opened last month.

Jon is unaware of the specific functions the franchisor performs. He is wondering what would be provided in the way of training, equipment, supplies, and so forth.

Jon has not considered a location for his store. He also has not evaluated the size and saturation of the ice cream consuming market in his town to date. He does know, however, that he wants to go into business for himself operating an ice cream store.

Is Jon ready to open an ice cream store? What additional information might he need? How might a franchise feasibility study help him?

3-1 INTRODUCTION

If one is thinking about starting a franchised business, has a franchise and wants to expand, or simply wants to know more about franchising, then it is of critical importance for that person to understand and develop an appropriate franchise business plan. A carefully developed franchise system can provide phenomenal results for franchisor and franchisees; a franchising system not properly planned or implemented can lead to financial loss and business failure. Ray Kroc started McDonald's with a plan.

> Todd Graves is a guy who would work ninety-plus hour weeks as a boilermaker in Los Angeles, hitchhike to Alaska, sleep in a tent on the frozen tundra for a month, then work twenty hours a day on a sockeye salmon boat just so he could one day start a business and sell chicken fingers.
>
> To learn about business, Graves read business books, attended seminars, and talked with businesspeople. He was told he needed to write a business plan. Along with a friend who was enrolled in a business class at Lousiana State University, he decided to use the class as a springboard to write the plan. Ironically, the class project earned only a C grade. Following their business plan, they now have fifty-seven stores in twelve states. Go business plans.
>
> Source: *www.raisingcanes.com*

A new typical franchisor may be able to add three new franchisees in the first year of business, seven in the second, thirteen in the third, and twenty annually thereafter. However, this is only accomplished after the new franchisor has properly developed a business plan and the proper organization and operations associated with the new franchise system.

A prospective franchisor develops a comprehensive business plan to outline in detail the franchise operations and functions of the organization. As we will soon see, many areas need to be investigated during the process of developing a franchise business plan. A properly developed franchisor plan will have three major components or packages: a franchisor's business plan, a franchisee recruitment package, and a franchisee operations manual and success package. These components will be discussed at the beginning of this chapter. Then a detailed outline will be developed identifying the elements essential for determining the feasibility of entering a franchised business. The chapter will conclude with the presentation of a franchisor PERT chart illustrating the development steps and functions to be addressed prior to opening a franchisor business.

3-2 FRANCHISOR BUSINESS PLAN

A franchisor's business plan should include a detailed blueprint of operations. Such a blueprint would have the following primary components: management, organization, and administrative policy (Chapter 4); managing the marketing process (Chapter 5); sales and marketing research (Chapter 6); managing the operations process (Chapter 8); location and site selection (Chapter 9); accounting practices and fiscal responsibilities deemed appropriate, along with realistic financial projections (Chapters 10 and 11) based on the strategy to be followed and the market conditions anticipated; management information systems (Chapter 12); and legal documentation for determining the franchisor–franchisee relationship and anticipated activities of each party (Chapters 13 and 14).

WENDY'S FRANCHISEE—MARK GEORGE

Mark George, a Wendy's multiunit franchisee with sixty restaurants makes the following important points about the franchisor–franchisee relationship.

To become a good franchisee you need to do the following:

1. Read everything you can about the franchisor and business.
2. Get in and see the business work.
3. Talk to existing franchisees—check their backgrounds for similarity to your own.
4. Check on the franchisor's communications and how they really work.
5. Study the cost of becoming a franchisee. (Labor cost is 19 percent wages and 8 to 10 percent management—or about 30 percent of the sale price is labor cost.)
6. Find out what the franchisor has done when the franchisee has gotten into trouble.
7. Check and see if there are hidden charges.
8. Consider working for the company before becoming a franchisee.
9. Remember that you are in the people business—the most important aspect of the business—and there is a correlation between loyalty and profits.

3-2a Franchisee Recruitment Package

The second component of a franchise business plan is an articulated franchisee recruitment package which would include disclosure documents, recruitment and advertising brochures, and franchising agreements and contracts. The recruitment package is designed to show to a prospective franchisee what the franchisor has to offer and should contain clear statements about expectations and responsibilities of each party—franchisor and franchisee. This package should describe the business concisely through a logical flow of topics that identify (1) the objectives of the franchisor firm, (2) the initial capital and expected investment required of a potential franchisee, (3) personal and other qualifications a potential franchisee must have, (4) the training provided by the franchisor to the franchisee, and (5) the anticipated benefits and responsibilities of becoming a franchisee.

The disclosure document should be given to a prospective franchisee at the first personal meeting between the prospect and the franchisor, or ten days prior to the execution of a contract or a payment dealing with the franchising relationship between the franchisor and the franchisee, whichever occurs first.

The franchising agreement has to be presented to a franchisee five business days prior to any due consideration given by the franchisee to the franchisor. Due consideration is what the franchisor would demand and receive as the price for providing the elements of the franchising agreement (franchise fee—probably between $10,000 and $50,000). Similarly, the franchisee would demand, receive, or perform certain elements, duties, and responsibilities with respect to the franchisor. In essence, due consideration constitutes the agreed upon elements of the franchising relationship between the franchisor and franchisee that impose liability or create duties between the two parties.

The franchise brochure is simply a typewritten or printed booklet provided to a prospective franchisee that has responded to the franchisor's advertisement or seeks information based on a word-of-mouth inquiry. The brochure and recruitment flowchart help explain the product and service format the franchisor is using and identify the steps or processes one should follow to become a franchisee in this particular franchise system. The recruitment flowchart illustrates the steps of the franchisee development process as prescribed by the particular franchisor.

3-2b Franchisee Operations and Success Package

The third component of the franchise plan is the franchisee operations package, which generally contains elements of the following items: operations manual, financial and bookkeeping systems, advertising and promotional packages, sales manuals, the franchisor or franchisee support package, and the training manual.

The operations manual is often identified by the franchisee as the bible of the business. This manual describes in detail each function and subfunction with procedural guidelines and standards for operating the business. For example, an operations manual for a fast-food franchise would cover a wide range of topics, such as planning menus, setting up the required machinery (ovens, broilers, etc.), sanitation standards and procedures, safety procedures, cash register use and procedures, food preparation and cooking procedures, and methods of inventory control, purchasing, and analysis. The purpose of an operations manual is (1) to impart specific information about the franchisor's system or approach, (2) to develop the values and knowledge of the prospective franchisee toward the franchise approach and procedures, and (3) to develop skills in accordance with the system of operations for the franchised unit. In essence, the franchisee should become knowledgeable about each facet of the business and how they fit together to ensure the successful operation of the franchised unit.

The franchisee will not actually get a copy of the operations manual until after signing the franchise agreement. The operations manual is then "loaned" to the franchisee for the duration of the contract. The book is generally kept in a three-ring binder to allow for easy access and edits.

The franchisee also needs to know the **accounting system** for the business. An appropriate recordkeeping approach is generally developed by the franchisor and explained to the franchisee. A franchisee needs to know about each reporting form required by the franchisor, as well as any approaches to financial analysis, which will assist the franchisee in becoming an effective financial controller of the franchised unit.

The **advertising, promotion, and sales programs** typically address, among other issues, the amount of advertising and promotional support available prior to and at the time of a grand opening, cooperative advertising arrangements between franchisor and franchisee, under what conditions direct mail is worthwhile, and any "required" participation in national or regional franchisor-sponsored advertising campaigns. It is important that both franchisor and franchisee have a clear understanding of the amount and type of advertising, sales promotion, and public relations themes, including which party is responsible for development and to what degree each activity is meant to generate sales, heighten visibility, and improve the franchise's image within the local community.

The **franchisor support package** is a rather nebulous term that typically refers to the measures franchisors adopt to maintain wholesome relationships between themselves and their franchisee(s). Very often expectations are set forth in writing which indicate the degree to which franchisees are responsible to develop their specific market(s), the level of performance to be maintained in internal operations, and what steps would normally be followed to eliminate or at least minimize legal problems in trademark, brand or trade name, or antitrust areas. On all counts, the franchisee needs to understand what is expected prior to acquiring the franchise. A clear understanding is beneficial to both parties—franchisor and franchisee—to avoid potential problems within the franchisor–franchisee relationship. The franchise, once acquired, is the centerpiece of a continuing relationship.

Training manuals need to be prepared so that not only can prospective franchisees be trained but also future employees within the franchised unit. Training is necessary to fill the gaps between a franchisee's (and employees') existing knowledge and skills and the levels of performance expected by the franchisor. The training manual for employees can be quite different from that of the

---

SMOOTHIE KING: STEPS TO BECOMING A FRANCHISEE

Step 1: **Complete the Online Request for Consideration**: The information will be reviewed. Upon preliminary approval, you will be notified of our interest.

Step 2: **Visit the Home Office of Smoothie King**: A franchise development representative schedules an interview with you at their headquarters in Covington, Louisiana. During this visit, you will get an in-depth introduction to the Smoothie King operation, receive your Uniform Franchise Offering Circular (UFOC), meet the executive staff, and have an opportunity to visit several existing franchise locations.

Step 3: **Receive Smoothie King UFOC**: The UFOC contains valuable information to help you analyze our franchise system.

Step 4: **Complete Personal Information Forms and Submit to Smoothie King**: We evaluate your information forms, financial statements, credit forms, and background information. Upon a mutual decision to proceed, if necessary you are scheduled for a second interview.

Step 5: **Approval**: We evaluate your information forms, financial statements, credit forms, and background information. Upon a mutual decision to proceed, if necessary you are scheduled for a second interview.

Step 6: **Enter into a Franchise Agreement**: By this point, you should have enough information about Smoothie King to make a prudent decision. If you are approved, you may sign a franchise agreement. After receiving it and waiting five working days you will be able to sign. Your notarized agreements and check for the franchise fee will be completed prior to the next step.

Step 7: **Orientation**: As soon as possible you will attend a one-day orientation class. At this class you will be oriented on all of the steps involved in opening your store. This will include budgeting, financing, planning, site selection, ordering, construction, and much more. After orientation, our real estate department will work with you to find the perfect site.

Source: *Smoothie King, Online franchise information, 2007.*

---

recruited franchisee. The franchise employee training is often focused heavily toward skill development, clerking, counter behavior, and the specific task to be performed by the employee—donut making, egg preparing, hamburger preparing, or setting and timing an engine. Along with having the business skills honed, the franchisee often receives training in facts, attitudes, beliefs, values, and opinions which comprise the so-called indoctrination of an auto dealer, fast-food restaurateur, muffler shop owner, or electronics store franchisee.

3-3 FRANCHISE FEASIBILITY STUDY

The first step in establishing a comprehensive integrated franchise plan is to determine the feasibility of developing an existing business into a franchise operation. The **feasibility study** should contain sufficient information to enable either a franchisor or a franchisee to make a "go or no go" decision.

The franchisor's position must be properly analyzed to determine if the franchisor will or will not be able to (1) properly administer the franchising system, (2) support franchisees through home office functions appropriate to the type of business being analyzed and do so in a profitable fashion, and (3) benefit more through franchising than by operating a separate, independent business. If these questions can be answered affirmatively, the prospective franchisor should pursue the next step in making the decision about being a franchisor.

Both the franchisor and the franchisee will deal with the marketplace; the franchisee, however, will do so on more of a day-to-day basis. It is important that the franchise feasibility study show that (1) a prospective franchisee will or will not be profitable given the format proposed in relation to the market forces being confronted, (2) the proposed product or service has or does not have sufficient "utility" or customer demand or preference in light of alternative purchase possibilities, (3) the business operation at the proposed location(s) will attract the consuming public, and (4) the prospective franchisee will be more successful providing this particular product or service through a franchised unit than through an independent business. As with the franchisor decision, if the answers to these questions are in the affirmative, the person should consider further becoming a franchisee within the proposed franchise system.

The franchise feasibility study should show that it is or is not beneficial to both parties to enter the franchising field. If only one party will benefit, then the particular franchise system is not likely to be successful in the long run. When the basic criteria for success of both parties are met, then franchising can be a rewarding relationship. The franchisor and the franchisee will remain separate and independent businesspeople although they will have interdependence in their business dealings and objectives. It is important to understand that the failure of one would generally result in the failure of the other.

A well-prepared franchising feasibility study will address critical areas found in most business plans. The feasibility study, however, will usually contain certain elements not found in plans for other proposed businesses, such as the following six content sections.

1. Executive summary

2. Marketing segment

3. Management segment

4. Finance, accounting, and taxes

5. Legal requirements

6. Appendix

Each of the four "substantive" areas (i.e., items two through five) should spell out the franchising approach to be followed so that an individual would know whether the proposed business could potentially be successful. Each of these six areas is outlined in Table 3-1 and will be described in the sequence shown.

3-3a   Executive Summary

The most crucial part of any business plan is the executive summary, because it tells the story of the franchise venture and sparks the interest of any outsiders. The professional tradition states that this summary must not be more than three pages in length. Attached to the summary is generally the complete business plan or proposal, but many outside financial investors prefer not to go through the details of the business plan until they understand the business as described in the executive summary. The summary generally consists of the company name, type of business, company description, key personnel, start-up schedule and competition, funds requested, funds use statement, and fund repayment ability. Thus, the executive summary

TABLE 3-1   THE FRANCHISOR BUSINESS PLAN

I. Executive Summary
   A. Company Name
   B. Type of Business
   C. Company Description
   D. Key Personnel
   E. Start-up Schedule and Competition
   F. Funds Requested
   G. Funds Use Statement
   H. Fund Repayment
II. Marketing
   A. Major Marketing Objectives
   B. Market Plan and Pricing Strategy
   C. Franchisee Recruitment Plan and Flowchart
   D. Franchisee Prospectus
   E. Franchisee Sales and Advertising
   F. Franchisee Location Criteria Selection
   G. Grand Opening Plan
   H. Customer Advertising (Ongoing)
III. Management
   A. Headquarters
      1. Organizational Structure
      2. Policies
      3. Personnel (Wage and Salary)
   B. Franchise
      1. Organizational Structure
      2. Policies
      3. Personnel (Wage and Salary)
   C. Operations Manual
   D. Training Manual
   E. PERT Chart
IV. Financing and Accounting
   A. Headquarters
      1. Start-up or Turnkey Costs (Itemized)
      2. Financial Position for Securing Franchise
      3. Pro Forma Income Statement
      4. Pro Forma Balance Sheet
      5. Projected Cash Flow
      6. Breakeven Analysis
      7. Ratio Analysis
      8. Provision for Taxation
   B. Franchisee
      1. Start-up or Turnkey Costs (Itemized)
      2. Financial Position for Securing Franchise
      3. Pro Forma Income Statement
      4. Pro Forma Balance Sheet
      5. Projected Cash Flow
      6. Breakeven analysis
      7. Ratio Analysis
      8. Provision for Taxation
V. Legal Aspects
   A. Business Structure
   B. Contracts, Licenses, Trademarks
   C. Insurance: Type and Cost
   D. Disclosure Document—UFOC
   E. Franchise Agreement
   F. Franchisor–Franchisee Conditions
VI. Appendix
   A. Building Plans
   B. Layout Design
   C. Graphs
   D. Working Papers
   E. Diagrams
   F. Layouts
   G. Charts

highlights the type of business, key personnel, and financial requirements necessary to open and operate the business.

3-3b Marketing

The marketing process concerns the distribution of goods and services to existing and potential customers to satisfy some want or need. The marketing section of the feasibility study should investigate the major marketing objectives of the franchisor, the basic market plan, the pricing strategy, the franchisee recruitment plan and flowchart, the franchisee prospectus, franchisee sales and advertising, the franchisee location and criteria selection plans, any grand opening plan, and continuous ongoing customer advertising. The marketing section is of critical importance to the success of the franchise. Often, eight elements are included in the marketing section of a franchisor business plan, as identified here. It is important to remember, however, that each business organization is unique and therefore will place more emphasis on certain elements of the marketing section and less on others.

1. Major marketing objectives
2. Market plan and pricing strategy
3. Franchisee recruitment plan and flowchart
4. Franchisee prospectus
5. Franchisee sales and advertising
6. Franchisee location criteria selection
7. Grand opening plan
8. Customer advertising

Major Marketing Objectives

Major goals and objectives of the organization will explain what the franchisor ultimately wants to do and when the franchisor plans to do this. The franchisor should list three to six major goals and objectives to achieve, for example, the sale and opening of four franchise units during the first year of operation. This objective has the major elements important in an "operational objective." These include: (1) the definition or description of activity (sales), (2) a quantitative measurable number, and (3) a time period of one year. This form of an operational objective allows the franchisor to understand the extent of the goal or objective and how they can evaluate the completion or satisfaction of that goal or objective.

Market Plan and Pricing Strategy

Creating the market plan and pricing strategy is an encompassing step in the business plan. This section needs to include a description of the products or services. It is important to list in detail the products or services. Additionally, this section should describe and discuss the target market—who? where? and how many? The target market information should also contain the basic demographics including age, gender, income, education, and marital status of the target market consumer. Additionally, the price lists should be included. This generally will also allow you to develop the pricing strategy (percent markup or beating the competition).

Target Market Analysis

It is important to properly identify the target market and analyze that market's primary characteristics, to determine the potential buyer power available through that market. For example, if one is examining a market to determine the potential for a clothing or shoe store, then basic demographics and apparel buying trends must be understood in order to develop an overall profile of the targeted customer group. The type of information one might seek includes the following:

1. Age: 0–4, 5–11, 12–18, 19–25, 26–35, 36–45, 46–65, and over 65

2. Gender: male or female

3. Family income: under $12,000, $12,000–$17,999, $18,000–$24,999, $25,000–$34,999, $35,000 and over

4. Geographical area of the city: northwest, northeast, southeast, southwest

5. Education: high school not completed, high school completed, some college, college graduate, additional education

6. Number of children living at home: 0, 1, 2, 3, 4, 5 or more

7. Marital status: single, married, divorced, widowed

These kinds of information, when considered together, will tend to profile a certain type of customer. Then, it is important to determine the density or concentration of that type of person within the overall market area in which the product or service will be offered. Particular types of demographic data that might be helpful to forecast the market potential for product or service include age ranges, gender, or disposable income. One should be aware, however, that a successful firm develops customer profiles from a variety of sources and uses factors that have tended to be accurate and reflective of the particular market niche and customer tastes associated with that niche. Thus, it is hard to generalize about what information would be reflective of any business.

Pricing Strategy

The price at which a product or service is offered must cover relevant costs and ensure an adequate profit for the franchisee and the franchisor. Prior to making final determination about a specific price, it is important to determine cost schedules at various levels of anticipated production, promotional costs per unit, and profit desired per unit, and to compare this "ideal" price with the price offered by direct competitors for the same or similar product or service. It is wise to develop a pricing structure, as opposed to ironclad prices, for the items to be sold. A pricing structure provides the franchisee the flexibility to meet competitive shifts and changes in consumer preference and provides latitude for promotions without the need to establish a new price each time a change is necessary.

Markup Pricing

An illustration of markup pricing is appropriate since it is a common practice. Markup pricing is one of the easiest forms of price determination, which may explain in part why it is popular. The steps are to determine actual costs of the product (including all overhead) at the anticipated production/ sales volume, and to add the profit margin. The final figure is referred to as a markup price. Many fast-food meat restaurants, for example, have 60 percent of the final price allocated to food and wage costs. If the average cost of the elements used to produce a hamburger is thirty-five cents, and the wage cost associated with the preparation of the hamburger is twenty-five cents, then the total direct cost is sixty cents. If overhead cost (building, utilities, debt service, etc.) is estimated to be twelve cents per hamburger (based on the anticipated number of burgers to be sold in the year divided by the anticipated total overhead cost), then by adding the direct and indirect costs one gets a total of seventy-two cents. If the industry standard is a 40 percent markup (i.e., $40\% \times \$0.72$), then the anticipated cost of the hamburger would be one dollar. If market conditions suggest that the average price for a hamburger in the market is eighty cents, not one dollar, then it would be advisable for this potential fast-food franchisee not to enter business in this particular market unless the costs could be significantly lowered.

Franchisee Recruitment Plan and Flowchart

The franchisee recruitment plan and flowchart should also include a basic description of the franchisee profile describing who you are trying to recruit. Additionally, it would be important to understand what locations and from where you are trying to recruit these individuals. It is also important to provide a recruitment flowchart (see Figure 3-1) which explains the steps to follow in working with prospective franchisees. This is important because many times you will need to follow up on prospective franchisees within a five-day period after they have contacted you in various stages of their franchising development.

The recruitment brochure is a vehicle of assistance in working through the initial personal interview between franchisor and prospective franchisee. The brochure informs prospective franchisees about primary attributes of the particular franchise system from a franchisee's perspective and provides points the two parties can discuss to determine level of interest.

The recruitment flowchart outlines the steps a franchisee needs to take in order to be (1) accepted as a prospective franchisee, (2) interviewed, trained, and assigned as a franchisee, and (3) authorized as the operator of an opened franchised unit. The flowchart provides the overview and steps a franchisee needs to complete in order to operate as an authorized franchised unit operator within the particular franchise system.

Franchisee Prospectus

The franchisee prospectus discusses the franchise opportunity. This is basically the sales brochure or the franchisee prospectus which the franchisor has put together to explain to prospective franchisees what the business is about and to encourage them to become franchisees of the system. The prospectus should also include basic start-up costs and in many cases includes information about the history, training, and opportunities of the franchising system. Included in the back of this brochure or prospectus is generally a confidential application inviting the prospective franchisee to apply for a franchise.

Franchisee Sales and Advertising

The sales and advertising section will explain how to promote the franchise opportunity to prospective franchisees. This will also include a discussion of the media mix (newspapers, direct mail, magazines, and point-of-purchase displays). The franchisor needs to write down the different methods they will use to promote the sale of franchisees to the prospective franchisees.

Franchisee Location Criteria Selection

The section regarding location criteria selection allows the franchisor to describe where and why they are going to locate a franchise. The franchisor should list the criteria which they are going to use to select the best possible franchise location. This may be simply a corner location close to another fast-food store, gasoline service station, or shopping center. However, most often this would also include the demographics of the target market customers including the age, gender, income, education, and marital status of the end consumers. This information is important to have so that you can find the best possible location close to the customer.

Site Location

One of the most important factors in the success of a retail business is to have a properly determined location. Location theorists suggest the three most important factors in the success of a business are location, location, and location!

Two, three, or perhaps even five sites need to be initially analyzed and screened by the franchisee to determine the best alternative sites for the proposed business. Before choosing the

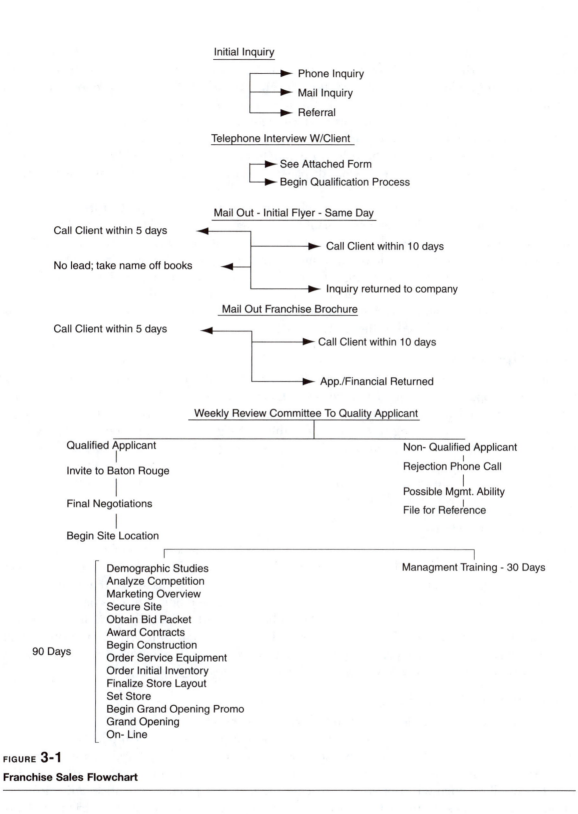

FIGURE 3-1

Franchise Sales Flowchart

specific location, it is important to have determined the location of all competitors and the concentrations of potential customers by the "profiling" completed in the previous step. One can develop rough approximations concerning the primary service area for each competitor and for the proposed site through drive or walking time analysis.

In urban areas, it is suggested that approximately two-thirds of a store's business is done by people who live or work within a five-minute drive or walk of the location, if the product or service offered is in what is considered a convenience goods and service category. (More will be said about categorizing types of goods and services in Chapter 9.) The drive or walk time analysis can be used to develop approximate **primary service areas (PSAs)** for the proposed business site and for each existing competitor. Using this technique to identify zones of probable coverage across the market area, a prospective business can determine areas where the market is basically underserved as well as areas where it is highly competitive. The goal is to find a location with convenient access that does not have heavy competition (cross-lapping PSAs) within a market sector with sufficient numbers of people displaying the "profile" which the business wishes to attract.

Once the preferred location is found, purchase or lease may be an important factor. Although lease terms should not be the sole determinant in selecting a site, a franchisee may decide to move out of a particular location solely because of increased rent or lease agreements. However, a proposed new location may not have the same accessibility, targeted customer density, or complementary store clustering as the original site. Thus, it is important to consider each of these factors carefully, remembering that location is critical to but not the sole determinant of proper site selection. All factors should be reviewed before a final location is chosen or a change of location is made. (This topic is developed further in Chapter 9.)

Grand Opening Plan

The grand opening plan is important. One franchisor met with the franchisee and experienced a terrible grand opening. The city dignitaries were there, the ribbon cutting occurred, the balloons were sent aloft, the band played, and no customers came. Both the franchisor and franchisee forgot to advertise the grand opening to the general public. The grand opening should explain who is doing what, when, where, how, and why. This grand opening plan should also explain the costs to both the franchisor and the franchisee. This plan would include the information about how many representatives from the franchisor will be on site during the grand opening and all the advertisements and promotions which will be used at that time.

Customer Advertising

In addition to marketing to the prospective franchisee, it is also important to advertise and market the product and services to the end consumer. This section should include all the promotions, direct selling, public relations, and advertisements which will be used by the franchisee to encourage the customer to purchase the goods or services. In addition, a discussion of the media mix as well as some original advertisements should be developed and included within this section.

Many franchisors, such as Ruth's Chris Steak House, have their own advertising manual with prepared page slicks for newspaper and yellow page advertising. In addition, Ruth's Chris Steak House provides their franchisees with ten- to thirty-second television ideas.

Promotion and Advertising

Sales promotion and advertising are two differing concepts. Sales promotion is associated with specific time-related efforts to improve sales of a specific product, line of products, or services. Advertising, on the other hand, concerns more general factors of the brand, trademark, or product and service of the business. Advertising is often "institutional" in orientation, promoting the franchise itself as opposed to offering a specific product at a promotional price. Advertising is meant, in many cases, to promote the overall goodwill of the franchise or the attributes of the product line. For example, McDonald's spends millions every year to make certain the consuming public is aware of its product quality, prompt service, and store cleanliness. These types of promotions have their purpose and should be developed with sufficient detail within the proposed franchise plan so that the franchisor and the franchisee have a clear understanding and cooperate appropriately in their use.

Marketing to the Franchisee

To have a successful franchisee recruitment program, a franchisor should develop a recruitment book designed to present to prospective franchisees the benefits a franchisee would gain by joining the particular franchise system. For example, the central features of a three-page recruitment package of West Coast Auto Parts franchise system include having ten dealers that use auto parts obtained for the franchisee (parts distributor) from tire stores, garages, service stations, and new car dealerships; the merchandise needed to service these ten accounts; and a minimum investment of $7,150. The support features of this franchise include no experience needed in the auto parts business, a 60 percent markup, no "dead" stock, free warehousing, and an inventory exchange mechanism.

3-3c   Management

Management can be simply defined as "getting things done through people." However, management is one of the most critical factors in determining the success or failure of any business. The two main reasons for failure in business are poor management and lack of capital. The management section of the franchise feasibility study is designed to identify and explain the organizational structure and system of operation established by the franchisor to help the franchise system to be successful.

A franchisee, as owner-manager of a franchise unit, should be able to design and operate an efficient organization within the guidelines established by the franchisor and by using the policies and practices developed by the franchisor for dealing effectively with employees and customers. The franchisee needs to be able to respond to changing environmental conditions, making good use of the franchisor's support to manage the resources available in order to ensure that the basic thrust of the organization does not get sidetracked or become dysfunctional. The management section of the franchise feasibility study should include detailed information on the following five elements.

1. Headquarters' organization

2. Franchisee organization

3. Operations manual

4. Training manual

5. PERT chart

Successful development of these topics is consistent with the theme of the business format used by the franchisor which allows a prospective franchisee to properly plan, manage, and control a franchised unit. (This general topic area is addressed more fully in Chapter 18.)

Headquarters' Organization

Every organization, whether it is a family household or a complex giant corporation, requires commonly understood organizational relationships to function effectively. A franchising system is divided into two major and different sections—selling to prospective franchisees and operations. Two distinct and separate people need to be in charge of these vital activities, which will help determine the success and failure of the franchising business.

In business, management relationships should not be left to chance, particularly if differing motivations exist for why such organizational relationships exist in the first place. A chart, diagram, or table of organization should be developed to illustrate and clearly identify the position required, authority and responsibility vested in each position, and the placement of each position in regard to the functions and overall thrust of the organization (see Figure 3-2). A president or chief executive officer (CEO) is identified as the head of an operating organization. However, a CEO is unable to perform all the functions of most organizations unless the organization is of the simplest form and has a very limited scope of operations. Therefore, it is important that the various positions,

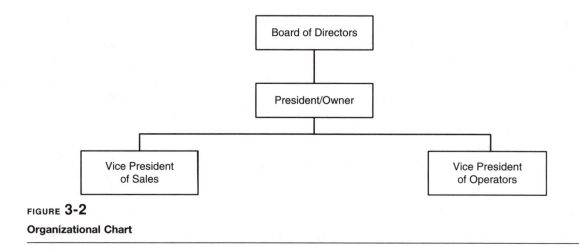

FIGURE **3-2**

Organizational Chart

assignments, and functions within an organization be unified toward achieving the objectives sought and that those staffing the positions understand their assignments and have sufficient authority to carry out their responsibilities.

Each franchisor needs to keep the franchise organization structurally consistent with the ever-changing objectives of the franchise system. As the system grows, the product line is modified, and new products and services are added and others deleted. The organization needs to keep structurally current with such changes, or else staffers will begin to ignore the "formal" approach to running the organization, often leading to severe consequences as the organization becomes more and more informally managed (or mismanaged).

Policies and Procedures

One franchisor noticed that in many of the company-owned units as well as the franchised outlets, overall food costs were rising. Upon investigation, the franchisor realized the policy of allowing employees to take home pizzas not eaten at the end of the day was causing an excessive number of pizzas to be baked during the last hour of business operation. Food costs had risen 4 percent above expected levels. The franchisor changed the policy—no longer allowing employees to take home unused prepared foods—which led to a reduction of 6 percent in food costs, an additional 2 percent below normal expectation.

Policies serve as guidelines for employee actions. As the previous example about the pizza franchise shows, when a policy is not given enough consideration initially, it can be abused to the detriment of the organization. **Procedures**, on the other hand, identify the steps or elements within a process that are considered appropriate for performing assigned tasks. Of course, procedures can also be abused; as we all know, it can be difficult working with or managing an employee who does only what is required in the manual. Policies exist for the benefit of the organization and its employees. Similarly, procedures should be used to identify how tasks are to be performed, while recognizing that at times variance may need to be allowed for; otherwise, organizations could not accommodate the changing supplier, media, customer, or general community conditions without constantly rewriting the policies and procedures of the franchise system.

Personnel Management

The franchisor should define and describe the personnel practices of the organization. The franchise organization should have job descriptions and policies relative to the operations and functions of each employee, guidelines for wage and salary administration, and established methods of evaluating performance and determining how raises and/or bonuses are to be administered. In the feasibility study, it is important that personnel needs be addressed and explained. Policies on tipping or gratuities in restaurants, for example, need to be carefully set forth along with their relationship to existing pay schedules, and how such information is to be reported to the IRS and appropriate state departments of revenue must also be explained. In addition, bonuses, commissions, or fringe benefits should be explained by the franchisor for prospective franchisees and their franchised unit operations. (Additional discussion of this topic is presented in Chapters 7 and 18.)

Franchisee Organization

Sufficient direction should be provided by the franchisor so that each franchisee will know what is expected concerning operations and management of the franchised unit, as well as what elements are essential to the franchisor–franchisee relationship.

The franchisee organization also needs to include organization structure, policies, and personnel management. This is similar to the headquarter's organization, but now this is an organizational structure designed for the franchisee. The franchisee will often have managers, assistant managers, and workers. These people need to have their policies, procedures, and personnel practices outlined and developed for them similar to those which have been developed for the headquarter's organization.

Operations Manual and Training Manual

Included in the operational instructions should be an operations manual and a training manual for the franchisee.

As we noted earlier, the operations manual describes the functions of the franchisee's business in detail. It provides a step-by-step illustration and description for each set of required activities within the store's operation. The training manual may be separate from or part of the operations manual. It provides the information necessary to train unit employees to perform the required functions and operations within the specific business environment of the franchise. For example, the training manual may explain to convenience food store clerks how to operate the cash register, account for cash, account for inventory, and stock food supplies. Training manuals, while often almost too detailed, are needed to help each employee understand the tasks that constitute the responsibilities of the job.

PERT Chart

The project evaluation review technique **(PERT) chart** (see Figure 3-3) is a simple, clearly delineated set of related events presented in sequence. Often, time periods are identified to reflect expectations for completion of each set of activities or events identified in the sequence. Identifying normative times for each event is beneficial in estimating the length of time through the "critical path" that is necessary to complete the project. A PERT chart can be a useful tool for a franchisor in establishing franchised units. Such charts illustrate the required steps from initiation of the franchise idea to the grand opening of the unit by a franchisee. Since each franchise system is unique and can be involved in any of a variety of business activities, such a charting can take anywhere from six months to two years to satisfactorily complete. Seldom does a franchise successfully start up and show a profit in the first 180 days of operation.

PERT charts can be used as a guide (plan) as well as an implementation tool for both the franchisor and the franchisee. Using the PERT concept, the franchisor can determine those steps absolutely essential (not just desirable) for the development and start-up of a franchised unit. The franchisee can see the steps with their requirements and time periods for accomplishment and can thus plan how to best use the time prior to opening the franchised unit.

3-3d Finance and Accounting

The priests of Ur in Mesopotamia around 3200 BC kept records of the transactions between the priests and the public. Since that time, people have been keeping records to account for financial transactions in their business dealings. These records can and should be valuable tools for assistance

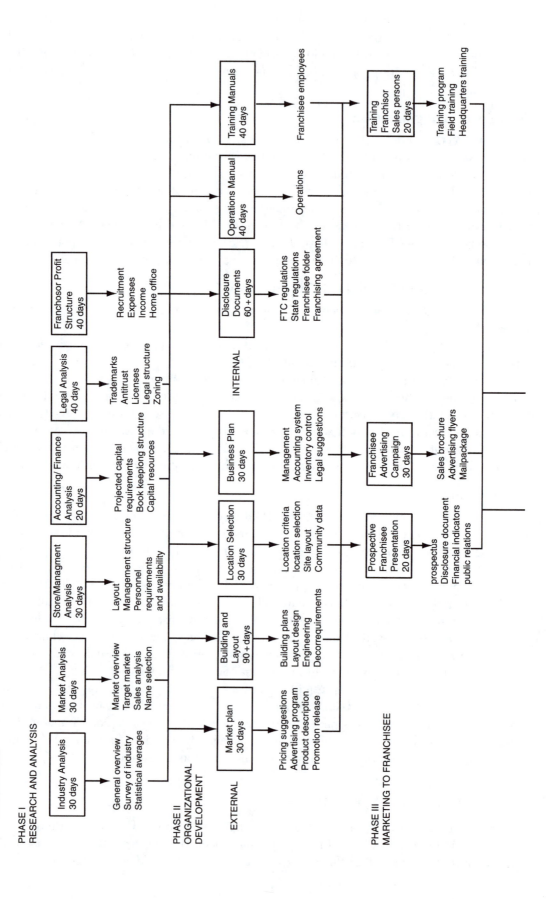

START

Franchise Plan
Start

PHASE I
RESEARCH AND ANALYSIS

| Industry Analysis 30 days | Market Analysis 30 days | Store/Managment Analysis 30 days | Accounting/ Finance Analysis 20 days | Legal Analysis 40 days | Franchosor Profit Structure 40 days |

General overview
Survey of industry
Statistical averages

Market overview
Target market
Sales analysis
Name selection

Layout
Management structure
Personnel requirements and availability

Projected capital requirements
Book keepiong structure
Capital resources

Trademarks
Antitrust
Licenses
Legal structure
Zoning

Recruitment
Expenses
Income
Home office

PHASE II
ORGANIZATIONAL
DEVELOPMENT

EXTERNAL

| Market plan 30 days | Building and Layout 90 + days | Location Selection 30 days | Business Plan 30 days | Operations Manual 40 days | Training Manuals 40 days |

Pricing suggestions
Advertising program
Product description
Promotion release

Building plans
Layout design
Engineering
Decorrequirements

INTERNAL

Location criteria
location selection
Site layout
Community data

Management
Accounting system
Inventory control
Legal suggestions

| Disclosure Documents 60 + days |

FTC regulations
State regulations
Franchisee folder
Franchising agreement

Operations

Franchisee employees

PHASE III
MARKETING TO FRANCHISEE

| Prospective Franchisee Presentation 20 days | Franchisee Advertising Campaign 30 days | Training Franchisor Sales persons 20 days |

prospectus
Disclosure document
Financial indicators
public relations

Sales brochure
Advertising flyers
Mailpackage

Training program
Field training
Headquarters training

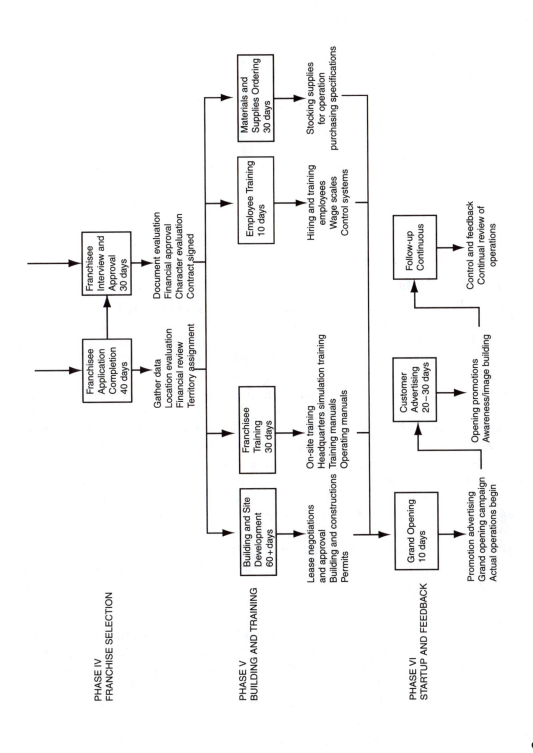

FIGURE **3-3**

Franchise Plan PERT Chart

in making effective management decisions. In a franchise system, it is important that proper financial records be kept by both franchisor and franchisee. In assessing the feasibility of a franchise, it is essential that financial projections be made for or by the franchisor to estimate income, expenses, cash flow, assets required at various levels of business activity, debt capacity, and equity requirements anticipated for each potential level of business activity.

The major accounting records to be kept by a franchisor and a franchisee would at the very least include the following:

1. Start-up or turnkey costs (itemized)
2. Financial position for starting franchisor's system
3. Pro forma balance sheet
4. Pro forma income statement
5. Pro forma cash flow statement
6. Breakeven analysis
7. Ratio analysis
8. Provision for taxation

Start-up or Turnkey Costs

Before the franchisor begins operation, it is important to develop a start-up or **turnkey cost** for the franchisor. This would generally include items such as land, building, furniture, fixtures, equipment, and personnel costs which are required to begin the franchise business. The franchisor needs to itemize all these costs to be able to determine the necessary start-up costs for the franchise system.

One of the most important parts of the franchising feasibility study is the development and presentation of the total costs necessary to open a franchised unit. These start-up (or turnkey) costs include all expenses required so that all elements of the business are in place and the operation is ready for the first customer who comes in the door. In many franchised businesses, this would include real property costs, building, advertising, utility hookups, internal fixtures, product inventory, commodities and supplies, and initial salary and wages. These costs should be itemized, providing a complete picture to the franchisee and franchisor of the resource commitment required to start a franchised unit business. Although not all expenses may be foreseen, it is important to develop as exhaustive a list as possible. An accurate and current listing will assist the franchisor in planning the start-up of future franchised units. Also, these costs can be compared with those of other nonfranchised as well as franchised competitors' new businesses as this information becomes available.

Financial Position

The franchisor needs to look at his or her own financial position to determine the availabilities of money to start a franchising program. It is important to realize that if a new building needs to be constructed or land purchased, tens of thousands of dollars may be required just to start a franchising operation. In addition, the legal requirements will generally cost between $15,000 and $30,000 to begin a franchising system. The franchisor needs to know how much money will be required to start a franchising system, and if the money is available.

The following three financial statements will provide valuable information to make financial decisions concerning initiation, growth or expansion, or even termination of specific franchise operations. We describe each of these accounting records briefly in a context useful to a franchise operation. (These topics are addressed more fully in Chapters 10 and 11.)

Balance Sheet

The balance sheet is a snapshot of the financial condition of the franchised business. This financial statement, once called a statement of financial position, shows how a business utilizes its resources and assets in comparison with the debt and ownership (or equity) of the business. The balance sheet is developed around the following accounting equation.

$$\text{Assets} = \text{Liabilities} + \text{Ownership Equity}$$

The balance sheet differentiates between money used by the franchise business for a short term (current assets) and money utilized for the long term (fixed assets). It indicates the difference between the monies received from creditors or loans (liabilities or debts) and the funds injected by the owners of the business (owner's initial equity or investment, plus retained earnings).

Income Statement (Profit and Loss Statement)

A business will reap a profit in a given period if revenues exceed expenses. Profit is shown on the income statement through identification of expenses (resources expended or used) to make the sales (which are expressed as total revenue). The expenses are subtracted from the revenue and this figure is considered gross profit. The figure is "gross" because other subtractions from the figure are likely to be made, such as withholding for reserves or taxes.

Usually, the income statement is prepared on a monthly, quarterly, or at least yearly basis in order to indicate the profit–loss relationship resulting from the use of the assets available in that accounting period and the expenses incurred. Revenues into the business are sales made through the franchise's product and service line, plus other forms of revenue such as, for example, rental income from the adjacent building owned by the franchised unit. Expenses are the outflow of resources required to produce and sell the product and service line, including direct cost of production as well as overhead.

Cash Flow Statement

The cash flow statement shows the sources from which the firm obtained its income during an accounting period and how it was spent. The cash flow statement is probably the most important of all financial documents used by a franchisor and a franchisee because it illustrates the flow of cash through the business across time. It is not like a balance sheet, which captures a picture of the business on a particular day of the year, say December 31, 2009. Rather, the cash flow statement often depicts the business over a period of six months or more, through which the history of revenue income and expenses can be traced and projected into the future. With these comparisons, future cash needs and projected availability of cash can be estimated during different sales highs and lows. Because most business activity is not constant during all twelve months of a year, it is important for an organization to conserve cash shortly after periods of high sales in order to maintain production, promotion, and normal levels of operation when sales are less than optimal.

The cash flow statement as a projection (or pro forma statement) is meant to anticipate the shortfalls of the franchise's business during different periods or seasons of the business cycle. The cash flow statement should indicate when funds are expected to be short and when they are expected to be in excess. When excess funds are available, they are often put into a short-term investment vehicle (securities or savings instruments) to generate additional income. In this way, any surplus cash can be working for the firm instead of being idle. In general, the cash flow statement helps the franchisee anticipate cash needs and adjust expenses as well as possible to ensure a smooth outflow of payments, even though income (revenue) tends to come in seasonally or cyclically. Thus, the franchise operator can maximize the use of resources in handling the uncertainties of consumer demand and the certainty of accounts payable.

Other factors for consideration in developing an accurate financial picture and proposing appropriate accounting and financial controls include several topics we will briefly discuss. A particular franchise system may find some of these factors less important than others; however, some consideration should be given to each before any of the concepts are rejected.

Equity, collateral, and loans constitute the capital that can be applied to the business at a given time. Any equipment brought to the new business should be documented and listed along with some measure of value for each piece at the time of the business start-up. Any collateral arrangements made to secure loans should be noted not just by one's banker or other source of the loan, but by the franchisee as well. If loans are needed by the franchisee to start up the business, each loan must be documented in the balance sheet, and the appropriate interest rate and approach to be used for its calculation, the length of the loans, and any other conditions that have been stipulated in the loan package should be filed in a secure location.

Working capital is simply an accounting expression that refers to how much cash or capital is available or can easily be made available to pay current debts. Working capital is determined by subtracting current liabilities from current assets.

Breakeven Analysis

Breakeven analysis refers to a determination of that point in the franchised business activity where revenues (income) exactly equal expenses (costs of doing business). This financial condition can be expressed in mathematical equations or depicted in line graphs, with separate lines representing the costs and the revenues of the firm. At the point of their intersection, the business is neither making nor losing money. Up to the point of intersection the firm is losing money, and after the point of intersection, the firm is making a profit.

Ratio Analysis

Ratio analysis is a method of determining the various financial relationships which would suggest the degree of financial health of a firm. The common marks to determine financial health include liquidity, profitability, and debt/equity position. The ratios are designed to compare the current business activity (1) with that of prior time periods or (2) with that of similar firms in the same industry. The franchisor develops a series of financial ratios on each of the franchisees for purposes of comparison. Such analyses help the franchisor understand the variances in different geographic sectors as well as the differing market/competitive intensities of the various franchisees in the franchise system. (More will be said about ratio analysis and its use in Chapter 10.)

Provision for Taxation

Provisions for taxes are an important consideration. Both franchisor and franchisee must recognize and understand the various tax filings required by federal, state, and local governments. Generally, the four main areas of taxation in which requirements of reporting about the business's activity and the resulting tax liability must be met are as follows:

1. Sales taxes

2. Business taxes

3. Property taxes

4. Employee-related taxes

The franchisor and the franchisee need to understand the filing requirements and obligations of each type of taxation as applied to their line of business and incurred through operation. If taxes are not filed and payments are not made as required, the business can incur civil as well as criminal liability.

Financial Records for the Franchisee

In addition to considering the financial and accounting requirements for a franchisor, it is also appropriate to develop a set of financial figures for a prospective franchisee. Important financial records or position statements for a franchisee would include:

1. Start-up or turnkey costs (itemized)

2. Financial position for starting franchisor's system

3. Pro forma balance sheet

4. Pro forma income statement

5. Pro forma cash flow statement

6. Breakeven analysis

7. Ratio analysis

8. Provision for taxation

Prospective franchisees need to understand what the total start-up or turnkey costs of a new franchise will be, as well as the prospective gross sales, typical direct and indirect costs, prospective profits at various levels of sales/output, the recordkeeping system required by the franchisor, and the filing requirements, as well as any financial requirements such as franchising fees, royalty payments, advertising cooperative payments, or consultant or service fees expected by the franchisor from an existing franchisee. The more information a prospective franchisee develops before the final decision is made whether to open a franchised unit, the wiser the decision. In the long run, fewer problems, misunderstandings, and potential litigations are likely to take place.

3-3e   Legal Requirements

Certain legal requirements of a franchised operation must be satisfied. Such requirements usually rest on legal opinion versed in franchising law. Typical factors covered in the legal agreement include:

1. Business structure

2. Licenses, contracts, and permits

3. Types and anticipated costs of insurance

4. Disclosure documents (Uniform Franchise Offering Circular—UFOC)

5. The franchising agreement itself

6. Conditions integral to the franchisor–franchisee relationship

7. Possible termination

Business Structure

Franchising is a highly competitive and legally controlled business operation. It is important that the franchisor develop a proper business structure which generally would be either (1) a sole proprietorship, (2) a partnership, (3) a corporation, (4) an L.L.C. or (5) a holding company.

An anomaly about franchising is that it is generally a highly competitive business activity, but is also a legally "controlled" business relationship. A franchisor has various options to consider for the structure of the business as a sole proprietorship, partnership, corporation, L.L.C., or holding company. In addition, depending on the type of franchise activity, various licenses, contracts, and legal permits may be necessary in order to operate within the boundaries of a particular state. Many states require the listing of the business name, filed through a specific department such as the office of the secretary of state or department of registration and licensing. Some franchised firms find it difficult to operate nationally because their name is already in use elsewhere; that is, it has been licensed by another business for use in a particular state. Because of this, it is important that a franchisor register the trade name and any brand names in every state if franchise system development on a national level will be even remotely contemplated.

Insurance is a similarly important factor for the franchise. The franchisee should have proper coverage in the areas of property insurance, liability insurance, and personal insurance. Insurance is important to cover natural disasters, accidents, emergencies, or other contingencies which can arise and alter the normal course of business activity. Without insurance coverage, the financial health of the firm could be destroyed.

Disclosure Documents

The Federal Trade Commission (FTC) has a requirement called the Franchise Rule, more specifically entitled, "Disclosure Requirements and Prohibitions Concerning Franchising and Business Opportunity Ventures" (16 C.F.R. No. 436). This rule requires that all franchisors engaging in franchising practices disclose their business activities through a disclosure document or **Uniform Franchise Offering Circular (UFOC)**. Rule 436 has helped reduce the fraudulent or improper use of the franchising concept to the detriment of unwitting prospective franchisees. A prospective franchisee should request a copy of the franchisor's disclosure document or UFOC prior to signing a franchising agreement. (Detailed discussion of this document is presented in Chapter 13.)

Franchising Agreement or Relationship

The franchising agreement, or contract, between franchisor and franchisee should be drawn up by lawyers, and franchisor and franchisee should have separate legal counsel. This document is the foundation for the franchisor–franchisee relationship and will continue to be central to the relationship between the parties. (Detailed discussion of this document is presented in Chapter 13.)

3-3f Appendix

The appendix is an important visual aid, containing illustrations, diagrams, analyses, and exhibits referenced throughout the franchise feasibility study. An expanded appendix would include the complete training manual, operations manual, advertising and promotion packages, sales manual, site and store layouts, franchisee recruitment presentations, charts, graphs, diagrams, layouts, and other materials which may enhance the franchise activities. A well-prepared appendix can enhance the possibility of successful recruitment of prospective franchisees.

3-4 THE FRANCHISE PERT CHART

The franchise PERT chart outline (Figure 3-4) presents a visual sequence illustrating each developmental step and function to be completed before a franchisor should open a franchised business. A complete franchise PERT chart would include the following phases.

1. Phase 1 Research and Analysis

2. Phase 2 Organizational Development (external and internal)

3. Phase 3 Marketing to Franchisees

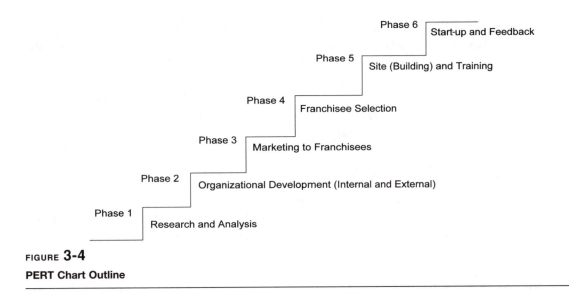

Phase 6 | Start-up and Feedback

Phase 5 | Site (Building) and Training

Phase 4 | Franchisee Selection

Phase 3 | Marketing to Franchisees

Phase 2 | Organizational Development (Internal and External)

Phase 1 | Research and Analysis

FIGURE **3-4**
PERT Chart Outline

4. Phase 4 Franchisee Selection

5. Phase 5 Site (Building) and Training

6. Phase 6 Start-up and Feedback

The chart identifies the steps necessary to begin a franchise system. When these steps are followed by a franchisor, some modifications are likely because of the unique characteristics of any particular business organization. It is probable, however, that the basic format as identified, if followed faithfully, will have superior results for the franchisor. Each of the phases is briefly described in this section.

3-4a Research and Analysis

The research and analysis phase is meant to develop those analyses which are necessary for a wise decision about whether to start a franchise. An obvious area for analysis is the industry, identifying its strengths and weaknesses and charting the industry cycle, if applicable. Also, an in-depth analysis of the intended market would be necessary for measuring current demand and forecasting future demand, as well as for identifying desired market segments, target markets, and market positioning objectives.

The store prototype should be analyzed and the management philosophy critically evaluated. If the store and general management style are not highly successful in existing franchised units, there may be need for change in operational processes, organizational policies, or perhaps management style.

A complete accounting and financial review is in order for the franchisor to understand the overall fiscal limitations or constraints as well as the current financial strengths and weaknesses of the existing organization. In addition, legal analysis should be utilized to determine if the trade name and/ or branded items can be registered in each of the states, and to make sure all legal requirements can be met in order to register within the states to qualify for initiating franchisee operations.

3-4b Organizational Development (Internal and External)

The second phase of the franchise PERT chart focuses on internal factors necessary in order to develop a franchise system. The legal documents, operating documents, training manual, recruitment brochure, and so forth, need to be well developed and approved by the franchisor and by legal counsel when appropriate. Such counsel applies with regard to disclosure documents, contractual relationships, agreements, trademarks, and other components that the franchise system intends to use in the development of the franchise network. The focus is then shifted to such external factors as development of the overall marketing plan, franchisee recruitment strategy, location analysis criteria, and specific elements desired within the franchise feasibility study for a particular location and prospective franchise.

3-4c Marketing to Franchisees

The third phase involves an in-depth analysis and compilation of the marketing package to be used to attract prospective franchisees to the franchise system. A franchisee profile can be very helpful, as it lists the desired attributes of a franchisee of this franchise system. As candidates are recruited, they can be compared to the "ideal franchisee" and judged as to their probability of success in the franchise system. Appropriate mass advertising through audio, video, or print media, as well as word-of-mouth approaches, should be considered in terms of their likelihood of attracting this ideal franchisee. Seminars advertised in local newspapers, or displays at major trade shows, or strictly word of mouth, or some combination thereof may constitute the right approach. Ultimately it is the judgment of the franchisor and advisers that will determine the specific approach to be taken. Whatever tactic is used, all salespeople and executives of the franchising organization need to be trained to handle franchisee prospects in a similar manner while properly representing the interests of the franchisor.

3-4d Franchisee Selection

Obviously, the process of selecting franchisees is of critical importance to the franchisor. As in the draft processes followed in professional sports, proper selection of franchisees can have outstanding results, whereas poor choices can result in problems for the firm. If the franchising organization has carefully developed its approach, however, requesting appropriate information on the application, conducting a well-designed informative interview, establishing solid criteria for acceptance or rejection of an application, deliberating and deciding about territorial restrictions as they might apply, and determining any particular legal restrictions or covenants applicable to any particular franchisee prospect, then the organization will likely succeed in acquiring people with the talents, capacity, and motivation to be successful in the system.

3-4e Site (Building) Selection and Training

Some franchising organizations focus more on site selection and building design than others. McDonald's Corporation, Holiday Inns, and Midas International Corporation have been known for exceptionally good site selection methods. In theory, good site selection requires three steps.

1. Determining markets in a geographical area or region that possess the customer demographics closely associated with existing successful businesses in the same field

2. Selecting the market area with the best combination of demographics that exists within the region or area analyzed, and then studying the specific locations in this area that are most likely to produce high volume sales

3. Examining a number of sites in terms of their "need" for an outlet or store, and forecasting the demand through an appropriate method of trade or primary service area delineation

Once a site is selected and sales volume is estimated, an appropriate building size and layout can be determined. While the site is being prepared and the building is under construction, most franchisees are undergoing training by the franchisor. Such training will be followed by training for employees, delivery of inventory, and promotions to begin announcing the grand opening.

3-4f Start-up and Feedback

One of the most exciting moments in any franchise business is the grand opening of a new outlet. Following the grand opening, the franchisor needs to follow up with activities that assist the new franchisee during these early days, as well as to collect information about start-up business activity to apply toward the next grand opening. Feedback can be as unwelcome as reminders to make tax payments, but appropriate and regular feedback is essential to a smooth franchisor–franchisee relationship. When the feedback and the franchisor response to such feedback are accurate and helpful, problems rarely become insurmountable.

In summary, the benefits of the PERT chart can be significant to both the franchisor and the franchisee. Proper use of the chart and the associated analyses and judgments to be made require that the franchisor carefully define what information and events are necessary for the initiation and successful operation of a franchised unit. This sequence can be followed over and over again, modified to meet local conditions or particular characteristics of the prospective franchisor–franchisee relationship. The basic ingredients, however, should remain the same.

Paul Hogan

HOME INSTEAD SENIOR CARE

President and cofounder Paul Hogan launched Home Instead Senior Care in 1994 from a single pilot operation in Omaha, Nebraska. In 2006, the company generated $550 million in revenues through a network of over 720 franchises operating in forty-nine states (excluding Hawaii) and in eleven foreign countries including Japan, Canada, Portugal, Australia, Ireland, New Zealand, Switzerland, United Kingdom, Spain, and Taiwan. The company has been featured in the Wall Street Journal, Kiplinger's Personal Finance, *and was recently recognized by* Entrepreneur *as one of the top hundred franchise companies in the world.*

Home Instead Senior Care is the nation's leading provider of nonmedical companionship and home care services for the elderly. These services include companionship and social interaction, meal preparation, light housework, errands, and shopping. The company's unique service offering is an affordable solution for many elderly who prefer to remain in the comfort and familiar surroundings of their home instead of being institutionalized.

Hogan is a 1985 graduate of the University of Nebraska–Lincoln with a BS degree in finance. After graduating from UNL, Paul went to work with Merry Maids in Omaha. There he learned the world of franchising. He was amazed at the number of senior citizens who wanted Merry Maids to visit, but once there, seniors wanted the "Maids" to talk rather than work. His advice on how to become the president of your own company—quit your job. Paul started his business in his mother's front living room. Grandmother told Paul that she liked the older caregiver applicants better—therefore the average age of Care givers is 50 years old. Several clients will spend $800 to $1,000 per month for Home Instead Senior Care services. Paul Hogan found a niche. He and his wonderful wife, Lori, are the parents of four children.

SUMMARY

One of the most fascinating experiences is to watch the development of a franchise business from the origin of the product and service idea through to the grand opening of the first franchised unit. The evolution of that idea into a successful franchise system requires time, careful analysis, patience, and extensive planning. The franchisor should develop a franchise feasibility study to understand the various aspects of the proposed franchise business and how each major factor relates to the others. In the first two-thirds of this chapter, where we identified and described the central elements of a franchise feasibility study, we have also made specific reference to other chapters for further development and elaboration of the concepts presented. In essence, much of this text is meant to assist the reader to develop a franchise feasibility study and PERT chart and to understand the sequence of events associated with the inception of the first franchised unit through to its grand opening.

These elements constitute the franchise plan. When the plan is prepared carefully and accurately, it should help the franchisor and franchisees realize their respective dreams. The notion behind the franchise plan is to "plan the work, and then work the plan."

KEY TERMS

Accounting system: an approach to recordkeeping developed by the franchisor and explained to the franchisee; includes aspects of both financial reporting and financial analysis

Advertising, promotion, and sales programs: address the amount and type of advertising and sales promotion a particular franchise plans to pursue

Feasibility study: determines the likelihood of success that would result from developing an existing business into a franchise operation; should contain sufficient information to enable either a franchisor or a franchisee to make a final decision

Franchisor support package: measures taken by franchisors to maintain wholesome franchisor-franchisee relationships

PERT chart: a simple, clearly delineated set of related events presented in sequence; outlines the "critical path" necessary to complete a project, such as the establishing of additional franchised units

Policies: guidelines for employee actions

Primary service area (PSA): an area from which a retail goods or service provider can expect to attract two-thirds or more of its business activity for the proposed business; needs to be large enough to sustain business activity and turn a profit; helps evaluate possible locations for a prospective business, identifying locations with convenient customer access and no heavy competition; determined using a drive or walk time analysis to determine zones of probable coverage

Procedures: the steps or elements within a process that are considered appropriate for performing assigned tasks

Training manual: a guide for teaching operating procedures and personnel management used in formal and ongoing training programs; ideally fills in the gaps between the knowledge of a prospective franchisee or future employee and the level of performance expected by the franchisor

Turnkey cost: also called start-up cost, any expense incurred by the franchisor when readying a new franchise for its first customers, such as land, building, furniture, fixtures, equipment, and personnel costs

Uniform Franchise Offering Circular (UFOC): a disclosure document outlining business activities which the Federal Trade Commission (FTC) requires from all franchisors

REVIEW QUESTIONS

1. What is meant by a franchisor business plan?

2. What are the elements of a franchisee recruitment package?

3. What is included in a franchisee operations package?

4. Why is it necessary to complete a feasibility study of the franchise before entering business?

5. What is the most important element of the franchise feasibility study? Why did you choose that element?

6. What is the purpose of the Federal Trade Commission Rule 436?

CASE STUDY

Neighborhood Foods, Inc.

Jim opened his Neighborhood Foods store three years ago and has been very excited about the growth and prosperity he has found. This past year's sales were over $890,000, with gross profits of $380,000 and realized net profits, after owner's draw, of $95,000. His store area of approximately 2,600 square feet with ample parking has been more than adequate for his store's activities. He now wants to franchise the idea of his store to others.

Jim's store is currently open 365 days a year, 24 hours a day. The store stocks a complete line of top name, national brand merchandise commonly used daily in most households. Jim located his store in a relatively new residential area and has found that residents within a one-mile radius provide the greatest pool of patrons for his business. Jim has always been interested in the proper locations of businesses. He believes that location is of utmost importance to the success of his own personal business. He believes that it is a good idea to locate in densely populated residential areas, preferably inhabited by the middle to higher economic groups. Jim prefers a store that can be seen from at least two, if not three, directions and is close to business traffic with convenient parking lot entrances and exits. Jim has also found that it is important for the speed limit on his stretch not to exceed thirty-five miles per hour, and he prefers being in a location where a large sign may be displayed outside, close to the highway.

Jim discovered after a period of time that the cash registers needed to be located close to the entrance to allow maximum visibility within the store as well as to and from the outside. He also prefers that the entire front be covered with windows to develop a friendly and cordial atmosphere and to allow people from the outside to see all the activities inside. He believes his checkout counter location has reduced theft and shoplifting.

Jim is thinking of establishing an initial franchising fee of $30,000 for the franchise of a Neighborhood Foods store. An additional store opened by the same franchisee would cost

NEIGHBORHOOD FOODS, INC.

Income Statement for the Year Ended December 31, 2008

		Percent (%)
Total Sales	$596,320	100
Cost of Goods Sold	418,616	70.2
Gross Sales	177,704	29.8
Operating Expenses		
Payroll (not including owner's draw)	55,372	9.3
Advertising	1,056	0.2
Taxes and insurance	4,300	0.7
Maintenance	3,426	0.6
Janitorial	2,000	0.3
Equipment rental	820	0.1
Returned checks	248	0.1
Auto	1,240	0.2
Telephone	430	0.1
Utilities	3,268	0.5
Supplies	2,004	0.3
Totals	$74,164	12.4
Less Owner's Draw	$30,000	5
Net Profit	$44,164	7.4

Start-up Costs

NEIGHBORHOOD FOODS, INC.

Land		$ 120,000
Building		185,000
Site Preparation Cost		30,000
Working Capital		18,000
Equipment	56,000	
Signs		11,000
Inventory	5,600	
Subtotal		$ 425,600
Franchising Fee		$ 30,000
Total Estimated Costs	$	455,600

$25,000, a third store, $20,000, and every store thereafter, $15,000. He is thinking of a franchising royalty of 4 percent and an advertising fee of 2.5 percent.

Jim realizes he has a long way to go, but he believes he can provide those ingredients which will make the business a success. Jim also believes he will be able to help the franchisees with merchandising, equipment, location, real estate development, training, bookkeeping, and even personnel insurance.

NEIGHBORHOOD FOODS, INC.

Inventory

Item	Gross Profit Margin, %
Baby Foods	25–30
Baking Supplies	20–30
Beer	40–46
Beverages	25–35
Breads/Pastries	5–15
Candy/Gum	15–25
Canned Fruits	25–35
Canned Meats	20–30
Canned Seafood	30–40
Canned Vegetables	30–35
Cleaners	25–35
Coffee/Tea	35–40
Dairy Products	5–10
Deli Items	35–40
Dessert Toppings	30–40
Dry Foods	25–35
Frozen Foods	25–35
Housewares	30–35
Ice Cream	25–35
Juices	30–35
Paper Products	20–30
Pet Foods	35–40
Snacks	25–35
Tobacco Products	30–40
Wine	40–50

CASE QUESTIONS

1. Develop a feasibility study for Neighborhood Foods.

2. What are the major problems?

3. Is this a feasible franchise?

4. What are the steps necessary in developing a franchise system?

REFERENCES

Adelman, Philip J. and Alan M. Marks, *Entrepreneurial Finance: Finance for Small Business*, 2nd ed. (Upper Saddle River, NJ: Prentice-Hall Inc., 2001).

Allen, Kathleen, *Launching New Ventures, An Entrepreneurial Approach* (Chicago: Upstart Publishing, Inc., 1995).

Bangs, David H. Jr., *The Business Planning Guide*, 7th ed. (Chicago: Upstart Publishing Company, Inc., 1995).

Bangs, David H. Jr., *The Market Planning Guide*, 4th ed. (Chicago: Upstart Publishing Company, Inc., 1995).

Kotler, Philip and Gary Armstrong, *Principles of Marketing*, 9th ed. (Englewood Cliffs, NJ: Prentice-Hall, Inc., 2001).

Longenecker, Carlos, G. Justin, W. Moore, and J. William Petty, *Small Business Management*, 11th ed. (Cincinnati: South-Western Publishing Co., 2000).

Scarborough, Norman M. and Thomas W. Zimmerer, *Effective Small Business Management: An Entrepreneurial Approach*, 6th ed. (Upper Saddle River, NJ: Prentice- Hall, 2000).

Seltz, David D., *Franchising: Proven Techniques for Rapid Company Expansion and Market Dominance* (New York: McGraw-Hill Book Co., 1980).

Thompson, John S., *Site Selection* (New York: Lebhar-Friedman Books, Chain Store Publishing Corp., 1982).

ADDITIONAL INFORMATION

For additional information about starting, organizing, or developing your franchising system, contact Bob Justis at the International Franchise Forum at Louisiana State University.

APPENDIX

Franchisor Feasibility Business Plan Outline

I. EXECUTIVE SUMMARY (maximum 1,000 words or three pages)
   A. List company name, address, phone, contact person, and title.
   B. Describe type of business in a one-sentence summary.
   C. Describe company in a one-paragraph summary of activities, products, and customers.
   D. Name key personnel in a sentence or paragraph description of top two to four executives, and discuss their qualifications.
   E. Mention dates of start-up schedule and competitors' names in a one-paragraph description.
   F. List funds requested and collateral provided in a two-sentence statement. Explain all money needed or requested to start.
   G. Provide a fund use statement in a one-paragraph description, list fund use (how all funds requested will be used).
   H. Provide fund repayment or exit schedule, and explain repayment or public offering.

II. MARKETING
   A. List major marketing objectives and goals: What do you ultimately want to do? When do you plan to do this? Goals are general, and span three to ten years. Objectives include definition, measurement, and time frame.
   B. Develop market plan and pricing strategy: What is your competitive advantage? What is your product and service description in detail? How does it function? What is its use? Also describe and discuss target market: Who? Where? How many? What are the demographics (age, gender, income, marital status)? What are the recommended prices? Do they beat the competition? What is the markup percentage?
   C. Develop franchisee recruitment plan and flow chart. In the franchisee profile, who are we trying to recruit? From where? What is the flowchart plan and follow-up?
   D. Create a franchisee prospectus. The sales brochure should discuss franchise opportunity, start-up costs, and confidential application.

E. Develop franchisee sales and advertising. How do you promote franchise to prospective franchisees? What is the proper media mix (newspapers, direct mail, magazines, etc.)?

F. Determine franchisee location criteria selection. Where are you going to locate a franchise, and why? What are the demographics (age, gender, income, marital status, etc.)?

G. Plan grand opening. Who will do what? when? where? how? and why? What are the costs to franchisor and franchisee?

H. Develop customer advertising (ongoing) through promotions, direct selling, public relations. What is the correct media mix? Develop two original advertisements.

III. MANAGEMENT

A. Outline operations manual in detail.

B. Outline training manual for franchisee.

C. Determine franchisor system headquarters.

1. Develop organizational structure, including chart, and describe organizational relationships.

2. Create policies.
   - Internal: sales, employee, general, financial controls
   - External: credit, checks, layaway, returns, general

3. Determine personnel (wage and salary), including recruiting, job descriptions, performance evaluations, wage and salary structure, benefits, incentives.

D. Determine franchise unit.

1. Develop organizational structure, including chart, and describe organizational relationships.

2. Create policies.
   - Internal: sales, employee, general, financial controls
   - External: credit, checks, layaway, returns, general

3. Determine personnel (wage and salary), including recruiting, job descriptions, performance evaluations, wage and salary structure, benefits, incentives.

E. Develop PERT Chart, including project evaluation review technique, activity and time chart

IV. FINANCING AND ACCOUNTING

A. Headquarters

1. Explain and itemize turnkey costs.

2. Determine equity or unencumbered cash, collateral, current loans (amounts and types).

3. Complete projected case flow for first 36 months, with yearly totals, and explain in narrative the rationale for your figures.

4. Complete pro forma income statements for the first year by month and by quarter for next two years, with yearly totals, and explain in narrative the rationale for your figures.

5. Complete pro forma balance sheets for start-up and first through third years, and explain in narrative the rationale for your figures.

6. Provide breakeven analysis (in units and/or dollars).

7. Provide ratio analysis—calculate and explain selected useful ratios and compare to industry averages.

8. Provide provisions for taxation (federal, state, social security, workmen's comp, etc.).

B. Franchisee

1. Explain and itemize turn-key costs.

2. Determine equity or unencumbered cash, collateral, current loans (amounts and types).

3. Complete projected case flow for first 36 months, with yearly totals, and explain in narrative the rationale for your figures.

4. Complete pro forma income statements for the first year by month and by quarter for next two years, with yearly totals, and explain in narrative the rationale for your figures.

5. Complete pro forma balance sheets for start-up and first through third years, and explain in narrative the rationale for your figures.
6. Provide breakeven analysis (in units and/or dollars).
7. Provide ratio analysis—calculate and explain selected useful ratios and compare to industry averages.
8. Provide provisions for taxation (federal, state, social security, workmen's comp, etc.).

V. LEGAL ASPECTS
   A. Provide disclosure documents: UFOC, contracts, licenses, trademarks.
   B. Provide business structure.
   C. Determine type and cost of insurance.
   D. Determine provisions for termination.

VI. APPENDICES
   A. Building plans
   B. Layout design
   C. Graphs
   D. Working papers
   E. Diagrams
   F. Layouts
   G. Charts

PARENT COMPANY (FRANCHISOR) DEVELOPMENT CHECKLIST

ACTIVITY	PERSON RESPONSIBLE	FINISHING DATE
SALES	_____	_____
Advertising		
Initial Announcements	_____	_____
Franchise Advertisements	_____	_____
Run Advertisements	_____	_____
Preliminary Information Folder	_____	_____
Response System to Initial Inquiries	_____	_____
Telephone Inquiry Qualification Guide	_____	_____
Application Forms	_____	_____
Form Letters and Paragraphs—prospects	_____	_____
Form Letters and Paragraphs—franchises	_____	_____
FINANCE	_____	_____
Franchisor Pro Forma Cash Flow Statement (5 yrs)	_____	_____
Franchisor Pro Forma Income Statement (5 yrs)	_____	_____
Franchisor Pro Forma Balance Sheet	_____	_____
Franchisee Pro Forma Cash Flow Statement (5 yrs)	_____	_____
Franchisee Pro Forma Income Statement (5 yrs)	_____	_____
Franchisee Pro Forma Balance Sheet	_____	_____
MANAGEMENT	_____	_____
Organization Chart	_____	_____
Location Selection	_____	_____
Store Design and Decor	_____	_____
Operations Manual	_____	_____
Training Program	_____	_____
Headquarters Training	_____	_____
Inventory Control	_____	_____
Personnel Selection	_____	_____
Field Support Programs	_____	_____
Field Crew	_____	_____
LEGAL	_____	_____
Uniform Franchise Offering Circular	_____	_____
Financials	_____	_____
Earning Claims	_____	_____
Site Criteria	_____	_____
Acknowledgment Form	_____	_____
Franchise Agreement	_____	_____
Trademark Registration	_____	_____
Trade Name Registration	_____	_____
Compliance	_____	_____
Registration State	_____	_____
MARKETING	_____	_____
Franchisee Store Advertising	_____	_____
Initial Advertising	_____	_____
Grand Opening Campaign	_____	_____
Continuous Support	_____	_____
Advertising Manual	_____	
Public Relations	_____	_____
Promotion	_____	_____
Pricing	_____	_____
Sampling	_____	_____
MARKETING RESEARCH	_____	_____
Target Market Research and Identification	_____	_____
New Product Research	_____	_____
Franchisee Profile Development	_____	_____
Manager Profile Development	_____	_____
Competition Analysis	_____	_____
ACCOUNTING	_____	_____
Franchisor Chart of Accounts	_____	_____
Accounting Controls	_____	_____
Franchisee Chart of Accounts	_____	_____
Franchisee Accounting System	_____	_____
Computer System	_____	_____

FRANCHISEE APPLICATION

Date: _____

PERSONAL DATA:

Name : _____ Social Security No: _____

Address : _____ Years there: _____

City: _____State:_____ Zip:_____

Business Phone: _____ Home phone: _____Best time to call: _____

Your email address: _____ Would you like to communicate by email? Yes_____ No _____

Date of Birth:_____ Marital Status: _____ Spouse name: _____

Number of Dependents: _____ Ages: _____

How did you become aware of this franchise opportunity?_____

_____

_____

BUSINESS EXPERIENCE:

PRESENT/MOST RECENT POSITION _____

_____

_____

PREVIOUS POSITION:

_____

_____

HAVE YOU EVER OWNED A BUSINESS: Yes_____No _____

IF YES, WHAT TYPE?_____

OTHER BUSINESS AFFILIATIONS (OFFICER, DIRECTOR, PARTNER, ETC.) _____

_____

_____

GEOGRAPHICAL PREFERENCE: _____

BUSINESS AND PERSONAL GOALS:

Do you plan to devote full time to this business? Yes_____ No_____

Do you have partners? Yes____ No ____

IF YES, PLEASE IDENTIFY ALL PARTNERS

NAME	ADDRESS	TELEPHONE NUMBER	EQUITY

PERSONAL FINANCIAL DISCLOSURE:

Assets:_____ Liabilities: _____ Net Worth:_____

Unencumbered Liquid Assets Available:

Equity in: Personal Residence $ _____ Other Real Estate: $ _____

ADDITIONAL INFORMATION:

Why do you believe you can successfully operate a store with this company?
_____
_____
_____

How will this franchise opportunity help you in achieving your business and personal goals?
_____
_____
_____

Additional information or comments that you might like to share with us in evaluating your Request For Consideration:
_____
_____

PLEASE ATTACH RESUME IF AVAILABLE

SIGNATURE: _____ **DATE:** _____

FRANCHISOR MANAGEMENT: ORGANIZATION AND ADMINISTRATIVE POLICY

In studying this chapter, you will:

- **Learn about the functions of franchisor management in a franchise system.**
- **Understand franchisor management practices and their importance to a franchisor.**
- **Learn the ten commandments of a successful franchise organization.**
- **Investigate leadership principles important to franchising.**
- **Understand the importance of quality and quality controls in franchises.**
- **Learn about franchisee advisory councils and how they operate.**

INCIDENT

Fred has been franchising a burger-and-fries drive-up restaurant for the past four years. He presently has a chain of fourteen franchised restaurants in three states. Six of these restaurants have been added in the last six months. Fred's franchising fee to the franchisees is relatively high compared with fees for other drive-up restaurant franchises, but Fred believes the higher fee is justified because of the well-known name, recognition, and management he provides the franchisees.

He helps a new franchisee begin operation by supplying financial, location selection, promotion, and operations guidelines, to which a new franchisee is required to adhere closely. Fred established strict policies and guidelines to ensure that each franchise is operating efficiently and effectively.

Once franchisees begin operations, they must follow Fred's guidelines for managing the business, as well as his financial and administrative controls. He contends that the less flexibility a franchisee has in operating the franchise, the greater the chance the franchised unit will be profitable.

Fred has received only a few complaints over the years on the policies by which he requires his franchisees to operate; however, several prospective franchisees have decided to go with another drive-up franchisor to enjoy more flexibility in managing and to avoid being subject to the strict controls imposed by Fred.

Is Fred correct in his assumption that a franchisee should be given as little flexibility as possible? Should he continue his stringent control strategy or allow for more flexibility?

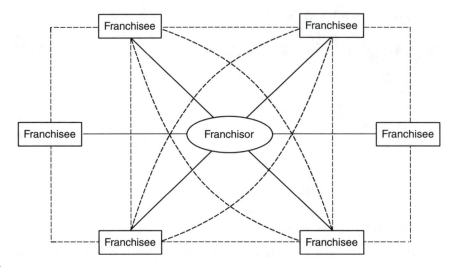

FIGURE 4-1

The Newer Look of the Franchisor–Franchisee Relationship

4-1   INTRODUCTION

A franchisor, like any other business owner, must determine goals and objectives to achieve results in order for the franchise system to survive. A franchise system will not last long unless the franchisor plays the central role in guiding the organization and evaluating performance. Gone are the days when the franchisor could "rule from the top," or when the franchisor–franchisee relationship was a vertical relationship.

To guide a franchise network, the franchisor must have more than just legal authority.[1] The franchisor will not be able to control franchisees merely by pointing to a line in the franchising agreement and demanding rigid compliance. Carefully developed programs to motivate franchisees and gain their cooperation in achieving the franchise system's objectives need to be established and implemented.[2] The newer look between franchisor and franchisees is something like that shown in Figure 4-1.

With franchisors and franchisees operating on a relatively equal level, and with the franchisor presuperimposed in the center, the real authority held by a franchisor in the franchised network rests in the managerial assistance that can be provided to the franchisees. To the extent this assistance and organizational guidance is effective, the franchise network, as well as the independent franchised businesses, becomes profitable and payment of residual fees to the franchisor is justifiable.[3]

This chapter will address two primary themes. First, good management is a prerequisite to long-term profitability, growth, and survival. It can mean the difference between success and failure. Second, primary services provided by the franchisor to franchisees are discussed, as well as points for a franchisor to consider when attempting to motivate franchisees.

4-2   BEING A SUCCESSFUL FRANCHISOR

What does it take to be a successful franchisor or franchisee? Perhaps the starting point should be to ask the question a little differently. What does it take to be a successful entrepreneur? The first requirement is managerial ability. Dun & Bradstreet suggests that over 90 percent of business failures are attributable to lack of managerial ability.[4] Clearly, a franchise entrepreneur needs the ability to conceptualize, organize, and manage a business (see Figure 4-2).

FIGURE **4-2**

Success in an Entrepreneurial Business Venture

Entrepreneurs typically tend to work harder and take greater risks than the person working as an employee in someone else's company. They tend to have high motivation to achieve, versatility, self-confidence, and a sense of adventure.[5] The entrepreneur must have a *genuine* business opportunity. A business opportunity is genuine when new businesses open up or when existing providers are ineffective in providing a product or service that meets consumer wants and needs. A genuine opportunity requires that people (potential customers) express economic or market need for the proposed product or service. With hard work, and perhaps some luck, an entrepreneur can be successful.

4-3 FRANCHISOR DEVELOPMENT

To properly develop the franchise system, the franchisor must create three levels of administration including strategic, administrative, and operations development. See Figure 4-3.

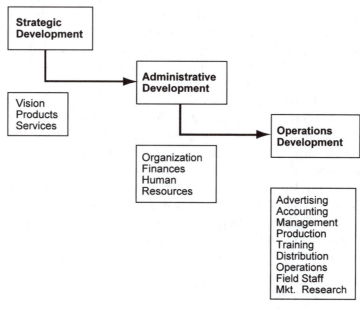

FIGURE **4-3**

Franchisor Development Process

4-3a   Franchisor Development Process

Strategic

The strategic development is focused around the vision of the franchisor, plus the products and services that the franchisor will provide. This may sound easy, but is probably the most difficult of all the franchisor's tasks. The franchisor needs to actually write down the vision, goals, and objectives to be accomplished by the franchise organization. Try doing this to see how difficult it actually is. Then, the franchisor needs to determine the products or services that the franchisee will provide the customer.

Administrative

Administrative development is centered around the organization of the business, necessary finances, and required human resources. This organization is generally divided into two major functions: franchise sales (selling of franchises to prospective franchisees), and operations (training, marketing, finances, advertising, and management). The financial section is concerned with how much money it takes to start the headquarters franchise system. The human resource management section is focused around the staffing and human resources needed to run the franchisor business.

Operations

Now the franchisor needs to turn to the functions and operations of the headquarters organization. This includes advertising, accounting, pricing suggestions, marketing, production, training, distribution, operations, field staff, market research, and management. The franchisor must put together an organization that will optimize the delivery of services to existing and prospective franchisees. These operations systems are needed to encourage and promote unity, harmony, and direction throughout the franchise system. In addition, the franchisor should develop an incentive system that will encourage and support the franchisees.

4-3b   Franchising is a Two-Way Street

The most important ingredient for success of a franchise system is the interdependence between franchisor and franchisee. The franchisor develops the profitable way to produce, sell, or distribute a product, and must monitor or oversee every unit within the franchise system. On the other hand, the franchisee, looking for a limited-risk entrepreneurial opportunity, desires a business venture that can be managed effectively and profitably. The franchisee expects to receive an accepted business name, a product to sell or distribute that has a positive image, and ongoing training and other assistance from the franchise system.

The franchisor is responsible for each unit in the franchisee system. The system itself is no stronger than its weakest link. To achieve effective and profitable results requires controls at many levels, and the controls must be balanced by incentives to—and receive support from—the franchisees. Characteristics of a successful franchisor would typically include a high degree of managerial ability, extensive knowledge of competition and market conditions, keen sensitivity to operating costs and quality control, and the ability to motivate people.[6]

Making the transition from an entrepreneurial single-unit firm to a multiunit professionally managed franchise system requires the franchisor to make several transitions in the development of the organization. An overview of a successful organizational development plan is illustrated in Figure 4-4.

The franchisor of a rapidly growing franchise system has to cope with the day-to-day problems of being in business while keeping a constant eye on new developments and the intended growth plan for the system. It is likely that the franchisor is going through this process for the first time,

IHOP ANNOUNCES NEW LONG-TERM STRATEGIC GROWTH PLAN

International House of Pancakes (IHOP) Corp. announced a new strategic growth plan in January 2003. By transitioning from company-financed development of new restaurants to a traditional franchise development model, IHOP believes it can significantly increase its free cash flow by reducing investment in fixed assets and franchisee receivables. IHOP intends to pursue the number-one position in family dining. Their new model provides the financial flexibility to build the business while enhancing shareholder value.

IHOP has determined that the cash flow benefit of shifting to a traditional franchise development model creates greater value than an earnings model fueled by company-financed restaurant development. The new model is designed to do the following:

Generate positive cash flow

Reduce capital expenditures

Achieve brand penetration through new restaurant openings

Leverage the entrepreneurial base of franchisees while extending franchising options for IHOP

In 2003, IHOP began brand-building initiatives in quest of its vision to become number one in family dining. These initiatives are meant to increase guest traffic counts, raise comparable sales, and create greater brand awareness.

IHOP has been serving breakfast, lunch, and dinner selections for forty-five years. Offering eighteen types of pancakes, as well as burgers, omelets, chicken, and steak entrees, IHOP's diverse menu appeals to people of all ages. As of December 2002, there were over 1,100 IHOP restaurants in the chain in forty-six states and Canada.

Source: Adapted from "IHOP Corp. Announces New Long Term Strategic Growth Plan," 20 January 2003, Bison1.com.

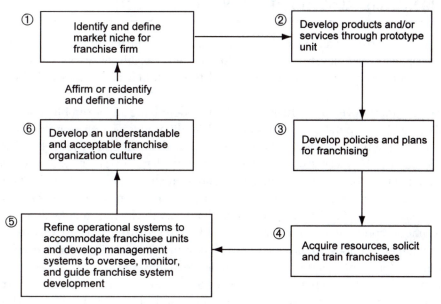

FIGURE **4-4**

Six Major Organizational Development Tasks

which requires thinking about the franchise organization as a whole and planning for changes in the key areas as a progressive set of events or activities to achieve successful growth. The six major organizational developmental tasks identified in Figure 4-4 show how to convert from an entrepreneurial to a professionally managed franchise system.

Identifying and defining the market niche is the fundamental step for the franchisor to develop a competitive advantage in providing the product or service to customers. The second task is designing the product or service to meet the wants, needs, and expectations of the targeted customer group. This also means the franchise firm must be able to produce the product through the franchise delivery system through internal processes that ensure the product meets customer needs.

The third task involves problems and challenges associated with growth—seeking franchisees, opening franchised units, increasing sales, and facing seemingly endless operational problems associated with product, purchasing, collections, payables, and delivery. Developing the policies and plans for controlling the anticipated growth can keep any problems manageable while allowing the firm to continue development toward meeting its growth objectives.

The fourth step is the implementation phase of step three: acquiring the financial and human resources necessary to implement the planned course of development of the franchise system, including recruitment, selection, training, and supervising the grand openings of the first franchised units.

Fifth, the operational systems of the prototype unit, warehousing, and distribution systems must be carefully examined to ensure that the policies and procedures are followed and can, in fact, provide sufficient support to the new franchisees. Appropriate monitoring and control procedures must be established so the franchisor can guide further franchised system development as well as ensure consistency in product and service offerings to the public.

Sixth, the organizational culture can be a critical factor in developing an aura of success and can have profound impact on the behavior of franchisees and employees within the franchise system. Major franchise systems in the automobile, restaurant, and electronic product industries often remind the customer through media advertisements about their corporate images, such as "quality is job one" or "the pause that refreshes" and other positive statements about the corporate culture of the franchise system.

4-4   FRANCHISE ENTREPRENEUR AS MANAGER

Each franchisor is in some way an entrepreneur, and each entrepreneur is to some degree an innovator. A franchisor, as innovator, is seeking to find newer or better ways to meet the customer's needs. The ultimate test is customer satisfaction. If the customer is not satisfied, the business will ultimately fail.

The franchisor must develop an efficient method of identifying and assembling necessary supplies and materials, provide an operational method for efficiently producing or assembling the product and service, and determine the effective methods of selling or delivering the product and service to the customer. Ultimately, the success of the franchise system, large or small, will rely heavily on the capabilities and ingenuity of the system's management—franchisor and franchisees. The management responsibilities can be generalized through discussion of the management process; however, the particular focus and extent of activity required in each area by the management will be conditioned by the size and unique operating characteristics of the franchised firm. It is for this reason that what works best in a large firm does not necessarily work best in a smaller firm, nor does what works best within restaurants work best in auto service or home cleaning services.

More than 50 percent of all marriages fail, over 80 percent of all new products introduced into the marketplace are not accepted and are withdrawn, and about 75 percent of U.S. adults are unhappy with their work. This is a sad commentary, but true. With perspective toward the entrepreneur, one finds a similar rate of failure. About every one minute a new business is started in North America, but unfortunately, three of five (60 percent) will die within the first five years.

The typical reasons stated for business failure are lack of business know-how and under-capitalization. However, the real underlying reason for business failure resides in the concept of "fit." People excel in activities that use their natural talents and abilities, but struggle or fail in activities that rely on talent or skills not possessed by the person.

The central question for entrepreneurs should be: "Does the business venture I am considering match the skills, interests, and abilities of who I am?" Start-up businesses remain marginal or fail because business owners make poor choices that eat up time, energy, and financial resources. Starting a business venture or changing a business venture into a franchise system can be compared, in a limited sense, to a marriage. The entrepreneur is virtually wedded to the business. If the relationship between the owner and the business is not healthy, the business will not be healthy.

The success of your business venture hinges upon what is going to make you, the entrepreneur, happy. Even hot business opportunities are not likely to succeed if the ownership is not happy with the work involved. Therefore, ask yourself: "What is going to make me happy?" Before you change your business into a franchise network, paint a picture of your work-future that will produce overall satisfaction for you; only then look to see if creation and development of a franchise system will fit your needs.

The franchisor should consider developing an approach consistent with the strengths and weaknesses of its ownership/management, to determine what needs to be done and by whom in order to accomplish the objectives of the franchise organization. This requires planning. Figure 4-5 depicts an approach a franchisor can use to systematically and comprehensively plan the development of the organization.

A new, small-sized franchising firm should start with an uncomplicated approach. The approach suggested in Figure 4-6 provides flexibility for the franchisor and management team and franchisees to start out simply and increase sophistication as their planning skills develop.

According to Figure 4-6, the first step is *scanning/assessing the environment* from each of two perspectives: external and internal. External influences on the firm, such as customers, lenders, stockholders, competitors, suppliers, and government regulatory agencies, can help the firm clearly identify the competitive issues it confronts. Being alert to changes in national and international economic conditions, change and advances in technology, and changes in social conditions or in the

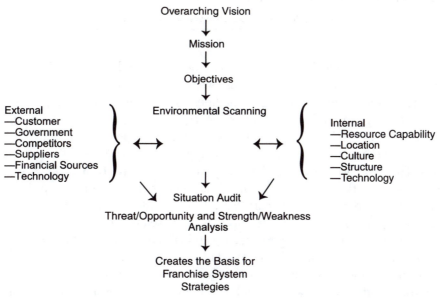

FIGURE **4-5**

Organizational Development

Steps in the Strategic Process	Factors/Variables under Consideration	Outcomes/Results of Assessment
Scanning/Assessing the Environment External	Influence of major groups: customers, lenders, stockholders, employees, the community, competitors, suppliers, government Changes in national and international economic conditions, in technology, in social conditions, in the business climate	Competitive issues in industry Stress points in relationships Trends affecting industry/ firm Discovery of untapped markets
Outcome:	An understanding of opportunities and threats facing the firm	
Internal	The firm's capabilities in functional areas of business, its facilities, location(s), and business image The firm's management, structure, and culture	The firm's ability to compete as is or to change Management's core values and how the firm operates
Outcome:	An understanding of the firm's strengths and weaknesses	
Developing Strategic Plans	Outcomes from above The firm's mission and analysis of past strategic results Firm's objectives	Definition of business and its strategic mission Updated objectives
Outcome:	Appropriate strategies with long-, medium-, and short-range plans	
Implementing Strategic Plans	Resource attraction and allocation Operating system (policies, methods, procedures) Control system (standards, monitoring, comparison) Management Information Systems	Funds to operate Innovation Control of costs Market response
Outcome:	Operating results with objectives achieved	
Continuing Review	Review results and fine-tune plans	
Outcome:	Strategic plans responsive to changing markets	

FIGURE 4-6

A Strategic Planning Process Useful to Franchisors

Source: Figure developed by Professor Jerry Geisler, Metro State University, Denver, Colorado

business climate enables the franchising firm to understand the trends affecting the industry as well as the firm, and can help the management team to discover untapped market opportunities. Factors about the franchise organization itself, including capabilities in each functional area of the business, its facilities, locations, image, as well as the firm's management, organization structure, and culture, should be carefully assessed. This internal and external analysis provides objective information for the management of the franchised business to make appropriate choices and develop tactics to reach the firm's goals. This two-part analysis is what many would call a **situation audit**. A situation audit is the attempt to determine the franchised business's current operating situation in the context of the environmental factors (external and internal) that affect operations. Practically, the small franchisor would identify the objectives and analyze the importance of each to the firm in the short and long run, ranked in priority; analyze current sales performance and sales trends by product or service and by unit or location; analyze current available resources; and identify strengths and weaknesses within the firm. The general purpose of this analysis is to stimulate a consciousness within the franchised business to identify problems, opportunities, strategies, and market tactics to determine future courses of action.

The second step is *development of the strategic plans* for the franchised business. The firm's mission and analysis of past results should be carefully assessed and refined if necessary. The firm's objectives can then be updated and a particular course of action determined to exploit potential opportunities while remedying existing or anticipated problems.

The third step, *implementation of strategic plans*, can be categorized as long, medium, or short range, depending on the time frame in which it is to take place. The overall purpose of this step is to allocate the firm's resources to achieve the best possible market response given the market conditions and the resource capabilities of the firm. Reallocation of resources among existing functional areas may be necessary to complete this step.

The fourth step is *continuing review* of the operating results and market results of the strategic plans. Careful use of the data provided by the information retrieval system as well as feedback from internal operations will help in fine-tuning the plans and modifying policies and procedures to help the business become as efficient as possible. The goal of this fourth step is to ensure that the strategic planning process, as developed and utilized within the franchised firm, keeps the business responsive to the ever-changing needs of the market and alert to the social, cultural, political, and economic factors influencing the firm's environment.

4-5   SET PRIORITIES FOR STRATEGIC DECISIONS

The franchise system entrepreneur must concentrate on multiple perspectives to avoid myopic thinking through a single-lens trap and thus maintain a strategic view across and within the franchise network. Six desired or targeted outcomes can generate balanced decisions, manage risk, and build an effective communication network within the franchise system. The strategic priorities are as follows:

- Build a franchise system and its infrastructure to establish and maintain high performance at the home office as well as corporate and franchisee locations.

- Be state of the art in products and services; look for continual product and service development.

- Seek to gain and maintain market share with quality service to customers.

- Continually improve processes and procedures to ensure efficiency, standards of high quality, and strong financial return.

- Develop a competent and committed workforce within the corporation and build a supportive environment and identity for franchisees.

- Position the franchise system for the long term by identifying issues and trends that may provide opportunities or produce threats to the franchise.

The most brilliant strategy will take you nowhere if you cannot execute the plan. The real value of strategy is gained through execution. When a strategic decision is made, the entrepreneur and senior management must make the business commitment to provide a direct connection with the targeted results to be achieved with the actions that must take place. Creating "results" targets or outcomes leads to a culture of accountability in which people are measured by the strategically aligned results they produce. This requires not only senior management, but also corporate unit managers, franchisees, and other employees to think in terms of outcomes instead of everyday activities.

4-5a   Know What You Are Not Going to Do

Often, strategic initiatives will fail because they are seen as extra work to be accomplished in addition to existing work. A successful strategy does not "add to," it replaces. In implementing a strategic initiative, decide what initiatives are no longer going to be pursued and communicate that message clearly. This allows the franchise system to focus resources and place attention on the new initiative.

Once the new strategic initiative is deployed it should reshape individual and unit performance assessments, without bogging down the franchise system by endless reorganization or resource shuffling. The franchise system leadership should automate status and progress reporting so that franchisees, corporate managers, and home office executives can have real-time field information. Such data can increase effectiveness by addressing critical execution issues. For example, how effective is the initiative in acquiring new customers and determining average dollar size of sale, type of sale, products cross-sold, year-to-date revenue, year-to-date revenue annualized, and actual variance from targeted outcomes.

4-5b   Strategic Process Is Circular

Successful strategy execution is a dynamic process. It begins as a set of agreements among the home office, corporate units, and franchisees about markets, revenues, products, growth rate, and so on. The rest is execution. Without execution, the initiative dies.

Evaluation of execution requires input from both the inside and outside of the franchise system. Internal information often needs answers to questions such as: What's on track? How is this initiative in relation to other initiatives and commitments and their key measures? What's important today? Has there been any change from yesterday? Have there been changes in the past week or month? The external perspective encompasses research and information collection about what is taking place outside the company: economic and social trends, competitor actions, industry trends, and others. Collectively, the franchise systems needs accurate and current information about what trends are taking place relevant to its strategy, what resource commitments need to change, and what actions are required at the home office, corporate units, and franchised units.

4-5c   Growth Opportunities during Tough Times

When times are tough, it is tempting to think that strategies for growth are out of the question. Instead, some franchise systems focus on mere survival, waiting for "good times" to return. The benefits of growth are clear. Nothing contributes to greater shareholder value and improves performance and morale than generating higher levels of growth in the franchise system's core business.

Make a careful examination of the franchise to search for every possible opportunity to increase sales and share of market in the franchise's core market. There are four types of growth opportunities for consideration.

- Retain your existing customers. Reducing attrition is the same as growth.

- Stimulate more purchase/use of your product/service by existing customers to satisfy the basic needs to be met—but more often.

- Generate increased sales with existing customers by cross-selling complementary products or services that meet a new or different combination of the existing customers' needs.

- Bring in customers from your competitors or those who are totally new to your type of product/ service offering.

Some franchise systems may lack the kind of data on customers or end users that enable the franchise system to figure out which approach will result in the most growth for the system. Begin then by gaining as much of a fine-tuned understanding of your customer segment as possible. This is indispensable if the franchise system wishes to influence existing or new customer behaviors. The goal is to examine your customer segment so carefully that you can (figuratively) "crawl inside the heads" of your customers. The rationale herein is, "If I know my customer in detail, I will know not only how to market to him/her but also how to please him/her." For example, two toy companies hope the small hands riffling through Burger King Kids Meals to find toy cars and tiny dolls will remember the toys they received and bug their parents to buy more in stores long after the burgers and fries are gone.[7]

Organize your market research and data collection about your customers around segments that your franchise can act upon. If your franchise does not or cannot isolate onto a particular desired customer segment, you will not be able to influence the franchise's behavior, no matter how hard you try or how intimately you know the customer profile. Therefore, know *who* your customers are as well as *how* you can reach them. Growth-oriented franchise systems work on the previous four approaches at all times. Sounds like hard work? Sure, but it proves out to be well worth the effort.[8]

4-6 PLANNING SHOULD BE ORGANIZED

Planning helps the franchisor keep a proper perspective on individual whims and personal aspirations. Consistent growth and development usually requires an approach other than the proverbial shooting from the hip. Formal planning is the initial process, the completion of which enables the remaining elements of the process of management to be utilized.

4-6a The Process of Management

The franchisor must provide direction that can be described through the management functions. A small franchisor must perform the same general management functions as the CEO of a large franchise system. The management process described here primarily involves day-to-day business operations, although a franchisor or franchisee, as owners of their respective businesses, are also concerned with strategic planning as discussed in the preceding section.

4-6b Planning

Planning is the primary responsibility of the owner-manager. Planning concerns the following:

- Determining the overall goal, mission, and objectives of the franchise
- Formulating policies, plans of action, and procedures (when appropriate) for attaining the objectives of the franchise organization
- Developing standards for costs, sales targets, and performance for incorporation into a budget and sales forecast, which can be used as an operating control
- Developing the franchise's line of products, services, and processes in the long run to ensure continuity for the organization as well as adaptability to the ever-changing needs of the marketplace

Solid strategic planning demands that all the pieces of the franchise development plan fit together. Copying off of another franchise system's approach or play book is usually a mistake, because the personalities and the driving influences underlying the copied portions of some other franchise system may make a very poor fit for a new franchise company. When one copies another franchise plan, one rarely gives sufficient thought to the rationale behind it and, ultimately, there is no reason for it to be part of one's own offering. In franchising, you either own your strategy for system development or you do not. If you are blurred by copying other systems' tactics or features, you will not be operating on a solid footing when trying to explain your system to prospective buyers—as investors or potential franchisees.

As a franchise system, the franchisor typically relies on two income streams: (1) franchise fees and (2) royalties based on franchisee sales. Franchise fees need to be sufficient to cover costs of marketing the franchise system to prospective franchisees, site selection and approvals, pre–grand opening setups, franchisee and employee training, and so forth. For many successful franchise systems, franchise fees are not designed to be a profit center for the franchise system. Most if not all the funds generated by franchise fees are expensed in the marketing of franchises and the development of successful start-up ventures by new franchisees. As a franchise system grows, royalties should pay for the franchisor's administrative and support programs as well as profit as the return on investment for helping franchisees become and remain successful. Many franchise systems have concluded that without strong royalty flow, there will be little income to pay for the needed research and development of new products and services and programs to keep the franchise system fresh and of high quality.[9] Therefore, central to the administrative planning function is determining the amount of funds from franchise fees and royalties that the franchise system needs in order to carry forth a quality program of franchise system development.

4-6c Organizing

Organizing is the coordination of human, financial, and physical resources deemed necessary to reach the objectives set forth in the planning phase. Activities in the organizing function include identifying the jobs required to be performed, staffing each job with qualified people, determining how much authority and responsibility each person should have as an employee of the business, and clearly defining the authority–responsibility relationships to avoid confusion and overlap of authority. Job descriptions and an organization chart describe and graphically represent these relationships.

Organization Chart

An organization chart is particularly useful for showing these relationships as well as indicating the formal decision-making and communications channels. Usually, the organization chart is simple because of the small size of many franchised businesses. However, business growth implies change to reflect new franchisees, territories, and required staff assistance. These relationships should be reflected in the formal organizational chart. Figure 4-7 illustrates the franchisor organization prior to the sale of the first franchise. Figure 4-8 shows a franchise organization at full development. Table 4-1 identifies a job title with some of the duties and responsibilities that could apply to a franchise sales position.

Multiunit Franchising

A major movement in the franchising field is the utilization of multiunit franchises. A **multiunit franchisee** is one who owns and operates more than one franchise, often in an urban area. Most generally, multiunit franchisees are granted geographical areas, primarily designated market areas (DMAs) as developed by the A. C. Nielsen station index. As we will address in Chapter 9, the DMA is a television market coverage area rating system, and is a common method of allocating geographical territories based on a market's media for advertising and promotion. The DMA is simply a map that outlines television viewing markets exclusive of one another based on measurable viewing patterns.

The multiunit franchisee generally will begin with one unit and utilize the proceeds and profits to expand into the second, third, and fourth units. Many franchisors wish to limit a franchisee to one, two, or three units; however, some franchisors seeking rapid development and expansion may encourage a franchisee to expand to as many as five, ten, or even twenty or more franchised units.

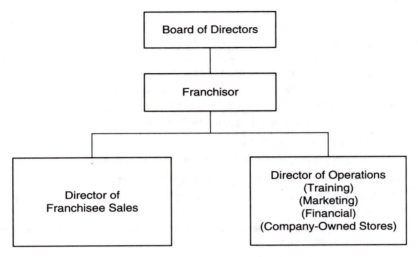

FIGURE **4-7**
Franchise Organization Chart Prior to Sale of First Franchise

A study was conducted to determine the propensity of multiunit franchisee ownership in the United States. International Franchise Association (IFA) members were sent surveys asking about multiunit ownership in their particular system. Eighteen percent of IFA members responded. About 80 percent of franchisees are single-unit franchisees and they operate almost half of the franchised units. Multiunit franchisees account for 20 percent of the franchisees but operate just over half of the franchised units. The primary reason that franchisors have multiunit franchisees is to grow their respective systems, as a reward for good franchisees, for economic and efficiency reasons, and to grant franchisees' request for more units.[10] Table 4-2 identifies the primary reasons for multiunit franchising.

Single-brand franchise system franchisees comprise 94.3 percent of multiunit franchisees. Multiple-brand franchise system franchisees comprise 5.7 percent of multiunit franchises and own 7.5 percent of the multiunit franchisee units. On average, multiple-brand franchise system

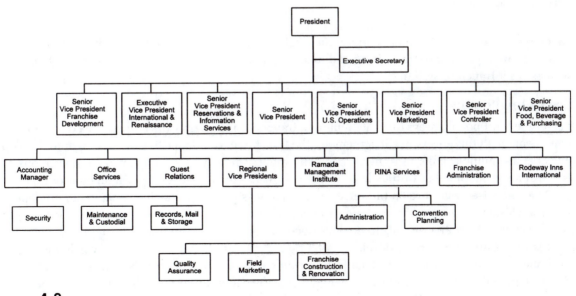

FIGURE **4-8**

Organization Chart (Ramada Hotel Group)

TABLE 4-1   DIRECTOR OF FRANCHISE SALES

Responsible to:	Direct responsibility to the Franchisor Board of Directors
Authority:	Functional authority for all phases of franchisor sales activities as overseen by the franchisor's directives and policy statements of the franchisor organization.
Responsibility:	Line of responsibility to include, but not be limited to:
X	Advertising and promoting the franchise
X	Performing the franchisor representations to prospective franchisees
X	Setting forth and administering franchisee qualification procedures
X	Performing as the sole, or when with others the primary, negotiator of franchisor–franchisee contracts
X	Submitting reports on advertising and promotion, as well as prospective franchisee recruitment and contract negotiations
X	Participation, as desired, in franchisee training
X	Submitting all executed documents and down-payment monies to Franchisor Board of Directors

TABLE 4-2   PRIMARY REASONS FOR MULTIUNIT FRANCHISING

Reason	Percent of Total Responses (%)
System Growth	22.6
Reward for Good/Selected Franchisees	15.1
Economic/Efficiency	14.1
Franchisee Requests	14.1
Market Penetration Strategy	10.4
Miscellaneous	10.4
Attract Potential Franchisees	7.5
Easier to Manage Franchisees	4.7

franchisees own about 1.5 more units than single-brand franchise system multiunit franchisees. However, multiple-brand franchising did not begin until after about seven years of being in business as a franchise system.

Area Developer

One of the most popular ways to create multiunit franchises is to simply draw up an area development agreement. With this development agreement, the franchisee (developer) is given the right to develop and operate multiple units in a given area. This right generally is accompanied by obligations to establish a specific number of franchises in the designated territory over a given amount of time.

The franchisee will develop the territory as rapidly as possible, utilizing separate and independent franchising agreements for each new franchised outlet. An area development agreement would usually cover the number of units to be developed in a given time, site selection, approval methods, any restrictions on transferring developmental rights, and any specific conditions which may cause the franchisee-developer to be in default. For example, if the franchisee fails to meet the schedule of development, then the franchisor would have the right to reduce the area or revoke the exclusivity granted under the original development agreement. In any case, however, all existing franchising agreements would remain in effect.

The developer may have to pay initial development fees to retain the geographic area for the reserved geographic area. In addition, the franchisee will often need to meet unit quotas and abide by the predetermined developmental schedule.

Master Franchisee

Another major method of developing multiunit franchises is through a **master franchisee** or subfranchisor. This individual has the right to offer and sell franchised units, collect fees, and provide services within a given territory. Often this individual is not a franchisee, but an agent who is directly responsible for selling franchises in a given geographic area.

The master franchisee makes a subfranchising agreement with the franchisor. This agreement allows the franchisee to act as an intermediary who will collect royalty fees, advertising fees, and even initial franchising fees. Only a portion of these fees, according to the subfranchising agreement, are paid back to the franchisor. The subfranchisor is generally responsible for enforcing the terms of the franchising agreement and the operations manual, collecting all franchising fees, and providing initial and continuing training, evaluation, and reports on each franchised unit.

The franchisee will sign a franchising agreement with the subfranchisor which obligates the subfranchisor to fulfill most functions and obligations of the franchisor. The subfranchisor may often retain a majority of the fees, providing only a limited portion back to the headquarters organization.

Area Representative

Another method of developing multiunit franchising is through development of an **area representative**. This person is generally an employee of the franchisor who has the right to solicit for prospective franchisees but does not have the right to contract with franchisors. The area representative acts in essence as a sales representative for the franchising company, but also often has responsibilities for training franchisees, providing periodic inspections, controlling standards, setting up marketing and advertising schedules, and sometimes consulting.

Franchise Broker

The **franchise broker** is generally an independent third party who simply solicits prospective franchisees for the franchisor. Franchise brokers generally work for several franchisors at the same time and provide information to prospective franchisees concerning many franchising opportunities. Once a contract has been developed, the franchise broker will contact the franchisor for a disclosure meeting and possible signing of the prospective franchisee.

Strategy must drive organization structure. The organization structure and the particular approach for franchise development should have clear criteria to ensure strategic alignment between mission, planning, organization, direction, control, and evaluation.[11] Between the white spaces on the organization chart, superior business processes get the work done to offer a first-class product or service.

The planning and organization processes should ensure the following:

- Consistency with the one-two-three core processes that facilitate the workflow of the franchise system and support the overall strategy

- Support from corporate headquarters for the central functions necessary to support the geographic nature of the franchisor's market area and market penetration

- Compatibility with the franchise system's market tactics and competitive advantage(s)

- Compatibility with the franchise system's culture and leadership style

TABLE
4-3 **SAMPLE OF CRITERIA FOR FRANCHISEE SELECTION**

Firm	Franchisee Selection Considerations
McDonald's	Entrepreneurial spirit and strong desire to succeed Ability to motivate and train people Ability to manage finances Willingness to personally devote full time and best efforts to day-to-day operation as on-premises franchisee Willingness to complete comprehensive training and evaluation program Financial qualifications[1]
Boston Pizza	Necessary capital investment and/or financial requirements Manpower commitments including management personnel Business experience in local market Willingness to adhere to Boston Pizza system Strong desire to succeed, work hard, and be part of winning team[2]
Jungle Jims	"We will accept only those franchisees whom, upon reasonable investigation, appear to possess the requisite skills, education, personal qualities, and financial resources to meet the needs of a successful restaurant operation. We will provide reasonable supervision over the activities of franchisees to protect the integrity of the franchise system for the benefit of the public, other franchisees, employees and suppliers."[3]
Gelare	"There is no particular experience required to own a Gelare franchise. Gelare franchisee selection process focuses more on the character and personal qualities of the applicants. At Gelare we believe that a successful franchisee is a team player that understands and adheres to the franchise system, has commitment and strong belief in Gelare products and system, good PR and customer relations, ambition, integrity and a passion for success with ability and energy to work hard to achieve it. It is important for all applicants to realize that Gelare Franchise is not a passive investment and they must be willing to be hands on."[4]
Wendy's (Australia)	A positive attitude An ability to provide outstanding customer service and to relate well with employees A strong desire to achieve and succeed A willingness to become actively involved in their Wendy's franchise A high level of energy and enthusiasm To be able to take directions, be willing and able to change, be a team player as part of a franchise system[5]

[1] http://www.mcdonalds.com/countries/usa/corporate/franchise/faq/faq.html
[2] http://www.bostonpizza.com/franchising/partner.cfm
[3] http://www.junglejims.ca/franchise.php
[4] http://singalpore.franchiseopportunities.com/franchise,d,fid,m,12234 5,t,et,m,6,t,cid,m,O.asp
[5] http://www.wendys.com.au/html/fran6.html#successful

4-7   FRANCHISEE SELECTION

Some franchise systems will openly disclose their criteria for franchisee selection. A convenience sample of criteria for franchisee selection, based on a search of selected franchise websites, is shown in Table 4-3.

As can be readily identified from Table 4-3, personal and financial consideration are significant in describing their franchisee selection processes. For a more definitive examination of franchise selection processes by Clarkin and Swaverly, 1,206 franchise systems were categorized.[12] The ratings of importance assigned to each evaluation criteria are extracted from each website. Table 4-4 identifies the level of importance of characteristics in franchisee selection.

Generally, the importance of financial net worth in franchisee selection is considered as most important by 34 percent of franchisors. Over 60 percent of respondents rated the personal interview as being the factor of highest importance. General business experience was rated at level four, the second highest rating, by 36 percent of respondents. Specific industry experience, formal education, and the prospective franchisee's psychological profile were ranked lower than financial net worth, general business experience, and personal interview.

| TABLE 4-4 | LEVEL OF IMPORTANCE OF CHARACTERISTICS IN FRANCHISEE SELECTION |

Criteria	FNW		GBE		SIE		FE		PP		PI	
Rating	N	%	N	%	N	%	N	%	N	%	N	%
5 (Most)	330	34.0	218	22.5	106	10.9	24	2.5	114	11.9	588	60.6
4	291	29.9	350	36.0	140	14.4	115	11.9	255	26.7	261	26.9
3	253	26.0	299	30.8	253	26.0	453	46.7	329	34.4	94	9.7
2	80	8.2	83	8.5	228	23.4	272	28.0	151	15.8	14	1.4
1 (Least)	18	1.9	21	1.0	246	25.3	106	10.9	107	11.2	13	1.3
Total	972	100	971	100	973	100	970	100	956	100	970	100

FNW = Financial Net Worth
GBE = General Business Experience
SIE = Specific Industry Experience

FE = Formal Education
PP = Psychological Profile
PI = Personal Interview

4-7a Directing

Direction is used to achieve the franchise organization's objectives while building an organizational climate conducive to encouraging superior performance. The five major activities associated with the directing function are giving directives, supervising, leading, motivating, and communicating.

Giving Directives

Directives can be given in either written or oral form. Written directives, or orders, may be in the form of memos sent directly from the franchisor to those in the next hierarchal level of the franchise organization, notices placed on bulletin boards for all employees to read, or instructions included prominently within the narrative of the operating manual for use in the pilot or, perhaps, in the franchisee unit. Oral directives involve face-to-face contact and are specifically designed for the two or more persons involved in the communication.

Supervising

Supervising is about the training—and disciplining if required—of personnel employed in the franchise organization. Supervision is a set of activities to ensure prompt and proper execution of directives. Supervising duties are for every managerial employee. For example, the pilot or proto-type unit manager supervises personnel of the unit in accordance with the franchisor's directives, and the franchise system's policies and set procedures, consistent with solid business practice for the operation of the unit.

Leading

Leadership behavior is meant to influence others to willingly provide effort and cooperation in order to achieve the objectives of the organization. The franchisor and each manager in the organization should be aware of techniques helpful for influencing others to do their work well.

Motivating and Communicating

A natural by-product of effective leadership is a good work environment. Within a work environment, the most important resource is the people. Understanding people and how and why they behave as they do is a vital part of a franchisor's and franchisee's job. It is easy to oversimplify or stereotype employees' attitudes and behaviors. It is a wise franchisor or franchisee who recognizes individual differences in people and communicates effectively with employees in light of these differences.

TABLE 4-5

COMPARISON OF NEEDS: ENTREPRENEURS VERSUS MANAGERS

McClelland's Theory	Maslow's Theory	Needs	Entrepreneurs vs. Managers
	Physiological	Minimum income needs/base salary; basic working conditions, e.g., heat, facilities	Initially, entrepreneurs might have higher tolerance for adverse conditions; with seniority, or longevity, managers are more tolerant of adverse condition.
	Safety and Security	Job security; safe working conditions; stable demand for employable skills; pension	Entrepreneurs have high risk propensity; managers have higher needs for job security, being more willing to "stay put," hoping to become more secure and to have more economic value in the organization in time.
Need for Affiliation	Social	Compatible work group members; teamwork; professional friendships	Entrepreneurs often "go it alone"; managers often have higher needs for, and place higher value upon, affiliation and work-related friendships.
Need for Achievement / Need for Power	Self-Esteem	Overall responsibility and authority held/exercised; job title/position in firm; Importance of promotion	Entrepreneurs might fulfill need from seeing their names on business marque; managers might fulfill need from job title and/or status factors available in the organization.
	Self-Actualization	Autonomy; challenges of the job/task; creativity	Entrepreneurs create their own success, often with their firms being a reflection of their personalities and values; managers create autonomy and challenge within the constraints of the employing firms

Source: Figure developed by Dan Gallagher, Professor of Business, University of Illinois at Springfield. Figure used with permission, 1997.

Like the employee, the franchisor and subsequently the franchisees within the franchise chain should be examined in a motivational context. Is there a set of entrepreneurial motives as compared to managerial motives to which a person can address particular interests as a potential franchisor or franchisee? Table 4-5 lists the essential elements of two famous motivational theorists and suggests differences between entrepreneurs and managers in terms of the respective theories.

Choosing to become a franchisor or franchisee involves consideration of both types of career options—entrepreneur or manager. As Table 4-5 indicates, there are some clear distinctions between entrepreneurs and managers. The primary difference is the degree to which specific needs are to be satisfied. Comparison of the McClelland and Maslow theories suggest that entrepreneurs have opportunity for more self-expression, more income, more job security, and greater freedom in choosing what to do and when to do it. On the other hand, managers have greater security by having a regular income, less risk, and less worry when away from the job.

The task of creating and implementing strategy is difficult. It requires vision, discipline, commitment, leadership, and superior execution skills. The leaders in the franchise system must carefully track implementation progress. Implementation may show that the strategy needs updating or changing, or more effort or other resources may be required to ensure that the implementation tactics are in line and consistent with the strategy and the time frame for completion.

Subway Restaurants is the world's largest submarine sandwich franchise, with more than 20,000 locations worldwide. It is also the second largest fast-food chain in the world and has surpassed McDonald's in number of locations in the United States and Canada. Subway was recently awarded the "#1" designation in the Franchise Top 500 for the third year in a row.

Source: *www.bisoni.com/press/prl_21_03subway.html, 2006.*

4-7b Controlling

Controlling involves the determination of standards and methods of evaluating performance against those standards to appraise operating results. Evaluation should be followed by prompt praise, concurrence, or punitive action when the results significantly deviate from the standard. Evaluations are required in each functional area of the franchise organization, whether formally or informally determined. A franchisor would likely have an interest in making the following types of appraisals.

- Appraisal of performance of subordinate managers (e.g., directors of training, purchasing, franchise sales, and pilot unit manager)

- Appraisal of policies associated with franchisee recruitment, franchisee screening and selection, franchising contracts, franchisee training, franchisee operations, minority group franchising opportunities, site selection practices, etc.

- Appraisal and analysis of financial transactions

To be effective in the long run, the franchisor will need controls and methods of determining appropriate performance in such areas as costs, output, sales, profits, quality, employee morale, and labor turnover. In essence, the control process helps the franchisor stay abreast of what is currently happening in the business by providing continual feedback in important areas so the firm can stay on a course to achieve its objectives. The three basic steps in the controlling process are determining standards, comparing performance to standards, and taking corrective action.

Lack of monitoring and control can lead to misuse of a franchised system. Good management practice requires that the franchisor create and use adequate monitoring and control programs to reach quality goals and objectives. Marginal and poor franchise systems either do not care about network quality or lack the wherewithal to achieve it. It requires time, money know-how, and motivation to provide sound training and support, which in turn produces control and a quality brand on a consistent basis over time. *Continuity* and *uniformity* are two adjectives that describe quality franchise operation. They result from constant training, review, supervision, and care. The best franchises assign significant resources, personnel, and financial to ensure similarity across their network, which ultimately leads to customer satisfaction with the products and services.[13]

Determining Performance Standards

Standards for each person in the organization identify what performance levels are expected to achieve the franchise's goals. Not only should overall firm goals and objectives be set, but also realistic standards for individual performance. Otherwise, objectives may not be achieved. A form of management by objectives (MBO) can be effectively utilized here.

Comparing Performance to Standards

By comparing actual performance to standards, franchisors can determine if employees are operating at acceptable levels. Performance standards can be checked at various times and in various ways. The key is that the control standard must be measurable and comparable to actual performance. Performance can be checked hourly, daily, weekly, or monthly. It can be checked against activity (phone calls made, customers visited, slide presentations made, etc.) or by outcome (sales quota expected, or sales by product or service category, by territory, or by franchised unit).

By having predetermined standards, the franchisor can monitor activities without continually having to personally oversee the specific activities of each employee. Most employees do not like close supervision if they have clear standards and goals. Employees need some degrees of freedom to do what is requested by the leader (franchisor or franchisee); the franchisors and franchisees need to bear responsibility for activities such as planning, monitoring economic and technological changes, and competitive positioning.

To summarize, the essentials of management—planning, organizing, directing, and controlling—apply to the franchise organization as much as to any business enterprise. The planning function concerns formulation of the franchise's goals and objectives and overall policies for internal operation. The organizing function addresses the structural requirements of the firm, identifying jobs by functional or divisional arrangement with associated authority and responsibility for each position. Directing involves an overlap of processes and activities such as supervising, issuing orders, leading, and motivating subordinates to achieve individual and franchise objectives. The controlling function includes determination of performance standards, appraising performance with standards, and providing rewards or taking corrective action.

4-7c   Franchisor Policies

A franchise often starts out small and because of its size is usually a highly centralized operation. In time, emphasis shifts from seeking and acquiring franchisees to maintenance of the ongoing franchise distribution network. To assist the franchisor in making this transition is the set of organizational and operational policies. Policies guide operation work activity, assist in coordination of effort across functional lines and areas of the business, and help reduce conflict between individuals and units. Policies provide statements about certain areas of the business and how these areas should be addressed in order to achieve the overall franchise objectives. Examples of such policies are product features, promotional strategy of approach, franchising fees, license fees, rental lease fees, sale of materials or semifinished products or goods, royalty fees, and policies associated directly with services as provided by the franchisor to the franchisees.

Enhanced communication between central offices and franchisees in the field can have merit. For example, if the resident or director of sales was to make two or three telephone calls per week to the franchisees of the chain, it is likely that within a manageable period of time all franchisees would receive a personal call from the central office. This helps the morale of franchisees and provides an open channel to identify and resolve grievances early before they become major points of contention. For example, franchises surveyed by the Conference Board believed their respective companies should be spending more money on advertising the franchised products and services and less on efforts to recruit new franchisees.[14] In the early stages of developing a franchise network or chain, this is a difficult line for a franchisor to walk, trying to build the franchise network through recruitment while needing an ever-larger portion of the budget to generate brand recognition and patronage.

Franchisor advertising, if exaggerated or deceptive, can result in criticism and complaint by franchisees, as well as by the general public. It can also draw criticism from other franchisors who are reasonably meeting the needs of their respective franchisees and the consuming public.

Franchisors or directors of franchise sales can feel pressure from the board of directors to generate new franchised outlets. When this is the case, they may be hasty in selecting new franchisees or simply lower the screening standards. These practices often lead to increased franchisee terminations, poor market representation, and depending how the arrangements were handled, increased litigation for the franchisor. The common error or omission seems to be in not thoroughly checking applicants' references and personal data. A potential franchisee's past experience, experience in the line of business of the franchise, reference checks on each named person to be identified as owning the franchise, financial condition, and educational background should be carefully examined.

4-7d   Ten Commandments of a Successful Business

Jim Peterson, chairman, CEO, and president of Bojangles' Restaurants Inc., has developed the ten commandments of running a successful business. These ten points are as follows:[15]

1. Leadership

2. Staying with the business one understands

3. Developing and maintaining a unique niche

4. Keeping firsthand touch with the customer

5. Relentless pursuit of management principles and fundamentals

6. Organization

7. Freedom from government intervention

8. Strong fiscal responsibility

9. Strategic development

10. Picking winners

Leadership

Peterson lists leadership as the first commandment and states that it is absolutely necessary to ensure the success of any franchising organization. Four factors are required for a successful leader. These include that the person must (1) have a sense of vision, (2) be able to articulate vision, (3) be able to develop agenda to accomplish strategic vision, and (4) have the self-confidence to make it happen. The leader must have flexibility to learn and change. All leaders make mistakes and mistakes can be corrected. Leaders need to be able to accept advice and to correct their blunders. A leader must have a good sense of vision, to see where the business can be ten years later. A leader needs to understand the problems of growth and how to overcome difficulties when developing, creating, and building the business.

A leader needs self-confidence to function effectively. The leader should train employees so that they will become self-confident. Self-confidence comes from developing self-esteem and having a good feeling about oneself. Self-confidence comes from asking questions, learning, continued reading, and questioning the entire operation and business processes. Employees should think of their job opportunity as a beginning. They should endeavor to communicate and gain information about the organization over their tenure in the firm. The franchisee should set up networks of information, convert the information to knowledge, and then convert the knowledge to action.

Information ! Knowledge ! Action

An individual needs to be honest. It is important that the franchisee and employees are open and help customers get what they desire. If honesty is compromised, there will be trouble. If there is a question about the weight requirements of a product, a business should always exceed the requirements rather than fall short.

Stay in the Business You Understand

Franchisors should be in a business they understand. Almost all successful businesspeople follow this principle. They create and expand upon business opportunities within their spectrum of knowledge and experience.

Develop and Maintain a Unique Market Niche

The franchisor should develop and maintain a unique marketing niche, serving that niche with a high-quality product. The primary advertising and promotional activity by the franchisor should be to promote quality. For example, in food service business it is important to provide consistently fresh, made-to-order, quality products.

Keep in Touch with Customers

The franchisor should have firsthand knowledge of the customer by going into franchised outlets and talking with customers. For two days, Jim discovered that in one particular location there were no senior citizen discounts for early dining hours. Upon learning this, it was an easy step to provide the discounts and improve the organization's image within that community. Further questions revealed that diners felt the highchairs were not safe and were fearful of putting their children in them. Additionally, one customer complained about finding gum underneath a booth. These were all matters which were quickly corrected.[16]

Maintain Management Principles and Fundamentals

The franchisor must maintain a relentless pursuit of management principles and fundamentals for the franchise system. Jim Peterson will write to or visit with an unsatisfied customer within thirty days of a complaint. He picks up litter around the outside before going into a store, thereby setting an example for employees, franchisees, and staff members. People follow examples, so if an owner does something, others will follow suit.[17]

Develop and Maintain Strong Organization

It is the franchisor's responsibility to develop and maintain a strong organization. The organization exists so that people will know their responsibilities and how to respond to management directives. Management should inform employees about how they will be evaluated and rewarded. The organizational structure is meant to allow for a smooth flow of business operations.

Remain Free from Government Intervention

The franchised business should remain free from government intervention. Jim Peterson often spends up to one week per month in Washington, D.C., working to ensure freedom of business opportunities from government intervention.[18] Regulations to ensure health, property, and personal safety are essential, but it is important to keep that government intervention and regulations limited to those areas of utmost necessity. The greater the freedom of operation, the greater are the chances for success and development.

Develop Fiscal Responsibility

The franchisor should develop strong fiscal responsibility. Franchisors must understand their financial picture and their financial responsibilities. For example, most fast-food, nonmeat franchises will operate with a cost of goods sold plus labor cost of 50 percent to total sales volume. This ratio of food costs plus labor costs to gross sales may be increased to 60 percent in meat service businesses.[19] Other ratios are important for different industries and operations. Deviations from correct ratios often illustrate problem areas.

Develop Strategic Program

The franchisor is responsible for identifying and explaining the vision of the franchise system. This vision should be strategically oriented. Based on the strategic vision, the firm establishes the objectives and from these objectives develops departmental plans which can accomplish the strategies proposed. These objectives and programs need to be reviewed at least yearly to update and develop future strategy. Environmental and social changes may require changes in business to deviations over time.

Pick Winners

One of the greatest needs of a successful franchise is good, honest, hard-working people. There is no need for individual stars, but a tremendous need for good people who are willing to work hard to develop the right franchising concepts and develop and encourage an image of integrity and honesty within the organization. The greatest resource an organization has is the people within that organization. Quality people build success.

4-7e   Motivation

Jim Peterson also reports five basic steps on motivating and developing employees. These steps are as follows:[20]

1. Improvement-oriented attitude

2. Measuring everyone's performance

3. Evaluation

4. Feedback

5. Recognition

Employees' attitudes are important to customer satisfaction and the perceived quality of the business. Each employee's performance should be measured on a regular basis. This evaluation should be face to face between the immediate supervisor and the employee. Honest feedback should flow between the franchisor and employees. When an employee is dissatisfied, the reasons for dissatisfaction should be brought into the open. If mistakes occur, then they should be properly pointed out and corrected.

Recognition is important as well in motivating employees. Many times this recognition provides status, a feeling of self-achievement, and can help build self-esteem. Individuals have a tendency to work harder and better when they have been recognized for their accomplishments and suitably rewarded for their good performance. Everyone in the organization should be able to grow and develop.

4-7f Quality

It is important for the management of the franchise to know how customers honestly perceive the quality of the product or service. Quality is the customer's perception of the product, and the customer's perception is greatly influenced by the employee or server. Jim Peterson points out that the attitude of the customer is made up of three key factors.

1. "70 percent—the way the customer is looked at;

2. 29 percent—based on the tone of the server's voice; and

3. 1 percent—exactly what the employee (server) says."[21]

The employee is there to make the customer feel comfortable, not to win an argument. If there is a problem, the employee may simply say, "This is our fault; let us correct it for you."

The quality of the product will also be influenced by the condition of the premises. If the office or store is clean and bright, then quite often a positive feeling will prevail. Friendly employees often provide a feeling of security and warmth to the customer.

The availability and convenience of a product also reflects on the quality of that product. Another factor is the completeness of the service. It is estimated that 35 percent of customers are never thanked before leaving the store. The business has not been completed until a "thank you" is offered the customer. Also, packaging must be properly identified. Also, there is no need to ask, "Is that all?" A more complete question would be, "Would you like something else?"

Timeliness is also important to ensure the quality of the product or service. It may be acceptable to take fifteen minutes for the purchase of an airline ticket, but if it takes more than three minutes to receive a fast-food order, then the quality or service may be deemed poor or inferior. Food service for a restaurant with table service may take up to twelve minutes for appropriate delivery of the order, but if more than five minutes is taken to deliver a car rental agreement, then the service may be deemed inadequate. Finally, the degree of personalization or name recognition is also important to ensure the quality and reputation of the store.

Franchisors need to collect information from their franchisees in a timely report (see Table 4-6). Many franchisors collect information from their franchisees regarding gross sales,

TABLE 4-6 FREQUENCY WITH WHICH FRANCHISEES REPORT SALES TO THEIR FRANCHISORS*

Frequency of Franchisee's Sales Reports	Total, All Companies	Fast-food & Beverage	Nonfood Retailing	Personal Services	Business Products/Services
	Franchisors Reporting				
Weekly	29.5%	26.3%	31.1%	32.1%	28%
Monthly	48.7	56.1	28.9	59	44
Yearly	8.0	7.0	17.8	1.8	8.0
Not required to report	13.6	10.5	22.2	7.2	20
TOTAL	~100%	~100%	~100%	~100%	~100 %

*Note: Based on information reported by 183 franchised companies. Includes 57 franchisors of fast foods and beverages, 45 of nonfood consumer products, 56 of personal services, and 25 of business (or industrial) products and services. Column totals may not add to exactly 100 percent due to rounding.

cost of goods sold, and labor costs on a weekly basis. Long John Silver's collects such information from its company-owned stores on a daily basis via a computer system.[22]

4-7g   Franchisee Advisory Council (Joint Council)

There is a great need for strong communication lines between franchisor and franchisee. Coupled with the franchisor–franchisee relationship is the need for the development of a franchisee advisory council or joint council between the two parties. The franchisee advisory council is not the only means for improving franchisee relations. An advisory council is often advantageous for both franchisor and franchisee. It provides the opportunity for franchisees to work with and provide counsel to a franchisor. It may also be a key source for developing advertising and marketing campaigns in conjunction with the franchisor. This council may also hear the grievances of the franchisee and may suggest managerial actions for the franchisor. It is designed to help and promote a strong relationship between the franchisor and the franchisees.

Franchisors have often found franchisee advisory councils to be effective in helping develop mutual trust, improved communications, policy changes, product introduction, program development, feedback, improved sales, improved motivation, and opportunity to work together to improve the entire franchise system. Many councils have proved effective by strengthening the franchisor–franchisee relationship while increasing sales throughout the system.

Franchisee councils have usually developed along one of three paths, as follows:

1. The franchisor has called together a group of appointed or elected members and conducts the council according to the franchisor's format and dictates.

2. The franchisees of a specific franchisor have met with other franchisees to form a council to provide advice and suggestions for the franchisor. The franchisor is often, later, invited to join under the terms and conditions the franchisees have established.

3. The advisory councils are initiated and formed jointly by both the franchisor and the franchisees. They have worked together to establish the bylaws for the councils and have mutually agreed upon the operations and structure of the council.

The bylaws or ground rules of the franchisee councils are generally established to allow for the free interchange of ideas between franchisor and franchisees and they are developed to protect both sides. The bylaws of the organization generally discuss council membership and officers, frequency of meetings, dues, quorum size, and responsibilities. They may be periodically changed to reflect the conditions of the council and the interaction between the franchisor and the franchisees. The council executives representing the franchisees and the franchisor generally will determine the council's exact purposes and limitations.

Council Membership and Officers

Membership in a franchise council generally occurs in one of two ways. Members are either elected by franchise peers or appointed by the franchisor. Some franchisee advisory councils may even include all franchisees of the franchise system and even managers of company-owned stores, each owner-manager having one vote in determining council positions.

In addition to the franchisees represented on the council, it is important that the board chairman, company president, or other top management personnel from the franchisor's office be invited to participate. This allows for the proper interaction between franchisor and franchisee organizations.

Officers for councils may be elected by the council or appointed by the franchisor. Many franchisors name an executive vice-president as the president of the council or franchisee system. Other organizations allow the franchisee to elect or appoint the president (or chair), one or two vice-presidents, and a secretary-treasurer. These officers are responsible for organizing and convening meetings, appointing committees, developing agendas, and working with the franchisee and franchisor organizations.

Council Functions

Many councils create five basic standing committees, including:

1. Operations

2. Marketing

3. Products and services

4. Finance

5. Grievances

These committees play an important role in handling the proper functions and interactions between the franchisees and the franchisor. Most of the problems associated with the franchisor–franchisee relationship can be worked out by these standing committees. The use of advisory council committees often places the responsibility for harmonious and strong working relations on the franchisees. At times, the franchisor may ask the council members to help resolve problems with a particular franchisee. After hearing the situation, the committee may choose to work with both the franchisee and the franchisor to resolve the conflict or dispute.

Most councils hold national council meetings once a year. A council may invite all franchisees to participate in such meetings. This practice allows the opportunity for all franchisees to assemble and meet other franchisees and to work with the franchisor.

In addition to the national council, regional councils may be established. A regional council generally comprises three to seven states and meets once a year approximately six months after the national council meeting. Regional council agendas often include reviews of the marketing, management, operations, finance, and legal aspects of operating a franchised unit within the respective franchise system. In addition, all products and services are reviewed. Any new products to be offered by the franchisor are presented and demonstrated to the franchisees. The expenses for the franchisee council are generally shared by the franchisor and the franchisees.

Advisory councils are important for the strength and unity of the franchise system. The council provides a vital input mechanism for the franchisees to the franchisor management staff at the control office. The franchisor needs input to ensure the proper function and operation of the franchise system. A properly operating franchisee advisory council can provide the suggestions and advice necessary to ensure the continuation and development of the entire franchise system.

4-7h   Innovation in Franchising

To innovate or not innovate is not the question. All successful franchise systems innovate. Franchise systems must continually examine and modify their core product and service offerings to maintain competitive advantage in their industry, continue their current customer base, and attract new customers to their product and service line. In general, small firms have difficulty innovating; and even when they do, they may find the potential new product or service to their market offerings too expensive to implement. According to the NFIB Research Foundation, National Small Business poll on innovation:[23]

- Eighty-eight percent of small firms do not purposefully innovate.

- Sixteen percent of small firms avoid technology when possible.

- Five percent of small firms own a patent used in the business.

These figures confirm that innovative small firms are unusual and that the "serial innovators" are very rate indeed. There are a variety of sources from which innovations can emanate, including:

- The unexpected—a "Eureka" or here-to-for unrecognized insight

- A process need—to simplify or make a production process more efficient, less costly

- Changes that take place in industry or market structure (e.g., offering of sizable rebates for new care purchases by Chrslyer Corporation that was quickly matched by most all other producers within the industry)

- Shifts in demographics (e.g., more women in the workforce giving rise to dramatic increases in

- domestic cleaning services, or the dramatic increase in monitored senior living establishments)

- Changes in perception, meaning, or mood that bring forth "enlightened" perspectives

- New knowledge

Whether a franchise system is a leading Fortune 500 company or has only a few franchisees, all franchise systems have one thing in common: They confront roadblocks to innovation on a daily basis. One great challenge facing a franchise system is finding the type of innovative thinking the firm needs to survive, to find the right approach and uncovering the strategic leadership capabilities within the home office staff and franchisee network. Charles Fleetham suggests five key ways to unleash the potential in a business to achieve high levels of success.[24]

1. Think two generations ahead. Work the firm's vision plan in ten-year increments. Ask the "who, what, where, and how" questions about your business. For example, in ten years who will be your target demographic; what will be your core products and services; where will your home office be located (regionally, nationally, globally); when will key business milestones by achieved, such as signing the fiftieth, hundredth, five hundredth, or one thousandth franchisee be achieved? Perhaps the most intriguing question to confront is, Why will my business matter in ten, twenty, or fifty years, and how am I going to achieve my business goals for those time-targets?

2. Work with your conscience. It is the conscience that provides over 90 percent of a person's valuable insights.

3. Aim to increase energy, not just efficiency. Look to determine what actually energizes your employees and franchisees. Talk with them. Ask for their insights and, particularly, what it is about their work and responsibilities that bring satisfaction and happiness. If you understand what energizes your employees and franchisees, then you will be able to implement actions that motivate them and increase productivity.

4. Establish the freedom to innovate. Creativity drives change. Allow for tinkering with process possibilities or with new ideas. Realize that many new product ideas did not stem from the home office, that many highly successful products and services have "bubbled up" from franchisees, such as the Big Mac burger at McDonald's.

5. Start all problem-solving tactics by taking responsibility. Any problem that the franchisor is directly involved with reflects on your role and the responsibility related to that problem.

6. Take the leadership, even if the problem is directly associated with your own performance. Your employees and franchisees will respect you for your openness, candor, and willingness to address the issues head on.

In franchising, innovative franchise systems tend to fall into one of the four following categories as a taxonomy of innovative small firms, as shown in the Table 4-7. The categories are specialized subcontractor firms, providers of product solutions, providers of service solutions, and consumer goods suppliers.

TABLE 4-7	TAXONOMY OF INNOVATIVE SMALL FIRMS

Specialized Subcontractor Firms. Firms that develop unique, one-of-a-kind items for a specific buyer or for niched buyers with very low volume produced for them. Typically, these are small firms that excel in highly specialized technologies for which applications need to be customized and/or integrated in what may be highly complex products (e.g., manufacturing subsystems, aircraft component systems, security systems for "intelligent" buildings, etc.). The potential sources of competitive advantage for these types of innovative franchise organizations are:

- Flexibility
- Firm's track record and reputation
- Product and service with high-quality, unique features
- Customization capability to integrate within a complex system

Product Solutions Providers. Typically, this is a small franchise system that identifies a market need that should be addressed holistically, and provides a turnkey solution for the same problem confronted by a number of other firms or individuals (e.g., home security systems, commercial maintenance supply, auto muffler and brake shops, auto parts stores, etc.).
The potential sources of competitive advantage for these types of innovative franchise firms are:

- High degree of vertical integration through inventory systems across parts and product lines
- Strong customer service skills
- Strong internal systems

Service Solutions Providers. Typically, these are franchised firms that can tailor a service to the needs to a large group of customers who have highly similar or the exact same needs. Basically, these franchise systems serve as technical consultants to their clients (e.g., tax services, chip design services for wafer foundries, software development for specific client needs, etc.).
Potential sources of competitive advantage for these types of innovative franchise firms are:

- Close relationships with clients
- Potential for long-term supply and maintenance contracts
- Strong customer service skills
- Strong engineering and production process implementation skills

Consumer Goods Suppliers. Usually, these are franchise systems that create and manufacture niche consumer products for their clients (e.g., a variety of sporting goods products supplied to retailers and professional franchise teams).
Potential sources of competitive advantage for these types of innovative franchise firms include:

- Strong brand reputation
- Flexible production systems
- Targeting of niche markets with high-quality products

William Rosenberg

Dunkin' Donuts

William Rosenberg's life has been a true Horatio Alger success story: A self-made man who had to leave school in the eighth grade to help support his family during the Depression. At age twenty-nine, he founded Dunkin' Donuts and, through hard work and risk taking, has become a senior statesman not only to his own company but to the entire franchise industry.

Born in Boston, Massachusetts, and educated in public schools, Rosenberg left school after the eighth grade to work full time for Western Union. At seventeen, he joined a company that distributed ice cream from refrigerated trucks. There his hard work and skills were rewarded. At twenty, he was promoted to assistant manager, at twenty-one to branch manager and then to national sales manager.

At the start of World War II, he joined the Bethlehem Steel Company at the Hingham, Massachusettts, shipyard. He was elected union delegate and then appointed by management as contract coordinator.

When the war ended, Rosenberg borrowed $1,000 to add to his $1,500 in war bonds and began an industrial catering business conducted from trucks. Within a short time, he had 140 catering trucks plus twenty-five in-plant cafeterias and a vending division. When he discovered that 40 percent of his business was coffee and doughnuts, he established a shop that specialized in those products and Dunkin' Donuts was born.

After opening six shops, he decided on franchising a method of expansion and the rest is history. Dunkin' Donuts is now an international

company with over 6,000 shops in the United States and throughout the world.

In 1959, while attending a "Start Your Own Business" show, it occurred to Rosenberg that he and other companies in the fledgling franchise industry needed a united group to educate legislators and the general public—a clearinghouse organization for the industry. To meet that need, he and a group of exhibitor's founded the International Franchise Association. Over the years, the association has become the voice of franchising and has set the standards for the industry. Rosenberg served one term as president and several terms as director. He was honored as the first recipient of the IFA's Hall of Fame award in recognition for his contributions to the franchise system of distribution. In 1990, he was unanimously voted founder and chairman emeritus of the IFA by its board of directors. The IFA honored him with a special dedication of the thirty-third annual IFA convention in 1993.

CASE STUDY

Yvonne knows that home construction is riding a dramatic trend in hard flooring materials; hardwood, brick, and tile are back with a vengeance. The area rug market is on fire, and the established providers cannot handle the flames. Indeed, Oriental rug traders, impersonal warehouse stores, and wall-to-wall carpet marts leave consumers looking for an alternative.

Yvonne Kelleher started "The Rug Place" in 1997 in Baton Rouge, Louisiana. The Rug Place is an exciting, unique rug business opportunity, custom tailored to this rapidly growing market. Yvonne's business is customer friendly by design, simple to operate, and proven in the real world. Best of all, this opportunity has come at the right time, in the right place; and now Yvonne wants to franchise. They have proven experience, raw buying power, and top-notch market research. They provide innovative display technology, software, and thorough training and support to get the franchisee going and keep them growing. The Rug Place also keeps it simple: no irritating accounts receivable, no costly warehousing, and no reinventing the wheel.

The Rug Place is an exciting design studio–style retail environment, stocked with a great selection of affordably priced area rugs in the latest styles and colors.

Now Yvonne wants to franchise. Does she need an accountant, marketing expert, and financial advisor? What should she do to set up her organization correctly?

CASE QUESTIONS

1. How should Yvonne organize her franchise system so that she can sell new franchises and support the franchisees once opened?

2. What three levels of development should Yvonne accomplish before starting her franchise program?

3. What else does Yvonne need to know before franchising?

4. What can Yvonne learn from Jim Peterson that would help her to become a better franchisor?

SUMMARY

A prospective franchisor will need more than a legal agreement and a hot idea to be successful in franchising. The franchisor, like most other entrepreneurs, must be self-motivated, willing to work long hours, and eager to provide the product or service in a market niche that can be considered a genuine business opportunity.

The franchisor should be well versed in the art of managing—planning, organizing, directing, and controlling—the franchise operation, as this is of critical importance in the relationship between the franchisor and the franchisee. Policies should reflect the strengths of the franchising concept and organization approach to effectively deliver product or service to the target market. In applying the management concepts, problems can take place. Jim Peterson has developed the ten commandments of a successful business; these include leadership, staying with the business one understands, developing and maintaining a unique niche, keeping firsthand touch with the customer, pursuing management principles and fundamentals, organization, freedom from government intervention, strong fiscal responsibility, strategic development, and picking winners for employees. Motivation and quality control are important management functions. Franchisee advisory councils are a valuable mechanism to assist in the effective operations of a franchise system. Innovation and long-range vision are becoming increasingly important to the success of franchise systems.

KEY TERMS

Area Developer: An area developer, as a franchisee, is given the right to develop and operate multiple units in a given area. This right is usually has an obligation to establish a specific number of franchises in the designated territory over a given period of time.

Area Representative: One who is usually an employee of the franchisor with the right to solicit for prospective franchisees but does not have the right to contract with franchisees Also, often the area representative has responsibility for training franchisees, provide periodic inspections on franchised units, sets marketing and advertising schedules and may provide consulting to franchisees.

Franchise broker: An independent third party who solicits prospective franchisees for the franchisor.

Master franchisee: One with the right to offer and sell franchised units, collect fees, and provide franchise system services within a given territory. This person is not a franchisee but an agent who is responsible for selling franchises in a given geographic area.

Multiunit franchisee: one who owns and operates more than one franchised unit. Who have often be granted geographic areas within or near urban areas.

Situation audit: An attempt to determine the firm's current operating situation in the context of its external (environmental) and internal factors and conditions that affect its operations.

REVIEW QUESTIONS

1. Explain the functions of management in a franchising context. How might your explanation differ from the functions of management when considering a typical, large bureaucratic business organization? A large, company-owned chain-store organization?

2. Illustrate a franchise management practice for each of these functions of management: planning, organizing, staffing, and controlling.

3. Why are quality and quantity controls of such importance in franchised firms?

4. What is a franchisee advisory council? How do franchisee councils operate? How do such councils relate to the formal hierarchy of a franchise parent firm?

FRANCHISING QUIZ: FACT OR FICTION?

1. T F McDonald's restaurant system is the largest user of fresh eggs in the United States.

2. T F Blue Chip Cookies is renowned for creating the first white chocolate macadamia cookie in the United States.

3. T F According to the American Bagel Association, bagels are one of the fastest growing breakfast foods in the United States.

4. T F Though bagels are one of the hottest franchise concepts, the history of the bagel dates back to the late seventeenth century.

5. T F Of over 3,000 U.S. franchisors, at least 15 percent have franchise units in operation overseas, with another 10 percent planning entry into foreign markets.

6. T F A & W is the oldest franchise restaurant chain in the United States, founded in 1913.

(If you answered "True" to all the questions above, you are correct.)

REFERENCES

Besanko, David, D. Dranove, and M. Shanley, *Economics of Strategy* (New York: Wiley, 1996).
Bibby, Nick. "Ask Our Experts," 20xx, ww.bison1.com/articles/expert9-02.html.
Boroian, Donald and Patrick Boroian, *The Franchise Advantage* (Schaumburg, IL: National Best Seller Corporation, 1987).
Broom, H. N. and Justin G. Longenecker, *Small Business Management*, 6th ed. (Cincinnati: South-Western Publishing Co., 1983).
Certo, Samuel C., *Modern Management*, 7th ed. (Upper Saddle River, NJ: Prentice Hall, 1997).
Clarkin, John and Steven Swaverly, "How Franchisors Choose Franchisees: A Comparison of Prospective Franchisee Evaluation Criteria," in *International Society of Franchising Proceedings* (San Antonio, February 2003), 417–439.
Day, George S., *Strategic Market Planning* (St. Paul: West Publishing Co., 1984).
Flandes, Raymund, "Toy Makers Hit It Big with Burger King Deal," *Wall Street Journal* (6 March 2007): B-1.

Fleethan, Charles, "Unleash the Innovator Within," 3 February 2007, Entrepreneur.com/grow your business/waystoinnovate/article83284.html.

"Franchising Fever," *Time* (31 August 1987) 36–38.

Freedman, Mike, "The Genius Is in the Implementation," *Journal of Business Strategy* (March/April 2003) 26–31.

Glueck, William F., *Management Essentials* (New York: The Dryden Press, Holt, Rinehart and Winston, 1979).

Guiltinan, Joseph P., U. B. Rejob, and W. C. Rodgers, "Factors Influencing Coordination in a Franchise Channel," *Journal of Retailing* (Fall 1980) 41–58.

Hicks, D. and D. Hegde, "Highly Innovative Small Firms in the Markets for Technology," in *Research Policy* (Washington, DC: U.S. Small Business Administration, Office of Advocacy, July 2005).

Hisrich, Robert E. and Michael P. Peters, *Entrepreneurship*, 5th ed. (Chicago: McGraw-Hill Irwin, 2002).

Hunt, Shelby D. and John R. Nevin, "Power in a Channel of Distribution: Sources and Consequences," *Journal of Marketing Research* (11 May 1974) 186–193.

Ivancevish, John, Peter Lorenzini, Stephen Skinner, and Philip Crosby, *Management: Quality and Competitiveness* (Chicago: Irwin Publishing, 1994).

Justis, Robert T. and Richard Judd, *Franchising* (Cincinnatti: South-Western Publishing, 1989).

Justis, Robert T., and Richard Judd, "Master Franchising," *Journal of Small Business Management* 24(3) (July 1986) 16–21.

Justis, Robert T., Richard Judd, and David B. Stephens, *Strategic Management* (Englewood Cliffs, NJ: Prentice-Hall, Inc., 1985).

Justis, Robert T. and Richard Judd, "Strategies for Multi-Level Franchising," unpublished working paper presented at Society of Franchising annual meeting, San Francisco, CA, January 1988.

Lewis, Mack O., *How to Franchise Your Business, A Quick Step-by-Step Guide* (New York: Pilot Industries, Inc., 1974).

Lewis, Pamela, Stephen Goodman, and Patricia Fandt, *Management: Challenges in the 21st Century* (New York: West Publishing, 1994).

Lovelock, Christopher H., *Services Marketing* (Englewood Cliffs, NJ: Prentice-Hall, Inc., 1980).

McClelland, David, "Achievement Motivation Can Be Developed," *Harvard Business Review* (November-December 1965) 6–8.

Lurie, Bob and Toby Thomas, "Growth Strategies for Tough Times," *Journal of Business Strategy* 23(1) (Jan/Feb 2002) 18–24.

McGuire, E. Patrick, Conference Board: Franchised Distribution.

Mendelsohn, Martin, *The Guide to Franchising*, 4th ed. (New York: Pergamon Press, 1985).

Peterson, Jim, Whataburger, Inc. material presented in Visiting Executive lecture at the University of Nebraska-Lincoln, April 16, 1987.

Porter, Michael E., *Competitive Advantage: Creating and Sustaining Superior Performance* (New York: The Free Press, A Division of Macmillan, Inc., 1985).

Pride, William M. and O. C. Ferrell, *Marketing: Basic Concepts and Decisions* (Boston: Houghton Mifflin Company, 1987).

Seltz, David D., *How to Get Started in Your Own Franchised Business* (Rockville Centre, NY: Farnsworth Publishing Company, Inc., 1980), 1.

Stoner, Charles L. and Fred L. Fry, *Strategic Planning in the Small Business* (Cincinnati: South-Western Publishing Co., 1987).

The Dun & Bradstreet Failure Record (New York: Dun & Bradstreet, Inc., 1981), 12–13.

Vaughn, Charles L., *Franchising*, 2nd/rev. ed. (Lexington, MA: Lexington Books, 1979).

Vesper, Karl, *New Venture Strategies* (Englewood Cliffs, NJ: Prentice-Hall, Inc., 1980).

Wadsworth, Frank and Kathryn B. Morgan, "Multi-Unit Franchisee Ownership Study," *International Society of Franchising Conference Proceedings* (San Antonio, February 14–16, 2003), 261–268.

Weinrauch, J. Donald, "Franchising an Established Business," *Journal of Small Business Management* 24(3) (July 1986) 1–7.

Wheelen, Thomas and J. David Hunger, *Strategic Management and Business Policy*, 8th ed. (Upper Saddle River, NJ: Prentice- Hall, 2002).

NOTES

1. Joseph P. Guiltinan, Usmail B. Rejob, and William C. Rodgers, "Factors Influencing Coordination in a Franchise Channel," *Journal of Retailing* (Fall 1980) 41–58.
2. Shelby D. Hunt and John R. Nevin, "Power in a Channel of Distribution: Sources and Consequences," *Journal of Marketing Research* (11 May 1974) 186–193.
3. David D. Seltz, *How to Get Started in Your Own Franchised Business* (Rockville Centre, NY: Farnsworth Publishing Company, Inc. 1980), 1.
4. *The Dun & Bradstreet Failure Record* (New York: Dun & Bradstreet, Inc., 1981), 12–13.
5. David McClelland, "Achievement Motivation Can Be Developed," *Harvard Business Review* (November-December 1965) 6–8.
6. E. Patrick McGuire, *Franchised Distribution*, a Research Report from the Conference Board, 17.
7. "Toy Makers Hit It Big with Burger Deal," *Wall Street Journal* (6 March 2007).
8. Bob Lurie and Toby Thomas, "Growth Strategies for Tough Times," *Journal of Business Strategy* 23(1) (Jan/Feb 2002) 18–24.
9. "Ask Our Experts," 20 January 2003, www.bisonI.com/articles/expert/cuffent/franchising.
10. Frank Wadsworth and Kathryn B. Morgan, "Multi-Unit Franchisee Ownership Study," *International Society of Franchising Conference Proceedings* (San Antonio, February 14–16, 2003), 1–7.
11. Mike Freedman, "The Genius Is in the Implementation," *Journal of Business Strategy* (March/April 2003) 26–31.
12. Adapted from John Clarkin and Steven Swaverly, "How Franchisors Choose Franchisees: A Comparison of Prospective Franchisee Evaluation Criteria," *International Society of Franchising Proceedings* (San Antonio, February 2003).
13. Nick Bibby, "Ask Our Experts," www.bisonl.com/articles/expert9_02.html
14. Ibid, 29
15. Jim Peterson, Bojangles' Restaurants, Inc. material presented in Visiting Executive lecture at the University of Nebraska-Lincoln, April 16, 1987.
16. Ibid.
17. Ibid.
18. Ibid.
19. Winn Sanderson, Piece of the Pie, Inc. material presented in Visiting Executive lecture at the University of Nebraska-Lincoln, December 11, 1986.
20. Peterson.
21. Peterson.
22. Eugene Getchell, Long John Silver's Inc. material presented in Visiting Executive lecture at the University of Nebraska-Lincoln, February 19, 1987.
23. Adapted from D. Hicks and D. Hegde, "Highly Innovative Small Firms in the Markets for Technology," in *Research Policy* (Washington, DC: U.S. Small Business Administration, Office of Advocacy, July 2005).
24. Adapted from Charles Fleethan, "Unleash the Innovator Within," 3 February 2007, Entepreneur.com/grow your business/waystoinnovate/article83284.html.

THE FRANCHISING MARKET PROCESS

In studying this chapter, you will:

- **Learn the steps involved in strategic market planning.**
- **Learn about strategic planning in franchising through examining the market function and activities.**
- **Understand how a hierarchy of objectives and strategies can be developed within a franchise organization.**
- **Learn how to develop a marketing mix for the franchise.**
- **Understand the role and use of channels of distribution.**

INCIDENT

Six years ago, after finishing college with a degree in exercise physiology, Amy opened her own exercise studio. While in school, Amy worked as an assistant trainer on the men's and women's basketball teams. With this background, Amy has a good understanding of the human body and what types of exercises might do more harm than good.

In those six years, the exercise studio has become so busy that Amy is considering expanding. One of her options is to franchise. The market possibilities are endless, especially since the national interest in good health has become a way of life for many people. Amy believes her exercise studio can capitalize on that interest because it offers a "fun" way to get, and stay, in shape.

Several of Amy's instructors have expressed interest in participating in her plans to expand. With help from Amy they could select and decorate a studio. Most importantly, Amy could train prospective franchisees in appropriate and correct exercise techniques as well as provide concise information about health issues.

Amy believes she has a good chance for success through growth as a franchised business. She has a valuable service to offer prospective exercise studio owners, who in turn have a valuable service to offer customers. She senses that once her chain of studios becomes established, the franchise name will be associated with quality exercise programs and conscientious instructors.

Amy's next step is to determine exactly how to market the business. What considerations are essential as she begins to develop a marketing plan? What strategies might she consider? Can she accomplish her business objectives through the marketing function and activities involved in a franchise system?

5-1   INTRODUCTION

The most notable characteristic of franchising is the intent to increase revenues by creating new business units. In a practical sense, though, the most fundamental element of franchising involves marketing. Franchising requires bringing the product or service to the customer at the right time, at the right place, and at the right price. The concepts of product, place, price, and promotion within an appropriate time frame for the purchaser constitute the classic principles of marketing for a business venture.

As a prospective franchisor, Amy should be aware of the characteristics of the market for her studio's service. What is the estimated size of the market? What is a reasonable estimate of her share of the market? Conditions in the market can determine the success or failure of Amy's or anyone's business. It is essential to develop an overall marketing strategy that focuses the efforts of the business on satisfying the customers' needs, at a profit.

Amy should know what her customers like and dislike. She should ask such questions as, Is the buyer the user of her exercise classes? Is the person who makes the decision to buy a membership in her studio the same person who actually pays for the membership? Who else influences the purchase? Within a household, because the decision to purchase or use (and perhaps to continue purchasing or using) can be made by different persons, the roles played are not always easy to identify. For example, when a family goes to a fast-food restaurant for lunch, does the driver choose the particular restaurant? Who else influences this decision? Is the decision linked to other factors such as how close the restaurant is to the workplace or to major shopping areas? What is ordered and by whom? What effect do location, convenience, price, service, product quality, and restaurant atmosphere have on the decision?

Marketing involves everything that it takes to get a product or service into the buyer's hands. Successful marketing requires careful thought and an action plan. The franchisor must be certain to get the right product or service to the right customer at the right price and at the right time and place. To do so requires research, creative thought, and planning.

Using a marketing concept, a prospective franchisor can develop an orientation to focus on consumer needs, and then put together an effective marketing strategy using the basic components of a marketing mix. A **marketing strategy** consists of identifying one or more target markets and creating a marketing mix. In our example, Amy must determine the customers most likely to purchase memberships and use her exercise club.

Once a target market has clearly been established, the next step is to develop an appropriate marketing mix. The **marketing mix** consists of controllable factors to be considered in combination to satisfy the needs or wants of customers in the target market. These factors include the four Ps: product, price, place, and promotion.

Two general concepts—marketing strategy and marketing mix—are essential components of this chapter. Initially, we will discuss strategy from an overall business perspective to identify how the market orientation fits into a general strategy for the business itself. Then we describe the four components of the marketing mix. The product and service life cycle will be explored through appropriate advertising and promotion strategies, as well as product and service innovation and business-to-business (B2B) franchising. Finally, we explain a marketing effectiveness matrix to show how to link strategic market planning to effective tactical execution for franchise system growth.

5-2   STRATEGIC PLANNING IN FRANCHISING

According to Kenneth Franklin of the Franchising Law Group of Piper, Marbury, Rudnick and Wolfe, a firm that decides to enter franchising must have a clear understanding of four essential factors: (1) how it will support the franchise system's operations, (2) how it will foster communications with franchisees, (3) what financial results the firm and its franchisees can anticipate, and (4) how it will market its franchise once the franchise program is in place.[1]

The support program provided by the franchisor to the franchisees often includes market research, marketing surveys, site selection, operational layout and store design, help with lease negotiation as necessary, an accurate and understandable operations manual, training programs for franchisees, and possibly financial assistance. These factors should be addressed and the franchisor's program made ready for implementation *prior* to development of the marketing program.

The marketing program is the key for success of the franchise system and the franchised units independently owned and operated within that system. The franchisor's principal responsibilities with regard to the marketing function center on the following core marketing issues: (1) business image, (2) determining the market direction, (3) recruitment and selection of franchisees, and (4) grand opening, and ongoing advertising programs in support of the local franchisees' units.[2]

The **business image** is the image that the franchisor "packages" for public consumption. It is the key attraction for potential franchisees and customers to the franchise system's products and services. The image sought must be distinctive and appealing and have appropriate graphics, colors, logo, trademarks, and exterior and interior designs and colors to project the image sought by the franchise system. For example, the core colors used by McDonald's are the three primary colors of red, yellow, and blue. These colors are the most identifiable by toddlers who are yet to develop sophistication in color identification and attraction. These colors work well in supporting the long-term image of McDonald's as a family restaurant. In addition, the McDonald's playland rooms are supportive of bringing the kids to McDonald's. In contrast, Wendy's has chosen colors that may be considered more adult, or mature. Brown, orange, soft almond, and other shades of cream present an interior coloration that is more pleasant to the eye and mood of adults than the bright red/yellow/blue of McDonald's. Notice also, the menu items at Wendy's seem to support adult taste and desired options such as chili and baked potatoes.

Successful franchise systems know that the image presented to the public—franchisee and customer—is vital to ensure consistency and customer expectations throughout a franchise's market territory.

Determining the market direction is a crucial decision in the early stages of the development of a franchise system. Where will the first expansions take place? How will they be served by head-quarters? What locations or territories are targeted to be entered next? To what extent does the franchise system intend to become a multistate, regional, national, or international system? Franchisors tend to cluster franchised locations internal to established market areas because these markets, typically, have been known to be successful for franchised firms. Adding franchised locations within an established market area can generate additional funds for advertising in that market, which can enhance market share, minimize advertising cost per franchised location, and help deter competition for entry.

When you consider locating franchised units in areas where there are no existing units for the franchise system, several factors must be taken into account. How well can corporate service and supply product to the new territory or area? What is the sales potential of the new area? Is it likely to be profitable enough to extend the franchise distribution system? What is the level of competition that currently exists at the new territory? Is it likely to increase, be stable, or decline? What are the population, income, retail sales, and other statistics for the new area? Do they support the current type of franchise? How much with franchisor advertising be needed to support the new territory and can it do so effectively?

Recruitment of franchisees should be based on the profile of the type of people desired, their goals and aspirations, skills, financial capability, motivation, and level of commitment required of a franchisee owner-operator. The characteristics of the franchised business will likely dictate the profile of the person needed to become a franchisee. The franchisor must identify the franchise system's unique features, benefits, core competencies, and competitive advantage; and then express these concepts through carefully worded and graphically designed advertisements, brochures, mail programs, and even video presentations. All this effort is meant to obtain interviews with qualified prospective franchisees.

Franchisee entrepreneurs are a diverse pool of individuals. Over the next ten years we are likely to see the most diverse pool of entrepreneurs entering in business in general, and in franchising specifically. The following types of people will likely take the plunge into franchising.

- *The Immigrant:* Bilingual, bicultural background, has international contacts; knows many people; is likely to have been educated in the United States and is attuned to the opportunities available—often better than persons native born; understands, appreciates, and is motivated toward entrepreneurial capitalism. According to the U.S. census, immigrant entrepreneurs are the fastest growing segment of small business ownership today. Immigrants turn to entrepreneurship to get around traditional barriers of entry into the U.S. workforce. Immigrants often lack corporate contacts, larger company experience, and smooth English-language skills. Thus, starting a business is often easier than finding a job in the United States.

- *The Mompreneur:* Will be with you in just a moment, as soon as she finishes multitasking; is the perfect person for a "personal business," i.e., a one mom, part-time shop; is looking for increased intellectual stimulation and sees franchising as a superior means to develop and then hone her talents and skills; is online savvy as she one-clicks her way to the outside world starting and running her business confidently and effectively. Workforce participation of women with children has reached an all-time high. In 2005, 72 percent of mothers participated in the workforce. Life is a continual juggling act for most mothers as they try to balance quality work in their jobs and quality care for their children. Many also need additional income. The "mompreneur" often enters business through a part-time at-home business approach. The approach provides for flexibility and work–life balance. These women will be increasingly looking to entrepreneurial careers to fulfill their goals.

- *The Baby Boomer:* Save the rocking chair for another ten to twenty years, this person who is nearing retirement is still looking for the next adventure; has a nice sized nest egg but needs additional income to really live out the retirement dream; has devoted her career to someone else's company or a government agency; is ready to build own business. The demographics of business ownership, particularly small business ownership, is rapidly changing. Baby boomers account for over 25 percent of the U.S. population. They are the largest population cohort. Within that age grouping, those between ages forty-five and fifty-four form businesses at an above average rate. The sheer size of the baby boom generation indicates that business formation will grow over the next decade. The baby boomers are at a life stage where starting a business is perceived as less risky and increasingly attractive to achieve a work–life balance.

- *The Professional Woman:* She has climbed around the glass ceiling and, tired of the old boys club, is ready to start her own business; has high interpersonal skills and a strong IQ; has strong entrepreneurial skills; is not afraid of budgets, is adept at bargaining, and is not distracted in her work by video games or solitaire while in the office; is a prime audience for franchise ownership. Because women outnumber men as college graduates, can women entrepreneurs be far behind? Women make up 46 percent of the American workforce, according to U.S. census statistics, but hold only 6.4 percent of the top earner positions. Entrepreneurship offers an alternative to women with corporate experience and ambition. Mid-career women have sharp business acumen and solid managerial experience, but have had little luck in pursuit of top corporate positions in relation to their numbers in the workforce. Many mid-career women have good networking skills, want to further develop themselves, and are looking for a way to invest in further professional growth without letting go of family ties.

- *The Gen-Yer:* This person do not seek a corporate career; has watched parents suffer through corporate mergers, downsizing, and layoffs; hasn't "been there" but has the experience from it; doesn't want that for a career; is flexible and has a social network that is constantly in flux; has been groomed through grade and high school that entrepreneurship is a viable and attractive career calling; is ready to develop own case study about business. The Gen-Yers (ages five to twenty-five) will be the most entrepreneurial generation. As the first generation to grow up with digital technologies, they have a unique approach to information, society, and the workplace. They are not afraid to take risks, try new approaches, make mistakes, and learn from them. These traits are important seeds for entrepreneurship. Members of the Gen-Yer cohort have strong conceptual abilities, build on ideas to formulate and reformulate, and adapt or reinvent as needed.

Having the "right" franchisee in place is of extreme importance to the success of both the franchise system and the individual franchised units. Figure 5-1 shows a typical franchisee recruitment process followed by franchisors to recruit, screen, and select appropriate people to become franchisees of their franchise system.

---

1. Franchise brochure

2. Franchise solicitation advertising
   A. Establish profile of your prospective franchisee
   B. Select media which attract the most subscribers that meet your profile
   C. Website

3. Hire a public relations firm
   A. Press releases
   B. Appropriate targeted advertisements

4. Attend trade shows
   A. International Franchise Association–sponsored expositions
   B. Industry trade shows

5. Conduct franchise seminars

6. Blind franchisee solicitation advertising
   A. Purchase business mailing lists appropriate to your ideal franchisee profile
   B. Design and produce attractive mailer

7. Track each form of contact and advertisement; measure the results

---

FIGURE **5-1**

Typical Process for Recruitment of Potential Franchisees

Ongoing advertising and grand openings constitute extremely important services provided by the franchisor. Though a franchisee may be able to create some advertising, it is not likely that individual franchisees will be able or capable of funding sophisticated, carefully designed advertising programs. Usually, the advertising program is funded locally but run on regional and/or national bases. The franchisor usually has a contractual obligation to spend a certain amount in each market area or local level. Ongoing advertising and grand openings will also be addressed in Chapters 17 and 20.

These four market-based factors are essential for the effective development of well-designed and implemented marketing programs for the two target groups of a franchise system, the franchisees and the ultimate customers group. Knowing the profiles of the prospective franchisee and the customer, the franchisor is ready to begin strategic planning, with particular focus toward the marketplace.

Strategic planning is the process of formulating and maintaining organizational objectives and operational capacities to allow the franchise organization to function effectively within its ever-changing environment. The steps of this process are shown in Figure 5-2. The resulting plan is a

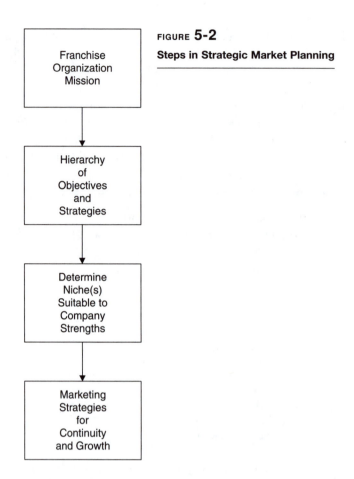

FIGURE **5-2**

Steps in Strategic Market Planning

comprehensive and integrated approach to the production and distribution of goods or services which recognizes existing environmental pressures and opportunities. Planning becomes "strategic" when the business owner realizes that most of the planning activity involves examining the business and deciding what should be maintained, what should be dropped, and what should be added to ensure the continuing success of the firm.

5-2a   The Changing Marketplace

The twenty-first century promises to be full of surprises. A franchisor today must design a company with products or services that can withstand shocks. Economic forces, both long and short term, have produced an unstable marketplace and unpredictable competition. The influx of women into the labor force, the economic maturation of the baby-boom generation, revolutionary technological innovations, the Internet, increased foreign competition—all these realities have changed traditional U.S. business practices. In a dynamic marketplace, independence, adaptability to sudden change, and acceptance of risks can provide the edge a business will need to stay competitive.

The franchisor and the franchisee need to be sensitive to the changing habits, tastes, desires, and spending patterns of their customers to ensure the profitable continuance of the business. Strategic planning is a tool a franchise firm can use in a dynamic marketplace to keep the firm adaptable, to face new opportunities, to avoid or minimize effects of negative pressures or threats, and to build upon the firm's strengths. In simpler terms, strategic planning allows a franchised business to attain and then maintain competitiveness in its target markets. Because franchisor and franchisee desire both short-term and long-term profitability, they of course intend the business to have continuity, to survive over time. Strategic planning makes it more likely that they will succeed, because it involves making decisions in the present that will help to ensure the success of the business in the future.

5-2b   Problems in Applying Strategic Planning to Smaller Businesses

Strategic planning is used by many major corporations and is generally recognized as a valuable tool to determine the best strategies to increase market share or profit margin on a firm's products or services. But there are some problems in applying strategic planning in smaller businesses. Since the vast majority of franchised firms are not large corporations, we should first clarify what we mean by smaller businesses. Characteristics to consider typically include size of workforce, amount of assets, and total profits, although primary characteristics of a business are often not immediately discernible. Typical qualities are shown in Table 5-1.

FOREIGN FRANCHISES COMING TO U.S. SHORES

Franchise concepts such as Inter-Continental Hotel Group (U.K.), Mend-A-Bath Int'l (South Africa), Pollo Campero (Guatemala), and Automotive Art (Barbados) are a few franchise brands appearing in the United States. This developing trend is likely to continue.

Adapted from Mathew Shay (president of International Franchise Association), "Franchising— It's Developing beyond U.S. Shores," USA Today (7 February 2007): 8B.

Typically, the owner of a small business, like Amy in our opening example, has limited resources and as a result operates on a rather small scale. Small business performance (profits and costs) can be highly susceptible to changes in consumer buying patterns. Government regulations and compliance requirements can have a significant impact on operating costs. Also, the small firm usually lacks specialized staff personnel readily available to address legal questions, personnel issues, or tax questions. Perhaps most importantly, the small business owner often lacks the time to step back and evaluate, plan, and objectively determine what should be the next step to achieve the market, profit, and operational goals of the business.

Strategic planning may be inappropriate or difficult for a smaller business to implement for other reasons as well. Typically, strategic planning has been used by companies that have several or many product lines. Some larger firms keep the situation manageable by forming a holding

TABLE 5-1   TYPICAL CHARACTERISTICS OF SMALLER FIRMS

Limited resources are available to achieve business objectives.

Scale of operation is smaller, which can mean a higher cost structure because firm lacks size to be able to purchase in large, discounted quantities.

Governmental regulations and compliance requirements can significantly increase operating expenses.

Business performance is highly susceptible to changes in customer buying behavior.

Minor changes in operating efficiency can affect availability of resources and business profitability.

Firms are often without specialized staff to address legal, accounting, and other needs of the business.

Owner often lacks objectivity needed to evaluate and plan activities efficiently, or lacks ability to delegate responsibility effectively.

Business often fails to have sufficient working capital, financial controls, or materials or inventory on hand, or has not adequately analyzed the impact of fixed overhead on the cost of products or services.

company that has separate business entities under it which are held accountable for their performance by the holding company, each entity controlling its particular product or service lines. For example, large franchise system PepsiCo, Inc. has three divisions: soft drinks, snack foods, and restaurants. PepsiCo's soft drinks division markets Pepsi-Cola, Mountain Dew, and Slice in U.S. and international markets. This division also has joint bottling ventures with Ocean Spray, Lipton Tea, Avalon Spring Water, A&W Root Beer, Squirt, Vernor's, and other brands in specific North American, Asian, and European markets. Its snack foods division makes and distributes products throughout the world such as Lay's Potato Chips, Cheetos, Doritos, Ruffles, Rold Gold Pretzels, Fritos, and a line of salsa and picante sauces.

This is a situation not normally found in smaller franchise firms. Therefore, developing the overall business mission, objectives, and strategies from a multibusiness perspective is obviously not realistic for most small businesses. Several tools are appropriate for use by smaller firms and can be effectively utilized in franchising: analysis of market share, competitive analysis, competitive advantage–disadvantage analysis, and analysis of direct and indirect costs of production or operations. Thus, the process of strategic planning and some tools are appropriate and will be helpful to the great majority of existing franchised businesses as well as to budding franchisors.

5-3   STEPS IN STRATEGIC PLANNING

A successful franchisor takes several steps in the strategic planning of a franchised business. These steps are the topic of this section.

5-3a   Franchise Organization Mission

Establishing the franchise mission is the first step in strategic planning. The franchised business exists with the aim of accomplishing something within and through its economic environment. The methods to be used to accomplish the overall mission should be clearly set forth by the franchisor before any franchisees are recruited; otherwise, the mission may become blurred as growth takes place and goods or services become varied, or if marketplace conditions change sufficiently to make the original mission inappropriate. The simple-sounding questions to be addressed are perhaps the most difficult for the franchisor to answer: What is my business? Who is my customer? What are the needs of my customer? What do I want my business to be in the long run?

A successful franchisor asks and answers these questions in order to formulate a carefully prepared mission statement. The mission statement must provide a shared sense of opportunity, challenge, and motivation for the owners, franchisees, and employees of the organization. It should define the target markets or business areas in which the franchisor intends to operate; a target market can be described in terms of products or services offered, customer groups targeted, customer needs or wants to be fulfilled, or some combination of these.

In the past, a firm's mission statement was expressed in concrete and rather narrow terms, such as "we are in the typewriter business" or "we are in the steel-making business." More recently, as a result of more dynamic, less stable economic conditions, mission statements have been expressed in terms that address the customer, not the product. For example, "meeting the information processing needs of our customer" might be the mission statement today that once was "we are in the typewriter business," the main difference being that the old statement does not allow for market and technological change. The typewriter company could quickly go out of business if the firm failed to offer electronic calculators, word processing, and other forms of information processing desired by customers.

FIGURE 5-3
Hierarchy of Objectives for a Franchised Exercise Studio (Hypothetical)

5-3b   Hierarchy of Objectives and Strategies

The second step in strategic planning is for the franchisor to use the mission statement to formulate a detailed set of supporting objectives for the major functions of the business and the distribution network being established, maintained, or further developed. Objectives should be determined for functions such as marketing, finance, human resources, and operations, and then arranged in a hierarchy according to importance; the marketing objectives provide the overall direction for the franchised business in clear, understandable terms (see Figure 5-3). From this hierarchy, specific plans to implement the marketing strategy need to be spelled out so as to provide as many quantifiable targets or "hoped-for" results as possible. In so doing, the entrepreneur gains a stronger sense of what should take place in terms of planning, organizing, and controlling the management activities of the franchise organization.

5-3c   Determining Niche(s) Suitable to Company Strengths

This third step in strategic planning is useful to all franchised businesses, whether they provide only one or more than one product or service. The step involves choosing a propitious niche within which the franchise can target its operations in its industry. The niche may be a segment of the total line of products and services offered by competitors within the industry, or it may be a predetermined group of customers targeted according to characteristics such as size of group, income level, and location. In either case, the reason for seeking a niche is to identify the target group to whom the product or service is to be offered. If the franchised firm chooses wisely, its niche will be unserved or underserved by competitors, in which case the niche can provide profitability as well as growth. The firm should choose a market niche in which it can favorably strive in the daily competition to serve its customers.

Of course, the strategic advantage of carefully choosing a niche does not preclude the franchised company from seeking to develop more than one market niche. As a firm grows and gains experience within its industry and markets, it may choose to make additions to its product or service

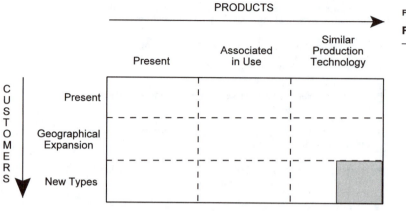

FIGURE 5-4

Franchise Expansion Matrix

Source: Adapted from: Wm. H. Newman, James P. Logan, and W. Harvey Hegarty, *Strategy, Policy & Central Management*, 9th edition (Cincinnati: South-Western Publishing Co., 1985), p. 94.

line that can be offered efficiently and effectively to its customers. For example, an accounting and business services firm specializing in payroll, accounts payable/receivable, and inventory accounting systems may decide to add other services, such as auditing, tax preparation, or consulting on management information systems. Likewise, a fast-food restaurant franchise may expand its scope of operation to include serving breakfast, while a domestic cleaning franchise may provide broader options for cleaning homes, including lawn care or minor household repairs.

The decision by a franchisor to try to boost profits typically involves some form of expansion. The question becomes whether to expand along customer lines or along product or service lines, or both. Figure 5-4 presents an expansion matrix for a franchised firm seeking to grow. The franchisor may seek to expand by providing the same product or service in new locations to attract a greater number of currently targeted customers, or it may seek new types of customers to whom to offer the current product or service. Or, the franchisor may choose to expand the product or service line. Such expansion typically includes providing products or services to complement the line already being offered to the customers.

5-3d   Products and Services

A franchised business often opts to expand in order to achieve synergistic results for the business. Synergy occurs when two separate actions performed together produce a greater effect than either can separately. This is sometimes called the "1 + 1 = 3" effect. For example, having a restaurant inside a franchised motel makes the motel a more convenient place for travelers to stop. The intention is clearly to increase sales over what they would be if the restaurant and motel were independently owned and operated or located one or two miles apart. Another, somewhat different example is franchised restaurants that expand their business to include serving breakfast. With this approach, the aim is to get the lunch or dinner customer to patronize the restaurant more than just once a day.

> Denny's Corp. has announced the completion of its systemwide rollout of a non-trans fat alternative fry shortening for all 1,545 restaurants. The new non-trans fat oil also enhances the flavor, appearance, and texture of fried foods. Denny's also introduced trans fat-free margarines in its restaurants in mid-2007.
>
> *Adapted from "Denny's Finalizes Switch to Trans Fat-Free Oil in All Restaurants," 16 March 2007, www.TradingMarkets.com.*

Because synergy is often part of the expansion goal of the franchisor, the approaches should be carefully considered. Figure 5-4 also presents the cells within which the intended expansion options can fall. As the franchised business moves further away from its present customers or its current product or service, the benefits of synergy diminish. At the extreme (lower right corner of the matrix in the figure), new customers are needed and a new product or service must be provided; here the benefits of synergy to the franchise can virtually disappear. A franchisor considering this type of expansion (that is, involving both a new customer group and a new product or service) is effectively seeking expansion through conglomeration. Typically, a franchised firm looking to expand will consider combinations of niches that supplement or reinforce one another in a synergistic way. Before expanding, the franchisor should plan carefully in order to avoid losing benefits the firm has accrued by concentrating on its present product or service and customer group.

Once the market niche is determined and related to the firm's primary strengths (the unique characteristics or methods of the business), the mode of expansion—along product and service or customer lines—can be examined when the franchisor considers expansion. An expansion decision should always bring the franchisor to reexamine the next and final step in strategic market planning.

5-3e   Marketing Strategies for Continuity and Growth

Several basic options are available to a business trying to enter a market and grow. Whether the business is large or small, we want to consider these basic options in terms of how a franchised firm would "fit" or interact with its market. Table 5-2 proposes four generic or natural marketing strategies with factors typical to the ownership decision orientation as well as descriptive characteristics associated with the market strategy. Some franchisors, particularly those with highly innovative businesses, would tend to choose the initiator strategy. This strategy is expensive, however, and since many new franchised businesses do not have large amounts of capital available to them, it is

TABLE 5-2   FOUR MARKET-FOCUSED BUSINESS STRATEGIES

Strategy Type	Business Profile	Characteristics
Initiator	Entrepreneurial; growth oriented; high risk-taking (comfortable gambling in all-or-nothing situation).	Knowledge of current customer needs/wants in order to stimulate demand for product/service; access to capital; good timing.
Early Imitator	Has good market sense; introspective; intuitive; risk-taking; willing to commit to change without full knowledge of costs/benefits of product development or modification of manufacturing facilities.	Flexibility in relation to current product and/or production; speed and efficiency in making necessary product/service modifications; ability to differentiate product/service from that of competition in such a way as to ensure uniqueness of product/service to customer (i.e., high sensitivity to customer.)
Follower	Externally dedicated (to market), yet internally focused (on production); seeks to produce high-volume or high-value product/service; carefully examines new opportunities for costs/benefits in relation to known strength of firm; looks for market trends to be established before committing resources.	Knowledge of market pricing and demand levels; desire to maximize market share based on known strengths of firm; entry into market when strong opportunity exists for providing product/service at attainable level: i.e., low product/service cost, low overhead, and efficiency of operation.
Market Segmenter	Seeks niche or opportunity for market skimming; market-dedicated, but lacking capacity for high volume at present; willing to take only minimal risk; avoids head-to-head competition.	Goal of discrete segments with promise of strong demand; flexibility; concentration of firm's resources.

more commonly used by large, established franchising firms with already strong or even dominant positions within a particular industry or market, as is evident in restauranting and in the automotive after-markets (that is, firms offering products or services to keep the car running and in good repair). For example, Honda reentered an almost forgotten motorcycle market aggressively, capturing the interest of youth as well as other potential customers who would not ordinarily make this sort of purchase.

> McDonald's Restaurants averages $3 billion per year from sales through more than 31,000 stores. McDonald's draws more than 50 million people in 119 countries daily. Yet, the men and women operating seven of ten stores are local, independent small business owners and operators.
>
> *Adapted from Mathew Shay (president of International Franchise Association), "Big Name, Small Business,"* USA Today *(4 October 2006): 6B, USA Today.marketplace.*

The second strategy, early imitator, is usually not used by a franchised business for an extended time. Trying to expand the number of franchised units and enter additional markets usually requires that the franchisor reduce flexibility, thus stabilizing product or service offered and developing operational consistency, effective advertising, better field service to existing franchisees, and high-quality training to recently signed franchisees.

The third strategy, follower, is perhaps the most accommodating strategy for a budding franchise firm. The characteristics of this strategy can be positive in the short term: Market demand is strong; existing firms in the market appear to be growing as consumer demand increases; methods of operation are tested to enable the firm to determine the most effective and efficient ways to deliver product or service; and new competitors are entering the marketplace almost daily. The long-term scenario is not so accommodating. As more and more competitors enter the market seeking to be profitable while demand is strong, price competition begins to take place and the market becomes mature—that is, the number of suppliers is sufficient to meet demand. As one or more firms try to deepen their penetration in the market, price competition inevitably increases. This ultimately forces out of business producers that are inefficient or that do not have sufficient capital resources to survive a period of heavy price competition.

Some budding franchised firms might choose the fourth option, to be a market segmenter, as their initial strategy for market entry and growth. Market segmentation is actually an excellent choice, but it requires the franchisor to be particularly aware of customer needs and target market dynamics. Many new franchised businesses fail because they do not have sufficient experience and market knowledge to successfully follow this strategy. The market segmentation approach has been used effectively in the automotive aftermarket industry. There are franchises to service virtually every part of an automobile, including radiators, seat covers, mufflers, and transmissions, or to do such work as rust-proofing, bodywork, diagnostic tests, and lube and oil changes. The restauranting business has also become a segmented industry, with franchises offering full menu or specialty menu, with full or limited service, in ornate or merely functional surroundings.

Before choosing a market strategy, a franchisor must consider the following points about the franchisor–franchisee relationship. First, franchisees deserve professionalism and expect the franchisor to develop marketing strategies with the highest degree of competence. Second, franchisees also want to participate in planning for their own future. Third, a franchisee has the market expertise; it is up to the franchisor to tap this expertise. When their advice is sought and their ideas, problems, and market information considered in the planning of the business, franchisees are likely to feel more a part of the business and thus be better motivated and more loyal to the franchise system.

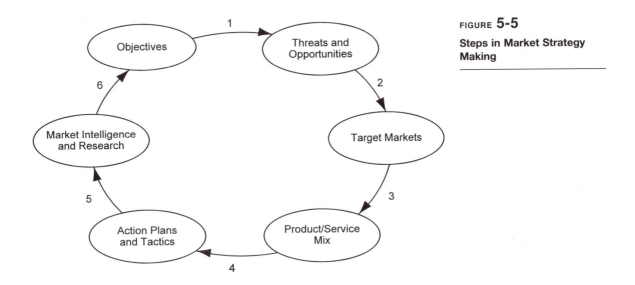

FIGURE **5-5**

Steps in Market Strategy Making

The franchisor should consider a six-step approach to marketing strategy. First, objectives are formulated. Second, the threats and opportunities of the marketplace need to be identified and assessed. Third, the target market(s) are determined. Fourth, the product mix is determined. Fifth, the marketing places of action are developed. Sixth, market research is conducted to provide market intelligence. Figure 5-5 illustrates these six steps which we will now discuss more fully.

Objectives

The franchisor should develop a set of objectives based on the mission of the franchise organization that are consistent with the scope of the business. Figure 5-3, earlier in this chapter, identifies the mission and specific objectives our example franchisor, Amy, intends to pursue for her exercise studio. The objectives of a franchised business should be specific and quantifiable, or closed ended, in order to be clearly conveyed and understood.

Threats and Opportunities

The franchisor should monitor the external environment to identify factors which may pose major threats to or provide significant opportunities for the franchised business and its products. The purpose of this external monitoring and evaluation is to counterbalance the human tendency to become so engrossed in day-to-day activities that one fails to recognize developments in the marketplace that can have significant impact on the firm. The franchisor should regularly examine the external environment, listing then updating threats and opportunities to keep current with market trends. This assessment can be invaluable when developing action plans to capitalize on opportunities to prepare for impending threats to the business. Figure 5-6 lists external factors that can have immediate or long-term impact on a franchised business.

Examining the questions in Figure 5-6 and supplying the information pertinent to each question, if it applies to the particular business, can help the franchisor stay "on the pulse" of events or conditions that can affect the business. In reviewing the questions, one could respond that a particular item would have a great impact but a low probability of occurring and so would not be worth the firm's time or resources to collect or analyze information about it. Or the response could be that even though an event is likely, it would occur so far off into the future that there is probably little need for immediate concern. The purpose of examining these factors and making such assessments is to provide the franchised business time to react and to develop contingency plans to accommodate major changes that will affect the firm's market, customers, or suppliers.

Competition

To what extent is competition increasing/decreasing? In what ways?

Are there any new developments in the market? Product substitutes? Costs? Prices?

Is there change in strategy by a competitor? What type is it? What does it mean?

Target Market(s)

Are there any demographic trends taking place that will affect market size?

Are there any changes in submarkets?

What demographic trends can mean opportunity? Threat?

Are there any new developments in the distribution channel? Reliability? Cost?

Are changes in advertising or promotion necessary? What? How effective?

Is there any change in market potential? Market strength? Market share?

Is there further need for product differentiation? From where is it likely to come?

Government

Are any changes in regulation possible? Probable? What will be the impact?

Is there any change in tax law or other incentives that might affect strategy?

Are there any political risks in existing franchise territories? Next expansion?

Technology

Are existing technologies for my business stable? Maturing?

What technologies are being considered? Is there a likelihood of breakthrough?

How fast is the impact of a change in technology for my business? Industry?

Suppliers

Is availability of substitutes on the horizon? When are they available? Are there potential cost savings/increases?

Are supplies to franchisees timely? Cost effective? Profitable? Increasing or decreasing?

Sociocultural

Are there any emerging trends in fashion, lifestyle, preferences?

What are the possible implications and their immediacy?

Overall Economy and My Industry

What are the prospects of change in the current situation of relative economic health?

What is the economic health of my industry? Submarkets of the industry?

FIGURE **5-6**

Environmental Factors to Monitor and Assess

Target Markets

Based on the objectives and the knowledge of environmental factors and market threats and opportunities, the franchisor develops the broad marketing strategy for achieving those objectives. The overall strategy includes clear descriptions of target markets or market segments on which the franchisor intends to focus. Each specific market or market segment will have unique characteristics, usually couched in terms of consumer preferences and spending patterns. A franchisor should determine the attributes of each segment and develop strategies that can best serve the franchise from a competitive standpoint. These attributes can be categorized in accordance with common buying factors such as price, and consumer sensitivity to it; product quality, standardization, and features; product or service delivery—modes, cost, speed; and marketing support and service required with and after the sale. The franchisor wants to find the product- or service-specific factors that address customer requirements and response to the firm's marketing approach.

Product Mix

The marketing strategy should include considerations of the product line to be offered to the customer and it should consider this set of products in light of all products that compete for customers in the target markets. For example, in the fast-food restaurant industry, major franchising firms pay special attention to their product line, raising questions of whether a particular food item should be featured, whether the product line should be expanded by adding similar items, or whether the line needs a more extensive overhaul, replacing one or more items or modifying others. For example, given the increased demand for white meat products, many franchised restaurants have added chicken and/or fish items to their product lines. Several franchised restaurants have added breakfast menu products, modified store hours, and added to and deleted from the product line during certain seasons of the year. In conjunction with the product mix offered by the franchised business, the type of advertising and any sale promotion, pricing, packaging, and distribution methods should be incorporated into the marketing strategy. Once a firm becomes large and has locations widely dispersed throughout a geographic area, certain modification may be necessary because of differences in lifestyle, climate, or other geographic or sociocultural characteristics.

Plans of Action

In developing the franchised business plan, the franchisor should turn the marketing strategies into specific plans of action or tactical programs that provide answers to the following questions: What exactly is to be done in each market segment offering the product? When will the activities be started and completed? Who is responsible for these activities and their outcomes? How much will it cost to implement this plan of action?

Most franchise systems want to expand into new geographic areas to tap into new markets. This can be of high risk for a franchise organization and its existing franchisees. One or a combination of the following marketing strategies are often used by franchise systems to lower the risk of expansion. Careful and accurate collection of the demographics, employment, and income data of the market area under consideration should be made in order to determine the number of stores the market area can support. Prevailing wisdom of experienced franchisors clearly shows not to open a territory with three new franchisee units when the market area can justify twenty to thirty units. Seek to attract potential franchisees who can generate multiple store locations within a reasonable time frame to achieve the overall targeted number of store units to effectively cover the new market area.

Once the appropriate number of franchisees are committed and their growth plans determined, develop an opening launch program to help the new franchisees achieve—and even exceed—break-even point for each store opening during the agreed upon expansion program. In addition, an annual local store marketing plan should be developed and implemented immediately following the opening launch program to assist the new franchisees to achieve even higher sales levels. When these strategies have met with positive results, then establish an advertising co-op plan. Do not start the co-op advertising plan until the critical (minimum essential) number of stores are open. See further information and explanation about this in Chapter 9.

For example, efforts to promote a new product in a market where the franchise firm has a foothold would differ from those directed at a market segment in which the franchise's products have not yet appeared. The approach to be taken varies depending on the target audience, the

Medium	Jan.	Feb.	Mar.	Apr.	May	June	July	Aug.	Sept.	Oct.	Nov.	Dec.
Television: "evening news" "game of the week"		/////	/////	/////	/////	/ / /	/ / /	/ / /	/////	/////	/////	
Newspaper: (national distribution) sports section	/	/	/	/	/	/	/	/	/	/	/	
Magazine: weekly news magazine	/					/		/				/
Cooperative:* Radio—jingle with message Newspaper—mats available			(Franchisee develops schedule, breadth, and depth of coverage using local media mix with some franchisor cooperative cost sharing and assistance in development or presentation of advertisements.)									

*Franchisor agrees to pay a portion of the franchisee's advertising costs and may supply materials, audio or video tapes.

FIGURE 5-7

Media Schedule of a Franchised Auto Body Repair Firm

objective of the promotion, and the amount of money available to promote the product. The tactical elements of the promotional campaign for use by the franchisee would include such elements as point-of-purchase displays; national or regional advertising by the franchisor, including advertising copy and the times, days, and dates when the advertisements will appear on air; and any available information about what the competition might be doing in their promotional campaigns during the same period.

The various plans of action for each product, location, type of promotion, and running dates can be organized on a monthly, quarterly, semiannual, or annual basis through use of a table with weeks or months identified in columns and market action plans or tactics identified in rows. Figure 5-7 illustrates a media schedule for a franchised auto body repair firm. The schedule shows that the "evening news" will be used each weekday from February through May and September through November. From June through August, one advertisement will be aired between the fifth and seventh innings of the "game of the week" on one network. A nationally distributed daily newspaper will carry an advertisement in the sports section on the first three working days of the month. An advertisement will appear four times, once per quarter, in a nationally distributed weekly news magazine.

Typically, the market objectives (anticipated sales results) and budgets are developed on a monthly or quarterly basis. This allows the franchisor to monitor the progress of each product by location and type of promotional effort once the cooperative advertising method has been selected. This approach helps the franchisor and franchisee plan advertising costs and, over time, learn the benefits of such expenditures by evaluating type of advertisement in terms of sale performance at the time of the advertisement.

Market Research and Intelligence

To properly guide a franchise network, the franchisor needs a great deal of information. Much of the information can be hard to acquire, is not available at all, or comes too late for the franchisor to act on an opportunity. Market research and intelligence can be viewed from both an internal and an external perspective.

Internal market information is data from controllable activities of the franchise system. A well-designed internal market information system tracks the primary elements of the franchise distribution mechanism and the important facts about product sales. Such a system could include (1) a list of equipment by type and age at each franchise location, (2) supply and inventory levels by location, (3) sales performance by type of service performed or goods sold, (4) relevant profit and loss data by location and/or product categories, (5) promotional costs per unit sold by type of promotion utilized, and (6) daily accounts receivable and accounts payable data. These types of information are critically important in evaluating performance in light of market objectives, determining strong or weak points in the marketing plans of action; and proposing future marketing strategies or tactics including estimated budget requirement.

External market information needs are outside the realm of activities controlled by the franchise system. These information needs are usually associated with market issues, problems, and threats or opportunities. Researching problems of the market involves several steps. First, the problem, issue, threat, or opportunity must be carefully defined. Once it is defined, it must be determined what information about the problem is necessary so that a judgment or decision can be made. Second, a data collection plan is determined. The plan identifies the types of information needed from primary and secondary sources. Primary data collection (direct observation, field experiment, customer survey) requires developing instruments, determining sample size, and choosing a contact method to retrieve the desired information.

Market research and competitive intelligence are important responsibilities of the franchise system. With the huge, growing retail and B2B markets, it can be difficult for a franchise to stand above the crowd, especially on a light (or tight) budget. It has become essential for successful franchise systems to regularly conduct research on the following key points.

- *What do your customers want?* Customers want you to develop unique ideas for future products and services, and obtain feedback from your customers. Involve them in regular online chats, group discussion, mail or e-mail surveys, and listen to what they have to say.

- *What is your competition really doing?* Not only is it important to follow industry trends, but it is also necessary to study your competition. By observation and "street" knowledge, it is fairly easy to learn what your competition is doing now. Review radio and TV commercials, print advertisements, news announcements, and current events taking place within your franchise system's competitive marketplace. This will help you keep on track with your customer in terms of what they (and you) are doing now; however, what are their intentions into the future? Online newsrooms, annual reports from competitors' corporate headquarters, and recent marketing materials can reveal insight into plans of action for their future goals and growth intentions.

- *Do you have a competitor plan?* When a franchise system does the appropriate research, it knows its customer base and has the right technology, facilities, and team members in place to develop an effective marketing plan. Create a team of people from the home office and franchisees across your franchise network. Share market research and competitive intelligence with them on a regular (weekly, monthly, and annual) basis. Keeping these people "in the know" can spark creativity and unique approaches for the growth and further market penetration of your franchise system. Dunkin' Donuts utilizes such an approach across their brands to better understand their customers, competitors, and industry trends.

- *What does it take to truly promote your business model and product or service line?* Take the time to reevaluate current strategies and market tactics on a regular basis. Review all areas of your franchise system's exposure. To develop and maintain current, attractive, and meaningful marketing advertising and promotion, spend the money to hire experienced graphic designers, technicians, copywriters, and publicists to make sure your messages are on target and create the best impression possible in the marketplace.

To illustrate the above points, an example is in order. In 1998, McDonald's unfolded a modified mission for its chain of restaurants as: "Hot Food. Served Faster. To Order. Every

Time." For the first time in decades, McDonald's became determined to make better food—to put hotter, fresher food first. Telephone surveys of their customer base showed one common complaint: McDonald's food did not taste as good as it used to taste. Further customer research identified that the complaint did not concern the recipes. Customers wanted the food hotter. Two-thirds of the take-out customers consumed their purchases *at least five minutes* away from the franchised restaurant. Thus, it became important that the food be provided hot and stay hot. How hot is a closely held secret. McDonald's had allowed its food preparation system get out of date with how their customers were living their lives. They determined they would regain customer satisfaction by delivering on the promise to deliver hot food. In addition, McDonald's developed a system to deliver hot buns—heated in just ten seconds with radiant convection heat, juicy meat in high-tech holding cabinets with moisture controls to keep patties hot and moist for up to twenty minutes, and faster service through new computer software to project what items will be ordered during heavy times of the day by placing extra orders of a few best-selling items such as Big Macs.[3]

Secondary data collection (through trade publications, government publications, periodicals, books, or commercial surveys) usually provides the starting point of data collection and offers the advantage of low cost and quick availability. It will often happen that the precise information needed is not available from secondary sources, or if it is, the information is incomplete, unreliable, or obsolete. When this is the case, the franchise firm must use primary data collection methods, which typically cost more and require more time to complete. However, primary data collection is often more relevant and reliable because it enables the franchisor to obtain the precise information needed to address the problem at hand. The third step is the actual collection and analysis of information to determine the relationships within the data as they apply to the problem. Finally, judgments must be made about the information analyzed to assist the franchised firm in making decisions about the market problem or issue.

Often, a franchisor will seek outside help from a university or private market research firm to perform studies when primary research is required. However, some larger franchisors operate their own market research departments in order to build statistical data banks to improve their analytical capabilities as well as increase their knowledge of their particular markets and the industry on the whole.

What is the number of advertising messages to which the average U.S. resident is exposed to on a daily basis? In 1960: 1,500; in 1990: 3,000; and in 2000: 5,000.

Adapted from Nora Aufreiter, David Elzinga, and Jonathan Gordon, "Better Branding," The McKinsey Quarterly (21 August 2006): 1, www.mckinseyquarterly.com/article.

5-4 DETERMINING THE MARKETING MIX

As we have already demonstrated, marketing strategy is important to an entrepreneur. Finding opportunities and developing marketable products or services for those opportunities are the primary functions of all budding business ventures. To achieve success, the franchisor will need to understand the marketing mix. As mentioned earlier in the chapter, the marketing mix is that set of controllable elements the franchisor and franchisee put together (or integrate) to reach the target market. To be successful, the franchise organization must have a product that addresses a want or need of a group of people, is available where these people want it, and is priced within an acceptable range. Also, the product must have qualities or characteristics that can be communicated or promoted to the targeted

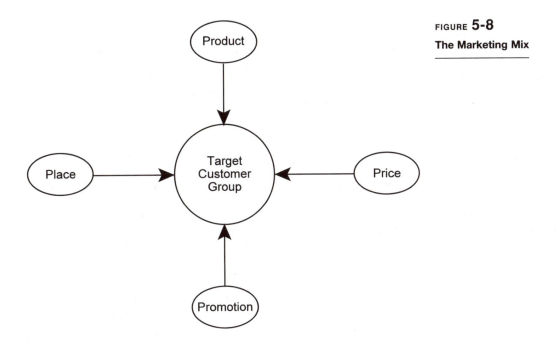

FIGURE **5-8**

The Marketing Mix

group of people. The elements that constitute the marketing mix are otherwise known as the four Ps of marketing—product, promotion, price, and place (see Figure 5-8).

The franchising concept is not often cited or compared to other types of firms in a marketing distribution system. Often, a holding company or parent firm may seek to achieve the "place" objective through several alternatives to franchising. It could develop company-owned retailers or distributors, or establish units that are jointly owned by the parent and a local entrepreneur in a stock or partnership arrangement. Or perhaps it could establish a freestanding relationship between independent distributors or retailers, in which the retailer or distributor would handle several lines with a diversity of brands from a wide variety of companies. In any event, the parent firm or holding company considering these alternatives must face the same reality as the budding franchisor: If the qualities or unique characteristics of the product do not meet customer needs, then the franchising attempts of distributors or retailers to meet the "place" objective will be for naught. The other marketing mix factors—price, promotion, and product—must be put in proper balance by the franchising organization; otherwise, the whole endeavor may fail.

Generic Categories of Goods and Services

Traditionally, there have been four generic categories to classify consumer goods and services. Each category has typical pricing, promotional, and distribution strategies associated with the type of goods or services. By thinking about this classification scheme, a budding franchisor can use this information to help build a logical, realistic marketing mix to reach the specific target market or customer niches.

Convenience goods or services are frequently purchased, usually are low to competitively priced, and are staples, emergency, or impulse buys. The convenience/gasoline store is a classic example of a convenience seller.

Homogenous shopping goods or services are purchased less frequently than convenience products. The customer typically "shops" for the best bargain among goods or services that are considered highly similar if not the same quality. Thus, price tends to be the motive for purchase. Retail clothing and accessories are typical examples of homogenous shopping goods.

TABLE 5-3	GENERIC CATEGORIES OF GOODS OR SERVICES AND STRATEGIC MARKETING MIX OPTIONS		
Type of Goods or Service	Place/Location/ Strategy	Pricing Strategy	Promotion Strategy
Convenience	Intensive	Odd-even	Brand loyalty themes; full communication mix used; intensive advertising
Homogenous Shopping	Intensive	Odd-even; low price	Intensive advertising; Brand conscious; Focus on building customer traffic
Heterogeneous Shopping	Limited; selective	Full range; focus usually not on price	Full range of communication mix; differentiation; focus on building customer traffic
Specialty Shopping	Selective-to-exclusive	Prestige price; skimming is possible	Limited; niche focused; image building

Heterogeneous shopping goods or services category is the one where most franchise systems see themselves. The focus is on product or service qualities or characteristics with prices being a second-level or a lower-order concern to the purchaser. Auto dealerships, flower shops, legal or accounting services, coffee shops, landscaping, and architectural firms are common examples of this category.

Specialty products or services include a wide array of possibilities. Franchised custom software services, wedding gowns, other formal wear, exclusive shoe wear, jewelry, optical services, consulting services, optical and oral surgery clinics, custom catering, and other service providers are few in number within a general market area, may be hard to find, offer unique features to the customer, and charge higher prices. Their promotional mix may be the most singular and focused of any—word of mouth with occasional news articles or public service sponsorships to keep the name of the firm in front of the community.

It is important to realize that there can be a significant amount of *crossovers*. The categories in Table 5-3 are not meant to be mutually exclusive of one another. Therefore, the franchisor must carefully match the marketing mix variables to be used with the perceptions and expectations of the target market group.

5-4a   Product

The first P to be considered in the marketing mix is product. **Product** is not just the item or service itself. Rather, it carries with it a unique set of physical and psychological characteristics or attributes designed to satisfy the wants or needs of a group of people. For example, a Big Mac is not just a McDonald's hamburger; it is designed to carry with it the attributes that the company name suggests—clean environment, prompt service, and competitive price. Likewise, a Corvette has a host of attributes connected with it, apart from the warranty, sales approach, and road performance estimates.

Psychological and social factors are so important, in fact, that a franchisor requires its franchisees to follow certain prescribed practices consistent with the product's purpose, characteristics or attributes, and image in the targeted market. For each product, a franchisor must answer the following: How should the product be designed? What unique characteristics should be included and what options allowed? How should the product be named, labeled, and packaged? What type of warranty or service guarantee should be offered? The franchisor must determine the importance of each product characteristic and then establish specifications to ensure homogeneity for marketing and distribution through the franchise network.

Consistent quality in product is an identifiable characteristic of successful franchise systems. Customers like to feel they are getting their money's worth, and they like to know what to expect, whether they are having a transmission repaired, staying in a hotel, or having their photos finished. The success of such firms as Aamco Transmissions Inc., Holiday Inns, Inc., and Moto Photo suggests in part that some customers will bypass competent independents to deal with a franchise chain because they believe they will receive a consistent, quality product.

By failing to recognize the importance of product consistency to the customer, one franchisee can immeasurably hurt the business of other franchisees in the same distribution system. As we have said, a bad cup of coffee served by one donut shop affects other franchisees and thus sheds an unfavorable light on the franchise system itself. The underlying principle is to establish guidelines for maintaining product consistency and then to make sure these guidelines are followed throughout the franchise system.

5-4b When the Product Is a Service

In the United States, the production and sale of services accounts for about 53 percent of total gross domestic product (GDP). In terms of jobs, the services sector accounts for about 70 percent of total employment in the United States. Between 1992 and 2005, employment in the United States experienced a net increase of about 27 million jobs. The service sector is likely to generate almost 90 percent of those new jobs, with the greatest amount of concentrated growth taking place in health services and business services. Other sectors anticipating large gains are government, finance, insurance, real estate, and retail trade. A major reason for the sharp growth increase in these areas is the movement to an information age—the computer and telecommunications technologies (see Table 5-4).

Characteristics of Services

Four qualities are inherent to services only, not in goods. These characteristics create real challenges for the providers of services to attract customers and keep them coming back for additional services. These characteristics and brief descriptions are listed here.

TABLE 5-4 OFFERING A PRODUCT: A SERVICE: OR BOTH?

Criteria	No/Low Tangibility	Both to a Degree	High Tangibility
Tangibility	Fully intangible	Partially tangible	Fully tangible
Buyer and seller inseparable	Both must be present	Distant/remote exchange is possible	Remote transactions easy
Difficulty to measure and control quality	Measure and control processes and people, not product	Measure and control processes, people, and product	Measure and control product specifics and its quality
Customize the offering to the buyer	Can enhance buyer perception of perceived quality	Customizing can have marginal effect on perceived quality	Customizing will increase costs; not likely to affect buyer perception of product quality
Perishability	Need on site, on demand, or no sale	Extent of buyer need and patience before receiving offering	Buyer usually can wait to receive product
Inventory	Cannot store or warehouse the offering		Easy to inventory product offering
Buyer–seller relationship	Relationship is at least as important as the service provided	Relationship can be important	Focus is on product; personal relations often minor in importance to the transaction

Perishability means that a particular service cannot be inventoried or stored for a period of time. Sporting events, concerts, booking service, dental hygienic cleaning, and the purchase of a burger, fries, and malt are examples of perishability. To reduce the negative impact of perishability of services, franchised systems of medical, dental, and business services have developed strategies to cope with fluctuating demand to achieve some balance between the so-called supply of the service sought and its demand. Note how fast-food restaurant chains have been positioning themselves toward a three-meals-a-day context to keep their kitchens and counters at optimal efficiency while increasing cash flow.

Intangibility refers to the lack of tangibility of a product or service such as what can be seen, touched, smelled, tasted, or heard prior to purchase. Child care, education, sporting events, a music DVD, a prepared tax return, and a financial audit are examples of services that are considered within the range of intangibility. Some services offer tangibility with the intangible. For example, a restaurant provides the food as the outcome, but is paid as much for the availability of the service, quality of the service and food provided, convenience, and ambiance. The quality of the service is based on the intangible as much, if not more, than the tangibles of the food service.

Variability means the random, or unwanted, levels of quality that the customer can receive as they purchase, receive, and consume the service. Typically, variance in the level of quality provided is centered in the human element. Two employees can perform the same service differently, even after following the same directions. Or, quality of service delivery may vary over time, where the outcomes differ each time the customer comes in for the ten-minute oil change. Because of the human element and varying conditions within a business when a particular service has been ordered, standardization and quality control are more difficult to achieve than when the purchaser is buying a bowling ball or loaf of bread. Burger King has applied industrial engineering and organization concepts to their food processing and customer servicing techniques to increase productivity and efficiency in their business. For example, prior to peak demand times, hamburgers, fries, and other foods can be prepared and placed in warming ovens or bins. Thus, peak demand can be met efficiently while quality of product serviced can remain constant and standardized. Employees are trained to follow specific procedures when pre-preparing such foods.

Inseparability refers to the simultaneous production and consumption of a service. Tangible goods, such as cars, can be produced in Detroit in January, inventoried there until May, shipped on consignment to Los Angeles in June, and sold by a franchised dealer in July or August. When a service must be produced and consumed at the same time, the quality of the service is strictly dependent on the ability of the service provider and the quality of the interaction with the customer during the service delivery. For example, franchised dental practices place great emphasis on comfort, ease, professionalism in demeanor, efficiency, and friendliness. These concepts do not have to be in conflict with one another. Pearle Vision, Inc. provides optical services that, like dentistry, have a high degree of inseparability. The customer is present and involved in the production of the service while other customers may be observing. It is not possible to mass produce this service delivery. Each person's optical needs are unique and must be dealt with on a one-to-one basis. To overcome inefficiencies, Pearle Vision, like many franchise service systems, developed a process. A receptionist greets the customer on entry, information is provided to the optometrist, while the customer is taken to a comfortable waiting area that may have a radio, television, and reading material and soft drinks. While some customers are having their eyes examined, others are having their new glasses fitted, and others still may be examining the various types of frames and prices that are available. Pearle Vision seeks to manage the customer service delivery process every step of the way.

Life Cycle

Every product has a life cycle. Even though different products have different cycles, life cycles always have four stages: introduction, growth, maturity, and decline. A product life cycle is illustrated in Figure 5-9.

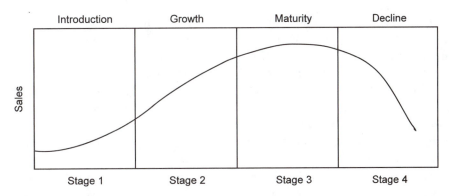

Media Schedule of a Franchised Auto Body Repair Firm

The first state, the *introduction,* is a period of slow, gradual sales growth. During this state, the product does not have much name recognition or customer loyalty. The product itself may be completely new, or it may be an old product with new features. Sales and profits tend to be low. If the product is targeted properly and meets consumer acceptance, the *growth* stage begins. In the growth stage, the life cycle curve takes a dramatic upward surge. This sharp increase reflects the product's recognition and acceptance as it is sought by growing numbers of consumers in the target market. As more consumers seek more of the product, market demand increases and sales and profits may seem to soar. The income to the franchisor is typically enough to cover research, market development, and promotional costs as well as yield substantial profits. The *maturity* stage occurs when the rate of sales growth slows and, ultimately, sales level off. For some products in highly competitive franchise industries, such as fast-food restauranting, sales may actually decline as competition intensifies for the customers in the target group. But sales of the product are still usually at a relatively high level with reasonably predictable production and inventory schedules. The franchise organization reaps the benefits of operational efficiency through high-volume processing. Franchisors may also try to create increased sales by penetrating deeper into existing markets, expanding into new locations, entering new markets in various ways, or broadening the scope of business activity within the target market through the addition of new products or services. Some examples follow:

1. Expanding into complementary segments of the market (as some fast-food franchises have by serving breakfast and/or late-night service)

2. Changing the packaging or image (such as using two-liter plastic bottles of soda, or claiming "orange juice isn't just for breakfast anymore")

3. Finding new uses for the product (such as by informing households that baking soda can be used to keep the refrigerator odor free)

4. Finding new ways to deliver the product to deepen market penetration (such as the Burger King mobile units that can park at university campuses, along a beach, or on the fairway of a state fairground)

During the *decline* stage of the product life cycle, it is typical for sales volume to drop as demand shifts to other products. Inevitably, new products become available and gain the favor of consumers. Under decline conditions, maintaining the franchise network and seeking to meet ever-shifting market demand are critical to the survival of the franchised firm.

The franchisor must determine if the decline is due to a temporary fluctuation in the market, or if it is the result of a permanent change in the target market population. Typical courses of action for a franchisor are (1) to cease to produce the product; (2) to change or improve the product and offer it to the market segment that is shifting (as with the McDonald's conversion from chicken sandwich to Chicken McNuggets); or (3) to phase out the product gradually, replacing it with a new one that will appeal to the shifted market. This last option suggests that the franchised firm should maintain the product within the line for perhaps six months or longer, waiting until the shift in customer preferences has been completed before entering the market with a new product. The reason for a stalling tactic is obvious: A franchised firm will probably not want to risk having another product "failure" that the consuming public might remember and associate with the franchise.

The decline stage can create a difficult set of circumstances for a franchised firm. Because a franchisor will want to change the product to keep pace with the changing preferences of the target market, conflicts can arise with some franchisees. Signs will need to be replaced with new logos, menus changed, pictures of models or products or services updated, or costly interior renovations completed. Often a franchisee may not see the need to spend money to make the changes called for by the franchisor. In some cases, franchisees feel strongly that such changes should be paid for by the franchisor, or at least that the franchisor should share the costs of the changes through some sort of cooperative plan. Some franchisees refrain from making any changes until absolutely essential, agreeing to change only when sales fall or when it is apparent that other franchised units have benefited from the change. Some franchisees are content with a gradual decline in sales, as long as it eventually settles at a satisfactory level and can be maintained there. Others may even try to sell their franchised business, while still others are content just to close up shop! Some franchisors faced with sustained decline in demand and reluctant franchisees may withdraw from franchising altogether, choosing instead to operate only company-owned establishments.

With the introduction of the Egg McMuffin in 1975, McDonald's turned breakfast into a fast-food meal. Now it is moving to capture the rest of the day. More than 90 percent of the 13,700 McDonald's units have extended their hours beyond the basic 6 A.M. to 11 P.M., and nearly 40 percent of these restaurants operate nonstop, up from less than 1 percent in 2002.

Adapted from Michael Arndt, "Special Report: McDonald's," BusinessWeek (5 February 2007): 66.

Product Life Cycle in Franchise Marketing Strategy

The product life cycle model is a theoretical construct that can help a franchisor understand the industry cycle and the cycle of specific products in the franchise system's product line. This theoretical model can be interfaced with practical marketing in a franchise system, with particular view toward the advertising and promotion needs of the firm and its products. Table 5-5 identifies how a franchise system's marketing strategy should change as the industry and product life cycles unfold over time.

The first product stage is called introduction and early growth—growth at an increasing rate. This time period is when the majority of prospective franchisees and ultimate consumers are unfamiliar with the franchise system and its products and services. The second stage is near the upper part of the life cycle curve, when sales continue to grow but are increasing at a decreasing rate until sales become stable (maturity). One knows they are in this stage when competition is keen and the majority of the franchise's customers have tried one or more competitors' products. The third stage is called the retention and evaluation stage. This stage coincides with stability, even sluggishness in industry and firm product sales with decline in sales as likely, if not imminent. This

TABLE 5-5	ADVERTISING/PROMOTION STRATEGY BY LIFE CYCLE STAGES		
Introduction and Early Growth	**Decreasing Growth to Stability**	**Stability/Maturity to Decline**	
First: Inform/educate consumers	Build brand quality in image and practice	Retain existing customer base	
Second: Encourage trial use; samples and coupons	Position against competitors based on core competencies	Build customer relationships; target customer groups and one-one ones	
Third: Build distribution system: horizontal then vertical	Penetrate target market; capture a major market share	Improve quality; improve again and again	
Fourth: Focus on market niches; segment market to better serve customer needs	Improve quality; improve service; learn more about customer needs	Upgrade service; upgrade product; modify product if needed	

stage is known in practice by its most outstanding negative feature: Finding new customers costs more than retention of current or past customers. By careful analysis of the franchise system's sales records and industry data providing aggregate sales and demand figures, a franchise system can position itself, correspondingly, to choose the most effective use of the advertising and promotion budget (see Table 5-5).

By studying Table 5-5 and staying focused on how your product meets customer needs and how their tastes and preferences change, the details of the franchise system's marketing tactics will become clearer, simpler, and accurate to the target customer group.

Target Marketing

An explosion of customer segments, media choices, products and services, and distribution channels has made franchise system marketing more complex, more costly, and harder to be effective. Subbrands and trademarked products multiply and so the media required to sell them multiplies also. For a marketer to "meet every need" is becoming virtually impossible to accomplish. A "prevailing wisdom" is developing among major franchise systems to focus on a few of the available customer segments and serve them with fewer brands (instead of more) to reduce the impact of complexity from product development to promotion.

Rethinking brands, and target markets are just two of the challenges facing franchisors to successfully grow their franchise organization. Franchise marketing must also address the overall cost of serving their customer segments and franchisee businesses. Surely, the customer comes first, but providing effective marketing support to individual franchisee units must be a close second. In the overall, franchise marketers need to develop a segment-driven approach to build stronger, distinctively positioned brands and products and services to increase the return on the investment made in marketing.

New Product Development

A franchised firm cannot rely in the long run on its initial products. Customers want and *expect* new or improved products, so the firm must introduce new products to replace those with limited or declining consumer interest. For this reason, a franchised firm needs to have objectives and plans of action to develop new ideas and assess, test, and distribute new products through the franchise system.

New product (or new service) launches may or may not correlate with improvement in a brand's revenue growth. Truly innovative product breakthroughs have been found to provide a 2.7 percent improvement in revenue growth as reported in a study which analyzed 480 product launches associated with high growth categories.[4] Breakthrough products were found to be rare with only 15 (3 percent) of the 480 launches qualified in this category.

TABLE 5-6   TYPICAL MARKETING TACTICS BY TYPE OF INNOVATION CATEGORY

Marketing Tactics	Description	Example
Incremental Innovation	Innovation to product or its packaging using existing technology that provides an incremental consumer benefit	Adding chicken or fish strips or fruit to a fresh salad
Line Extension	Slight "tweaks" to existing products that provide no true incremental consumer benefit	New size, flavor, or new packaging
Repositioning the Product	Target new customers, uses, or occasions with focus on benefits not previously identified with the product/service	Grape juice as antioxidant Tools for various uses
Premium Pricing or	Premium price to raise perceived value	Interior components or rich textiles in autos
Value-based Pricing	Value pricing to increase demand	99-cent sandwich

A franchise system that is not bursting with new products coming through their pipeline can have impressive revenue growth through repositioning products for new consumer segments, offering new uses or additional occasions for use when complemented with solid marketing tactics. A study found that the use of existing technology to enhance a current product through incremental innovation improved revenues as much as they did for breakthrough products.[5] What innovative behavior did not spur revenue growth? The study found that line extensions such as a new flavor, color, or wordage such as "new and improved," when not supported by other marketing tactics, were associated with minimal (0.5 percent) revenue growth.[6] Overall, the findings suggest that consumer goods executives should continually look for opportunities to reposition their products which can require big changes in product development priorities, targeted objectives within existing customer segments, and new markets for entry. Achieving rapid growth of a franchise system is never easy, particularly in the broad array of retail businesses providing consumer goods and services. However, rapid growth is possible when the product, price, promotional appeal, and place are in balance.

Marketing tactics and types of innovative behavior by franchise firms can be identified and described in a straightforward way as shown in Table 5-6. Numerous examples can serve to illustrate the application, although only a few are noted herein.

Assess the Marketing Program's Effectiveness

The marketing budget should provide a realistic identification of the action plan for marketing the franchise system's products and services in the current year and project effectiveness of expenditures for the forthcoming year. The crucial question for the franchisor is: Does this mix of marketing activities meet the franchisee and customer sales objectives? A quick, though poignant picture may tell the story. As the old adage goes, "A picture can be worth a thousand words." (See Figure 5-10.)

From Strategic Marketing Planning to Effective Tactical Execution

Franchise systems today are not sitting on their backsides. Strategic planning completed at the company's headquarters and filtered down through the organization to the franchisee units is going by the wayside. The current "buzz" phrase is tactical planning and execution. Franchise systems are becoming tactical companies, where strategic planning is performed by interdisciplinary teams of people who have to do the execution. The idea is to push the company out of its comfort zone—to think out of the box—looking at itself objectively to challenge any sacred cows. Tactical planning and execution requires that decisions be made quickly, in accordance with the mission throughout

	Limited Success	True Success
High	Lost customers are replaced by new customers	Profit and sales grow at maximum feasible rate
	Total Failure	**Partial Failure**
Low	Total sales and sales units fall as customers leave	Sales stagnate or fall due to lack of new customers

Customer Attraction to Products and Services

FIGURE **5-10**

Marketing Effectiveness Matrix

the organization—including the franchisee locations. In a number of franchise systems, individual franchisees and/or franchisee advisory councils (FACs) are playing an important role in strategic and tactical planning. The new values being stressed in the franchise industry seem to be as follows:

- Strategies are to be crafted, not calculated.

- Learning, flexibility, and adaptability are critical (new) norms.

- Headquarters and franchisees truly believe in the franchise system's vision and mission.

- Franchise system's culture is of crucial importance, the central focus of the franchise system.

- A feeling of brand ownership and loyalty to the company is paramount in the franchise system's culture. The franchise system will learn what customers want and what the competition is doing.

- The franchise system will trust in its team to formulate changes in tactics quickly, bring forth effective new product or services offerings, and stay consistent with the changing tastes and needs of their customer groups.

- The franchise system will have a structure in place that provides for, and encourages, effective communication across and within all levels of the organization.

Individual franchise systems have their particular market imperatives, distinctive missions, and diverse cultural norms and values. These previous seven values about firm strategy and tactical execution, however, are somewhat common to successful franchise systems early in the new millennium.

SUMMARY

Effective marketing is essential to the success of a franchise system, whether it is at the start-up, growth, or maturity stage of development. In franchising, the intent is to increase revenues by creating new business units. Effective marketing requires bringing the product or service to the customer at the right time, at the right place, and at the right price. Determining the market direction is crucial in the early stages of a franchise system's development, including the marketing tactics with regard to the marketing mix of price, place, product, and promotion. Marketing strategy and tactics need to be understood and proven to be effective for the franchise system to successfully recruit franchisees.

In the first generation of the twenty-first century, the demographics of business ownership will be diverse. By 2020, baby boomers will account for over 25 percent of the U.S. population. The sheer size of the baby boom generation suggests that business formation will grow substantially between now and 2020. The Gen-Yers will be the most entrepreneurial generation since the 1930s. They have strong conceptual abilities, will be well educated, be critical thinkers, and can readily adapt or reinvent as needed. Mid-career women have sharp business acumen, managerial experience, and have a strong work ethic. Many mid-career women will want to continue to build on their corporate experiences by developing businesses of their own. Immigrant entrepreneurs are the fastest growing segment of small business ownership in the first seven years of this new century. Immigrants often lack contacts into large business firms, experience in large business ventures, and smooth English-language skills. Thus, starting a business is often easier for an immigrant than it is to find a good job. In addition, the mom who wants to work part time, yet control her destiny by have a home-based business venture, is also part of a rising tide of home-based woman-owned start-up businesses. In effect, today's marketplace is ripe for expression of entrepreneurship through a diverse group of demographics. Having the "right" franchise opportunity, depending on a person's particular background and needs, is of extreme importance to the diverse population of potential entrepreneurs in today's America. Having the right type of advertising and promotional materials will be crucial to tap into each type of potential entrepreneur, as described in the chapter.

Successful franchise systems must employ strategic planning to be successful in both the short and long run. The first step is to establish the franchise organization's mission, which provides a shared sense of opportunity, challenge, and motivation for the owners, franchisees, and employees within the franchise system. It is upon a firm understanding of the mission of the franchise system that objectives and strategies about what will be done and how it is to be done are based. Suitable market niche(s) must be determined and effective approaches to continue market development must be developed and evaluated to assure continuity and growth of the system. To this end, market research and competitive intelligence are important to guide the franchise network in its continued development. Internal market information about the system's products or services, efficiency norms, product development, and promotional and advertising plans become important to balance with external market information. It becomes crucial for a franchise system that operates under strong competitive conditions to know precisely what the customers want; what the competition is doing; what your next tactical market plans are to be; and what it takes to effectively promote your franchise system's business model and product or service line. In addition, product life cycle as well as business and industry cycles, or swings, can affect the future growth, maturity, and decline of a franchise system. Therefore, it is important for new product and service development to be taken seriously. Innovation and change is in the domain of the franchisor. A system should not rely on new ideas, methods, products, or service variations to come from disgruntled franchisees. The system itself should provide the resource support and manage the effort to develop a stream of operations improvements and product options.

KEY TERMS

Business image: The image the franchise system "packages" about itself for public consumption.

Convenience goods or services: Goods frequently purchased that are usually low-to-competitively prices, are staples, emergency or impulse buys.

Heterogeneous shopping goods or services: The focus is on product or service qualities or characteristics with price being a second-level or lower-order concern to the purchaser.

Homogenous shopping goods or services: Goods purchased less frequently than convenience goods. The customer typically shops around for the best bargain among highly similar goods or services.

Inseparability: The simultaneous production and consumption of a service; for example, franchised dental service.

Intangibility: The lack of tangibility of a product or service such as what can be seen, smelled, tasted or heard prior to purchase.

Marketing: Involves everything it takes to get a product or service into the buyer's hands.

Marketing mix: Controllable factors to be considered in combination to satisfy the needs or wants of customers in the target market.

Marketing strategy: Consists of identifying one or more target markets and creation of a marketing mix to reach the targeted customer group.

Perishability: Means that a particular good, component or service cannot be inventoried or stored over a period of time.

Product: A unique set of physical and psychological characteristics or attributes designed to satisfy the wants or needs of a targeted customer group.

Specialty products or services: Include a wide array of possibilities. Generally providers are fewer in number than shopping goods providers and usually offer unique features to the customer and charge higher prices.

Variability: The random, or unwanted, levels of quality that the customer can received as they purchase, receive and consume the product or service.

Louis DeAngelo, Jr.

DeAngelo's Pizzeria Company

DeAngelo's Pizzeria Company was founded in Baton Rouge, Louisiana, in October 1991 by Louis DeAngelo, Jr. Louis is originally from New Jersey and honed his culinary ability in a friend of the family's pizza shop. He began working at the age of ten by washing dishes, bussing tables, working the counter, and eventually making pizzas. By the time Louis was seventeen, his passion for pizza became an inevitable part of his future.

Louis spent less than a semester in college before deciding that his goal was to open his own pizza restaurant, which was fueled by the support and enthusiasm of his parents. His grandfather loaned him the initial capital to buy equipment, signs, and utensils. From there he was headed to Baton Rouge to give the town what it really needed—quality pizza! Before opening the doors at the first store, Louis promised himself that he would only serve the best

pizza possible and hold everyone to that promise everyday. The restaurant was a success three to four months after opening because of his passion and commitment to quality. The philosophy of the restaurant quickly grew from great pizza to great service, which eventually led into great teamwork.

Following the first location in the Hammond Aire Shopping Center, DeAngelo's continued to grow. In 1996, DeAngelo's Pizzeria opened up on Bluebonnet Boulevard. Following that, in 1997, DeAngelo's Pizzeria in Mandeville opened up, in which Louis's brother Tim is a managing partner. In 1998, DeAngelo's Pizzeria on West Lee Drive opened; and, in 1999, development of a franchise package began. In March 2000, DeAngelo's Pizzeria on Coursey Boulevard at Hickory Ridge opened.

The mission and values that developed out of these initial goals are at the very center of this company.

When talking about franchising, the biggest obstacle was how to transfer what DeAngelo's is all about. That "feeling" is what makes the restaurants so special, and without it, DeAngelo's is just another restaurant serving good food.

Louis redesigned the training program, refocused the trainers, and made transferring DeAngelo's Core Values priority "Number 1." Louis believes that this will always be a major key to success, but at the same time, will always represent the greatest threat to that success and to the people who stand for what DeAngelo's is all about.

Core values make up a large part of the Family Corporate Culture. When a new teammate is hired, they are taken through a two-step interview process, and then given a test on DeAngelo's nine core values. These values are the people, guests, teamwork, service, productivity, quality, communication, working environment, and commitment.

If Louis believes that they have what it takes to be a part of the team, and can contribute to the culture, regardless of their experience, then he gives them a chance. Louis provides them with all the proper tools, training, and most of all, the opportunity to make a success of their efforts. If they put forth their best intention, and care about what they are doing and who they are doing it for, then they have earned a place on DeAngelo's team. The one lesson Louis has learned is "the more you grow, the harder you must work at the fundamentals."

The next challenge was to develop a system where the franchisees would put the same care and concern into their food and their people as Louis has for the last ten years. To address the food issue, he decided that the franchisees would purchase core items labeled as "proprietary," which include dough, dressings, and sauces, so that Louis may help close the gap on any quality control issues that might arise from another interpretation of the company recipes. By doing this, Louis efficiently ensures that the food the cooks are preparing is the same as the fine company-owned restaurants.

In the final analysis, Louis has come to understand that business opportunities are made and lost on a daily basis. By orchestrating what he calls "controlled growth," DeAngelo's can help ensure that each franchisee is as successful as the first, and by pursuing such growth, the company can put the proper time and energy into them, helping to eliminate the mistakes and wasted motions experienced over time. Louis would rather have ten excellent quality franchisees, instead of fifteen or twenty average ones. Quality, not quantity, is what DeAngelo's will always be known for.

REVIEW QUESTIONS

1. Why must marketing fit in with other functions of a franchised business?

2. What is strategic planning in marketing? How is it used?

3. What are the four Ps of marketing? Provide an example of how each can be applied in franchised merchandise retailing; in franchised service retailing.

4. Explain the legal considerations associated with product pricing in the franchisor–franchisee relationship.

5. What is meant by a dual system in franchised product distribution?

6. Distinguish between sales promotion and mass advertising. How might the distinction be made in franchise retailing compared with franchise wholesaling?

7. It is said that products have "psychological" attributes. Explain.

8. Explain the potential conflicts between the franchise's decisions about customer orientation and resource allocation.

9. Discuss innovation in terms of its role in franchise product and service delivery.

CASE STUDY

Dunkin' Donuts*

Ramone walked out of a downtown Dunkin' Donuts and knew that this was the kind of franchise he wanted to open. He had been looking for a franchise for the last year and a half, and had raised approximately $38,000 to help start a food service business. He had looked at many different kinds of stores and had finally found the one he would like to operate.

Dunkin' Donuts has over 1,400 stores worldwide, more than any donut shop competitor. Dunkin' Donuts has a national advertising and promotional budget currently over $18 million annually. In addition to being the largest franchise chain of donut shops in the world, it also has the highest average sales per shop—approximately $400,000.

Dunkin' Donuts attributes its success to certain factors. First is the concept itself: superior products at the right price with prompt, courteous service in clean, well-designed, conveniently located shops. Second, and just as important, is the franchising system. Hundreds of dedicated franchise owners diligently maintain standards and upgrade work records to earn handsome financial rewards.

In addition to being able to meet the basic financial requirements, which excluded land or building, Ramone was excited about the required six-week training program at Dunkin' Donuts University in Braintree, Massachusetts. The training program is to teach product methods and to ensure product quality and freshness, proper training, employee motivation, merchandising techniques, accounting, budgeting, and recordkeeping. A great deal of this training time is spent in learning the operations necessary to ensure cleanliness and a good image.

Ramone was still uneasy about the marketing needs of the franchise. He was not certain who was the target market of a franchised donut shop. He did not know what kind of research was necessary to understand the marketing process or if Dunkin' Donuts would help with the marketing program. He read in the brochure that Dunkin' Donuts "concentrates on a single sales theme and directs the message to consumers who are likely to become regular customers." Ramone was hoping that Dunkin' Donuts might help him with advertising. He would also need help in finding a good location. Ramone was also wondering about new products and if there was a continuous effort to improve the product line. Ramone knew he could be a success, because Dunkin' Donuts is a corporation committed to the future and profitability of its franchisees. He wanted the opportunity to prove himself. If the franchisor would buy the land and put up the building, then Ramone believed that he could finance a new Dunkin' Donuts operation.

---

* Information provided courtesy of Dunkin' Donuts of America, August 1987.

ESTIMATED COSTS AND CASH REQUIREMENTS

Minimum Cash Required	Region I	Region II
Franchising fee	$40,000	$30,000
Working capital	$19,000	$19,000
Total minimum cash required	$59,000	$49,000

Estimated Cost Ranges	Region I		Region II	
Minimum cash required[1]	$ 59,000	$ 59,000	$ 49,000	$ 49,000
Equipment[2]	$ 65,000	$ 85,000	$ 65,000	$ 85,000
Signs[3]	$ 7,000	$ 14,000	$ 7,000	$ 17,000
Total estimated costs	$131,000	$158,000	$121,000	$151,000

[1] Minimum cash required refers to the amount of cash needed to acquire franchise rights. These funds must be unencumbered.
[2,3] Equipment and sign costs will vary for each shop.

CASE QUESTIONS

1. What does Ramone need to know before becoming a Dunkin' Donuts franchisee?

2. What marketing information should Ramone seek?

3. What marketing mix should Ramone look for with his business?

REFERENCES

Aaker, David, Nora Batra Aufreiter, David Elzinga, and Johnathan Gordon, "Better Branding," *The McKinsey Quarterly* (21 August 2006): 1, www.mckinseyquarterly.com/article.

Aaker, David, Rajeev Batra, and John G. Myers, *Advertising Management*, 4th ed. (Englewood Cliffs, NJ: Prentice Hall Inc., 1992).

Arndt, Michael, "Special Report: McDonald's," *BusinessWeek* (5 February 2007): 66.

Baghai, Mehrdad, Stephen Coley, and David White, *The Alchemy of Growth* (Cambridge, MA: Perseus Books, 1999).

Coulter, Mary K., *Strategic Management in Action* (Upper Saddle River, NJ: Prentice Hall, Inc., 1998).

Curry, J. A. H., et al., *Partners for Profit: A Study of Franchising* (New York: American Management Association, Inc., 1996).

"Denny's Finalizes Switch to Trans Fat-Free Oil in All Restaurants," 16 March 2007, www.TradingMarkets.com.

Dixon, Edward L., Jr., ed., *The 1980 Franchise Annual Handbook and Directory* (Lewiston, NY: International Franchise Opportunities Press, Inc., 1980).

"Entrepreneur's Franchise Special," *Entrepreneur Magazine*, P.O. Box 50368, Boulder, CO, 1998.

Fisk, Raymond, Stephen Grover, and John Joby, *Interactive Services Marketing* (New York: Houghton Mifflin Company, 2000).

Flanagan, Sharon and Cari-Martin Lindahl, "Driving Growth in Consumer Goods," *The McKinsey Quarterly* (13 November 2006), www.mckinseyquareterly.com/article-page aspex.

Franklin, Kenneth, Franchising Law Group of Piper, Marbury, Rudnick and Wolfe, http://franchise.org/resourceetcr/partII.asp, Chicago, 2001.

Justis, Robert T., Richard J. Judd, and David B. Stephens, *Strategic Management and Policy: Concepts and Cases* (Englewood Cliffs, NJ: Prentice-Hall, Inc., 1985).

Kotler, Phillip and Gary Armstrong, *Marketing*, 4th ed. (Upper Saddle River, NJ: Prentice-Hall, Inc., 1997).

Lamb, Charles W., Jr., Joseph F. Hair, Jr., and Carl McDaniel, *Marketing*, 4th ed. (Cincinnati, OH: South-Western Publishing, 1998).

Longnecker, Justin G., Carlos W. Moore, and William J. Petty, *Small Business Management; An Entrepreneurial Emphasis*, 11th ed. (Cincinnati, OH: South-Western Publishing, 2000).

Lovelock, Christopher H., *Managing Services: Marketing, Operations and Human Resources*, 2nd ed. (Englewood Cliffs, NJ: Prentice Hall, Inc., 1992).

McGuire, Patrick, E., *Franchised Distribution*, report no. 523 (New York: The Conference Board, Inc., 1971).

Mintzberg, Henry and James B. Quinn, *Readings in the Strategy Process*, 3rd ed. (Upper Saddle River, NJ: Prentice Hall, Inc., 1998).

Pride, William, M., and O. C. Ferrell, *Marketing: Concepts and Strategies* (New York: Houghton Mifflin Company, 2000).

Rhoton, Terry, "How to Increase Franchise Sales of Popeye's Famous Fried Chicken & Biscuits and Church's Chicken," presentation at International Franchise Association National Convention, 1991.

Shay, Mathew, "Big Name, Small Business," *USA Today* (4 October 2006): 6B.

Shay, Mathew, "Franchising—It's Developing beyond U.S. Shores," *USA Today* (7 February 2007): 8B.

Snepenger, David, ed., *Perspectives: Marketing Tactics* (Chicago: Coursewise Publishing, Inc., 1999).

U.S. Bureau of Census and Bureau of Labor Statistics, 2007, www.usbureauofcensus.gov.

U.S. Department of Commerce, *Franchising in the Economy, 1983–1985* (Washington, DC: U. S. Government Printing Office, 1985).

Vaughn, Charles L., *Franchising*, 2nd ed. (Lexington, MA: D. C. Heath & Company, 1979).

NOTES

1. K. Franklin, "Franchising Your Business: In What Way Is Franchising a Superior Expansion Method?" The Franchising Law Group of Piper, Marbury, Rudnick and Wolfe, http://franchise.org/franchise.org/resourceetcr/partII.asp, 1–9.
2. Ibid.
3. B. Horovitz, "Re-inventing McDonald's," *USA Today*, reprinted in *Perspectives: Marketing Tactics,* ed. David Snepenger (Chicago: Coursewise Publishing, 1999), 3–4.
4. S. Flanagan and C. M. Lindahl, "Driving Growth in Consumer Goods," *The McKinsey Quarterly* (13 November 2006): 1, www.mckinseyquarterly.com/article-page.aspx.
5. Ibid., 2.
6. Ibid., 3.

SELLING AND MARKETING RESEARCH

In studying this chapter, you will:

- **Learn about the uniqueness of selling in a franchise organization.**
- **Organize franchisee sales programs.**
- **Learn how to develop a sales package.**
- **Understand the first meeting between the franchisor and the franchisee.**
- **Discover the excitement of the sales playbook.**
- **Realize the importance of knowing the selling game.**

INCIDENT

Stan has just started franchising his bakery business. He is excited about the prospects of expanding his bakeries along the East Coast and then later expanding westward throughout the United States.

Stan is very motivated about the success which he has had with different breads and a breakfast cinnamon roll. He has fourteen varieties of breads and six different rolls, plus two kinds of cinnamon rolls, that he has been able to sell successfully on the East Coast, south of Washington, D.C. Stan has now opened a second store almost a year ago that has also been very successful. He has been working on his franchising program for the last nine months and feels like he is about ready to begin. Stan has spent considerable time working through the legal documents including the UFOC and the franchise agreement, and has completed the operations manual about five weeks ago.

Stan now is looking at developing the sales program which will launch his franchising business. He is concerned because he does not know how to go about this process. He knows that he could hire a sales firm to do it for him, but he also realizes that by helping develop the program himself he will have a much better understanding of what he is developing and why it is important. The manager of his second store asked him the other day if he was developing a sales program for the customer or for new franchisees. Stan just stood dumbstruck. He realized the manager was right. He needed to develop not only a sales program, but also a sales and marketing program for both the end consumer and the prospective franchisees.

6-1   INTRODUCTION

Every product, service, or idea has to be sold. Although the inventions of the automobile and airplane were fantastic, their use needed to be sold. People were originally scared of riding in an automobile or taking an airplane ride. Today, people clamor for new cars and larger jets with greater range.

Selling is simply encouraging the transfer of products or services from one individual to another. Selling is one of the most important functions of any business. The franchisor must be involved in the development of an image and a reputation that will encourage literally hundreds of thousands of people to purchase the company's products and services on a repetitive basis. The franchisor is a salesperson both to the franchisee and to the end consumer.

Salespeople, including the chairman, president, and secretaries, represent their companies every time they talk to someone else about their business. The salesperson is the representative of the company, and will work with the other officers and employees of the company to help develop new franchisees and to expand sales at the local franchise unit. It is important to recognize that the person taking the order at the cash register in the local McDonald's hamburger restaurant is a sales representative of the company. This person will help influence the purchasing decisions of the buyer.

In franchising, selling is divided into two different categories: selling to the prospective franchisee and selling to the end consumer. Before we influence these two target markets to purchase our products or services, however, we must understand the process and game of selling. Dunkin' Donuts must sell to prospective franchisees to expand and sell to end customers to increase overall sales.

6-1a   The Journey of Selling

Selling is the highest paid and first profession in the world. The leaders of business, governments, and the world are generally the top salespeople in their professions. Our culture thrives on and encourages skillful persuasion as an important part of any successful business. At some critical stage in one's life, a person has come to recognize the need to sell his or her ideas.

When David Thomas was still in his youth, he dreamed that one day he would own the best restaurant in the world. His customers would love his food and his employees would do everything they were supposed to do the right way and, most importantly, everyone would think that he was a good boss and people would be glad to see him when he came to work. He also learned that to be able to do this he needed to sell his ideas and dreams to others. Today, Wendy's is one of the giants in the fast-food industry and continues to expand based on the original ideas and dreams of a young orphan boy who took a chance and sold his idea.

> "When my daughter, Melinda Lou, was born, neither her brother nor her two sisters could pronounce her name. They started calling her Wenda, which then turned into Wendy. Her cleanly scrubbed, freckled face was it. I knew that it was the name and image for the business: 'Wendy's,' and I knew 'old-fashioned hamburger' had to be part of the image because that is the type of hamburger we'd serve. With the name Wendy's and the logo of a smiling, wholesome little girl, my restaurant would be the place where you went for a hamburger the way you used to get them, with fresh pure American beef. My experience with the Colonel taught me the importance of image and of having a personal identity tied to the restaurant."
>
> R. David Thomas, Dave's Way, A New Approach to Old Fashioned Success (New York: G. P. Putnam and Sons, 1991), 112–113.

The foundation of the sales experience is the image of the product, service, or business itself. Is the product being represented one of high quality, value, and important services? Is the product high priced or is there a low-quality, low-price discount appearance? Fast-food restaurants have been successful because they are offering a valuable product, with good quality, and at reasonable prices—this leads to success and repeat customers. It is important that the price of the product be matched with the product itself.

Perhaps one of the most difficult experiences in franchise selling is identifying the **target franchisee**. It is never easy to identify target customers. It is even more difficult in franchising to identify and properly locate the "right" franchisee. Several franchisors have looked at common characteristics among existing successful franchisees. This is beneficial but in no way will it guarantee the future success of prospective franchisees. The franchisor needs to look at successful characteristics, but the franchisor also needs to look at the history and the biographical data of each prospective franchisee to see if they have had experiences which will allow them to overcome difficulties and to have the drive necessary to be a success. Those individuals who have never had failures in the past and who have not had successful experiences generally do not know how to overcome difficult times nor do they understand the necessity of hard work to achieve success.

Probably the most important characteristics that franchisors are looking for in franchisees is not experience but a positive attitude and inner drive which will allow the franchisee to overcome obstacles and be successful in the operation. Many franchisors prefer that the prospective franchisees do not have prior experience in the field. Many franchisors will look at prospective franchisees and determine their probability of success based on two common attributes: personality and financial net worth. AlphaGraphics, which generally requires a $225,000 to $400,000 total investment, looks for a minimum net worth of $300,000 for each prospective franchisee. Century 21 Real Estate simply requires a minimum net worth of $75,000. Blimpie has a total investment of $114,000 to $341,000, with a requested minimum net worth of $150,000. This is somewhat in contrast to Subway which has a total investment between $92,000 and $222,000, and a requested minimum net worth of between $30,000 and $90,000.

6-2 SALES PACKAGE

How would you like the Indianapolis Colts to send their football team out on the playing field without selling a ticket to the game? Most franchisors develop a sales package which they can use as they build out the sales presentation to the prospective franchisee. This sales package generally consists of three parts: (1) an introductory folder, (2) a sales brochure, and (3) the Uniform Franchise Offering Circular. These three documents may be presented to the prospective franchisee all at the same time; however, they are generally presented separately and in the mentioned order.

SALES PACKAGE		
Introductory Folder	*Sales Brochure*	*Uniform Franchise Offering Circular*
Information on franchise business	Ongoing training and support from franchisor	Investment fees
Invitation to join franchising family	Brief explanation of franchising	History and background of the franchise
Information on training programs	Initial investment costs: financial overview	Earnings claims made by the franchisor
Initial announcement of all fees	Historical background and information of franchisor	Obligations of both franchisor and franchisee
Request for further information	Application form for franchisee	Most informative and concise document that the franchisee will receive

6-2a   Introductory Folder

The **introductory folder** is generally a single sheet which is trifolded and contains information on both sides about the franchising opportunity. This sales folder generally contains an introductory statement and an invitation to prospective franchisees to join the franchisor's family as they build out a wonderful business opportunity. This folder generally will describe what the franchise business consists of, the training programs, and often an initial announcement about the basic franchise fee, royalty fee, advertising fee, and initial start-up costs. The folder also will have an invitation and a tear-off section on which you can write your name and address and send for further information about the franchise opportunity from the franchisor.

6-2b   Sales Brochure

The second item that many prospective franchisees will receive is the **sales brochure**. This brochure is an in-depth explanation of the business which is presented to the prospective franchisee. This generally starts with a letter from the franchisor followed by a brief explanation of franchising, an invitation to become involved in the company's franchising business, a few testimonials from existing franchisees, an explanation of the initial training program, additional explanations of ongoing training and round-the-clock support, an explanation of the steps involved in franchising, and pictures illustrating a typical franchise operation. In addition, the sales brochure will contain loose-leaf pages that will discuss the initial investment, financing, minimum cash requirements, and a financial overview of the franchise opportunity. Historical background and information also may be provided to the franchisee; and in the back of the franchising presentation will be a confidential personal profile which you may fill out as an application to be a franchisee. This application form will contain information about you, your most recent employment, previous employment, reasons for wanting to become a franchisee, financial information including a personal net worth statement and total assets, as well as personal references.

The sales brochure is designed to entice prospective franchisees to look further into purchasing a franchise. In many of these brochures you will find question-and-answer sheets as well as the answers to many questions about the steps to owning a franchise business.

6-2c   Uniform Franchise Offering Circular

After the application is received and a preliminary approval has been granted based on the historical and financial background of the prospective franchisee, the franchisor will then send out the Uniform Franchise Offering Circular (UFOC), which the franchisor must give to a prospective franchisee ten days prior to the signing of any franchise agreements or payment in any form to become a franchisee. The UFOC contains twenty-three different items which will provide tremendous information to the franchisee including the history and background of the franchise as well as all investment fees, obligations, and any earnings claims made by the franchisor. It is important to realize right now that earnings claims are not required by franchisors and because of the requirements (supervised by the Federal Trade Commission) most franchisors (75 percent) will not disclose any earnings, sales, or income claims by the franchisees. All of this information and a franchise agreement are found in the UFOC.

The UFOC is the most informative and concise statement of operations that the prospective franchisee will receive prior to becoming a franchisee. Most UFOCs are approximately thirty pages, but because of the financial statements and contracts attached to them, they will easily go over sixty pages in length. The UFOC is a wonderful sales tool of the franchisor and the most informative document which the prospective franchisee will receive.

Probably more important than the UFOC to the prospective franchisee, however, is the discussion which the prospective franchisee should have with several different existing franchisees. Prior to becoming a franchisee, the prospective franchisee should discuss with at least ten or more other existing franchisees their experiences, both with the franchisor and with suppliers and customers. The prospective franchisee should take the time to find out about all aspects of the business, and the greatest resources available are current franchisees. Most existing franchisees are more than willing to talk to prospective franchisees if they are sincere, honest seekers of a franchising opportunity.

Initial Meeting

After the prospective franchisee has received the UFOC and there is still a desire on the part of the franchisor, it is best to hold an initial meeting between the franchisor and the prospective franchisee. This initial meeting is a "search and find" meeting on the part of both the franchisor and the prospective franchisee. The franchisor is anxious to meet the prospective franchisee to learn more about the person and to evaluate his or her potential as a franchisee. The prospective franchisee is also equally excited about meeting the franchisor to determine if this is the right fit for possibly a lifetime of business. Both parties are interacting to evaluate and approve the other party. This meeting is designed to allow both parties the opportunity to meet face to face and to discuss the intricacies and the requirements of becoming a bona fide franchisee.

6-3   THE SALES PLAYBOOK

It is difficult to imagine the Dallas Cowboys or the University of Southern California football players going into a game without having studied their football playbooks. It is almost equally amazing to think that a salesperson would endeavor to develop sales skills or enter into the sales experience without developing and studying the sales playbook. If you fail to create the playbook, then reading and studying about football or selling is primarily a waste of energy. To be a success, it is important to study, learn, practice, and use those skills to the best of your ability.

The development of a selling or training playbook for yourself and your company is easy if you use the following format. The **sales playbook** is a document designed to be altered by the individual based on personal preferences and characteristics. It should generally be developed and placed in a loose-leaf three-ring notebook and tabbed by the following subjects: (1) mission statements, (2) inquiries, (3) opening benefits, (4) listening, and (5) close. This playbook should go with you on every trip. It is designed to help you, the salesperson, reach out and help the customer. This manual can even be used when you are on the telephone and you can turn to the proper area and have several prepared answers for appropriate questions. After a period of time, it will be easy to memorize them, but initially you do not have to "wing it." You can become a professional salesperson or you can remain a novice throughout your entire career. That decision, to a great extent, will be based on the development and use of your sales playbook.

6-3a   Mission Statement

The first responsibility of a franchising salesperson is to survive the initial encounter and allow the interview to progress until you find a problem to solve. The next step is to solve the problem and close the sale as beneficially as possible for both the buyer and the franchisor.

The **mission statement** is simply your introduction to the buyer. This allows you to introduce yourself, your business, and even a benefit to the prospective franchisee in forty words or less. Specifically the mission statement will allow you to provide your name and company name, your business objective, what kind of problem you solve, and the benefits of your business. For example, the mission statement might be: "My name is Susan Zimmerman from Kwik Kopy Corporation. We help you copy your important documents while you wait." Another example may be: "I'm Richard Allen from Century 21 Real Estate. From all the numbers of homes on the market, I will help you match your needs and desires with just the right home for you and save you money, time, and irritation."

The franchisor may have a mission statement as follows: "I'm Bob Tracy from Smoothie King and I will help explain to you the exciting opportunities available to you by becoming a Smoothie King franchisee."

6-3b   Inquiries

One of the easiest ways to learn information about the prospective franchisee or customer is simply to ask the person questions. These probes are best done in a nonconfrontational fashion. The easiest way to inquire is to ask questions using *who, what, when, where, how,* or *why*. An easy introductory probing question would then be: "Why, Mr. Jones, are you interested in a McDonald's franchise?" If you are talking to a prospective franchisee who may be converting a real estate business to your franchise business, you may simply ask, "How have you enjoyed your experience with your prior real estate agency?" Another interesting probing question which often elicits a flood of response would simply be to ask, "Mrs. Prospective Franchisee, if you could design this transaction any way that you wish, how would you do it?"

The probing questions allow you to gather information from a prospective franchisee while providing the candidate an opportunity to explain personal wants, needs, and desires. This allows you to solve potential problems immediately.

6-3c   Opening Benefits

The **opening benefit** is based on the prospective buyer's problem or need. You now provide them an opportunity to improve themselves and their situation. Benefits are easily divided into four classifications, or **four Ps of selling**: power, profit, pleasure, and prestige. The secret of using benefits is to move from the features of the business to personal benefits which the buyer will receive. The features and benefits go hand in hand; however, features never sell. Benefits sell. The features of the business may include size, cost, activity, products, logos, or name recognition. The benefits in which the prospective franchisee has a true interest are personal and will improve the person's lifestyle.

Feature:	Health, Fitness and Wellness Clinic provides exercise machines and evaluation for an individual to become healthier and stronger.
Benefits:	Many exercise opportunities, pleasurable surroundings (pleasure)
Club membership:	(pleasure, power)
Prestige of membership:	(pleasure, prestige)

People buy features of products or services only when they see personal benefits.

6-3d   Listening

It is estimated that 50 percent of successful selling is listening. After the original probing and opening benefits are introduced, it is important to listen to find out if the prospective franchisee understands how their needs and desires will be met by becoming a member of your franchising family. People need to listen with their whole body. You must listen to what is being said, what is not being said, and what cannot be said. You need to listen with full attention and concern for the speaker. You can listen up to five times faster than the person who is speaking. You need to stay tuned in and not turned off.

6-3e   Close

Even though the most wonderful part of any selling process is the close, half of professional salespeople will not ask for the order at all. Eighty percent of all sales are obtained by 20 percent of the salespeople. Probably most damaging is the idea that only 2 percent of all salespeople in the United States know how to close a sale correctly.

It is easy to close a sale by simply assuming the close, and then going back to the probing questions using *who, what, when, where, how,* or *why*. Probably the easiest closes are simply: "When do you want to begin?" "Where would you like to locate your store?" "When will you be able to start the training program?" "How do you wish to make payment for the franchise fee?" "We want to be your franchise partner. What can we do to help you become a member of our franchising family today?" In the best of worlds, the easiest close would be: "How would you like for us to finalize this transaction?"

The sales playbook is a continuous development. You should start your own playbook by using the five aforementioned tabs. At first, develop one page for each tab and list the statements or ideas which you have for that subject. Review these periodically and use them in your face-to-face conversations and over the telephone. You will develop a wealth of knowledge and information which will allow you to become an effective and successful salesperson.

SALES APPROACH COMPARISON

Professional	Traditional
Benefits driven	*Features driven*
Customer needs based	*Product based*
Uses: Who, What, When, Where, How, Why	*Uses confrontations: Do you. . .? Will you. . .?*
Listens 70 percent of the time	*Listens 30 percent of the time*
Talks 30 percent of the time	*Talks 70 percent of the time*
Slower	*Faster*
Customer oriented	*Self-oriented*
Confident	*Tentative*
Enjoys the game	*Does not understand the game*
Truthful	*Whatever appears appropriate*
Appreciative	*Condescending*
Interdependent	*Independent*
Relaxed	*Pushy*

6-4   SELLING IS A GAME

Selling is a wonderful opportunity. When you realize that you are in the process of helping people solve problems, then you understand the essence of selling. You will need two trades as you develop professionally: (1) the work for which you have studied and practiced, and (2) the trade of selling. One CEO of a large franchised fast-food restaurant system answered the question of how he perceived his job by simply stating, "I am a salesperson. I have to sell my ideas to our executives and our staff, to our franchisees and their employees, and finally to the customers. I will need to do that for the rest of my life."

Was he a top administrator? Did he understand management? Did he understand the legal aspects of his business? Was he involved in the advertising and marketing of his business? Did he fulfill and satisfy his function as the CEO and president of his company? Yes to all of these question, and he was also a salesperson.

The strange thing about selling is that *successful salespeople realize that it is a game*. They are in the process of problem solving, not hustling or hassling people. They are involved in helping people. They are involved in a lifetime journey that is important. Selling is more fun than football, basketball, or even baseball. Selling is more fun than the Olympics or standing on the podium and having them drape the gold medal around your neck. Selling allows you to help other people satisfy their needs and desires.

6-4a   The Rules of Selling

Remember the following simple rules of selling as you become a professional salesperson. They will help you develop your sales skills and abilities.

1. Sell benefits not features.

2. Ask questions using *who, what, when, where, how,* and *why.*

3. Be honest.

4. Listen intently.

5. Do not refer to yourself.

6. Allow the other person to talk at least 60 percent of the time. (This is a tough one.)

7. Always be closing. (Most sales are made after the sixth effort to close.)

8. Always make an effort.

9. Be positive.

10. Enjoy the game, realizing it is a game.

6-4b   Selecting Target Markets

Developing the proper marketing and sales plan will help increase revenues and profits. This process in franchising begins by selecting the target markets for both prospective franchisees as well as end consumers. You need to be able to reduce the total universe of potential franchisees into a manageable group of target franchisees. To select the proper prospective franchisees, a series of screening decisions needs to be developed. While this decision process is not precise, it needs to be realistic and useful. To approach the two primary target markets and develop the proper screening process, these four steps need to be followed.

1. Targeting markets

2. Segmenting the markets

3. Profiling the customer

4. Qualifying the market segments

Target marketing is a simple, planned approach used to identify the winning customers whose needs can best be satisfied. Target marketing gives a competitive edge by helping better the marketing and sales opportunity. The goal is to win a market. You are looking for a niche which allows you to have a competitive advantage and allows you to be a leader in your market. For example, Home Instead Senior Care found a niche with the elderly by providing "part-time, full-time and live-in nonmedical service for the elderly who can manage their physical needs but require assistance, supervision, light housework and companionship to remain in their homes."

A **market segment** refers to the prospective franchisees or end consumers who are related by some common characteristics. Generally these target market segments will have common means, similar characteristics, will purchase for similar reasons, require similar products or services, and even operate in similar fashions. You need to find those segments which will allow you to make sales,

SELLING: THE NEW REALITIES

A revolution is occurring today because of the new realities in selling. Every customer is now unique and forms a market segment of one. This revolution is the result of believing in the customer and staying close to the individual.

Marketing research is staying abreast of the individual consumer and their information is current. Specific marketing and selling goals are set for a specific customer. The investment is made relative to the probability of consumers doing what they "should do." The old approach that "one-size-fits-all" simply meant that the product or service actually fit no one. The problem was that as soon as somebody knows how to do a better job, the product was obsolete.

Now a strong sustainable competitive advantage is found in a superior understanding of the customer. We need to know the customers' wants, needs, and values. The value of the product to the customer will now determine the price of the product. Losing businesses use financial cost models, whereas winning companies use investment models. We now need to spend our time developing high-quality relationships with our customers. The new reality: When somebody knows your customers better than you do, you're out of business.

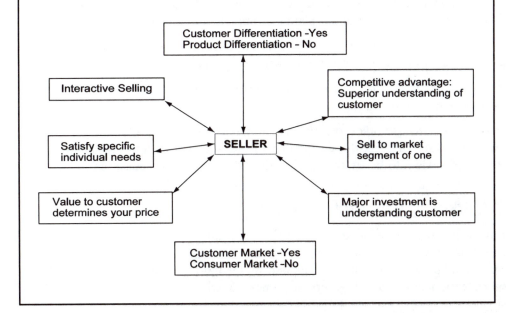

revenues, and profits. The ideal market segment is where you can satisfy the needs of the customers resulting in the desired revenues and profits. There is a simple focused objective in seeking the correct market segment—focus on the customer. After identifying market segments, it is important to profile the customers. For example, Subway provides a variety of meals for the different tastes of their discerning customers. To do this, it is critical to look at three different aspects of customer behavior.

1. *Customer needs*—the desired goal or objective which the customer wants to obtain.

2. *Customer benefits desired*—the result the customer wishes to achieve. This is the reason why the prospective franchisee or the end consumer will purchase the product or service.

3. *Purchase characteristics*—the behaviors and requirements affiliated with the customers' buying habits.

The only way to properly profile the customers, then, and learn about the customer needs, benefits sought, and purchasing characteristics is to simply ask the customers, that is, franchisees and end consumers.

You now need to qualify your market segments which will allow you to sell to prospective franchisees and your end consumers. To do this, consider the following three questions.

1. Can my franchising system satisfy the priorities and needs of my potential customer, that is, prospective franchisee and end consumer?

2. Will my franchising system sufficiently impact customers to allow them to reach their priorities?

3. Using my franchising system, products, and services, can I fully satisfy the customers' needs and provide the benefits sought?

6-5 MARKETING RESEARCH

The development of a good marketing information system focuses on the creation and use of four specific areas, as follows:

1. *Internal records*—information gathered from within the company and used especially for making day-to-day decisions about planning, implementation, and control decisions

2. *Marketing intelligence*—information about the development of the marketing environment and marketing systems often collected from company's personnel, suppliers, resellers, and customers

3. *Information analysis*—the analysis and reporting of information gathered from marketing intelligence and marketing research systems

4. *Marketing research*—studies of specific situations and areas of concern (The marketing research function will link the customer to the franchisee system and allow the franchising products or services to best satisfy the needs and desires of the consumer.)

6-5a   Marketing Research Process

Marketing research is intended to provide the information which the franchisor and the franchisee need to develop the marketing and sales strategies for the franchising system. This information may provide valuable insights and understanding concerning the needs and desires of prospective franchisees and the end consumers. Marketing research thus should provide the following:

1. Knowledge about prospective franchisees and end consumers' needs and benefits sought

2. Guidelines for the business and its employees

Marketing research may be easily designed and developed by any franchisor or any franchisee. Marketing research may be divided into the following four steps.

1. Define the problem and/or research objectives.

2. Develop the research design.

3. Implement research plan.

4. Analyze and report results.

MARKETING RESEARCH: HFS INC.

In 1990, Henry Silverman founded Hospitality Franchise Systems (HFS) Inc. and started buying national hotel chains, including Days Inn, Ramada, Super 8, Villager Lodge, Howard Johnson, Knights, and Park Inn International. Today, HFS Inc is the world's largest franchisor of hotels (over 6,000 locations) and residential real estate brokerage offices. In 1995, HFS Inc. purchased Century 21 from Metropolitan Life Insurance Co. for $200 million. That was followed by the acquisition of Electronic Realty Associates (ERA) for $37 million and finally Coldwell Banker Corp. for $740 million. In 1997, HFS was sold to Cendant Corporation and Henry Silverman became president, CEO, and chairman of the board in 1998. For travelers, Cendant owns Avis Group Holdings, which operates about 4,400 Avis car rental locations worldwide. They believe very strongly in franchising and desire to expand into areas where marketing research shows a number of independent agents who can convert to franchising. Cendant Hospitality is now Wyndham Worldwide Corporation, and Cendant Car Rental Group is now Avis Budget Group.

6-5b   Defining the Problem and/or Research Objectives

The proper marketing research questionnaire is not as difficult to develop as many people perceive it to be. The questionnaire is designed to provide that information about the products or services of the business and the attitudes of the customers or prospective buyers (see Figure 6-1). Common areas that are generally covered in most research designs include the following:

1. Where do shoppers go when making purchases?
2. Why do they go to that particular location?
3. How does this franchise compare with competitors?
4. How strong is the market potential for this franchise business?
5. How effective is the current advertising and are there ways to make it more useful?
6. Are there additional services which the business should provide?

THE COMPETITION ANALYSIS

Name of Competitor: _____

Product quality	Good	Average	Poor
Service	Good	Average	Poor
Store cleanliness	Good	Average	Poor
Price	High	Average	Low
Product selection	Large	Average	Small
Friendly employees	Good	Average	Poor
Employees	Knowledgeable	Average	Little knowledge
Financial position	Very Profitable	Ave. Profits	Possible losses
Management	Good	Average	Poor
Physical image	Good	Average	Poor

Where:

1. When considering a fast-food restaurant, where do you go most often?

2. What do you consider to be your primary convenience store—the convenience store at which you shop most often?

3. Which shoe store do you use most often or consider to be "your shoe store"?

Why:

1. Why that particular copying center? Or restaurant?

2. Please tell me what attracts you to that particular brand or piece of sports clothing?

3. Why do you drink _____?

	Very Important	Important	Not Important	Definitely Not Important
a. Taste	_____	_____	_____	_____
b. Brand loyalty	_____	_____	_____	_____
c. Calories	_____	_____	_____	_____
d. Availability	_____	_____	_____	_____
e. Price	_____	_____	_____	_____

What:

1. How many times in the last month have you purchased fast food?

2. What time of day do you usually make a purchase at a fast-food restaurant?

3. Within the last month, how many times did you eat food from a fast-food restaurant?

How:

1. How do you compare pizza restaurant A with the other pizza restaurants in the city?

2. How would you compare restaurant A and restaurant B concerning the following factors?

	Restaurant A	Restaurant B	Both Even	Do Not Know
a. Quality of food	_____	_____	_____	_____
b. Cleanliness of restaurant	_____	_____	_____	_____
c. Best price	_____	_____	_____	_____
d. Lowest price	_____	_____	_____	_____
e. Friendliness of employees	_____	_____	_____	_____
f. Presence of manager	_____	_____	_____	_____

3. How would you compare a McDonald's television commercial with a Wendy's television commercial?

	Better	Much Better	Worse	Much Worse
a. McDonald's	_____	_____	_____	_____
b. Wendy's	_____	_____	_____	_____

Advertising:

1. Have you read, seen, or heard any advertising for store A?

2. Can you tell me the slogan for bank A?

3. What would be the best way to ready you with an advertisement about a sale at store C?

Services:

1. Do you prefer a drive-thru window at your restaurant?

2. Do you prefer e-mail, catalog, or in-store purchasing for your clothes?

3. What would you suggest to restaurant A's manager if he asked how to improve his store's operation?

FIGURE **6-1**

Sample Questions

Certain techniques may be utilized in developing the proper methods for marketing research. The following information may be important to the franchisor and franchisee as they gather data from their prospective target markets.

1. Geographic—local, state, regional, national, and international

2. Demographic—age, gender, education, marital status, family size, income, race, occupation, nationality

3. Psychographic—social class, lifestyle, behaviors

4. Operating variables—frequency (light, medium, or heavy), purchasing criteria (service, price, and cleanliness)

MARKET SEGMENTATION METHOD

Geographic	The one-mile, two-mile, or total geographic area you will serve
Demographically	The age, gender, race, family income, and other data of your total market area
Psychographically	The lifestyle, values, and ethics of your customers (i.e., introverted, outgoing, athletic, partygoers, religious, academic, family-oriented)
Benefits buying	The benefits that the customers are actually buying: power, prestige, pleasure, profits, status, romance, comfort, entertainment, durability, self-indulgence, security/safety, convenience, etc.
Users	The profile and the percentage of your customers that account for the largest portion of your sales

---

Developing the Research Design

Generally speaking, it would be impossible to survey the entire population of a market with a questionnaire. A smaller market sample must be developed. Follow these three basic steps to adequately design your sample.

1. *Describe* the population for which the information is desired. For example, a quick service restaurant may desire information about customers age eighteen to forty-five as their primary target market group.

2. *Explain* the sample selection procedures. Will you be using telephone numbers from telephone books or in-person solicitation or questionnaires left at the store? It may be appropriate to call every eighth name on every other page of the white pages in the telephone book and then add to that a random number from one to nine which will allow you to contact unlisted phone numbers.

3. *Specify* all procedures required for contacting the respondents. How many times should each respondent be contacted? What is the total number of individuals you wish to contact? How long will it take for you to contact these individuals?

Your sample size may be as small as 100 individuals. Most professional marketing research organizations generally consider a sample size of 300 to be the most cost efficient. This 300-person sample size would generally provide a 94 percent confidence level with about five percentage points for maximum error.

Analysts from PIA Quarterly Print Market Survey, sponsored by Eastman Kodak, collected information about changing the marketing conditions for printers. They found that nearly 60 percent of printers collect marketing information about their customers. Approximately 18.1 percent categorize customers by industry groups such as hospitals, hoteliers, retailers, or auto dealers; 11.9 percent categorize their customers by product classification (books, brochures, automobiles); and 29.4 percent of the printers segment their customers by both industry groups and product classes. Utilizing this information, the printers can develop their strategic marketing plans and focus their sales and marketing efforts on current customer groups. The studies of the printing industry have shown that the profit leaders focus their efforts on specific industries whereas those with lower profits generally do not specialize.

6-5c   Implementation of Research Plan

The actual collection of data may be performed by the franchisor, franchisee, or employees either before, during, or after working hours. The data collection may be perceived as a fun experience or pure drudgery. It is important to realize that it may take several days longer to collect all information than originally considered. Three different methods of data collection include mail questionnaires—generally preferred by academics because of the low cost, phone call interviews, and in-person interviews. The person-to-person contact can create serious biased responses and is generally performed at a considerable cost. The phone call interview has become the best method because of the lower cost and the partial elimination of response bias interference. Many organizations have found that short questionnaires—ten to fifteen questions on one side of the page—may be easily answered by customers and other individuals in a short time without difficulty or frustration to the respondents.

6-5d   Analysis and Reporting of Results

Marketing research is a valuable tool when it is properly collected, tabulated, and analyzed. The collection of the data and its tabulation has provided the owners and operators an opportunity to better understand the end consumer.

Marketing research will be a valuable tool for both the franchisor and the franchisee. It will allow the owners to develop a competitive advantage over their competitors by better understanding the target markets. This will also help the franchisor to better understand prospective franchisees and to focus in on those characteristics and lifestyles which have proven to be more successful in a particular franchise system. At the same time, marketing research about customer preferences will also allow a better understanding of how to use advertising, promotion, location, and pricing considerations to enhance product or service desirability.

6-5e   Qualifying the Prospective Franchisee

The initial personal contact (generally on the phone) with a prospective franchisee is by far the most crucial step in establishing rapport and developing a sales relationship. This is the time to develop strong franchise relations with the prospective franchisee. Also at this time prospective franchisees will make their initial judgment about the franchisor. It is important to remember that you (as the franchisor) are what the prospective franchisee understands to be the franchise. The prospective franchisee's opinion and attitude about your franchise will be based on how they perceive you.

The initial contact will set the tone for all future interaction between the franchisor and the franchisee. A favorable first contact will often provide favorable and strong relationships in the

---

FRANCHISEES ARE ENTREPRENEURS

Most franchisees are bona fide entrepreneurs. Often the more fiery their entrepreneurial spirit the more successful franchisees they become. After you agree to follow the basic rules comes the enormous opportunity to be entrepreneurial.

Example 1: LeRoy Walker Jr., McDonald's franchisee, Jackson, Mississippi

LeRoy Walker owns and operates ten McDonald's restaurants in Jackson, Mississippi. One of his franchises is unique in that the guests frequently play chess while drinking coffee and biting on hot apple pies. They may have up to ten people playing, while many others watch. In 1989, Walker started his chess program by buying five chessboards and the accompanying chess pieces. The customers have been using them ever since.

Example 2: Isabelle Villasenor, McDonald's franchisee, Cypress, California

Isabella Villasenor has seven McDonald's restaurants in California. One of her restaurants is decorated in a floral motif from top to bottom. She uses paintings of irises and Calla lilies, coupled with bouquets of silk flowers decoratively placed throughout the store. Her restaurant has even earned the San Diego Region Decor Award. She is a unique entrepreneur.

---

future for both the franchisor and franchisee. This favorable relationship will allow the prospect to continue in a positive manner and allow them to strive to become friends with the franchisor.

People will buy a franchise to satisfy their needs, wants, or desires. Some of these are emotional and some logical. The franchisor should take the time to find out what these needs, wants, and desires are, because when you have satisfied the emotional and logical components you have made the sale. As you continue to satisfy these needs, wants, and desires, your positive relationships will continue to grow throughout the duration of the franchise agreement.

6-5f   Initial Call Process

When the initial call occurs, regardless of who made the call, it is important that an agenda has been established and the franchisor knows those questions to ask which will help the prospective franchisee as well as the franchisor. Almost all prospective franchisees have a personal agenda and want to find out what the franchise is about, its cost, and the opportunities to obtain a franchise. Many of them have already decided to buy a franchise—they just want to buy the best one. The franchisor should remember that the prospective franchisee is seeking a change in life or otherwise the person would not be looking to obtain a new business on a full-time basis.

The following list of questions may be helpful to the franchisor to inquire of the franchisee so as to learn about the individual's desires and wants.

1. (To self) What is the prospective franchisee looking for? Is this person trying to buy a job or looking for part-time work? Is this person looking for a lifetime career or something to do after retirement? Does this person want to work the business alone or want an investment?

2. (To prospective franchisee) Are you desirous of working for yourself or are you more comfortable when you are working for someone else? Have you ever worked for yourself? Do you feel like you are ready to own your own business or are you ready to be in business for yourself?

3. When do you wish to start working? Or when do you wish to start operating the franchise? Are you interesting in starting now or are you interested in starting in three or four years?

4. Why are you interested in our business? Or what attracts you to our business? Why are you inquiring about our business?

5. What has attracted you to our business? Or why is our business so attractive to you?

The main purposes of that initial call center on establishing a positive relationship with the prospective franchisee, determining if the prospective franchisee is qualified, and encouraging the prospective franchisee to continue searching and analyzing your company. Probably the most important aspect of that initial call is to encourage the prospective franchisee to fill out the franchise application as soon as possible. This franchisee profile will allow you to look at the person's background and financial fit with the franchising operation.

Prospective franchisees should realize that when the initial package is sent out with the application form that you are committing to the prospective franchisor the opportunity of becoming a franchisee. The completed application form is the prospective franchisee's commitment to the franchisor of his or here commitment to becoming a franchisee. That initial package includes literature, application, and possibly a UFOC. A UFOC may cost between $15 and $20. It is important that this material be a good representative of the franchising system.

A method of further qualifying a candidate focuses on two important questions, one of which has already been asked: When can you start to work? However, some franchisors generate more leads than they can handle and these individuals may follow with a second question after explaining the start-up finances required for owning the business: Are you prepared to finance this level of business operation? If they do not want to start for six months to a year, or if they just do not have the financial resources to handle the expenses, then most people will withdraw their inquiry and seek a different franchise system.

The four main areas of qualification for a franchise are as follows:

1. Common interests or desires

2. Trust/honesty

3. Availability

4. Financial capability

Most successful franchisees are individuals who have finally decided that they wish to try something on their own. They are willing to commit the time, energy, and finances necessary to become a success. They have needs, wants, and desires which can be satisfied by a successful franchising operation. They have a strong interest in the product or service which the franchisor is offering.

One of the great (most crucial) attributes of prospective franchisees is their trustworthiness and honesty. You need to find honest people to work with you. The name and reputation of your brand will be enhanced or destroyed by your franchisees. Honest people generally build the business.

The availability of prospective franchisees is vital. If they are interested in starting in the immediate future, then the opportunity is present. If they are only looking for part-time work or added income or not going to be able to start within the next year or longer, however, then their availability is seriously questioned.

Additionally, the franchisor needs to explain the franchising costs, including the initial franchise fee and the start-up costs of the franchise. Most franchisors require that the franchisee be able to pay the initial franchise fee out of pocket. In addition, many desire that they have an additional 50 percent of the remaining start-up costs which can be paid out of the current assets. Few franchisors are willing help finance part or all of the initial franchise start-up costs.

The serious prospective franchisees will generally be straightforward about their interest, availability, and financial resources. They are interested in getting started as soon as possible.

As the interest level continues to increase, their time frame will shrink. The franchise fee will take over and a lot of their rationality will leave as they become seriously engrossed in one of the greatest opportunities of their life—your franchise system.

Dallen Peterson

Merry Maids

In 1980, Dallen Peterson and his wife, Glennis, recognized a void in the field of professional home cleaning services and opened the first Merry Maids in Omaha, Nebraska. Since that time, Merry Maids has grown to become the nation's largest home cleaning company with over 1,500 franchised offices across the United States and in several foreign countries. Merry Maids cleans more than 300,000 homes, apartments, and condominiums each month in North America.

Each new Merry Maids franchise owner participates in a week-long training program at the company headquarters in Memphis, Tennessee. Here, they learn about the latest advances in customized home cleaning as well as the procedures to be followed in hiring and training personnel, marketing, and advertising their services, and managing and scheduling their business via the company's exclusive Data Management software system. In order to graduate, franchisees visit and actually clean several homes following Merry Maids professional home cleaning proce-

dures and using the cleaning products manufactured and distributed by the company.

Dallen Peterson foresees continued and significant growth in the professional home cleaning industry. Today, more than 60 percent of the working population consists of families in which both the husband and wife work. The traditional housekeeper, who performs such services as cleaning, laundry, and ironing, is becoming a rarity. Peterson believes that Merry Maids has only begun to fill this gap between the growing demand for home cleaning and the declining availability of reliable house cleaning help. "We haven't even scratched the surface," he says. "Our best estimates are that we are serving less than one-half of one percent of the potential market today."

Dallen Peterson is one of the original members of the University of Nebraska-Lincoln's Franchise Studies Advisory Council, and his company was one of the first to afford UNL students the opportunity to participate in a Franchise Studies summer internship program.

SUMMARY

Selling is one of the most fascinating and exciting aspects about franchising. Selling provides the franchisor the opportunity to meet with new prospective franchisees and to provide them with an opportunity to obtain a business unit. The franchisor will generally put together a sales package which includes three parts: an introductory folder, a sales brochure, and the Uniform Franchise Offering Circular (UFOC).

Many successful franchisors utilize a sales playbook which explains those activities that the franchisor needs to inform and excite the prospective franchisee. The sales playbook is generally divided into five areas.

1	*Mission Statement*
2	*Inquiries*
3	*Opening Benefits*
4	*Listening*
5	*Close*

The rules of selling are important but so is being honest, listening intently, and making sure you sell benefits and not features.

Marketing research is important for the franchisor. The process is generally divided into the following four areas.

- *Defining the Problem or Research Objective*

- *Developing a Research Design*

- *Implementing the Research Plan*

- *Analyzing and Reporting the Results*

Marketing research will allow the franchisor to forecast franchisor sales as well as the franchisee unit sales. Marketing research is important to ascertain the attitudes and behaviors of franchisees as well as end consumers.

KEY TERMS

Four Ps of selling: different types of benefits: power, profit, pleasure, and prestige

Introductory folder: part of the sales package given to the prospective franchisee by the franchisor; a two-sided information sheet about the franchising opportunity, including an introductory statement and an invitation to prospective franchisees to join the franchise

Market segment: a grouping of customers who will respond similarly to a given set of marketing promotions

Mission statement: an introduction to the buyer in forty words or less, should cover the following: (1) name and company name, (2) business objective, (3) the type of problem to be solved for the customer, and (4) benefits of the business

Opening benefit: begins the actual sale and moves toward the close, based on the prospective buyer's problem or need; provides an opportunity for them to improve themselves and their situation; divided into four classifications known as the 4 Ps of selling

Sales brochure: also part of the sales package, an in-depth explanation of the franchise, which may include a letter from the franchisor, an invitation to become involved in the franchising business, testimonials from existing franchisees, or pictures illustrating a typical franchise operation, as well as financing and background information; also includes an application to become a franchisee

Sales playbook: a flexible document developed by salespeople to help them reach out to the customer; generally includes sections for a mission statement, inquiries, opening benefits, listening, and close

Target: Target in marketing is that segment of the total universe of potential customers for your product or service which are most likely to provide the most revenue. In franchising, the target is divided into two different categories: the prospective franchisee and the end consumer.

REVIEW QUESTIONS

1. What is meant by the statement: "Every product, service, or idea has to be sold"?

2. What are the three components of a franchisor sales package? Discuss each component.

3. How do you develop the five components of a sales playbook?

4. Why is selling generally referred to as a game?

5. Why is marketing research important to the franchisor? Franchisee?

6. How should you qualify a prospective franchisee?

7. What are the four different areas of a marketing research program? Discuss each area.

CASE STUDY

Fairfield Inn by Marriott

Fairfield Inn by Marriott is the company's award-winning answer to the lower moderate lodging market. Fairfield Inn targets business and leisure travelers seeking clean, convenient, quality accommodations and consistently friendly hospitality at an economical price. Fairfield Inn began in 1987 and today has an occupancy rate of 76.6 percent—one of the highest in the market. More than 425 Fairfield Inn hotels span forty-eight states coast to coast—with a room rate of $49 to $79 depending on the location.

The new franchisee has a minimum capital requirement of $40,000 or $400 per room. The annual franchise fee is 4.5 percent of revenues with an additional marketing and advertising fee of 2.5 percent and a reservation fee of 1.5 percent.

In 2000, the brand launched a new brand extension, Fairfield Inn & Suites, reflecting a combination of guest rooms and suites to create a moderate-tier feel at existing and new build hotels. As part of the brand's expansion and repositioning, the following upgrades are being rolled out.

1. New guest suite amenities (in-room coffee makers, hair dryers) and suite design

2. New hotel exteriors (larger prototypes)

3. Reconfiguration of lobby and public space

4. Swimming pool and whirlpool spa

5. Complimentary continental breakfast served daily

6. Complimentary coffee and tea available in the lobby all day

7. Guest laundry

8. Meeting rooms in many localities

9. Exercise room

10. Facsimile service and high-speed internet

11. Same-day dry-cleaning service

12. Complimentary newspaper available in lobby

13. Vending machines offering snacks and beverages

14. Guest elevator

CASE QUESTIONS

1. Develop a sales program which Fairfield Inn could use to expand their sale of franchise hotel units.

2. What sales program might be best for Fairfield Inn to expand their customer awareness?

3. What kind of marketing research would be appropriate for Residence Inns or Courtyard motels?

4. Discuss how you would prepare a marketing research instrument for Marriott and their hotel systems.

REFERENCES

Advertising Age, 740 N. Rush St., Chicago, IL 60611.

Anderson, Ralph E., Joseph F. Hair, Jr., and Alan J. Bush, *Professional Sales Management*, 3rd ed. (New York: McGraw-Hill, 1996).

Bangs, D. H., *The Market Planning Guide*, 4th ed. (Dover, NH: Upstart Publishing, Inc., 1995).

Lamb, Charles W., Joseph F. Hair, Jr., and Carl McDaniel, *Essentials of Marketing*, 2nd ed. (Cincinnati, OH: South-Western Publishing, a division of Thomson Learning, 2001).

Ley, D. F., *The Best Seller* (Newport Beach, CA: Sales Success Press, 1990).

Mackay, Harvey B., "Humanize Your Selling Strategy," *Harvard Business Review* (March-April 1988).

Schultz, Don E., William A. Robinson, and Lisa A. Petrison, *Sales Promotion Essentials*, 2nd ed. (Lincolnwood, IL: NTC Business Books, 1994).

Thomas, R. David, *Dave's Way, A New Approach to Old Fashioned Success* (New York: G. P. Putnam and Sons, 1991), 112–113.

Totten, John C. and Martin P. Block, *Analyzing Sales Promotion: Text and Cases*, 2nd ed. (Chicago: Dartnell, 1994).

Vass, Jerry, *Soft Selling in a Hard World* (Philadelphia: Running Press, 1998).

CO-BRANDING*

In studying this chapter, you will:

- Learn the importance of branding in franchising.
- Understand the nature of co-branding in the franchising industry.
- Learn the motivating factors behind the co-branding phenomenon.
- Appreciate the different methods of co-branding.
- Recognize the importance of collaborating for success.

INCIDENT

Marcia Brown is a successful franchisee owning several units of a well-known sandwich shop in and around the metro area. One unit, just south of the city, is located in a declining neighborhood but some redevelopment in the area has begun recently. The site is positioned on a major U.S. highway just off the interstate and is on the morning traffic side of the street. The square footage of the land on which the building sits, as well as the building itself, are twice as large as what Marcia really needs for her sandwich store. Over the last two years, she has seen gross sales for the unit decline slowly but consistently. She realizes it is time to consider new growth options for the store and has noticed other fast-food franchisees incorporating co-branding into their local marketing strategies. Marcia has talked with several of the franchisees to learn about their co-branding experiences. She has also discussed this option with her current franchisor system manager. Although co-branding is not a top priority for the sandwich shop system at this time, the manager encouraged Marcia to further investigate the option. What factors should Marcia consider in making her decision and should she be seriously involved in co-branding at this time even though her existing franchise brand is not?

7-1 INTRODUCTION

A recent phenomenon has spread rapidly throughout the United States, as well as internationally, with franchising units. **Co-branding** occurs when two brands are combined in a business offering.

---

* The authors gratefully acknowledge Joyce A. Young, Indiana State University, and Audhesh K. Paswan, University of North Texas, as the writers of this chapter.

Each brand expects the other to be strong and will draw customers who have brand preference for the other brand. According to Ellen Shubart, co-branding columnist for *Franchise Times*, "No one is keeping tabs on the precise numbers, but growth in co-branded franchises appears to be higher than growth in franchising alone."

Labeled various names such as dual branding, multibranding, cross-system franchising, and even strategic alliance, co-branding is now considered a standard business practice that a franchisor should disclose in its UFOC. For many franchise systems, however, co-branding remains a new franchising format with relatively unknown properties that present many questions concerning long-term viability. The Federal Trade Commission (FTC) defines co-branding as an activity in which "two or more franchisors combine forces to offer a franchisee the opportunity to operate two or more franchises in one outlet." Co-branding can also be a franchisee-driven initiative. Franchisors tend to encourage co-branding when they own multiple brands while franchisees seek complementary opportunities with less concern for ownership of brand. Regardless, both franchisors and franchisees hope that two powerful and complementary brands can combine to produce an offering that is greater than the sum of the parts.

7-2   BRANDING

A franchisor's brand name is a critical element in the chain's success as its prominent display at each outlet signals to potential customers consistent quality at a given price level. Customers rely on brand names to help simplify choices and reduce risk. One of the great issues facing any franchisor is the development of an appropriate brand. The American Marketing Association defines a **brand** as "a name, term, sign, symbol, or design, or a combination of them, intended to identify the goods or services of seller or group of sellers and to differentiate them from those of competitors." The brand then is designed to identify the franchise system. A brand can then be a trademark, name, logo, or symbol representing the franchise. Under trademark law, the franchisor holds exclusive rights to the use of its brand or trademark for perpetuity. This brand becomes a major asset to the franchisor and easily identifies the franchisor's company and products. A familiar example of this is McDonald's—the trade name, the Golden Arches—its logo, and even the name of its sandwiches—Big Mac. All of these have been registered and are protected by the trademark laws both in the United States and many countries throughout the world.

"The idea behind co-branding is that several brands can command more power through customer awareness and traffic than can a single brand-name operation." Holiday Inn with T.G.I. Friday's, Ziebart with Speedy Auto Glass, Texaco Star Mart with Taco Bell, and MainStay Suites with Sleep Inn represent four co-branding relationships involving eight well-known brands. Co-branding efforts in the restaurant industry are prevalent with recent estimations that 20 percent of all food franchises are co-branded units. In addition, co-branded food service in the convenience store industry accounts for approximately 23 percent of total food service sales. Franchisors, however, within other industries such as automotive aftermarket and hospitality are teaming up also. Figure 7-1 shows three visual examples of co-branding partnerships.

Although initial results for several co-branding partnerships in the food service industry indicate revenue increases ranging from 20 percent to 100 percent, not all co-branding attempts have been successful. For example, the co-branding relationship between Jack in the Box and Ravioli's failed within just five months during the testing phase. The revenue generated by the venture was not sufficient to justify the investment for Jack in the Box units. Zu Zu's and Arby's co-branding effort disintegrated into a lawsuit by Zu Zu's against Arby's that sought millions of dollars in damages involving stolen trade secrets. McDonald's, one of the largest and most successful franchisors in the world, secured a captive audience in Wal-Mart stores, but found itself with limited exposure in the back of stores. As a result, many of the units have been removed. Such

The only one of its kind, this co-branded unit of Mrs. Winner's and Blimpie's is located in Jonesboro, Georgia. The existing Blimpie franchisee took the initiative in securing a second brand for the location.

Photo by Joyce Young

Ziebart International and Speedy Auto Glass joined together in 1998 to offer co-branded units that combine the offerings of two of North America's largest installers of automotive aftermarket products and services.

Photo by Joyce Young

Tricon Global Restaurants (TGR) OWNS BOTH THE KFC and Taco Bell franchise systems. TGR is bundling several of its own brands to create co-branded units for its franchisees.

Photo by Joyce Young

FIGURE **7-1**

Visual Examples of Co-Branding Efforts

highly publicized disappointments have led one writer for *Nation's Restaurant News* to ask the following about co-branding: "Is this building or hurting brand equity?"

By definition, a franchise system depends on its uniqueness, in other words, **brand equity**, for its competitive advantage in the marketplace. Brand equity consists of four dimensions: brand loyalty, brand awareness, perceived quality of brand, and brand association. Yet, little is known about whether co-branding has a positive or negative impact on a franchisor's brand equity. Some franchise systems, however, have experienced the **halo effect**, when a strong, well-known brand links with a lesser known one and the second brand is lost in the halo of the first. The problem occurs frequently in the convenience store and petroleum industry. While many convenience store systems attempt to build their brands, they are often kept "literally" under the canopy of the gasoline brand, according to franchising consultant Mark Siebert. For lesser known brands, co-branding may result in increased sales, but building brand identification may not occur if partnered with a significantly larger company. Results, however, from a foreign market entry study suggest that consumer evaluations of an unknown brand from one country were more positive when a brand ally was used. Thus, brand alliances can be effective. We may assume that if the co-brands both have strong brand equity, then most likely, the co-brand relationship may result in stronger brand equity for both parties if the franchising alliance is successful. On the other hand, if the relationship is unsuccessful, one or both of the brands may suffer. In addition, if one franchise system or unit falters independently of the other, then the second brand may also be affected (i.e., guilt by association).

7-3   EMERGENCE OF CO-BRANDING

Co-branding is becoming prevalent across the franchising landscape for several reasons. Following are the most common motivational factors among franchisors and franchisees.

Mature Markets—Many franchise sectors are mature markets that provide little opportunity for sales and profit growth through traditional outlets. Co-branding represents a new approach that can revitalize mature units. These new and improved versions of brand offerings have the potential to bring in extra cash flow that can result in greater overall new profits for the franchise system.

Labor Shortages—As the franchise world begins the twenty-first century, it faces unprecedented labor shortages that are predicted to continue far into the future. Many co-branded units that share space require only about one and one-half times the labor of a single unit, not double the amount.

Land Shortages—In franchising, as in brick-and-mortar retailing in general, location is often the key to reaching the desired target market. As franchise sectors reach maturity, fewer choice locations are available to support further expansion efforts. Retail sites that were previously passed over by a franchisor, because they were too large or traditionally inappropriate for a stand-alone unit, are now feasible with co-branded units.

Consumer Demands—Franchising customers today are looking for convenience. They are also looking for one-stop shopping. Co-branding allows franchisors to work together with their franchisees to bring several concepts together for the convenience of the customers. McDonald's, for example, has research data that shows approximately 75 percent of its customers decide to eat at a McDonald's unit just five minutes or less before their fast-food purchase. Thus, it is important to bring the brand to the customer rather than wait for the customer to find the brand.

Trade journals describe the basic pros and cons of co-branding for franchisors. Yet, the co-branding phenomenon may represent much more than just one franchisor partnering with another franchisor to take advantage of the current business climate as discussed. Take Cinnabon's attempt, for example, to redefine its image, "transforming itself from a single product to a contemporary baked goods retailer." The discipline may be witnessing the evolution of food service franchisors into "typical" mass merchandisers. Though certainly not a Wal-Mart nor Kmart, the merging of franchisor brands does lend itself to basic mass merchandising retailing concepts. Figure 7-2 shows the advantages and disadvantages of single versus multiple brand offerings. Any retailer, regardless of industry, should consider these issues when looking to expand its product offerings, and franchisors and franchisees are no exceptions. A case in point is the Tricon Global Restaurant tri-branded concept of KFC, Taco Bell, and Pizza Hut. Although the multiple brand offering will reach

---

SINGLE BRAND OFFERING

Advantages

- Specialist image
- Good customer choice in category
- Specialized personnel
- Customer loyalty

Disadvantages

- No one-stop shopping
- Too much emphasis on one category
- More susceptible to trends
- Greater effort needed to enlarge the size of trading area

MULTIPLE BRAND OFFERINGS

Advantages

- Broad market
- High level of customer traffic
- One-stop shopping
- Emphasis on convenience customers

Disadvantages

- Low variety within product lines
- General image
- Some disappointed customers
- Reduced customer loyalty

FIGURE **7-2**

Advantages and Disadvantages of Single versus Multiple Brand Offerings

Source: Based on a discussion of retail assortment strategies by Berman and Evans (1995). Reprinted with permission from Joyce A. Young, Robert D. Green, and Audhesh K. Paswan, "Co-Branding Approaches in the Franchised Food Service Industry," *Journal of Business & Entrepreneurship* (July 2000): 22.

---

a broader market, the depth of variety within each brand will be reduced. Only the most popular items from each of the three brands will be available. Thus, a traditional Pizza Hut consumer, for example, may be disappointed by the pizza selection offered by the tri-branded unit. Consumers, however, that are searching for convenience and some brand assortment may be quite pleased by the concept. Obviously, long-term success of the concept is dependent upon satisfying the second type of consumer while not alienating the traditional consumer.

Co-branding can also lead to a high-pressure situation at the store or unit level that the management staff may not be well equipped to handle. Often the increased velocity of business that may result can lead to burnout among key personnel. In addition, the skills needed to successfully manage, or juggle, two or more brands may not be characteristics found in existing store managers. Industry insiders suggest that franchisors and franchisees hire general managers that have prior co-branding experience, two to four years of college study preferably in business, and be willing to pay general managers significantly more than their counterparts at single brand units. Co-branded units should also be assigned more assistants and co-managers to prevent general manager burnout.

7-4   CO-BRANDING METHODS

7-4a   From the Franchisor's Perspective

Once a franchisor actually decides that co-branding is a viable option for its system, the franchisor must select an appropriate format. A co-branding relationship involving franchisors may develop through a variety of methods. The underlying motivation to engage in partnering activities is often a result of a firm's evaluation of its resources and expertise. Figure 7-3 presents a two-by-two matrix of resources by expertise and their resulting co-branding methods. The matrix is based on a thorough review of co-branding approaches documented in various trade and academic journal articles. Figure 7-4 depicts specific food service industry examples of each co-branding method discussed here. A franchisor must decide if it has the expertise and originality to create a second brand, as well as the financial and human resources to commit to the development of a second brand. If the franchisor does indeed feel that it can answer yes to both questions and does not

RESOURCES

	Yes	No
Yes	Internal Development Of Second Brand 1	Sell Its Brand To Acquisitor 2
No	Acquisition Of Second Brand 3	External Development Of Second Brand 4

(left vertical axis label: E X P E R I E N C E)

FIGURE **7-3**

Co-Branding Methods for Franchisor

Source: Reprinted with permission from Joyce A. Young, Robert D. Green, and Audesh K. Paswan, "Co-Branding Approaches in the Franchised Food Service Industry," *Journal of Business & Entrepreneurship* (July 2000): 22.

desire to partner with another franchisor, then it will develop the second brand internally as indicated by quadrant 1 in Figure 7-3. If the franchisor answers no to one or both questions, then it begins to search for a co-branding partner, and will place itself in one of the three remaining co-branding quadrants as shown in Figure 7-3. In quadrant 2, the franchisor has developed a brand with high equity but does not have the internal resources that will enable it to pursue co-branding on its own. Instead, the franchisor must look to an external source. One option is to offer its units to franchisees of other complementary franchisors. A more drastic option is to sell its entire system to another franchisor. In quadrant 3, the franchisor lacks the expertise to develop a second brand but does not have the resources to either buy the entire system of a complementary franchisor or simply enter into a franchising agreement with another franchisor and its franchisees. Finally, in quadrant 4, the franchisor lacks both the expertise and the resources to secure a second brand. While it does seek the assistance of another franchisor, the approach is different than those in quadrants 2 and 3 in that both firms remain separate entities with no financial equity exchanged for units.

7-4b   From the Franchisee's Perspective

The decision to open a co-branded unit has historically been a franchisee-driven initiative. While a franchisee may develop an overall co-branding strategy that it implements consistently from unit to unit, the owner can also approach each unit in isolation by considering its unique strengths and weaknesses, threats and opportunities. Franchising consultant Mark Siebert recommends that franchisees ask the following questions when considering co-branding.

- Do I get a competitive advantage?
- Do I need to co-brand for defensive reasons?
- Should I look for an exclusive relationship?

In addition, franchisees should follow an eight-step process when evaluating and choosing a co-brand.

- Identify your positioning strategy for your local market.
- Contact industry insiders to learn more about the nature of co-branding.

INTERNAL DEVELOPMENT

- **Creation of New Brand**—As recently as 1997, Blimpie International (BI) Inc. sought to acquire a second brand. BI Inc., however, decided to develop its own high-end quick serve Italian concept called Pasta Central. Between 200 and 300 co-branded Blimpie Subs & Salad/Pasta Central units are to open over the next five years.
- **Bundling of Existing Brands**—Tricon Global Restaurants Inc., parent company of KFC, Taco Bell, and Pizza Hut, recently unveiled its latest prototype of the three brands in one format. Only the most popular items from each of the three brands will be offered.

SELL TO ACQUISITOR

- **Sell Franchise System**—Long John Silver's (LJS) Restaurants Inc. had been searching for a buyer for its 1,275 units since it filed for bankruptcy in 1998. A&W Restaurants has agreed to acquire LJS. Though both systems will continue to operate as separate companies, plans are underway to make co-branding of A&W/LJS an important aspect of future strategy.
- **Franchise Units to Other System**—TCBY Enterprises is allowing approved Subway franchisees to sell a limited number of TCBY products in their stores. It is not known how many Subway units will add TCBY franchises since Yogen Fruz, a TCBY competitor, is also a potential co-branding partner for Subway.

ACQUISITION

- **Buy Franchise System**—In 1996, Arby's Inc. secured a franchise agreement with T. J. Cinnamon that would place T. J. Cinnamon products in approximately 2,500 Arby units. As a result, Arby's franchisees were given the opportunity to become T. J. Cinnamon franchisees. Arby's then took the co-branding effort one step further by actually acquiring the T. J. Cinnamon brand.
- **Become Franchisee of Other System**—In its first co-branding venture, White Castle Systems Inc. has become a franchisee of Church's Chicken. White Castle now has the right to develop Church's restaurants within its existing White Castle restaurants in the United States.

EXTERNAL DEVELOPMENT

- **Trade-Out Agreement**—When a proposed acquisition of Miami Subs by Arthur Treacher's Inc. collapsed (Treacher's lacked the financial resources), the two companies agreed instead to an extensive co-branding pact allowing each chain to offer the menu of the other.
- **Host Agreement**—Holiday Inn Worldwide entered into a relationship with T.G.I. Friday's to create numerous co-branded sites. With expectations of increased traffic and greater profitability for both, Holiday Inn focuses solely on accommodations while T.G.I. Friday's provides hotel guests with food and beverage.

FIGURE **7-4**

EXAMPLES OF CO-BRANDING METHODS IN THE FOOD SERVICE INDUSTRY?

Source: Reprinted with permission from Joyce A. Young, Robert D. Green, and Audhesh K. Paswan, "Co-Branding Approaches in the Franchised Food Service Industry," *Journal of Business & Entrepreneurship* (July 2000): 22.

- Define exactly what you want to do in terms of your co-branding partnership.
- Meet with principles from the second brand, as well as your first brand.
- Perform feasibility analysis to determine the potential return on investment.
- Make decision to co-brand or not to co-brand.
- Negotiate contract with second franchise system.
- Renegotiate contract with your first brand if necessary.

Once a franchisee decides that co-branding is a viable option for a given unit and/or multiple locations, the franchisee has several formats available for selection, although the actual format may depend on the franchisor's preference as discussed. Although a franchisee may look at co-branding from its own unique perspective, its actions may simply represent the implementation of the franchisor's strategy at the local level. Following are frequently cited formats.

Single Franchisee/Single Franchised Brand/Additional Nonfranchised Brand—occurs when a single franchisee obtains the rights to distribute a second (i.e., nonfranchised) brand, or vice versa. For example, Gingiss Formalwear has begun to co-brand its franchised formal-wear stores with local independent dry cleaners in various cities across the United States.

Single Franchisee/Dual Franchised Brands—occurs when a single franchisee obtains the rights to franchise a second system. Franchisee David Zagorski operates several combined Bellini Safe and Sound stores in New Jersey. The Bellini franchise system markets designer children's furniture. The Safe and Sound is a baby safety franchise. Both brands are owned by ASD Development, and according to Zagorski, the co-branding effort is "a winning combination for customers and the franchisee alike."

Dual Franchisees/Dual Franchised Brands—occurs when two local franchisees decide to coexist and build their stores together. For example, in Chicago, Mail Boxes Etc. franchisees operate in the hotel lobbies of many franchised hospitality systems. While both brands function relatively independent of the other in the same building, in this particular case, it is clear that Mail Boxes Etc. exists to serve the needs of the hotel customer, not vice versa.

Portfolio Management of Multiple Brands—occurs when a franchisee brings together numerous franchise systems to provide a comprehensive and market-tailored opportunity at the retail level. HMSHost Corporation is the leading provider of food, beverage, and retail concessions in travel venues in the world. The company currently holds licensing and franchising rights to over 100 internationally and regionally known brands representing franchisors from the United States, as well as Europe, Canada, and even the Orient. The company utilizes the portfolio approach in airports, colleges, entertainment venues, travel plazas, among others.

When a franchisee takes the initiative to co-brand within a system that has no prior relationship with the second brand, the franchisee is often charting new ground primarily on its own. For example, Vickey and Gary Shelton, owners of several Blimpie Subs and Salads units in the Atlanta metropolitan area, transformed one of their stores into a dual concept with Mrs. Winner's Chicken and Biscuits as shown in Figure 7-1. The Shelton's presented their proposal to Karen Spencer, vice president of franchise sales and administration for Winners International, the parent company of Mrs. Winner's. She agreed that the breakfast-strong Winner's brand created a good tie with Blimpie, which draws heavier lunch and dinner traffic. Neither brand had worked together previously. As a result, the Sheltons had to personally mesh the two brands by trial and error. In addition, they were somewhat surprised to learn that their regular Blimpie customers were somewhat intimidated by the co-branding concept. Not only did the Sheltons have to cross-train all the employees, but they also had to train the customers on how to place orders at the counters. Furthermore, by observing which door a customer would select to enter the store, the Sheltons noticed that many customers had already decided on the brand to purchase, resulting in few combined menu purchases. As a result, future co-branded units may have changes in the physical layout and appearance that address such weaknesses.

7-5 DEGREE OF COLLABORATION

Until recently, only in a few cases was co-branding being initiated from the franchisor level down, specifically when a franchisor owned more than one concept. More typically the decision to co-brand was driven by franchisees wanting to get involved on an individual basis. For example, two KFC franchisees approached A&W Restaurants to propose a co-branding concept because the franchise rights to open Pizza Hut and Taco Bell units were not available in their local markets. Today, however, more franchisors are including co-branding initiatives in their overall strategic marketing plans.

When a franchisor selects a co-branding method that involves joint marketing efforts across independent franchise systems, collaboration on franchise-related issues must occur. With different companies under one roof, working together can be challenging. Co-branding partners know that for success the brands must have some sort of natural synergy—be it with customers, product or service offerings, and/or day parts. Yet, some partners overlook critical factors such as equal representation of both brands in the store and the creation of new graphics that integrate both brands. Although co-branding may jeopardize the uniqueness of each franchise system by blending proprietary symbols and trademarks, operational concerns will also demand significant attention. Different hours of operation required by franchisors, managers who do not share the same business philosophy, paperwork involving two separate sets of books with common costs, design of employee uniforms, and store unit survival if one brand fails in the marketplace are potential collaborative pitfalls. Figure 7-5 lists issues for potential collaboration. Although important to franchisors, such issues will impact each system's franchisees, because many decisions must be implemented at the store or unit level. Some existing franchisees may not support a franchisor's decision to co-brand. For example, a Green Burrito franchisee recently sued its franchisor alleging that the co-branded

STRATEGIC ISSUES
- Organization mission statement
- Organization-wide objectives
- Long-range planning
- Market share objectives
- Financial objectives
- Capital investment
- Franchise fees
- Proprietary symbols and trademarks
- Expansion decisions
- Decision to resell

OPERATIONAL ISSUES
- Accounting methods
- Human resource needs
- Equipment needs
- Site location
- Operational procedures
- Hours of operation

PURCHASING ISSUES
- Supplier selection
- Inventory levels

RELATED ISSUES
- Test marketing
- New product planning
- Mix of products
- Guarantees
- Packaging of products

PRICE-RELATED ISSUES
- Prices of products
- Discounts offered

PROMOTIONAL-RELATED ISSUES
- Advertising expenditures
- Nonadvertising promotional expenditures
- Personal selling activities
- Public relations efforts

STORE DESIGN ISSUES
- Physical layout
- Physical appearance
- Atmosphere/ambience

FIGURE **7-5**

Franchise-Related Issues for Collaboration With Co-Branding Partner

units' menu shortcut diminished the value of the stand-alone units. Thus, co-branding partners should carefully craft their agreements and create co-branding checklists that address every aspect of the venture to assistance initial start-up, as well as day-to-day operations.

SUMMARY

Co-branding continues to increase in popularity. There is an absence, however, of available research that documents such partnerships. As discussed in the chapter, important differences in approaches to co-branding involving motivation, methods, and implementation do exist. Franchisors and franchisees that are considering co-branding as a possible approach to market expansion have various methods available. Before entering into a co-branding agreement, a franchisor should carefully evaluate its expertise in brand development and its available resources. The outcomes can determine whether the franchisor should attempt to develop a second brand in-house or whether it should begin to look for a co-branding partner. Obviously, internal development provides a greater element of control. Franchisors and franchisees must also realize that a variety of methods are available in terms of co-branding. Finally, the franchisor should expect to collaborate on numerous managerial and marketing issues, especially store design and possibly trade dress. Most co-branding relationships are more similar than they are different. The relationships are similar in that the common goal is for brands to share space while catering primarily to different target audiences. They are different in that franchisors tend to push co-branding when they own multiple brands while franchisees seek complementary opportunities with less concern for brand ownership.

Jim and Carole Britton

Working Their Way to the Top

It is a win-win situation at Express Personnel Services where both job seekers and business clients find success. Franchise owner Jim Britton says, "The approach involves a professional evaluation of the customer's needs and wants."

Husband and wife, Jim and Carole Britton have been in the staffing business in central Illinois since 1980. They became part of the Express Personnel franchise in 1986 and have offices in Springfield and Bloomington, Illinois. Raised in Springfield, the Brittons have developed an intimate knowledge of the communities they serve. This vested interest shows in the commitment and dedication they put into their work.

And work they do! The Brittons and their professional staff learn as much as they can about the client business, including standards, business personality, expectations of employees, the skills needed, and the demands of the job. On the other

hand, they also learn as much as they can about the job seekers, determining their employment needs, expectations, training, and skills. The match can then be made!

The Brittons began in a 660-square-foot, windowless office. In 1990, they moved to a 3,000-square-foot space and then added another 3,000 square feet expecting that to last a lifetime. In January 2001, they moved into a new, custom-designed building in south Springfield and are utilizing 15,000 square feet of space.

Recognizing and adapting to societal changes affecting employment has been important in the growth of the Britton's business. Personnel services have become an important way for both the employers and employees to get together. Rapid changes in technology as well as acquisitions and mergers keep many employers and employees in flux. No longer does the average employee expect to stay with one company throughout a lifetime of work, nor do businesses now commonly offer that kind of job security. Many employees are on the lookout for new challenges and variety in their work. Express Personnel Services has become an important way for both the employers and employees to adapt to these changes.

Express Personnel offers options in a diverse range of situations. Some job seekers prefer temporary or contract employment. Many of these people become career associates with Express and qualify for medical, retirement, vacation, and other benefits. They have many choices in the jobs they accept including full-time and part-time hours. They gain a broad range of experience and meet new people creating friendships, contacts, and future employment opportunities.

It could be that a career change is the goal of other job seekers. Express does the homework, saving time that might otherwise be spent looking through ads and knocking on doors. For the employer, Express does the screening and initial interviewing. A direct job placement may be the result. Sometimes an evaluation hire option is the best for the employer and employee. In this situation, both parties have the opportunity to evaluate each other while on the job, determining whether a situation is right for a more permanent full-time hire.

Carole and Jim offer businesses a full range of staffing services across a wide spectrum of employees including sales, accounting, office, customer care, and industrial workers. Jim states, "We have become the way that companies acquire their workforce, whether they need to hire employees or want to utilize temporary staffing." In the Britton's market area, a number of employers no longer maintain their own per-sonnel departments but depend on the professionals at Express Personnel to keep them fully staffed, while providing a full range of human resource support.

Express gives support and stability to the business community by providing contract or temporary workers at peak times, reducing the risk of future layoffs. In turn, these workers are not dependent upon one firm for work but instead look to Express for ongoing employment.

When layoffs do occur at a client firm, Express Personnel can provide workshops for that client's employees, with advice on updating resumes, guidance on securing new employment, and insight into opportunities available in the job market.

Express Services, Inc. has recognized Jim and Carole Britton with numerous awards for their sales and service. The Gordon Blair Heritage Award is particularly special to be Brittons because it is "presented to an individual or individuals possessing extraordinary enthusiasm, positive attitude, and integrity that has had a profound influence on the overall success and future growth of Express Personnel Services." Jim also serves as a regional developer of Express Personnel Services Franchise Company with responsibilities for developing Express offices throughout Illinois and Indiana.

The Brittons and their forty staffing professionals fill over 4,800 positions each year. When asked to what they attribute the extraordinary success of their Express Personnel franchise offices, Jim and Carole say, "That's simple, it's our great staff; they have a tremendous commitment to helping people succeed."

KEY TERMS

Brand: identifies the franchise system, can be a trademark, name, logo, or symbol representing the franchise

Brand equity: the uniqueness of a franchise system which is necessary for its competitive advantage in the marketplace, consists of four dimensions: brand loyalty, brand awareness, perceived quality of brand, and brand association

Co-branding: when two brands are combined in a business offering, also called "dual branding," "multibranding," "cross-system franchising," and "strategic alliance"; now considered a standard business practice for franchises

Halo effect: when a strong, well-known franchise system links with a lesser known one and the second gets lost in the "halo" of the first

REVIEW QUESTIONS

1. Why would you be interested in co-branding if you are a franchisor?

2. Why would you be interested in co-branding if you are a franchisee?

3. In your opinion, is co-branding a fad or does it reflect a long-term approach to the market? Explain your position on the issue.

4. Co-branding efforts are most prevalent in the restaurant industry. Can you think of other franchise industries that are appropriate for co-branding? Why?

5. What are the various co-branding methods discussed in the chapter? Explain each one.

CASE STUDY

Little Caesars and Kmart

Though Kmart is one of the world's largest mass merchandise retailers, it has sustained substantial revenue losses over the last decade. Primarily a take-out-only concept, Little Caesars, once financially strong and growing faster than its chief rivals Pizza Hut and Domino's, had less than half the units of Pizza Hut. As of mid-1995, there were over 600 Little Caesars in various Kmart units. The expansion by Little Caesars into mass merchandising sites provided access to a new market segment of dining in consumers that went previously untapped by the pizza franchise. The heightened brand awareness was also expected to result in increased sales at freestanding units. The relationship between Little Caesars and Kmart is that of the standard franchisor–franchisee contract. Kmart is a franchisee of the Little Caesars franchise system and thus must pay franchisee fees and royalties. The opportunity to own and operate a fast-food unit in a Kmart was not offered to any of the Little Caesars freestanding unit franchisees. Some franchisees openly expressed concern over the co-branding decision, fearing the Kmart units would cannibalize sales of existing freestanding operations. As both companies entered the year 2000, their individual struggles continued. Little Caesars announced the closing of many of its stand-alone locations due to a company restructuring effort. Kmart did likewise.

CASE QUESTIONS

1. Did Little Caesars make a mistake when selecting Kmart as its co-branding partner? Why or why not?

2. Conduct primary and secondary research to determine the current state of this co-branding partnership. Do both firms view the venture a success?

3. In your opinion, what does the future hold for Little Caesars in terms of its co-branding efforts?

REFERENCES

2000 State of the Industry (Alexandria, VA: National Association of Convenience Stores, 2000).

Bennett, Peter D., ed., *AMA Dictionary of Marketing Terms* (Chicago: American Marketing Association, 1995).

Bertagnoli, Lisa, "The Buddy System," *Restaurants and Institutions* (1 November 2000): 79–86.

Blackett, Tom and Bob Boad, *Co-Branding: The Science of Alliance* (New York: St. Martin's Press, 1999).

Boone, Juliette M., "Hotel_Restaurant Co-Branding—A Preliminary Study," *Cornell Hotel and Restaurant Administration Quarterly* (October 1997): 34–43.

Burns, Greg, "French Fries with That Quart of Oil," *Business Week* (27 November 1995): 86.

Cannon, Charles B., "Dependence and Reliance: Keys to Unshackling Co-Branding Alliances from Federal Franchise Rule Compliance," *Franchise Law Journal* (Fall 1997): 39–48.

Carlino, Bill, "A&W Fishes for Growth, Hooks Long John Silver's with Merger," *Nation's Restaurant News* (22 March 1999): 1, 93.

"Churchs/White Castle Form Franchise Partnership," *Franchising World* (January/February 1997): 52, 62.

Duell, Richard C., III, "Co-Branding Is It for You?" *Franchising* (2000), www.franchising.org.

Federal Trade Commission, "Advance Notice of Proposed Rulemaking," *Federal Register* (28 February 1997): 9115–9127.

Hamstra, Mark, "Arby's Rolls T. J. Cinnamons into Dual-Branded Stores," *Nation's Restaurant News* (14 July 1997): 5, 165.

Hamstra, Mark, "Operators See Potential in Tricon's Newest Prototype," *Nation's Restaurant News* (5 October 1998): 3, 170.

Kochak, Jacqueline, "Trick or Treat?" *Restaurant Business* (15 September 1998) 60-64.

Kramer, Louise, "Arby's Launches Alliance with T. J. Cinnamons," *Nation's Restaurant News* (5 February 1996): 1, 66.

"Like Some Yogurt with That Sandwich," *Arkansas Business* (7 April 1997).

"More Burrito/Carl's Jr. Co-Branding: Franchisee Files Suit," *Franchise Times* (January 1999): 4.

"RTM to Accelerate Co-Branding," *Nation's Restaurant News* (22 March 1999). Also based on interviews with the case principles conducted in Atlanta, Georgia, by the authors during June 2000.

Rubinstein, Ed, "Allied Domecq Unwraps First Togo's/Dunkin Donuts Units," *Nation's Restaurant News* (7 September 1998): 8, 80.

Sen, Kabir C., "Advertising Fees in the Franchised Channel," *Journal of Marketing Channels* 4(1/2) (1995): 83–101.

Sheridan, Margaret, "Room to Grow," *Restaurants and Institutions* (1 November 1998): 58–75.

Shubart, Ellen, "Co-Brands Can Get Lost in Halo Effect," *Franchise Times* (August 2000): 58.

Shubart, Ellen, "Financing Co-Branding: A Matter of Individuality," *Franchise Times* (January 2000): 25.

Shubart, Ellen, "Look How Far We've Come; Where Are We Going Next?" *Franchise Times* (November/December 1999): 40-41.

Shubart, Ellen, "Now More Than Ever, Franchises Adopt Co-Branding," *Franchise Times* (January 1999): 24.

Shubart, Ellen, "Safe and Sound Method of Expansion," *Franchising Times* (August 1999): 39.

Shubart, Ellen, "When Franchises Become a Candy Bar," *Franchise Times* (February 2000): 47.

Strate, Robert W. and Clinton L. Rappole, "Strategic Alliances between Hotels and Restaurants," *Cornell Hotel & Restaurant Administration Quarterly* (June 1997): 50–61.

Sullivan, Janet, "Arrivederci, Ravioli's," *Restaurant Business* (February 1997): 24.

Tannenbaum, Jeffrey A., "Blimpie Seeks to Gain Synergies from an Acquisition," *Wall Street Journal* (20 May 1997): B2.

Voss, Kevin E. and Patriya Tansuhaj, "A Consumer Perspective on Foreign Market Entry: Building Brands through Brand Alliances," *Journal of International Consumer Marketing* 11(2) (2000): 39–58.

Webb, Wendy, "Hotel Company Experiments with Two Brands under One Roof," *Franchise Times* (March 2001): 38.

Weingartner, Nancy, "Two-in-One Stores Can Be Adventure for Franchisee," *Franchise Times* (January 2000): 26.

Williams, Debra, "Franchise Operations See Boom in Co-Branding," *Air Force Times* (8 November 1999): insert.

"Wrong Turns Point in Right Direction," *Nation's Restaurant News* (29 September 1997): 42–46.

Yoo, Boonghee and Naveen Donthu, "Developing and Validating a Multidimensional Consumer-Based Brand Equity Scale," *Journal of Business Research* (April 2001): 1–14.

Young, Joyce A., Audhesh K. Paswan, John M. Buch, and Lori J. Ashby, "Fast-Food Franchisors and Discount Retailers: A Tale of Two Alliances and Beyond," in Mark Spriggs, ed., *1997 Society of Franchising Conference Proceedings—Winning Strategies for Franchising: Current Research and Future Direction* (Minneapolis, MN: St. Thomas University, 1997), paper 7.

Young, Joyce A., Robert D. Green, and Audhesh K. Paswan, "Co-Branding Approaches in the Franchised Food Service Industry," *Journal of Business & Entrepreneurship* (July 2000): 19–31.

Zuber, Amy, "A&Ws Rampant Co-Branding Heats up the 2nd 100's 11—Chain Sandwich Sector," *Nation's Restaurant News* (24 July 2000): 104-105.

Zuber, Amy, "Blimpie Eyes Higher-End QSR, Opens Pasta Central," *Nation's Restaurant News* (April 1999): 1, 6.

MANAGING THE FRANCHISOR'S OPERATIONS PROCESS

In studying this chapter, you will:

- Learn why a franchisor has a promotional and an operations process.
- Learn about the components of the promotional package.
- Learn about how to develop the operations process.
- Understand the purpose of the franchisor's brochure and what information is included in the brochure.
- Learn why franchisors develop informational manuals for franchisee trainees and for prospective franchisees.

INCIDENT

Betty would like to open a franchised coffee and donut business. She has sought information from large franchisors with well-known names and solid reputations and has narrowed the field to two franchise systems. She received disclosure documents, sample franchising contracts, and fee schedules along with information showing sample franchisee financial statements from several of the franchisors she contacted. Next, Betty intends to contact several coffee and donut franchisees to get their opinions about the franchising arrangements they have with their respective franchisors.

The franchisees told Betty that the leading advertisements, promotions, and marketing programs of the franchisor have helped achieve up to 97 percent recognition factor among Americans. As a franchisee, Betty will have the buying power and impact of powerful chains. Betty could also have an influence on many advertising decisions through her representation on the franchisor marketing and advertising councils.

What other type of information should Betty seek? Would a franchisor normally be willing to supply Betty with the type of specific information she is requesting? Are there sources of information Betty can use other than what is provided by franchisors in the donut industry?

> Typically, the most valuable source of information on any franchise system is its existing franchisees.

8-1 PROMOTIONAL PACKAGE

The written information provided in the franchise package represents the types of support a franchisor provides a franchisee. A franchise package is generally divided into two parts, the promotional package and the operations materials. The **promotional package** is the carefully prepared information developed and given by the franchisor to prospective franchisees in order to (1) solicit franchisee applicants to the franchise system, (2) provide basic information about the franchise, and (3) illustrate the follow-up forms used to sign franchisees. A promotional package should explain the basic purpose and substantial requirements of the franchise program, specifying intrinsic values and services provided to a franchisee, suggesting probability for franchisee success in the franchise system, and identifying a typical offer the franchisor makes to a franchisee.

The purpose of a promotional package is to solicit and sign franchisees. The promotional package should explain the overall operations and format (basic approach) of the franchise system. It will typically include items relative to disclosure documents required by law, essentials of the franchising agreement, and even explanations of the recommended information reporting and bookkeeping systems as well as certain advertising practices used by the franchisor. This package is designed by the franchisor to help a franchisee understand the responsibilities of both parties for the successful operation of a franchised unit.

---

1. Administrative Expenses
2. Recruitment Costs
   a. Advertising
   b. Sales
3. Promotion Costs
4. Training and Schooling Costs
5. Supplementary Services and Related Expenses
6. Administrative Cost Forms
   a. Personal contact (see Figure 8-1 later in the chapter)
   b. Follow-up (see Figure 8-2 later in the chapter)
   c. Personal data sheet
   d. Financial data sheet

To prepare for soliciting new franchisees, the franchisor needs to understand the costs associated with bringing a new franchisee into the franchising family and the control system needed to maintain effective information sharing between franchisor and franchisee to assure profitable results. When properly prepared, this package will enable the franchisor to have a controllable, tactical approach to franchisee recruitment, as well as an understanding of the total costs associated with starting a franchised business.

The franchisee is likely to view the promotional package somewhat differently. The franchisee is primarily interested in learning about the franchise system, including how it operates and what requirements or conditions a franchisee must meet with this company. The franchisee would be interested in learning about the items identified in the following list.

- A description of the business, its product, and/or services

- Background information about the franchisor and franchised company

- Historical information concerning development and operation of a franchised unit

- Amount of money required for acquisition of a franchise

- Assistance offered by the franchisor (financial, training, and service) to a franchisee

- Site, equipment, and building information

- Marketing factors associated with promotion and sale of the franchise system's products or services

- Financial information about franchisees and the franchise system

Notice how the needs of the two parties, franchisor and franchisee, differ when the information in the previous two lists is compared. Although both parties address virtually the same information, each has a separate perspective on that information. The franchisor needs to organize the information in a logical sequence that describes the franchising organization, its administrative reporting approach, its approach to recruitment and training of potential franchisees, and its support services to the new franchisee. The franchisee is seeking information from a different perspective, often for purposes of comparison. By examining the differences between franchising organizations, their training, approach to advertising, financial health, promotional and marketing approaches, and reporting requirements, the potential franchisee can determine the advantages of one franchise system over another.

A fundamental question for a franchise system is: "Why would anyone want to buy this franchise?" The deeper, or underlying, question is: "Why wouldn't someone simply do this business themselves—without a franchise agreement?"

To effectively promote, solicit, and sign quality franchisees, a franchise concept should have panache or sizzle. When a franchise concept is not well differentiated, clearly targeted to customer groupings, and effectively delivered, the franchise system is not likely to be successful in the long term. Factually, a number of franchise companies do not have their system, including their products and services, effectively differentiated from their competition.

According to Mark Seibert, the best franchisees are motivated adopters, that is, people willing to take on some level of risk and are willing to follow rules set forth by the franchisor. In effect, the prospective franchisee is buying a strong value proposition and a unique (differentiated) market position.[1]

It is the franchise company's "system" of all those things that make the ultimate difference between success and failure. (See Chapters 3 through 9 and 11 through 14.) For example, when someone buys a McDonald's franchise, they are not buying it to learn the recipe of the Big Mac sandwich. Instead they are buying into a system that offers superior value as a brand to a franchisee and quality products to its customers. Subway's success is not dependent upon its Italian meatball sandwich, nor are Burger King's or Wendy's long-term profitable development due to a particular hamburger or chili product.

> Prospective franchisees want to buy a consistent customer experience that is proven, day after day, to be successful in the marketplace.

A franchise system's central concept needs to be replicable at every franchised location, but to be successful in the long run, it will need to be differentiated from its competition if the franchise system hopes to achieve any significant level of success. For example, note how Burger King developed a unique tag line to their sandwich offerings by stating, "Have It Your Way"—a clear step away from the standardized format for what is expected at many fast-food businesses. Wendy's modified its product offerings to attract a more adult customer by having baked potatoes and chili as standards on their menu. Subway differentiates itself and clearly states its value proposition through the phrase: "A Fresh Value Meal." Some fast-food franchise systems have differentiated themselves through operational characteristics such as a double drive thru; others differentiate themselves on service—either high or low; while other systems have differentiated themselves by having a "low intrusion" into the franchisee's business, having minimal requirements upon how the product would be offered, the service provided to the customer, or size of geographic territory. In any event, successful franchise systems have found effective ways to clearly differentiate themselves from their competition, and to uphold the value proposition of the franchise concept itself.

Some will argue that competitive advantage, differentiation, and strong value proposition should be link-pinned into one or two of the following five approaches to the marketplace.

- Biggest: a dominant assortment (of products, or geographic locations)
- Quickest: orientation toward fast service—to be the fastest
- Cheapest: lowest prices on a day-by-day basis
- Hottest: quickest availability of newest fashion, newest technology, newest...
- Easiest: high service orientation: We'll do it all for you. You make the decision, we implement the solution until you are satisfied.

> There is one thing every franchise system knows. If you don't know how you want to be positioned in the marketplace and don't know the value proposition you uphold, you will be positioned in the marketplace and educated on that position by your competitors. And, that is not a good strategy to follow. Therefore, know Who you are, What you do, and Why you do it in developing the promotional package for attracting potential franchisees to your system.

Figure 8-1 illustrates a typical **personal contact information sheet**. Usually the name of the franchise system is at or near the top.

When someone makes a franchising inquiry to a field representative, an existing franchisee of a franchised business system, or a district or headquarters office, preliminary information about the nature of the contact should be recorded. The prospect's name, address, and phone number should be taken down, as well as how the contact was made—by phone, letter of inquiry, personal visit to the office, stopping at a trade show booth, or some other means. Also, the impressions of that initial contact are recorded by the person contacted. For example: "Mr. Jones appears to be seeking comparative information. I provided a disclosure document and discussed possible expansions for the Southwestern District. I will follow up in two weeks to assess if sufficient interest exists to make any further contact"; or, "Sal Walters of Roanoke, Virginia, appears to have strong interest in our hot tub franchise. Roanoke could use a franchisee. I will follow up with a personal visit." Typically, the bottom of the form is reserved for signatures, usually including that of the franchising representative first contacted by the interested party. There may also be other signatures or marks to identify where the inquiry contact sheet has been passed. Usually a copy of each contact sheet goes to the district or regional office, if the administration of franchisee development takes place at that level. If not, the inquiries are sent to the home office of the franchisor. It is these initial contact sheets that provide the basic information utilized by those involved in franchisee recruitment.

Figure 8-2 provides an illustration of a typical **follow-up contact information form**. The first part of the follow-up sheet provides basic information about the first contact. If the franchisor expresses an interest in the prospect, further processing takes place. Typically, the phone conversations and letter to set up an appointment, and every other step of the recruitment process, need to be recorded so that the interaction between the franchisor and the prospect can be efficiently and

NAME OF BUSINESS

Directions for Distribution:

    1st sheet to prospective franchisee master file
    2nd sheet to headquarters
    3rd sheet retained by salesperson

PERSONAL CONTACT

Date_____ Time_____ Prospect's Number_____

Prospect's Name_____

Address_____ Phone Number _____

City _____ State_____ Zip_____

How contacted: _____ Phone   _____ Letter   _____ Trade show

    _____ Internet   _____ Office   _____ Field

    _____ E-mail   _____ Fax   _____ Other

Results:_____

_____

_____

_____

_____

Signature_____ (Salesperson)

Signature_____ (Region or District)

Signature_____ (Headquarters)

FIGURE **8-1**

Sample Personal Contact Information Form

effectively managed. The next third of the form identifies the type of information provided and activities completed that comprise a step-by-step sequence leading to an agreement between the prospect and the franchisor. The last lines of the form indicate home office action on the application, noting when the agreement was signed and when notices were mailed, and containing any summary remarks about the application. The form thus provides a sequence of steps useful for a franchisor to develop a prospective franchisee from the point of serious inquiry to the signing and formalization of the franchising agreement.

8-1a   Administrative Expenses

The franchisor must develop a method of determining the expenses of administering a franchise program. The primary administrative costs are typically those of hiring and training salespeople to recruit or solicit prospective franchisees. In addition, the nonpersonnel costs of franchisee recruitment, such as costs of publishing brochures, advertising, or promoting the business through trade shows, should also be considered. Further expenses may be incurred in running background checks on prospective franchisees, performing analyses of their current or former businesses, and inquiring into their credit ratings. By estimating the number of franchisees expected to be signed in the next planning period—month, quarter, or year—and by estimating the costs of franchisee recruitment and selection, including the personnel and nonpersonnel costs directly associated with such recruitment, the franchisor can develop an administrative expense schedule that can be used in the future for both planning and control.

8-1b   Recruitment Package

The franchisee **recruitment package** usually consists of a recruitment brochure, a disclosure document, and other information about the benefits and opportunities of becoming a franchisee with the franchise system. This package is used as part of the franchisor's response to initial inquiries by a prospective franchisee. The annual report of the franchised business may also be provided by the franchising firm. A number of franchising businesses have superb annual reports and are happy to make them available to prospective franchisees. The franchising brochure briefly

NAME OF FRANCHISED BUSINESS

Prospective Franchisee's Name_____

Address_____ Phone Number _____

City _____ State_____ Zip_____

Prospect's Number_____

Original Contact Date_____

Original Contact By_____

HOME OFFICE USE

_____ Yes, Needs Further Processing   _____ No, Reject

By:_____

Reason:_____
_____

Initial inquiry received, date:_____

First response package mailed, date:_____

Date assigned:_____

Name of sales representative:_____

Master file started, date:_____

Initial phone contact, date:_____

Initial sales letter mailed, date:_____

Additional phone date:_____ Results:_____

Additional phone date:_____ Results:_____

Additional phone date:_____ Results:_____

Additional phone date:_____ Results:_____

Additional follow-up date:_____

Appointment letter mailed, date:_____

Appointment made for, date:_____

Accommodation_____ yes_____ no_____

Reservation_____ yes_____ no_____

Prospect_____ yes_____ no_____

Date of presentation made:_____ Those attending:_____
_____

Personnel data sheet evaluated, date:_____ By whom:_____

Financial sheet evaluated, date:_____ By whom:_____

Following recommendation:_____Positive _____ Negative_____

Closing agreements signed:_____ Check received_____ Credit form completed_____

Site report developed_____

FIGURE **8-2**

Sample Follow-up Contact Information Form

Successful franchise sales: Check when completed

Franchise agreements_____ Check received_____

Site report_____ Credit form_____

Corporate resolutions_____

Receipt of disclosure document_____

HOME OFFICE USE

Staff Recommendation	_____	Accepted	_____	Rejected
By Whom:_____			Date:_____	
Board of Directors	_____	Accepted	_____	Rejected
Agreement, By Whom:_____			Date:_____	
Notices mailed, Date:_____				
Acceptance_____	Rejection_____	Licensee_____	Sale representative_____	
Remarks:_____				

_____

_____

Source: Adapted from Pizza Inn Personal Data Sheet

FIGURE **8-2**

Continued

_____

discusses the major points about the franchise and the principal people involved in running the franchise system. Most brochures will include the types of information found in the following list.

1. Description of the business
2. The principal people in the franchise system (primary ownership)
3. The franchise system
   a. Territory covered
   b. Operating assistance
   c. What is needed for a franchisee to get started
   d. Ongoing assistance available through the franchisor
   e. Franchise system's regional or national advertising program
   f. Marketing programs utilized
   g. Credit card systems (if applicable)
4. Operating a franchise
   a. Location
   b. Training
   c. Insurance
   d. Assistance
   e. Management and planning
   f. Standards of performance

    g. Trademarks and trade names

    h. Duration of the franchising agreement

    i. Franchising and other fees

    j. Franchisee right to assign and/or transfer

    k. Business forms recommended/required and supplies

5. Investments

6. Franchise application (attached, or information how to receive one)

The franchise brochure is meant to address initial questions or concerns of prospective franchisees. Usually it is a well-developed color brochure describing the franchise concept, organization, operation, franchisor assistance, and nominal sales figures and projections. The brochure should also contain the initial application form for a prospective franchisee, as inclusion of an application encourages a prospect to make contact.

8-2 OPERATIONS PACKAGE

The second part of a franchise package is the operations package. The **operations package** is fairly extensive, and the materials are often put in the form of manuals. The information contained in the manuals is meant to assist the franchisee to properly conduct the operations of the franchise. Eliminating any one of the manuals or information packages may cause a breakdown in the financial flow, operational work activities, or required reporting procedures on which the success of the franchise system depends. There are at least ten major manuals or information packages which may make up the operations package.

- Operating Manual

- Training Manual

- Location Selection Criteria (and procedures, franchisor involvement in the choice and type of assistance provided, if any)

- Marketing Manual

- Advertising Manual (sometimes included in Marketing Manual)

- Field Support Manual

- Quality-Control Manual

- Pre-Opening Manual

- Site Inspection Manual

- Reporting Manual (including financial forms and approved procedures)

Beginning franchisors may have developed only the operations manual and after a few years will develop the additional materials as needed. Explicit statements in the manuals concerning each area of running the franchised business help franchisees understand the nature of the business they are entering, the reporting requirements, and proven procedures for efficient operation of a franchise. The manuals should be written clearly and concisely so that a person without experience in the particular business can learn the requirements and operating processes of the franchise system. Many prospective franchisees have experience in various types of employment or business;

but entering a franchising relationship is different, as there are separate and distinct activities and responsibilities for a franchisor and a franchisee as well as areas in which the two must work together. These factors, plus the franchisor's method of operation, must be understood by the franchisee if the franchise is to be a success.

8-2a   Operating Manual

The **operating manual** is often referred to as the bible of the franchise system. It is given to the franchisee only on loan, and is to be returned to the franchisor if the franchisee ever leaves the system. It should be thoroughly developed so that a franchisee can rely on it for ready and regular reference to address the vagaries and uncertainties of day-to-day operations of the franchised business. It should describe each major function and operating procedure of the business. Not only should the manual present a step-by-step explanation of operations, but it should also provide an overview of the major thrusts of the franchise system. The manual typically illustrates in graphs, charts, and/or pictures how the franchisor and franchisee conduct business together, and identifies each essential facet of the daily operations of a franchised business. The operating manual is also an instructional tool useful in the programs run by the franchisor for training new franchisees. Often, the operating manual covers the essential administrative, legal, and functional aspects of the franchise system. Because the system's procedures and policies may change with the changing business climate, the operating manual is probably best kept in a loose-leaf binder. Thus, as administrative policies, operating procedures, and personnel practices are changed, the franchisee and franchisor can update the particular section by removing the old pages and inserting the new. Topics often included in an operating manual are identified in Table 8-1.

The sections and items included in Table 8-1 are intended to present a comprehensive view of what might appear in a franchisor's operating manual. Obviously, each franchise system has its own unique set of operating procedures. Some items in this table might not be included in a manual for a carpet-cleaning franchise, for example, but that franchise system might include more detail for other items.

Procedures incorporated in the operating manual should be carefully developed and then tested "under fire" in the franchisor's prototype unit to ensure that they are understandable and that by reading the manual, employees and franchisees can learn precisely what constitutes the operating procedures of that franchised business. By having clear, understandable operating procedures available to them, both franchisor and franchisee will know exactly what is expected in the operations of the franchised business.

Existing franchisees are an important source of information when the franchisor seeks to improve the operating manual, because franchisees have gained practical experience in applying the concepts and procedures within the operating manual on a daily basis in their own businesses. Illustrations are often incorporated in the operating manual to display techniques or provide a picture of some facet of the operations, showing the best way to wash a dish, set up a display, stock a shelf, and so on. In addition to illustrations, definitions and descriptions provide instruction or sequencing of work activities necessary to ensure quality and consistency in preparation and delivery of products or services.

8-2b   Training Manual

A franchisor works closely with the franchise system's franchisees. The interaction between franchisor and new franchisees is primarily directed through a **training manual**, a guide for teaching operating procedures and personnel management. Franchise training programs can be classified into two categories: formal training programs and ongoing training programs.

TABLE 8-1   SAMPLE OUTLINE OF TOPICS INCLUDED IN THE OPERATING MANUAL

SECTION ONE: INTRODUCTION

    Company History

    Franchisor and Administrative Staff

    Franchisor/Franchisee Obligations

SECTION TWO: GENERAL RULE OF OPERATION

    Important Success Factors

    Quality Standards

    Warranties and Replacement Practices

    Customer Relations

    Inventory Systems

    Quality and Variety of Product

SECTION THREE: UNIT OPERATIONS

    Pricing

    Quality

    Franchise Image

    Customer Service, Courtesy

    Credit Policies

    Maintenance Requirements

    Store Hours

    Employee Discounts

    Community Relations

    Brand Policies

SECTION FOUR: MANAGEMENT

    Wages and Salaries

    Purchasing, Receiving

    Quality Control

    Advertising

    Legal Documents and Practices

    Accounting/Financial Reports

    Insurance Reports

    Customer or Employee Accidents

    Inventory

SECTION FIVE: STORE OPERATION

    Position Descriptions

    Individual Responsibilities

    Store Opening Procedure/Checklist

    Store Closing/Checklist

    Maintenance and Housekeeping

    Opening and Closing Out Registers

    Equipment Maintenance

    Inspections

MANAGING THE FRANCHISOR'S OPERATIONS PROCESS

TABLE 8-1 (CONTINUED)

SECTION SIX: SALES OPERATIONS (may be separate manual)

Selling Methods

Exchanges, Adjustments, Refunds

Order Taking

Check Cashing

Credit Accounts

Sales Tax

Supplies/Purchasing

The Customer Is Always Right, Except...

Promotional Activities: Display, Grand Opening, Mail, Sales and/or Seasonal Promotions, Weekly, Monthly
Promotions: TV, Radio, Newsprint, Direct Mail

SECTION SEVEN: INVENTORY

Purchasing

Receiving

Inventory Control

Loss Prevention, Shoplifting, Pilferage

Pricing Policies, Procedures

Order Forms

SECTION EIGHT: MAINTENANCE CONTROL

Restrooms

Parking

Utility Cost Control

Fire Protection

Repairs

Plumbing, Electrical, Mechanical, Construction

Pest Control

Fire Prevention/Control

Preventive Maintenance

Alarms, Locks, Keys, Entrances/Exits

Background Music

Formal training programs provide opportunity for the franchisor to help new franchisees develop specific knowledge about the franchise system and the business factors important to running a successful franchised unit. Administrative and operating functions are stressed. The training is typically given in a central location of the business, such as the prototype for the franchise system or a district or regional franchised unit operating by the franchised company or a franchisee. A well-known example of a formal training site is Hamburger University, founded in 1961 by McDonald's Corporation. Hamburger University has become an international management training center for McDonald's licensees, managers, and corporate personnel. It is accredited by the American Council on Education and offers a number of courses for college credit. More than 2,000 students graduate annually from this suburban Chicago, Illinois, facility. Many large franchise systems have such a facility, or two or three, in order to accommodate their franchisees. Having several regional training centers is of great advantage to a franchise system that is national in scope.

Many smaller franchisors find it convenient to use their first unit, the prototype, as the training facility. Often it is located near the franchise system headquarters and may even be housed within the same building. Close proximity provides the opportunity for a franchisor to closely scrutinize training content and methods and be involved in evaluating performance of new franchisees as they learn to become authorized representatives of the franchise system. A prospective franchisee should successfully complete all training offered by the franchisor prior to opening the franchise. In this way all franchisees are certain to have the same training, and therefore, the same opportunity for understanding the policies and practices of the franchise system. With this common set of norms for operating a franchised unit, mutual expectations between franchisor and franchisee can be upheld. Almost all franchisees agree that formal training is important and should be a prerequisite service provided by a franchisor. Formal training helps both franchisor and franchisee achieve success in the franchise system.

BLIMPIE TRAINING

Once you join the BLIMPIE system you will learn from people who are experts in the business: subfranchisors, other franchisees, and Blimpie International employees. BLIMPIE provides a tremendous training program so that you can take advantage of the knowledge at each level in our system.

The BLIMPIE University

Once you have signed your lease, you will need to attend BLIMPIE University at the BLIMPIE Franchise Support Headquarters in Atlanta, Georgia. The training is 10 full days of in-class discussion and hands-on experience all about operating a BLIMPIE business. You'll learn how you can be successful as an entrepreneur, the basics of operating a business, BLIMPIE operations, marketing at every level, and valuable information that you need to grow your business.

Hands-On Training

All new BLIMPIE franchisees spend a minimum of 80 hours in an operating restaurant. A minimum of 40 hours are spent learning the day-to-day operations of the store before you come to BLIMPIE University in Atlanta. After BLIMPIE University, you'll spend an additional 40 hours (minimum) in a BLIMPIE restaurant learning and developing the skills to successfully manage your BLIMPIE restaurant. An experienced franchisee and your sub-franchisor will conduct the in-store training.

Ongoing Training

BLIMPIE also provides a variety of ongoing training programs to franchisees, which are presented in a variety of methods. Training programs are conducted at national and regional conferences. In addition new training modules are continuously being developed. You will also be kept up to date on the latest and greatest in the BLIMPIE system through continuing communication from Blimpie International.

Source: Blimpie International Inc., "Franchise Opportunities," 2001.

Ongoing training is usually provided by field staff of the franchisor after the franchisee has entered business. Traveling field representatives provide on-site training for franchisees as well as for the franchisee's staff, when appropriate. Typically, the first ongoing type of training is provided just prior to the opening of the franchised outlet. This means training a complement of perhaps twenty to thirty people in new restaurants, perhaps fifty or more people in newly signed motels or hotels, or perhaps only one or two people in smaller, service-oriented franchised outlets. The franchisor's field representative also provides the continuous training to the franchisee and staff, depending on the franchisee's needs and/or the administrative and operative changes suggested by the franchisor. Many franchise systems also provide training manuals for use by the franchisee to help train new employees. This type of training brings the franchisee and staff closer together, providing them with the same information at the same time. Of particular benefit is training, provided by the franchisee, to staff of the same type provided by the franchisor to the franchisee. Thus, employees will be able to understand not only the operational facets of the franchised business, but also the overall perspective, the general goals of the franchise system, and the objectives and policies of the franchise system for profitability and growth.

Training Program Development

Training programs are generally developed based on the notion that new franchisees have little or no specific business knowledge about the franchise system. It is important for the franchisor to recognize that educating the franchisee is not based only on what the franchisor feels needs to be taught, but also on what the franchisee needs to learn in order to be a successful operator. Training franchisees in the business of the franchise system should be a blend of concept development and practical application of those concepts. Franchisees need to become familiar with all aspects of the business, including advertising, promotion, bookkeeping, management, reporting, inventory control, marketing, and other activities essential to the day-to-day operations of the franchised outlet. Also, franchisees should be instilled with pride of ownership in their business, loyalty to the franchise system, and a sense of confidence in the future.

A training program should develop basic management and business skills. Basic economics, profit motives and incentives, cost controls, management and leadership practices, financial tools, and marketing principles, as they apply to the franchised business, should be included in the training. The formal training program provided at the prototype or other designated facility should be as thorough but as concise as possible. Such programs can last from five days to a few months, depending on the amount of classroom (conceptual) and on-site (practical) training provided. Although the classroom is vitally important, the majority of what franchisees take back to their own units is usually the practical information acquired in on-site training. Franchisors have also found that group training is more effective than individual training. Three to five new franchisees are preferable for a training program, for in these small groups, franchisees can interact more closely with one another to discuss common experiences and personal insights grained through the training program. This opportunity to exchange ideas is important to the attitude development and knowledge formation of each franchisee.

After formal training at the franchisor's facility, the franchisee will typically receive from three days to two weeks of additional training at the franchisee's own location, providing an opportunity to apply the conceptual and practical training. This second stage of training focuses on actual operations at the particular franchised unit and utilizes the skills learned at the training facility. This unit training is usually handled by the franchisor's field representatives; it takes place just before and continues through the grand opening of the outlet. An outline of a formal training program is presented in Table 8-2.

Franchisor training is important. It can have a dramatic effect on the success or failure of a franchise system. The franchisor has the responsibility to train new franchisees so they are familiar with all aspects of the franchised business operations and the management functions associated with making the operation profitable. A good training program will allow sufficient time for questions to be asked and answered accurately and concretely and will allow for interactions between new franchisees. Trainees will likely learn the most useful information from hands-on exercises and operations rather than classroom instruction at the training facility. Each component, however, is important in the development of a firm grounding in the concepts of the franchise system as well as the tools and skills necessary to run a franchised unit.

TABLE 8-2   A TYPICAL FORMAL TRAINING PROGRAM FOR NEW FRANCHISEES

SECTION ONE: INTRODUCTION

Executive Summary of Business Facts

Information about Business Industry

Information about Franchisor

Required Activities with Franchisor

Contracts, Licenses, Permits, and Any Other Legal Requirements

SECTION TWO: FINANCE

Balance Sheet—how to develop, read, and use

Income Statement—how to develop, read, and use

Cash Budget—how to develop, read, and use

Pro Forma Income and Balance Sheets—how to use

Recordkeeping Procedures—a system and its procedures

Cash Register—how to use

Reading Cash Register Tapes

Procedures for Opening Register

Procedures for Closing Register

Inventory Control

Credit Sales

Check Sales

Petty Cash

Reconciliation

Cash Register

Bank Statements

Sales Slips versus Cash

Night Deposits

Payroll

Social Security Requirements

Federal, State (and County or City) Withholding Taxes

Lease

Insurance

SECTION THREE: MARKETING

Target Market

Advertising/Promotion

Pre-Opening Activities

Grand Opening

Post-Opening Activities

Merchandising

Customer Relations

Products—Definition and Description

TABLE 8-2 (CONTINUED)

SECTION FOUR: OPERATIONS

Personnel and Store Operations

Housekeeping and Maintenance

Management

Sales Operations

Inventory

Unit Operations (also, see Operating Manual)

SECTION FIVE: SERVICE/PRODUCTION

Equipment Ordering

Inventory Control

Ordering Control

- From franchisor
- From other suppliers

Cost Factors

Serving

Service/Product Preparation Methods

Warehousing Storage Methods

Sanitary Control

Kitchen Operation (or Production Floor Operation)

Portion (or Specific Weight, Color, Size, Thickness) Control

SECTION SIX: MANAGEMENT OF PERSONNEL

Job Specifications

Recruitment, Selection, and Training of Employees

Weekly Work Log/Monthly Schedules

Motivation

Personnel Development

Labor Laws and Regulations

Franchisor Assistance

8-2c Location Selection Criteria

One of the most crucial decisions confronting the franchisee (and the franchisor as well) is selection of the site for the new franchised business. Many franchised businesses depend heavily on walk-in traffic; others depend on drive-in/drive-thru traffic. Some need extensive advertising; others need merely to have their business name in the phone book. Franchised businesses also differ in how important the choice of location is to the success of the business. Based on the type of franchise business, the franchisor will prepare a list of factors to be investigated prior to making the location decision.

Location for a new franchised business is usually based on a variety of factors including economic strength and potential of a particular region; economic strength and potential of metro-politan area or market area; availability of transportation for supplies; employment trends and employment mix; demographic characteristics within the community or particular market segment in terms of usage or purchase of the product or service; traffic ingress and egress at sites being

Jiffy Lube has changed over the years. In 1987, Jiffy Lube was a stand-alone business with 561 units after eight years in franchising. In 2007, the franchise system has over 2,200 locations and has gone through two acquisitions, first by Pennzoil-Quaker State and then by Shell Oil Company. Both parent companies added to the products and services offered under the Jiffy Lube brand. Their growth and ownership changes are reflected in their territory definitions: In 1987, the definition of a *territory* was complete in one-half of a page; now it is more than a page.

Information adapted from Edith Wiseman, "Choosing the Right Territory," FRANdata Research e-Newsletter (Arlington, VA: FRANdata, March 13, 2007).

considered; land development and construction costs; and location of primary competitors within the primary service area.

Although a location selection manual may be developed to assist franchisees in determining optimal sites, the final determination often rests with the franchisor. A site must meet the criteria of the franchisor prior to any final decisions for purchase, development, and construction by the franchisee. Many franchisors will actually purchase the land, then lease it back to the franchisee on an intermediate- to long-term basis, for five to thirty years. Obviously, by owning the land, the franchisor gains enormous leverage on the franchisee. In many mall and shopping-center locations, the franchisor will obtain the lease and then sublease to the franchisee. For some franchising systems in which location is not as important for customer traffic, site selection is of little importance, but access to the intended target market may be of critical importance. In such instances, the selection criteria include availability of transportation and immediate access to the territory to be covered.

8-2d Marketing Manual

The **marketing manual** describes the franchisor's marketing philosophy. It discusses in detail the features and characteristics used to market the franchised business's offering, which may be consumer or industrial goods, durable or nondurable goods, or a service. The brand name is described, and the franchisor's quality concept is articulated as being higher, the same as, or lower than that of the competition. If there is a family of brands or if other products are to be given the same brand name, then this is also covered in the marketing manual. Sometimes the brand name is used horizontally to cover product differences, or else there may be individual brands in franchised businesses, such as the different sandwiches available at some franchised restaurants. Also, several products may be marketed under a family branding approach, such as with auto parts from major auto manufacturers. All these variances should be stated in the marketing manual.

Other factors discussed in the marketing manual include information about packaging, labeling, and consumer services that franchisees should make available. The manual might also contain information about appropriate ways to feature a product within a line, how to promote a featured product, or the right amount and quality of service to offer in order to minimize complaints and maximize customer satisfaction.

Along with product classification, product features, and customer services, the marketing manual should state the franchisor's pricing policies, including new-product strategies, product mix strategies, price-adjustment strategies, and how to initiate price changes and respond to price changes of competition. The marketing manual should state policies concerning physical distribution of the product as well as the conditions under which the product can be sold at wholesale, if the franchisee's business is retail.

The marketing manual should describe the market position the franchise system seeks, in terms of the market segment and customer groups targeted and the competitive position the franchise system wants to reach and/or maintain. Information about customers is provided in the form of a customer profile, identifying the typical gender, age, and income characteristics, what the customer seeks to derive by purchasing the product, and the price range most appropriate for triggering purchase decisions, as well as what services customers will want to accompany the purchase of the product. Sometimes a marketing manual will explain how to gather the appropriate information to develop a reasonable market share for the products offered, how to penetrate new market segments, and how to deepen penetration in established market segments. Some marketing manuals also contain basic information about how to perform market research within the franchisee's local trading area, from measuring general economic conditions of a community to testing consumer attitudes about products or services offered by the franchisee.

The marketing manual contains a wealth of information about how the franchise system attracts and maintains customers through the basic product, pricing, place, and distribution policies, as well as information about current customers and collecting market intelligence. It clearly identifies the marketing philosophy of the franchise system.

However, one major factor concerning the marketing of the franchised product or service—advertising and promotion—may not be included in this manual. Some franchise systems prefer to include advertising policies and promotional strategies in a separate manual. Advertising and promotion for many franchised systems involve regular participation by the franchisees. Separating the advertising policies and strategies from the rest of the marketing information allows for such information to be contained in one smaller manual and easily updated as market conditions dictate and as the franchise system modifies its approach to the market.

8-2e Advertising Manual

From a broad perspective, *advertising* means effective communication and promotion of the franchised product to the targeted audience. This means the franchisor must know who is the audience targeted and what response is sought, and so choose the appropriate messages, as well as be able to determine whether an advertisement or promotion is effective. The advertising and promotional strategies are then budgeted and appropriate cost-sharing arrangements are made between the franchisor and the franchisees.

An effective **advertising manual** covers at least four topics: advertising, promotion, graphics and signage, and public relations. As noted in the previous paragraph, the major decisions in advertising are to determine the objectives of the particular advertisement, what message is to be conveyed, the media most appropriate for conveying the message, the impact of the advertisement, and its anticipated cost. Plans to advertise by means of radio, television, and print media should describe to the franchisee what sales tool is appropriate for what market condition, suggesting which mix is most effective in attracting customers. An advertisement should express at the appropriate level of detail the usefulness and advantages of the product being offered. Recommended advertisements should be tested by the franchisor to ensure that advertisements to be used by the franchise system and by its franchisees have been found successful.

The advertising manual will also contain illustrations of direct mail pieces and newspaper display mats (with space for the franchisee to plug in the location of other necessary information), as well as audiovisual disk sampler presentations, brochures, and presentation booklets when personal selling is the primary means of making sales.

Promotion materials are designed to attract market response or enhance existing customer demand. Contests, cents-off coupons, rebate or refund offers, and product samples or demonstrations are sales tools used by many retail franchise systems. Sales promotions through the sales force of a franchisee would also be included when personal selling is the principal method of generating sales. Bonuses based on sales volume, or sales contests for trips, merchandise, or cash would be described in the manual.

The graphics program of a franchise system provides the franchisee with information about how, where, and when to use the trademarks, logos, and service marks. Both franchisor and franchisee need to be keenly aware of the signs of the franchise system, and must guard and protect all trademarks and logos. The franchisor is required to show the franchisee what is permitted in the use of registered trademarks. All trademarks, logos, and service marks must receive consistent use. The franchisor should take immediate action to stop any unauthorized modification or inappropriate use by franchisees or other parties. Franchisees are often requested to help the franchisor identify any copying or modifications of the franchise system's works. The franchisee should never be permitted to use the trademark of the franchisor without written consent.

Most franchisors insist on one unchangeable sign for the entire franchise system. Although different sizes and types of signs are usually permitted, the particular signage is unmodifiable and consistent regardless of location. Usually, this means all colors must be identical with the illustrations provided in the manual, using the same style or type, word order, and word authorization. Any changes or personalization of such signs may result in loss of trademark protection for the franchise system, which would also result in loss of "added value" or goodwill to the franchise system.

The last major topic usually covered in an advertising manual is public relations. The purpose of a public relations program is to generate favorable publicity for the franchise system as well as for the individual franchise locations. In this broad context, public relations is usually aimed toward building an image of good corporate citizenship for the franchise system. The tools discussed in the advertising manual should include the franchise system's approaches to product publicity, press relations, internal and external corporate communications, and lobbying if the franchise system has an interest in promoting or defeating government regulations or legislation. Franchisees are often encouraged to become involved in community activities such as community service projects, scout troops, sports team sponsorships, and other activities that tend to enhance the name of the franchise system as well as the local franchise as an active participant in promoting the community.

8-2f   Field Support Manual

Successful franchise systems have developed extensive field support systems for the franchisees. Franchisors have learned such support is necessary to help ensure their success, for when the franchisees are successful, the franchise system prospers. Instead of the vertical or top-down approach traditional in business relationships, the franchisor–franchisee relationship in many franchise systems had become horizontal. A sense of equity, fairness, and mutual respect is sought in the relationship. After all, the franchisor and franchisee are independent, yet interdependent, in their business agreements and practices.

The **field support manual** should identify and outline the services provided by the franchisor to each franchisee. This manual would likely include such services as training, inspection, record-keeping, financial planning, and quality-control standards and procedures, as well as recommend forms and procedures for use in evaluating the performance of the franchised business.

Most of the personal interactions between the franchisor and the franchisee occur through the franchisor's field representatives, who periodically (often monthly) visit the franchisee to discuss overall operations, sales performance, problems in production, sales promotions that were or were not effective, training needs, upcoming promotional campaigns, or any problems with the building, work process, or equipment. An inspection of the facility might also be included, or a review of records kept by the franchisee. Because the field representative is the mouthpiece of the franchisor, he or she must thoroughly understand operations procedures, comprehend the details of the franchising agreement, and have good human relations skills. Also, the field representative must serve as the promoter and motivation builder for the franchisor, lifting sagging spirits whenever they are evident in the franchised unit. A weekly telephone call or regular e-mail inquiries about "how things are going...and...how can I help you?" have proven to provide a morale boost to franchisees and their staff.

8-2g   Quality-Control Forms

Proper quality control helps the franchisee maintain desired standards of product quality, service performance, and presentation. Standards appropriate to the market niche targeted by the franchise system must be strictly adhered to by both franchisor and franchisee. Franchisors generally want the highest possible standards for their product and its delivery in the marketplace because they realize that consumers are becoming increasingly interested in product quality. A franchise system's reputation can be permanently tarnished by a greasy donut, a bad cup of coffee, a surly sales representative, or an indifferent counter clerk. The franchisor must address each point of contact between the franchised business and the customer and develop standards for product quality as well as for interaction with the customer. Policies and standards should exist for the following types of customer interactions: credit on product or service sold; technical services available; maintenance services available (if applicable); customer inquiries about the company; products, product features, delivery schedules, or other backlog policies; and how complaints or adjustments to purchases are to be made.

New franchisees might find the franchise system's field representative visiting the business weekly or perhaps even daily during the first weeks or months of operation with the dual purpose of helping the franchisee and grading the performance of the new franchised business. General areas of quality control will include at least the physical appearance of the business location, adherence to operating procedures and conformance to quality-control standards, and personal appearances of employees. Once the new franchised business is running smoothly, the frequency of visits tends to diminish, with visits made on a biweekly, monthly, or bimonthly basis.

The evaluation forms used by field representatives should be included in the field support manual, with an explanation of what is being evaluated and how the evaluated data will be used. Inclusion of such forms and their explanations is important to ensure an atmosphere of trust and openness between the franchisor and the franchisee.

8-2h   Pre-Opening Manual

Most franchisors prepare a **pre-opening manual**. Usually the manual is not lengthy or overly descriptive. The manual almost always includes checklists of activities and steps that must be completed before a grand opening can take place. The four time periods considered important prior to the grand opening of a franchised business are as follows:

1. Six months prior to grand opening

2. Three to six months prior to grand opening

3. One to three months prior to grand opening

4. Thirty days prior to grand opening

These checklists help the franchisee follow a logical plan to complete essential activities before opening the business. A time-balanced approach helps ensure that the franchisee has not forgotten to complete these activities or is not trying to accomplish too much before the grand opening. Table 8-3 presents checklists of activities to be completed six months and then three to six months prior to the grand opening.

From examination of the items included in Table 8-3, we see that the franchise feasibility study must be approved, and the necessary legal, financial, site, and building requirements must be fulfilled and approved. Also, the first "publicity" for the new business can take place with the

| TABLE 8-3 | TYPICAL CHECKLISTS FOR FRANCHISEES THREE TO SIX MONTHS PRIOR TO OPENING |

Six Months Prior to Grand Opening

_____ Yes	_____ No	Franchise feasibility study completed
_____ Yes	_____ No	Franchising agreement completed
_____ Yes	_____ No	Financing available
_____ Yes	_____ No	Site selection announced
_____ Yes	_____ No	Building blueprints approved
_____ Yes	_____ No	Franchisor–franchisee relationship developed

Three to Six Months Prior to Grand Opening

_____ Yes	_____ No	Instructions begun
_____ Yes	_____ No	Formal franchisee training completed
_____ Yes	_____ No	Fixtures and equipment ordered
_____ Yes	_____ No	Name registered
_____ Yes	_____ No	Bank account opened
_____ Yes	_____ No	Licenses applied for

announcement of the new site for the franchised business. These activities are followed by the less visible but essential activities of training new franchisees, ordering fixtures and equipment, registering the name of the business with the state, county, and city if necessary, opening a bank account, and applying for appropriate licenses.

Table 8-4 identifies typical activities during the three months prior to opening. Notice how the checklist items become more external and public-oriented as the opening date approaches. Also,

| TABLE 8-4 | TYPICAL CHECKLIST FOR FRANCHISEES THREE MONTHS TO THIRTY DAYS PRIOR TO OPENING |

One to Three Months Prior to Opening

_____ Yes	_____ No	Basic instruction completed
_____ Yes	_____ No	Fixtures received and installed
_____ Yes	_____ No	Early publicity developed
_____ Yes	_____ No	"Coming Soon" sign displayed
_____ Yes	_____ No	IRS forms and schedules, withholding schedules, and employment wage and hour regulations obtained
_____ Yes	_____ No	Inventory ordered
_____ Yes	_____ No	All utilities and services arranged
_____ Yes	_____ No	Hiring, bonding, and training of personnel begun

Thirty Days Prior to Opening

_____ Yes	_____ No	Staff training by field representative received
_____ Yes	_____ No	In-store franchisee training received
_____ Yes	_____ No	All construction and installation of fixtures and equipment completed and inspected
_____ Yes	_____ No	Merchandise displayed
_____ Yes	_____ No	Grand opening publicized/advertised
_____ Yes	_____ No	Grand opening program followed

the basic activities essential to opening a business are shown, such as installing fixtures, ordering inventory, arranging for utilities, initiating the bonding and training of persons selected as employees, training franchisees in the store, developing displays, and inspecting any construction that has been required as well as the fixtures or equipment to be used in the business.

8-2i   Site Inspection Manual

Part of the motivation for a franchisor to develop a franchisee system is to ensure consistency throughout the business units in the system. A franchisor should develop an approach to site inspection that helps the franchise system achieve consistency in the external features of the outlet. A **site inspection manual** for a franchise system that must attract customers to the business location is typically more detailed than a manual for a system that takes the service to the customer. Rather elaborate site inspection criteria are used for franchised businesses such as hotels or motels, auto repair shops, nursing homes and health care facilities, general merchandise stores, automobile dealers, furniture and home furnishing stores, and restaurants.

The items included in a site inspection will vary depending on the business being examined. Typically, an inspection will look at certain physical attributes as well as less-tangible factors such as store ambience, attractiveness of decor, cleanliness of restrooms and operating equipment, neatness of customer service and work production areas, and personal appearance of employees. Figure 8-3 presents an example of a form that might be included in a franchisor's site inspection manual.

The sample site inspection form identifies two major categories, appearance and maintenance. The appearance category lists items for inspection that are internal and external to the business facility. The maintenance category contains items by which to rate neatness and cleanliness of customer and employee work areas, as well as adherence by the franchisee to the recommended preventive maintenance program. From the completed form, one can readily see that the location being inspected is a newly constructed site at which some work on the grounds and parking area needs to be completed. The equipment and interior features receive high marks, as would be expected of a newly constructed building provided it has been built in accordance with the franchisor's specifications. Note the item "ceiling and lights." The field supervisor has recommended that the franchisee add more lighting under the soffit above the service counter in the hot tub showroom. With the business facing northwest, the lighting in the showroom could be improved during the morning hours by addition of a fluorescent lamp above the service counter whose fixture is hidden within the soffit. Such "differences" between one franchised business location and another are understandable. Not all businesses can face east or south in order to enjoy daylight in the customer service areas. The field supervisor has found the promotional items on the service counter in disarray and a life-size display promotion sign placed too close to the entrance, preventing customers from entering the business comfortably. Recommendations are indicated on the form. The work area of the franchisee passed inspection with flying colors. Each item for inspection was rated highly in accordance with specifications set. Also, the preventive maintenance program implemented by the franchisee was shown to be in accordance with the recommended time intervals, and internal records indicate that the maintenance has been performed.

A franchisor's site inspection manual will describe each item that is included in an inspection, along with the criteria used and procedures to be followed by the franchisee. Each maintenance item may have a daily or weekly log for the franchisee to complete. The appearance features are to be checked every day. The value of a site inspection for the franchisee is to help that person make changes that will enhance the image of the business to its customers and in the community in general. To the franchisor, the completed site inspection checklist provides regular, written information gathered by the field representative about important quality-control features of the franchise system. Another major category for inspection and evaluation is personnel. Information regarding appearance and behavior of employees, attitude of the franchisee, turnover rates,

APPEARANCE	Good	Satisfactory	Unsatisfactory	Comments
External:				
Building	X			New
Grounds			X	Sod to be placed
Access	X			Near major intersection
Parking			X	Lines to be painted
Overall		X		Deficiencies to be completely rectified within one week according to franchisee
Internal:				
Equipment	X			New
Walls	X			Freshly painted
Ceiling and Lights		X		Too dim in A.M.
Floors	X			Clean, bright
Counters and Fixtures	X			Clean, dust-free
Furniture	X			New
Signage	X			New
Overall	X			Request additional lighting around soffit of serving counter
MAINTENANCE	**Good**	**Satisfactory**	**Unsatisfactory**	**Comments**
Customer Areas:				
Entry		X		Sales display too close
Order/Purchase		X		Promo in disarray
Seating			X	Too tight
Exit	X			Good egress
Restrooms	X			Clean/neat
Overall			X	Promo displays to be put in front and side windows away from door; recommended modification in seating arrangement for better traffic flow
Work Area:				
Production		X		Clean
Storage		X		According to manual
Office	X			Orderly
Traffic-ways		X		Clear, uncluttered
Overall		X		Daily maintenance of work areas is evident. Well organized and clean.
Preventive:				
Adherence to schedule on equipment		X		Records approved
External/Internal:				
Signage		X		O.K.
Insect/Rodent		X		Records approved
Overall		X		First month of operation records are in order for each area.

Location: Cincinnatti   Date: 10/17/07   Field supervisor: Al Belz

FIGURE **8-3**

Sample Site Evaluation Form

absenteeism, and sick days used can be requested by the franchisor. The purpose of collecting information about personnel at a franchised location is to provide a vehicle for discussion between the field representative and the franchisee about any problems or issues involving employees and to help the franchisee encourage and maintain high-quality customer service.

8-2j   Recordkeeping Manual

The franchisor, working with an accountant, needs a **recordkeeping manual** in which to develop a standardized accounting and recordkeeping system. A well-planned system will provide a means of obtaining accurate financial information with a minimum of time and effort. The recordkeeping parts of the financial system should allow for weekly, biweekly, or monthly income statements reflecting sales and expenses, a cash budget which helps the business plan its financial activities, and a balance sheet on a monthly, quarterly, semiannual, or annual basis. Most franchisors require the reporting of the following on a weekly, biweekly, or monthly basis: total sales, cost of goods sold, and labor costs. The franchisor will also generally recommend the accounting package that the franchisee uses for recordkeeping purposes (and reporting information back to the franchisor). Seeing financial information in graphic form as Figure 8-4 enables the franchisor and franchisee to quickly monitor performance.

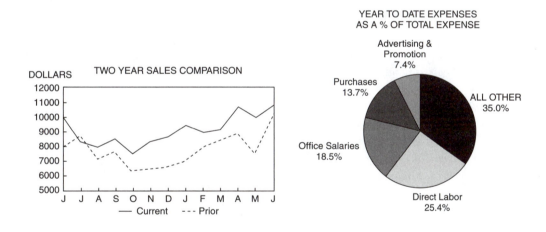

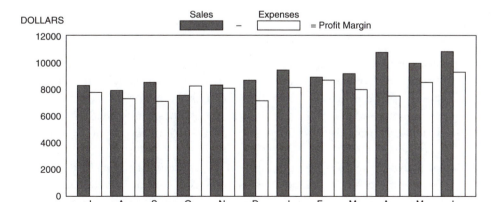

FIGURE 8-4

Operating Statement Performance Graphs

Source: ©1984 Copyright Comprehensive Accounting Corporation. ® COMPREHENSIVE is a service name

Bud Hadfield

Kwik Kopy Corporation

A truly successful entrepreneur must be familiar with the dark side of failure...a person who has tasted the bitterness of defeat but is possessed of the persistence, drive, ambition, and vision to rebound. F. C. (Bud) Hadfield is such a man.

In 1967, Hadfield discovered a new positive imaging camera. That was the very beginning of what later developed into Kwik Kopy Corporation.

Hadfield is now chairman of the board of the International Center for Entrepreneurial Development, the parent company which includes Kwik Kopy Printing (located in thirteen countries), American Wholesale Thermographers, The Ink Well, Copy Club, and Franklin's Printing. As a group, the companies comprise the largest quick printing chain in the world with annual sales in excess of $450 million. Just recently added to their growing family is their newest franchise, Parcel Plus.

Hadfield is the author of Wealth within Reach, *an inspirational and practical book about attaining success in business. No matter how people phrase the question—What was the most exciting or unforgettable moment in Kwik Kopy's history?—maybe Bud's answer requires no hesitation and is always the same. Here is his story:*

It began when a disgruntled franchise owner persuaded a number of other owners to join him in a $21 million suit, with treble damages—it totaled $63 million. They sued under the RICO provision of the law. In case the term isn't familiar to you, and I hope there is no reason it should be, this is the statute the Justice Department had enacted to more easily prosecute the Mafia and other elements of organized crime, including drug traffickers.

I can spin a joke about the suit now. I occasionally boast that we emerged stronger and more secure as a result of it. I do believe that until you have been tested, you can't know what kind of character you and your employees have. We found out. We were tested. And, at the time, I was angry, worried, bitter, fearful, uncertain, a walking ball of barbed wire. The thought of losing your company and good people losing their jobs does that to you.

At last the case went into pretrial hearings in Atlanta, and a federal judge ruled in our favor on virtually every point. In the end, the attorneys got together and a settlement was more or less brokered by the judge. On its face, the judgment very clearly absolved Kwik Kopy of any wrongdoing, denied all of the allegations in the plaintiffs' petition, and awarded Kwik Kopy compensation in the amount of $725,000.

SUMMARY

The promotional and operations package represents the support a franchisor provides a franchisee. Often these two forms of support are divided into two separate packages, the promotional package and the operations package. The promotional package contains the materials used by the franchisor to solicit prospective franchisees to the franchise system, the basic information concerning the franchise, and the follow-up forms used to trace to conclusion the actions and decision made on each prospective franchisee.

The promotional package contains the recruitment, promotional training and schooling, and supplementary services offered by the franchisor as well as the approach taken to developing administrative control over the recruitment, selection, and training process of franchisees. When carefully prepared, this package provides a franchisor with clear purposes, policies, and procedures for the recruitment, promoting, selection, and training of franchisees. Also, by incurring and documenting the actual costs in development of this package, the franchisor has a basis for forecasting the costs associated with franchisee recruitment in the future growth periods of the franchise system.

The prospective franchisee's view on the promotional package is different from the franchisor's view. The prospective franchisee is interested primarily in learning the requirements associated with owning a franchise, how it operates, and what services the franchisor provides, often for the sake of comparison. Specific information is often sought, including the financial requirements of purchasing the franchise, site, and equipment; building information; marketing factors and assistance from the franchisor; termination, cancellation, renewal, and restrictions that can be placed on a franchisee; and the financial solidity of the franchising system itself.

The operations package contains materials often separated into different manuals that address specific parts of the operations of the franchisor's approach to business, including operations, training, location selection criteria, marketing, advertising, field support, quality control, pre-opening, site inspection, and reporting/accounting forms and requirements. The material contained in the manuals is vitally important to a franchisee, helping reduce the risk of business failure because the errors and uncertainties have been worked out. The franchisee is guided and supported by the franchisor's proven methods of doing business in the particular industry.

KEY TERMS

Advertising manual: a guide to effective communication and promotion of the franchised product to the targeted audience covering at least four topics: advertising, promotion, graphics and signage, and public relations.

Field support manual: identifies the services provided by the franchisor to each franchisee, including such services as training, inspection, recordkeeping, financial planning, and quality-control standards and procedures, as well as recommend forms and procedures for use in evaluating the performance of the franchised business.

Follow-up contact information form: provides basic information about the first contact; including the type of information provided and activities completed that comprise a step-by-step sequence leading to an agreement between the prospect and the franchisor.

Formal training program: a structured program for the franchisor to help new franchisees develop specific knowledge about the franchise system and the business factors important to running a successful franchised unit.

Marketing manual: describes the franchisor's marketing philosophy; discusses in detail the features and characteristics used to market the franchised business's offering, including information about packaging, labeling, and consumer services that franchisees should make available.

Ongoing training: on-site training provided by field staff of the franchisor after the franchisee has entered business.

Operating manual: the bible of the franchise system that is a ready and regular reference to address the vagaries and uncertainties of day-to-day operations of the franchised business.

Operations package: the second part of a franchise package, usually fairly extensive and often put in the form of manuals; assists the franchisee to properly conduct the operations of the franchise.

Personal contact information sheet: form for recording preliminary information about a prospective franchisee, including the prospect's name, address, and phone number, how the contact was made, and an impression of that initial contact, recorded by the person contacted.

Pre-opening manual: includes checklists of activities and steps that must be completed before a grand opening can take place.

Promotional package: the carefully prepared information developed and given by the franchisor to prospective franchisees in order to (1) solicit franchisee applicants to the franchise system, (2) provide basic information about the franchise, and (3) illustrate the follow-up forms used to sign franchisees.

Recordkeeping manual: describes a standardized accounting and recordkeeping system that will provide a means of obtaining accurate financial information with a minimum of time and effort.

Recruitment package: consists of a recruitment brochure, a disclosure document, and other information about the benefits and opportunities of becoming a franchisee with the franchise system; used as part of the franchisor's response to initial inquiries by a prospective franchisee.

Site inspection manual: describes each item that is included in an inspection, along with the criteria used and procedures to be followed by the franchisee including a daily or weekly log for the franchisee to complete.

Training manual: a guide for teaching operating procedures and personnel management used in formal and ongoing training programs; ideally fills in the gaps between the knowledge of a prospective franchisee or future employee and the level of performance expected by the franchisor.

REVIEW QUESTIONS

1. What are the typical components of a franchisor's promotional package?

2. How does the information of interest to a prospective franchisee differ from what the franchisor puts into the promotional package?

3. What information is typically included in a franchisor's brochure?

4. Briefly describe each of the major manuals a franchisor may develop. What is the purpose of each? What are the primary elements contained in each?

5. Why should a franchisor develop manuals or information booklets for prospective franchisees and franchisees-in-training?

CASE STUDY

Certain-teed Rental System

In a midwestern city with a population of about 160,000, John Certain believes he has developed a wonderful idea for a franchising business. John has been the owner and operator of a late-model used car sales business for over ten years. The business has been successful, even though John has experienced several lean years.

Considering various ways to increase cash flow, John began thinking that renting used cars might be profitable. As a result, John has begun a rental business as a sideline to his used car sales business. The rental business has been quite successful during the first five months of operation and has led John to thinking about franchising. He is considering franchising his rent-a-car concept based on two primary factors: (1) the business would rent used rather than new cars; and (2) the lower rental fees would appeal to budget-conscious travelers and to government and business clientele. John wants to develop the franchise trademark and logo around his name, so he came up with "Certain-teed Rental System."

John obtained a list of used car dealers from his state's Used Car Dealer Association and is working on a franchise brochure to mail to this group of dealers. He sees the attraction to used car dealers to become franchisees as being their ability to increase utilization of current facilities by having a profitable secondary business with minimal additional expenses. Also, rental of used cars should increase floor traffic in the sales section, as well as be a good outlet for some hard-to-sell trade-in vehicles.

Considering today's budget consciousness, rental car users would be more concerned with daily cost of a car than with the car's vintage. John believes he could undercut the average price of new-car rentals by about 50 percent; and, the market is wide open, as literally thousands of cities are without a major new or used rental car company.

John knows he must create some administrative policies and develop operational procedures for prospective franchisees. Based on his experiences and recent conversations with friends in the used car business, he plans to address the following areas: an insurance liability pool for franchisees to join if they so desire; logos and trademark design and appropriate usage; design of the customer contact; tax benefit possibilities for a franchisee; maintenance/safety guidelines for rental cars; a computerized bookkeeping system; promotional kits for advertising; and a proposed schedule of gross income based on level of rental business activity.

CASE QUESTIONS

1. What else should John Certain consider?

2. Has he missed any major areas of administrative or operational policy?

REFERENCES

Bekey, Michelle, "How a Little Company Got Big," *Venture* (September 1985): 52–53.

Besanko, David, David Dranove, and Mark Shanley, *Economics of Strategy* (New York: Wiley, 1996).

Boroian, Donald and Patrick Boroian, *The Franchise Advantage* (Schaumburg, IL: National BestSeller Corporation, 1987).

Curry, J.A.H., et al., *Partners for Profit: A Study of Franchising* (New York: American Management Association, Inc., 1966).

Day, George S., *Strategic Market Planning: The Pursuit of Competitive Advantage* (St. Paul, MN: West Publishing Company, 1984).

Elgin, Jeff. "The Best Franchise Advice You'll Get," 15 March 2007, http://entrepreneur.com/franchise/buyinga/franchise/franchisecolumnist.

Hisrich, Robert D. and Michael P. Peters, *Entrepreneurship*, 3rd ed. (Chicago: Irwin Publishing, 1995).

Hodgetts, Richards and Donald Kuratko, *Effective Small Business Management*, 5th ed. (New York: Harcourt Brace Publishers, 1995).

Ivancevich, John, Peter Lorenzini, Stephen Skinner, with Philip Crosby, *Management: Quality and Competitiveness*, 2nd ed. (Chicago: Irwin Publishing, 1997).

Justis, Robert T. and Richard J. Judd, *Franchising* (Cincinnati: South-Western Publishing, 1989).

Justis, Robert T. and Richard J. Judd, "Master Franchising," *Journal of Small Business Management* 24(3) (July 1986): 16–21.

Lewis, Pamela, Stephen Goodman, and Patricia Fandt, *Management: Challenges in the 21st Century* (New York: West Publishing, 1994).

Lovelock, Christopher H., *Services Marketing* (Englewood Cliffs, NJ: Prentice-Hall, Inc., 1984).

Mendelsohn, Martin, *The Guide to Franchising*, 4th ed. (New York: Pergamon Press, 1985).

Megginson, William, Mary Jane Byrd, Charles Scott, and Leon Megginson, *Small Business Management*, 2nd ed. (Chicago: Irwin Publishing, 1997).

Siebert, Mark, "Can You Franchise an Unsexy Company?" 15 March 2007, http://entrepreneur.com / franchises/franchisingyour business/art.

Siebert, Mark. "The Importance of Brand Sizzle," 15 March 2007, http://entepreneur.com/ franchises/franchisingyour business/art.

Siropolis, Nicholas, *Small Business Management*, 5th ed. (Boston: Houghton Mifflin Company , 1994).

"The Franchise 100: The Most Profitable Franchises in America for the Franchisee," *Venture* (September 1985): 40–46.

Vaughn, Charles L., *Franchising*, 2nd ed. (Lexington, MA: Lexington Books, 1979).

Wheelen, Thomas and J. David Hunger, *Strategic Management and Business Policy*, 5th ed. (New York: Addison-Wesley Publishing, 1995).

Wiseman, Edith, "Choosing the Right Territory," *FRANdata Research e-Newsletter* (Arlington, VA: FRANdata, 13 March 2007).

NOTE

1. M. Seibert, "The Importance of Brand Sizzle," 15 March 2007, Entrepreneur.com.

LOCATION AND SITE SELECTION

In studying this chapter, you will:

- **Learn how site selection can mean the difference between success and failure for a franchised business.**

- **Understand how the site selection process fits into an overall growth plan for a multiunit franchised business.**

- **Learn an approach to allocating franchises within a geographic area and for selecting specific sites within those areas.**

- **Understand how the difference in type of business can influence location and site selection decisions.**

- **Recognize the importance of market share to site selection.**

INCIDENT

Eva and Carlos have made the decision to franchise their music store chain. Currently, they jointly own and manage four music stores in two state university towns. They credit their tremendous volume of business to the college student market. Eva and Carlos center their marketing strategy on the college community and they time their major promotions to coincide with the university calendar of events.

To adequately serve the college student market, a store manager needs to be aware of student tastes and trends. Because of this, Eva and Carlos believe they could not successfully operate a new business in other university towns outside their state. They have determined the logical alternative is to franchise.

First they want to find prospective franchisees in other state university towns. Once Eva and Carlos find the type of franchisee they feel would be capable of handling a business, that person will go through a six-week training period. Each potential franchisee will work in one of the existing stores and learn the ins and outs of the retail music business. Then the new franchisees will begin operating their own stores in their towns. All music ordering will be channeled through Eva and Carlos; however, the franchisee will have the freedom to determine the quantities and selections in demand in their local communities. The franchisee will also receive weekly window layouts and a page of promotional ideas. The franchisee will have the option to use these ideas when and if desired.

Eva and Carlos are convinced that franchising is the best plan for expansion of their music business. Franchisees will have the benefit of Eva and Carlos's experience but will be encouraged to make many of their own business decisions to profitably serve their community. The only problem is that Eva and Carlos are not sure which college town and which site within a town would be the best place to open a music store franchise.

9-1   INTRODUCTION

Whole books have been devoted to the topics discussed in this chapter. Although it is not the purpose of this book to exhaust the subject, we intend to provide some understanding about location, site selection, and layout considerations from a franchising perspective. First, the general considerations made by a franchisor prior to developing a franchise system are discussed, followed by a discussion of concepts and techniques useful for determining target trade areas, development map and market share, site selection considerations, and factors associated with types of real estate programs of franchised businesses. Franchisees' considerations about general location and specific site factors are presented. These considerations are combined into a checklist that can be used by a prospective franchisee to evaluate a proposed site. For the last topic, layout, we present material about layout characteristics for a manufacturing operation, warehousing or distribution center, and retail outlets with perspective on franchised businesses in each of these types of business activities and locations.

Selection of the right location for a proposed franchise outlet can mean the difference between success and failure and can be the crucial factor in whether a franchise will be a moderate or a big success. Location theorists often claim that the three most important criteria for success of any business are location, location, and location! This concept applies to franchised businesses as well. If a business person lacks the knowledge and skill appropriate to the particular business field and is also a poor manager, the franchise is most assuredly on the road to failure. If the franchise has a good location, however, there is a chance the business might succeed even in spite of the owner's shortcomings.

The franchisor should know better than anyone where successful franchise units should be located. Most franchise systems grow out of single-unit stores. The franchisor spends years developing the right criteria for a successful franchise location. One of the best solutions to correctly choosing the right location is to develop a staff that knows the business like the franchisor and chooses the location based on experience, not on the convenience to the franchisee.

Selection of a suitable location is of extreme importance to both franchisor and franchisee. Factors associated with a specific site can affect the initial cost of many franchises and profitability forecasts of a proposed franchised outlet and can also project the rate of growth of the business at the proposed site. A franchisor has the responsibility for planning the growth and development of the franchise system within a particular area, across areas, cities, states, and regions. Both franchisor and franchisee want the best possible site within a locale that displays the demographic characteristics and traffic patterns that will increase the chance for success in the organization's line of business. Further, some franchisees will want to expand at a particular site once they become established, or they'll want to add sites by opening a second or third location. Therefore, the growth plan of the franchise organization is of critical importance to the franchisor and the franchisee as well.

9-2   CONSIDERATIONS FOR LOCATION AND SITE SELECTION

The potential location and site selection considerations are endless. Does a franchisor wish to expand through single-unit franchisees and small geographic areas within cities, or is the franchisor looking for large geographical areas and multiunit franchisees? Will the franchisor have the financial capacity to purchase outright or acquire over time through a lease arrangement the sites that the franchisees will operate? If not, will the franchisee be required to purchase land or building? Will there be any shared equity arrangements between franchisor and franchisee? If the franchise is to be located within a shopping center or mall, will the franchisor be responsible for the lease contract?

Many franchise organizations have established specific retail site qualifications. Such franchises require certain population densities, income levels, and traffic patterns. Martinizing Dry Cleaners generally look for locations where the median household income is over $60,000; 5,000 households within two miles; 60 percent white collar, and mostly female. Other franchises, such as Manpower and Snelling and Snelling, may simply require that a franchisee locate in a downtown or business area. Still other franchise systems, such as those offering business services, may simply require space in the franchisee's home or other noncommercial location.

9-2a   Franchise Expansion

Frankly, site selection and other location considerations are looked upon by the franchisor and the franchisee quite differently. The primary topic addressed in this chapter is a location model for a franchisor specifically interested in the concept of developing territories with multiple-unit operations. A franchisor's plans for expansion would range from this concept, as used by some of the well-known companies (e.g., Ford Motor Co., General Motors Corp., Wendy's International Inc., McDonald's Corp., Midas International Corporation, Kentucky Fried Chicken Corp.) to a single-unit expansion stemming from the franchisor's base of operations and likely to be within the same geographic locale.

9-2b   Overhead and Distribution

Regardless if the intended expansion plans of a prospective franchisor are international or simply local, two points must be considered in developing the expansion plans: overhead and distribution. The plans begin with a determination of what level of operational support will be provided to a given zone, districts, territory, location, or specific site. Consideration should be given by the prospective franchisor to the types of operational characteristics of a functioning franchisor within a franchise distribution system.

A prospective franchisor has numerous details to work out prior to initiating the first plans for expansion. Sources of supply, distribution and inventory scheduling, warehousing (if required within the line of business activity), and costs and profit margins by type of product or service, as well as the cost of acquiring and maintaining the name, design, copyrights, and registration necessary to prepare franchisor–franchisee contracts, need to be worked out. Once determined, such services and their costs should be identified as **overhead** of the corporation, which are the fixed costs of doing business, or as costs associated with **distribution**, which are the services expected by a franchisee from a franchisor, to provide inventory, supplies, or products through the franchise distribution system.

Determining these factors—and their associated costs—is of extreme importance to the development of a franchise program. One of the keys to success in franchising is to have a package that does not require large-scale financing by the franchisor or the franchisee. Another key is to set up the distribution system to the degree that franchisees have faith in the franchisor's and the franchise system's ability to deliver. Therefore, a predictable distribution system that is efficient and responsive to a franchisee's needs, and the legal propriety of franchised names, marks, or brands that are not too costly for the franchisee to support, are considerations the franchising organization should address prior to actually expanding the franchise.

The particular topics listed in Table 9-1 are addressed in more detail in other sections of the book, under legal considerations, franchisor and franchisee financing, and managing the operations process. The purpose of addressing these topics here has been to highlight the importance of

TABLE 9-1   OVERHEAD AND DISTRIBUTION CONSIDERATIONS FOR A PROSPECTIVE FRANCHISOR

1. Determine the steps involved and costs of incorporation.

2. Determine the steps involved and costs of registering to do business in two or more states.

3. Determine the franchisor's corporate capital structure, including projected cash flow and profit–loss figures over the next two or three years.

4. Determine any short-term financing arrangements for selected franchisees to provide funding for building, land, equipment, or inventory.

5. Develop policies for site selection and franchisee involvement, if any, in selecting or approving a particular site.

6. Determine sources for raw or finished goods, inventory requirements, costs and projected profit margins, warehousing needs, or other factors associated with the franchisor's distribution system in order to identify the components and their costs.

7. Determine proprietary status of name, trade, and service brands or marks, corporate logo, and designs or other registrations necessary for the franchisor to operate legally within a particular state or states.

overhead costs and distribution factors and costs as primary considerations that underlie any proposed expansion by a franchisor. These costs can vary considerably, and the philosophy of expansion can also vary from franchisor to franchisor. For example, some franchisors use a shotgun approach, developing as many franchised units within a state or trade area as quickly, practically, and profitably as possible. Other franchisers use more of a rifle shot approach, identifying and establishing a master franchisee within a fairly large territory or district and relying on that franchisee to do the further development within the specified territory. Some franchisors have used the concept of a company store "seeding" as the method to enter a new trade area or state, as establishing a franchisor-owned (or company) store as the first in a trade area lifts the burden of operational support and distribution from the newly forming franchisees within a trade area placing it in the more controlled environment of the company operations of the franchisor.

Once overhead and distribution factors have been determined and their costs have been identified in relation to any proposed expansion, a franchisor can turn attention to the geographic questions of expansion.

9-3   GEOGRAPHIC SELECTION

For successful expansion, a franchisor needs to know what characteristics about the franchised product or service are measurable. The franchisor needs to learn what type of people patronize the franchisor's own operating unit as well as any franchised units. A franchisor would want to know about the people who are primarily from the immediate area around the store.

- Are they residents or do they work in the nearby office buildings?

- Are they male or female, young, old, or middle-aged?

- Do they come in alone, as couples, or with children?

- Where are they on the socioeconomic scale?

Identifying patron characteristics can be useful in estimating market potential and type of clientele for a proposed site as well as for prospective areas considered for expansion.

The Lifestyle Market Analyst, published annually by SRDS (Standard Rate and Data Service) available at most libraries, provides lifestyle market profiles and demographic characteristics of most marketing areas. The lifestyle index includes information about "home-good life; investing and money; sports, fitness and health; great outdoors; hobbies and interests; and high tech activities." In addition to profiling the franchised firm's customer, the franchisor should also analyze the competition and the cost of real estate if the franchisor has a real estate program, and from these analyses carefully develop estimates of the costs of serving any new franchised units in the proposed expansion area.

The overall objective of analyzing locations and determining particular sites for expansion is to forecast the sales volume (and therefore profit) that can be generated at a certain location. Certain areas and regions thus might be considered more attractive than others. The general business expansion taking place across the southern United States is a normal outcome of the population increases of recent years. As people have moved south, cities and even areas of a state have had increased activity such as road building, improvement/expansion of sewage facilities, expansion of power-generating capabilities, and various types of construction including commercial, governmental, and residential. Such activity naturally leads to expansion of businesses offering consumer products and services to meet the increased demand. Other areas of the country have also experienced population increases, but not on the same scale as the southern regions. Surely, every region of the country has interest in enhancing economic development and seeking the increased employment, tax revenues, and business sales volume associated with such development. Some very successful franchise systems have developed in northeastern, midwestern, and northwestern states. Franchise development should not be exclusive to southern states or to any single region. For development, a franchisor needs a logical method to establish what geographic areas should be considered for expansion. If a franchisor intends to become a nationwide distribution system and perhaps international franchise system, geographic market areas need to be examined and those that offer optimal opportunity for franchise system development need to be identified.

9-3a The Location Model

The **location model** is basically a three-step approach (Figure 9-1) to identification of areas for system expansion and determination of specific sites within a chosen area. These steps are as follows:

1. Selection of geographic areas for franchise system development

2. Determination of the number of franchises to be established within a specific geographic area

3. Individual site selection based on criteria used to distinguish between specific site alternatives

Location models can help franchisors take steps appropriate for developing expansion plans for their franchise system. Each step should be fully considered before any further step is taken. Accomplishment of these steps will generally yield a successful and profitable franchise system for the franchisor.

Step 1   Designated Marketing Areas

Step 2   Buying Power Index

Step 3   Individual Site Analysis

FIGURE **9-1**

Three-Step Approach to Identifying Areas for System Expansion

9-3b Distribution of Franchises

The first step in geographic selection is to determine the proper distribution of franchises within the total geographic area covered by the franchise organization. By example, if the United States is to be the total area, then it should be divided into geographic sections, and then into manageable subsections or franchise areas, depending on how extensive a distribution system the franchisor can set up. A franchise area could be an entire metropolitan area or portion thereof, a multicounty district, or perhaps a multistate region.

Designated Marketing Areas

One way of dividing the United States into franchise market or geographic areas is to use the A. C. Nielsen ratings map. The units of the map are determined by **designated marketing areas (DMAs)**. Since that time, the DMA system has gained general acceptance as a basic approach to structuring advertising and promotion as well as determining the extent of distribution systems. We suggest this approach to geographic area selection because a potential franchisor in any part of the country can get information on the particular DMA in which the franchised firm operates or information about other areas of the United States under consideration for franchise development.

The DMA approach divides the United States into dominant television market areas. Each county is assigned to a DMA, with no overlap, according to the market influence a local television media beams to its viewers. A particular DMA may be made up of counties in one, two, or more contiguous states. Criteria identifying the level of market influence as shown on a DMA map are based on viewership rather than political boundaries. The television viewing ratings provide a franchisor the opportunity to determine how the franchised firm's advertising budget might be spent most effectively, through concentrated advertising, dispersed advertising, or on-site promotions within a particular DMA area.

The DMA concept originated within the advertising industry and was designed to offer potential advertisers maximum dollar efficiency for customer/market penetration in a specific area. Advertisers were interested in knowing how much advertising expenditure would be needed to ensure a certain level of customer exposure for an advertised product. A certain percentage of people exposed to an advertisement would be influenced to buy, which would yield a particular level of sales revenue for the company paying for the advertisement.

Using the DMA as the sole criterion for allocating franchises might be more suitable for multiunit franchised distribution firms, where a master franchisee or area-wide franchisee would be established, than it would be for allocating single-unit franchises. The DMA concept is used to determine the overall number of individual franchisees considering forming franchise clusters to pool their advertising dollars in order to launch promotional campaigns. For example, franchises of a well-known pizza restaurant have been allocated in many instances based on DMA areas. This means that if a franchisee wished to establish five pizza restaurants in the state of Texas, the franchisee would be urged to cluster these restaurants within a specific DMA area rather than locate restaurants across DMA areas such as El Paso, Houston, Austin, Dallas/Fort Worth, and Lubbock. These five areas are in different DMA media markets. The cost of advertising for the five would be substantially higher than if the five stores were located in a single DMA market such as Dallas/Fort Worth, where the five stores could share the marketing media costs uniformly.

Population

Another approach often used in allocating franchises is simply identifying the number of people within a particular geographic territory. The U.S. Bureau of the Census tabulates population figures at the state, county, and census tract levels. A franchisor could attempt to maintain "parity" for franchisees by assigning territories based on population contained within a specific area. For example, NAMCO Systems, Inc. franchises territories for the sale and distribution of telephone book covers based on population within a specified territory. Other franchisors, such as Meineke Discount Muffler Shops, determine a specified service area or zone such as a two-mile radius around a particular muffler shop as that franchisee's territory. Other franchisors, such as Southland Corp., which franchises 7-ELEVEN convenience stores, and Midas International Corporation, do not grant exclusive areas or territories. Instead, a right to operate is granted for a specific location only and the franchisor has the right to establish other shops or stores at any other locations whatsoever.

As one can see, there are various approaches that can be used to determine territory for a franchise. The best approach is the approach that works best for the franchisor. The A. C. Nielson DMA concept is one criterion that may be useful to a franchisor considering area, state, or regional growth within the range of possibility. Such ratings and media audience concentrations can be helpful in developing advertising budgets and proposing cost-effective approaches to increasing visibility of the franchise's product or service.

9-3c   Number of Franchised Units

The second step in geographic selection is to determine the number of potential franchised units the franchisor would like to have within a specified geographic area.

Buying Power Index

A useful tool to assist in this determination is *Sales and Marketing Management*'s "Survey of Buying Power," in which a **buying power index (BPI)** is found for each of the geographic subunits of a particular DMA. The buying power index statistics suggest the consumer buying power available in a particular area, which can be compared to the buying power judged necessary for a single unit to operate profitably within a proposed geographic area. Once sales, income, and profitability standards have been established, the number of franchised units viable for a geographic area can be determined. The "Survey of Buying Power," published annually (generally in July), provides a variety of statistical data useful for a franchise location decision, such as population totals, age-group distribution, and retail sales analysis by county or standard metropolitan statistical area (SMSA). The BPI is a powerful tool for determining market potential and can be defined as:

> a weighted index that converts three basic elements—population, effective buying income, and retail sales—into a measurement of a market's ability to buy, and expresses it as a percentage of the U.S./Canada potential. It is calculated by giving weight of five to the market's percent of U.S./Canada effective buying income, three to its percent of retail sales, and two to its percent of population. The total of the weighted percents is divided by ten to produce the BPI.[1]

The buying power index offers a franchisor the opportunity to identify an area's potential buying power. Similar to the DMA, the BPI uses county boundaries for categorizing the market-based information. To use the BPI as an aid in decision making, a DMA is chosen wherein franchises have already been established and have proven profitable. The proportion of profitable units to all similar units within the specific DMA can be used to develop a normative ratio to suggest the number of franchised units that a similar DMA area could sustain. If a DMA geographic area is considered fully developed (saturated) according to the franchisor for the particular industry in question, then BPI information may be useful for maintaining, expanding, or possibly retrenching the number of franchised units within a particular market area.

As an example, a hypothetical franchisor, Anything Fast Food Company, located in Cincinnati, Ohio, conducts an analysis of its outlets in the metropolitan area. This franchisor believes that thirty franchised outlets is the extent to which this area can be developed for Anything Fast Foods. The population of the Cincinnati area of 1,403,500 is sufficient for this franchisor, with thirty units, and the other fast-food firms and their outlets to satisfy the demand for fast-food restaurants by consumers. The buying power index for the greater Cincinnati area is 0.6007.[2] Dividing the BPI (0.6007) by the number of existing stores (30 is the number beyond which the franchisor will not expand because the market is believed to be saturated) will yield a figure of 0.0200 BPI. This figure (0.0200) suggests the lowest buying power index this franchised firm believes necessary to meet the costs and market demands associated with a single Anything Fast Food outlet. In general, when a marketplace for a particular product or service is considered saturated, the addition of more outlets by any particular supplier will tend to hurt other existing suppliers, causing some to leave the market. An oversupply will exist, given the level of demand for the product or service. Therefore, Anything Fast Foods, with its thirty units in Cincinnati, which it considers a maximum penetration level for itself considering the remaining competition, can then apply this minimum amount of buying power (0.0200) it deems necessary to other metropolitan market areas in which it develops franchised outlets.

A franchisor would use the BPI information, provided on a county-by-county basis, in examining new areas for possible entry. While a county-by-county or statewide analysis can be quite useful, it often does not adequately reflect the promotional and advertising needs that a franchisor involved in consumer durable and nondurable sales and distribution would have. That is where the area of dominant influence information becomes helpful. By combining the BPI and DMA information, one can develop a broad scope of fairly concrete information about an overall market area as well as specific segments within that overall market. A franchisee, considering a selection of a second or third outlet to be owned and operated under the franchising agreement, could also use the DMA and BPI information, rather than just site selection factors. For example, an Anything Fast Food franchisee considering additional units within the Santa Barbara, California, area (which has a BPI of 0.1602) could seek approval from the franchisor for a total possible of eight franchise site approvals (0.1602/0.0200 = 8). The franchisee used the minimum BPI figure considered appropriate by the Anything Fast Food franchisor and divided that minimum figure (0.0200) into the BPI figure for the market area within which he or she resides, in this illustration Santa Barbara, with a BPI of 0.1602. Therefore, both franchisor and franchisee can utilize the same information and cooperate in the franchise development program of the firm.

Targeted Trade Area

Through the use of the A. C. Nielson ratings and the buying power index, a general trade area can be targeted for consideration. Some franchisors use this method exclusively, expanding only through the sale of multiunit franchises. This approach to expansion was pioneered in the franchised restaurant business by Wendy's International Inc. It has pursued this strategy nationally and has achieved significant success.

9-3d   Development of Target Trade Areas

The third step in geographic selection is development of **target trade areas** for consideration, which might include specific cities, counties, or sections within cities. Normally a franchisor will do a market analysis of a specific city or county to determine likely areas in which to open new franchised outlets. Some franchisors, especially large companies, such as franchising motel companies, automotive manufacturers, oil companies, and franchisors in the automobile aftermarkets, take extensive pains to examine transportation networks, industrial development patterns, and financial capabilities of the communities in question, and assess the overall economic condition of the community from a historical perspective in order to make judgments about the future economic and business health of the communities. The overall economic perspective relates to how well the local community being examined reacts to higher or lower interest rates, higher or lower unemployment, inflation, recession, and aggressive growth or decline. From this economic and market data, trade areas are judged worthwhile or not for entry. The definition of a targeted trade area may differ from franchised company to franchised company, as may the specific items used by franchising firms to develop their sales projections and particular cost schedules.

There are two basic approaches for delineating a target trade area. If it is the first site for a new franchisor locating what will be the pilot operation or facility, the target trade area is often determined through a "best guess" approach, particularly if the business deals with a unique line of product or new type of service not available elsewhere. On the other hand, the more common approach for proposing sites is to estimate, based on logic, experience, and available information, the site or sites where competitive advantage is most favorable. Stated another way, when one moves outward from a proposed site, at some point competitive advantage is lost to alternative shopping choices. It is within this delineated "ring" around the proposed site that competitive advantage exists. Therefore, a trade area can be considered as a circle from which a significant portion of the business will be derived. Obviously, trade areas are not precise circles; they often appear as amoeba-like forms, or are rectangular or triangular when natural boundaries or barriers elongate or dramatically shorten the area.

Primary Service Area

Whatever the particular shape of the target trade area, the objective is to determine a geographic space within which a **primary service area (PSA)** for the proposed business would be large enough to sustain the business activity and to help it to be profitable. A primary service area is an area from which a retail goods or service provider can expect to attract two-thirds or more of its business activity. The size of a PSA depends on factors such as traffic systems, traffic patterns and conditions, and physical barriers or boundaries such as rivers, undeveloped lands, railroad tracks, or limited-access superhighways. Also, the PSA for a particular franchised business depends on site, overall economic health of the trade area, size of the facility to be opened, and location of existing competition. Therefore, defining the PSA is basic to determining whether a specific area "needs" a particular franchised outlet, whether the area can support such an outlet (or the addition of one more outlet), and whether existing competitive conditions would allow another competitor to exist within the trade area.

A PSA should be selected only after careful consideration of the factors that reflect what the present buying habits of residents of the area are and how the buying habits might change if the franchisor opened a business within the trade area in question. The techniques which follow are directly related to retail products considered as convenience or shopping goods or services, which constitute a great part of the goods and services offered by franchises today. The factors important in determining size and shape of a PSA include the following:

1. *Alternative shopping choices*—that the drawing power of a shopping facility or convenience goods site is a function of the size of population around the facility and the distance to the nearest alternative shopping or convenience facility

2. *Barriers and pockets*—that the potential market is measured in terms of the total market less that share of the total market now absorbed by existing outlets, and that natural physical barriers separating the target trade area from alternative trade areas will determine the market potential

3. *Drive-time analysis*—that the number of customers a store can expect to attract depends on convenience factors such as the amount of time and trouble a customer must exert to reach the store, based on the accessibility of the location to people living nearby, using driving time as a basis for measurement

4. *Intuition*—that the use of a given shopping facility is largely a matter of habit and traditions within a community, which means relying heavily on judgments of people knowledgeable about the economic and market characteristics of the targeted trade area and of people knowledgeable about the particular business activity

Population

Through use of Arbitron ratings, the Lifestyle Market Analyst, Survey of Buying Power, and the buying power index or other appropriate methods, a general trade area can be targeted for consideration. Once this broad delineation of a proposed target trade area is determined, the next step is to estimate and forecast the population for the trade area. Why? Because population is a fundamental source of information about a target trade area upon which site selection decisions are made. The primary data source is the U.S. Bureau of the Census, which conducts a census every ten years. But ten years is a long time, and census data can become obsolete quickly. Sometimes special censuses are made by counties or cities, and usually this information can be acquired at little or no cost from the appropriate governmental office. However, the information is not always uniform with the U.S. census data, as it may only involve fundamental counts associated with housing units and population. The more extensive data from the Bureau of the Census divides the United States into a number of subdivisions: states, regions, SMSAs, and counties. Information is collected and is available to provide the detailed information about population, housing, and income within the uniformly defined geographic area called a census tract.

Other sources that can provide population estimates during the ten-year span from one census to the next include local planning departments of a county or city, local chambers of commerce, and even the U.S. Post Office. When population estimates are obtained from sources other than the U.S. Census Bureau, it is wise to ask about the method used in arriving at the estimates. One should try to learn if estimates are predicted on number of possible postal deliveries, building permits, and building demolitions, or the basis used if a regression model was developed to make the estimates.

Competition

The second consideration is the amount of competition in the proposed site. In evaluating competition in the proposed site, one should first locate all the competition by type or category of competitiveness on a map. For example, fast-food competition might include fried chicken outlets, ice cream parlors, traditional restaurants, snack bars, pizzerias, baked potato shops, and coffee shops. Therefore, when undertaking a study of locating a hamburger-oriented restaurant with drive-thru capability, it can be important to look at all of these types of fast-food retailers as potential competitors. However, restaurants similar to the type being proposed clearly provide the most direct and strongest competition. As a result, one would not give as much weight to ice cream parlors, baked potato shops, or coffee shops, or perhaps even pizzerias, snack bars, traditional restaurants, and fried chicken outlets, as one would to other hamburger-oriented fast-food outlets in the same trade area. When there is wide variation in considering one competitor to another, other factors should be considered such as the square footage of competitors' outlets or the level of sales each competitor might be generating, to reflect how strong the competition is in relation to the outlet location being considered. Further, the image of each competitor should be considered, in terms of how it relates to the market it is serving. For example, in franchised businesses such as auto parts/repair/replacement, some franchises project a high-quality image, stressing service and dependability, while others emphasize price discounting. Therefore, giving the same weight to all existing competitors in the target trade area, even though they may be trying to appeal to different segments of the market, would tend to distort the market analysis.

Three other points should be mentioned in our discussion about location and competition. First, a competitor's square footage is not as important a factor when there is little variance in what the consuming public expects from a certain type of retail business as it is when there is wide variance in customer attitude about company logo, trademark, and level of product selection. For example, when a franchised convenience store is competing with other convenience stores, franchised or not, simply the existence or absence of competition within a certain geographic section of the trade area will enable one to evaluate the strength of the competitive environment.

Second, locating competitive stores or outlets within one area, such as "clustering" of franchised auto dealerships, furniture stores, or fast-food outlets along a business strip or inside a shopping mall, tends to improve potential sales for all competitors because of the added attraction for the consuming public of variance in choice. However, retail outlets that offer very similar product choices (such as convenience stores) tend to dilute the market, dividing up the retail pie into thinner slices as additional business enters the trade area or cluster of stores.

Third, the specific location of the competition in relation to the proposed business site can be extremely important. A site should be chosen that gives one a competitive advantage. For example, being two blocks away from a major intersection when the competitor is at or near the intersection can be a disadvantage. On the other hand, if the store is located more conveniently than that of the primary competitor, and closer to the specific neighborhood or other population concentration from which the customers are to be drawn, the site is likely to be viewed more favorably than the competitor's. The reason is simple: The site is closer to the customer, and in business activity where convenience is a factor, this may provide the advantage over the competitor.

9-3e   Demographic Map of Trade and Primary Service Area

The determination of a PSA is based on careful consideration of factors which reflect the present purchasing habits of consumers within the trade area. A map of the general area under consideration should be used to determine (1) the alternative shopping choices for the proposed product or service; (2) the barriers or pockets of the trade area, as natural or man-made physical barriers that identify the target trade area from alternative trade areas; (3) the extent to which the "convenience" factor (the amount of time and trouble a customer must exert to reach the location) affects the purchase decision, using drive time as a basis for measurement; and (4) the habits and traditions within a community that suggest which trade areas within a community would be preferable to other trade areas within the same community.

Drive-Time Analysis

Drive-time analysis is a study of driving time that uses a proposed location and alternative or competitive locations as the points of reference. A drive-time analysis helps answer questions about the need for and convenience of a retail outlet offering a product or service that has convenience as one of its primary attractions. There is no absolute criterion by which to judge one location as being better or worse than another. However, a generally accepted drive-time limit can be determined by examining the nature of the shopping facility proposed and the nature of the product or service offered to the public. Drive-time analysis helps suggest convenience of one location over that of alternative locations. Convenience is a function of a consumer's discretionary purchasing power and leisure time. More specifically, the amount of trouble a consumer will go through to get to a given location or to make a given purchase depends on how familiar the customer is with the product, how much money is available for purchase, and how much time the customer has to travel to alternative locations offering the product or service. Further, the more important leisure time is to customers, the less effort they will exert to patronize a particular location for the product or service.

As suggested, convenience can be as important a factor associated with a proposed facility as the attributes of the product or service offered for sale. Therefore, traffic conditions, parking, ease of entry and exit, business operating hours, and the mix of products and services available all affect the relative convenience of a particular site. A five-minute drive time suggests trade area for convenience goods such as food and personal services. In contrast, shopping goods such as clothing or specialty services such as jewelry repair, health services, and mechanical replacement or repair can have a trade area that extends to between fifteen and thirty minutes in drive time.

Demographic Data

The habits, patterns, and traditions of a community represent the more subjective information about a proposed site and its trade area. In order to solidify judgments about the worth or quality of a proposed site and its primary service area, a franchised company will often want demographic data about the primary service area or trade area and contrast that information with the overall community data. Such information typically collected includes population, age characteristics, housing, distribution of families by income classification, distribution of heads of households in the PSA by occupational category, retail sales by the county/city/trade area, industrial activity, and perhaps other data comparisons. Some franchised companies, particularly in restaurants, motels, and auto dealerships and service centers, will do extensive research beyond the items listed, considering other factors such as transportation networks, financial capabilities of the communities, and a historical economic reaction rating. A historical economic reaction rating is an indication of how well the business community reacts to recession, inflation, interest rates for short-term and long-term financing, volatility of local interest rates in relation to national trends, unemployment level, and overall rate of economic growth of the community in relation to other communities the firm is considering.

9-4   FRANCHISE SITE SELECTION

Often it is the responsibility of the prospective franchisee to develop the market information. For franchised retail locations, a franchisor normally tells a new franchisee that the company will assist in site selection and must have approval of the final site. Wendy's International Inc. has a single person responsible for the approval of locations; Burger King Corporation has an extensive board-of-review procedure.

Whatever the number of steps and degree of control by the franchisor in the site selection process, a franchisor will typically address approval of a site from three distinct viewpoints: (1) real estate, (2) operations characteristics and sales forecast, and (3) marketing. The real estate view considers the specifics of appropriate zoning, local ordinance clearances, land purchase or lease, property development and facility building, site ingress and egress, and flow of traffic. Operations characteristics include size of unit proposed, breakeven point of sales in relation to cost of operation, and calculations of one-year, three-year, and five-year financial return on investment (ROI). It is of extreme importance that marketing considerations also be addressed in a site selection process to determine who the customers will be (based on demographic profiles) and what are their tastes and preferences. Such preferences or specific desires indicate the "hot points" between the franchisee and the customer.

Often a prospective franchisee is much like the typical person considering entry into business as an independent business owner-operator. In many cases, the franchisee has little understanding about what is required to develop location or to assess existing properties as potential business locations. As a result, the franchisee usually seeks advice from different people, some professional, in addition to seeking the advice of the franchisor. It is important that both the franchisor and the franchisee understand who are the professionals the franchisee is likely to deal with in examining alternative sites and selecting the site appropriate for the business location. These professional parties typically include the following:

1. The franchisee's banker, who will usually lend from 65 to 80 percent of the cost of site development

2. An attorney, who will provide consultation on tax matters, leases, contracts, zoning restrictions, and any other general business developments particular to the community and site being selected

3. A real estate broker, who usually provides advice concerning prime or "hot" commercial areas as well as the relative costs within these areas of the community

1. Name Recognition	19. Traffic
2. Type of Site	20. Competition
3. City/Town Description	21. Direct Competition
4. Area Description	22. Cannibalism
5. Visibility	23. Restaurant Activity
6. Prototype Look	24. Retail Activity
7. Sign Quality	25. Entertainment Activity
8. Access	26. Evening Activity
9. Access Time	27. Students
10. Office Access Corridor	28. Offices
11. Resident Access Corridor	29. Surrounding Area
12. Trade Area Access	30. Surrounding Retail
13. Strategic Position	31. Major Discount Stores
14. Parking	32. Mall Information
15. Drive-By Influence	33. Retail Trade Zone History
16. Travel Influence	34. Retail Trace Zone Age
17. Commuter Potential	35. Retail Clusters
18. Public Transportation	36. Critical Factors

FIGURE **9-2**

Site Evaluation Questionnaire

4. An accountant, who will determine the amount of cash available to the franchisee that can be used for development of the property, as well as advising about the tax considerations (important for all investors or business owners)

In the site selection process, the franchisee is much like a student in the real-world classroom. The quality of information available, the accuracy of the analyses made, and the wisdom of ultimate decisions made by the franchisor and the local professionals may well determine the success or failure of a particular site. However, in most franchise location decisions, the franchisee has the ultimate responsibility for the decisions. Therefore, the franchisee should actively *make* the final decision and not just be held responsible for the decision. See Figure 9-2 for a list of factors that must be considered in this decision.

9-4a Site Profile

Finding the appropriate location involves careful analysis of more than just one site. As the franchisee is collecting information from the CPA and lawyer and is visiting sites, the analysis of consumer demographics for each site being compared and the costs of each site should be considered. A detailed examination of a site should be based on specific factors that address both the sites' characteristics and the nature of the business to be located at the sites. When a high volume of traffic is important, a good arterial street, preferably without a median strip, or a marked highway with a substantial traffic count is superior to a side street, divided highway, or interstate highway. Traffic speed limits of twenty-five to thirty-five miles per hour are preferable to lower or higher limits. Location within a particular block or shopping strip can also be important. Generally,

- ✓ What is the average traffic count in front of the store?
- ✓ What is the average speed of traffic passing the store?
- ✓ What is your primary trading area?
- ✓ What is your secondary trading area?
- ✓ What are the zoning laws?
- ✓ What are the parking ordinances? How many spaces are available?
- ✓ For how far is the site visible upon approach?
- ✓ What is the demographic data for your site?
- ✓ Is the site easily accessible? Can you easily leave?
- ✓ How close is the competition?
- ✓ What are the sign laws for the community?
- ✓ Are there architectural laws for the area?
- ✓ Is the area a new or older area?
- ✓ Is the area financially strong?
- ✓ What is the quality of life for the area?

FIGURE **9-3**

Checklist for Franchisee Retail Outlet

a far corner or a mid-block location that has good visibility is preferable to other locations within a given block. Adequate frontage is a necessity for most retail businesses. Store and driveway frontage of less than 100 feet should be avoided if possible. Typically 100 to 200 feet of frontage is considered sufficient. A width of 35 to 45 feet is adequate for most retail locations.

The homeward side of the street is often considered superior to the side of the street on which the majority of people drive to work. Demographic factors that are given significant weight typically include:

- Concentration of young families with children
- Proximity to schools, high schools, junior colleges, or universities
- Twenty-four-hour institutions, such as hospitals or industrial plants
- Median-family-income households within the primary service area

For some types of businesses, proximity to shopping centers or being located within a shopping center can be of extreme importance to provide sufficient walking traffic in front of the store.

A checklist can be developed by the franchisee that identifies pertinent information about the type of customer sought, the physical site characteristics, and the desires, preferences, and habits of the target customer group. Figure 9-3 illustrates such a checklist. Obviously, a checklist for an auto service center would differ from a checklist for a coffee shop or home decorating business. Table 9-2 is a useful too to evaluate a prospective location.

9-4b   Types of Franchised Businesses

The type of business and how the product or service is presented to the customer can make all the difference in the world in shaping the decision about site selection. There are three types of

TABLE
9-2

LOCATION ANALYSIS EVALUATION

Personality Profile Characteristics	**Potential Impact**
Population size	5 4 3 2 1 x 5 4 3 2 1 =
Age group	5 4 3 2 1 x 5 4 3 2 1 =
Household income	5 4 3 2 1 x 5 4 3 2 1 =
Number of children at home	5 4 3 2 1 x 5 4 3 2 1 =
Gender	5 4 3 2 1 x 5 4 3 2 1 =
Employment	5 4 3 2 1 x 5 4 3 2 1 =
Children	5 4 3 2 1 x 5 4 3 2 1 =
Number of families	5 4 3 2 1 x 5 4 3 2 1 =
Number of single adults	5 4 3 2 1 x 5 4 3 2 1 =
	Subtotal =

Physical Site Characteristics	
Area image	5 4 3 2 1 x 5 4 3 2 1 =
Visibility	5 4 3 2 1 x 5 4 3 2 1 =
Access	5 4 3 2 1 x 5 4 3 2 1 =
Parking	5 4 3 2 1 x 5 4 3 2 1 =
Traffic count	5 4 3 2 1 x 5 4 3 2 1 =
Trade barriers	5 4 3 2 1 x 5 4 3 2 1 =
Site value	5 4 3 2 1 x 5 4 3 2 1 =
Rent value	5 4 3 2 1 x 5 4 3 2 1 =
Population	5 4 3 2 1 x 5 4 3 2 1 =
1 mile	5 4 3 2 1 x 5 4 3 2 1 =
2 miles	5 4 3 2 1 x 5 4 3 2 1 =
3 miles	5 4 3 2 1 x 5 4 3 2 1 =
Distance from office	5 4 3 2 1 x 5 4 3 2 1 =
Distance from home	5 4 3 2 1 x 5 4 3 2 1 =
Construction	5 4 3 2 1 x 5 4 3 2 1 =
Evaluation	5 4 3 2 1 x 5 4 3 2 1 =
Sign/light acceptability	5 4 3 2 1 x 5 4 3 2 1 =
Nearby competition	5 4 3 2 1 x 5 4 3 2 1 =
Nearby shopping center	5 4 3 2 1 x 5 4 3 2 1 =
Nearby offices	5 4 3 2 1 x 5 4 3 2 1 =
Nearby college	5 4 3 2 1 x 5 4 3 2 1 =
Building code	5 4 3 2 1 x 5 4 3 2 1 =
Frontage street	5 4 3 2 1 x 5 4 3 2 1 =
Secondary street	5 4 3 2 1 x 5 4 3 2 1 =
Utilities	5 4 3 2 1 x 5 4 3 2 1 =
	Subtotal =

Frequency Pattern	
Breakfast	
Daily	5 4 3 2 1 x 5 4 3 2 1 =
Weekly	5 4 3 2 1 x 5 4 3 2 1 =
Group size	5 4 3 2 1 x 5 4 3 2 1 =
Lunch	
Daily	5 4 3 2 1 x 5 4 3 2 1 =
Weekly	5 4 3 2 1 x 5 4 3 2 1 =
Group size	5 4 3 2 1 x 5 4 3 2 1 =
Dinner	
Daily	5 4 3 2 1 x 5 4 3 2 1 =
Weekly	5 4 3 2 1 x 5 4 3 2 1 =
Group size	5 4 3 2 1 x 5 4 3 2 1 =
Coming/going home	5 4 3 2 1 x 5 4 3 2 1 =
Coming/going work	5 4 3 2 1 x 5 4 3 2 1 =
	Subtotal =
	Total =

businesses, and their general characteristics should be considered before a checklist is developed by the franchisee.

Unique Business

The **unique franchised business** typically has a craft or high-quality image associated with the product or delivery of the service. Customers are "drawn" to the location from a community as compared to living in the immediate geographic area of the business location. The reason for the wider draw is the uniqueness of the product or service and the limited number of competitors. Examples of unique or specialty franchised businesses include franchised garden centers, picture framing shops, automobile undercoating businesses, or upscale franchised restaurants. There are usually limited choices available within a community for such services or products. Also, there is often a craft or high-quality connotation associated with the product or service in this category. These types of businesses can usually do very well in many locations within the community, even on the outskirts of town, as long as the customers continue to feel that the product or service is worth the inconvenience of going to a business that is "off the beaten path."

Competitive Business

A **competitive franchised business** offers the same or similar kinds of products or services that other franchised or independent businesses provide within the community. Convenience is a major factor in determining site for the business. Convenience food stores, ice cream shops, fast-food restaurants, donut shops, and pharmacy/variety stores typify the competitive franchised business category. They are often located throughout a community with particular concentration in high-traffic and high-consumer-density locations such as established business strips, shopping centers, downtown areas, or near offices or plant locations. It is desirable to have heavy walking as well as driving traffic in the vicinity since the business activity is usually price competitive and convenience oriented. A business trade area is usually limited geographically as determined by convenience factors and amount of direct competition and its location in relation to the business's location. Nearness to direct competition is usually seen as undesirable.

Comparative Business

With **comparative franchised businesses**, such as catalog stores, and businesses selling cosmetics, home furnishings, shoes, sporting goods, hardware and paints, consumer electronics, computers, as well as auto repair shops, lube-and-oil-change centers, printing centers, diet centers, and travel, recreation, and leisure businesses, location should normally be near competitors so that potential customers can compare products. As a result, the franchisee and any employees must be able to explain or demonstrate the advantages of the product or service over competing products or services. Comparative type businesses often locate along business strips, within shopping centers or malls, or on neighboring street corners. High-rent locations are not essential but can encourage sales growth by virtue of the usually higher traffic and consumer density at such locations. Thus, the two keys for these types of business are location near competition for customers to comparatively shop and effective assistance to the customer in explaining advantages and determining value of the product or service.

Obviously, any of the product or service examples cited in the previous three illustrations can conceivably be within any of the three business categories. For example, a convenience store can be classified as a unique business when only one exists within a community. The same can be said for the examples identified in the comparative business category. In essence, the availability of like products or services, the relative nearness to direct competition, and the degree to which customer assistance is of importance tend to suggest the business category in which a particular franchised business activity would be classified.

9-5   LOCATION SELECTION RATIO: SALES/COSTS

One of the more interesting ratios for franchising is the location selection ratio or sales/costs. This ratio is best when it equals one (1) or better.

$$\text{Location Selection ratio} = \frac{\text{Sales}}{\text{Costs}} = 1.0 \text{ or higher}$$

Simply explained, if it costs $650,000 to open a store (turnkey costs including land, building, equipment, fixtures, and furniture) then you should have sales of $650,000 for that start-up year. One franchisor's ideal ratio is 1.2, which is good profit. This franchisor was looking for a new quick service restaurant location, but could not come close to a 1.0 ratio so he was forced to pull out. This ratio will vary from one franchise system to another, but the guideline is important for both franchisors and franchisees.

9-5a   Market Share

Before the final determination is made on a specific site, it is important to ascertain the appropriate market share forecast for the proposed franchised business. **Market share** refers to the portion of total market volume a business would likely have under normal operating conditions. If a market area has expressed demand of $7 million for women's clothing, and there are twenty women's clothing stores competing in the area, the "normative" gross sales for a single store would be approximately $350,000. This would be an average or normal market share for each women's clothing store in that market area and would not reflect consumer preferences, share of market of a particular store, competitive practices of the stores, or their size or attractiveness.

There are different ways to ascertain market share. Whatever the approach, three major variables will likely be considered: population, average amount of money spent by consumers, and buying power of the community.

Number of Facilities and Total Population

An easy (and common) method of estimating market share is to determine the number of facilities and total population within a specific trading area from the census tracts or local chamber of commerce data. Once the population figure is known, and the franchisor determines the average amount of money spent on the proposed product category, multiplying these figures together will yield the area's annual sales. For example, if Sally were interested in starting a fast-food restaurant franchise, she could determine a basic trade area within the community. If this trade area contained 30,000 people and the average person spent $750 per year at fast-food restaurants (as determined from the "Survey of Buying Power" or the "Economic Census of Retail Trade"), then the area's total estimated sales would be $22.5 million. The formula can be stated as:

Individual purchases of fast food × Population = Area's estimated annual sales, or

$$\$750 \times 30,000 = \$22,500,000.$$

$$\frac{\$22,500,000 \text{ (estimated annual sales)}}{25 \text{ (number of competitors)}} = \$900,000$$

Because the business is new, Sally would probably not have sales as strong as existing local competitors. She may subjectively determine that her annual sales level would be roughly $600,000 (two-thirds of the average in the first year of operation). Subsequent sales projections and estimates of market share will have actual sales data on which to base the projections.

Dollar Amounts

A second method of determining market share is to find the exact dollar amounts spent per year on the specific products or services that Sally intends to offer in the trade area. Sources of this information include the *Economic Census,* published by the U.S. Department of Commerce, and the "Survey of Buying Power," published by *Sales and Marketing Management,* or trade publications that deal with the particular products or services. In the example of Sally's fast-food restaurant, the trade association for food restaurateurs in the state identified the average individual expenditure on fast food as $771 per year. With a population of 30,000 in the trade area, the total sales for that area would amount to $23,130,000. However, the estimated sales (or market share) would be approximately $925,200.

$$\frac{(\text{population})(\text{individual annual purchase})}{\text{number of competitors}} = \text{estimated sales per store}$$

$$\frac{(30,000)(771)}{25} = \$925,000$$

This figure suggests the average or typical market share for one unit (restaurant) in the trade area. Because Sally's business is new, she may not be able to expect a full market share for perhaps the first several years. As in the first example, Sally should estimate her sales at a figure somewhat less than average, perhaps somewhere between 40 and 60 percent of the average for a restaurant in the trade area in her first year of operation. This estimate would suggest Sally would have a sales estimate somewhere between $370,000 and $555,000. Actually, tighter estimates should be made, and would be based on the strength of competition, the nearness of the restaurant to other restaurants of similar type, pricing structure, and ambience, as well as the overall strength of the competition within the restaurant activity in the trade area.

A method that includes the three critical sales estimating variables—population, number of competitors, and either individual purchases made or overall purchases made within a community—can provide a reasonable estimate of a typical market share for the average competitor of a particular product or service within a trade area. Unless a franchisor has national brand recognition, coupled with significant amounts of advertising, and good location, a franchised unit in a new market area is not likely to achieve the average sales level for the existing competitors within the marketplace. The checklist suggested in Table 9-2, knowledgeable judgments of local professionals, and prior history of the franchising company upon entry into similar markets will suggest the sales that can be achieved within the first, second, and third years of business. Before a final site selection is made, a map can be used to pinpoint each competitor in the market area. The map is useful in determining where conditions would appear to be most competitive and may identify areas that have been underdeveloped or overlooked by the existing competition. A new, developing, or redeveloping area within the community may be favorable for a new franchise.

9-6 KIOSKS, SATELLITES, AND CARTS

Satisfying the wants and urges of individuals is the driving force behind the increasing popularity of kiosks, satellites, and carts franchise locations. The Coffee Beanery is looking for franchisees who desire more than just one outlet. They are looking for franchisees who want a cluster of stores.

Satellites add a tremendous amount to the franchise system and many franchisors now expect franchisees to establish as many satellite locations as possible. The satellite sites generally have no production facilities. The pretzel oven is generally located at the main franchise store in the mall. The satellites are there as simple vending sites. These satellites have the possibility of boosting profitability and keeping the brand before the customer's eyes. Malls, strip centers, sports arenas, movie theaters, airports, train stations, colleges, and even automotive dealers have proven to be successful satellite locations for the Coffee Beanery.

Some specialty food franchisees have found that running a kiosk in a nearby gas station plus three or four additional store front satellites being supplied by the freestanding site nearby is the easiest way to make significant profits. The satellites need to be within a three- or four-mile radius of the main store and this makes it fairly easy for the franchisee to manage and visit regularly the satellite units. The nearness of the satellite units ensures product quality and freshness.

An example of costs illustrates the advantages of the satellite locations. Generally a full Dunkin' Donuts site costs about $400,000 to build and furnish while each storefront satellite costs only $125,000 to open. This low investment coupled with low overhead means additional profits for the franchisee.

There are some difficulties associated with the kiosk or satellite unit. One of the main worries is the diversion of sales from the main store resulting in a decreased profit picture. An additional factor is determining the costs as well as the employment requirements. When the satellite is initially opened, generally the experienced employees will be sent to start up and handle the first phases of the business. It is important to properly adjust the production levels at the main store. This often means changes in schedules and hiring of new employees for the different units. The satellite units also need to protect against stale goods, limited quantities, or assortments. The satellite could undermine the image and strength of the brand.

Because of limited space, menus and offerings are generally much smaller. A Dunkin' Donuts airport kiosk typically offers only twelve kinds of donuts with several varieties of muffins and coffee instead of the fifty-five kinds of donuts available in the standard store.

The opportunities with kiosks, satellites and carts are tremendous. But you have to look before you leap. It is wise to be cautious before developing a satellite system.

9-6a   Layout

Considerable time and effort will be spent in selecting a proper location or site for development. Similarly, a franchised business should give serious consideration to effective exterior and interior design. With existing buildings, exterior factors can severely limit the normal decisions to be made about structural shape, exterior composition, atmosphere, or image, as well as parking and walking traffic entrances and exits. Typically, the sign identifying the business, the window treatments, and the lighting of the exterior of the business comprise the major decisions a franchise owner would confront in the identification of the business within the immediate trade area. Obviously, each of these factors may be constrained by the landholder or by local ordinance. Determining what is allowable for creating sufficient identification of the proposed business can be of critical importance in the site selection process.

Inside the building, the critical questions concern sufficiency of space and the franchised business's ability to use that space efficiently. Some businesses, typically those that rely on heavy walk-in traffic, seek to construct their own buildings to ensure that the franchisor's preset internal design or layout can be accommodated.

Generally, retailers, service firms, and distributors or manufacturers should carefully design and develop effective interior designs. Appropriate layout can be a major undertaking. A layout needs to be neat, clean, and attractive enough to draw people into the business. Many hours can be spent in analyzing space and in changing and assessing alternative use of interior space before a proper layout is determined. A proper layout will provide for ease of customer movement in the store and allow for efficient work flow. Interior layout should facilitate sales, be attractive, and provide an appropriate atmosphere that makes customers feel comfortable while making a purchase.

Retail Stores

Retail store layout should be attractive and have a positive influence on customers. Characteristics necessary for an effective retail outlet for consumer durable or nondurable goods include the following:

1. Adequate entrance and exit space and doors for normal customer traffic at near-peak times

2. Appropriate service available to the customer, based on the type of decision required in making a purchase, such as assistance in identifying or determining a need, assessing available alternatives, making the decision to buy, or perhaps simply order-taking

3. Appropriate displays, counters, or racks that assist traffic flow and encourage browsing where desired

4. Sufficient aisle space

5. Attractive decor

6. Effective lighting for the atmosphere sought

7. Control of cash registers, goods, and exits

8. Overall attractive atmosphere or ambience

When determining the store layout, it is important that two concepts receive primary consideration: customer traffic and employee traffic.

Customer Traffic

The customer should be able to move freely through shopping areas without feeling hindered or constrained. It may also be important for customers to be able to "feel " the merchandise prior to selection, choose the items they want unassisted, and pay for the items at a cash register prior to departing the store. This enables customers to choose a variety of goods at their own pace, requiring only one stop for actual purchases to be recorded at a cash register or check-out counter.

Another factor important to interior layout is customer traffic flow. The franchised business should determine how a customer's space should be provided to primarily meet the needs of destination traffic or shopping traffic. A customer who has already decided on what to purchase and simply needs to place the order or present the goods at a checkout station goes directly to the area where the purchase can be made. In retail stores this customer typically moves against the normal customer traffic flow. This person is a destination traffic customer with the purpose of making a particular purchase. In contrast, shopping traffic customers seek to "shop" the store, moving from aisle to aisle, counter to counter, or department to department to scan the merchandise available for sale. Most shopping-traffic-oriented stores develop an interior design to move customers from right to left, or left to right, following a pattern of aisles through the store. The shopping-oriented customer will usually follow the main flow of traffic through a store, usually in a right-to-left pattern. This pattern runs counter to the left-to-right movement of a destination-oriented shopper. Point-of-purchase displays, consistency in merchandise display location, and grouping of similar product categories can help reduce problems of traffic flow. Thus, the destination-oriented shopper, who wants to minimize time in the store, as well as the shopping-oriented customer, who wants to use time to examine merchandise and scan the product available, can both be served well by a carefully designed store layout.

Employee Traffic

The second concept addresses the difficulty employees can encounter carrying out their assignments to assist customers. Work flows vary considerably, from sales representatives being with the customer constantly to assist in making purchases, to unassisted customers selecting merchandise from inventory on open shelves for presentation at a check-out counter. Some of the most difficult work flow patterns occur in the restaurant industry. A flow pattern that causes one employee to cross another employee's path while both try to serve customers can be nerve-racking, counterproductive, and potentially dangerous. An employee should not have to interfere with another

TABLE 9-3	WORK ACTIVITY AND PRODUCTION PLANNING CONSIDERATIONS

Work Activity Questions

1. Why is the activity being performed? Is it essential or can it be eliminated?
2. Who is performing the activity and where is it performed in the overall work space available for use?
3. Can the activity be performed in another way? Is another location in the work space available?
4. Can the activity be combined with another operation or set of work tasks?
5. Can the work sequence be changed in such a way that the overall volume of work activity is reduced?
6. Can the work sequence be simplified to reduce or eliminate unnecessary delays?

Production Planning Alternatives

1. Produce goods at a constant level in order to equal the average monthly demand of the product for the year. (Inventory would increase when demand is lower than average and would decrease when demand is higher.)
2. Produce goods only after order is taken. (Produce to meet demand as it occurs; results in no inventory of finished goods.)
3. Produce goods to a certain level to meet expected consumer demand. Subcontract any production beyond that level.
4. Produce complementary products that fit the work-area design and skills of employees to balance out the fluctuations in demand. Attempt to achieve a constant product level.
5. Use sales estimates and prior experience to initiate special sales inducements (e.g., lower prices) when sales volume is expected to be low.
6. Do not expand production beyond a certain level, regardless of demand. Expansion of production capacity should be carefully considered before commitment to expand is made.

employee while serving a customer. This important factor is sometimes overlooked in planning work stations, work processing, and delivery routes to the customer. A common problem is that one employee has to wait to receive the remainder of an order before completing the transaction or otherwise serving the customer. While it may not be possible to eliminate all employee "crossovers" or "waiting lines," it is important to try to reduce or eliminate as many of these flow problems as possible through careful design of the product or service work processes and work flow. Table 9-3 lists points about work activity and production plans a franchisor and franchisee should consider in designing store layout.

Stephen Kuhnau: The Father of the Nutritional Smoothie

A Passion for Healthy Living Positioned

Ask Stephen Kuhnau if he ever dreamed he'd be known as the "Smoothie King" along with spearheading the booming smoothie drink industry and you get a resounding "no!" But his wife, Cindy, is far from surprised. "Stephen is an incredibly determined person and that contri-

butes to his success," she says. "He is committed to a healthy lifestyle and is passionate about spreading the word that good nutrition improves your health, your well-being, and your life."

With nutritional sales exploding, that unique combination of determination, knowledge, and passion has transformed Stephen from a teenager plagued with hypoglycemia, chronic allergies, and skin problems into a successful entrepreneur and the proud founder of the New Orleans–based Smoothie King, a chain that combines their popular great-tasting healthy Smoothies drinks, along with a vast offering of nutritional products and supplements. The Smoothie King chain is so successful that they currently have more than 430 franchises across thirty-two states with more than twelve units in Korea. Kuhnau claims that it was destiny that led him to where he is today, and that his success couldn't have come without the health struggles he faced in his youth. "As I look back on all the challenges and opportunities that I was exposed to in my life," he says, "I realize that they were all pointing me in this direction."

As a teenager in the early 1960s, trips to doctors and allergists brought him no relief and left him frustrated and determined to find an alternative cure for his ailments. Working as a soda jerk at a local Hoppers Drive-In, he began experimenting with the many ingredients he had at his disposal—bananas, pineapples, strawberries, and more. However, there was a twist to his shakes. Knowing that he needed additional proteins, vitamins, and minerals to combat his low blood sugar and to build his immune system, Kuhnau began adding nutritional formulas. In addition, believing he had an allergy to whole milk, he concocted his drinks without the standard milk ingredients. The result was shakes that tasted delicious, boosted his energy, and elevated his blood sugar without requiring him to consume large amounts.

Time passed and Kuhnau found himself in the army reserves and stationed at Fort Sam Houston in Texas where he worked as a nurse for the Brooks Burns Center. The position gave him plenty of opportunities to learn about nutrition and the effect of diet on body tissue. He followed his stint in the service with a position as a leasing executive at Ford Motor Co. in Dearborn, Michigan. When Ford opened a satellite leasing office in New Orleans, the company asked Kuhnau to be in charge. Throughout his successful years with Ford, Kuhnau continued to study nutrition and experiment with protein drinks. When he decided to go into business for himself,

he realized it was natural for him to combine his business skills with his passion for nutrition. In 1973, he mortgaged his home for $65,000 and opened Town and Country Health Foods in Kenner, Louisiana, where he offered smoothies on the side for ninety-nine cents.

Twelve years later, Kuhnau met and hired Cindy Zimmer who had worked for another local health food store for many years. Cindy's interest in nutrition stemmed from her desire to improve the health of her son who had allergies similar to Stephen's. Working together, they realized they not only shared a passion for natural foods and healthy living, they also shared a passion for each other. A few years later, they were married.

It was Cindy who had a hunch that Stephen's hallmark smoothies—formulated on the spot by blending real fruits and fruit juices with an impressive array of wholesome nutrients that Kuhnau researched and tested, along with a nutritional product store—had the potential to be more than a sideline. In 1989, they opened their first Smoothie King franchise on Baronne Street in New Orleans. Three other stores soon followed. Over the years, the steady stream of franchises have helped the company grow to 430 units open. Smoothie King has over $60 million in franchise revenues and over 25 million Smoothies sold in the past year. Smoothie King is also the only business of its kind that carries the endorsement of Heart-Smart Restaurants International for forty-seven of their sixty Smoothie drinks; and the Kuhnaus are positioning themselves for smooth and steady growth long into the future.

"Our ultimate goal is to have Smoothie Kings wherever people gather throughout the world," says Kuhnau with an energy and enthusiasm that is contagious.

Smoothies may have brought Kuhnau great wealth, but the richest reward, he says, comes from the satisfaction he gets when customers become converted to maintaining a healthy lifestyle with the help of his Smoothies and nutritional products. "When customers tell me they have more energy and feel better," he says, "it's the best feeling in the world."

SUMMARY

Site selection and location considerations are usually critical to the successful expansion of a franchise system. Selecting the right location can mean the difference between success and failure not only for a particular franchisee's business but also for the franchise system. This chapter has been written primarily from the perspective of the franchisor, specifically one interested in developing multiple territories with multiple-unit operations.

The location model we have developed utilizes a three-step process. The first step is selection of a geographic area appropriate to the development of the particular franchise system. The designated marketing area (DMA) is a helpful tool for structuring marketing advertising and promotion as well as distribution systems. Second, once a general market has been determined, the buying power index (BPI), a tool utilizing information from *Sales and Marketing Management*'s "Survey of Buying Power Index," can suggest the consumer buying power available in the area under examination. The franchisor would use this information on a county-to-county basis, examining the proposed areas for possible entry and using the buying power information for comparison against the market characteristics and sales levels required for the franchisor to enter a specific market area.

Specific site consideration is the third step in the location process. Specific sites are proposed and examined in a variety of ways. The approach proposed recommends examination of alternative shopping choices, barriers, and pockets that tend to separate the targeted trade area from alternative trade areas, and drive-time analysis.

Ultimately, two or more desirable sites should be profiled for a comparison and contrast of the strengths and weaknesses of the specific sites under review. The site that meets the criteria better than the others would probably make the best choice for the franchised business location.

Once a site is selected, building and layout considerations become important. Effective exterior and interior design can considerably affect the overall growth and success of the franchise system. Ready identification, easy ingress and egress, and appealing atmosphere can help the franchised business on its road to success. Also, an interior layout ensuring customer convenience, traffic flow, and efficient utilization of production space is essential. Clearly, location and site selection decisions can make or break the franchise.

KEY TERMS

Buying power index (BPI): statistics found for each of the geographic subunits of a particular DMA which suggest the consumer buying power available in a particular area; can be compared to the buying power judged necessary for a single unit to operate profitably within a proposed geographic area; determined using three basic elements: population, effective buying income, and retail sales.

Comparative franchised business: should normally be located near competitors so that potential customers can compare products.

Competitive franchised business: offers the same or similar kinds of products or services that other franchised or independent businesses provide within the community; convenience is a major factor in determining site location.

Designated marketing areas (DMAs): units on the AC Nielsen ratings map, which divides the United States into franchise market/geographic areas based on dominant television market areas; help determine the number of potential franchised units the franchisor would like to have within a specified geographic area; may be made up of counties in one, two, or more contiguous states.

Distribution: the costs of services expected by a franchisee from a franchisor, such as providing inventory, supplies, or products through the franchise distribution system.

Location model: a three-step approach which helps franchisors take steps to develop expansion plans for their franchise system and determine specific sites within a chosen area: (1) designated marketing areas, (2) buying power index, and (3) individual site analysis.

Market share: refers to the portion of total market volume a business would likely have under normal operating conditions.

Overhead: the costs of doing business, such as sources of supply, distribution and inventory scheduling, warehousing, and the cost of acquiring and maintaining the name, design, and copyrights of the franchise.

Primary service area (PSA): an area from which a retail goods or service provider can expect to attract two-thirds or more of its business activity for the proposed business; needs to be large enough to sustain business activity and turn a profit; helps evaluate possible locations for a prospective business, identifying locations with convenient customer access and no heavy competition; determined using a drive or walk time analysis to determine zones of probable coverage.

Satellites: additional vending sites which generally have no production facilities; need to be within a three- or four-mile radius of the main store so the franchisee can easily manage and visit the satellite units regularly.

Target trade areas: likely areas in which to open new franchised outlets, where competitive advantage is most favorable; can include specific cities, counties, or sections within cities.

Unique franchised business: typically has a craft or high-quality image associated with the product or delivery of the service; the uniqueness of the product or service and the limited number of competitors draws customers from a wider geographic area than other business types.

REVIEW QUESTIONS

1. What are the major reasons why site selection is such an important decision for both the franchisor and the franchisee?

2. What is the three-step approach to the allocation of franchises within a geographic area?

3. What is a designated marketing area (DMA)? How is the DMA concept used in geographic area selection?

4. What is the buying power index (BPI) as developed by *Sales and Marketing Management*? How is it used by franchisors in area selection?

5. Describe the use of a demographic profile for a specific area by a prospective franchisor. How are the demographics related to marketing the product or service? How does the demographic profile assist a franchisor in choosing a site?

6. Explain the concept of market share. How would a franchisor use this concept to assist in choosing specific sites?

7. Describe basic approaches used to determine market share.

8. Describe how "layout" factors can vary in retail stores.

CASE STUDY

Nina's Mexican-Style Restaurant

Nina's is a casual style, full service restaurant. The average meal ticket is $14.63 per person. The waiters serve some of the finest Mexican-style food in the United States. They are primarily located in the South. The hours of service are 11:00 A.M. to 11:00 P.M. Sunday through Friday and 11:00 A.M. to 1:00 A.M. Saturday.

Nina's, surprisingly, currently prefers to take over well-located existing restaurant facilities and convert them into Nina's restaurants. This has resulted in lower start-up costs and has provided a faster entry into an area. A few restaurant facilities which are suitable for conversion to the Nina's concept are available for purchase or lease at attractive prices. Nina's major criteria for a great site location include the following:

1. *Building Size*—3,000 to 6,000 square feet to allow for 120 to 180 seating capacity; lounge seating for 30 to 50 people and parking for 70 to 110 or acceptable overflow

2. *Site Criteria Guidelines*—(A) strong traffic count of 20,000 plus, (B) excellent access to and from the site, (C) outstanding business/office employment in immediate trade area, (D) distant visibility of building and signage, (E) traffic generators, and (F) major retail shopping center

3. *Demographic variables*—(A) population of 35,000 to 50,000+ in primary trade area, (B) medium to upper income area (large percentage of white-collar workers), (C) age 20 to 45, with a median age of 35 or less, (D) good mix of single family homes and apartments, and (E) high education levels

Nina's is ready to build out across the southern states. What additional criteria should the company employ before building in your city?

CASE QUESTIONS

1. What might be a good location for Nina's Mexican-Style Restaurant in your town?

2. How many Nina's restaurants would you put in your town?

3. How would you determine where to locate the Nina's restaurants in your town?

4. What location criteria do you believe to be appropriate for a restaurant in your town?

5. Is a good location important to a business? Why?

REFERENCES

Arbitron Ratings: Television, 1992–1993 University Estimates Summary.

Green, Charles N., Everett E. Adam, and Ronald Ebert, *Management for Effective Performance* (Englewood Cliffs, NJ: Prentice-Hall, Inc., 1985).

Longenecker, Justin G., Carlow W. Moore, and J. William Petty, *Small Business Management: An Entrepreneurial Emphasis* (Cincinnati: South-Western College Publishing, 1997).

Philips, Debra, "25 Best Cities for Small Business," *Entrepreneur* 22(10) (October 1994): 107.

Schwartz, George, *Development of Marketing Theory* (Cincinnati: South-Western Publishing Co., 1963).

Selt, David D., *Franchising* (New York: McGraw-Hill Book Company, 1980).

"Survey of Buying Power," *Sales and Marketing Management* 145 (July 1997).

Thompson, John S., *Site Selection* (New York: Lebhar-Friedman Books, 1982).

Vaughn, Charles L., *Franchising*, 2nd ed. (Lexington, MA: Lexington Books, 1979).

NOTES

1. "1983 Survey of Buying Power," *Sales and Marketing Management* 131(2) (25 July 1983).
2. "1985 Survey of Buying Power," *Sales and Marketing Management* 135(2) (22 July 1985).

LOCATION AND SITE SELECTION

APPENDIX

Request for Site Approval

DATE: _____

Following the regulations set forth in the TRACY'S RESTAURANT INC. Franchise Agreement, I am submitting the enclosed site evaluation. This site lies within my franchise area according to my franchise agreement.

Site Address: _____

City and State: _____

Country: _____

Submitted by: Name of franchisee: _____ Phone: _____

Address: _____

Corporation Name: _____

Corporation Address: _____

The approval of this site request by TRACY'S RESTAURANT INC. does not in any way create or imply any assurance of the success of this business venture; rather such approval implied that this particular location meets TRACY'S RESTAURANT INC. minimum site standards based upon past experience, research, and knowledge of similar food operations.

This site survey form does not constitute official approval and I (the franchisee) will only purchase, or lease, this property only after the written approval of the franchisor, TRACY'S RESTAURANT INC.

Attachments

_____Site plan (preliminary)
_____Aerial photos (approximately 1″ = 300′)
_____Surface photos (per instruction)
_____Area diagram
_____Area development map—update
_____City street map (approximately 5-mile radius)
_____Demographic report (1-3-5 mile ring)
_____Survey (if applicable)
_____Tax assessor's plat map

Location of Site

_____ and _____
(Front Street)   (Side Street)
City _____ County _____ State _____

Street Address (if available) _____

Far Corner _____ Near Corner _____ Inside Lot _____ Shopping Center Pad _____

Site Characteristics

1. Dimensions: _____ × _____ = Total Area _____

   Net Usable Area _____

2. Grade: _____ feet above/below/same as (circle one) street level

3. Soil Conditions (Describe if unusual) _____

4. What are building setback requirements? Front _____ Side _____ Back _____

5. What are parking setback requirements? Front _____ Side _____ Back _____

6. Existing improvements to be demolished or removed (buildings, UG tanks, asphalt paving, foundations, trees, etc.) _____

   _____

7. Existing improvements to be used or converted (building, paving, driveways, landscaping, etc.) _____

   _____

   If building conversion, give details on separate sheet (include as-built floor and site plans).

Visibility of Site

1. Describe any obstructions to the visibility of the site upon approaching from both the <u>near</u> and <u>far</u> side traffic (adjacent buildings, billboards, trees, etc.)

   Near side: _____

   Far side: _____

2. Is there any freeway visibility? _____ Describe: _____

   _____

Accessibility to Site

1. Describe left-turn access (median cut, middle 'suicide' lane, left-turn lane, protected left-turn lane, median barrier, no left turns, etc.) _____

   _____

2. Is site on "going home" side of street? _____

3. Describe traffic control at or near site (signal, stop sign, none, etc.) _____

   _____

4. Is site in proximity to freeway access? _____ How far? _____

5. Describe any congestion at site (backed-up traffic, conflicting traffic patterns, etc.) _____

Traffic

1. Average daily (24 hour) traffic (ADT) or other available count:

   Primary street _____ Secondary street _____

   Date and Source _____

2. Describe intensity of traffic (heavy, moderate, light)

   Weekday 11 AM - 2 PM _____

   6 PM - 9 PM _____

   Weekend 11 AM - 2 PM _____

   6 PM - 9 PM _____

3. Posted speed limit _____ MPH

4. Estimated actual speed of traffic _____ MPH

5. Is the primary street a major <u>commercial</u> artery? _____

6. Number of traffic lanes: Near Side: _____ Far Side: _____

Activity Generators

1. Describe the <u>shopping</u> activity associated with the site (regional mall, community shopping center, neighborhood shopping center, strip commercial, etc. and its location:)

   _____

   _____

2. Have you talked with some of the merchants and other restaurant people in the area? _____

   Are there signs of vacant retail store space in the area? _____

3. Is the shopping activity the <u>primary</u> activity generator for the market? _____

4. Is the site on the primary commercial street of the market area? _____

5. Is the site located <u>between</u> the major shopping area and the primary market population?

   _____

6. Describe employment centers in the market area (office parks, strip office, downtown, high-rise office building, light industrial, etc.)

   _____

   _____

7. Number of white-collar employees in 3-mile radius? _____ Source _____
   square feet of occupied office space in a 3-mile radius. Source _____

8. Other significant activity generators (hospital, college, amusement park, etc.)

   _____

   _____

Competition

1. Straight-line distance to nearest <u>existing</u> or <u>proposed</u> (circle one) TRACY'S RESTAURANT, INC.

   _____ miles, driving time _____ to _____ location

2. List <u>all</u> direct and indirect competitors within a one-mile radius of proposed site. Include <u>any</u> Mexican restaurant and <u>all</u> national, regional, or local <u>chain</u> restaurants (fast food, coffee shop, cafeteria, smorgasbord, BBQ, Mexican, pizza, budget steak or seafood, theme or dinner house). Make every attempt to obtain the <u>actual</u> sales volume of two or three well-operated competitors.

Name	from Site	Street	Sales Volume
1 _____	_____	_____	_____
2 _____	_____	_____	_____
3 _____	_____	_____	_____
4 _____	_____	_____	_____
5 _____	_____	_____	_____
6 _____	_____	_____	_____
7 _____	_____	_____	_____
8 _____	_____	_____	_____
9 _____	_____	_____	_____
10 _____	_____	_____	_____

Seasonality

Is the site location subject to seasonal population shifts which would cause "peaks and valleys" in sales? _____ If yes, explain: _____

_____

Radius	Population	Med Age	Median Family Income	Persons Per Household	Black %	Latin %
1 mile	_____	____	_____	_____	___	___
3 miles	_____	____	_____	_____	___	___
5 miles	_____	____	_____	_____	___	___

Attach copy of actual demographic report.

Zoning

1. Present zoning: _____

2. Does this zone allow restaurant use? _____

   If not, explain proposed rezoning action: _____

   _____

3. Are there any variances, conditional use permits, special use permits, etc. required? _____

   If yes, explain: _____

   _____

4. Is there any problem in obtaining a liquor license? _____

5. Are Sunday liquor sales permitted? _____

Easements

Describe any easements which may affect the use of the property such as reciprocal parking, driveways, etc:

_____

_____

Signed: _____ Date: _____

Photographic Presentation No.1

Franchisee _____

Location _____ Date Taken _____

Instructions

Photos A and B shall clearly show relationship of adjacent property and existing structures to subject property.

Photo C shall be taken from front center of site looking left along the front.

Photo D shall be taken from front center of site looking right along the front.

Photo E shall be taken from the back center of site looking towards street.

Photo F shall be taken from the front center of site looking from street towards subject property.

ACCOUNTING AND FINANCIAL STATEMENTS: PRESENTATION AND USES

In studying this chapter, you will:

- **Learn about the usefulness of financial records within a franchised business.**

- **Learn about the measuring and reporting of the financial information of the franchise.**

- **Develop an understanding of the purpose, components, and use of the three key financial statements: income statement, balance sheet, and cash flow statement.**

- **Learn about the five primary types of financial ratios and what they measure.**

- **Develop an understanding of the importance of financial statement analysis for planning and control within a franchised business.**

INCIDENT

Tracy operates Tracy's Sandwich Shoppe, a successful deli and sandwich franchise system. After only two years as a franchisor, she has fourteen successful franchised units. Different accounting procedures are being used by a number of her franchisees as a result of their unfamiliarity with financial statements and accounting procedures. Tracy is worried. As the number of her franchisees increases, this problem could compound itself. More specifically, Tracy is considering whether to obtain additional bank financing and this accounting/financial statement problem could jeopardize the loan process.

Tracy believes the solution is to develop a standardized accounting system with software for use on a personal computer. She could then require her franchisees to attend a training session to learn how to use the package, after which they would purchase the software and run the accounting system at their own stores.

Tracy knows the accounting procedures she would like her franchisees to follow, but she knows relatively little about financial analysis and financial planning. She believes computer software or models could greatly assist the standardization effort. Should she attempt to develop new accounting software or adapt an available software package to her needs? What type of accounting software would best suit Tracy and her franchisees? What can Tracy do to find answers to these and similar questions?

10-1   INTRODUCTION

Every franchisor and franchisee must keep a set of financial records. Too often the franchisor or franchisee is a beginner, opening a business for the first time, and is not fully aware of what it takes to run a business, particularly from the point of view of managing the finances. Like many other businesspeople, a franchisor or franchisee may see financial statements as complicated, technical documents prepared by professional accountants and understood only by loan officers. The prevailing attitude may be that financial records are useful only for filing taxes, borrowing money, and reporting to regulatory agencies.

Accounting and financial records are basic to any business, franchised or otherwise. Simply put, **accounting** is a process of measuring and reporting the financial information of the franchise. It is the process by which money, assets, and resources are measured and their flow through the company is recorded. Financial accounting is important, because it provides owners and managers with the information often necessary for making appropriate business decisions. This information should be reviewed by management each fiscal quarter.

The **financial flow** is the heartbeat of a franchised business. It is a written documentation or recording of business transactions shown through financial statements. The financial statements provide a franchisor and franchisees the basic format to report the financial activities of a franchise network or franchised unit. A business owner is ultimately responsible for the functions and operations of the business. Therefore, the owner must keep financial records in accordance with commonly held principles of accounting. Such rules are referred to as **generally accepted accounting principles (GAAPs)**. They include widely agreed-upon definitions, procedures, conventions, and forms, and are used to develop financial statements which may be used by anyone. Because the statements are written to follow standard procedures, anyone familiar with basic accounting principles should be able to read and understand them. Often the format of these statements is specifically mandated by federal or state regulatory agencies, such as the Federal Trade Commission, the Internal Revenue Service, or the Securities and Exchange Commission.

10-2   FINANCIAL STATEMENTS

Financial statements are informational pictures of the financial status of a particular business firm for a certain period of time. Private corporations usually will not be required to publicly disclose these informational pictures. However, the franchisor may be obliged to publicly disclose selected financial statements to obtain outside financing, such as bank loans or lines of credit, or to offer private stock placements (Regulation D stock) such as intrastate offerings (Rule 147), Regulation A offerings, and Rule 144 sales. Generally, any investor or creditor willing to assume capital risk for the franchisor will want to analyze the financial statements. These statements should be audited each year but must be reviewed by the firm's manager each month.

Franchisors capitalizing or financing their businesses are generally required to disclose three key financial statements.

1. Income Statement—or operating statement

2. Balance Sheet—or statement of financial position

3. Cash Flow Statement—or cash budget statement

All of these key financial statements are used by a financial decision maker. We will now discuss each of these statements, with special emphasis on the income statement, the balance sheet, and the cash flow statement.

10-3 OPERATING OR INCOME STATEMENT

The **income statement** (profit and loss, or statement of earnings) is a record of revenues versus expenses for a stated period, such as a day, week, month, quarter, or year. (See Figure 10-1.) The income statement shows the accounting profits or losses of a business through accounting of receipts or revenues minus the expenses (costs of business, goods sold, or related expenses). Once expenses are deducted from business revenue, the result is profit (or loss) for that particular period of time.

An annual statement (often used for tax reporting or for disclosure to stockholders and prospective franchisees) illustrates the financial activities of the franchise for the fiscal year of operation. A fiscal year may or may not coincide with the calendar year. For example, a fiscal year may be April 1 through March 31, or July 1 through June 30, rather than January 1 through

---

TRACY'S SANDWICH SHOPPE INCOME STATEMENT
YEAR ENDING DECEMBER 31, 2008

Revenue		
Gross sales	$ 900,000	
Other	100,000	
Net sales	1,000,000	
Less Cost of Goods Sold	$ 420,000	
Gross Profit	580,000	
Expenses		
Office equipment rental	8,000	
Rent, leases	40,000	
Insurance	15,000	
Depreciation	25,000	
Selling expenses	55,000	
Wages, salary	139,500	
Other	13,500	
		716,000
Net Operating Income or Earnings before Interest and Taxes		$ 284,000
Deductions for Interest Charges		
Interest on bank notes	3,000	
Interest on notes payable	2,000	
Interest on private loan	2,500	
Interest on long-term debt	4,500	
		12,000
Earnings before Taxes		$ 272,000
Taxes (36% tax rate)		98,000
Net Income after Taxes		$ 174,000

FIGURE **10-1**

Hypothetical Consolidated Income Statement

December 31. The income statement can be easily compiled when the appropriate financial data has been collected and recorded.

Usually, income and expense figures are initially entered in an accounting book referred to as the journal. The invoices (bills) are entered into a journal as an "original book of entry." Items not normally entered on a daily basis, such as depreciation, are entered into the journal as adjustments at the end of the month or reporting period. After all entries have been journalized, each transaction is posted (transferred) to the general ledger, which may be a bound book, a computer printout, or even a set of file cards. The general ledger keeps track of all financial transactions by category (wages, telephone, rent, supplies, etc.). Once amounts have been posted or ledgered, they are balanced, credits versus debits. These balanced amounts are then used to prepare the financial statements. This process, while not necessarily difficult, requires time and skill to accurately report the financial activities and the resulting financial condition for the period.

The income statement generally identifies the revenues first, followed by all expenses. The expenses are deducted from revenues to show the profit (or loss). Therefore, the income statement summarizes the revenues and expenses of the franchise during the specific month or fiscal year and reveals a net profit or loss.

A brief explanation of the items included in the income statement is helpful to understand the critical elements and value of such a financial statement. The income statement presented in Figure 10-1 is somewhat abbreviated for purposes of analysis. A large franchised company will have many more items presented on its income statement, whereas a small firm is likely to have fewer items to record and analyze.

10-3a   Revenue or Income

Sales, fees, or revenues flowing into the franchised business are recorded as **income** to the franchise. Revenues generated from normal, day-to-day business (sales) are considered "operating income." Revenues such as dividends or interest from investments are considered "other income." It may happen that certain products become damaged. The business would use the heading "allowance for sales returns" to account for such occurrences. The price associated with sales returns is subtracted from the gross sales. After adjustment, the result is the "net sales" of the franchise.

10-3b   Operating Expenses

The **operating expenses** reflect all the expenses incurred in the operations of the business. They may be summarized from adding the general/administrative expenses, selling expenses, and depreciation expenses.

General/administrative expenses are expenses of the franchisor and of operating the main headquarters. This category may include such items as rent, salaries, wages, employee benefits, insurance, taxes, utilities, and other general expenses. Selling/operations expenses are those costs directly associated with the "selling" of the product. Often these costs fluctuate; that is, as production (or service) activities increase, costs usually rise. Conversely, as production activities decrease, these costs should fall. Items often included here are costs of sales, wages, salaries, commissions, advertising, supplies, travel, car or delivery expenses, dues, insurance, and other selling expenses.

10-3c Net Income before Interest and Taxes

To derive this figure, we subtract the operating expense figure from the revenues. This will show what each franchised unit or franchise system (when figures are available for all units) earned during a given time period (month, quarter, or year).

10-3d Taxes and Interest

Almost all businesses will have to pay some type of tax. Generally, taxes are subtracted from the pretax earnings if the business is a corporation. Corporate taxes are not paid on proprietorships or partnerships; rather, the income is reported on the owner's personal tax return. The taxes paid are based on federal and applicable state taxation levels and regulations. Interest paid on a principal to produce a business revenue is tax deductible. Interest payments are usually considered the highest form of debt in the firm and must be paid when due. This is why debt service reduction is very important to the income statement analysis.

10-3e Net Profit (Income)

The final, or **net profit**, represents the sum of all revenues minus the sum of all expenses and is the profit figure which a franchise reports. This sum is commonly called the "bottom line." Net profit is the amount of earnings available which may be used to reinvest in the business, pay dividends to shareholders, provide bonuses, or provide additional product and service research and development for the franchise system. Overall, net profit is a measurement of the performance of the franchise over a period of time. Usually, an income statement is developed to reflect performance during the month, quarter, or year. It identifies and accounts for income, expenses, and profit. The income statement, when compiled on a monthly basis, will show how much was "cleared" or "overspent" for that month.

10-3f Reinvested Earnings

Often the franchisor will plow growth funds or reserve funds back into the business, and these are usually considered **reinvested earnings** or retained earnings. However, reinvested earnings, unlike other income statement items, are often subject to significant IRS regulations.

A franchisor should be able to demonstrate the franchise system's profitability through data and trends on the income statement. Data trends showing the system's profitability would be:

- More revenues derived from royalties and overall system income than from the selling of new franchises;

- Revenue trends that tend to be increasing, generally greater than 15 percent;

- Increasing net income trend, usually greater than 15 percent; and

- Increasing net income per share, usually greater than 15 percent.

10-4 BALANCE SHEET

A **balance sheet** is an accounting statement which illustrates the value of the assets, liabilities, and equity (net worth) of a franchise at a specific time (see Figure 10-2). The balance sheet (also referred to as a statement of financial position or condition) is simply a snapshot of the fiscal condition of the franchise at a given instant in time. This statement is divided into two

<table>
<tr><td colspan="2" align="center">**TRACY'S FRANCHISEE SANDWICH SHOPPE**
YEAR ENDING DECEMBER 31, 2008</td></tr>
</table>

ASSETS:	
Current Assets:	
Cash	$ 18,000
Accounts receivable	22,000
Inventory	20,000
Total current assets	60,000
Fixed Assets:	
Land	0
Building	0
Office equipment	34,284
Accumulated depreciation	5,716
Total fixed assets	40,000
Total Assets	$100,000
LIABILITIES AND EQUITY:	
Current Liabilities:	
Accounts payable	$10,000
Current portion notes payable	5,000
Current portion long-term debt	2,500
Short-term borrowings	2,500
Total current liabilities	20,000
Long-Term Liabilities:	
Notes payable	2,500
Long-term debt	17,500
Total long-term liabilities	20,000
Total Liabilities:	40,000
Retained Earnings	0
Equity	60,000
Net Worth	60,000
Total Liabilities and Net Worth	$100,000

FIGURE **10-2**

Hypothetical Balance Sheet

counterbalancing sections: (1) assets (what the business owns) and (2) liabilities (what the business owes) and owner's equity (owner investment capital). This accounting equation states:

$$\text{Assets} = \text{Liabilities} + \text{Owner's Equilty}$$

These sections are generally divided into a two-column "T" account format with the assets on the left equaling the liabilities and owner's equity on the right. A one-column statement form would list the assets at the top and the liabilities and equity at the bottom. The assets of the business can be divided into two major categories, current assets and fixed assets. These assets represent the properties of the business which are used to provide for future benefits or sales for the franchise.

10-4a Balance

The concept of balance can be illustrated simply. If a franchise owner purchases $1,000 worth of new merchandise (or supplies) by using credit, the franchise's assets are increased by the value of the new inventory of merchandise or product. At the same time, liabilities are increased $1,000 by virtue of the franchised business incurring an account payable by buying the merchandise on credit. On the other hand, if the franchise owner spends $1,000 cash to buy the new merchandise, assets would be increased by the $1,000 increase in merchandise inventory, but the "cash" account would be decreased by the cash outlay. Therefore, total assets would be unchanged. Liabilities and equity would also remain the same since this transaction would not involve either an equity or a liability account.

10-4b Current Assets

Cash, accounts receivable, and inventory that can be changed into cash within a brief period of time (usually twelve months from the date of the balance sheet, or one cycle of the business's operations) are considered **current assets**.

- Cash—money in hand and on demand, as available in checking or savings accounts
- Short-term or temporary investments, including interest or dividends that can be expected to be converted into cash within one year, marketable securities, stocks, bonds, certificates of deposit
- Time deposit savings that are valued on the balance sheet at either original cost or market value, whichever is less
- Accounts receivable—amounts due from customers or clients in payment for merchandise or services received
- Inventory—raw materials on hand, finished goods available for sale, and any work in process, which usually has a value determined on a "unit" basis
- Prepaid expenses—goods or services bought or rented in advance of their actual use, such as office supplies, office space, insurance protection, or taxes

10-4c Fixed Assets

Fixed assets, often called "plant and equipment," include the resources the firm owns or acquires for use in running the business. Such assets are generally not intended for resale. Land would be listed at its original purchase price, while other fixed assets would be listed at cost, less any depreciation. Also, fixed assets can be leased. When fixed assets are leased, it may be necessary to list both the value of the assets and the liability of a leased property item.

10-4d Long-term Investments

Long-term investments, often called **long-term assets**, are holdings the franchised firm intends to keep for at least one year. Such investments typically yield an interest accrued or dividend paid back to the firm. Examples of such long-term investments are bonds, stocks, other marketable securities, or special savings accounts set aside for specific purposes such as to build a cash reserve, to purchase a new building or remodel an existing business location, or to reduce debt.

10-4e   Other Assets

Resources of the business not otherwise identifiable in a preceding category are listed as other assets. These assets are created from superior entrepreneurial capacity (know-how) or granted as exclusive privileges by governmental authorities. Usually, such assets are intangibles such as trademarks, labels, and copyrights often associated with franchised businesses. The trademark "Big Mac" is a good example.

10-4f   Liabilities

Liabilities of the franchised business include all monetary obligations the firm has created and any claims creditors may have on the firm's assets. They are usually categorized as current or long-term liabilities. **Current liabilities** are debts or obligations payable by the franchised firm within a normal cycle of the business, or twelve months. Usually the following types of liabilities are found in a franchised business.

- Accounts payable—amounts owed to the franchisor or other suppliers for goods or services purchased by the franchisee for use by the business

- Short-term notes—short-term, borrowed funds, often necessary to purchase inventory (The amount shown in the account is the balance of the principal due to such creditors. This is often contractual debt incurred to ensure that essential supplies or functions of the business continue uninterrupted.)

- Current portion of long-term notes—current amount due on notes owed to creditors when the terms of the notes exceed twelve months (Mortgage payments on the business building illustrate the amount owed and payable this year and the amount owed in total for the extended year note.)

- Interest payable—accrued fees or interest charges due for use of both the short-term and long-term borrowed funds and credit that has been extended to the franchised business

- Taxes payable—amounts estimated to have been incurred during the accounting period, as well as taxes mandated to be collected, such as gasoline, retail sales, and worker's compensation taxes

- Accrued payroll—salaries of the owners and nonowners who are employed in the franchised business, as well as any hourly wages currently owed

10-4g   Long-term Liabilities

These are debts usually used to finance capital assets such as buildings, machinery, or fixed assets. **Long-term liabilities** are then balance sheet items entered as mortgage payments, bonds, or long-term notes. These liabilities are fixed cost to finance fixed assets and are contractual obligations which must be paid when they are due. Generally, long-term liabilities are obligations owed over a period that exceeds twelve months or one cycle of business.

10-4h   Equity

Equity is often called the net worth of the business. It is the owner's claim on the assets of the business. In a corporation, the owners are shareholders—that is, persons who have invested capital (as cash or other assets) into the business in return for shares of stock. A franchised corporation's equity would be the sum of the contributions made by the shareholders, plus earnings of the business retained within the firm after paying dividends. On the other hand, a proprietorship or partnership arrangement would have as its equity the sole owner's original investment (or the partner's original investment), plus any earnings after ownership withdraws.

10-4i   Total Liability and Equity

The sum of the total liabilities plus equity must always equal the sum (or total) of the assets.

The things that an investor into a franchise system or prospective franchisees into the system would want to see on the franchise's balance sheet would be financial data that demonstrate a balance of strength, growth, and stability, such as the following:

- Increasing assets
- More cash than debt
- Amount of current debt less than one-half of total assets
- Amount of current debt less than one-third of the stockholders' equity
- Increasing stockholders' equity

Potential investors as well as prospective franchisees should want to see audited statements of the franchise system. The financial statements provided should contain at least two and more likely three years of financial data.

10-5   CASH FLOW STATEMENT

During months of peak sales, generally November and December in retail business, the cash flow position should be quite high; however, during months of slow sales, January and February, the cash flow position for the month may be very low. Also, during months of heavy inventory purchasing, such as September and October, the cash flow position may be low. Cash will flow through a franchise as a result of customer purchases and operating expenses required of the franchised business to make the sales. Additional capital may be received through new equity financing or equity injections. On the other hand, assets may be decreased when inventory, equipment, land, buildings, or even accounts receivable are sold, resulting in a cash increase. This would simply reduce the asset account and increase the cash flow profile. Additionally, most increases in liabilities result in an increase of cash to the business account.

10-5a   Importance of the Cash Flow Statement

The **cash flow statement** (see Figure 10-3) may be the most important financial tool available to both franchisor and franchisee. This statement allows the separate business owners to understand the cash position and to know when each may need to borrow money to meet obligations or invest money because of excessive cash flow. By using a cash flow statement, an owner is alerted to the financial strengths and weaknesses of the franchise and may react accordingly. In addition, seasonal periods and broader cyclic trends can be identifiable. A franchisor or franchisee should always be concerned about the relationship between sources of funds and application of funds.

The franchisor or franchisee, as well as the banker, creditor, tax preparer, and prospective investor, will find data in the financial statement to help them make decisions. Financial decision makers have a variety of financial tools available to analyze business financial statements. Perhaps the most useful of these tools is ratio analysis. The franchisor's comparisons of various items on the business's financial statements provide a clearer informational picture. Specifically, the general purpose of ratio analyses of financial statements is to determine the success of the franchise in meeting its overall business objectives. These objectives are to meet current obligations and to meet interest costs and repayment of long-term obligations while earning a specific return on invested funds.

Although the income statement and the balance sheet are important, they fall short in one critical area: They do not show or explain much about cash flow—the lifeblood of the business. The income statement does a good job of measuring the operating results over a specific period of time, and the

Hypothetical Monthly Cash Flow Statement
Tracy's Franchisor Headquarters
2008

Description	Month 1	Month 2	Month 3	Month 4	Month 5	Month 6	Month 7	Month 8	Month 9	Month 10	Month 11	Month 12	Year Total
FRANCHISOR													
Number of UNITS SOLD						1	0	1	0	1	1	1	5
Number of UNITS OPENED								1		1			2
CASH FLOW:													
Franchise Fees						16,000	0	16,000	0	16,000	16,000	16,000	80,000
Royalties									167	146	317	358	988
Interest Income	0					0	0	0	0	0	0	0	0
TOTAL CASH AVAILABLE						$16,000	$0	$16,000	$167	$16,146	$16,317	$16,358	$80,988
DISBURSEMENTS:													
Salaries - Executive	4,000	4,000	4,000	4,000	5,000	5,000	5,000	5,000	5,000	5,000	5,000	5,000	56,000
Salaries - Administrative													0
Salaries - Sales					4,500	4,500	4,500	4,500	4,500	4,500	4,500	4,500	36,000
Payroll Taxes													
FICA	306	306	306	306	727	727	727	727	727	727	727	727	7,038
Unemployment	60	60	60	60	143	143	143	143	143	143	143	143	1,380
Rent	1,000	1,000	1,000	1,000	1,000	1,000	1,000	1,000	1,000	1,000	1,000	1,000	12,000
Advertising													0
Legal				2,000	2,000	2,000	2,000	2,000	2,000	2,000	2,000	2,000	18,000
Travel - Executive	1,000	1,000	1,000	1,000	2,000	2,000	2,000	2,000	2,000	2,000	2,000	2,000	20,000
Travel - Administrative													0
Travel - Sales					2,000	2,000	2,000	2,000	2,000	2,000	2,000	2,000	16,000
Manual Preparation			2,000	2,000									4,000
Printing					3,000				3,000				6,000
Sales and Commissions									2,000		2,000		4,000
Bonus													0
Dues and Subscriptions						200		200		200		260	860
Loan Repayment							2,142	2,142	2,142	2,142	2,142	2,142	12,855
Insurance	500			500			500			500			2,000
Other Cash Outflows													
Utilities	200	200	200	200	200	200	250	250	250	250	250	250	2,700
Gas/Water/Sewerage	250	250	250	250	250	250	300	300	300	300	300	300	3,300
Phone	100	100	100	200	200	200	200	200	200	250	250	250	2,250
Miscellaneous	250	250	250	250	250	250	250	250	250	250	250	250	3,000
Seminars and Meetings		2,000			1,000				2,000				5,000
TOTAL DISBURSEMENTS	7,666	9,166	9,166	11,766	22,269	18,469	21,012	20,712	27,512	21,262	22,562	20,822	212,383
NET CASH FLOW	($7,666)	($9,166)	($9,166)	($11,766)	($22,269)	($2,469)	($21,012)	($4,712)	($27,345)	($5,116)	($6,245)	($4,463)	
CUMULATIVE CASH FLOW	($7,666)	($16,832)	($25,998)	($37,764)	($60,033)	($62,503)	($83,514)	($88,226)	($115,571)	($120,687)	($126,932)	($131,395)	

FIGURE 10-3

Hypothetical Monthly Cash Flow Statement

Hypothetical Monthly Cash Flow Statement
Tracy's Franchisor Headquarters
2009

Description	Month 1	Month 2	Month 3	Month 4	Month 5	Month 6	Month 7	Month 8	Month 9	Month 10	Month 11	Month 12	Year Total
FRANCHISOR													
Number of UNITS SOLD	2	2	2	2	2	2	3	3	3	3	3	3	35
Number of UNITS OPENED	3	4	5	7	9	11	13	15	17	20	23	26	26
CASH FLOW:													
Franchise Fees	32,000	32,000	32,000	32,000	32,000	32,000	48,000	48,000	48,000	48,000	48,000	48,000	480,000
Royalties	600	883	1,208	1,838	2,550	3,346	4,225	5,188	5,985	7,042	8,098	9,154	50,117
Interest Income	0	9	0	8	0	0	6	64	61	63	53	64	328
TOTAL CASH AVAILABLE	$32,600	$32,893	$33,208	$33,845	$34,550	$35,346	$52,231	$53,251	$54,047	$55,105	$56,151	$57,218	$530,444
DISBURSEMENTS:													
Salaries - Executive	5,000	5,000	5,000	5,000	5,000	5,000	5,000	5,000	5,000	5,000	5,000	5,000	60,000
Salaries - Administrative	5,500	5,500	5,500	5,500	5,500	5,500	5,500	5,500	5,500	5,500	5,500	5,500	66,000
Salaries - Sales	4,500	4,500	4,500	4,500	4,500	4,500	4,500	4,500	4,500	4,500	4,500	4,500	54,000
Payroll Taxes													
FICA	1,148	1,148	1,148	1,148	1,148	1,148	1,148	1,148	1,148	1,148	1,148	1,148	13,770
Unemployment	225	225	225	225	225	225	225	225	225	225	225	225	2,700
Rent	1,000	1,000	1,000	1,000	1,000	1,000	1,000	1,000	1,000	1,000	1,000	1,000	12,000
Advertising													0
Legal													0
Travel - Executive	2,000	2,000	2,000	2,000	2,000	2,000	2,000	2,000	2,000	2,000	2,000	2,000	24,000
Travel - Administrative	2,500	2,500	2,500	5,000	5,000	5,000	5,000	5,000	5,000	7,500	7,500	7,500	60,000
Travel - Sales	2,000	2,000	2,000	2,000	2,000	2,000	2,000	2,000	3,000	3,000	3,000	3,000	28,000
Manual Preparation		2,000	2,000										4,000
Printing				3,000				3,000				3,000	9,000
Sales and Commissions	2,000	2,000	2,000	4,000	4,000	4,000	4,000	4,000	4,000	6,000	6,000	6,000	48,000
Bonus												10,000	10,000
Dues and Subscriptions						200		200		200		260	860
Loan Repayment	2,142	2,142	2,142	2,142	2,142	2,142	2,142	2,142	2,142	2,142	2,142	2,142	25,709
Insurance	1,000			1,000			1,500			1,500			5,000
Other Cash Outflows													
Utilities	250	250	250	250	250	250	300	300	300	300	300	300	3,300
Gas/Water/Sewerage	300	300	300	300	300	300	300	300	300	300	300	300	3,600
Phone	250	250	250	250	250	250	250	250	250	250	250	250	3,000
Miscellaneous	300	300	300	300	300	300	350	350	350	350	350	350	3,900
Seminars and Meetings	2,500			1,000					2,500				6,000
TOTAL DISBURSEMENTS	30,115	33,615	31,115	37,615	34,615	33,815	35,215	36,915	37,215	40,915	39,215	52,475	442,839
NET CASH FLOW	$2,485	($722)	$2,093	($3,770)	($65)	$1,531	$17,016	$16,336	$16,832	$14,190	$16,936	$4,743	
CUMULATIVE CASH FLOW	($128,910)	($129,632)	($127,539)	($131,309)	($131,373)	($129,843)	($112,827)	($96,490)	($79,659)	($65,469)	($48,533)	($43,790)	

FIGURE 10-3
Continued

Hypothetical Monthly Cash Flow Statement
Tracy's Franchisor Headquarters
2010

Description FRANCHISOR	Month 1	Month 2	Month 3	Month 4	Month 5	Month 6	Month 7	Month 8	Month 9	Month 10	Month 11	Month 12	Year Total
Number of UNITS SOLD	3	3	3	3	3	3	4	4	4	4	4	4	77
Number of UNITS OPENED	29	32	35	38	41	44	47	50	53	57	61	65	65
CASH FLOW:													
Franchise Fees	48,000	48,000	48,000	48,000	48,000	48,000	64,000	64,000	64,000	64,000	64,000	64,000	672,000
Royalties	10,210	11,267	12,323	13,379	14,435	15,492	16,548	17,604	18,660	20,069	21,477	22,885	194,350
Interest Income	18	65	64	79	66	57	90	147	147	152	143	157	1,187
TOTAL CASH AVAILABLE	$58,228	$59,332	$60,387	$61,458	$62,502	$63,549	$80,638	$81,752	$82,808	$84,221	$85,620	$87,042	$867,537
DISBURSEMENTS:													
Salaries - Executive	5,000	5,000	5,000	5,000	5,000	5,000	5,000	5,000	5,000	5,000	5,000	5,000	60,000
Salaries - Administrative	5,500	5,500	5,500	5,500	5,500	5,500	5,500	5,500	5,500	5,500	5,500	5,500	66,000
Salaries - Sales	4,500	4,500	4,500	4,500	4,500	4,500	4,500	4,500	4,500	4,500	4,500	4,500	54,000
Payroll Taxes													
FICA	1,148	1,148	1,148	1,148	1,148	1,148	1,148	1,148	1,148	1,148	1,148	1,148	13,770
Unemployment	225	225	225	225	225	225	225	225	225	225	225	225	2,700
Rent	1,000	1,000	1,000	1,000	1,000	1,000	1,000	1,000	1,000	1,000	1,000	1,000	12,000
Advertising													0
Legal													0
Travel - Executive	2,000	2,000	2,000	2,000	2,000	2,000	2,000	2,000	2,000	2,000	2,000	2,000	24,000
Travel - Administrative	7,500	7,500	7,500	7,500	7,500	7,500	7,500	7,500	7,500	10,000	10,000	10,000	97,500
Travel - Sales	3,000	3,000	3,000	3,000	3,000	3,000	3,000	3,000	3,000	3,000	3,000	3,000	36,000
Manual Preparation													0
Printing				3,000				3,000				3,000	9,000
Sales and Commissions	6,000	6,000	6,000	6,000	6,000	6,000	6,000	6,000	6,000	8,000	8,000	8,000	78,000
Bonus												20,000	20,000
Dues and Subscriptions						200		200		200		260	860
Loan Repayment	2,142	2,142	2,142	2,142	2,142	2,142	2,142	2,142	2,142	2,142	2,142	2,142	25,709
Insurance	1,500			1,500			2,000			2,000			7,000
Other Cash Outflows													
Utilities	300	300	300	300	300	300	300	300	300	300	300	300	3,600
Gas/Water/Sewerage	300	300	300	300	300	300	300	300	300	300	300	300	3,600
Phone	300	300	300	300	300	300	350	350	350	350	350	350	3,900
Miscellaneous	350	350	350	350	350	350	350	350	350	350	350	350	4,200
Seminars and Meetings		3,000			8,000				3,000				14,000
TOTAL DISBURSEMENTS	40,765	42,265	39,265	43,765	47,265	39,465	41,315	42,515	42,315	46,015	43,815	67,075	535,839
NET CASH FLOW	$17,463	$17,067	$21,122	$17,693	$15,237	$24,084	$39,323	$39,237	$40,493	$38,206	$41,805	$19,967	
CUMULATIVE CASH FLOW	($26,327)	($9,259)	$11,863	$29,556	$44,793	$68,877	$108,200	$147,437	$187,929	$226,135	$267,940	$287,908	

FIGURE 10-3

Continued

balance sheet measures the assets carried forward into the next time period while showing the liabilities and equities in those assets. But neither statement measures the actual cash flow of the business.

This fact escapes many franchisors. Even though the franchise business may be earning profits, this does not mean that they are financially sound. The franchise system may be having soaring profits, but the franchisor is busy trying to obtain a loan to pay the bills. For example, one franchisor was very proud because of a $12,000 profit the previous month. However, the next day her banker called and told her that she did not have sufficient money left to pay her checks. "How can I be out of cash when I made $12,000 last month?" she replied. She later found out that her missing cash was tied up in accounts receivable and inventory.

The cash flow statement covers a given period of time (usually a month and/or year), and it reflects the increases or decreases in the cash position of the business. The cash flow statement is similar to the gas gauge in our cars as it shows the amount or fuel (cash or gas) available to run the business or car. The cash flow statement monitors the flow of cash in a business by showing the sources and uses of cash for the business during a specific time period.

The cash flow statement is divided into four major areas: (1) cash receipts, (2) cash disbursements, (3) net cash flow, and (4) accumulative cash flow. The cash revenue or receipts is a total of all cash receipts, including cash sales, franchise fees, royalties, and other income. The total of all receipts yields the total cash available.

The cash disbursements reflect all expenditures of the business for that time period. This would include all salaries, wages, benefits, travel, rent, advertising, accounting and legal fees, utilities, insurance, loan repayments, and all other cash payments.

The net cash flow is the result of subtracting the disbursements from the receipts. This figure shows how much cash is available to pay the bills and invest in new business programs such as advertising, expansion, or new products and services.

Finally, the accumulative cash flow shows us how much cash we have on hand for a longer period of time. Tracy's accumulative cash flow indicates that there will be a negative accumulative cash flow until the third year of operation—very common with many beginning franchisors. This account also shows how much total money will be needed during the start-up phase of the business.

It is important to remember that even good accounting records cannot measure the exact worth of a franchise (see Figure 10-4). A common belief is that accounting records are exact—they are not. Neither the income statement nor the balance sheet is able to give more than a rough picture of a business. The figures they contain are rough estimates, because all businesses are highly dissimilar and complex and the actual cash, materials, land, buildings, inventory, incentives, and morale make it impossible to develop a precise financial picture of the franchise. Accounting cannot put a value on the individuals, their creativity, patents, or even teamwork.

However, even with all the limitations, the accounting statements enable the franchisor to draw a picture around many complex events into a handful of useful financial statements—notably the income statement, the balance sheet, and the cash flow statement. This is a remarkable achievement.

FRANCHISE ACCOUNTING SYSTEM

Income Statement	Balance Sheet	Cash Flow Statement
• How efficiently is the business being run?	• Is the franchise properly financed?	• Is there sufficient cash to pay the bills?
• Is the business profitable?	• What is the franchise worth? (At least on paper)	• How much cash will the franchise need to meet sales projections?

10-6   FINANCIAL RATIO

The five major categories of financial ratios are liquidity, profitability, activity, coverage or leverage, and market. Several of the most commonly used ratios are discussed in this section. Table 10-1 presents a general description of these ratios.

10-6a   Liquidity Ratios

Liquidity ratios indicate how well the franchise meets its short-term debts or financial obligations. Two measures are commonly used: the current ratio and the acid test. The **current ratio** is current assets divided by current liabilities, with both figures coming from the balance sheet.

$$\text{Current ratio} = \frac{\text{Current Assets}}{\text{Current Liabilities}}$$

This relationship illustrates the ability of the franchisor to pay current debts using only current assets (cash, inventory, accounts receivable). The higher this ratio, the better the franchisor is able to pay off these short-term liabilities or debts. A general rule is that the current ratio should be 2 to 1 ($2 to every $1, or 200 percent). However, many businesses operate with a current ratio of 1.5 or even 1.2 to 1, and are highly successful. For any business venture being considered, it would be wise to find out the industry averages, and more particularly, the averages for the franchised businesses within the particular industry before making judgments about what ratio is "good" or "insufficient." The current ratio of Tracy's Sandwich Shoppe is calculated as $60,000 to $20,000 or 3 to 1 and the working capital is $40,000 ($60,000 current assets ? $20,000 current liabilities).

The **acid test** or quick ratio is developed by subtracting current inventory from total current assets and dividing that figure by current liabilities.

$$\text{Acid Test} = \frac{\text{Current Assets - Inventory}}{\text{Current Liabilities}}$$

Each of these figures is found on the balance sheet. This ratio indicates the extent to which a franchisor can pay current debts without relying on future sales of inventory. A general rule of thumb is to maintain a ratio of 1 to 1, or $1 of current assets minus inventory to $1 of current liabilities. When the acid test ratio dips below a ratio of 1 to 1, there is a developing "dependency" on inventory, rather than other current assets such as cash and accounts receivables, to help pay debts. The acid test or quick ratio for Tracy's franchise is as follows:

$$\frac{\$\,60,000 - \$\,20,000}{\$\,20,000} = 2{:}1$$

TABLE 10-1   PRIMARY RATIOS AND WHAT THEY MEASURE

Liquidity	Ability of the franchised business to pay its short-term debts
Profitability	Overall effectiveness of the franchise leadership and management team to generate a profit
Activity	How effective the franchised business is in using the available resources; focus is on the generation of sales in relation to an asset base
Leverage (or Coverage)	The amount of long-term debt the franchised business carries and its ability to meet these debt obligations
Market	The performance of the common stock of the franchised business if the stock is not significantly owned by insiders

10-6b   Profitability Ratios

Profitability ratios are generally developed from the income statement and measure the ability of the franchise organization to turn sales into profits and to generate profit from assets. The two most common profitability ratios concentrate on operating income and the effects of taxes and fixed expenses on operating income.

The net profit margin is found by dividing net income after taxes by the total sales for the period:

$$\frac{\text{Net Income After Taxes}}{\text{Total Sales}} = \text{Net Profit Margin}$$

This ratio describes the net or "real" profitability of the business. It is of interest to note that the average net profit margin of most businesses is between 3 and 7 percent. When a net profit margin rises above 12 percent, more and more competitors are attracted to the arena to share in the market demand because of the high net profits available. As more competitors enter the market, profits tend to decline because of the increasing competition for the customer.

Therefore, the net profit margin for Tracy's Sandwich Shoppe may be calculated as:

$$\frac{\$174,000}{\$1,000,000} = 7.4 \text{ percent}$$

This indicates that Tracy's franchise was able to generate more than seventeen cents of operating profit on each dollar of sales.

A second important profitability ratio is the net return on assets calculation. This ratio measures the firm's ability to generate an after tax return on assets.

$$\frac{\text{Net Profit After Taxes}}{\text{Total Assets}} = \text{Net Return on Assets}$$

Specifically, Tracy's net return on assets is $174,000 ÷ $100,000 = 1.74 percent.

10-6c   Activity or Efficiency Ratios

Activity or **efficiency ratios** measure the franchise's ability to use capital and assets to maximum efficiency. Generally, three ratios are calculated to measure business efficiency—inventory turnover, collection period ratio, and the fixed asset turnover.

$$\frac{\text{Net Sales}}{\text{Inventory}} = \text{Inventory Turnover}$$

More specifically, this ratio indicates the number of times the average inventory expenditure of the franchise is turned into dollars. The basic objective is to increase this ratio overall. The inventory turnover for Tracy's firm is $900,000 ÷ $20,000 = 45 times.

Determining the average collection period for accounts receivable tells the franchisor the average length of time it takes from the point of purchase to the point of payment for a particular sale. To determine this figure requires using net sales figures from the income statement and accounts receivable figures from the balance sheet, as follows:

$$\frac{\text{Accounts Receivable}}{\text{Net Sales}} \times 360 \text{ (days)} = \text{Average Collection Period}$$

Generally, a favorable decline in this ratio indicates increased efficiency in the collection of accounts receivable. The average collection period of Tracy's Sandwich Shoppe is calculated as follows:

$$\frac{\$22,000}{\$900,000} = 8.8$$

Therefore, Tracy's average age of receivables is 8.8 days.

As indicated, the correct way to view financial ratio analysis is by an industry approach. In our example, a review of the average collection period of 8.64 days may indicate Tracy's Sandwich Shoppe is doing very well in collecting its accounts receivable. Businesses usually pay their receivables within thirty-five to sixty-five days, while customers often take thirty to forty-five days to make payment. This set of days-for-payment by business and by customer will, of course, vary from industry to industry.

Other operating ratios also require information from both balance sheet and income statement. The fixed asset turnover ratio indicates the extent to which the business's fixed assets are used in generating sales, while the total asset turnover ratio shows how efficiently the franchised firm is utilizing its assets to generate sales. The ratios are as follows:

$$\frac{\text{Total Sales}}{\text{Fixed Assets}} = \text{Fixed Asset Turnover}$$

$$\frac{\text{Total Sales}}{\text{Total Assets}} = \text{Total Asset Turnover}$$

The fixed asset turnover of Tracy's Sandwich Shoppe is $\$1,000,000 \div \$40,000 = 25$ times, or for each dollar invested in fixed assets Tracy's firm earns $25. The total asset turnover is $\$1,000,000 \div \$100,000 = 10$ times.

10-6d Leverage Ratios

Leverage ratios measure long-term debt and the franchisor's ability to take care of the obligations associated with this type of debt. Various ratios using balance sheet information can be computed, such as the debt ratio, debt–equity ratio, debt-to-capital ratio, and the short-term liabilities-to-total-debt ratio. One leverage ratio, the times-interest earned ratio, is generated from the income statement as follows:

$$\frac{\text{Net Income Before Taxes} + \text{Interest Expense}}{\text{Interest Expense}} = \text{Times Interest Earned}$$

This ratio indicates the proportion that interest expense constitutes in relation to the net income of the firm. This proportion gives a quick indication of what income obligation is associated with long-term debt. The banker is quite interested in the times-interest-earned ratio in that it measures solvency, the ability to pay back interest. Following is the times-interest-earned ratio for Tracy's Sandwich Shoppe.

$$\frac{\$272,000 + \$12,000}{\$12,000} = 23.6 \text{ times}$$

Tracy's franchise thus earns more than $23 for every dollar the firm must pay in interest.

The debt/equity ratio can be used to estimate the amount of debt a franchisor can carry based on the equity invested in the business. This is estimated as follows:

$$\frac{\text{Total Current Liabilities} + \text{Long-term Debt}}{\text{Total Stockholders' Equity}} = \text{Debt/Equity Ratio}$$

Specifically, Tracy's debt–equity ratio would be 0.66 to 1:

$$\frac{\$20,000 + \$20,000}{\$60,000} = 0.66$$

The debt-to-asset ratio, another leverage or debt ratio, is found by dividing total debt by total assets. This would indicate that Tracy's business assets are financed by 66 percent debt and 34 percent stockholder equity.

10-6e   Market Ratios

Market ratios are useful in assessing the performance of the common stock of the franchised firm, if it is a corporation. A franchised corporation may be closely held with limited or no stock being traded by virtue of being an actively traded public corporation. The ratios often used to assess the performance of this stock of such firms are as follows:

$$\text{Dividend Yield} = \frac{\text{Dividend Per Share of Common Stock}}{\text{Price Per Share}}$$

$$\text{Earnings/Share} = \frac{\text{Net Income After Taxes} - \text{Preferred Dividends Paid}}{\text{Number of Shares of Common Stock Outstanding}}$$

$$\text{Dividend Payout} = \frac{\text{Dividend Per Share of Common Stock}}{\text{After} - \text{Tax Earnings Per Share}}$$

$$\text{Price Earnings Ratio} = \frac{\text{Current Market Price Per Share}}{\text{After} - \text{Tax Earnings Per Share}}$$

Generally speaking, these market ratios are evaluation ratios. The supply and demand relationships upon the security or "market value" of the security have significant effects on that security market ratio.

10-6f   Location Selection Ratio: Sales/Costs

One of the more interesting ratios for franchising is the location selection ratio or sales/costs. This ratio is best when it equals 1 or better.

$$\text{Location Selection Ratio} = \frac{\text{Sales}}{\text{Costs}} = 1.0 \text{ or higher}$$

Simply explained, if it costs $650,000 to open a store (turnkey costs including land, building, equipment, fixtures, and furniture), then you should have sales of $650,000 for that start-up year. One franchisor's ideal ratio is 1.2, which is good profit. The firm was looking for a new quick service restaurant location, but they could not come close to a 1.0 ratio so the firm was forced to pull out. This ratio will vary from one franchise system to another, but the guideline is important for both franchisors and franchisees.

10-7   USES OF FINANCIAL STATEMENT ANALYSIS

As indicated, many outsiders, such as the banker, creditor, and investor, may be interested in the financial picture of a franchise. Our discussion of the various financial statements has indicated that the key financial ratios of liquidity, profitability, activity or efficiency, leverage, and market are useful in analyzing this picture. Generally, these ratios may be viewed as analyzing the "bottom line," which is the return to the franchised business owner.

10-8   HOW IMPORTANT ARE FINANCIAL RATIOS?

Financial ratios do not have much significance unless they can be compared with other financial ratios. First, within the franchised business, comparisons with ratios from previous years provide an indication of the current state of the firm's financial affairs. Second, comparisons of the business with like businesses within the industry help provide an understanding of how well this firm serves its customers in contrast to the average firm. For example, it would be of little use to examine the financial ratios of a single Midas Muffler franchise without looking at Midas's position in the industry and the average performance ratios in the muffler industry in general. Table 10-2 presents an overview of the meaning of financial ratios.

Ratio analysis involves interpreting a relationship between two financial figures. This relationship is commonly expressed as a ratio, percentage, or fraction. For example, the current ratio is developed by dividing total current assets by the total current liabilities. If total current assets of $20,000 are divided by total current liabilities of $10,000, the current ratio is (2:1), a percentage (200 percent), or a fraction (2/1). Current ratios often encompass the entire corporation's or firm's product line. Therefore, we should understand that ratios may not be mutually exclusive to "our" product line. For example, if we were to analyze Mobil Oil's financial ratios and compare these ratios to Exxon's, we should be familiar with the "nonconsolidated" statements. These statements include a breakdown of individual product lines. Mobil Oil's product lines include Montgomery Ward's, which is a retail merchandising operation. Exxon includes office machines and home/office computers in its product lines, not just petroleum products. Therefore, the reader must be aware of appropriate use of financial statement and ratio analysis. After all, the purpose of financial statement and ratio analysis is to "red flag" key fiscal areas for further analysis and review.

TABLE 10-2 FINANCIAL RATIOS USEFUL FOR ANALYZING A BUSINESS WITH INTERPRETATIONS AND NORMATIVE EXPECTATIONS

Ratio	Interpretation	Norm
Return on Investment	The rate of return on total assets employed; a measure of management's overall performance in generating a profit.	Should at least be equal to the market rate of return on Treasury bills during the time period in question.
Return on Equity	The rate of return on stockholder's investment in the company; a measure of management's performance in generating a profit for the owners of the company.	Same as above.
Net Profit Margin	The amount of after-tax profits per dollar of sales.	None exists.
Gross Margin	The amount of gross profit generated per dollar of sales.	None exists.

Source: Adapted from Manab N. Thakur, Memphis State University, "How to Conduct Financial Analysis for Policy Casework," in R. T. Justis, R. J. Judd, and D. B. Stephens, *Strategic Management and Policy* (Englewood Cliffs, NJ: Prentice-Hall, Inc., 1985), 620–621.

Terri Bears

eModel.com

Terri Bears has been a part of the entertainment industry since before she was able to walk. At four weeks old she won a "Cutest Baby" contest. By the age of twelve, a model scout and her parents allowed Terri to pursue her dreams. Ms. Bears continued modeling while attending the University of Central Florida where she got a degree in English education. After eight years of part-time modeling, Terri was booked on a job in Paris, which was the start of an illustrious career. The next four years saw her traveling among Paris, Miami, Milan, and Manhattan working the catwalk, fashion magazines, as well as commercials and music videos.

She modeled extensively with many of the top agencies in her field, including Elite, Vogue, Flame, LA Models, City, and American. After four years, Terri returned to school, received her master's degree in education, and became a teacher; but the allure of the industry was a strong one, and when Terri saw an ad to become a model scout for eModel, she could not resist. Soon she was promoted to the position of talent executive, interviewing the next generation of potential models.

eModel was formed in Los Angeles in 1996, and then was purchased by a group of investors who moved the headquarters east to Washington, D.C., with an operations center based in Orlando. Terri was quickly promoted to vice president of new business development. eModel has quickly grown from a company of half a dozen in Los Angeles to a company of over sixty operations staff plus thousands of scouts worldwide and dozens of franchise partners. It is currently the largest model scouting network in the world, offering its models a digital portfolio of pictures that can be accessed twenty-four hours a day by over 5,500 registered modeling agencies, photographers, ad agencies, casting directors, and other clients. With plans to expand internationally by early 2002, eModel joined the International Franchise Association and at their most recent convention, won the unofficial "Rookie of the Year" award.

It is truly revolutionizing the way the modeling industry operates, slowly replacing the paper composite cards with digital composite cards and portfolios. By using the computer, clients can use a high-speed search engine to narrow their search to criteria such as height, shoe size, hair and eye color, languages the model speaks, or sports or musical instruments in which the model has a proficiency. In addition, the 5,500 clients can book models directly or sign them to agency agreements, and models that are already professional can be listed through their agencies to increase their visibility to clients around the globe.

In her current position, Terri is responsible for all new business development, as well as having a primary role in all advertising campaigns and franchise operations. Ms. Bears has developed such a unique sales department that she and her staff have sold over fifty franchises in six short months. EModel, with Terri Bears's expertise and leadership, is poised to take advantage of a surge in advertising to the baby boom generation and over the Internet with its worldwide network of scouts, models, clients, and franchises.

SUMMARY

Calculating key financial ratios is not difficult. However, the analysis and managerial interpretations may be significantly difficult, especially for a franchise, because most financial ratio data are collected for larger firms (i.e., corporations). Yet for many industries, including various wholesaling, retailing, manufacturing, and service categories, ratios are compiled and published on an annual basis. These reference figures are available through sources such as the Robert Morris Associates Annual Statement Studies, Moody's, Standard & Poor's Corporation Records, Value Line

Investment Survey, and Industry Surveys. Such sources provide fact sheets on companies, editorial comments on corporations, and information about industry averages and ratios for comparative purposes. Using available published compiled ratios and industry data, a franchisor can compare a franchise's financial data to national averages for that industry. In addition, a franchisor can compare company-owned competitors to franchisee-owned stores, or any single franchise to the industry average or to the average of all franchises combined.

KEY TERMS

Accounting: the process of measuring and reporting the financial information of the franchise; the measurement and record of money, assets, and resources and their flow through the company.

Acid test: also called the "quick ratio"; another type of liquidity ratio; developed by subtracting current inventory from total current assets and dividing that figure by current liabilities.

Activity or efficiency ratios: measure the franchise's ability to use capital and assets to maximum efficiency; generally consist of three calculations: inventory turnover, collection period ratio, and the fixed asset turnover.

Balance sheet: also called "a statement of financial position or condition"; an accounting statement which illustrates the value of the assets, liabilities, and equity (net worth) of a franchise at a specific time.

Cash flow statement: allows separate business owners to understand the cash position and to monitor seasonal periods and broader cyclic trends, as well as identify the business's strengths and weaknesses.

Current assets: a business's cash, accounts receivable, and inventory that can be changed into cash within a brief period of time, usually twelve months from the date of the balance sheet or one cycle of the business's operations.

Current liabilities: debts or obligations payable by the franchised firm within a normal cycle of the business, or twelve months.

Current ratio: one type of liquidity ratio; current assets divided by current liabilities, with both figures coming from the balance sheet.

Equity: also called "net worth"; the owner's claim on the assets of the business.

Financial flow: a written documentation or recording of business transactions shown through financial statements, which provide a franchisor and franchisees the basic format to report the financial activities of a franchise network or franchised unit.

Fixed assets: also called "plant and equipment"; the resources the firm owns or acquires for use in running the business, generally not intended for resale but can be leased.

Generally accepted accounting principles (GAAP): widely agreed-upon definitions, procedures, conventions, and forms which are used to develop financial statements which may be used and understood by anyone.

Income: sales, fees, or revenues flowing into the franchised business.

Income statement: also called "profit and loss," or "statement of earnings"; a record of revenues versus expenses for a stated period, such as a day, week, month, quarter, or year; shows the accounting profits or losses of a business through accounting of receipts/revenues minus expenses.

Leverage ratios: measure long-term debt and the franchisor's ability to take care of the obligations associated with this type of debt; use balance sheet information.

Liquidity ratios: indicate how well the franchise meets its short-term debts or financial obligations.

Long-term assets: also called "long-term investments"; holdings the franchised firm intends to keep for at least one year, typically yield an interest accrued or dividend paid back to the firm.

Long-term liabilities: debts normally used to finance capital assets such as buildings, machinery, or fixed assets; contractual obligations which must be paid when due, generally after a period that exceeds twelve months or one cycle of business.

Market ratios: useful in assessing the performance of the common stock of the franchised firm, if it is a corporation.

Net profit: also called "final profit" or the "bottom line"; the sum of all revenues minus the sum of all expenses; the profit figure which a franchise reports; the amount of earnings available which may be used to reinvest in the business, pay dividends to shareholders, provide bonuses, or provide additional product/service research and development for the franchise system.

Operating expenses: all the expenses incurred in the operations of the business; may be summarized by adding the general/administrative expenses, selling expenses, and depreciation expenses.

Profitability ratios: developed from the income statement and measure the ability of the franchise organization to turn sales into profits and to generate profit from assets.

Reinvested earnings: also called "retained earnings"; funds which the franchisor pumps back into the business which are often subject to significant IRS regulations

REVIEW QUESTIONS

1. What is the importance of developing and maintaining financial records in a franchised business?

2. What is the importance and use of a balance sheet? What are its primary components?

3. Describe the importance and use of an income statement. What are its primary components?

4. Explain the cash flow statement. What are the types of "flows" in such a statement?

5. What are the major ways a franchised business can increase the cash position of the firm?

6. Identify and describe the five major types of financial ratios.

CASE STUDY

The Hair Emporium

Rolando and Rosa have been operating their own hair salon for the past six years. They have been very successful and now are interested in franchising their particular hair system throughout the United States. They are aware that the hair care industry is a $16 billion activity in this country. Rolando and Rosa specialize in hair care for women, men, and children, and believe they can provide their services on a profitable basis for other franchisees.

Rolando and Rosa have estimated that the total cost for a new location would be between $65,000 and $136,000. This includes the following:

Franchise Fee	$20,000
Leased Deposit	$ 5,000
Leased Improvements	$15,000 - $65,000
Real Estate Rental Costs	$ 2,000 - $ 5,000
Equipment and Trade Fixtures	$17,000 - $30,000
Opening Supplies	$1,000
Working Capital	$5,000 - $10,000

They would expect that a new franchisee should have one-fourth to one-half of the total investment in cash and should be able to finance the balance through some lending source.

Franchisees would have the opportunity to open multiple stores after successfully operating the first Hair Emporium salon for a sufficient length of time and generating sufficient profits. It is anticipated also that the franchisee would be in operation approximately six months after the initial signing of the franchising agreement. Additionally, they plan to offer a one-week course in hair care, cutting, hair forming techniques, settings, hair sculpturing, and management.

Rolando and Rosa have a major concern about the accounting methods and recordkeeping. They have hired a local bookkeeper to keep track of their own records, but find it more difficult each year in dealing with the local accounting firms and taxes.

They are concerned about what kind of accounting service they should provide for the franchisees and whether they should also utilize a computer system. They have kept a basic journal but have never developed an itemized general ledger.

CASE QUESTIONS

1. What type of accounting records and/or financial statements should Rolando and Rosa keep themselves and also offer their franchisees?

2. Are balance sheets and operating statements important or necessary on a monthly or yearly basis?

3. Should they recommend a common accounting procedure for all franchisees?

4. Discuss the following financial/accounting records for the Hair Emporium: journal entry, detailed general ledger, bank account reconciliation, monthly payroll register, accounts receivable, comparative operating statements, taxes, and monthly business/accounting consultation.

REFERENCES

Annual Statement Studies (New York: Robert Morris Associates, 1997).

Carey, Theresa W., "Bean Counting Made Easy," *PC World* 13(9) (September 1995): 164–176.

CCH Business Owner's Toolkit, 2004, www.cch.com

Fess, Philip E., and Carl Warren, *Accounting Principles*, 14th ed. (Cincinnati: South-Western Publishing Co., 1984).

"Financing Small Business," *Small Business Reporter*, Bank of America, 1996.

Ronstadt, Robert, *Entrepreneurial Finance: How to Take Control of Your Financial Decision Making* (Wayland, MA: Lord, 1989).

Seitz, Neil, *Financial Analysis: A Program Approach*, 3rd ed. (Reston, VA: Reston Publishing Company, Inc., 1984).

Small Business Administration, "The Profit Plan," *Business Basics* (Washington, DC: U.S. Government Printing Office, 1996).

Wilcox, Kirkland A., and Joseph G. San Miguel, *Introduction to Financial Accounting*, 2nd ed. (New York: Harper & Row Publishers, 1984).

FINANCIAL MANAGEMENT AND FISCAL PLANNING TOOLS AND TECHNIQUES*

In studying this chapter, you will:

- **Learn about potential sources of financing utilized in franchised businesses.**

- **Develop an understanding of the financial function within a franchised business.**

- **Learn about objectives and evaluating factors for making choices about sources of capital for the franchised business.**

- **Be able to identify the capital requirements confronting any franchised business.**

- **Learn about financial ratios useful in analyzing the financial condition of a franchise operation.**

INCIDENT

Tracy's Sandwich Shoppe has been very successful after just three years of operation, so she has decided to expand. Yet many of her franchisees are having difficulty planning and managing financial resources, especially cash. For example, financing in the short run—from whom, when, and at what cost—has been difficult to plan. From the normal course of running the business, current cash assets and net working capital are being managed. At month's end, however, the cash available is just not sufficient. The timing differences, or synchronization, between cash outflow due to the costs of franchise and the sales of products and services usually do not require short-term financing; however, there are times when outflow exceeds inflow.

One particular franchisee of Tracy's Sandwich Shoppe is meeting with the bank Monday morning to try to arrange a short-term loan to cover the temporary cash shortage. Three types of interest rates are available to the franchisee: *add-on, simple,* or *discount* rates. Which type of interest is most advantageous to the franchisee? Also, what unneeded assets or liabilities may be eliminated in the future so that the franchisee can better manage the working capital?

---

* Prepared in part with Robert C. Maple, independent financial consultant, Springfield, Illinois

11-1 INTRODUCTION

In this chapter we continue our discussion about the financial matters of a franchised business. In Chapter 10 we addressed financial statements—what accounts and categories are needed and how to analyze financial statements—and introduced ratio planning. In this chapter we look at the ability of a franchised business to manage working capital, develop a cash budget, evaluate financial performance, and forecast future financial needs.

Financial planning and management are essential to any business. Both franchisor and franchisee need to understand the tools of financial planning. Working capital management and cash budget management are keys to the continuing success of the business, as is the ongoing and timely review of all financial statements.

11-1a   Sources for Financing Your Franchised Business

What are the best sources for financing your business? For most businesspeople, piecing together the financial package is challenging. In fact, the majority of franchisees do not receive all their funding from one source; rather, they utilize a combination of sources to finance their businesses. Foremost, franchisees must determine how much they can commit from their personal savings. Then, most prospective business owners turn to family, relatives, and friends to be investors in their business. Often the next source is from the franchise system itself, bank loans, government programs, and home equity loans.

Why multiple sources of funding? The prospective business owner needs to take a realistic look at the initial and working capital costs of entering business. For example, it is not uncommon for a fast-food franchise to require an investment of $750,000. Auto aftermarket franchises such as Valvoline or Jiffy-Lube generally require franchisees to have a net worth of about $200,000, with about $100,000 of that in cash, marketable securities, or other liquid assets. Some franchised casual restaurant systems require prospective franchisees to have a minimum worth of $500,000 or more with liquidity assets of between $200,000 and $250,000, excluding one's personal residence.

Obviously, not all franchisees require financial commitments into the hundreds of thousands of dollars, but some require much more, such as hotels, motels, auto dealerships, and beverage distributing companies. Some franchised systems may require a financial commitment from prospective franchisees to be in the $5,000 to $15,000 range. However, it is generally true that the more successful franchise systems require a substantial financial commitment from the prospective franchisee.

If you borrow the money, you are using debt financing and, as mentioned, probably borrow from one or a combination of family, friends, commercial banks, government-sponsored bank loans, franchise system loans, home equity loans, or credit card loans. On the other hand, equity financing is a way to raise money, although debt financing is far more prevalent for franchise investments. In equity financing, you are giving up part of the control of the business to the investor. They can, and often do, claim some control of the business operations and will demand some of the earnings. The investor will be at risk as to when and how much of the investment to recoup, and whether there will be a return on the investment.

Partnerships provide opportunity for the prospective business owner to share the ownership and responsibilities of the business with another person. If you enter a partnership, it is strongly suggested that you formulate a written agreement that clearly details each partner's rights and obligations. Though the primary intent of a partnership is based on mutual trust and confidence in one another, your capital and personal assets can be at risk due to the actions of your partner. Whether your business is successful or fails may depend largely on your choice of one or more partners.

Leasing may be an attractive arrangement to have in your start-up financial planning package. Leasing, sometimes from the franchise system itself, entails paying a monthly fee to rent equipment, furnishings, and fixtures for your franchised location. Usually, the lease contains a buyout provision at the end of the leasing period, where the business owner can buy the leased equipment, fixtures, or furnishings at a prearranged price. In many industries, equipment may become worn, obsolete, or have but a minimal value within five to ten years, so that at the end of a lease period, it may be more effective for the firm to enter a new leasing arrangement than operate with the older, worn equipment or interior furnishings.

An often asked question is: Which franchise systems have franchisees that get Small Business Association (SBA) backed loans? According to the SBA Franchise Registry, franchise systems that facilitate SBA loans are in a broad array of business categories. Franchises that use SBA financing options tend to be smaller than larger franchise systems. Almost 60 percent of franchise systems that apply to be listed on the SBA Registry had less than 100 franchised units. Note, however, franchise systems such as Burger King, Dairy Queen, Dunkin' Brands, and Subway are included in the 40 percent that are larger. The value proposition of the SBA loan program appeals to a broad spectrum of franchise systems. Small and large, as well as young and mature systems, have found the SBA loan programs to help their plans for growth.

11-2 MANAGING WORKING CAPITAL

Successfull management of the working capital in franchised businesses may be the key to maintaining the profitability. **Working capital** refers to all the current assets of the firm; more specifically, net working capital equals current assets minus current liabilities:

$$\text{Current Assets} - \text{Current Liabilities} = \text{Net Working Captial}$$

Working capital for Tracy's Sandwich Shoppe is $60,000 - $20,000 = $40,000. These funds are generated from the operation of the franchised business. Sales of goods and services bring into the business new working capital (current assets), and expenses incurred in order to create sales (current liabilities) reduce working capital.

Generally, responsibility for "managing" working capital means one must keep track and understand the position of cash, marketable securities (investments), and inventory, as well as accounts receivable, current assets, accounts payable, and other current liabilities. Understanding these concepts and keeping an appropriate balance between cash inflow and outflow are essential to effective net working capital management. Managing net working capital is critical to enhancing business profits. An owner should keep in mind that working capital is generally 50 percent of total assets and liabilities.

Timing is essential to effective capital management. The key is to maximize cash inflow while minimizing cash outflow. In practice, this means one should try to buy resources at the lowest possible cost, while selling the products at the highest possible price (given competitive conditions), and at the same time collecting as early as possible from accounts receivable. In other words, working capital management is an attempt to achieve a balance by maintaining as low a level of cash on any given day (minimizing idle funds) in relation to current liabilities (claims against cash that are to be paid) in order to have sufficient funds available to avoid nonpayment of these obligations.

Often, timing of cash income and outflow is predictable. For example, Tracy's Sandwich Shoppe franchisees can forecast a fourteen-day working capital cycle based on past business practice. Figure 11-1 illustrates a Tracy's franchisee with a cash flow period (capital cycle) of fourteen days. This period of time is a normative (or average) period for the franchisee to (1) order food from suppliers, (2) receive the food, (3) store the food, (4) prepare the food, and (5) generate a customer order. Working capital management is the attempt to minimize the cash "gap" between ordering the food and receiving payment. This cash gap is narrowed through the management of inventory to the management of cash to pay for the inventory. The balance sought here is the risk trade-off between anticipated level of sales (customer demand) and amount of inventory to be purchased.

To reiterate, working capital management is managing the flow of funds into and out of the franchised business. More specifically, it is managing the gap between purchasing the product

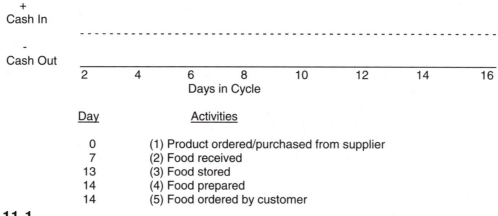

FIGURE **11-1**

Working Capital Cycle for Tracy's Sandwich Shoppe

materials and selling the product or supplying credit to the customer. Businesses by nature are cash deficient and must manage working capital—especially cash. Managing cash is perhaps the most dynamic element of running a business.

11-2a   Cash Management

Cash may be the most critical financial component of working capital, and as a result it is the item watched most carefully. Operational policies and managerial actions of the franchised firm should be aimed toward effective accumulation, expenditure, and control of cash. The franchisee should seek to minimize the risk of running out of cash. Sales are the main source of cash inflow. Cash in low levels must be balanced against the outflows due to purchases of inventory in order to make the sales and other expenses of the business. Yet, if the franchisee simply allows cash to remain idle, then no opportunity gain (earned interest) can be made.

There is another way to achieve the balance or synchronization associated with managing cash. The franchised business must ensure that bills due (accounts receivable) are collected in a timely manner. The franchise owner may develop policies and practices to expedite payments from customers for purchases made. The well-worn reason of "the check is in the mail" can cost the franchise an opportunity to earn interest on marketable securities or it can cause a loss of sales as a result of unpurchased inventory or insufficient stock to make sales. Methods to help synchronize cash inflow with outflow are cash discounts and lockbox systems to assist in the inflow of cash and the timely investing of idle cash through marketable securities or time-deposit accounts that earn interest. The goal of the franchised firm should be to keep its available cash working at all times. The following examples are part of a viable cash management program.

Cash Discounts

Cash discounting means reducing the price of the product or service if payment is made earlier than what is typical business practice for making payment. For example, the policy of 2/10 net 30 is a common cash discounting practice. This means the seller will allow a 2 percent discount off the purchase price if the customer pays for the product or service in full within ten days instead of the thirty days normally taken to make payment in full. For example, a customer who would buy a $800 desk could settle the debt owed by paying $784 within 10 days of making the purchase, or by paying the full $800 within thirty days. The **lockbox** concept means the business has a post office box for receiving payments that is managed by a commercial bank. Customers who owe accounts payable to the franchised business send their payment to the post office box instead of to the place of business.

This practice facilitates the collection of cash, because the commercial bank is directly collecting payment and making the deposit to the account of the franchised business. Lockboxes are practical and are used by a number of large, high-volume businesses. Smaller chains and franchises may find the costs of maintaining a lockbox system prohibitive and so may rely primarily or solely on offering cash discounts to encourage early payment. Franchise systems in areas such as auto parts, auto service or repair, tires, home cleaning, lawn service, and business services may wish to have a policy known to their customers which rewards early payment. Other franchises, such as those which have a high volume and a low unit price per product or service (fast-food restaurants, beverage or snack shops, etc.), typically collect cash or require a credit card at the point of purchase. These types of businesses usually have little need for cash discounting or other early remittance policies.

Marketable Securities

Marketable securities or other liquid investments can also be significant components of the cash assets or net working capital of the franchised business. Typically, marketable securities are very liquid, interest-bearing, low-risk financial assets. Examples of marketable securities are bank certificates of deposit (CDs), government securities (T-bills), and commercial paper held by the franchised business as short-term investments.

Sound financial planning for the franchised business owner is to hold only enough cash to ensure the availability of sufficient working capital, while investing all excess cash. These excess funds, invested at "market" (i.e., competitive) rates, can be used by the business during times when working capital has become unexpectedly short. For example, if a sales promotion planned between the franchisor and the franchisee necessitates purchasing more inventory than normal, then the franchisee could sell marketable securities to have the cash to spend for the additional inventory. Financing the inventory by selling the marketable securities may be significantly "cheaper" than extending the line of credit with the franchisor or other supplier or by seeking a short-term loan from a bank.

Idle cash resulting from excess working capital does not earn a return. Idle cash will not have a compounding effect for the franchisor (or the franchisee); that is, it does not work to increase the amount of cash available to the business. Investing the idle cash in marketable securities is an effective way to manage the cash account to the best advantage of the business. The following equation illustrates this concept and indicates how a franchisor or a franchisee can calculate earned interest on marketable securities:

$$\text{Annual Interest Rate} \times \frac{\text{Number of Days Invested}}{365} \times \text{Amount Invested} = \text{Earned Income}$$

For example, if a Tracy's Sandwich Shoppe franchisee has idle cash of $15,000 available for two months or sixty-one days, the cash may be invested at the market rate, say 8.5 percent, to earn interest for the franchisee.

$$0.085 \times \frac{61}{365} \times 15,000 = 213.08$$

The *opportunity cost* of cash in this illustration is $213.08. It is the amount the franchisee would forgo—or not earn—by having the $15,000 remain idle for those sixty-one days. The $213.08 should not be used to supplement the regular cash account. Rather, it should be used to create a reservoir of cash for unscheduled or unanticipated cash outflows.

11-2b   Accounts Receivable Management

Accounts receivable management addresses the firm's policies and activities associated with the selling of product or service on credit. Credit in this situation means the cash the franchisee is using to finance the sale. If the franchisee has a credit policy of "forty days same as cash," the customer has forty days to make the payment for the purchase. This policy also means the franchisee must be willing to finance the customer for forty days. To effectively manage working capital, the franchisee should attempt to make sure the customer will pay in full within these forty days.

A franchisee should realize that there is a direct relationship between sales volume and credit. The more generous (or liberal) the franchisee's credit policy, the more the sales volume increases. Yet, the more purchases made because of generous or lenient credit terms, the greater the risk of "bad debts" as a result of these credit sales. As credit terms are relaxed or lowered, more and more people find they can purchase products or services by scheduling out the payments. Unfortunately, some of these people become too extended in their credit purchases and find themselves unable to pay. Thus, the seller can increase sales volume through liberal credit policies, but a certain portion of those sales will be made to people who will be unable to pay. This results in the creation of bad debt for the franchisee as the seller, because the product or service has been provided or sold, but payment has not been received. This condition can destroy the balance sought through management of working capital.

Managing working capital is not easy, but experience with customer credit and planning sales volume will greatly increase effective management of accounts receivable. It is important to remember that the ultimate goal for the franchisee is to reduce cash commitment (or financing investment) in accounts receivable, which in turn increases the effectiveness of working capital.

11-2c   Inventory Management

Inventory management is another way to significantly reduce working capital requirements. Every franchisee should know that when inventory is low, the possibility of lost sales increases. If the franchisee does not have the materials to cook, assemble, combine, and so forth, to make a sale, then a sale cannot be made. The franchisee can take a number of actions to enhance inventory control, to minimize the risk of losing sales, but in general a franchised business should try to keep inventory investment costs at a minimum while being certain not to run out of product. Other factors to manage are costs of making orders, carrying costs (financing of inventory), and related costs attributable to inventory such as insurance, storage, taxes, and, of course, obsolescence. The franchisor will often develop an approach to inventory management, test it, and then recommend it to franchisees to help them minimize their inventory costs. There are models such as the economic order quantity (EOQ) approach that can help the franchisor and the franchisees manage inventory more effectively.

11-2d   Current Liability Management

Accounts payable are short-term obligations created by the franchisee in buying supplies, materials, or services associated with running the business. The franchisee does not pay cash for the supplies, but rather purchases the products or services on credit extended by the seller. Accounts payable are liabilities of the business. Liabilities must be managed as effectively as the assets (cash, marketable securities, inventory) in working capital. Generally, current liability management involves the financing of current assets. Figure 11-2 illustrates the difference between current liability management and the capitalization of the business.

Let's say that Tracy's franchisee purchases a $6,000 computer system for use by the business to develop and maintain the franchisee's records as well as to assist in financial planning and control. The purchase will be financed by a one-year bank note, which is a short-term liability for the business. On the other hand, if the franchisor were to build a new office or add a new showroom, it is likely the financing would be either through a mortgage (as a long-term liability) or through issuance of bonds or stocks in the company (from the equity portion of the franchisee's balance sheet). The rule of thumb for accounts payable management is to finance the current assets in such a way as to ensure that the asset is bought and paid for before the asset is fully depreciated.

	ASSETS	**LIABILITIES & EQUITY**	
Financing Current Assets (e.g., Inventory)	Current Assets	Short-term Liabilities Long-term Liabilities	Financing for Short Term
Financing Long-term Assets (Office, Building, Showroom, etc.)	Long-term Assets	Stocks Retained Earnings	Financing for Long Term

FIGURE **11-2**

Role of Current Liabilities for Financing the Franchisee's Asset

Accounts payable management is an important consideration when the franchised business is seeking to obtain a short-term loan. If net working capital is not properly managed, or seasonal sales dictate, the business owner may find it necessary to borrow for the short term in order to have sufficient cash to purchase inventory or pay salaries. The cost of borrowing can be significant and can cause a drain on working capital. The franchised business owner not only forgoes the opportunity to receive interest earned from invested funds (that otherwise would be idle cash), but also has to pay interest—out of working capital—for the funds borrowed.

Borrowing funds is a normal and appropriate activity for a business. From time to time funds will be borrowed for a number of reasons such as meeting short-term obligations of running the business, purchasing equipment, constructing a building, or purchasing vehicles for delivery. These actions are part of the typical capital requirements of being in business. It is the unexpected, unplanned borrowing of funds that runs counter to effective management of working capital.

Methods for borrowing funds in the short term can vary significantly. The most common methods involve borrowing at simple, add-on, or discount interest rates. Table 11-1 illustrates the differences between these methods of computing interest. For instance, if a franchisee borrows $4,200 to pay for a shipment of inventory needed for the next season of merchandise, the stated annual percentage rate (APR) in each example is the same, but the annual interest rate differs depending on the approach taken by the lender. The annual interest rate is 22.32 percent for the add-on approach, 25.4 percent using the discount method, and 12.5 percent using the simple interest approach.

In the add-on approach, the interest charged is "added on" to the amount borrowed, meaning the balance of the loan is $4,725 for the year. Monthly payments are $393.75, and the franchised business receives the $4,200 to pay for the inventory. Using the simple interest method, the interest charge is $289.80, which is added to the $4,200 borrowed, for a balance of $4,489.80. Monthly payments of $374.15 will clear the loan in one year. The discount method has interest of $525, which instead of being added to the amount of the loan is deducted from the proceeds of the loan. The franchised business receives $3,675, has a balance of $4,200, and will pay $350 per month to clear the loan in one year.

So we can see that getting the best rate of interest is not the critical question; rather, it is what method is being used to finance the funds to be borrowed. Within a local marketplace, the rates of interest for short-term loans are likely to be the same or similar. The method used to calculate the interest for the loans makes the primary difference. Therefore, it is to the advantage of the franchise owner to seek simple interest borrowing if at all possible, and to avoid the discount method, as it is usually the most costly for the borrower.

TABLE 11-1	INTEREST COMPARISONS BY METHODS		
	Add-on	**Discount**	**Simple**
Amount Financed	$4,200	$4,200	$4,200
Stated APR*	12.5%	12.5%	12.5%
Loan Maturity	I year	I year	1 year
Repayment Terms	monthly	monthly	monthly
Interest Charges	$ 525	$ 525	$ 289.80
Loan Proceeds	$4,200	$3,675	$4,200
Balance Due	$4,725	$4,200	$4,489.80
Monthly Payments	$ 393.75	$ 350	$ 374.15
Annual Simple Interest Rate	22.32%	25.4%	12.5%

*According to the Fair Credit in Reporting Act, nominal interest rates are stated in annual percentage rates.

As shown in Table 11-1, the franchised business can minimize the number of times it confronts opportunity costs of cash. If the franchised business owner does not effectively manage the cash, then the firm will either quickly, or gradually, deplete its cash, and its costs of doing business will increase. The costs may increase because of the interest payments that must be made to acquire cash to cover the short-term obligations incurred. If the market conditions confronting the franchised business are highly competitive, then the firm may only survive in the short run.

To summarize this section on working capital, franchisors or franchisees should keep two objectives in mind regarding cash management. First, the franchise owner should maintain a keen interest in the level of cash available in the business in order to determine and maintain the level of cash that could be invested to maximize the time value (opportunity gain) of funds. Second, the franchise owner must understand working capital and its components in relation to the business in which the franchise is engaged and the competitive conditions confronted. This is important in order to forecast accurately the minimum cash balances needed at a given time within the firm. By keeping minimum cash balances available, the short-term as well as long-term obligations can be met in a timely manner. Any excess cash can be invested and can reap a return on the investment prior to the time when that sum of cash is needed by the business.

To achieve these two objectives, the franchised business owner must be able to forecast cash needs or balances. This is usually accomplished by development and use of the *cash flow statement*. Figure 11-3 illustrates a cash budget set up on a monthly basis for the first year of operations. This figure reveals the monthly cash receipts (cash in) and cash disbursements (cash out) for Tracy's franchisor headquarters.

The cash flow statement, as illustrated for Tracy's franchisor headquarters, is a significant financial planning document. The sales and other income are estimated for the period, in this example a quarter of a year. Cash disbursements such as salary or wages, rent or lease payments, insurance premiums, and utilities are usually more predictable than income because these expense items are relatively fixed. Variable expenses typically are accounts payable, inventory purchases, taxes (based on sales made as well as income or withholding taxes), and other costs attributable to the specific activities of the business venture. These costs will fluctuate with the level of sales experienced by the firm.

In a franchised business, there may be a cooperative advertising fee, a percentage of sales that a franchisee remits to the franchisor to assist in developing and paying for mass media advertisements.

FRANCHISOR	Month 1	Month 2	Month 3	Month 4	Month 5	Month 6	Month 7	Month 8	Month 9	Month 10	Month 11	Month 12	Year Total
Number of UNITS SOLD						1	0	1	1	1	1	1	5
Number of UNITS OPENED								0	1	1	2	2	2
CASH FLOW:													
Franchise Fees				0	0	16,000	0	16,000	0	16,000	16,000	16,000	80,000
Royalties									167	146	317	358	988
Interest Income	0	0	0	0	0	0	0	0	0	0	0	0	0
TOTAL CASH AVAILABLE					$0	$16,000	$0	$16,000	$167	$16,146	$16,317	$16,358	$80,988
DISBURSMENTS:													
Salaries - Executive	4,000	4,000	4,000	4,000	5,000	5,000	5,000	5,000	5,000	5,000	5,000	5,000	56,000
Salaries - Sales					4,500	4,500	4,500	4,500	4,500	4,500	4,500	4,500	36,000
Payroll Taxes													
FICA	306	306	306	306	727	727	727	727	727	727	727	727	7,038
Unemployment	60	60	60	60	143	143	143	143	143	143	143	143	1,380
Rent	1,000	1,000	1,000	1,000	1,000	1,000	1,000	1,000	1,000	1,000	1,000	1,000	12,000
Advertising													0
Legal				2,000	2,000	2,000	2,000	2,000	2,000	2,000	2,000	2,000	18,000
Travel - Executive	1,000	1,000	1,000	1,000	2,000	2,000	2,000	2,000	2,000	2,000	2,000	2,000	20,000
Travel - Sales					2,000	2,000	2,000	2,000	2,000	2,000	2,000	2,000	16,000
Manual Preparation			2,000	2,000									4,000
Printing					3,000				3,000				6,000
Sales and Commissions									2,000		2,000		4,000
Dues and Subscriptions						200		200		200	260		860
Loan Repayment							2,142	2,142	2,142	2,142	2,142	2,142	12,855
Insurance	500			500			500			500			2,000
Utilities	200	200	200	200	200	200	250	250	250	250	250	250	2,700
Gas/Water/Sewerage	250	250	250	250	250	250	300	300	300	300	300	300	3,300
Phone	100	100	100	200	200	200	200	200	200	200	250	250	2,250
Miscellaneous	250	250	250	250	250	250	250	250	250	250	250	250	3,000
Seminars and Meetings		2000			1,000				2000				5,000
TOTAL DISBURSMENTS	7,666	9,166	9,166	11,766	22,269	18,469	21,012	20,712	27,512	21,262	22,562	20,822	212,383
NET CASH FLOW	($7,666)	($9,166)	($9,166)	($11,766)	($22,269)	($2,469)	($21,012)	($4,712)	($27,345)	($5,116)	($6,245)	($4,463)	
CUMULATIVE CASH FLOW	($7,666)	($16,832)	($25,998)	($37,764)	($60,033)	($62,503)	($83,514)	($88,226)	($115,571)	($120,687)	($126,932)	($131,395)	

FIGURE **11-3**

Hypothetical Monthly Cash Flow Statement—2008

11-3   FINANCIAL PLANNING

Financial planning is a logical next step from the development and use of a cash budget and other financial tools mentioned in the preceding section. Generally, the term **financial planning** refers to the business owner's ability to plan and forecast the appropriate use of funds for the business. Financial planning helps the franchisor and the franchisee make independent judgments for their own businesses concerning cash surpluses, cash shortages, levels of sales to be sought, and those fixed and variable costs essential to produce the sales. Financial tools combined with financial ratio analysis can be used to assess the franchised business's performance.

Financial planning takes into account the long-range and short-range goals of the franchised firm, as well as the economic factors associated with the competitive conditions in the industry and the overall state of the economy. Our immediate task here is to review techniques or tools used to make financial forecasts, particularly in franchised businesses.

11-4   PRO FORMA STATEMENTS

Once again, the starting point of any financial planning system is the cash flow statement. The cash flow statement identifies the activities of the business in terms of cash receipts and cash disbursements and identifies the trends or changes occurring month to month and quarter to quarter. Usually, after two or three quarters (six or nine months), the franchised business owner may be able to accurately predict or project changes in the firm's cash position. More important than predicting changes in cash, however, the owner must understand the relationships peculiar to the type of business and the level of marketplace competition and must learn to predict sales and costs with some degree of accuracy. After eight or twelve quarters (two or three years), the history of the business's activity as depicted through the cash budget and its changes allows for more accuracy in forecasting. After specific trends are revealed within the cash budget, the franchised firm can estimate financial statements for periods into the future. These financial statements are called **pro forma statements**. Technically, pro forma means "in form only." Practically, pro forma financial statements are financial planning documents for the business to use as it tries to expand into new products or markets and/or deepen its market penetration.

Pro forma statements are planning tools which are always adjusted for accuracy after the facts (business activities/sales performance) are known. Therefore, these statements are never formally evaluated by an independent auditor or certified public accountant to attest to the accuracy of the business's activities. The three pro forma statements usually developed are the cash flow statement, income statement, and balance sheet forecasts.

Up to this point, only the "cash" perspective of the pro forma statements has been reviewed. Once the cash flow statement is developed, it can be used by the franchised business to project a more comprehensive view of the financial future of the business. The pro forma income statement and balance sheet can be prepared. Each is a separate budget plan which helps the franchisor or the franchisee see where expected revenues will come from and in what amounts on a month-to-month basis. A budget plan can be extended into the future to indicate one, two, three, or more years of planned sales revenue and operating expenses. The primary value of such a plan is to help the business keep on target with its intended rate of growth and evaluate this growth on a regular basis. The pro forma income statement and balance sheet can also be very helpful to a franchisor who intends to phase down or out of a particular district or area. The budget plan would show how the franchise system plans to retrench and in what stages that retrenchment will take place over a period of time.

> Of interest to note: Although franchising has existed in the United States for over 200 years, particularly in product and trade name franchise categories, it did not have substantial notice by the consuming public until the 1950s to 1960s with the rapid development of franchised food service. Now only about 30 percent of franchises are in the food service industry. Other areas of business-format franchising have had rapid growth since the 1970s in areas such as business services, auto repair, home maintenance, health care, beauty, and personal fitness.
>
> Adapted from www.clarioinledger.com/apps/pbes.dll/2007/311/BIZ, March 13, 2007.

11-4a Pro Forma Income Statement

The first step in setting up a pro forma (or operating plan) income statement is to develop sales projections. The initial sales projections are taken from the cash flow statement. The cash receipts section of the cash flow statement reveals the sales on a month-to-month basis. Although a pro forma income statement can be prepared monthly, it is most commonly prepared as a quarterly statement; that is, activities over three months are recorded together. Four quarterly periods equal one year's income and expense activity for the business (see Figure 11-4).

To bridge from the cash flow statement to the pro forma income statement, some basic questions must be asked about the data in the cash budget. For example, will trends (sales, costs, etc.) identified in the cash budget on a month-to-month basis continue? Will other noncontrollable economic factors (the nation's money supply, rate of inflation, interest costs, etc.) create deviating trends? More specifically, the overall economy could be entering or coming out of a recession, which is a noncyclical trend; or other noncyclical factors could affect the economy, such as insurrection in a foreign country, forming or dissolving of cartels of critical resources, assassination of a world leader, or major changes in a business regulation or tax law.

After the basic assumptions about the overall economy, as well as the local economy where the franchised business operations are located, have been made, then the historical trends presented in the cash budget may be used for developing future projections.

> You can find a franchise to buy for almost any budget. The key is to find something you love to do and can make a career out of doing.

11-4b Economic Assumptions in Financial Planning

Making valid, logical assumptions concerning the economies of the United States and the particular local community is significant to the franchised firm's financial planning. For example, let's assume that the local economy of a given town is not growing. In fact, conditions are sluggish and the local economy is actually slumping. Young people are moving out of the area and disposable income is generally decreasing. In this type of economy, the local Tracy's Sandwich Shoppe should reduce projected sales. A franchised unit's sales reflect the effort of the franchisee to produce sales and make a profit within a particular market area; however, overall economic conditions can also shape the sales that will be made. Boosting sales efforts will not always result in dramatic sales increases if there are fewer people willing or able to buy. Therefore, factors such as effective buying income, construction starts, utility usage rates, and general retail sales levels can be used and compared with the same statistics for earlier years to determine overall rate of growth, stability, or decline within a local economy.

FRANCHISOR	Month 1	Month 2	Month 3	Month 4	Month 5	Month 6	Month 7	Month 8	Month 9	Month 10	Month 11	Month 12	Year Total
INCOME:													
Franchise Fees	0	0	0	0	0	16,000	0	16,000	0	16,000	16,000	16,000	80,000
Royalties	0	0	0	0	0	0	0	0	167	146	317	358	988
Other Income	0	0	0	0	0	0	0	0	0	0	0	0	0
TOTAL INCOME	$0	$0	$0	$0	$0	$16,000	$0	$16,000	$167	$16,146	$16,317	$16,358	$80,988
EXPENSES:													
Salaries & Wages - Executive	4,000	4,000	4,000	4,000	5,000	5,000	5,000	5,000	5,000	5,000	5,000	5,000	56,000
Salaries & Wages - Sales	0	0	0	0	4,500	4,500	4,500	4,500	4,500	4,500	4,500	4,500	36,000
Payroll Taxes													
FICA	306	306	306	306	727	727	727	727	727	727	727	727	7,038
Unemployment	60	60	60	60	143	143	143	143	143	143	143	143	1,380
Benefits	360	360	360	360	855	855	855	855	855	855	855	855	8,280
Rent	1,000	1,000	1,000	1,000	1,000	1,000	1,000	1,000	1,000	1,000	1,000	1,000	12,000
Advertising	0	0	0	0	0	0	0	0	0	0	0	0	0
Legal	0	0	0	2,000	2,000	2,000	2,000	2,000	2,000	2,000	2,000	2,000	18,000
Travel - Executive	1,000	1,000	1,000	1,000	2,000	2,000	2,000	2,000	2,000	2,000	2,000	2,000	20,000
Travel - Sales	0	0	0	0	2,000	2,000	2,000	2,000	2,000	2,000	2,000	2,000	16,000
Manual Preparation	0	0	2,000	2,000	0	0	0	0	0	0	0	0	4,000
Printing	0	0	0	0	3,000	0	0	0	3,000	0	0	0	6,000
Sales and Commissions	0	0	0	0	0	0	0	0	2,000	0	2,000	0	4,000
Dues and Subscriptions	0	0	0	0	0	200	0	200	0	200	0	260	860
Loan Repayment	0	0	0	0	0	0	2,142	2,142	2,142	2,142	2,142	2,142	12,855
Insurance	500	0	0	500	0	0	500	0	0	500	0	0	2,000
Utilities	200	200	200	200	200	200	250	250	250	250	250	250	2,700
Gas/Water/Sewerage	250	250	250	250	250	250	300	300	300	300	300	300	3,300
Phone	100	100	100	200	200	200	200	200	200	250	250	250	2,250
Depreciation	476	476	476	476	476	476	476	476	476	476	476	476	5,716
Miscellaneous	250	250	250	250	250	250	250	250	250	250	250	250	3,000
Seminars and Meetings	0	2,000	0	0	1,000	0	0	0	2,000	0	0	0	5,000
Total Operating Expenses	8,502	10,002	10,002	12,602	23,601	19,801	22,343	22,043	28,843	22,593	23,893	22,153	226,379
Operating Income	($8,502)	($10,002)	($10,002)	($12,602)	($23,601)	($3,801)	($22,343)	($6,043)	($28,676)	($6,447)	($7,576)	($5,795)	($145,391)
Corporate Taxes	0	0	0	0	0	0	0	0	0	0	0	0	0
Net Income	($8,502)	($10,002)	($10,002)	($12,602)	($23,601)	($3,801)	($22,343)	($6,043)	($28,676)	($6,447)	($7,576)	($5,795)	($145,391)

FIGURE 11-4

Hypothetical Monthly Income Statement—2008

TRACY'S SANDWICH SHOPPE PRO FORMA BALANCE SHEET

	Year Ended	Quarter Ended
ASSETS		
Current Assets		
Cash	$18,000	$15,000
Investment	2,000	1,700
Accounts receivable	20,000	16,700
Raw materials	8,000	6,700
Finished goods	12,000	10,000
Total Current Assets	60,000	50,100
Fixed Assets	55,000	54,200
Less Depreciation	(15,000)	(29,200)
Total Assets	$100,000	$75,100
LIABILITIES AND EQUITY		
Current Liabilities		
Notes payable	10,000	8,300
Accounts payable	5,000	4,200
Due franchisor	2,500	2,100
Interest payable	2,500	2,100
Total Current Liabilities	20,000	16,700
Long-term Liabilities	20,000	16,700
Stockholders' Equity	35,000	24,400
Retained earnings	25,000	17,300
Total Liabilities and Equity	$100,000	$75,100

FIGURE **11-5**

Hypothetical Pro Forma Balance Sheet

The basic and most essential variable of the financial planning tools is the **sales forecast**. The percentage of sales method is a common device to project sales in the next period or year. It is simply an extrapolation of past sales set in terms of the general economic conditions confronting the local economy. However, a franchisor or franchisee can use three other sales forecasting techniques.

1. Extrapolation or trend analysis, including "grass roots" input

2. Executive decision making—setting sales goals by the management team

3. Sophisticated econometrics or statistical modeling methods

The percentage of sales method is an extrapolation technique that requires the executive or management team to make key assumptions about the overall and local economies. Large franchised systems, such as fast-food restaurants, auto parts/services, or major rental companies, often use all three techniques. The most commonly used technique is extrapolation or trend analysis, including "grass roots" input, in which the franchisor calls local franchisees or requests written estimates to evaluate future sales potential.

11-4c   Pro Forma Balance Sheet

The cash flow statement is used to plan liquidity. The income statement is used to plan profitability for the franchise business. The **pro forma balance sheet** is a budget or plan of the assets and liabilities of the business. It is a natural extension of the cash flow and income statement. Figure 11-5 presents a hypothetical pro forma balance sheet for Tracy's Sandwich Shoppe.

The data contained within the pro forma balance sheet comes from the cash flow statement, any changes in taxes or retained earnings (the pro forma income statement), and the *actual* balance sheet variables contained in the last quarter's balance sheet. The pro forma balance sheet is not an audited financial statement, but a *planning tool* which provides an analysis of what funds are needed to operate and effectively manage the franchised business.

Therefore, the various assumptions used in the cash flow statement and pro forma income statement affect the pro forma balance sheet. The inverse of this is true also. That is, the pro forma balance sheet affects the pro forma income statement and cash flow statement. The planned sales revenue, operating costs, asset development/depreciation, and liabilities are linked through these statements about future efforts planned within the franchise business.

Al Copeland

Copeland's

In 1972, entrepreneur Al Copeland opened the first Popeye's Famous Fried Chicken restaurant in the suburbs of New Orleans. His unique spicy recipe, created out of his love for the foods of south Louisiana, launched a hospitality industry career that today includes restaurants and comedy clubs, a food manufacturing and supply company, and hotels.

At the start, Copeland had little more than the rags to make his own rags-to-riches story come true. Living with his grandmother in a housing project, the man who would revolutionize the fast-food industry by introducing the world to zesty Cajun foods first delivered papers for a few pennies then divided his time between bagging groceries in a supermarket and making donuts at a shop owned by his brother.

"All you have to do is believe in yourself," says Copeland, who found inspiration in the success stories of his day. The values he read about in Horatio Alger tales—hard work, imagination, ability to survive disappointment—became the principles by which he lived. His formula for success is simple: "I owe it to 16-hour days, working two and even three jobs at a time, self-confidence, taking calculated risks, setting goals and pursuing them and learning something new every day about the business I'm in."

He began franchising Popeye's in 1976 and eventually grew the company to more than 800 outlets around the world. With the highest per-unit volume in the segment, by 1991 revenues reached $500,000. While Popeye's has been owned by America's Favorite Chicken since 1992, Copeland retains ownership of several franchises and received the company's Lifetime Achievement Award in 1993.

In 1983, he founded Copeland's of New Orleans, a casual full service restaurant he created to give diners far from the city he loves the enjoyment of authentic Louisiana dishes, made fresh from the best ingredients. Starting in 1993, he began a unique franchise program that gives other entrepreneurs the Copeland's of New Orleans opportunity. By 2000, there were seventeen company-owned locations in Louisiana, Mississippi, Maryland, Virginia, and Texas, and twenty-four franchise locations in Alabama, Arizona, Kansas, Louisiana, Florida, Georgia, Mississippi, North Carolina, South Carolina, Ohio, and Tennessee. With several other locations in development, Copeland's of New Orleans continues to spread exciting flavor to cities around the country.

Al Copeland spends long hours in the test kitchen developing the recipes that garner rave reviews and earn top rank in restaurant ratings year after year. He is also proud of his home-town's famous hospitality, which is an important ingredient in his recipe for success.

Copeland's Cheesecake Bistro restaurant, featuring a bakery along with a menu of nearly 100 selections, and Improv Comedy Clubs are Al Copeland's newest concepts. With the purchase of Improv in 1999, Al entered an entirely new and exciting venture that combines live comedy entertainment with famous Copeland's food and hospitality. Including franchise locations, plans call for the development of as many as twelve Improv Comedy Clubs in as many cities.

The hotel business is a natural extension of Al Copeland's spirit of hospitality. The luxury Straya Grand Boutique on St. Charles Avenue is his third hotel property in the New Orleans area.

Diversified Foods & Seasonings, which Al established in 1972, manufactures and supplies proprietary food products for his own restau-rants as well as Popeye's and other food service, industrial, and restaurant clients. In 2001, Diver-sified move into a modern new $22 million facil-ity near New Orleans.

SUMMARY

Financial planning allows the franchisor and the franchisee as independent business owners to develop solid accounting systems and budgeting systems which are synchronized (or linked) with the sales goals of the franchised business. Financial planning enables the franchisor and franchisee to evaluate performance of the franchise system for the franchisor, and the franchised unit for the franchisee.

Figure 11-6 provides an overall view of the financial process, illustrating the financial planning and budgeting process through the various financial tools necessary to complete this essential type of planning.

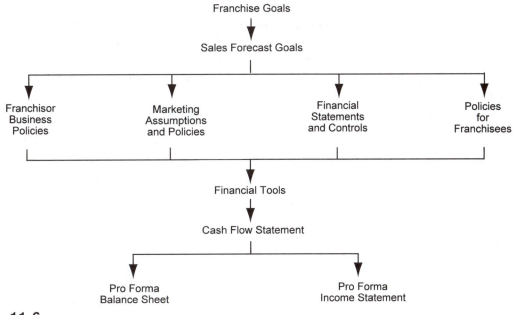

FIGURE **11-6**

Overview of Financial Process in a Franchised Business

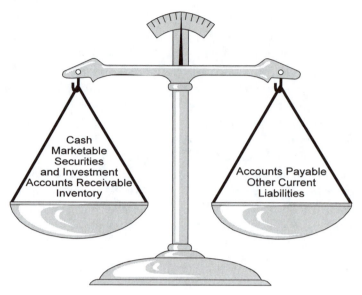

FIGURE **11-7**

"Balancing Act" Current Assets = Current Liabilities

The financial planning process illustrated in Figure 11-6 begins with the franchise owner's goals and assumptions about how well the business can do given the economic and competitive conditions it confronts. The marketing, financial, and operating objectives of the franchise should be integrative and comprehensive for the franchise to be truly effective in following a strategy for success in the marketplace. The financial policies and objectives help establish the financial controls. The financial controls and financial statements help management understand what the past period's performance means in relation to what is planned for the future. This requires the franchisor or the franchisee to understand the use of financial tools. It is through the financial tools described in this chapter and the essentials of business finance presented in Chapter 10 that a cash flow statement, pro forma balance sheet, and pro forma income statement can be developed.

Appropriate use of these financial statements allows the franchised business to pursue effective working capital management, accounts receivable management, inventory management, marketable securities and liquidity management, and short-term and long-term debt management.

Figure 11-7 illustrates the balancing act a franchised business owner must perform. The owner seeks to achieve a balance between the inflow and outflow of cash through the accounts described in this chapter.

The financial planning process involves the development of a cash flow statement, followed by essential pro forma statements. These pro forma financial statements are useful to plan, coordinate, evaluate, and control the franchised business's operations. The overall planning documents are essential for financial forecasting and effective management of the franchised business.

KEY TERMS

Accounts receivable management: addresses the firm's policies and activities associated with the selling of product or service on credit.

Financial planning: refers to the franchisor and franchisees abilities to plan and forecast the appropriate use of funds for the franchise system and any particular franchised unit.

Lockbox: means the franchise business has a post office box for receiving payments from franchisees (and others) that is managed by a commercial bank.

Net working capital: refers to current assets minus current liabilities.

Pro forma balance sheet: is a budget or plan about the assets and liabilities of the business. It is a natural extension of the cash flow and income statement.

Pro forma statements: are estimated financial statements for future periods.

Sales forecast: means to project sales in the next period or year. It is simply an extrapolation of past sales set in terms of the general economic conditions for the local economy. Four different approaches are commonly utilized by franchise systems.

Working Capital:

REVIEW QUESTIONS

1. What is a cash flow statement?
2. What is a pro forma balance sheet?
3. What is a pro forma income statement?
4. How are each of these statements used in a franchised business?
5. What interrelationships exist between these statements?
6. Why should a franchised business be interested in financial planning?

CASE STUDY

Your Franchised Business's Cash Flow

Figure 11-8 identifies a projected cash flow for "Your Franchised Business." Sources of cash and anticipated disbursements for the next twelve months have been projected. Net profit amounts, loan payments, withdrawals, depreciation, and income tax payments have been carefully determined. The result is that a net cash flow as well as a cumulative cash flow is available as a planning or control tool as well as a projection of cash sources and disbursements that can help others identify anticipated results of your business in its first year. After carefully examining the projected cash flow figures, answer the following questions.

CASE QUESTIONS

1. Why is a cash flow projection considered an important tool to both the franchisor and the franchisee?
2. Explain why the net cash flow figure is negative in October, November, and April of the projected year.
3. Given the total amount of cash available, does the anticipated disbursement of cash appear to be realistic?

	Preoperating	Oct	Nov	Dec	Jan	Feb	Mar	Apr	May	June	July	Aug	Sept	Total
Cash Sources														
Equity	$20,000	—	—	—	—	—	—	—	—	—	—	—	—	$20,000
Loan	$65,000	—	—	—	—	—	—	—	—	—	—	—	—	$65,000
Net Profit	0	478	1,001	2,234	1,738	1,491	1,745	1,749	1,752	2,008	2,010	2,264	2,267	$20,737
Depreciation	0	300	300	300	300	300	300	300	300	300	300	300	300	$3,600
Total	$85,000	778	1,301	2,534	2,038	1,791	2,045	2,049	2,052	2,308	2,310	2,564	2,567	$109,337
Disbursements Purchase of Business	$50,000	—	—	—	—	—	—	—	—	—	—	—	—	$50,000
Franchise Royalty Fee	$9,200	—	—	—	—	—	—	—	—	—	—	—	—	$9,200
Improvements and Equipment	$17,000	—	—	—	—	—	—	—	—	—	—	—	—	$17,000
Deposits	$1,400	—	—	—	—	—	—	—	—	—	—	—	—	$1,400
Loan Payments (Principal)	0	400	405	410	415	420	425	430	435	440	445	450	455	$5,130
Owner's Draw	0	1,000	1,000	1,000	1,200	1,200	1,200	1,200	1,200	1,200	1,200	1,200	1,200	$13,800
Income Taxes	0	—	—	—	—	—	—	$1,047	—	—	—	—	—	$1,047
Total	$77,600	1,400	1,405	1,410	1,615	1,620	1,625	2,677	1,635	1,640	1,645	1,650	1,655	$97,577
Net Cash Flow	$7,400	(622)	(104)	1,124	423	171	420	(628)	417	668	665	914	912	$11,760
Cumulative Cash Flow	$7,400	6,778	6,674	7,798	8,221	8,392	8,812	8,184	8,601	9,269	9,934	10,848	11,760	

FIGURE **11-8**

Your Franchised Business Projected Cash Flow—2008

4. Explain how this franchised business can have a total net profit in excess of $20,000, while the net cash flow is less than $11,760.

REFERENCES

Bank of America, "Buying a Franchise," *Small Business Reporter*, 1996.

Bank of American, "Financing Small Business," *Small Business Reporter*, 1996.

Beals, J. and T. Muris, "The Foundations of Franchise Regulation: Issues and Evidence," *Journal of Corporate Finance* 2 (1995): 157–197.

"Business Update," *The Clarion Ledger*, 13 March 2007, www.clarionledger.com/apps/phes.dll/2007/311/BIZ.

Caffey, Andy, "Are You Franchisee Material?" 4 April 2007, www.entrepreneur.com/article/printthis/17204.html.

"Cash Flow: Who's in Charge," *Inc* 15(11) (November 1993): 140.

Ernst & Whitney, *Deciding to Go Public—Understanding the Process and the Alternatives*, Ernst & Whitney no. 42323, 1984.

Henward, DeBanks M. and William Ginalski, *The Franchise Option* (Phoenix: Franchise Group Publishers, 1979).

International Franchise Association, *200l Benchmarking Report (2000 data)* (Boulder, CO: Profit Planning Group, 2001)

Justis, Robert T., Richard J. Judd, and David B. Stephens, *Strategic Management and Policy: Concepts & Cases* (Englewood Cliffs, NJ: Prentice-Hall, Inc., 1985).

Norton, S., "Is Franchising a Capital Structure Issue?" *Journal of Corporate Finance* 2 (1995): 75–101.

PriceWaterhouseCoopers, *Economic Impact of Franchised Businesses: A Study for the International Franchise Association Education Foundation* (Washington, DC: IFA Education Foundation, 2004).

Sen, K., "The Use of Initial Fees and Royalties in Business-format Franchising," *Managerial and Decision Economics* 21 (1993): 175–190.

Thakur, Manab N., "How to Conduct Financial Analysis for Policy Case Work," in Robert T. Justis, Richard J. Judd, and David B. Stephens, *Strategic Management and Policy: Concepts & Cases* (Englewood Cliffs, NJ: Prentice-Hall, Inc., 1985), 617–639.

The State of Small Business: A Report of the President (Washington, DC: U.S. Government Printing Office, 1996).

U.S. Small Business Administration, *Franchise Registry* (Washington, DC: SBA), www.sbaregistry@frandata.com.

Vaughn, Charles L., *Franchising*, 2nd ed. (Lexington, MA: Lexington Books, 1979).

"Working Capital," *Inc.* 17(6) (May 1995): 35.

INFORMATION SYSTEMS IN FRANCHISING*

In studying this chapter, you will:

- Typical information systems used typically by a start-up franchise.
- Typical information systems used typically by midsize franchise.
- Typical information systems used typically by a large franchise.
- The importance of using Application Service Providers (ASP) as a part of strategies for information systems investment.

INCIDENT

John is twenty six years old and just earned an MBA degree with a concentration in marketing. During his college years John worked part to full time at several restaurants. John wants to go into business for himself. He realizes that signing up with a franchise system will give him a better chance to succeed. Based on the Franchise Trends for 2001 published by Entrepreneur.com and his restaurant experiences, John is considering either a chicken wing restaurant or a family-style restaurant for his business. While in school, John read Bill Gates's (2000) book, *Business @ the Speed of Thought: Succeeding in the Digital Economy,* and was impressed by the following statement in the book: "Information Technology and business are becoming inextricably interwoven. I don't think anybody can talk meaningfully about one without talking about the other." John is wondering how information systems and the Internet are used in restaurant franchises. Will the size be a factor in using the information systems and the Internet? How about the costs of the information systems and e-business? Shall the franchisor or he build the information systems and e-business in-house or outsource them to application service providers?

12-1   INTRODUCTION

This chapter addresses five questions:

1. What kinds of information systems does a start-up franchise need?

2. What kinds of information systems does a midsize franchise need?

---

* The authors gratefully acknowledge Ye-Sho Chen, Louisiana State University, as the writer of this chapter.

3. What kinds of information systems does a large franchise need?

4. How do you deploy the e-business strategy in franchising?

5. How can a franchise invest in information systems and e-business wisely?

12-2   INFORMATION SYSTEMS FOR A START-UP FRANCHISE

In this section, we discuss the kinds of information systems needed in the two areas of a franchise business: the franchisor headquarters and the franchisee unit. The major goal of information systems at this stage is to provide solutions to increase franchise efficiency and productivity.[1][2] In the process, information systems can also help the franchise to develop working knowledge upon which the business can grow and expand.

12-2a   Information Systems for the Franchisor Headquarters

Before discussing information systems for a start-up franchisor, one must first observe the daily functions in the franchisor's headquarters. In general, we need to consider four crucial parties when running the franchisor's headquarters: the business units owned by franchisees or company, the prospective franchisees, the suppliers, and the government. Figure 12-1 depicts this business environment of the franchisor headquarters. Running the franchisor's headquarters office involves four major activities: (1) helping and supporting business units, (2) marketing and advertising to prospective franchisees for franchise development, (3) managing people who perform franchise

FIGURE 12-1

Business Environment at the Franchisor Headquarters

support and franchise development, and (4) dealing with financial issues such as accounting and finances.

The center of attention for all these activities should be the business units, because they are where tires meet the road. The three categories of business units are **start-up franchisees**, the ones the franchisor headquarters should do its best to support; **established franchisees**, the ones the franchisor headquarters needs to provide incentives to encourage expansion; and **company units**, the ones the company owns and wants to use as the role models for the franchisees.

The prospective franchisees contact the franchisor headquarter in various formats: (1) referrals that recommend their associates, friends, and relatives to contact the franchisor headquarters for the franchise opportunities, (2) current customers interested in owning and running the franchise units, and (3) leads generated from various marketing channels including advertisement, website promotion, community services, and public relationships.

Suppliers provide more to a franchisor headquarters than just the raw materials for producing goods and services at the business units. These suppliers may include marketing agents, accountants, insurance providers, attorneys, information systems vendors, real estate agents, and human resource management companies. Lastly, the franchisor headquarters is subject to the regulations of the government, including taxes and various business laws such as worker compensation.

Based on the business environment illustrated in Figure 12-1, information systems that can improve basic franchisor headquarter operations fall into five major categories (Table 12-1): (1) **franchise support system**, supporting business units using applications software for tasks such as help desk, performance tracking marketing and auditing; (2) **franchise development system**, contacting and building relationship with prospective franchisees using applications software for tasks such as marketing, contact management, and real estate management; (3) **franchisor headquarters office management system**, helping the franchisor deal with office issues using

---

TABLE 12-1   WHAT INFORMATION SYSTEMS CAN DO FOR THE FRANCHISOR HEADQUARTERS

Business Units

Franchisor Office

- Franchise Supports
  - Help Desk
  - Performance Tracking
  - Marketing
  - Auditing
- Franchise Development
  - Marketing
  - Prospective Franchisees Contact Management
  - Real Estate Management

Prospective Franchisees   **Government**

- Headquarters Office Management
  - Human Resources
  - Accounting
  - Financing
- Suppliers/Government Contact Management
  - Suppliers
  - Government
  - Communications with Business Units, Prospective Franchisees, Suppliers, and Government

Suppliers

TABLE 12-2	TYPICAL INFORMATION SYSTEMS FOR THE FRANCHISOR HEADQUARTERS				
Typical Information Systems Used	Franchise Support	Franchise Development	Office Management	Contact Management	Communications
Accounting			x		
Contact Management	x	x		x	x
Database Management	x	x		x	x
Desktop Publishing	x	x		x	x
E-Mail	x	x		x	x
Help Desk Management Systems	x			x	x
Presentation Programs	x	x			x
Spreadsheets	x	x			
Web Browsers	x	x		x	x
Web Site Development and Management	x			x	
Word Processing	x	x		x	x

applications software for tasks such as human resource management, accounting, and financing; (4) **suppliers/government contact management system**, contacting and building relationship with suppliers/government using applications software for tasks such as scheduling and reminders; and (5) **communication system**, helping the franchisor communicate efficiently and effectively with business units, prospective franchisees, suppliers, and government.

For supporting these five major functions, the franchisor's headquarters may use information systems listed in Table 12-2. Because of the fierce competition today, many software vendors are moving toward integrating those commonly used information systems into one office suite to reduce costs.

12-2b   Information Systems for the Franchisee Unit

Before determining the type of information systems a franchisee needs, one must first observe what may take place in the franchisee's unit every day. In general, when operating a unit, the four crucial parties that need to be considered are the customers, franchisor headquarters, suppliers, and the government. Figure 12-2 depicts this business environment of the franchisee unit. Running a unit involves four major activities: making sales to customers, managing people who make sales to the customers, marketing and advertising to customers, and dealing with financial issues such as accounting and finances.

It is clear that the customers should be the center of the attention. Customers can be classified into three categories: **frequent customers**, the ones a store should do its best to keep; **infrequent customers**, the ones a store needs to provide incentives to encourage them to buy more; and **potential customers**, the ones a store wants to start buying. Franchisor headquarters provides support to store operations for franchisees in various formats: (1) help desk services on issues happening during the store operations, (2) personal demonstrations from visiting field representatives, and (3) training and continued education from the management group of the franchisor.

Based on the business schema illustrated in Figure 12-2, information systems that can provide the basic functions are summarized into three major categories at franchisee unit (Table 12-3): (1) Front office operations, including point-of-sale transactions and marketing; (2) back office

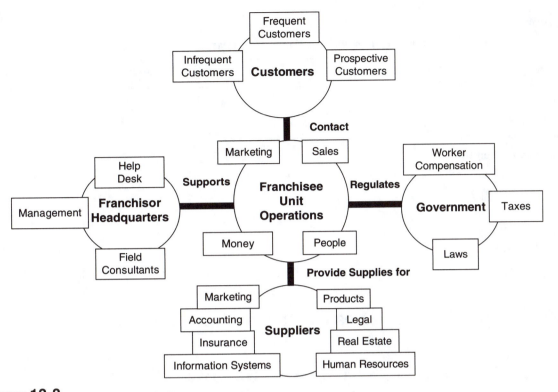

FIGURE **12-2**

Business Environment at the Franchisee Unit

TABLE
12-3   **WHAT INFORMATION SYSTEMS CAN DO FOR THE FRANCHISEE UNIT**

Customers

Franchisee Store

Franchisor Office

- Front Office Operations
  - Point-of-sale transactions
  - Billing
  - Customer tracking
  - Inventory control
- Labor
  - Marketing
  - Back office operations
  - Accounting
  - Financing
- Communications with Customers, Franchisor Office, Suppliers, and Government

Government

Suppliers

---

operations, including accounting and financing; and (3) communications with customers, franchisor headquarters, suppliers, and government. For supporting these three major functions, a franchisee unit may use information systems listed in Table 12-4.

TABLE 12-4 **TYPICAL INFORMATION SYSTEMS FOR THE FRANCHISEE UNIT**

Typical Information Systems Used	Front Store Operations	Back Store Operations	Communications
Point of sale Systems	x		
Accounting		x	
Contact Management		x	x
Presentation Programs	x		
Database Management		x	x
Desktop Publishing		x	
E-Mail		x	x
Spreadsheets		x	
Web Browsers		x	x

12-2c   Information Systems for the Franchisee Community

12-3   INFORMATION SYSTEMS FOR A MIDSIZE FRANCHISE

Although a midsize franchise system has learned how to strive and survive in the franchise business, a major challenge ahead is how to preserve the working knowledge learned over the years and be able to share and disseminate it over the company's intranet (Chen et al. 2000b). In this section we discuss the importance of building working knowledge profiles and an easy-to-use methodology to build, share, and disseminate the profiles.

12-3a   Building Working Knowledge Profiles

Working knowledge is generally accumulated from information that is deciphered from data analyses. A franchise system generates voluminous data every day from various information systems such as the front office operation system at the franchisee unit shown in Table 12-3. Every business transaction, billing, customer tracking, inventory control, and labor adds to the enormous amount of data generated each day. At the end of a day, a report is sent through the communication system to the franchisor headquarter to summarize the daily business transactions such as total sale, total cost of raw materials, and total cost of labor. If the report is not received after a predetermined time, a triggered message requests prompt actions.

Once daily sales reports are received from all the business units, they are converted into information using a variety of analytical methods. For example, a company may use statistical data modeling, including regression analysis, correlation analysis, time series analysis, forecasting, Pareto analysis, and quality assurance. Recently, data mining modeling, including decision tree analysis, cluster analysis, market segmentation analysis, cross-sell analysis, and association analysis, is also becoming popular.

These statistical data analyses can also help generate many business intelligence reports. For example, a business unit may receive its performance ranking report along with the report of the top ten best-performing business units. This information generation process may also incorporate some sort of reward system. For example, the owner of a business unit may receive a free trip to Hawaii when on the top ten list for a number of consecutive times.

The information contained in the daily business intelligence reports becomes the foundation-pon which a franchise system builds its working knowledge profiles. For example, consider the following three important profiles.

- *Site Profiles.* Selecting a good site is perhaps the most important decision in the franchise business. A well-run franchise system will have the working knowledge in the form of **site profiles** to help prospective franchisees select good business sites. The profiles enlist vital elements of value and risk for sites, which are identified based on several years' experiences. For example, sales data at each site may be analyzed daily to determine the best and worst performers on the previous day immediately. Long-term analyses of such data can exhibit vital value and risk elements of sites, which in turn becomes the working knowledge of site selection of the franchise.

- *Personality Profiles.* A successful franchise knows well that franchisees must have strong work ethic, self-esteem, relationship extension (the desire to become friends with the customers), a commitment to service, team orientation, and exactness and cleanliness.[3] The information on the best and worst franchisees can be identified through comprehensive analyses of sales and performance reports with respect to these traits. The analyses over the years will exhibit the vital value and risk elements of personality, which in turn becomes the working knowledge for franchisee recruitment in the form of **personality profiles**.

- *Customer/Product Profiles.* According to the 80/20 principle, we may observe that (1) 80 percent of sales come from 20 percent of total products; and (2) 80 percent of business comes from 20 percent of customers. We can see immediately that in order to be successful, we need to be market led in those few right products and be customer centered for those few right customers. Thus, we need to build **product profiles** that focus on the vital few product groups, that is, 20 percent of the total products that generate 80 percent of product sales, and **customer profiles** that focus on the vital few customer groups, that is, 20 percent of customers generating 80 percent of total sales.

12-3b   Building the Site Profile: An Example

"Location, location, location." Selecting a good business site is perhaps the most important decision in the franchise business. A prospective franchisee typically investigates several candidate sites before choosing the best one among them. This prospective franchisee may seek professional advice from the franchisor, real estate agents, attorneys, and the like. Thus, a complicated decision-making process becomes even more complicated as the number of participants and choices increase. The following **value-cost-risk (VCR) procedures** may be used to simplify the process of comparing the alternative sites. These procedures can be easily implemented on any spreadsheet program such as Microsoft Excel.

1. Form a location and site selection team that includes managers from the franchisor headquarters and the franchisee as well as other stakeholders. If needed, the team may also include other professionals and experts.

2. Develop a consensus on how values and risks associated with location and site selection can be evaluated. *Value* is defined to be the attributes that may increase the profit potential of a site; *risk*, on the other hand, is defined as the attributes that may decrease the profit potential of a site. Table 12-5 is a simplified example.

3. Assign weights to value and risk factors using a scale of 1 to 10. The assignment of values, risks, and weights are based on several years' working experiences of the franchise.

4. Calculate the total of the weight score, and then calculate the weight percentage by dividing weight assigned in step three by this total weight. The weight percentages should total 100 percent.

5. Rate alternative sites using a scale of 1 to 5 for each element, 5 being the best.

6. Multiply the rating with the assigned weight for all sites.

7. Sum the value-risk pair for each site; the example in Table 12-5 shows the value-risk pair of (3.12, 0.25) for site 1, (1.05, 0.5) for site 2, and (1.18, 0.75) for site 3.

8. Estimate the cost for each site. See Table 12-6 for an example.

9. Draw a value-cost-risk diagram. Figure 12-3 is an example. The value-risk pair represents the center and the cost is the radius of the circle.

10. Compare the alternative circles and make the decision. For example, site 1 in Figure 12-3 is the best choice, because it has the highest value, the lowest risk, and the lowest cost.

TABLE 12-5 EVALUATING ALTERNATIVE SITES USING VALUES AND RISKS

	Weight (1)	% of Weight (2)	Site 1 Rate (3)	Site 1 (2)x(3)	Site 2 Rate (4)	Site 2 (2)x(4)	Site 3 Rate (5)	Site 3 (2)x(5)
Values								
Buying Power Index	8	13.3%	5	66.5%	1	13.3%	2	26.6%
Sales Potential	10	16.7%	5	83.5%	1	16.7%	2	33.4%
Population in 1 mile radius	8	13.3%	5	66.5%	1	13.3%	2	26.6%
Ingress/Egress of site	10	16.7%	3	50.1%	1	16.7%	1	16.7%
Parking	9	15%	3	45%	3	45%	1	15%
Total				**3.12**		**1.05**		**1.18**
Risks								
Workforce inventory	9	15%	1	15%	2	30%	3	45%
Suppliers services	6	10%	1	10%	2	20%	3	30%
Total	60	100%		**0.25**		**0.5**		**0.75**

TABLE 12-6 ESTIMATING THE TOTAL COST (x1000) FOR ALTERNATIVE SITES

	Site 1	Site 2	Site 3
Land cost	25	35	27
Design/building cost	10	15	22
Utilities/communications cost	10	15	8
Equipment purchase cost	15	12	9
Safety cost	15	16	30
Periodic site management cost/month	10	25	20
Miscellaneous cost	5	15	9
Total	**90**	**133**	**125**

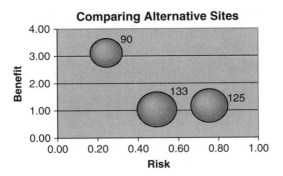

FIGURE 12-3

The Value-Cost-Risk Diagram for Alternative Sites

12-4 INFORMATION SYSTEMS FOR A LARGE FRANCHISE

To work at the heart of a large franchise system is to leverage and market the working knowledge behind the successful brand name of the business. The new products or services coming out of the process of leveraging the working knowledge may transform the franchise business into a more, sometimes surprisingly, profitable enterprise. For example, McDonald's real estate business, Franchise Realty Corporation, became the real money-making engine as can be evidenced from the following quotation in the book, *McDonald's: Behind the Arches*: "What converted McDonald's into a money machine had nothing to do with Ray Kroc or the McDonald brothers or even the popularity of McDonald's hamburgers, French fries, and milk shakes. Rather, McDonald's made its money on real estate and on a little-known formula developed by Harry J. Sonneborn."[4] Ray Kroc, founder of McDonald's, further commented months before he died: "Harry alone put in the policy that salvaged this company and made it a big-leaguer. His idea is what made McDonald's rich."[5]

Thus, the major goal of the information systems for a large franchise is to leverage the proven working knowledge and transform the business into a more profitable enterprise. A useful model for accomplishing this goal may be described as an airplane with the working knowledge profiles as the main body of the plane and "new markets" and "other companies" serving as its two wings. The airplane is powered by the franchise's research and development team, which gets its thrust from the cooperative work of the franchisor, the franchisees, and the franchise community. The plane's elevation, distance, and direction are controlled by the following six strategies adapted from the process-driven business strategies of Hammer:[6]

1. **Intensification**—improving the working knowledge profiles to serve the current customers better. Considering the site profiles for a franchise in the juice-bar industry, one may classify the sites into location categories such as subway stations, health clubs, and college campuses. By doing so, the procedures for assigning values, risks, weights, and rates will be much more refined and accurate. As such, the site selection team can make a better decision in identifying a location for a targeted location category.

2. **Augmentation**—expanding the working knowledge profiles by adding new services to current customers with the goal of increasing the value-added services to the customers. Using the site profiles example again, one may want to enhance the procedures to enable the site selection team to compare a candidate site with the best and worst sites of the company in similar areas. Figure 12-4 shows that the VCR approach enables the site selection team to make the decision easily.

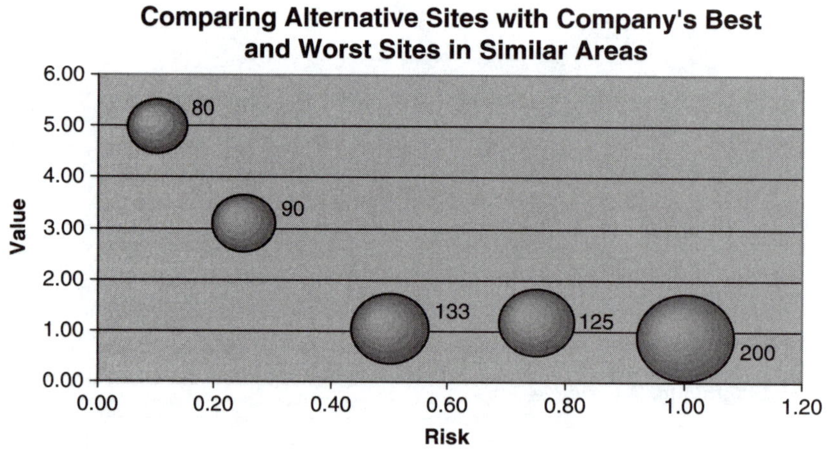

Comparing Alternative Sites with Company's Best and Worst Sites in Similar Areas

FIGURE **12-4**

The Value-Cost-Risk Diagram for Comparing Alternative Sites with Company's Best and Worst Sites in Similar Areas

3. **Conversion**—taking a proven working knowledge profile as a service for other franchise companies with the goal of converting the working profile into a salable service. Since standardization and replication are two essential ingredients in franchising, the proven working profiles of a successful large franchise will be very salable to start-up or midsize franchise companies. A quick and easy way for conversion is to write a know-how book showing how your company grows to such a large franchise. This strategy can be evidenced from so many know-how books by large franchises such as McDonald's,[7] Subway,[8] and Blimpie.[9]

4. **Extension**—using proven working knowledge to enter new market with the goal of extending current successful knowledge to serve new customers in the new market. A large international franchise company has a lot to offer to those domestic retailing companies who are interested in going abroad to, say, China. Thus, the the going international working knowledge profile developed by the franchise company over the year will be very useful to the retailing companies, and thus profitable to the franchise company. A word of caution has to be made here regarding the strategies of *conversion* and *extension*. One may argue that selling the hard-earned working experiences of the franchise may expose the company to the competitors. The fact of the matter is that in today's ever-changing world, companies need to strive for innovations. As evidenced by many examples, when a system or method works, it will become obsolete sooner or later. For example, the just-in-time inventory method pioneered by Wal-Mart is now a common practice by modern retailing businesses. Thus, the JIT method is no longer a competitive advantage to Wal-Mart. A balance act for the strategies of conversion and extension is to release the old versions of the working knowledge profiles with the intension of tracking and analyzing the valuable comments and critics from the outside customers. By doing so, the company gains additional profits and fresh new ideas from outside which may plant the seed for future innovation. It is a one-stone-two-birds strategy indeed!

5. **Innovation**—applying successful working knowledge to provide different products or services with the goal of applying existing proven knowledge to new products or services. Consider the International Center for Entrepreneurial Development (ICED) (www.iced.net) as an example. ICED is home to a variety of franchise systems, including Kwik Kopy, American Wholesale Thermographers, Copy Club, Franklin, Inkwell, Women's Health Boutique, and Parcel Plus. To find a location to house the training programs and related activities for the variety of

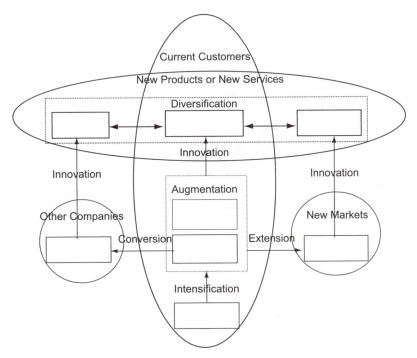

FIGURE 12-5

Visualizing the Six Strategies Adapted from Hammer[10]

franchises is a big challenge. Over the years, ICED has developed its own training center and learned how to host large conference events for its franchisees. Now, ICED has created a new line of services, Northwest Forest Conference Center (www.northwestforest.com), catering training and meeting events for corporations.

6. **Diversification**—creating new markets to provide new products or services with the goal of creating new working knowledge to support new products or services in current or new markets. Using ICED as an example again, it started with a single franchise company, Kwik Kopy, and through its subsidiary companies has broadly expanded its products to a comprehensive spectrum of printing, copying, and thermography. Using its knowledge and experience in running a large international franchise in printing, copying, and thermography, ICED has expanded its business into a diversified portfolio of franchise opportunities, including Women's Health Boutique in the health care industry and Parcel Plus in the shipping industry.

Figure 12-5 summarizes the intrinsic essence of the six strategies as applied in a franchise business setting. The strategies allow a franchise company to excel in the current market *vertically* by providing an excellent service to current customers and expand the services *horizontally* to new markets, other companies, and new products and services through process diversification.

12-5   E-Business Strategy in Franchising

With the advancement of Internet technology, franchise companies are adapting emerging information systems for e-business to their basic business operations. Figure 12-6, adapted from McKenna's virtual community in electronic commerce,[11] is a visual depiction of typical e-business

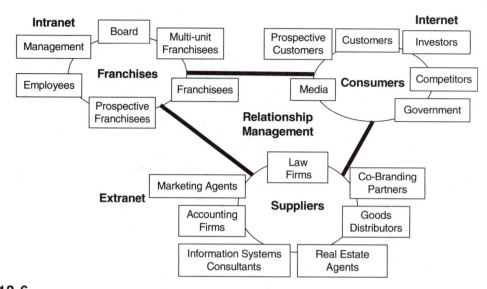

FIGURE **12-6**
Typical E-Business Deployment in Franchising

deployment in franchising. This community of franchise companies, consumers, and suppliers can be virtually connected through Web technologies for relationship management, as follows:

- Intra-enterprise collaboration through Intranet, enabling the franchisor to build up relationships with the board of directors, franchisees, prospective franchisees, franchisor management, and employees

- Collaboration with consumers through Internet, enabling the franchisor and the franchisees to build up relationships with customers, investors, competitors, media, and government

- Collaboration with suppliers through extranet, enabling the franchisor and the franchisees to build up relationships with law firms, co-branding partners, goods distributors, real estate agents, information systems consultants, accounting firms, and marketing agents

Table 12-7 shows a customer-service-life-cycle (CSLC) e-business strategy[12] to deploying Web technologies for relationship management as is presented in Figure 12-6. Here we define the franchisee as the customer of the franchisor and the franchisee's customer as the customer's customer of the franchisor. The stages of CSLC are based on two well-known franchising books by Justis and Judd[13] and Thomas and Seid.[14] Guiding by the CSLC approach to managing the franchisor/franchisee relationship, we can implement e-business strategy with technologies such as Internet, intranet, and extranet to better serve the franchisees and their customers. The table enlists some practical guidelines for deploying the e-business.

12-6 INFORMATION SYSTEMS AND E-BUSINESS INVESTMENT

Although information systems add many benefits to the franchise business, the immediate question is "at what cost?" The information systems investment could be quite expensive, and most franchise companies, especially small ones, find it unaffordable. However, a new type of service called **Application Service Providers (ASP)** promises to make information systems investment more economical and affordable to the franchise community. According to

TABLE 12-7   THE CUSTOMER-SERVICE-LIFE-CYCLE (CSLS) E-BUSINESS STRATEGY IN FRANCHISING

Stages of CSLC	Internet Strategy	Intranet Strategy	Extranet Strategy
Understanding How Franchising Works	Using the Internet website as the friendly customer relationship management tool to address customer concerns at various stages, e.g., providing useful on financing and showing how the franchise system may help finance the franchise investment		Partnering with suppliers to enhance the various stages of CSLC continuously, e.g., a franchise system may need to partner with banks to deliver good services at the stage of "Financing the Franchise Business."
Investigating Franchise Opportunities			
Obtaining Franchisee Prospectus			
Making the Choice			
Preparing Business Plan			
Financing the Franchise Business	Benchmarking and enhancing the Internet website continuously, e.g., identifying frequently the best practices of Web deign in the industry and improving the website accordingly	Helping the franchisees make sales and serve their customers with proper policies dealing with the Internet encroachment issues	Aligning the Internet and intranet strategy with reputable Application Service Providers (ASP) having focused businesses reengineering around the stages of CSLC. For example, Statability.com is a "visionary Web-based Reporting" portal for the hospitality industry. It has the focused business reengineering around the stage of "Managing the Franchise System." Its focused service is being respected by franchise companies in the hospitality industry, as is evidenced from the ever-increasing list of its client base, including Hilton and Marriott.
Signing the Contract			
Marketing and Promoting the Franchise Products or Services			
Managing the Franchise System		Cultivating the franchisor-franchisee relationship with effective knowledge management tools, e.g., basic communications support, distance learning, and centralized franchise applications such as employee recruitment and online ordering	
Building the Relationship between the Franchisor and the Franchisee			
Becoming a Professional Multiunit Franchisee or Retiring from the Franchise System			

the ASP Industry Consortium (www.aspindustry.org), ASP delivers and manages applications and computer services from remote data centers to multiple users via the Internet or a private network.

The ASP concept has additional appeal in the franchising industry. An ASP providing excellent services to its client can duplicate the success to other similar franchises quickly and inexpensively. For franchising companies, an ASP can offer the benefits[15] of reducing focus on the information technology issues; reducing total cost of ownership of information technologies; reducing time to deploy applications; reducing the risks to develop, implement, and maintain the applications; and reducing cost of recruiting, training, and retaining skilled information technology staff.

Although the ASP in the franchising industry is relatively new, there are success stories already. For example, as a Web-based reporting ASP for the hospitality industry, Statability (www.statability.com) provides statistical reporting for hotels, restaurants, and retail stores.[16] Examples of reports include Mystery Shopping, Customer Feedback, Marketing, Purchasing, Quality Assurance, and Budgeting. Its hotel client list includes those large franchises such as Days Inn, Hilton, Holiday Inn, and Ramada. Statability also has the "one-stop-shopping" alliance partners that assist Statability in providing a variety of services for its customers.

TABLE 12-8   EVALUATING ALTERNATIVE ASPs USING VALUES AND RISKS

	Weight (1)	% of Weight (2)	ASP 1 Rate (3)	ASP 1 (2)x(3)	ASP 2 Rate (4)	ASP 2 (2)x(4)	ASP 3 Rate (5)	ASP 3 (2)x(5)
Values								
Meet Business Requirements	8	13.3%	5	66.5%	1	13.3%	2	26.6%
User Friendly	8	13.3%	5	66.5%	1	13.3%	2	26.6%
Flexible	8	13.3%	5	66.5%	1	13.3%	2	26.6%
Support Training Process	10	16.7%	3	50.1%	1	16.7%	1	16.7%
Time Plan	9	15%	3	45%	3	45%	1	15%
Total				**2.95**		**1.02**		**1.12**
Risks								
Stability of the Vendor	9	15%	1	15%	2	30%	3	45%
Technical Architecture	6	10%	1	10%	2	20%	3	30%
Resources	2	3.4%	1	3.4%	2	6.8%	3	10.2%
Total	60	100%		**0.28**		**0.57**		**0.85**

TABLE 12-9   ESTIMATING THE TOTAL COST (x1000) FOR ALTERNATIVE ASPs

Cost Elements	ASP 1	ASP 2	ASP 3
Cost of hardware, software, and peripherals needed at the unit level	50	40	32
Cost of hardware, software, and peripherals needed at the multiunit level	35	20	27
Cost of hardware, software, and peripherals needed at the corporate level	25	20	13
Ongoing costs of hardware/software upgrades and maintenance at each level, including licensing fees	15	17	14
Installation testing and training costs	15	21	35
Costs of customization to achieve proposed solution	10	30	25
The basis for charges and rates	5	20	14
Total	**155**	**168**	**160**

Choosing a trustworthy ASP vendor, however, is not an easy task. There are many critical issues to address. For example, how can an ASP be sure that the important data of the franchise company is well protected and not being shared with a competitor?[17] A franchisor typically investigates several candidate ASPs before choosing the best one among them. This franchisor may seek suggestions from franchisees and professional advice from information systems consulting firms. Thus, a complicated decision-making process becomes even more complicated as the number of choices and participants increase. The VCR procedures shown above may be used to simplify the process of comparing the alternative ASPs. The elements of value, cost, and risk shown in Tables 12-8 and 12-9 serve as simple templates for those readers who are interested in adopting the VCR methodology. Comparing the alternative circles in Figure 12-7, one can easily find ASP 1 as the best choice, because it has the highest value, the lowest risk, and the lowest cost.

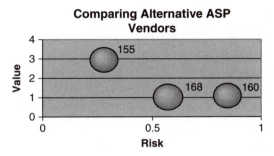

FIGURE **12-7**

Comparing Alternative ASP Vendors

SUMMARY

Developing good relationship between the franchisor and the franchisees is the most important element of a franchise business. This relationship is developed while a franchisee learns how the business operates from the franchisor. Through this learning process, both the franchisor and the franchisee gradually build a "family" relationship. This relationship consists of five crucial elements:[18]

1. Knowledge—proven abilities to solve business problems

2. Attitude—positive and constructive ways of presenting and sharing the working knowledge

3. Motivation—providing incentives for learning the working knowledge

4. Individual behavior—understanding and leveraging the strengths of the participants to learn and enhance the working knowledge

5. Group behavior—finding the best collaborative way to collect, dissimilate, and manage the hard-earned working knowledge

It is obvious that working knowledge is the base of the "family" relationship. Depending on the stage of a franchise, this chapter showed how information systems and the Internet can be used to help a start-up franchise to develop working knowledge, a midsize franchise to preserve working knowledge, and a large franchise to leverage working knowledge.

The use of Application Service Providers (ASPs) as a strategy of information systems and e-business investment was also discussed.

KEY TERMS

Application Service Provider (ASP): a new type of service provider which promises to make information systems investment more economical and affordable to the franchise community by delivering and managing applications and computer services from remote data centers for multiple users via the Internet or a private network.

Augmentation: expanding the working knowledge profiles by offering new services to current customers with the goal of increasing the value-added services to the customers.

Communication system: helps the franchisor communicate efficiently and effectively with business units, prospective franchisees, suppliers, and the government.

Company units: business units which the company owns and wants to use as role models for franchisees.

Conversion: taking a proven working knowledge profile as a service for other franchise companies with the goal of converting the working profile into a salable service.

Customer profiles: help franchises stay customer centered by finding the right customers, that is, 20 percent of customers generating 80 percent of total sales.

Diversification: creating new markets to provide new products or services with the goal of creating new working knowledge to support new products or services in current or new markets.

Established franchisees: business units which the franchisor headquarters needs to provide with incentives to encourage their expansion.

Extension: using proven working knowledge to enter new markets with the goal of extending current successful knowledge to serve new customers in the new market.

Franchise development system: helps the franchisor contact and build relationships with prospective franchisees using applications software for tasks such as marketing, contact management, and real estate management.

Franchise support system: supports business units using applications software for tasks such as help desk, performance tracking, marketing, and auditing.

Franchisor headquarters office management system: helps the franchisor deal with office issues using applications software for tasks such as human resource management, accounting, and financing.

Frequent customers: the customers a store should do its best to keep.

Infrequent customers: the customers a store needs to provide with incentives in order to encourage them to buy more.

Innovation: applying successful working knowledge to provide different products or services with the goal of applying existing proven knowledge to new products or services.

Intensification: improving the working knowledge profiles to serve the current customers better

Personality profiles: working knowledge to help franchisors recruit potentially successful franchisees with personality traits such as a strong work ethic, self-esteem, and a commitment to service; identified through comprehensive analyses of sales and performance reports with respect to these traits.

Potential customers: the customers a store wants to start buying.

Product profiles: help franchises stay market-led by focusing on the right products, that is, the 20 percent of the total products that generate 80 percent of product sales.

Site profiles: working knowledge to help prospective franchisees select good business sites; enlist vital elements of value and risk for sites identified based on experience.

Start-up franchisees: new business units which the franchisor headquarters should do its best to support.

Suppliers/government contact management system: helps the franchisor contact and build relationships with suppliers and the government using applications software for tasks such as scheduling and reminders.

Value-cost-risk (VCR) procedures: used to simplify the process of comparing the alternative sites for a potential franchised unit when building a site profile.

Success Story

Michael Wohl

Experience Matters

Statability (www.statability.com) was cofounded by two entrepreneurs who have spent their professional careers working in the service industry. Throughout, founders Michael Goldenberg and Michael Wohl saw a need for a way to present information in a way that it could easily be understood and analyzed at all levels of management in an organization. Together, they developed processes for packaging raw company data into usable information that helped management gain the knowledge and confidence to make better business decisions.

MICHAEL GOLDENBERG, COFOUNDER

Mike Goldenberg has held positions in information technology, unit and corporate level operations, financial analysis, and strategic systems. His background includes field and headquarters–level experience along with the creation of company-wide reporting and budgeting systems. Goldenberg's background provides Statability with a technology vision and understanding of the options available in capturing data and transforming it into useful information.

MICHAEL WOHL, COFOUNDER

Mike Wohl has a unique combination of lodging and retail level sales, marketing, and operations expertise. He has held positions in regional management, national sales, and brand marketing. This multiunit management experience has enabled him to develop solid economic and business skills. Wohl's combined experience provides a senior-level approach in helping Statability provide clear, focused data in a way that is easily understood by unit managers as well as senior management.

CASE STUDY

Smoothie King®

We will use the "Steps to Becoming a Franchisee at Smoothie King®" to illustrate how the information systems are used to perform the business process (Table 12-10). Smoothie King sells quick service food and juice bars. The company has been in business since 1987 and became franchised in 1988. Currently Smoothie King has more than 200 franchised units. The company was ranked 194 among the top 500 franchises in 2001 and ranked number 1 in the juice bars category from 1997 to 2001 by *Entrepreneur* (www.entrepreneur.com.).

> *Step 1: Obtain a Franchisee Information Packet*—The information packet may be requested by submitting an inquiry.
>
> *Step 2: Submit Information Forms, Financial Statements, and Resume*—The forms in the packet are completed and submitted to Smoothie King for review by the executive staff. If preliminary approval is given, a confidential notice is sent to the applicant.
>
> *Step 3: Attend Interview and Presentation*—An interview is scheduled by a Franchise Development Representative at Smoothie King's headquarters in Kenner, Louisiana. This interview includes a complete introduction to Smoothie King's operations, a meeting with the

TABLE 12-10 SMOOTHIE KING®—STEPS TO BECOMING A FRANCHISEE

Step	Activities	Information Systems Used
1	Obtain Franchisee Information Packet	• Web Pages on Company's Website
2	Submit Information Forms, Financial Statements, and Resume	• Web Pages on Company's Website E-mail
3	Attend Interview	• Appointment Software Presentation Programs
4	Review UFOC	• Web Pages on Company's Website • E-mail • Desktop Publishing • Word Processing
5	Meet with Existing Franchisees	• E-mail
6	Information Review	• Prospective Franchisee Profiles Database • E-mail
7	Second Interview	• Appointment Software • Presentation Programs
8	Sign the Franchise Agreement	• E-mail
9	Orientation Session	• Presentation Programs • Training Software • Site Selection System
10	Training Session	• Presentation Programs • Training Software
11	Completion of Construction	• Project Management • Site Management
12	Store Opens for Business	• Help Desk Management • Customer Relationship Marketing System

executive staff, a review of their Uniform Franchise Offering Circular (UFOC), and visits to several operating franchises.

Step 4: Review UFOC—The circular contains all the information needed to help a prospective franchisee to analyze Smoothie King's franchise system.

Step 5: Meet with Existing Franchisees—Meeting with some of Smoothie King's existing franchisees to learn more about their operations is recommended.

Step 6: Information Review—The information forms, financial statements, credit forms, and background information is evaluated by Smoothie King, and if a mutual decision to proceed is determined, a second interview may be scheduled.

Step 7: Second Interview—If necessary, a second interview at Smoothie King headquarters is scheduled by the Franchise Development Representative, which includes a meet with their franchise support staff and a visit to their training center in Metairie, Louisiana.

Step 8: Sign the Franchise Agreement—The prospective franchisee now has enough information about Smoothie King to make a decision about joining the Smoothie King operation. If approved, the prospect signs the franchise agreement.

Step 9: Orientation Session—As soon as possible after signing, the franchisee is invited to attend a one-day orientation session. This session covers all of the steps involved in opening a new store, including budgeting, financing, planning, site selection, ordering, and construction. After the orientation, Smoothie King's real estate department works with the franchisee to select find the ideal site for a new Smoothie King store.

Step 10: Training Session—The new franchisee and management staff attends the appropriate training at Smoothie King's training center.

Step 11: Completion of Construction—When construction is completed and the new store set up, more training is offered on site.

Step 12: Store Opens for Business.

CASE QUESTIONS

1. Is it safe to send important documents through the e-mail? How can you make it safe?

2. How do you design the company's website to serve the visitors better?

3. What shall a good prospective franchisee profiles database do?

4. What shall a good site selection system do?

5. What shall a customer relationship marketing system do?

CASE STUDY: FANCY FAST FOOD

Problem

To survive in the highly competitive quick service food market, Fancy Fast Food (3F), a major fast-food chain, must distinguish itself from its competition.

Background

As the one of the largest quick service food companies, 3F was in a difficult market position. The largest companies in 3F's market were involved in a price war that was further fragmenting an already divided and stagnant market. 3F management believed that they could not compete on price or name recognition, but they could compete on service and quality. Improving service was seen as required for *survival*.

After extensive analysis, they concluded that the single biggest factor in sustained success is the service provided by the customer-facing counter personnel. If they serve the customers well, sales will increase and 3F will remain competitive. Their analysis also showed that the biggest influence on the quality of customer service is the enthusiasm and support that their restaurant manager has for their team. Using the terminology and concepts from *The Service Profit Chain*,[19] 3F set out to implement an "Internal Service Program" in which each manager provides direct reports with great service, ultimately enhancing service for the customer.

Although it was relatively easy for the vice president of operations, the two division managers (each responsible for half the country), and the fifteen regional managers to understand the internal service message and "walk the talk," it was much harder for the 125 area managers and 1,000+

restaurant managers to understand the value of the message and commit to a powerful service program. There were too many geographically dispersed managers for simple, direct conversations.

3F tried writing extensive operations manuals to describe the desired service environments, which proved to be too complex and rigid to be useful. 3F also tried field training courses, which were too short and general to be effective. The management team needed to find a way to facilitate the internal service initiative with every manager.

Solution

3F used Cerebyte services and Infinos™ software to successfully implement their internal service initiative. The solution includes:

- Cerebyte used the Key Initiative Filter to guide the 3F executive team to define the internal service initiative in way that created strong organizational commitment.

- Cerebyte used its unique Positive Deviant identification process to identify the twelve most highly respected restaurant, assistant restaurant, and district managers.

- Cerebyte's specialized knowledge harvesting using Infinos™ Professional gathered best practices for implementing internal service, including all of the tips, rules of thumb, decision-making processes, and actions required to provide extraordinary internal service.

- Cerebyte's guided coaching using Infinos™ Coach and Manager enabled all 1,400 restaurant managers to work with their 140 district managers to create implementation plans for putting great internal service into each restaurant.

- Cerebyte's Live Action capability guided restaurant, district, and regional management to monitor progress of each implementation progress in each restaurant in a way that produced immediate improvements and long-term extraordinary internal service.

Results

- The entire senior management team was able set a clear, specific expectation that every restaurant would have a plan for implementing internal service based on the best available practices.

- In just one hour, the 3F management team was able to agree on the list of highly respected, Internal Service positive deviants.

- In just three days, working with just twelve positive deviants, 3F generated a consolidated set of great internal service best practices that were described as the most complete, realistic, and effective ever.

- The management team was able to quickly identify districts and restaurants that had completed their plans and determine if the plans were based on best practices.

- Each district manager used the Cerebyte system to guide each restaurant manager, in just two hours of coaching, to develop an in-depth understanding of internal service, including creating strong emotional commitment to the program and a detailed action plan for implementing internal service.

- The management team was able to quickly and easily determine the progress of every restaurant and district in implementing internal service, enabling fast and more meaningful management support.

Service and Financial Impact

- An estimated 10 percent increase in sales due to the internal service program[20]
- A significant and almost universal increase in quality of district and restaurant manager moral and performance[21]

REVIEW QUESTIONS

1. Which activities at the franchisor's headquarters office should be the center of attention?

2. What is the primary purpose of information systems in a start-up franchise?

3. Which activities at the franchised unit should be the center of attention?

4. Where does working knowledge originate?

5. What is the primary purpose of information systems in a midsize franchise?

6. The information contained in the daily business intelligence reports becomes the foundation upon which a franchise system builds what?

7. What helps to simplify the difficult site selection process?

8. What is the primary purpose of information systems in a large franchise?

9. What are the elements of virtual relationship management in e-business strategy?

10. Why might it be a good idea for a franchisor to investigate several ASP vendors before choosing one?

REFERENCES

Chen, Y., C. Ford, R. T. Justis, and P. Chong, "Application Service Providers (ASP) in Franchising: Opportunities and Issues," *Proceedings of the 15th Annual International Society of Franchising Conference*, Las Vegas, February 24–25, 2001.

Chen, Y., P. Chong, and R. T. Justis, "E-Business Strategy in Franchising: A Customer-Service-Life-Cycle Approach," *Proceedings of the 16th Annual International Society of Franchising Conference*, Orlando, February 8–10, 2002.

Chen, Y., P. Chong, and R. T. Justis, "Franchising Knowledge Repository: A Structure for Learning Organizations," *Proceedings of the 14th Annual International Society of Franchising Conference*, San Diego, February 19–20, 2000.

Chen, Y., P. Chong, and R. T. Justis, "Information Technology Solutions to Increase Franchise Efficiency and Productivity," *Proceedings of the 2000 Franchise China Conference and Exhibition*, Beijing (November 6–7), Guangzhou (November 9–10), and Shanghai (November 13–14), China, 2000, www.franchise.globalsources.com.

Conza, T., *Success, It's a Beautiful Thing: Lessons on Life and Business from the Founder of Blimpie International* (Hoboken: John Wiley & Sons, 2000).

Deluca, F. and J. Hayes, *Start Small Finish Big: Fifteen Key Lessons to Start and Run Your Own Successful Business* (New York: Warner Books, 2000).

Gates, B., *Business @ the Speed of Thought: Succeeding in the Digital Economy* (New York: Warner Books, 2000).

Hammer, M., *Beyond Reengineer* (New York: Harper Business, 1996).

Haskett, J., E. Sasser, and L. Schlessinger, *The Service Profit Chain* (New York: Free Press, 1997).

Justis, R. T. and Judd, R. J. *Franchising* (Cincinnati: Thomson Custom Publishing, 1998).

Keen, P., C. Balance, S. Chan, and S. Schrump, *Electronic Commerce Relationships: Trust by Design* (Upper Saddle River, NJ: Prentice-Hall, 2000).

Love, J., *McDonald's: Behind the Arches* (New York: Bantam Books, 1995).

McKenna, R., *Real Time: Preparing for the Age of the Never Satisfied Customer* (Westport, CN: Harvard Business School, 1997).

McKenzie, K., "Multi-units Can Turn Data into Usable Information," *Franchise Times* (June–July 1999): 51.

Thomas, D. and M. Seid, *Franchising for Dummies* (New York: IDG Books, 2000).

Webb, Wendy,"Personality Profiles: Next Best Thing to 'Cloning,'" *Franchise Times* (September 1999): 24.

NOTES

1. Y. Chen, P. Chong, and R. T. Justis, "Information Technology Solutions to Increase Franchise Efficiency and Productivity," *Proceedings of the 2000 Franchise China Conference and Exhibition*, Beijing (November 6–7), Guangzhou (November 9–10), and Shanghai (November 13–14), China, 2000, www.franchise.globalsources.com.

2. Chen et al., "Franchising Knowledge Repository: A Structure for Learning Organizations," *Proceedings of the 14th Annual International Society of Franchising Conference*, San Diego, February 19-20, 2000.

3. W. Webb, "Personality Profiles: Next Best Thing to 'Cloning,'" *Franchise Times* (September 1999): 24.

4. J. Love, *McDonald's: Behind the Arches* (New York: Bantam Books, 1995), 152.

5. Ibid., 152–153.

6. M. Hammer, *Beyond Reengineer* (New York: Harper Business, 1996).

7. Love, *McDonald's.*

8. F. Deluca and J. Hayes, *Start Small Finish Big: Fifteen Key Lessons to Start and Run Your Own Successful Business* (New York: Warner Books, 2000).

9. T. Conza, *Success, It's a Beautiful Thing: Lessons on Life and Business from the Founder of Blimpie International* (New York: John Wiley & Sons, 2000).

10. Hammer, *Beyond Reengineering.*

11. R. McKenna, *Real Time: Preparing for the Age of the Never Satisfied Customer* (Westport, CT: Harvard Business School, 1997).

12. Chen et al., "E-Business Strategy in Franchising: A Customer-Service-Life-Cycle Approach," *Proceedings of the 16th Annual International Society of Franchising Conference*, Orlando, February 8–10, 2002.

13. Justis and Judd, *Franchising* (New York: DAME, 1998).

14. D. Thomas and M. Seid, *Franchising for Dummies* (New York: IDG Books, 2000).

15. Chen et al., "Application Service Providers (ASP) in Franchising: Opportunities and Issues," *Proceedings of the 15th Annual International Society of Franchising Conference*, Las Vegas, February 24–25, 2001.

16. K. McKenzie, "Multi-units Can Turn Data into Usable Information," *Franchise Times* (June–July 1999): 51.

17. P. Keen, C. Balance, S. Chan, and S. Schrump, *Electronic Commerce Relationships: Trust by Design* (Upper Saddle River, NJ: Prentice-Hall, 2000).

18. Judd et al., *Franchising.*

19. J. Haskett, E. Sasser, and L. Schlessinger, *The Service Profit Chain* (New York: Free Press, 1997).

20. Total increase is extrapolated from an initial, representative sub-process called Speed of Service.

21. Based on comparison of standardized 360-degree evaluation scores with corresponding scores from previous evaluations.

FRANCHISE LEGAL DOCUMENTS*

INCIDENT

Julie and Lynn had successfully developed the first small chain of cinnamon roll specialty shops in Southern California. The sticky, sweet buns were getting a lot of attention in the press and customers lined up a dozen deep on Saturday mornings. Their four shops were each generating a substantial profit, averaging $120,000 before taxes.

Julie and Lynn have both been approached by friends and customers who wanted to open similar shops in other parts of the country. They loved the gooey product and thought it would be fun to be in a business that seems to bring such pleasure to its customers. "How can you put me in this business?" they asked.

The women's business lawyer, who quickly assured them that she was not a franchise specialist, told Julie that franchising was heavily regulated, and that it required the development of some lengthy and complex documents, including a long-term contract and a disclosure document registered with the California Corporations Commission. Julie understands that she and her partner must develop a disclosure document; they now want to know what is involved. They also learned from a book about franchising they found in the library that audited financial statements must be included in the disclosure statement so they made an appointment with their accountants.

There's more, their lawyer tells them. It may be inappropriate to tell their friends and customers interested in this business how well Lynn and Julie's shops do financially. This didn't sound right to them: Current shop profitability would be the first question that any franchise investor would ask, at least any investor that they would *want* in business with them. Why should any franchisor be restricted from answering such a fundamental question?

Lynn and Julie realize from their brief research that they must develop a strong contract and a disclosure document before they can begin to offer franchises.

13-1 INTRODUCTION

Franchising has its roots in the business expansion boom that occurred in the years following World War II. In the 1950s and early 1960s, a number of companies were riding the growth of the Eisenhower years, expanding through the use of independent owners and developers uniform services and the familiar trademarks of a newly mobile society.

---

* The authors gratefully acknowledge Andy Caffey of the Law Offices of Andrew A. Caffey, Bethesda, Maryland, as the writer of this chapter, and David G. Ross of The Ross Law Firm, also of Bethesda, Maryland, for his assistance in updating this chapter.

Franchising was born on the highways and nurtured in the adolescent years of the television age. As peacetime America built out its extraordinary interstate highway system, entrepreneurs built such roadside empires as Holiday Inns, McDonald's, and Dairy Queen.

These early franchising success stories spread through U.S. economic culture and became the stuff of dreams. Overnight hamburger millionaires added fact to the new myth of instant franchising success. On the heels of these real success stories came the scam artists, promising wide-eyed opportunities for eager but gullible investors to cash in on the franchise craze. Hundreds lost their investments in paper-thin franchise organizations. On the CBS program *60 Minutes*, franchises were seen being sold by con men driving rented Rolls Royce cars and wearing ostentatious gold jewelry. It is an image and association that haunts the franchise community to this day.

In the early 1970s, state and federal authorities began adopting laws to protect franchise investors. By the end of that decade, more than a dozen states had adopted laws regulating the sale of franchises, the Federal Trade Commission had adopted a national disclosure standard, and even more states had adopted laws to protect franchise owners from being arbitrarily terminated in their relationships with franchisors. Franchising had arrived at an important stage of maturity as a form of business, and it was also delivered into a new era of strict legal requirements.

California adopted the first modern franchise investor protection statute which became effective in 1971. This law, and the several state laws that quickly followed California's lead, impose two basic requirements on franchisors: They must deliver full, detailed presale disclosure of material information to prospective investors, and they must register their offering documents with state authorities before they can offer or sell franchises in the state. As part of the registration process, state officials review the company's disclosure documents to make sure that they are complete and that they follow the format requirements of the law.

Many states adopted franchise relationship laws. These were designed to protect franchise owners (not buyers) from arbitrary termination or nonrenewal of their franchise contracts. The franchise relationships laws establish minimum standards that a franchisor must meet in order to terminate a franchise contract, fail to renew a franchise contract, modify an existing contract, or refuse to permit a franchise owner to transfer their rights in the business.

The Federal Trade Commission (FTC) provided investors with additional protection in 1979, when it enacted a formal Trade Regulation Rule entitled "Disclosure Requirements and Prohibitions Concerning Franchising and Business Opportunity Ventures." That rule, commonly known as the **FTC Rule**, traditionally applied to all franchise sales in the United States—though amendments made to the FTC Rule in 2007 create an exemption for certain sales involving large investments and for certain experienced, well-heeled franchisees.

The FTC Rule is built on a single idea: *that investors armed with key information will be able to make well-informed and wise investment decisions for themselves.* Consistent with that theory, the FTC Rule requires the franchisor to make certain written disclosures to the prospective franchisee well before a franchise agreement is signed. The disclosure requirement not only assures the delivery of facts that are material to the franchise investment, but also works to prevent the fraudulent misrepresentation of those facts by sales representatives (whether they drive rented Rolls Royce automobiles or not!). The FTC Rule does not control the franchisor's business practices in any other way, however. This "noninvasive" approach to regulation allows the marketplace to work without heavy-handed government interference.

13-2   DISCLOSURE REQUIREMENTS

Disclosure under the FTC Rule comes in the form of a detailed and rather extensive **disclosure document**, or "offering circular," which must be delivered to each prospective franchisee. pursuant to the FTC Rule's pre-2007 terms–which franchisors may still voluntarily elect to follow until July

2008, when compliance with the updated version becomes mandatory – delivery is to occur *at the earlier of*:

a. the parties' first personal, face-to-face meeting to discuss the sale or possible sale of a franchise; or

b. at least ten business days before the franchisee executes a binding legal document or makes payment of any consideration for the franchise.

Further, the older version of the rule requires the franchisor to deliver the franchise agreement and any related documents (such as development agreements, leases, promissory notes, and personal guarantees) to the prospective franchisee in final form, ready for signature, at least five business days before they are executed.

However, the amended FTC Rule, which franchisors may opt to follow even before the mandatory compliance date of July 2008, does not require that an offering circular be delivered to the franchisee prior to the first "face-to-face meeting." On the other hand, it does mandate that delivery occur at least ***fourteen calendar*** days – not ten business days – before the franchisee signs a binding legal document or pays consideration for the franchise.

The revised FTC Rule also alters the franchisor's responsibility with regard to delivery of the final franchise agreement and related documents. In the new version of the rule, the requirement that the documents be delivered at least five business days before signing is eliminated altogether, as long as (a) these final documents are identical in all material respects to the "form" versions contained in the offering circular, or (b) all variations between the "form" and "final" versions arose from negotiations initiated by the franchisee. In the event that the franchisor unilaterally causes the franchise agreement or a related document to vary from its "offering circular" counterpart in a material way, however, the franchisor must deliver the final documents at least ***seven calendar*** days prior to their execution.

Another way in which disclosure requirements have evolved over time is with regard to the **form** of the disclosure document. Whereas the documents were traditionally delivered to franchisees in "hard copy" paper form, the Internet revolution and advances in other electronic media recently spurred a successful movement toward electronic disclosure. In 2000, Congress passed the Electronic Signatures in Global and National Commerce Act (E-SIGN), a statute that permits the use of electronic versions of signatures, contracts, and "other" transaction-related records in all types of commercial transactions. As acknowledged by an FTC staff report issued in 2004, E-SIGN apparently authorized electronic disclosure of offering circulars – via Internet, CD-ROM, or otherwise. Regardless, the express terms of the revised FTC Rule remove all doubt that electronic disclosure is permitted. According to the 2007 version of the rule, an offering circular may be presented in paper form or in any other form capable of being preserved in tangible form and read, including computer disk, CD-ROM, e-mail, or Internet.

13-3   CONTENTS OF THE OFFERING CIRCULAR

The contents of the offering circular are mandated by the FTC Rule; it must contain information that responds to the list of disclosures contained in the twenty-three topic sections. Under the pre-2007 version of the FTC Rule, the franchisor may use one of the two available formats for disclosure: the format prescribed by that version of the Rule, or, alternatively, the Uniform Franchise Offering Circular (UFOC). The FTC Rule allows use, in its entirety, of one or the other; the franchisor may not pick and choose between them on a piecemeal basis.

The UFOC was developed originally by securities administrators preparing the first state registration and disclosure laws in the 1970s. It is now administered by the North American Securities Administrators Association (NASAA), a national group of state securities law enforcement officials. Many state franchise laws are administered by the same offices that regulate the sale of corporate securities.

In 1993, NASAA approved for national use a newly designed UFOC format. The document now must be in plain English, free of legalese, antique phrases, technical language, and unnecessary detail. The format now requires the use of charts and tables to provide handy cross references to the franchise agreement and eliminates the wholesale regurgitation of contract provisions.

While all registration states accept the Uniform Franchise Offering Circular, not all states accept the format set forth in the pre-2007 FTC Rule. For this reason, the great majority of franchisors have used the UFOC format for disclosure. The UFOC is as close as the franchise community has come to a universally accepted document. In fact, the 2007 version of the FTC Rule essentially adopts the UFOC's standards and format as its own, with only a few relatively minor substantive variations. Because the FTC has expressed its desire for NASAA to revise its own standards to comply with those now contained in the Rule – and because the two standards are nearly identical already – the summary that follows highlights the twenty-three items as set forth in the revised FTC Rule.

Cover Page

The FTC cover page displays required language admonishing the investor to investigate the offering carefully and contact authorities if there is anything missing from the document.

Item 1. *The Franchisor and Any Parents, Predecessors, and Affiliates.* This section will give you a general sense of the franchisor, the franchise offering, the franchisor's prior business experience, and the length of time it has been offering franchises.

Item 2. *Business Experience.* This section lays out the business experience of the company's directors, principal officers, and other executives who have management responsibility for the franchise program. This will include the chief executive officer, the financial officers, marketing managers, training supervisors, and key employees who provide services to franchisees. The listing will show each person's five year employment history.

Item 3. *Litigation.* Three types of litigation must be disclosed in this Item: (1) pending adminis-trative, criminal, and material civil actions; (2) concluded criminal or material civil actions during the 10 year period before the date of the offering circular, and (3) currently effective restrictive orders from a court when the order relates to the franchise, or under US or Canadian franchise, securities, antitrust, trade regulation or trade practice law resulting from an action brought by a public agency. If the franchisor, its predecessor, an affiliate operating under the same trademark, or any person listed in Item 2 has one of these types of legal action against him, the details of the case must be disclosed. The FTC Rule standard requires litigation disclosure looking back seven fiscal years.

Item 4. *Bankruptcy.* This section will reveal if the franchisor, its or any of its officers have been involved in a bankruptcy in the prior 10 years.

Item 5. *Initial Fees.* Item 5 requires the franchisor to disclose all of the initial fees and other charges to be paid by the franchisee prior to opening the business. This will include the initial franchise fee, whether paid in a lump sum or in installments, and, if the fees are not set as flat dollar figures, the formula by which the initial fees are determined.

Item 6. *Other Fees.* This item shows in chart form the various other recurring or isolated fees and expenses that the franchisee is required to pay to the franchisor. It might include such fees as the continuing monthly royalty, advertising contributions, cooperative adver-tising contributions, training fees and expenses, transfer fees, audit costs, and renewal fees.

The chart shows the amount of the fee, its due date, and any remarks that might explain key information about the fee.

Item 7. ***Estimated Initial Investment***. This item summarizes the franchisee's total initial investment and displays it in chart form. The chart will break down the expenses into the categories such as the initial fee, expenses incurred during training, lease or purchase of real estate and improvements to that real estate, equipment, signs, grand opening advertising expenses, opening inventory, advertising fees, and any "additional funds" that might be required during the start-up phase of the business.

Item 8. ***Restrictions on Sources of Products and Services***. Item 8 discloses details about the supply arrangements for franchisees. If the franchisee is required by the Franchise Agreement to purchase only approved products, or goods and services only from approved suppliers, or from only those suppliers designated by the franchisor, it will be described here. The disclosures will notes what products or services are involved in the supply restrictions and the manner in which the company issues specifications or grants supplier approvals. The franchisor also must disclose the precise basis by which it will receive revenue as the result of purchases by franchisees, and estimate the percentage of the franchisee's expenses represented by the supply purchases.

Item 9. ***Franchisee's Obligations***. This item presents a cross reference table, highlighting the sections of the Franchise Agreement and the UFOC where various franchisee obligations, such as buying insurance and reporting information to the franchisor, are located.

Item 10. ***Financing***. If the franchisor offers financing for any part of the franchisee's investment, the details of the financing will be discussed here. The disclosure will include the items for which financing is available, such as equipment, the annual rate of interest, whether the franchisee waives any defenses under the financing program, whether the franchisor has any intent to sell the financing to a third party, and whether the franchisor or its affiliates receive any payments for the placement of the financing. Sample copies of the financing documents must be attached as an exhibit to the UFOC.

Item 11. ***Franchisor's Assistance, Advertising, Computer Systems, and Training***. This is the longest narrative section of the document, detailing the contractual commitments that the franchisor makes to the franchisee, both before and after the opening of the business. This includes such pre-opening obligations as selecting and approving site location for the franchisee's business and assistance in the construction of the premises, hiring employees, and pre-opening training. During the operation, the disclosure items include any assistance promised in operations such as product offerings, hiring and training employees, pricing, and accounting. The franchisor's advertising program must be described in detail: limitations on advertising content, the source of the advertising, whether the system has established an advertising council of franchisees, and whether the franchisee must participate in any regional advertising cooperatives. The item also calls for the disclosure of any computer systems the franchisee is required to use, the typical length of time between signing the Franchise Agreement and opening the business, and the franchisor's training program.

Item 12. ***Territory***. The franchisor will describe any territorial rights the franchisee is granted under the Franchise Agreement, whether the franchisor may establish another franchisee who may also use the trademarks, whether the franchisor may establish a company-owned outlet or other channels of distribution using the *same* trademarks, and whether it may establish a system distributing the same products and services using *different* marks.

Item 13. *Trademarks*. Information about the "principal trademarks"—not all of the company's trademarks—must be disclosed. This includes registration, litigation, and any restrictions on the franchisee's trademark use.

Item 14. *Patents, Copyrights and Proprietary Information*. The UFOC requires a detailed description of any copyrights or patents that are material to the franchised business.

Item 15. *Obligation to Participate in the Actual Operation of the Franchise Business*. In this item, the franchisor must disclose whether the franchisee is required to participate personally in the operation of the franchised business, and, if not, whether the franchisor recommends participation.

Item 16. *Restrictions on What the Franchisee May Sell*. Here the document reviews any restrictions or conditions imposed by the franchisor which limit the goods or services the franchisee may sell or the customers to whom the franchisee may sell.

Item 17. *Renewal, Termination, Transfer and Dispute Resolution*. This item calls for a table presentation of 23 separate subjects that appear in typical franchise agreements. The subjects relate to the duration of the contract, renewal rights, whether renewal involves the execution of a new and possibly different Franchise Agreement, conditions for transfer, termination and any restriction on competitive activity during and after the term of the Franchise Agreement. It provides a convenient cross reference to where the topics appear in the Franchise Agreement and the table provides a short description of the provision.

Item 18. *Public Figures*. If a public figure is used by the franchisor to promote the franchise program, the company must disclose the extent of the public figure's involvement in the actual management of the franchisor and the public figure's total investment in the franchisor.

Item 19. *Financial Performance Representations*. If the franchisor wants to show a prospective franchisee how he or she might perform financially, or how other franchisees in the system have performed, then the information must appear in this Item 19. It is not required to deliver this information; but if the company does provide these representations (formerly referred to as "earnings claims"), they must appear here. The claims must have a "reasonable basis" in fact and must disclose the material assumptions underlying their preparation and presentation. The FTC Rule requires much of the same information in a separate disclosure document if earning claims are disclosed.

Item 20. *Outlets and Franchisee Information*. Item 20 includes tables summarizing (1) three years of statistical data about the number of units that have been added or subtracted in the franchise program; (2) three years' worth of statistical data regarding franchised units that have been transferred from one franchisee to another; (3) the three-year statistical status of company owned-stores; and (4) a state-by-state breakdown of the projected franchised and company-owned unit openings in the coming year. This item also requires the franchisor to enclose as an exhibit a list of the names, addresses, and telephone numbers of those franchisees who have left the system for any reason in the franchisor's preceding fiscal year. In addition, the franchisor must list any trademark-specific franchisee association (i.e., a franchisee association devoted to the particular franchise) that (1) the franchisor itself sponsors or endorses, or (2) is organized under state law and makes a timely request to be listed for the particular year. Finally, the franchisor must disclose whether it entered into confidentiality agreements with any franchisees within the past three years.

Item 21. *Financial Statements*. This item requires disclosure of the franchisor's audited financial statements for the prior three fiscal years. This includes balance sheets for the last two fiscal years, and statements of operations, stockholder's equity, and cash flows for the past three fiscal years. The financials must be prepared by an independent certified public accountant, using Generally Accepted Accounting Principles. The FTC Rule and some states allow some franchisors to use unaudited statements only in limited circumstances.

Item 22. *Contracts*. This item requires the franchisor to enclose as an exhibit a sample copy of the Franchise Agreement, all related documents, and any other agreements that the franchisee will sign, including leases, options, and purchase agreements.

Item 23. *Receipts*. This item contains two identical copies of a receipt for the delivery of the Uniform Franchise Offering Circular. One is designed to be retained by the franchisor; the other by the franchisee. The receipt also contains warning language about the requirements of disclosure under state law.

13-4   CONTRACT

At the core of the franchise concept is a legally enforceable **contract**. A franchise agreement is a complex contract, representing the binding understanding between the franchisor and the franchisee. The principles of contract law will apply to this contractual relationship, as well as a variety of state and federal laws that govern business practices. The antitrust laws, discussed in Chapter 14, will also have a direct legal impact on the way business is conducted by the parties.

13-4a   Area Development Contracts, Subfranchising Programs, and Other Variations on the Theme

How does a franchisor grant the right to develop a whole town, a state, or a region of the country? After all, if the idea of a single unit franchise works well, using other people's capital to develop a business format franchise, then the idea of granting well-heeled investors the right to build multiple units should also work well.

Some franchise programs feature variations on the basic single unit franchise relationship. The most common of these is the **area development agreement**. This contract will allow a developer to build a number of franchised businesses in a particular market area and each one will be governed by the terms of a franchise agreement granted by the franchisor.

Some franchise systems, most notable Wendy's Hamburgers, expanded quickly through the use of **subfranchising contracts**. In these programs, a subfranchisor is granted the right to locate and sell individual franchises to individual investors in a defined region.

13-4b   The Franchise Agreement

Modern franchising documents are in many ways driven by the way franchising has come to be regulated by federal and state law. The following summary of contract components highlights the provisions used by a number of franchisors, and almost all of them are the subject of specific disclosure under the FTC Rule.

Remember, also, that franchising occupies an extraordinarily broad spectrum of businesses. It includes relationships created in order to distribute a single specialty product, as well as full business-format programs for the establishment of freestanding retail businesses. The franchise agreement used by any one of these businesses will change to reflect the needs of that particular relationship.

1. ***Introductory Preliminaries (or "Recitals")***. This portion of the agreement recites the parties who are entering into the contractual commitments, and lays out the basic mutual benefits of entering the contract. It will state the basic intention of the parties to enter into a continuing franchise relationship, and identify the distinctive components of that relationship. The Recitals often include a definition of the "System" of standards and operational details that comprise the heart of the franchise, and identify the trademarks that will be licensed to the franchisee to identify the franchise business.

2. ***Grant of the Franchise***. This key provision actually grants the franchise rights to the franchisee. The franchisee accepts the grant of right, and acknowledges here that the franchise must be operated only in conformity with the company's standards of operation, usually conveyed in operations manuals.

3. ***Term and Renewal***. The duration of the contract will be specified; it can range from three to twenty years. Most franchise contracts also allow the franchisee to extend the relationship by renewing the contract. This section will state the conditions to be met before renewal is allowed (such as being in compliance with the expiring franchise agreement, signing a then-current contract, releasing any legal claims against the franchisor the franchisee may have, and paying a renewal fee).

4. ***Territorial Rights***. Most traditional, freestanding franchise businesses feature a grant of territorial rights. These take the form of a promise by the franchisor that it will not establish another franchised business within a certain geographic area. The area may be defined by a radius emanating from the location of the unit, or by political boundaries such as counties or towns, or by clusters of zip codes. Some programs, especially those that are distribution systems or mobile businesses, specify the marketing activity that the franchisee is allowed to conduct inside and outside of the defined territory.

5. ***Training and Guidance***. These provisions detail the training to be provided by the franchisor, where it will be provided, and who is required to attend. The franchisor may also promise to provide a level of continuing guidance and advice about the operation of the franchised business.

6. ***Trademarks and Copyrights***. Trademarks have been called the cornerstone of the franchise relationship. These important commercial symbols are part of every franchise program, and their use (but not ownership) is licensed to the franchisee for the term of the franchise agreement. These provisions restrict use of the marks to follow the exacting standards provided by the franchisor. Franchisees are often required to assist in the franchisor's defense of the marks if they are legally attacked by another trademark user. Copyrights are protected as well as original expressions of an idea such as the contents of an operating manual or the copy appearing in an advertisement. As with trademarks, the franchise agreement will strictly limit the franchisee's use of the copyrighted materials.

7. ***Fees to Be Paid by the Franchisee***. Typically, the franchisee must pay an "Initial Franchise Fee" in a lump sum of as much as $30,000 or more when the franchise agreement is executed. Then each month the franchisee pays a royalty fee measured as a percentage (between 3 and 8 percent, usually) of the gross sales of the unit. That means that when the franchisee sells $10,000 of goods or services in one month, regardless of whether the business makes a profit that month, the franchisee must send to the franchisor a check for $500 to cover a 5 percent royalty requirement. Other fees that may appear here include advertising fund contributions (for pooled advertising activities), renewal fees, transfer fees, and any fees related to additional training for the franchisee and his/her staff.

8. ***Image and Operating Standards***. Business-format franchise programs require the franchisee follow every detail of the prescribed business operation, everything from the uniforms to be worn by counter staff to the number of seconds the fries must cook at 527 °F. Operational standards will be adopted for the equipment and decor of the business, the menus, the music, the words used by front line sales representatives. Almost every conceivable aspect of a business operation may be reduced to the franchisor's written operational standards and this portion of the franchise agreement will make it clear that the franchisee must comply with them all. The great bulk of this know-how is transferred to the franchise owner during training and through the use of a comprehensive operations manual, as it may change over time.

9. ***Advertising and Other Promotional Activity***. These sections will regulate the content and appearance of advertising. If the franchisee wants to run an advertisement for the business, she will have to clear it through the franchisor. If the owner wants to promote the business on a local cable channel or rent a booth at a local craft fair, in most franchise systems it would have to receive advance approval from the franchisor.

10. ***Recordkeeping and Reporting***. In any franchise system where continuing royalty fees are based on the franchisee's gross sales, the reporting of sales activity will be of prime importance to the health of the entire franchise network. These provisions generally require that the franchise owner provide detailed reporting of its sales activity and that it maintain records in an electronic or computerized form that is compatible with the franchisor's equipment. Most new franchise programs are fully computerized; reporting, and often the payment of royalty fees, is accomplished through computer modems and electronic funds bank transfers. The franchise agreement will specify exactly how this is to be handled.

11. ***Inspections and Audits***. This provision allows the franchisor to physically inspect the premises of the franchised business and to review the franchisee's financial books and records. This provides an indispensable tool to the franchisor to assure that the franchise owner is complying fully with all aspects of the franchise agreement.

12. ***Site Selection***. The franchisor reserves the right to approve the location of the franchised business, often after going through an exacting review of traffic count, community demographics, and town development plans. Careful and competent site selection is one of the keys to retail marketing success; the franchisor's judgment is vital, although the ultimate decision usually remains with the franchise owner.

13. ***Confidential Information***. A trade secret may be protected as such only when is kept confidential. In this provision the franchisee acknowledges that he will be receiving confidential information such as the contents of an operating manual and the information delivered during training. This provision often requires that the franchisee provide confidential information to store employees only on a "need to know" basis and only where steps are taken to protect the information, such as asking the employees to sign confidentiality agreements.

14. ***Transfer of Franchise Rights by the Franchisee***. This provision generally allows the franchisee to sell his business to another person, who will then become the franchisee, only after the franchisor approved the transaction. A series of conditions for the franchisor's approval may be imposed: The buyer must meet the same qualifications as other franchisees, a new franchise agreement must be signed, along with a release of any legal claims.

15. ***Termination***. The classic franchise agreement termination provision allows the franchisor to end the relationship only in several specified circumstances. Some of the specified circumstances will allow for termination immediately, without any opportunity to cure the problem. These include situations where the franchisee provides false information on his application for

the franchise, the franchisee is convicted of a crime that will injure the reputation of the franchise system, the franchisee files for bankruptcy, or the franchisee abandons the location. The second tier of situations that may lead to termination include all other situation where the franchisee fails to comply with some aspect of the program and does not cure the problem within a reasonable time after receipt of written notice from the franchisor. Regardless of the sta seventeen states may preempt the effect of the provision and impose termination standards adopted by the legislature.

16. ***First Refusal Rights to Purchase***. Many franchise agreements reserve to the franchisor the right to buy back a franchise if the franchisee receives to purchase it. The repurchase is usually required to be on the same financial terms as the offer received from the third party.

17. ***Obligations of the Franchisee on Termination or Expiration***. If the relationship comes to an end, the franchise agreement usually requires the franchisee immediately to cease using the trademarks, take down the signs, and remove all forms of decor, interior signs, color schemes that identify the franchise, and assign to the franchisor the telephone numbers used by the business while it was part of the system. The franchisor may agree to purchase any inventory that may be in resalable condition.

    Most contracts also restrict the departing franchisee from engaging in a competing business for a period of time, like a year or two of leaving the franchise system, within the immediate market of the franchised business. These "Covenants against Competition" are controversial in franchising; in some states, such as California, the courts have refused to enforce them because they place an "unreasonable" restriction on the right of every American to pursue a living. Franchisors believe such restrictions are necessary for them to re-establish another franchisee in the market, and that it would be unfair for a terminated franchisee to remain in the same town and, with insider knowledge, compete with the former franchisor.

18. ***Enforcement and Miscellaneous "Boilerplate" Provisions***. This section of a franchise agreement addresses a number of arcane legal subjects that clarify how the parties agree to have the contract interpreted and enforced. These sorts of provisions are common to most commercial contracts, they vary little, are often of little consequence, and so are described as "boilerplate": they are like the cast iron plating of a heat generating boiler, available in mat or plate form for the contract. This section may specify the state law that will govern the interpretation of the contract; where notice must be delivered to be effective; how "days" are counted where the contract specifies an action occur in a number of days; and so forth. The boilerplate provision may also address how and where disputes between the parties under the franchise agreement are to be resolved. They may require the parties to submit their disputes to binding arbitration and may specify where any litigation or arbitration must take place.

Andrew A. Caffey

Attorney-at-Law

Andrew A. Caffey practices law in Bethesda, Maryland, a suburb of Washington, D.C., in the boutique law firm he founded in August 1993. He specializes in franchise, trademark, business opportunity, and distribution law. Andy was Chair of the 1992 ABA Forum on Franchising held in Hilton Head, South Carolina, and is formerly General Counsel of the International Franchise Association (1983–1985). He is a member of the bar in Maryland and the District of Columbia.

Andy received his law degree from the University of Maryland School of Law in 1977 and his BA, cum laude, *from Amherst College. He is a member of the International Franchise Association's Legal Legislative Committee and a former member of the ABA Forum on Franchising's Governing Committee. Andy served as the industry advisor representing the interests of franchisors during the four-year development of the Uniform Franchise Law by the National Conference of Commissioners on Uniform State Laws. He has appeared on numerous franchise programs and is a frequent lecturer and author on subjects of franchise and business opportunity regulation. He has written two books:* Stay Out of Court! The Small Business Guide to Preventing Disputes and Avoiding Lawsuit Hell, *published in March 2005 (Entrepreneur Press); and* Franchises and Business Opportunities: How Find, Buy and Operate a Successful Business *(Entrepreneur Press 2002).*

His work history includes the positions of Director, State Government Affairs for the International Franchise Association in Washington, D.C., the leading trade association of franchisors (1978 to 1981); associate attorney specializing in franchise law with the Washington, D.C., law firm of Brownstein, Zeidman and Schomer (1981–1983); General Counsel of the International Franchise Association (1983–1985); partner in charge of the Washington, D.C., office of Kaufmann, Caffey, Gilden, Rosenblum & Schaeffer, specializing in franchise law (1986–1988); and partner with the Washington, D.C., office of Venable, Baetjer, Howard & Civiletti where he was cochair of the franchise practice group and partner in charge of the trademark practice group (1988–1993). He has practiced in his own law office, the Law Offices of Andrew A. Caffey, since 1993.

Andy served as official Industry Advisor from the International Franchise Association and represented the views of the franchisor community during the four-year development of the Uniform Franchise and Business Opportunities Act promulgated by the National Conference of Commissioners on Uniform State Laws (1983–1987). He served as a member of the Governing Committee of the Forum on Franchising of the American Bar Association (1989–1993), and served as Chair of the 1992 Annual Forum on Franchising Symposium. As Chair of the Symposium, he was responsible for selecting facilities, program topics, and faculty members, and reviewing the papers to be presented to a three-day Franchise Law Symposium attended by more than 500 attorneys from around the country.

During his service as a staff counsel and General Counsel for the International Franchise Association, he was involved in the development of many state and federal franchise investment laws, franchise relationship laws, and state "business opportunity" legislation. As General Counsel, he prepared policy position statements, evaluated the impact of proposed legislation, presented testimony to state and federal regulators, and managed a staff of three professional lobbyists and attorneys responsible for representing the views of the franchisor community to state and federal legislative bodies and agencies.

His law practice has concentrated on the representation of franchisors, distributors, and business opportunity sellers. He has represented numerous franchisors during the course of practice. These include ExxonMobil Oil Corporation, Holiday Inn Worldwide, Institutional Financing Systems, Inc., Decorating Den Systems, Inc., CM IT Solutions, Inc., Liberty Fitness Holdings, EconoLodge, Snap-on Tools Corporation, Choice Hotels, Logan Farms Honey Glazed Hams, Great Harvest Franchising, Inc., Priority Management Systems Inc., Cellular One Group (now part of AT&T), and a host of other companies involved in franchising.

KEY TERMS

FTC rule: a trade regulation rule adopted by the Federal Trade Commission in 1979 to regulate all franchise sales in the United States; built on a single idea: that investors armed with key information will be able to make well-informed and wise investment decisions for themselves;

requires the delivery of a detailed and rather extensive disclosure document to a prospective franchisee but does not otherwise control the franchisor's business practices.

Disclosure document: also called an "offering circular"; the FTC rule requires the delivery of this document to a prospective franchisee for a franchise purchase anywhere in the United States; must contain information that responds to the list of disclosures contained in the twenty-three topic sections.

Contract Area development agreement: a variation on the basic single-unit franchise relationship; allows a developer to build a number of franchised businesses in a particular market area; each franchise will be governed by the terms of a franchise agreement granted by the franchisor.

Subfranchising contract: an expansion program in which a subfranchisor is granted the right to locate and sell individual franchises to individual investors in a defined region.

TRADEMARKS, COPYRIGHTS, PATENTS, AND TRADE SECRETS*

CHAPTER

14

In studying this chapter, you will:

- Learn about trademarks and copyrights, and how to protect them.
- Learn about trade secrets and the role they play in franchising.
- Learn about patents and how to protect them.
- Gain an overview of intellectual property and its importance in business.
- Learn about the basics of antitrust laws and the role they play in franchising.

INCIDENT

Alexander is starting up a new mobile sales franchise, offering a unique and popular line of espresso-based drinks and frozen confections. Since creating his first service vehicle—placing a simple operations kiosk on the back of a converted classic roadster through the use of four conversion couplers and a spring suspension system, all of which he invented—he has had much success with the sales at air shows, community fairs, and high foot-traffic locations around his metropolitan location. Alexander now has three vehicles in full-time operation and has recently been approached by five separate investors who want to buy franchises from him to build a similar mobile business.

Alexander named his business:

> ***EspressO***
> ***On The GO***

and has painted the name on the side of his vehicles and had cups printed showing the name as his service mark. He also asked a buddy in art school to design a logo—a mug with a cartoon smiley face on speeding wheels—and has reproduced the colorful design on his vehicles and cups.

He is thinking about using the phrase:

> ♥♥♥♥ *Jump-Start Your Heart!* ♥♥♥♥

* The authors gratefully acknowledge Andy Caffey of the Law Offices of Andrew A. Caffey, Bethesda, Maryland, as the writer of this chapter.

as a catch phrase under the logo because he thinks it is clever and his customers seem to respond to it with a smile.

A customer who is a lawyer urged Alexander to register his trademarks with the U.S. Patent and Trademark Office. He is concerned about the rules surrounding trademark use and licensing as he begins to franchise the operation. Alexander is also concerned because his designing buddy recently mentioned that he still owns the copyright on his speeding mug design and should be receiving a royalty from EspressO On The GO.

Alexander wants to find out whether he can patent his couplers and suspension system, what steps he should take to protect his marks, whether his catch phrase can be a trademark, and whether he is going to have a serious copyright problem with his art school buddy.

14-1 INTRODUCTION

The term **intellectual property** describes a collection of intangible rights, including trademarks, copyrights, patents, and trade secrets. These are intangible assets that are formed not of bricks and mortar, but are expressions of the human imagination. If handled properly, ownership of these forms of intellectual property will be protected by the law, as are other forms of private property. In an information age, the ability to legally protect the output of one's creativity and imagination is of vital importance.

Intellectual property can represent enormous business value. The General Counsel of The Coca Cola Bottling Co. once stated that if every building, delivery truck, and physical asset of the company were to burn to the ground overnight, the company could go to its bankers and in a matter of days borrow every dollar the company would need to rebuild the entire business on the strength of the value of the *Coca-Cola* trademark alone!

Intellectual property rights are the basic legal building blocks of a franchise system. Trademarks are particularly important to franchising.

Here are brief definitions of the various types of intellectual property that will be discussed in this chapter.

- A **trademark** is a word, name, phrase, symbol, or in some cases a design that is used by a manufacturer or merchant to identify and distinguish its goods from those sold by others and to indicate the source of a product or the quality of a product.

- A **service mark** is the same as a trademark but identifies an intangible service instead of a product.

- A **copyright** is a property right provided by the government in an original work of authorship that is fixed in a tangible form. It protects an author's exclusive right to use and exploit literary, dramatic, musical, artistic, and certain other intellectual works. An author cannot protect ideas but can claim copyright in the original *expression* of an idea. (Most operation manuals are copyrighted.)

- A **trade secret** is confidential business information that is treated in a confidential or secret manner and that would have independent economic value if it were in the hands of a competitor.

- A **patent** is a protectable property right granted by the government that protects an invention, new device, or innovation.

14-2 TRADEMARKS

As defined, a trademark is used by a manufacturer or merchant to identify and distinguish its goods from those sold by others and to indicate the source or quality of a product. As an example,

XEROX® is a registered trademark of the Xerox Corporation, and is used by that company to identify its famous copier machines and other products and services.

Similar to a trademark, a service mark identifies an intangible service instead of a product. The mark *Pizza Hut*® is used by its owner, PepsiCo, to identify the restaurant services of its pizzerias.

A trademark or service mark is not always limited to a word or name phrase. Distinctive logo designs, such as the famous golden arches of the McDonald's Corporation; occasionally colors, such as the distinctive pink color of Corning's insulation (not to mention its Pink Panther!); and even sounds, such as the three-note chime ("bong, BONG, bong") of the NBC television network, can be protected as trademarks.

The first trademarks were craftsmen's marks stamped on their products. The early Roman brick makers identified their personally designed bricks by their shop's insignia. Paul Revere silverware pieces bore his personal mark of authenticity. In modern times, the trademark can still represent an indication of source but more often it represents a standard of quality. For instance, a McDonald's Big Mac hamburger can be purchased at any one of thousands of independent franchised restaurant owners around the world. Customers stepping up to buy a Big Mac sandwich do not assume they are buying a product manufactured for them by McDonald's Corporation of Oak Brook, Illinois. Instead, the mark tells us what to expect from the product and we know immediately from the company's advertising how to request the double-decker specialty. Most adults in this country can tell you what goes into a Big Mac® sandwich:

TWOALLBEEFPATTIESSPECIALSAUCELETTUCECHEESEPICKLESONIO NSONASESAMESEEDBUN.

That's right, another trademark.

14-3 CREATING AND PROTECTING TRADEMARKS

The rights one enjoys as a trademark owner stem entirely from use of the mark in commerce. A trademark has value because the buying public associates the mark with a certain source of the product. This can only come about by use of the mark in commerce.

Using the mark in commerce creates a "common law" right of exclusivity. That is, it is not created by statute or filing or registration. The common law rights of a trademark owner are based on this individual being the first to use a mark and extend to the trading areas in which it is actually used. Under the common law, the owner has the right of exclusive use and may file with a court to enforce that right.

Federal and state trademark statutes provide additional protections. The most important of these is the federal Trademark Act of 1946,[1] also known as the **Lanham Act**. This law provides a national system of registration and public notice of trademark rights, administered by the **Patent and Trademark Office (PTO)** in Washington, D.C. Registration of a trademark with the PTO gives the trademark owner the benefit of nationwide protection, access to federal courts to protect those rights, and "constructive notice" to everyone that the mark is protected. In additional, the Lanham Act prohibits deceptive practices in the marketing of goods and services.

The Lanham Act provides for a registration process by which the trademark owner may secure these rights for its mark. The owner must file a written application with the PTO, providing the name of the applicant, his citizenship and address, the goods or services identified by the mark, a drawing of the mark, specimens of actual use of the mark (if the application is based on prior use of the mark, as opposed to a future intent to use the mark), and a filing fee.

The PTO staff will review the application, and in a few months advise the applicant if there is any deficiency or other problem with registering the mark. If the drawing is inadequate, or the proposed mark is likely to cause confusion because it is the same or similar to another registered mark, the examining attorney will reject the application, giving the applicant an opportunity to respond as to why the application should proceed. Once approved, the PTO will publish the proposed registration in the *Official Gazette*, a widely circulated government publication. This gives a thirty-day opportunity to any member of the public to review proposed marks and file an opposition. If no opposition is filed, the PTO will issue a Certificate of Registration. The entire process takes from twelve to eighteen months, on average.

14-3a   Selection of a Trademark

Selecting a strong and durable trademark is one of the most important decisions that any business can make. From a legal perspective there are two vital questions to answer when selecting a new mark: First, will the selected name subject the business to an infringement action from a prior owner of the same name or a confusingly similar version of it? Second, how "strong" is the new mark and how much protection can the owner expect if the mark is attacked by other users of a similar mark in the future?

As to the first question, before a trademark is adopted, the new owner must search through all existing marks to see if the new name is already in use. Certain service companies will conduct such a search and report the results. Trademark counsel will review the results and advise the business if the mark it has selected is available for registration, or if there are problems, such as prior users of the same or similar marks, that may result in legal challenges down the road.

If the mark is available for registration, the company will proceed with the registration process as described. If it is not available for registration, the company will be forced to think up another word, phrase, or slogan for registration and protection.

As to the second legal concern, the potential strength of the mark will depend largely on how distinctive it is and where it falls on the spectrum of trademark strength. A mark is distinctive, and therefore strong, when it is easily distinguished from other marks for similar goods or services, and does not directly describe the product or service it is used to identify. The four categories of the strength spectrum are (1) fanciful, coined marks, (2) arbitrary marks, (3) suggestive marks, and (4) descriptive marks.

At the strong end of the spectrum are **fanciful** or **coined marks**. The courts will provide these marks the greatest protection. Coined terms such as KODAK® for cameras and EXXON® for petroleum products have no meaning apart from their trademark usage and through advertising and frequent display have come to be associated with particular products and services.

Arbitrary marks are also considered strong marks on this spectrum, including such names as CAMEL® for cigarettes, APPLE® for computers, and CREST® for toothpaste. These are dictionary words that have been used arbitrarily to identify the products and services; the word APPLE describes no quality or other aspect of the computers manufactured by the Apple Computer Corporation.

Suggestive marks describe a feature or quality of the product or service, but require some imagination to make the connection. This category includes such famous marks as IVORY® for soap products, MUSTANG® for automobiles, and CHEERIOS® for breakfast cereal. IVORY® suggests the white and pure color of the soap; MUSTANG® suggests the unbridled, untamed excitement of a sports car. They do not describe the product, but require some ingenuity to connect the mark with an aspect of the product. It is the requisite exercise of imagination that separates these protectable, suggestive marks from names that are "merely descriptive." Sometimes it is difficult to draw this line, and the courts have often struggled to analyze the likely intellectual thought process of the consumer.

Descriptive marks, which merely describe their goods or service, are weak marks. The mark BED & BREAKFAST REGISTRY merely describes the service it provides and was therefore held to be unenforceable as a trademark.[2] Descriptive marks will receive little or no protection from the courts unless they have become recognized in the marketplace and thus have acquired "secondary meaning." A mark such as HONEY BAKED HAM® falls into this category; it is a relatively weak mark but has acquired secondary meaning as identifying a particular source of baked ham products.

Generic terms can never become trademarks or service marks. These are dictionary words or other common expressions that describe in common fashion a product or service. *Sandwich, bed,* and *table* are all generic terms and are unavailable for trademark protection.

The courts have allowed the combination of two otherwise generic terms to form a protectable trademark. PIG and SANDWICH are both generic terms, but once combined into PIG SAND-WICH, they may acquire protectable status.

The trademark landscape is also littered with former trademarks and service marks that have become generic through improper use. When people start to refer to a product by its brand name rather than using the mark to distinguish one product from others, the owner of the mark may lose all rights in the trademark. Examples include *aspirin, thermos, cellophane,* and *nylon.* Xerox Corporation has become famous for its work to resist this fate for its famous XEROX® mark for copiers. Their concern is that the term *xerox* will become synonymous with *copy.* People might start saying, "Please make a xerox of this for me," using it in a generic sense. The company's advertising states: "When you use 'Xerox' the way you use 'aspirin,' we get a headache....All because some of you may be using our name in a generic manner....Which could cause it to lose its trademark status the way the name 'aspirin' did years ago. So when you do use our name, please use it as an adjective to identify our products and services..."

14-3b   Proper Use of Trademarks and Service Marks

The fastest way to lose one's trademark to the graveyard of generic terms is to abandon the mark through improper use. Following are fundamental rules of proper trademark use.

1. ***Distinguish the Mark from its Surroundings.*** The first rule is to set apart a trademark from its surroundings so that it is distinguished from its common word neighbors. Trademarks are special terms, not ordinary words. They are royalty among commoners and should never be confused with the common folk. Use all capital letters, bold or italicized highlighting to let the mark stand out from the crowd.

   Correct: "You can't go wrong with AJAX® widgets."

   Incorrect: "Ajax widgets last a long, long time."

2. ***Use Only as an Adjective.*** A trademark should always be used as an adjective, never as a noun, verb, or adverb. This simple rule often surprises businesspeople, but it reflects a fundamental truth about trademarks: A trademark is a brand name and it is used to describe an underlying (generic) product.

   Correct: "Please pass those delicious AJAX® muffins."

   Incorrect: "Have fun at your next beach party, pick up a few AJAX®." (noun).

   Incorrect: "Really let yourself go, AJAX your next block party." (verb).

   Incorrect: "My hair was AJAXed until it took on this wonderful shine." (verb)

   The same rules apply to a service mark. Use it only as a proper adjective to describe the services it represents.

3. ***Use Notice Symbol.*** Your trademarks should carry the appropriate notice symbol. Here is the meaning of the available notice symbols.

   ™   Can be placed on any trademark as soon as it is used as a mark. You need no registration of the mark to display ™ and it may be used immediately. Note: It does not appear in a circle.

   SM   Can be used just like ™ but for service marks.

® Indicates that the mark has been registered (not merely applied for, but effectively registered) with the U.S. Patent and Trademark Office. This symbol should be used only when the PTO has issued the Certificate of Registration.

14-3c Enforcement Standards and Remedies

A trademark owner may seek to prevent another user from using a mark that is "confusingly similar" to his own mark. If the two marks are likely to confuse the consumer regarding the source or qualities represented by the mark, the court will order that the junior user cease using the mark and causing the potential for marketplace confusion. A court may order that the infringer destroy all products or packaging that display the infringing mark, order that there shall be no future infringement, and pay the owner's costs associated with the infringement. In some circumstances where the infringer had appropriate notice of the other mark, or there is evidence of bad faith, the court may also award damages resulting from the infringement.

14-4 COPYRIGHTS

Our federal copyright laws protect the rights of authors and creators of writings, artworks, crafts, manuals, brochures, sculptures, plays, computer software, motion pictures, sound recordings, and works of architecture. As noted earlier in the chapter, copyright is a property right provided by the government in an *original work of authorship that is fixed in a tangible form*. It protects an author's exclusive right to use and exploit literary, dramatic, musical, artistic, and certain other intellectual works.

An author cannot protect ideas, but can claim copyright in the original *expression* of an idea. So, the author of a short story has a copyright in the telling of the story but not in the underlying ideas that comprise the story. A television journalist may have a right to the image and the words used to describe a newsworthy incident, but not the incident itself. The author of a technical manual has a copyright in the original expression of the how-to guidelines, but the copyright will never extend to the process or the technical concepts being described. There may be other ways to protect that technology, either as a patent or as a trade secret, as we discuss below in this chapter, but an idea apart from the expression of that idea can never be subject to a copyright.

What rights does a copyright holder actually have? We mentioned above that the owner of a copyright has the *exclusive* right to use and exploit the work. This concept includes (1) the exclusive right to reproduce the work in copies or musical tapes or CDs, (2) the exclusive right to prepare "derivative works" based on the copyrighted work, (3) the exclusive right to distribute copies of the work to the public, (4) the exclusive right to perform the work in public, and (5) the exclusive right to display the work in public.

14-4a Creating and Registering Works Subject to Copyright

It is not difficult to protect the rights an author has in original works. Since Congress updated the copyright laws in 1989, a copyright attaches to the work the instant it is created. The author does not have to register the work, file it with any public agency, attach a notice, or say any magic words. The moment the original work is fixed in a tangible form of expression, the author's legal rights come into being.

Under copyright laws, it is the author or coauthor of a work, or a person to whom the author has assigned legal rights, who is protected by the copyright. The only exception to this rule—and it is a limited exception—is for "works made for hire."

A **work made for hire** is typically a work created by an employee in the scope of the job. The copyright will be owned by the employer when it is a work made for hire, for instance, when an employee of a restaurant franchisor creates a new, fun menu design; or the employee of a publishing house designs a book illustration. There can often be a question of ownership where the author is not an employee but an independent contractor. Unless the copyright ownership rights are specified in a written contract as a work made for hire, the law will usually presume that the copyright in a given work is owned by the author.

When Should an Author Register a Copyright?

Registration of a copyright is done with the Copyright Office in Washington, D.C., and is easy and inexpensive to accomplish. By simply submitting the work with an application form and a $20 fee, the registration is complete. Registration affords the author additional protections under the copyright statute, not the least of which is the right to bring an infringement lawsuit. Registration also directly affects the damages that may be awarded by a court against an infringer.

How Long Does a Copyright Remain in Effect?

Generally, the copyright remains in effect for the life of the author, plus fifty years following his or her death. The rules are different for works made for hire, anonymous works, or "pseudonymous" works: The copyright will be effective for seventy-five years from the date of publication, or one hundred years from the date of creation, whichever expires first. As most copyrights held by corporations are considered works made for hire, the seventy-five years from publication/one hundred years from creation rules will generally apply.

How to Use Correct Copyright Notices

Although formal notice is not required in order to benefit from copyright protection, there are many advantages of applying appropriate notice to the copyrighted work. It gives notice of the claim of right, displays the owner of the right, and may save legal costs down the road associated with protecting the copyright. Following are two examples of proper copyright notices.

> Copyright 2004 Acme, Inc.
> © 2004 Jane X. Smith

What Steps Are Available to Enforce a Copyright?

A copyright owner may bring a lawsuit in federal court for damages suffered as a result of the infringement. The court may calculate the owner's financial loss from the infringement and may award statutory damages. If the court finds the infringement to be willful, it may increase the award up to a maximum of $100,000.

14-5 TRADE SECRETS

If a business has particularly sensitive and important information that it does not want to fall into the hands of competitors, the law of trade secrets provides an effective and efficient means of protecting that information.

What is a trade secret? It is generally defined as information, including a formula, pattern, compilation, device, method, technique, or process, that (1) provides a competitive advantage, and would have economic value if it fell into the hands of a competitor, and (2) is subject to reasonable efforts to keep it secret. This broad definition sweeps in a variety of confidential business information: the secret ingredients in a food recipe, a secret production method, software program designs, a secret marketing plan, and the list goes on.

Secrecy is essential to the existence of a protectable trade secret. The law does not require that the owner keep the information in *absolute* secrecy, but reasonable steps must be taken to ensure that it does not become generally known or available to those who are not authorized to receive it.

In most business situations several people—sometimes dozens of people—may be involved in developing and securing the trade secret. There are two ways that a trade secret owner can protect the information while sharing it with other people: by contract or by the existence of a special relationship, such as with an employee, where a duty of confidentiality and loyalty exists.

The contract, known as a confidentiality agreement, will first acknowledge that the confidential information is owned by the company, and that the recipient will keep it in confidence, will use it only in the manner authorized by the company, and will not disclose the information to any third parties with the company's consent. This type of confidentiality provision may also appear in employment agreements to be signed by company employees when they first begin their employment.

Any business that has confidential information it does not want in the hands of its competitors should take steps to protect its trade secrets. Among the measures available are the following:

- *Conduct a trade secret audit*. This a regular, internal review of trade secret information and the procedures that are used to protect them.

- Clearly mark all confidential documents: "Confidential and Proprietary Information—Do Not Reproduce or Divulge without the Written Permission of XYZ, Inc." Depending on the type of materials, the owner may want to sequentially number and log all copies created, so that they may be retrieved.

- Train employees so that they understand the importance of trade secrets, and understand the procedures adopted by the company to keep them secret.

- Use written confidentiality agreements for employees and independent contractors who work in confidential areas.

- Take steps at the time an employee leaves to make sure that all confidential information is returned to the company and get a written acknowledgment that all such material has been returned.

- Use noncompetition agreements with employees. Although these contracts are not enforceable in all states, many states will enforce an individual's promise not to engage in competing activity for a period of time after leaving a job, selling a business, or terminating a franchise relationship.

Does a Trade Secret Need to be Registered Anywhere to be Enforceable?

No, unlike patents (to be discussed), a trade secret need not be filed with any federal agency. State laws generally allow the owner of a trade secret to bring a lawsuit for injunctive relief by which a court might order the infringer to cease the infringing activity and/or for damages.

What is the Duration of a Trade Secret?

Unlike copyrights and trademarks, a trade secret has no defined life. It may continue on in perpetuity; so long as the information continues to meet the definition of a trade secret it will continue to be enforceable. The formula for Coca-Cola® has been kept as a closely held trade secret for decades and will likely continue to be held in the strictest of confidence for so long as it gives the Coca-Cola Company a competitive advantage.

14-6 PATENTS

U.S. patent laws offer a fascinating deal to an inventor. In exchange for revealing publicly how the invention works, society grants the inventor up to twenty years in which to exclude others from making, using, or selling, offering to sell, or importing the invention in the United States.[3] This approach nicely balances the need of the inventor to benefit from personal cleverness and industry and the needs of society "to promote the progress of science and useful arts," according to the U.S. Constitution.[4]

What Can Be Patented?

Generally, in order to be entitled to a utility patent, the invention:

I. Must fall within broad statutory categories, defined as follows: "[W]hoever invents or discovers any new and useful process, machine, manufacture of composition of matter, or any new and useful improvement thereof, may obtain a patent."[5]

II. Must be new.

III. Must be useful.

IV. Must be non-obvious to one of ordinary skill in the art to which the subject matter pertains.

A number of steps should be taken by an inventor in order to protect the invention, and its patentability, once the invention is conceived. Careful records are essential. The inventor should record every detail of the invention in writing, using photographs and drawings, and these records should be witnessed in writing by someone who is not a co-inventor. As the invention is tested and applied in practical situations, the inventor should continue to record descriptions of the invention and how it performs in testing.

The inventor must exercise great care not to make the invention public in any way, either through writing articles, selling it, or advertising it, prior to filing for a patent. If the inventor reveals the invention to the public and fails to keep it a secret, he or she may after a short period of time lose all rights to patent the invention.

Filing a patent application is a complex process that in most cases should be handled by a professional, like a patent attorney or patent agent. Prior to filing the application, the attorney or patent agent will usually conduct a patentability search at the Patent and Trademark Office by reviewing the "prior art" disclosed in existing patents and publications. If the review of the prior art reveals that the invention is not novel, is obvious based the prior art, or there is some other problem revealed, the inventor may decide not to proceed with the application for a patent.

The application itself consists of a detailed description of the invention and its uses, an oath or declaration attesting to certain aspects of the application, drawings of the invention if necessary to illustrate how it works, and a filing fee. The application is reviewed by a staff patent examiner assigned to the filing, first to determine if the application is complete, and second to review existing patents and publications to determine if the application should be approved and whether the invention is patentable. The examiner will issue any comments or objections, and the applicant will have an opportunity to respond to any concerns raised. The entire process can take an average of two years before a patent is issued to the applicant.

A patent right is the grant of a lawful monopoly extending to the claimed subject matter of the patent. However, the authority conferred by the patent process is essentially a negative right: the holder may exclude others from making, using, or selling the invention; he or she receives no affirmative grant of right to make, use, or sell the device. When another person violates the holder's right to exclude all others, the patent is infringed, and the infringer may be ordered by a court to cease the infringing activity, and held liable for compensatory damages. In some circumstances, the damages may be increased by the court and attorneys fees awarded if the plaintiff can show that the infringement was willful.

14-7   INTELLECTUAL PROPERTY RIGHTS IN FRANCHISING

The types of intellectual property discussed in this chapter are at the heart of the legal relationship between a franchisor and franchisee.

> Trademarks are the "cornerstone" of the franchise relationship. The trademark emblem is used to identify the franchised business in the eye of the public, and comes to represent all of the operational units in a franchise system. In fact, it is the families of famous trademarks—McDonald's®, Subway®, Holiday Inn®, Pizza Hut®—that most readily identify the most famous franchising programs.
>
> The know-how that is transferred to franchisees in the form of training usually constitutes a trade secret of the franchisor, and may be protected as such.
>
> The printed operations manual that the franchise owner uses to understand the details of daily operations may be copyrighted.
>
> The unique products distributed through many product franchises may be patented.

Care must be taken in any franchise relationship to delineate the rights of the parties to the various forms of intellectual property that comprise the franchise program. The franchise agreement will typically address these subjects, stating that the franchisor has rights to the trademarks, copyrights, patents, and trade secrets, and that the franchisee must use them in a limited fashion and only during the term of the agreement. Use by the franchisee will be subject to the terms and conditions set forth in the franchise agreement.

14-8   ANTITRUST LAW AND FRANCHISING

The antitrust laws of the United States have developed over the past hundred years to set the broad rules of economic fairness in business. Antitrust laws had their genesis in the powerful business organizations (or "trusts") that emerged from the Industrial Revolution in the late nineteenth century and monopolized many basic industries. On the strength of a populist movement to rein in the trusts, the U.S. Congress passed The Antitrust Act introduced by Senator John Sherman of Ohio, and signed it into law on July 2, 1890. This law, now known as the **Sherman Act**, has governed U.S. business and prohibited its excesses for the entire twentieth century.

The Sherman Act adopted a few sweeping concepts. Its basic aim was to eliminate the economic and political problems caused by monopoly power, and it prohibited monopolization, and combinations and conspiracies to monopolize.[6] The Sherman Act also addressed and prohibited pernicious activity on a smaller business scale by targeting all concerted action that might injure competition. Section 1 states:

> Every contract, combination in the form of trust or otherwise, or conspiracy, in restraint of trade or commerce among the several States, or with foreign nations, is declared to be illegal.[7]

The courts have struggled to adapt and apply these broad principles to business circumstances since the adoption of the Sherman Act. Virtually all contracts might be said to "restrain trade." If one party agrees to sell something or provide service to another by definition, it means that those parties will not be doing business with other parties. A literal reading to the restrictive language might prohibit most contracts in business relationships. The courts, therefore, ruled that "every" as it is used in Section 1 means those contracts, combinations, and conspiracies that *unreasonably* restrain trade. This approach has become known as the *Rule of Reason* and is one of the analytical touch stones of antitrust law.

Another judicial standard for legality under the antitrust laws is the *Per Se Rule*.[8] This standard will apply to those antitrust violations that the courts believe are so detrimental and "plainly anti-competitive" that they are presumed to be illegal without a detailed analysis of the business factors that might otherwise justify the practice. A *per se* unlawful practice, such as two competitors agreeing to fix prices, will be condemned once the elements of the conspiracy are proved and the court will hear no evidence as to procompetitive circumstances that might justify the conspiracy. In the eyes of the law, there is no justification and no redeeming virtue of such a "per se" illegal practice.

Most per se illegal practices are agreements among competitors, so called "horizontal" agreements. They are called horizontal agreements because they take place at the same level of distribution, among competitors. Vertical agreements—those that take place at different levels of distribution such as exists between a seller and a buyer, or a franchisor and a franchisee—are generally tested under the Rule of Reason.

Two other aspects of the antitrust laws should be noted. In 1914, the Sherman Act was supplemented by passage of the **Clayton Act**.[9] The Clayton Act prohibits certain practices between sellers and buyers and its provisions are particularly relevant to the business practices of franchisors and franchisees, as discussed below. Finally, rounding out the sweep of federal antitrust laws, the **Robinson-Patman Act of 1936** prohibits price discrimination by sellers in the prices they charge to similarly situation buyers.

Why is antitrust law so important to franchising? It is because the franchisor and franchisee are independent of one another. Unlike an employment relationship that involves individuals working for a single business entity, the franchise relationship involves two entities or businesses that are linked to one another only by contract; they must follow the same antitrust rules as all businesses and will run into severe legal trouble if they forget it. Franchisors must walk an often narrow path between the goal of uniformity in the appearance and operation of all franchises and the limitations that the law imposes on the dealings between independent businesses in order to protect competition.

We now turn to examining a few situations in the franchising context that might lead to a concern about the application of the antitrust laws.

14-8a   Selling Products to Franchisees

Perhaps the most common antitrust situations encountered by franchisors and franchisees surround the franchisor selling goods and services to franchisees.

Tying Arrangements

The Clayton Act prohibits a seller from conditioning the sale of one product on the purchase of another product, if that **tying arrangement** injures competition. This is called an unlawful tie because the seller has tied together the sale of the two products, saying in essence, "If you want to buy X, you've gotta buy Z." One is a desirable product (the "tying product") and the other is undesirable to the buyer (the "tied product"), but the buyer buys the second product because it is the only way the buyer can acquire the desirable product. A tying arrangement will be found to be unlawful when a court finds that (1) there are two distinct and separate products involved, (2) the seller has sufficient economic power in the tying product (product A) to restrain competition in the tied product (product B), and (3) the arrangement substantially lessens competition in the market of the tied product.

In franchising, a concern about tying arrangements arises when the franchisor conditions the sale of the desirable product (for instance, a well-known restaurant franchise) on the purchase from the franchisor of other products (such as printed cups, napkins, and other paper goods to be used in the operation of the restaurant). From the franchisee's perspective, these questions take on immediate importance. Is the franchisor simply taking advantage of the relationship by requiring franchisees to buy overpriced supplies only from the franchisor? The franchisee will naturally want to buy lower cost products from competing vendors. Why else would a franchisor demand that it be the exclusive seller of these supplies except to extract an unreasonable profit on the supplies?

When such challenges have been made in court, the first question is whether there are really two separate products involved: Is a franchised ice cream shop truly separate from the ice cream product served to customers?[10] Are printed cups and napkins a separate product from the chicken restaurant franchise itself?[11]

The answers to these questions probably lie in the nature of the franchise itself. The stronger the relationship between the trademark displayed and the product the mark represents, the more intertwined—and most likely a single product for tying analysis—they are. Where the tied product becomes more removed from the products represented by the trademark, the more likely they will be considered two separate products for tying analysis.

There are few clear, easy answers in tying situations. The response of franchisors to the uncertainties created by the tying cases has been to sell products to franchisees at acceptably low prices, perhaps contracting with a supplier who offers discount in prices when a high volume of product is purchased. Many franchise systems assure product quality by approving those suppliers who are authorized to sell to franchisees in the system. Some approve the products themselves, requiring that certain specifications be met before they may be sold through the franchise.

Pricing Issues

Few antitrust problems are more dangerous than those surrounding prices to be charged for franchisee goods and services. It is a per se violation of the Sherman Act for two competitors, such as two or more competing franchisees, to agree on the prices they will charge for their products. As they are direct competitors, it would be a horizontal price fixing agreement and a criminal violation of federal antitrust law. For this reason, franchisees are cautioned at conventions and regional meetings never to discuss prices or their pricing strategies with one another or in any group meeting.

Franchisees are free to set their own prices, regardless of the pricing suggestions of the franchisor. Pricing restraints between franchisors and franchisees are vertical in nature. Franchisors may certainly suggest the prices that the franchisee charges, but franchisees are not bound to follow the suggestions. A number of situations can arise in the business life of a franchisor that will have antitrust implications.

KEY TERMS

Arbitrary mark: a dictionary word that has been used arbitrarily to identify particular products and services, such as CAMEL® for cigarettes, APPLE® for computers, and CREST® for toothpaste; also considered strong trademarks.

Clayton Act: a supplemental law to the Sherman Act of 1914; prohibits certain practices between sellers and buyers; its provisions are particularly relevant to the business practices of franchisors and franchisees.

Copyright: a property right provided by the government in an original work of authorship that is fixed in a tangible form; protects an author's exclusive right to use and exploit literary, dramatic, musical, artistic, and certain other intellectual works; protects the original *expression* of an idea, not the idea itself.

Descriptive mark: weak trademark which describes a good or service; receives little or no protection from the courts unless it has become recognized in the marketplace and thus has acquired "secondary meaning".

Fanciful or coined mark: strong trademark which the courts will provide with the greatest protection; term that has no meaning apart from its trademark usage, and through advertising and frequent displays has come to be associated with a particular product and service.

Generic term: dictionary word or other common expression that describes in common fashion a product or service and can never become a trademark or service mark, although the combination of two otherwise generic terms can form a protectable trademark.

Intellectual property: a collection of intangible rights including trademarks, copyrights, patents, trade secrets; intangible assets that can be protected by the law like other forms of private property.

Lanham Act: the federal Trademark Act of 1946, which provides a national system of registration and public notice of trademark rights, prohibits deceptive practices in the marketing of goods and services, and provides for a registration process by which the trademark owner may secure these rights for its mark.

Patent: a protectable property right granted by the government that protects an invention, new device, or innovation.

Patent and Trademark Office (PTO): administers the national system of registration and public notice of trademark rights as provided by the Lanham Act; registration gives a trademark owner the benefit of nationwide protection, access to federal courts to protect those rights, and "constructive notice" to everyone that the mark is protected.

Robinson-Patman Act of 1936: prohibits price discrimination by sellers in the prices they charge to similarly situation buyers.

Service mark: like a trademark, but identifies an intangible service instead of a product.

Sherman Act: the Antitrust Act of 1890, introduced by Senator John Sherman of Ohio; aimed to eliminate the economic and political problems caused by monopoly power and prohibited monopolization and combinations and conspiracies to monopolize; addressed and prohibited pernicious activity on a smaller business scale by targeting all concerted action that might injure competition.

Suggestive mark: trademark that does not describe a product or service but rather a feature or quality of the product or service; requires some imagination for the consumer to make the connection between the mark and the aspect of the product or service being sold.

Trademark: a word, name, phrase, symbol, or a design that is used by a manufacturer or merchant to identify and distinguish its goods from those sold by others and to indicate the source of a product or the quality of a product.

Trade secrets: confidential business information that is treated in a confidential or secret manner and that would have independent economic value if it were in the hands of a competitor.

Tying arrangements: prohibited by the Clayton Act; when a seller conditions the sale of one product on the purchase of another product and thus "ties" the products together.

Work made for hire: a work created by an employee in the scope of the job and to which the employer owns the copyright; an exception to copyright laws which say that only the author or coauthor of a work, or a person to whom the author has assigned legal rights, is protected by the copyright.

Jim L. Peterson

Chairman and President, Apigent Solution

Jim L. Peterson is the chairman and president of Apigent Solutions and the past chairman, president and CEO of Bojangles' Restaurants, Inc. Apigent Solutions is headquartered in Oklahoma City. The firm is a software provider for real-time end-to-end technology solutions for businesses with a concentration on food service.

Prior to that, Mr. Peterson was president and CEO of Whataburger, Inc. for twenty years, growing that chain of restaurants across the Sun Belt from Texas to Arizona and making it one of the largest regional companies in food service specializing in made to order products. Whataburger also gained recognition for being one of the best franchises in the Sun Belt with over 250 franchise restaurants.

Jim Peterson started his career at age thirteen as a car hop. He went on to be a waiter, assistant chef, chef, musician, and athlete. He graduated from the University of Missouri in 1957. During his career, he has held the office of president of three major restaurant chains and has also franchised catalogue order stores, truck stops, gasoline and convenience stores, supermarkets, and drug stores. He is the immediate past chairman of the International Franchise Association Education Foundation. He is one of the original members of the University of Nebraska Franchise Study Advisory Council. He has received numerous awards and national recognition in the food industry as well as for his country. He is a leader in representing the food service industry in Washington, D.C., his involvement lasting over twenty years. He has been awarded the Golden Chain Award, the MUFSO Multi Unit Operator of the Year, and Man of the Year, Silver Plate Operator of the Year from the International Food Service Manufacturer's Association, and the Restaurant Business Leadership Award. He is past chairman and president of the National Restaurant Association and the Educational Foundation of the Food Service Industry. In the state of Texas, he has been recognized as Restauranteur of the Year and Hall of Fame Restaurateur. He has served as chairman of numerous state and local organizations as well as several business, utility, and hospital board of directors. He has been honored by the Boy Scouts of America and was named Boy Scout of the Year and Distinguished Citizen of the Year. He was awarded Leader of the Arts and also received a humanitarian award from the Fellowship of Christians and Jews. Mr. Peterson in a lay minister, and writes poetry and music. He still participates in tennis tournaments and running events around the country, running at least two marathons a year as well as numerous races promoting and selling his theme of the healthful and active lifestyle. He also is a cattle rancher in South Texas where he raises Semitol and Brangus cattle and quarter horses.

NOTES

1. 15 U.S.C. §1051, et seq. (1982 & Supp. 1989). The Lanham Act was amended in 1988 by the Trademark Revisions Act of 1988, H.R. rep. no. 100–515, 100th Cong., 2d Session 5–7, *reprinted in* 1988, U.S. Code Cong. & Admin. News 5577, 5581–5583.
2. *In re Bed & Breakfast Registry*, 791 F.2d 157 (Fed. Cir. 1986).
3. The terms of both utility patents, for machines, compositions, and new processes, and plant patents, for the asexual reproduction of a distinct and new variety of plant, is twenty years from the date of filing; the life of a design patent, granted for new, original, and ornamental designs for a manufactured product, is fourteen years from the date of issue.
4. Art. I, §8, cl. 8.
5. 35 U.S.C. §101.

6. 15 U.S.C § 2.
7. 15 U.S.C § 1.
8. "Per se" is a Latin phrase that means "through itself" or "by means of itself."
9. 15 U.S.C. §12 to §18.
10. In *Krehl v. Baskin-Robbins Ice Cream Co.*, 664 F2d 1348 (9th Cir 1982), a federal court ruled that the two are so inextricable intertwined in the mind of the consumer that they constitute a single product and therefore could not be bound together as an unlawful tie.
11. See *Siegle v. Chicken Delight, Inc.*, 448 F2d 43 (9th Cir 1971), where the court found that such printed paper goods did constitute a separate product for tying analysis.

INVESTIGATING FRANCHISE OPPORTUNITIES

In studying this chapter, you will:

- **Learn what is involved in choosing a franchise.**
- **Evaluate yourself as a prospective franchisee.**
- **Learn how to investigate and compare franchisors.**
- **Be able to develop questions about franchise opportunities.**
- **Understand what should be included in the disclosure document.**
- **Learn where to find information about franchisors and franchises.**

INCIDENT

Ramona has just finished college and wants to start her own business. Having heard about the success rate of franchises, she has decided to investigate the possibility of opening her own franchised business. She is very interested in a donut, yogurt, or popcorn business.

Ramona has taken the time to drive around and talk to several local franchisees. The result of her research was discouraging. She found that start-up costs were high, some profits were not as high as she had expected, and the workdays were very long.

Ramona learned that the average franchising fee was $32,000, with total start-up costs averaging $120,000. Estimated sales approached $365,000, with profits ranging between 8 and 16 percent of annual revenues. Some of the franchisors mentioned that they spend more time training franchisees in how to keep the store clean than in how to make a better product.

15-1 INTRODUCTION

Selecting the right type of franchised business may be the most important step taken by a prospective franchisee. A poor selection may create terrible problems for both the franchisee and the franchisor. Currently, because there are no laws requiring a franchisor to grant a franchise, the franchisor has the freedom to choose whoever would appear to be best for the franchised company. Therefore, it is up to the prospective franchisee to carefully investigate all possibilities and determine the best opportunity before signing on with a franchise company.

Answering the following questions will help a person into the right mindset to begin the necessary introspection for determining whether becoming a franchisee is the right thing to do.

- Do I need to control everything and make all decisions by myself?
- Can I handle the day-to-day operation of a franchise business, which may include performing the duties of an absent employee?
- Is success in business one of your primary goals in life?
- Is buying a franchise the same as "buying a job" to you?
- Are you prepared to work long hours to make a business succeed?
- Are you motivated to work without supervision and without a support staff?
- Do you set priorities and organize your time accordingly?
- Have you ever hired, assessed, or fired employees?
- Have you ever trained personnel? If yes, what was the outcome?
- How do you feel about being the primary salesperson in a small company?
- Do you have sufficient capital to get through the start-up phase of a new business venture?
- Is your spouse a strong supporter of you starting a business?
- If things don't go well for you, do you give up easily?

Questions adapted from "Franchise Quiz," 23 April 2007, http://franchisehelp.com/execfb/publc/quiz.

15-2   BECOMING A FRANCHISEE

Franchising is a risk, but very different from the risk of investing money in the stock market. One invests by buying shares of stock in the company, and after a given time, that company either will or will not provide a good return on the investment. In a franchised business, however, more than just money is invested. Time, energy, effort, and one's lifeblood are poured into the business. Some franchises also are less risky than others; some are "blue chip" franchises and have a tremendously successful track record; but they are also fairly expensive in terms of franchising fees and start-up costs. Other, newer franchises, without a proven record, are often less costly but may be more risky.

By joining a solid franchise system, much of the guesswork of running a business is removed. Further, many of the mistakes made by a brand new independent entrepreneur in a start-up business are not experienced. That success, venturing forward in a start-up business with minimal mistakes and a well-tuned operating system, is what a person buys when purchasing a franchise from a mature franchise system. The "kinks" of running a business have already been worked out. The franchisor has taken care of many of the headaches of opening a new business. What the new franchisee needs to do is follow the direction, guidelines, and procedures as developed by the franchisor.

15-2a   Inform Yourself about Available Franchises

Before committing to a particular franchise system, a prospective franchisee should investigate the opportunities available in franchising. Gathering information about various franchise systems is a crucial step in the business planning process.

At the very beginning of your search, start a journal. For each franchise system you consider, write the names of the people you talk with, the names of the sources of information you examined to get information on each franchise system, and your "gut" feelings or observations about each franchise system you are considering. Remember, looking for the right franchise system is much like the search made when looking for a new home. After a person has visited three or four houses, the particulars of each house toured become foggy or distant. It can be hard to remember which house might need a new roof in the next five years, which house would likely need a heating and cooling system very soon, and the size of the kitchens and second bedrooms. In the journal you record the specific information about each franchise system. The journal will help you recall which system had its highest priority for new franchises in the Midwest, which has the most extensive training program, which may have the simplest franchise contract, and which franchise had the 130-page operations manual!

There are many ways to collect information about franchised businesses. Many sources are in print and readily available, other sources of information are available at franchise trade shows and the newest source is the Internet. Take advantage of every source you can to get the best and most accurate information possible, to get a complete picture of each franchise system you are examining.

- **Over-the-Counter Business Publications.** Several magazines and a few newspapers regularly include franchise-related information as opinion pieces, stories, factual industry statistics, and even sections that contain articles and advertising about franchising. Several of these readily available sources are:

  - *The Wall Street Journal*

  - *USA Today*

  - *New York Times*

  - *Franchise Times*

  - *Franchising World*

  - *Entrepreneur*

  - *Franchise Update*

- **The Internet.** Quickly, the Internet is becoming a must-see location for examining franchise companies. Many franchise systems have their own website and list their site's address in various forms of advertisement and brochures. A number of mature franchise systems also link to the International Franchise Association's website. Fundamentally, websites provide some company information about its history, geographic distribution, products and services provided into the marketplace, management philosophy, number of franchised and corporate locations, general description of their franchise concept, and how to get additional information. Also, one can use the websites to make direct contact with the sales department of franchise companies. Some companies even allow a person to complete a franchisee application online, which can speed up getting additional information from the franchise systems a person has of primary interest.

- **Franchise Trade Shows.** Trade shows are typically held in major cities across the nation. Most metropolitan areas will have a franchise trade show or exposition at least once in a year. Check your newspapers and other sources of franchise information. Try to attend the nearest trade show to your home. Franchise trade expositions provide the opportunity to meet face to face with representatives of many franchise systems at one time.

- **Directories.** Several published franchise directories list most of the franchise companies operating not only in the United States but also worldwide. Typically, a directory will not guarantee information provided by a franchise system. It is up to individuals to verify any information contained therein. The franchise directories may be the best place to begin if interested persons are not sure what they are looking for in a franchise, because the directories provide capsules of information about literally thousands of franchised companies. The directories provide basic information, which individuals can take and then, through follow-up contact or looking up additional sources, fine-tune the information to get an accurate picture of each franchise system being considered before making an investment. Popular franchise directories include *The Franchise Annual, The Franchise Handbook, The Executive Guide to Franchise Opportunities, Bond's Franchise Guide*, and *The Franchise Opportunities Guide.*

15-2b   The Ten Basic Steps for Entering Franchising

To feel self-fulfilled, have a need to work, and a desire to get ahead are just a few of the many reasons budding entrepreneurs state for making the decision to enter franchising. Men and women of all ages, ethnicities as well as social and economic classes start their own franchised business and become more successful than they ever imagined. There are ten basic steps that budding entrepreneurs should carefully address before entering franchising, as indicated below.

1. Self-evaluation

2. The business arena

3. The franchise (the four "Ps" of franchising)

4. Disclosure documents

5. Profit/earnings claims

6. Professional advice

7. Legal rights

8. Disclosure meeting

9. The signing

10. Training/grand opening/operations

By following these steps, franchisees will assure themselves of being selective and hopefully wise in choosing their new line of business. In this way, risks may be identified and the franchisee can move forward with the greatest understanding of the limitations and potential for each franchise option.

A franchisor is not obligated to grant a franchise to every applicant; however, the refusal to grant a franchise to a qualified prospect, if such refusal is part of a conspiracy or a group boycott, is a violation of the Sherman Antitrust Act and is therefore against federal law. A prospective franchisee does not need to obtain permission from existing franchisees to open a new outlet in a specific area. If such permission is sought and refused, and the franchisor does not grant a franchise, then a group boycott may have been formed, which would be in violation of the Sherman Act.

In addition, if company-owned outlets are set up to be in direct competition with existing franchises, this also may be a violation of the Sherman Act.

The franchisor must make these kinds of decisions alone without including existing franchisees in territorial agreements and limitations. The law also requires that franchised outlets receive the same pricing schedules and any other cost advantages made available to company-owned stores. Anytime a franchisor holds a competitive advantage over its franchisees, the franchisor is likely to run afoul of the law.

It is not always necessary for the franchisor to "sell" the franchise to the franchisee; rather, it is frequently the case that the franchisee must be able to meet certain qualifications in order to be granted a franchise. At the beginning of the sales or disclosure meeting between the franchisor and the prospective franchisee, the franchisor may indicate that the prospect needs to prove oneself worthy of and eligible for a franchise. The disclosure or sales meeting is primarily a chance for the franchisor to explain the operations and opportunities of the franchise. It is during this meeting that the franchisee needs to demonstrate qualifications to the franchisor.

Franchising still remains the least risky method of business ownership. It provides entrepreneurs a relatively safe opportunity to be their own boss and develop their talents. Franchising is not for everyone, however. It is for individuals who are willing to take some risk in becoming an entrepreneur and feel they can work within the confines of a business system.

15-2c Self-Evaluation

The first step in the process of becoming a franchisee is to take a good look at oneself. It is necessary to ask whether one is willing to make a personal and business sacrifice to spend long, hard hours developing and starting a franchise. Individuals must know if they have sufficient energy, maturity, and managerial experience, the right leadership characteristics, and the ability to work with others—prerequisites of becoming a good franchisee (see Figure 15-1).

In the most pragmatic way, one should assess personal strengths and weaknesses, interests, personality type, and work skills. This is a good start-point to deepen the understanding of one's own interests and capabilities with the reality of being a franchisee business owner. Several focused questions are as follows:

- What kind of business will provide opportunity for you to maximize on your existing skills?

- What do you want to achieve by owning and operating your own business?

- By making this ($ amount) investment, how is my financial situation affected?

- How will this investment ($ amount) affect my family? Short term? Long term?

- How will this investment and business ownership/operation affect my desired quality of life?

- Are the rewards I see great enough, given that I could lose my entire investment?

Perhaps, the most important question is: By buying this franchise and running it, will this really make me happy? Will it keep me happy? Obviously, the answers here should provide clarity for the person such that one desires to pursue an opportunity through franchising that is compatible with one's own personality, interests, and skills.

By making a thorough examination of oneself with regard to the franchise opportunities under consideration, the person will know "what they have been looking for" when they find the right franchise. The right franchise is the one that fits the prospective franchisee's interests, capabilities, needs, and financial capacity. Asking deep questions of oneself helps a person avoid a haphazard major decision that could prove to be a strong source of regret for years to come.

It is so important to examine oneself to identify one's own unique traits and needs. For example, some people need a lot of structure. Others want a lot of freedom in decision making. Some want to be a small piece of a very big firm. Others want to be a "big fish in a little pond." Some want to get into a franchise system after all significant risks have been minimized. Others want to get in "on the ground floor." What are your unique traits and needs? The prospective franchisee needs to determine what factors about a franchise system are most important now and in the long term. Table 15-1 identifies some of the primary factors considered most important to prospective franchisees.

Date of Evaluation   Score

RATING
5 = Excellent
4 = High
3 = Average
2 = Low
1 = Poor

_____   _____
_____   _____
_____   _____
_____   _____

Directions: Mark the square which most accurately represents your own characteristics.

	5	4	3	2	1
ACTIVITY LEVEL					
Drive					
Energy					
Endurance					
MATURITY LEVEL					
Self-Motivated					
Self-Confident					
Common Sense					
Stability, Composure					
MANAGERIAL EXPERIENCE					
Motivation					
Problem Solving					
Skills					
Use of Resources					
OWNER CHARACTERISTICS					
Goal Setting					
Long-Term Involvement					
Taking Initiative					
Seeking Responsibility					
DEALING WITH OTHERS					
Use of Feedback					
Communications					
Adaptability					
Sense of Ethics					
WORKING WITH SELF					
Dealing with Failure					
Tolerance of Ambiguity					
Internal Focus of Control					
SELF AS FRANCHISEE					
Desire					
Accept Heavy Workload					
Motivate Others					

OVERALL RATING (TOTAL SCORE)_____

GENERAL COMMENTS_____

_____

SHALL I BECOME A FRANCHISEE?_____

WHY?_____

Score: 105-125 Do It Now; 95-104 Go For It; 85-94 Think Twice; 75-84 Be Very Careful; Below 75 Try Something Else

FIGURE **15-1**

Franchise Self-Evaluation Form

TABLE 15-1	**PRIMARY FACTORS TO LOOK FOR IN A FRANCHISE SYSTEM**

You likely want a franchise company that:

Is committed to franchising and is vitally interested in meeting the wants and needs of its ultimate customers.

Can transfer the product, process, and business knowledge to the franchisee.

Has strong name identify or recognition.

Has strong to excellent growth possibilities.

Has a mission and goal structure that is compatible with your own long-term vision.

Provides excellent training to its franchisees

Will assist a new franchisee in finding a location appropriate to the needs and is consistent with the competitive marketplace.

Truly operates as a partner with the franchisee providing the support necessary to achieve success.

Has an adequate home office staff and financial resources to succeed.

Provides for effective franchisor-to-franchisee communications that is at least consistent with the best competitor in the industry.

Has happy franchisees, that is, a franchise system that validates itself well.

Demonstrates willingness and capability to keep franchisees in business successfully.

Additional factors that franchisees, after being in business for several or more years, have indicated that could also be important include:

Is the franchise system a leader or a follower?

Does the franchise system offer needed and affordable products and services?

Does it encourage visitation with current franchisees to learn the "real story" about owning a franchise in that system?

Does the franchise system allow you to earn the amount of money you want and still enjoy life?

Is the franchise system ethical in its decision processes and supportive of its franchisees?

The prospective franchisee should determine the time that will be required to operate the franchise. Work weeks of sixty or more hours may be necessary, which obviously will have some effect on the franchisee's family or social life. The franchisees should find out if the family is also willing to sacrifice or get by with the franchisee out of the house so much.

Some franchisors will help prospective franchisees take a good look at the franchise opportunity and their individual potential. Other franchisors will simply find out if sufficient money is available without looking at the capabilities and personality of the prospective franchisee. The prudent franchisor—who is often the most successful franchisor—will determine whether the franchisee possesses those managerial and leadership characteristics which will help ensure the success of the business. If the business involves personal contacts with customers, then the franchisor should select franchisees with a friendly and congenial personality and a demonstrated ability to work closely with customers and employees.

Prospective franchisees also need to examine their physical, social, emotional, and learning capacities. Will the franchisee be able to work under the controls and guidelines of an authoritarian franchisor? Does the franchisee have the ability to work closely with the franchisor as well as with potential customers?

One of the biggest and hardest questions for a prospective franchisee to answer is: Can I afford the franchise I want to buy? Once I have the franchise fees covered, am trained, have the equipment and a good location, the deep penetrating question becomes: Can I afford to keep running the business? Can I keep the doors open and still have enough for me and my family?

There are three central financial questions the prospective franchisee must answer and have comfort with the answers. First, do I have enough cash to pay the fees and cover somewhere between 20 and 100 percent of the total amount required of the franchisee prior to opening? Second, can I find some one (or more) who will finance the amount that I cannot cover? Remember, the riskier the industry (or business arena) that you will operate within, the more collateral that lenders will require of you for loans. Third, what additional sources of capital will I need? Having one or more agreed upon sources to ensure that sufficient working capital is available particularly in the first one to three years is very important. Working capital is needed to cover cash shortages, to be a cushion to draw upon to cover operating expenses and income fluctuations. (See Chapter 11 for further discussion.)

Qualification

When prospective franchisees apply for a franchise, they generally need to complete an application form, which becomes a confidential qualification report, in which they agree that any information provided may be verified by the franchisor. Franchisors should check this information thoroughly, because the responsibility of granting franchises affects not only the franchisors themselves, but also the consuming public, the prospective franchisee, the franchised company, and those franchisees already in business. These personal qualification forms may request the following:

- Personal information

- Education

- Reason for becoming a franchisee

- Personal references

- Specific information about site location

- Personal characteristics

- Employment history

In addition to the personal qualification forms a confidential financial report is also required. Most franchisors have found that the prospective franchisees need sufficient nondebt capital to ensure the success of the franchise and to see that the debt burden of the franchise is not too great. Franchising fee payments almost always must be of a nondebt nature.

So that the franchisor can determine the financial position of the franchisee, a complete financial report is required of every potential franchisee. Any misrepresentations are grounds for nullification of subsequently signed agreements or contracts. The financial report generally requires a listing of personal assets, liabilities, and net worth. In addition, these reports often require information about current sources of income, contingent liabilities, supplementary schedules, banking relations, loans, life insurance, stock and bonds, real estate, credit accounts, and bank and finance company statements. The confidential financial report and the personal information form give the franchisor some information by which to properly evaluate the personal and financial status of the prospective franchisee. Although this information is very important, the final decision to grant or not grant a franchise is often based on the character of the franchisee (see Figure 15-2).

15-2d   The Business Arena

The prospective franchisee needs to decide which type of business and which type of franchise distribution system are most desirable. A franchisee should look at different industries to determine

Applicant's Name_____Date_____

Address_____

Interview with	Date	Score
1. _____	_____	_____
2. _____	_____	_____
3. _____	_____	_____
4. _____	_____	_____

RATING
5 = Excellent
4 = High
3 = Average
2 = Low
1 = Poor

Directions: Mark the square which most accurately represents applicant's characteristics. A total score of 90-100 is outstanding.

	5	4	3	2	1

EDUCATIONAL BACKGROUND
Appropriate/Sufficient
Intelligent
Ability to Reason

MANAGERIAL EXPERIENCE
Skills
Motivation
Past Accomplishments

INDIVIDUAL IMPRESSIONS
Appearance
Positive Attitude
Expression, Diction

POTENTIAL ABILITY
Organized, Self-Managed
Financially Strong
Responsible
Realistically Ambitious
Works Well with Others

MATURITY
Self-Confident
Self-Motivated
Common Sense

ABILITY TO WORK WITH FRANCHISOR
Communicate
Adaptable
Sense of Ethics

OVERALL RATING (TOTAL SCORE)

GENERAL COMMENTS_____

_____

DO YOU RECOMMEND THIS PERSON TO BECOME A FRANCHISEE?_____

WHY?_____

FIGURE **15-2**

XYZ Franchise—Franchisor Interview Form

what type of business or franchise is most attractive. The franchisee should determine if the product or service is seasonal or cyclical, what type of competition is present, and if governmental standards and regulations reduce the probability for success and profitability in that business.

The U.S. Department of Commerce has published a book entitled, *Franchise Opportunities Handbook*, by Andy Kostecka, which lists different categories of franchises available to interested prospects. The categories include the following:

Automotive Products/Service

Auto/Trailer Rentals

Beauty Salons/Supplies

Business Aids/Services

Campgrounds

Children's Stores/Furniture/Products

Clothing/Shoes

Construction/Remodeling—Materials/ Services

Cosmetics/Toiletries

Dental Centers

Drug Stores

Educational Products/Services

Employment Services

Equipment/Rentals

Foods—Donuts

Foods—Grocery Specialty Stores

Foods—Ice Cream/Yogurt/Candy/Popcorn/ Beverages

Foods—Pancakes/Waffles/Pretzels

Foods—Restaurants/Drive-Ins/Carry-Outs

General Merchandising Stores

Health Aids/Services

Hearing Aids

Home Furnishings/Furniture—Retail, Repairs, Services

Insurance

Laundries, Dry Cleaning Services

Lawn and Garden Supplies/Services

Maintenance/Cleaning/Sanitation—Service/ Supplies

Motels, Hotels

Optical Products/Services

Pain and Decorating Supplies

Printing

Real Estate

Recreation/Entertainment/Travel—Services/ Supplies

Retailing Not Elsewhere Classified

Security Systems

Swimming Pools

Tools, Hardware

Vending

Water conditioning

Wholesale/Service Business—Miscellaneous

Entrepreneur magazine publishes once each year the "Franchise 500" in its January issue which provides valuable information and insights into many franchising organizations. *Entrepreneur* also publishes an annual yearbook which includes a listing of nearly all franchised companies, and also discusses franchising opportunities and how to select franchises. The *Franchise Handbook* also provides an alphabetical list of franchisors according to industry and is published semiannually by CESA Publications, Inc. These publications and others such as *Money Magazine* provide information of value to prospective franchisees in their investigation of the different business arenas in franchising.

After having looked at the various opportunities available and deciding on a particular industry, the prospective franchisee should contact the appropriate franchisors in that industry. A prospective franchisee should probably choose the top two or three franchise systems and investigate each of them before making any final determination. Remember, before actually signing the franchising contract, a prospect may always choose another business opportunity which better suits his or her personality. It is always a good idea to investigate before investing.

DID YOU KNOW?

Today there are more than 10 million women-owned businesses. Approximately 57 percent of women business owners have a business line of credit and over 80 percent have a satisfactory banking relationship. In addition, since the 1980s, women-owned businesses have grown at twice the rate of all businesses.

Adapted from report by the Center for Women's Business Research, 23 April 2007, www. entrepreneur.com/article/177302.html.

15-2e   The Franchise

As mentioned earlier, choosing the best possible franchise involves investigating and analyzing the four Ps of franchising.

Product

Profitability

Process

People

Product

One of the first steps in choosing a franchise is for prospects to analyze the product or service they wish to sell. The quality, value, and demand for the product are very important. Continuing availability of the product is critical and needs to be assured. Consumer awareness of the product should be high, although with start-up franchises there may be a lack of awareness or acceptance that may be a severe limitation to the success of the franchise. Prospective franchisees should also understand the requirements of maintenance, upkeep, and handling of the product. If the product is technical in nature, this may exclude some technically unsophisticated franchisees.

Rating: 5=Excellent, 4=High, 3=Average, 2=Low, 1=Poor

	5	4	3	2	1
Product or Service:	_____	_____	_____	_____	_____
Positive reputation	_____	_____	_____	_____	_____
Customer need	_____	_____	_____	_____	_____
Growing market	_____	_____	_____	_____	_____
Safe	_____	_____	_____	_____	_____
Patented/guaranteed	_____	_____	_____	_____	_____
Self-interest	_____	_____	_____	_____	_____
Identified with known personality	_____	_____	_____	_____	_____
Future need	_____	_____	_____	_____	_____
Strongly desirable	_____	_____	_____	_____	_____

Process

Before choosing a business, prospective franchisees need to understand the process or business format of operations which they should employ to achieve success. In addition to knowing sales methods and service and repair procedures, the prospects should understand the accounting, financial, marketing, and management systems to be employed by the franchisor, and should understand how the products will be distributed and specifically what kind of selling is involved. Franchisees also should be aware of the training and continuing services available from the franchisor. Some franchisors offer extensive continuing services whereas others offer little support once the franchise process has begun. The prospective franchisees should determine the number of franchises and company-owned outlets, as well as the length of time the franchisor has been in business. The prospects should also find out if the franchised company belongs to the International Franchise Association whose members must meet high standards and follow a stiff code of conduct.

Rating: 5=Excellent, 4=High, 3=Average, 2=Low, 1=Poor

	5	4	3	2	1
Business-Format Process:	_____	_____	_____	_____	_____
Marketing	_____	_____	_____	_____	_____
Promotion	_____	_____	_____	_____	_____
Brand recognition	_____	_____	_____	_____	_____
Management	_____	_____	_____	_____	_____
Training	_____	_____	_____	_____	_____
Accounting	_____	_____	_____	_____	_____
Site selection	_____	_____	_____	_____	_____
Headquarters held	_____	_____	_____	_____	_____
Service/repairs	_____	_____	_____	_____	_____
Financial support	_____	_____	_____	_____	_____
Number of franchisees	_____	_____	_____	_____	_____
Advertising	_____	_____	_____	_____	_____

Profitability

Prospective franchisees should evaluate the profitability of any franchise opportunity. Some franchisors provide earnings claims or profitability statements for their businesses. (See Figure 15-3.) These statements, in accordance with Federal Trade Commission requirements, must stipulate the franchise system's sales or earnings, plus the percentage of franchises that earn above and/or below the stated sales or earnings. Indications of potential earnings plus working capital requirements are often found in the basic disclosure documents. In addition, the prospective franchisee may calculate a rough estimate of earnings by obtaining, from the corporate consolidated financial statements in the disclosure document, the total revenue from franchised units in the system. This would reveal the franchisor's average revenue per franchised unit. Knowing the franchising royalty fee percentage (e.g., 5 percent royalty fee) enables one to make a guesstimate of the total sales for that particular business. For example, if the royalty fee is 5 percent of annual gross sales and the average royalty payment per franchise is $17,500, then the annual sales average per unit would be $350,000. If the average revenue per unit to the franchisor is $40,000, then dividing $40,000 by 5 percent (0.05) gives average sales per unit of $800,000. But probably the best method of determining sales profitability and operating expenses is to call existing franchisees and ask them for information and

Rating: 5=Excellent, 4=High, 3=Average, 2=Low, 1=Poor

	5	4	3	2	1
Profitability:	_____	_____	_____	_____	_____
Profits	_____	_____	_____	_____	_____
Revenues	_____	_____	_____	_____	_____
Cost of goods sold	_____	_____	_____	_____	_____
Labor costs	_____	_____	_____	_____	_____
Expenses	_____	_____	_____	_____	_____
Return on investment	_____	_____	_____	_____	_____
Earnings claim	_____	_____	_____	_____	_____
Forecasted revenues	_____	_____	_____	_____	_____
Start-up costs	_____	_____	_____	_____	_____
Franchising fee	_____	_____	_____	_____	_____
Royalty fee	_____	_____	_____	_____	_____
Advertising fee	_____	_____	_____	_____	_____
Other fees	_____	_____	_____	_____	_____

	Total No. of Reporting Locations	Gross Sales Less than $75,000	Number of Reporting Stores—Percentage With Gross Sales Exceeding:				
			$75,000	$150,000	$250,000	$520,000	$750,000
All Reporting Franchise Stores	729	63–8.6%	62–8.5%	66–9.0%	125–17.2%	171–23.5%	242–33.2%
Gross Sales Achieved Measured by Years in Operation							
1 to 2 Years	147	34–231.0%	113–76.9%	82–55.8%	62–420.2%	32–21.8%	10–6.8%
2 to 4 Years	139	9–6.5%	130–93.5%	116–83.5%	100–71.9%	75–53.9%	31–22.3%
4 to 6 Years	121	7–5.8%	114–94.2%	106–87.6%	94–77.7%	73–53.9%	40–33.0%
6 to 8 Years	88	2–2.3%	86–97.7%	82–93.2%	78–85.2%	58–65.9%	38–43.2%
8 to 10 Years	61	4–6.6%	57–93.4%	54–88.5%	54–88.5%	45–73.8%	26–42.6%
10 to 14 Years	173	7–4.0%	166–96.0%	164–94.8%	153–88.4%	130–75.1%	97–56.1%

Schedule of Gross Sales for Calendar Year 20XX

Under $ 75,000	63	8.6%
$ 75,000–$150,000	62	8.5%
$150,000–$250,000	66	9.0%
$250,000–$500,000	125	17.2%
$500,000–$750,000	171	23.5%
Over $750,000	242	33.2%
ALL STORES REPORTING	729	100.0%

The above schedule reflects the gross sales achieved, within the range indicated, by franchised stores that reported sales volumes for the full calendar year 20XX and the percentage of the total stores reporting.

FIGURE **15-3**

A Printing and Copy Franchise System
Number and Percentage of Franchised Stores Achieving Gross Sales at Levels Indicated During Calendar Year 20XX

advice. However the information is obtained, the current financial condition and situation of the franchisor should be analyzed.

People

Perhaps the most important aspect of choosing a franchise is understanding the people with whom the prospective franchisee will be working. Any prospect should meet, interview, and discuss the franchising process with each executive of the franchise system. Franchising, because of its contractual nature, is similar to a marriage in that it demands a great deal of interaction and cooperation between the two main parties, franchisor and franchisee. The strength of the franchise, and its most important resource, is the people involved in the franchise. The prospective franchisee should investigate everyone connected with the business, including the franchisor, officers, and directors, and should find out if the franchisor has a reputation for making a rush sale to obtain a quick franchising fee and commission.

Rating: 5=Excellent, 4=High, 3=Average, 2=Low, 1=Poor

	5	4	3	2	1
People:					
Franchisor chairman					
Franchisor president					
Franchisor operations executive					
Franchisor sales executive					
Other principals or directors					
Service departments					
Advertising and promotions					
Finance and accounting					
Sales and marketing					
Site selection					
Personnel and training					
Manufacturing and operations					
Field support					

It is important to study each franchisor and each operation as thoroughly as possible. One of the best ways to accomplish this is through comparative shopping. A prospect should look at several franchises at the same time, just as one would look at several cars or houses before making the decision to purchase.

The prospective franchisee should formally inquire of the franchisor about the franchise. This contact is very important. The franchisor will generally send a "kit" in response to the inquiry, which includes promotional material for all prospective franchisees. This kit may also contain the franchisor disclosure documents, confidential qualification forms, and confidential financial report forms. If the prospective franchisee is serious about discussing further details with the franchisor, then he or she should fill out the personal application and financial information forms and send them to the franchisor. Upon receipt of these confidential records, the franchisor or sales representative will generally make a personal appointment with the interested prospect.

In addition, the franchisee should seek out other information about the franchise through various sources generally found in libraries, such as Dun & Bradstreet's credit ratings, *Value Line, Entrepreneur,* and other business publications that include information about franchised businesses. Also, area franchisees may be contacted, as well as chambers of commerce and the local Better Business Bureau. These resources often provide valuable information about a franchise or firm.

15-2f   Disclosure Documents

Most earnest inquiries to a franchisor will result in the prospective franchisee being sent information about the franchised business as well as a disclosure document (or Uniform Franchise Offering Circular). If a disclosure document is not provided initially by the franchisor, the franchisee should be sure to ask for one. The disclosure document was developed as the result of Congress enacting FTC Rule 436 in 1979. This franchise rule is formally titled "Disclosure Requirements and Prohibitions Concerning Franchising and Business Opportunity Ventures." It was created in an attempt to curtail widespread abuse, deception, and unfair practices by certain unscrupulous franchisors. The franchise rule has enabled prospective franchisees to properly analyze and investigate the business and activities of all reliable franchisors. Any franchise operating in the United States has to provide information in the disclosure document outlining the affairs and practices of the franchise.

This disclosure document is of great assistance to a prospective franchisee for comparing one franchise with another, enabling the prospect to learn what to expect from different franchisors before making a decision to invest. The disclosure document contains detailed information on twenty different subjects which are vital to an understanding of the operations of the franchised business. These subjects include identification, litigation, bankruptcy, fees, business description, and basic operations.

After having read three or four disclosure documents from different companies in the same industry, the prospective franchisee should check the accuracy of the information. One of the best ways to begin this investigation is to contact different franchisees listed in the disclosure document and ask them about their experiences in the business. These franchisees are generally very willing to talk to prospective franchisees and provide verification of the information given in the disclosure document.

It is important for a prospect to talk to several franchisees from different locations throughout the country. It is also valuable to talk to new as well as veteran franchisees to discuss the training programs, potential earnings, franchisor–franchisee relationship, and personal satisfaction with the franchise (see Figure 15-8 later in the chapter). Newer franchisees will be able to explain the problems associated with training, grand opening, and first year of operations. They will also be able to help the prospective franchisee understand the support system that the franchisor will provide during the initial training and start-up period. If the franchisor has recommended certain franchisees for the prospective franchisee to consult, it is best that the prospect contact additional franchisees not recommended by the franchisor.

15-2g   Disclosure Activities of Franchisors

A study was conducted of 114 franchise companies by Justis, Tuunanen, Chen and Castrogiovanni to identify what kinds of information was being disclosed by major franchise systems.[1] The information was collected from the respective franchise systems and UFOCs, and was divided into five classifications, as follows:

- Administrative operations (Figure 15-4)
- Financial obligations (Figure 15-5)
- Contractual obligations (Figure 15-6)
- Earnings claims (Figure 15-7)
- Obligations required by franchisor

As shown in Figure 15-4, a large proportion (80 percent) of the companies examined were involved with litigations during the past seven years. Franchisees should seek to learn why a specific franchisor is suing or being sued by their franchisees. It was found that 32 percent of the firms or their officers have been involved in some form of bankruptcy in the prior ten years. In addition, 92 percent of the franchisors have restrictions placed on franchisees. Most franchisees will be allowed to sell only those products or services previously approved by the franchisor. A majority of franchisors (52 percent) do not provide financial support to their franchisees, but some support may be available through a third

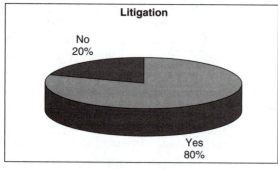

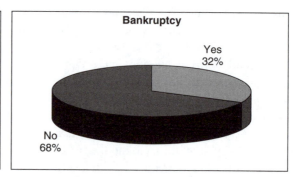

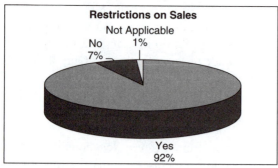

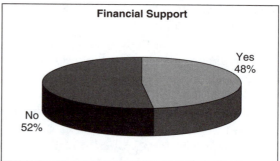

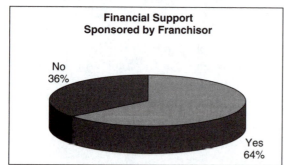

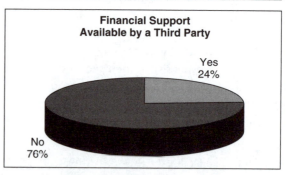

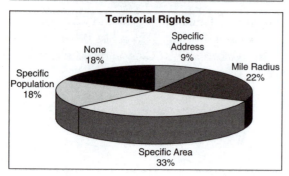

FIGURE 15-4

party or an outside resource to the franchisees in 24 percent of the franchise systems. Eighty-two percent of franchisors do not provide territorial guarantees to the franchisees; however, when a franchisee is given an exclusive territory, the restrictions and all boundaries are included.

In Figure 15-5, financial factors and obligations are identified. The great majority of franchisors (93 percent) charge a fixed dollar amount as their initial franchise fee. In contrast, the great majority of franchisors charge a fixed percentage royalty fee which is on average 5.48 percent.

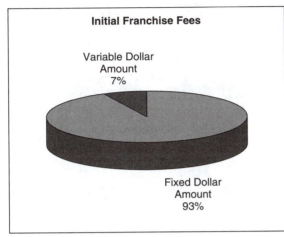

Initial Franchise Fees

Variable Dollar Amount 7%

Fixed Dollar Amount 93%

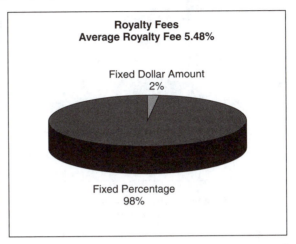

Royalty Fees
Average Royalty Fee 5.48%

Fixed Dollar Amount 2%

Fixed Percentage 98%

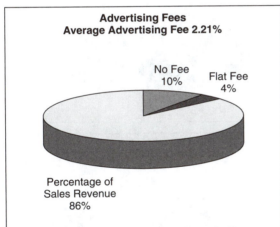

Advertising Fees
Average Advertising Fee 2.21%

No Fee 10%   Flat Fee 4%

Percentage of Sales Revenue 86%

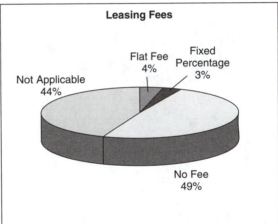

Leasing Fees

Flat Fee 4%   Fixed Percentage 3%

Not Applicable 44%

No Fee 49%

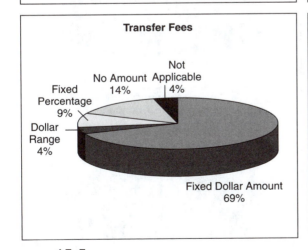

Transfer Fees

No Amount 14%   Not Applicable 4%

Fixed Percentage 9%

Dollar Range 4%

Fixed Dollar Amount 69%

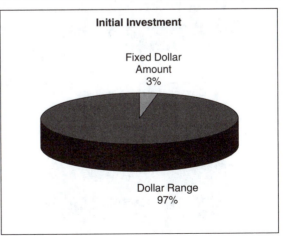

Initial Investment

Fixed Dollar Amount 3%

Dollar Range 97%

FIGURE 15-5

Financial obligations

Eighty-seven percent of franchisors in the study charged a percentage of sales/revenue advertising fee, while 4 percent charged a flat fee. Nearly 120 percent of franchise systems examined charged no advertising fee. In 97 percent of the time, the initial investment required of prospective franchisees is within a dollar range, with only 3 percent holding to a fixed dollar amount.

Figure 15-6 identifies contractual obligations between franchisor and franchisee. Fifteen years is the most common length of contract obligation, required by 35 percent of franchisors, whereas twenty

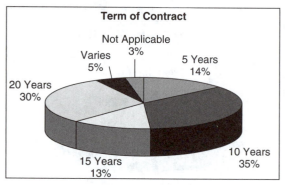

Term of Contract

Not Applicable 3%
Varies 5%
5 Years 14%
20 Years 30%
10 Years 35%
15 Years 13%

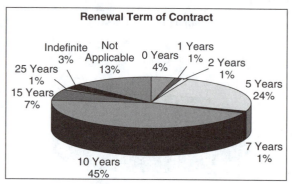

Renewal Term of Contract

Indefinite 3%
Not Applicable 13%
0 Years 4%
1 Years 1%
2 Years 1%
25 Years 1%
15 Years 7%
5 Years 24%
7 Years 1%
10 Years 45%

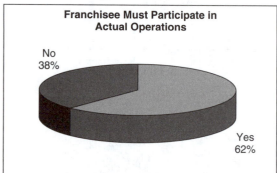

Franchisee Must Participate in Actual Operations

No 38%
Yes 62%

Franchisee Must be a Full-Time Operator

Yes 19%
No 81%

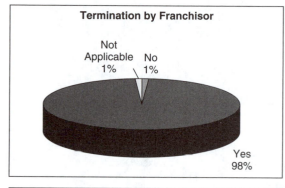

Termination by Franchisor

Not Applicable 1%
No 1%
Yes 98%

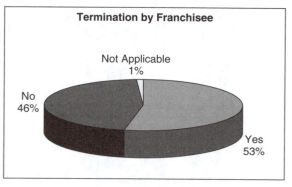

Termination by Franchisee

Not Applicable 1%
No 46%
Yes 53%

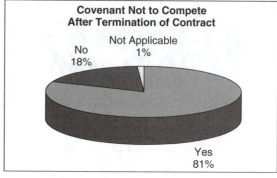

Covenant Not to Compete After Termination of Contract

No 18%
Not Applicable 1%
Yes 81%

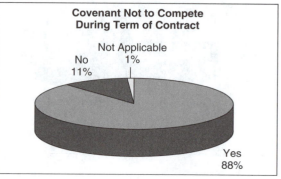

Covenant Not to Compete During Term of Contract

Not Applicable 1%
No 11%
Yes 88%

FIGURE **15-6**

Contractual obligations

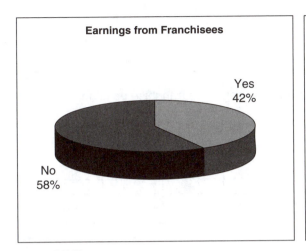
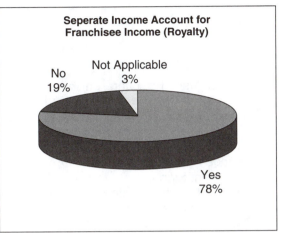

FIGURE **15-7**

Earnings Claims

years is required by 30 percent of franchisors. Remaining franchise systems examined had contract obligations that ranged from no contract term being required up through a fifteen-year contract duration. Sixty-two percent of franchisors require the franchisee to participate in the actual operations, whereas 19 percent require the franchisee to be a full-time operator. Eighty-one percent require a covenant not to compete after termination of contract clause, but 88 percent require a covenant not to compete in complementary or substitutable lines of business during the term of the contract.

Figure 15-7 identifies the position taken by these franchise systems regarding earnings claims. By law, franchisors may or may not provide projected earnings claims for prospective franchisees. This is, potentially, the most sensitive area of the franchise UFOC document as well as the franchise sales program. Under Federal Trade Commission rules or the UFOC, any written, visual, or oral representation of financial information must be included in the disclosure documents. Because of the rigid requirements, only 42 percent of the franchisors examined provide some form of earnings claims for franchisees.

Though not shown in a figure, 62 percent of the franchisors' UFOC documents studied required the franchisee utilize specific proprietary software with 46 percent requiring period upgrades for the software required. This form of policy allows the franchisor and franchisees to keep current with software requirements that link together the information technology of the franchisor with franchisees. In addition, 67 percent of franchisees are required to use models, 75 percent to use laser printers, and 88 percent to use color printers in providing numeric and graphic revenue, inventory, and customer-based information.

Litigation

The franchise rule requires that any litigation involving the franchise system be reported in the disclosure document. A description of any and all lawsuits in which the franchisor, officers, director, or management personnel have been or are involved should be included. This becomes important because some state laws prohibit selling certain items such as firearms, tobacco, and ammunition to convicted felons. The prospective franchisee may also be interested to know if any actions have been taken against the franchise's officers for fraud, embezzlement, restraint of trade, or unfair or deceptive business practices.

Franchise Costs

The prospective franchisee should investigate all costs associated with the franchise. This would include, but would not be limited to, the initial franchising or licensing fee; periodic royalties;

NAME OF FRANCHISOR_____ DATE_____

ADDRESS_____

Directions: Mark the square which most accurately represents the franchise position.

RATING: 5=Excellent, 4=High, 3=Average, 2=Low, 1=Poor

EXISTING FRANCHISEE

	5	4	3	2	1
Average Profitability (5 units) $_____					
Investment Startup $_____					
Favorable Relations with Franchisor					
Strength of Operations					
Reliability of Franchisor's Promises					
Required Sales Quotas					
Training Programs					
Favorable Contract					
Favorable Territory					
Promotion/Advertising					

Subtotal = _____

FRANCHISOR

	5	4	3	2	1
Fees					
Initial Franchise Fee $_____					
Royalty Fees $_____					
Advertising Fees _____%					
Other Fees _____%					

Values					
Value of Product or Service					
Value of Training					
Value of Trademark					

Activities

Franchisor's Experience					
Franchisor's Litigation					
Exclusive Territory					
Renewal/Termination Rights					
Contract Length					
Disclosure Document (U.F.O.C.)					
Restrictions					
Market Potential and Acceptance					

Subtotal = _____
TOTAL = _____

Score: 110-125 Superior; 100-109 Excellent; 90-99 Very Good: 80-89 Good; 70-79 Average; Below 70 Substandard

FIGURE **15-8**

Franchise Checklist Evaluation

advertising fees; service fees; bookkeeping, accounting, and data processing fees; and any additional management assistance fees to be paid to the franchisor. The franchisee should be able to determine these initial costs and be able to understand when and how fees are to be paid to the franchisor. The franchisee should realize too that these initial costs do not generally include the start-up costs of actually building and opening the franchise. Estimates of these costs may or may not be provided by the franchisor to the prospective franchisee. If they are provided, they are only guesstimates of what franchisees have paid to start their franchises. The prospective franchisee should contact other franchisees to determine what their actual start-up costs were and what help they received from the franchisor in starting the business.

One additional cost that may be associated with the franchise is the cost of the land and/or building. Many long-established franchise systems require that new franchisees lease the land from the franchisor. This means that the franchisor has either purchased and built the property (if freestanding) or signed the lease with the property owner and is subleasing the space to the new franchisee. These costs should be determined and discussed with the franchisor and with other franchisees.

Training/Start-up Assistance

Most franchisors regard the training of franchisees as vital to their success. Training programs will last from three days to eight weeks to ensure that franchisees are sufficiently knowledgeable about every aspect of the business operation.

If the franchised business requires some sort of technical expertise such as that needed to prepare food items or use cleaning equipment, then the franchisor should provide training to develop the technical skills required. The franchisor should also provide training in appropriate selling techniques and proper ways of handling customers.

The franchisee should determine how much training and support will be available in the actual start-up of the business. Quite often the franchisor will send experienced staff employees to help with the grand opening. The franchisee must be careful to anticipate the costs of this assistance. Sometimes the franchisee must bear not only the cost of the training, travel, and meals at the franchisor's training facility, but also the payment of the salaries or wages of all franchisor staff members helping with the grand opening. This can get to be very expensive. The franchisee should make sure that all training obligations and continuing support programs—and who pays for them— are specified in the franchising agreement.

Territory or Location

Most franchisors will not guarantee an "exclusive franchise territory," though they may establish geographical territories within which they agree not to operate a company-owned facility, or a radius around one franchise within which they will not offer another franchise. The prospective franchisee should remember, however, that franchisors generally reserve all rights to establish additional franchises wherever they wish.

The franchisor often reserves the right of refusal for a specific site selection. The franchisor may often help by providing location suggestions and analysis for choosing specific sites, and often will have location standards and profiles of other successful site selections. Frequently the final site determination is made by the franchisee with approval from the franchisor. The prospective franchisee should remember that it is unlawful for franchisees and a franchisor to agree upon or enforce a territorial division policy. Generally, however, if additional franchises are to be granted within an area, the franchisor often provides the established local franchisee the first option to purchase and build the new franchise.

Term and Renewal

Almost all franchising agreements are set up for a specified term, generally from five to twenty years. Some franchisors have found that the agreement may be renewed for perpetuity without any objections on the part of either the franchisor or the franchisee.

At the expiration of the term, most franchisors provide a one-time right of renewal to the franchisee. The franchisee should understand the terms and conditions of the franchisee renewal, and such fine points as whether a "good cause" must be given for nonrenewal or termination by the franchisor, or if the franchisor has the option to purchase all equipment if the agreement is terminated or not renewed. The prospective franchisee should thoroughly review and understand the terms and renewal options and have them recorded in the franchising agreement.

15-2h   Profit/Earnings Claims

Any claims made by the franchisor regarding sales, income, or profits which can be expected from the franchise should be closely examined and analyzed. Earnings claims are simply estimates and cannot be guaranteed by the franchisor.

Most franchisors will not (in disclosure documents or in disclosure meetings with interested prospects) provide earnings claims to prospective franchisees. If earnings claims are provided, then they must be backed by audited statements and by information regarding the percentage of existing franchises that have actually achieved the results that are claimed.

When reviewing any earnings claims regarding sales, profits, or income, a prospective franchisee must ascertain how many franchisees showed those figures during the first year of operation, when operating results are normally not as good. First-year results of franchises throughout a system are generally similar. Such information is usually attainable only from franchisees recently completing the first year.

15-2i   Professional Advice

All prospective franchisees should seek the advice of a competent accountant, attorney, banker, or other professional before signing any agreements. It is wise for a prospect to review the financial statements with an expert in the field. A professional accountant, banker, or other experienced business advisor may be able to give counsel as to whether the franchisor's financial condition is sound and whether the franchisor will be able to fulfill it commitments to the franchisees.

The prospective franchisee should also contact an attorney before signing any franchising agreement. The disclosure document does not include everything the franchisee needs to know about the consequences of signing a franchising agreement and the related contracts. An attorney will be able to advise the prospect about the legal rights granted by the franchising agreement and the obligations assumed by franchisees. Although most franchising agreements are fairly rigid, an attorney may be able to suggest important changes in the contract which might provide better protection of the franchisee's interests. Legal advice at the outset generally saves on the cost of legal advice should problems later arise.

Any promise or representation made by the franchisor to the franchisee should be put in writing and incorporated into the franchising agreement. If such promises do not clearly appear in the contracts, then they are not legally binding upon the franchisor or the franchisee.

15-2j   Legal Rights of Franchisees

The franchise rule (Rule 436) issued by the Federal Trade Commission provides franchisees and prospective franchisees with certain legal rights under federal law. These rights include the following:

1. The right to receive a disclosure document at the first personal meeting with a representative of the franchisor to discuss the purchase of a franchise; but in no event less than ten business days before signing a franchising or related agreement, or paying any money in connection with purchase of a franchise.

2. The right to receive documentation stating the basis and assumptions for any earnings claims that are made at the time the claims are made; but in no event less that ten business days before signing a franchising or related agreement, or paying any money in connection with the purchase of a franchise. If an earnings claim is made in advertising, the prospect has the right to receive the required documentation at the first personal meeting with a representative of the franchisor.

3. The right to receive sample copies of the franchisor's standard franchising and related agreements at the same time the disclosure document is received, and the right to receive the final agreements to be signed at least five business days before they are signed.

4. The right to any refunds promised by the franchisor, subject to any conditions or limitations on that right which have been disclosed by the franchisor.

5. The right not to be misled by oral or written representations made by the franchisor or its representatives that are inconsistent with the disclosures made in the disclosure document.

No federal agency will have reviewed the disclosure documents and other franchisor legal instruments before the franchisee obtains them. If they appear to be inaccurate, or if the franchisee thinks he or she has been denied any rights under federal law, then the franchisee should send a letter describing the violation to Program Advisor, Franchise and Business Opportunities Program, Federal Trade Commission, Washington DC 20580 (also, see Appendix at end of this chapter).

Franchising is an increasingly popular method of doing business, and with increased popularity comes the increased chance of unscrupulous participants. The best protection for the prospective franchisee and the franchisor, before signing any documents or making any final commitments, is to obtain whatever legal counsel is needed to clarify which rights are protected—and which are not protected—by the franchising agreement and the federal laws pertaining to franchising.

15-2k Disclosure Meeting

One of the most exciting times for a franchisor and a franchisee is when they first get together to discuss the operations of the business, in what is generally referred to as a disclosure meeting. At the disclosure meeting the franchisor will "disclose" the general business practices and obligations of owning a franchise. The franchisor may often include a franchise sales presentation or flip chart (or even a movie or slide presentation) to discuss the operations of the franchise system. This sales kit generally explains the history, organization, and operations of the franchise system. Usually included in the sales prospectus are the following:

1. History of the franchise

2. What the franchise package includes (products and services)

3. Franchisee support services (to show continuing value)

4. Corporate structure (chart)

5. Photos of corporate officers

6. Photos of corporate offices

7. Marketing tools available

8. Training schedules

9. Target market

10. Insurance programs (if available)

11. Other pertinent information

After explaining the history and operations of the franchise, the franchisor or representative generally becomes a listener rather than a talker, using this time to assess the qualifications of the franchisee. The prospective franchisee should use this time to ask questions about franchise. We include the following lists of questions, grouped in four areas and stated from the perspective of the franchisee, to give some examples of questions you as a prospective franchisee might ask of yourself or of the franchisor's representative in the disclosure meeting.

The Franchise

1. Did your attorney meticulously study the franchising contract you are considering before approving it?

2. Does the franchise call upon you to take any steps which, according to your attorney, are unwise or illegal in your state, county, or city?

3. Does the franchisor give you an exclusive territory for the length of the franchise, or can the franchisor sell a second or third franchise in your territory?

4. Is the franchise connected in any way with another franchised company handling similar merchandise or services?

5. If the answer to the last question is yes, what is your protection against this second organization?

6. Under what circumstances can you terminate the franchising contract and at what cost to you, if you decide for any reason that you wish to cancel it?

7. If you sell your franchise, will you be compensated for your goodwill, or will the goodwill you have built into the business be lost?

The Franchisor

1. How many years has the franchisor been in operation?

2. Does the franchisor have a reputation for honesty and fair dealings among the franchisees?

3. Has the franchisor shown you any certified figures indicating net profits of franchisees, which you personally checked with the franchisees?

4. Will the franchisor assist you with:

   a. management training program?

   b. An employee training program?

   c. public relations program?

   d. Capital?

   e. Credit?

   f. Merchandising ideas?

5. Will the franchisor help you find a good location for your new business?

6. Does the franchisor have sufficient financing to carry out its stated plan of financial assistance and expansion?

7. Is the franchisor a one-person firm, or a corporation with an experienced, well-trained management team (so that it would always have an experienced person at its head)?

8. Exactly what can the franchisor do for you that you cannot do for yourself?

9. Does the franchisor investigate prospective franchisees carefully enough to ensure that they will be able to successfully operate a franchise and show a profit?

10. Does your state have a law regulating the sale of franchises, and has the franchisor complied with that law?

You—The Franchisee

1. How much equity capital will you need, to purchase and operate the franchise before your income equals your expenses? What are your sources of capital?

2. Are you prepared to give up some independence of ownership to secure the advantages offered by the franchise system?

3. Do you really believe you have the innate ability, training, and experience to work smoothly and profitably with the franchisor, your employees, and your customers?

4. Are you ready to spend much or all of the remainder of your business life with this franchisor, offering its product or service to your public on a continuing basis?

The Market

1. Have you prepared to give up some independence of ownership to secure the advantages offered by the franchise system?

2. In the next five years, will the consumer population in your territory increase, remain static, or decrease?

3. Five years from now, will the product or service offered by the franchise be in greater, similar, or less demand?

4. What competition already exists in your territory for the product or service you will be offering? Is this competition from nonfranchised firms or from other franchised firms?

It is improper and generally illegal for the franchisor to sign the franchisee to a contract at this disclosure meeting. The disclosure meeting usually must occur no less than ten days before the signing of the franchising agreement.

If earnings claims have not been made in the disclosure document, then the franchisor will most likely not make any earnings claims during the disclosure meeting. Most franchisors will refer the prospective franchisee to other existing franchisees to learn about such claims. Franchisees should ask whatever questions they desire during the disclosure meeting.

15-2l   The Signing

One of the most exciting moments for both the franchisor and the franchisee occurs at the signing of the franchising agreement. At this time, there may also be other agreements, including lease, location, and purchase agreements, which need to be signed.

The franchisor will usually require that the franchisee have an attorney witness the signing of the franchising agreement (the franchisor commonly requests the franchisee's lawyer to be present at all contract signings). This meeting may be held at either the franchisor's or the franchisee's offices. At this time all fees, payments, and royalties should be understood and agreed upon, and any major problems should be resolved. Training programs, site selection, architectural designs, and start-up activities also should be discussed and planned at this meeting.

> Today, there are more than 2,500 franchise companies, with business models that span across eighty industries—from accounting to weight watching. Historically, most franchises involved operating through a storefront, but today, many franchises can be started part time or from a kitchen table for $50,000 or less.

15-2m   Training/Grand Opening/Operations

Once the franchising agreement has been signed, it is time to start the franchised business. The location and site must be selected, and the franchisee must receive the training necessary to open the franchised unit. Successful franchisors consider proper training to be one of the most critical components of a successful franchise. The training should adequately instruct the franchisee in sales operations, management, and marketing techniques. It is important that the franchisee have a thorough grasp of all aspects of the franchised business.

Following the training program, the next major function is the grand opening or start-up of the business. Often the franchisor will send representatives who will help open the franchise. For a simple operation, one representative may be sufficient to get the business ready for the grand opening. In large, complex franchises, however, fifteen representatives may be sent to ensure a smooth opening for the franchise. Representatives of the franchisor will often stay from a week to a month to make sure that the operations are running efficiently. The franchisee will generally pay the salary or wages of those visiting from the franchisor's headquarters.

In addition, representatives of the franchisor often provide the initial training for new franchise employees; these representatives may even help in the hiring of all new franchise employees. This enables new franchisees to learn the hiring and training processes which they may use later in the business operations.

Just as it is a common belief of many bank loan officers that the character of the applicant is worth 50 percent of the loan application, so most franchisors believe personality and personal characteristics, or worthiness, of the franchisee are vital factors in the determination of whether to grant a franchise. Therefore, all meetings, discussions, and contracts between a franchisor and a franchisee are important for both parties in determining whether the franchising agreement would be a beneficial experience for everyone involved.

SUMMARY

Franchising is basically a licensing business through which the owner (franchisor) of a product or service licenses other, independent parties (franchisees) to market the licensed product or service. Typically, the agreement requires the franchisee to operate within a defined territory and to follow the established guidelines of the franchisor. Franchising has been a successful format for doing business in the United States for over 100 years. Typical benefits provided by the franchisor to the franchisee include training, start-up assistance, purchasing power for supplies and equipment, marketing programs, an efficient operating system, and continued support to ensure the continuing success of the franchised network.

The benefits that often accrue to the franchisee are as follows. First, you own an independent business that produces and markets a proven, known product or service that you can start with limited experience and capital. Second, you buy a proven franchise business to achieve a good return on your investment. Third, you are given the necessary training and support to operate a successful business enterprise. Fourth, you are provided guidance and materials for local advertising and promotions, which complement regional or national advertising by the franchisor. Fifth, you can save by utilizing the franchisor's (group) buying power for supplies, equipment, printing, and so forth, and often can enroll yourself and family in an excellent group health insurance plan.

However, as a person seeks to determine the most appropriate franchise system to join, several cautions are in order. First, do not take anyone's word. Find out the information you deem necessary yourself. Remember, it is your money, your risk, and your opportunity. Do your investigations firsthand. Take your time as you research various franchise systems. Short-cutting your research can increase the likelihood of failure. Second, avoid overextending yourself financially. Be realistic about your financial situation, perhaps even be conservative. Third, seek professional advice. The amount of money you may save on professional fees may deprive you of information critical to making a good decision.

The success of new franchisees is often determined by their knowledge and understanding of the franchise system. With proper training, sufficient capital, and a desire to succeed, many new franchisees can become successful and profitable. The franchisee must approach the opportunity with care and wisdom, and must use all available resources to ensure the greatest possibility of success for the new business.

The recruitment of new prospective franchisees is important to the success of the franchise system. In a sense, the franchisees become the children of the franchisor's business family.

The prospective franchisee who properly investigates and chooses the right franchise will be happy and more likely successful. This investigation and selection process includes the steps of self-evaluation, understanding the business arena, investigating the franchise (including the four Ps of franchising: product, process, profitability, and people), studying disclosure documents, verifying profit/earnings claims, seeking professional advice, understanding and knowing one's legal rights, utilizing the disclosure and signing meetings, and proper development of training, the grand opening, and the operations of the franchise. The successful franchisee will spend sufficient time investigating and researching the various franchises. The right selection comes only after meeting the people involved and understanding the franchising process.

KEY TERMS

Four "P's of Franchising: An analysis of the product or service to be franchised, including: product, process, profitability and people.

Judi Sheppard Missett, Founder and CEO, Jazzercise, Inc.

Judi Sheppard Missett has turned her love of jazz dance into a worldwide dance-exercise phenomenon. A fitness advocate and aerobic dance pioneer for almost thirty years, she continues to break new ground in the industry through innovative class formats, exciting student–instructor conventions, broad-reaching children's fitness programs, and the first comprehensive nutrition program offered by a fitness organization—the Jazzercise Know More Diet.

Her passion for bringing the joy of fitness to thousands of individuals has led not only to her great success but also to numerous honors as

well; among them the 1996 National Fitness Leaders Association Charles Bucher Memorial Award for her contributions to youth fitness, 1996 Soroptimist International of San Diego "A Woman of Accomplishment Award," 1995 Women Who Mean Business Award from the San Diego Business Journal, the 1991 IDEA (International Association of Fitness Professionals) Lifetime Achievement Award, and in 1992, induction into the IDEA Hall of Fame. Judi's success was also recognized by President Reagan in his 1986 White House Conference on Women in Business, and in 1988, she was named

Working Woman's *Entrepreneur of the Year*. Her contributions to the growth and advancement of the fitness industry have been noted by leading fitness organizations, such as the Aerobics and Fitness Association of America (AFAA), the American Council on Exercise (ACE), the President's Council on Physical Fitness & Sports, and the National Fitness Leaders Association (NFLA), of which she serves as executive director. Judi serves on the California Governor's Council on Physical Fitness & Sports' Executive Committee and San Diego Inner-City Games Board of Directors.

In addition to serving as president of her worldwide dance-fitness franchise organization, which employs 135 support personnel from its Carlsbad, California, headquarters, Judi continues to teach her own Jazzercise classes every week and to choreograph new routines every ten weeks for franchised instructors to teach. She also authors a weekly fitness column for the Los Angeles Times Syndicate, *and stars in and produces her own best-*

selling home exercise videos. She travels extensively each year for corporate functions and philanthropic causes around the world. Judi and her army of instructors have raised millions of dollars for a wide range of charities by leading special, large-scale workout classes.

A native of Iowa, Judi attended Northwestern University in Illinois and earned her degree in theater and radio/television in 1966. She worked as a professional dancer throughout college and after graduation. While teaching traditional jazz dance classes in Chicago, Judi turned her students away from the mirror and created a special "just for fun" class which marked the beginning of Jazzercise. After moving to Southern California, she began training other instructors in 1977 and the program began to spread around the globe.

Jazzercise has spawned several other successful businesses, including JM Television Productions, a full service video production company, and Jazzertogs, a multimillion dollar mail-order catalog business.

CASE STUDY

Sue's Southern Kitchen

Sue Zimmerman wants to start her own franchised business. She loves southern-style cooking, especially southern fried chicken, and is interested in opening a restaurant in her local Colorado community. She has more than $125,000 to invest and feels that now would be a good time to start a franchised business.

The main reason Sue wishes to establish a franchised outlet is that she lacks management and marketing experience as she has never been a manager or been in charge of any marketing or promotional activities. She knows it will take a great deal of time to develop these skills, but she believes that the correct franchisor will provide her with the necessary training and marketing tools to enable her to be a successful business owner.

Sue is particularly interested in the Popeye's Famous Fried Chicken and Biscuits franchise system. She has recently written to and received materials from Popeye's, and has learned that the system offers seven weeks of extensive training, in addition to having accounting, operations, marketing, advertising, and real estate expertise available to franchisees. The training is provided for two persons per store, and includes station training, the operation of every job in the restaurant from cashier to sanitation, management expertise, sales motivation, employee counseling techniques, personnel training, and goal setting. A "pro" crew is sent by the franchisor to get the new store off to a flying start. This team of experts will train restaurant employees and make certain that grand opening growing "pains" are turned into "gains." Evaluations are regularly made of each store with a detailed checklist, which helps keep franchised units operating at the high level of efficiency demanded by Popeye's because of its unique recipes and procedures.

The Popeye's advertising department will supply a complete, professionally produced series of creative advertising for local, regional, and national campaigns. Sue has also learned that Popeye's advertising has won many awards, including the coveted Silver "Addy" Award for the South. These advertising campaigns help generate consumer activity in all market areas.

The start-up costs include the following:

ESTIMATED CASH REQUIREMENTS FOR FIVE UNITS

Franchise License Fee	
First unit fee	$ 25,000
Second unit option fee	$ 10,000
Third unit option fee	$ 10,000
Fourth unit option fee	$ 10,000
Fifth unit option fee	$ 10,000
Total of Fees and Deposits	$ 65,000
EQUIPMENT AND FINES PER UNIT	
(Down Payment)	$ 15,000
Operating Capital	$ 15,000
Total Cash Required First Unit	$ 95,000
Cash Required for Each	
Additional Unit	
(Balance of Franchise)	$ 15,000
Equipment and Signs	
(Down Payment)	$ 15,000
Start-up Operational Capital	$ 5,000
TOTAL	$160,000

For a franchise that is purchasing land and building, the additional costs which might be incurred include:

Building with 45 Seats and a Drive-Thru	$135,000
20,000 sq. ft. of land estimate	$100,000
TOTAL	$235,000

Sue is very excited about starting her new business, but she is unsure of how to begin, and she is still apprehensive because of her limited background in management and marketing. She is wondering what she should do to overcome these fears and inhibitions.

CASE QUESTIONS

1. What kind of management and/or marketing assistance should the franchisor provide to Sue?

2. What specific areas of management training should Sue request of the franchisor?

3. What specific marketing assistance should she expect from a franchisor?

4. What else should Sue do before opening her franchised business?

REFERENCES

Anderson, Evan E., "The Growth and Performance of Franchise Systems: Company versus Franchisee Ownership," *Journal of Economics and Business* 36 (December 1984): 421.

Bresler, Stanley, "Franchising: Road to the American Dream; It Can Give the Budding Entrepreneur Decided Advantages Starting Out," *American Banker* 149 (16 March 1984): 54.

Carner, William J., "An Analysis of Franchising in Retail Banking," *Journal of Retail Banking* 8 (Winter 1986): 57.

Dailey, Michael J., "Assessing Franchises for Client Purchase," *Journal of Accountancy* 161 (March 1986): 120.

Davis, Howard A., "Road Map to Selecting a Franchise," *Entrepreneurs Franchise Yearbook* 2 (1987/1988): 318–319.

Dugan, Ann, ed., *Franchising 101* (Chicago: Upstart Publishing Co., 1998).

"Franchise Directory," *Entrepreneurs Franchise Yearbook* 2 (1987/1988): 32–282.

"Franchise Evaluation Checklist," *The Franchise Handbook* 3 (1986): ix.

Golden Square Services Limited, "Choosing a Franchise," *The Successful Franchise* (Aldershot, Hantz, England: Gower Publishing Company Limited, 1985).

James, Andrew, "Business Format Franchising: Making the Right Choice," *Accountant's Magazine* 90 (September 1986): 43(2).

Justis, Robert, Mika Tuunanen, Ye-Sho Chen, and Gary Castrogiovanni, "Disclosing the Activities of Franchisors," *Proceedings of the International Society of Franchising 17th Annual Conference* (San Antonio, TX: ISF, February 2003), 398–417.

Kostecka, Andrew, U.S. Department of Commerce, and International Trade Association, *Franchise Opportunities Handbook* (Washington, DC: Government Printing Office, November 1987).

Kostecka, Andrew, U.S. Department of Commerce, and International Trade Association, *Franchising in the Economy, 1986-1988* (Washington, DC: Government Printing Office, January 1988).

Marx, Thomas G., "The Development of the Franchise Distribution System in the U.S. Automobile Industry," *Business History Review* 59 (Autumn 1985): 465.

Mosser, Frederick W. and Connell Hotel & Restaurant, "Franchising and the Spirit of Enterprise," *Administration Quarterly* 26 (May 1985): 13.

Thomas, Dave and Michael Seid, *Franchising for Dummies* (New York: IDG Books, 2000).

Weinrauch, J. Donald, "Franchising an Established Business," *Journal of Small Business Management* 24 (July 1986): 1.

NOTES

1. R. Justis, Mika Tuunanen, Ye-Sho Chen, and Gary Castrogiovanni, "Disclosing the Activities of Franchisors," *Proceedings of the International Society of Franchising 17 th Annual Conference* (San Antonio, TX: ISF, February 2003), 398–417.

APPENDIX

Federal Trade Commission

Guide to the FTC Franchising Rule

Table of Contents

I. **Rule Overview**

A. **Basic Requirement:** Franchisors must furnish potential franchisees with written disclosures providing important information about the franchisor, the franchised business and the franchise relationship, and give them at least ten business days to review it before investing.

B. **Disclosure Option:** Franchisors may make the required disclosures by following either the Rule's disclosure format or the Uniform Franchise Offering Circular Guidelines prepared by state franchise law officials.

C. **Coverage:** The Rule primarily covers business-format franchises, product franchises, and vending machine or display rack business opportunity ventures.

D. **No Filing:** The Rule requires disclosure only. Unlike state disclosure laws, no registration, filing, review or approval of any disclosures, advertising or agreements by the FTC is required.

E. **Remedies:** The Rule is a trade regulation rule with the full force and effect of federal law. The courts have held it may only be enforced by the FTC, not private parties. The FTC may seek injunctions, civil penalties and consumer redress for violations.

F. **Purpose:** The Rule is designed to enable potential franchisees to protect themselves before investing by providing them with information essential to an assessment of the potential risks and benefits, to meaningful comparisons with other investments, and to further investigation of the franchise opportunity.

G. **Effective Date:** The Rule, formally titled "Disclosure Requirements and Prohibitions Concerning Franchising and Business Opportunity Ventures," took effect on October 21, 1979, and appears at 16 C.F.R. Part 436

II. **Rule Requirements**

A. **General:** The Rule imposes six different requirements in connection with the "advertising, offering, licensing, contracting, sale or other promotion" of a franchise in or affecting commerce:

1. **Basic Disclosures:** The Rule requires franchisors to give potential investors a basic disclosure document at the earlier of the first face-to-face meeting or ten business days before any money is paid or an agreement is signed in connection with the investment (Part 436.1(a)).

2. **Earnings Claims:** If a franchisor makes earnings claims, whether historical or forecasted, they must have a reasonable basis, and prescribed substantiating disclosures must be given to a potential investor in writing at the same time as the basic disclosures (Parts 436.1(b)-(d)).

3. **Advertised Claims:** The Rule affects only ads that include an earnings claim. Such ads must disclose the number and percentage of existing franchisees who have achieved the

claimed results, along with cautionary language. Their use triggers required compliance with the Rule's earnings claim disclosure requirements (Part 436.1(e)).

4. **Franchise Agreements:** The franchisor must give investors a copy of its standard-form franchise and related agreements at the same time as the basic disclosures, and final copies intended to be executed at least five business days before signing (Part 436.1(g)).

5. **Refunds:** The Rule requires franchisors to make refunds of deposits and initial payments to potential investors, subject to any conditions on refundability stated in the disclosure document (Part 436.1(h)).

6. **Contradictory Claims:** While franchisors are free to provide investors with any promotional or other materials they wish, no written or oral claims may contradict information provided in the required disclosure document (Part 436.1(f)).

B. **Liability:** Failure to comply with any of the six requirements is a violation of the Franchise Rule. "Franchisors" and "franchise brokers" are jointly and severally liable for Rule violations.

1. "**franchisor**" is defined as any person who sells a "franchise" covered by the Rule (Part 436.2(c)).

2. "**franchise broker**" is defined as any person who "sells, offers for sale, or arranges for the sale" of a covered franchise (Part 436.2(c)), and includes not only independent sales agents, but also subfranchisors that grant sub-franchises (44 FR 49963).

III. **Business Relationships Covered**

A. **Alternate Definitions:** The Rule employs parallel coverage definitions of the term "franchise" to reach two types of continuing commercial relationships: traditional franchises and business opportunities.

B. "**Traditional Franchises**": There are three definitional prerequisites to coverage of a business-format or product franchise (Parts 436.2(a)(1)(i) and (2)):

1. **Trademark:** The franchisor offers the right to distribute goods or services that bear the franchisor's trademark, service mark, trade name, advertising or other commercial symbol.

2. **Significant Control or Assistance:** The franchisor exercises significant control over, or offers significant assistance in, the franchisee's method of operation.

3. **Required Payment:** The franchisee is required to make any payment to the franchisor or an affiliate, or a commitment to make a payment, as a condition of obtaining the franchise or commencing operations. (NOTE: There is an exemption from coverage for required payments of less than $500 within six months of the commencement of the franchise (Part 436.2(a)(3)(iii)).

C. **Business Opportunities:** There are also three basic prerequisites to the Rule's coverage of a business opportunity venture (Parts 436.2(a)(1)(ii) and (2)):

1. **No Trademark:** The seller simply offers the right to sell goods or services supplied by the seller, its affiliate, or a supplier with which the seller requires the franchisee to do business.

2. **Location Assistance:** The seller offers to secure retail outlets or accounts for the goods or services to be sold, to secure locations or sites for vending machines or rack displays, or to provide the services of someone who can do so.

3. **Required Payment:** The same as for franchises.

D. **Coverage Exemptions/Exclusions:** The Rule also exempts or excludes some relationships that would otherwise meet the coverage prerequisites (Parts 436.2(a)(3) and (4)):

1. **Minimum investment:** This exemption applies if all payments to the franchisor or an affiliate until six months after the franchise commences operation are $500 or less (Part 436.2(a)(iii)).

2. **Fractional Franchises:** Relationships adding a new product or service to an established distributor's existing products or services, are exempt if (i) the franchisee or any of its

current directors or executive officers has been in the same type of business for at least two years, and (ii) both parties anticipated, or should have, that sales from the franchise would represent no more than 20 percent of the franchisees sales in dollar volume (Parts 436.2(a)(3)(i) and 436.2(h)).

3. **Single Trademark Licenses:** The Rule language excludes a "single license to license a [mark]" where it "is the only one of its general nature and type to be granted by the licensor with respect to that [mark]" (Part 436.2(a)(4)(iv)). The Rule's Statement of Basis and Purpose indicates it also applies to "collateral" licenses [e.g., logo on sweatshirt, mug] and licenses granted to settle trademark infringement litigation (43 FR 59707_08).

4. **Employment and Partnership Relationships:** The Rule excludes pure employer–employee and general partnership arrangements. Limited partnerships do not qualify for the exemption (Part 436.2(a)(4)(i)).

5. **Oral Agreements:** This exemption, which is narrowly construed, applies only if no material term of the relationship is in writing (Part 436.2(a)(3)(iv)).

6. **Cooperative Associations:** Only agricultural co-ops and retailer-owned cooperatives "operated 'by and for' retailers on a cooperative basis," and in which control and ownership is substantially equal are excluded from coverage (Part 436.2(a)(4)(ii)).

7. **Certification/Testing Services:** Organizations that authorize use of a certification mark to any business selling products or services meeting their standards are excluded from coverage (e.g., Underwriters Laboratories) (Part 436.2(a)(4)(iii)).

8. **Leased Departments:** Relationships in which the franchisee simply leases space in the premises of another retailer and is not required or advised to buy the goods or services it sells from the retailer or an affiliate of the retailer are exempt (Part 436.2(a)(3)(ii)).

E. **Statutory Exemptions:** Section 18(g) of the FTC Act authorizes "any person" to petition the Commission for an exemption from a rule where coverage is "not necessary to prevent the acts or practices" that the rule prohibits (15 U.S.C. § 57a(g)). Franchise Rule exemptions have been granted for service station franchises (45 FR 51765), many automobile dealership franchises (45 FR 51763; 49 FR 13677; 52 FR 6612; 54 FR 1446), and wholesaler-sponsored voluntary chains in the grocery industry (48 FR 10040).

IV. Disclosure Options

A. **Alternatives:** Franchisors have a choice of formats for making the disclosures required by the Rule. They may use either the format provided by the Rule or the Uniform Franchise Offering Circular (UFOC) format prescribed by the North American Securities Administrators' Association (NASAA).

B. **FTC Format:** Franchisors may comply by following the Rule's requirements for preparing a basic disclosure document (Parts 43 6. 1 (a)(1)-(24)), and if they make earnings claims, for a separate earnings claim disclosure document (Parts 436.1(b)(3), (c)(3), and (d)). The Rule's Final Interpretive Guides provide detailed instructions and sample disclosures (44 FR 49966).

C. **UFOC Format:** The Uniform Franchise Offering Circular format may also be used for compliance in any state:

1. **Guidelines:** Effective January 1, 1996, franchisors using the UFOC disclosure format must comply with the UFOC Guidelines, as amended by NASAA on April 25, 1993 (44 FR 49970; 60 FR 51895).

2. **Cover Page:** The FTC cover page must be furnished to each potential franchisee, either in lieu of the UFOC cover page in non-registration states or along with the UFOC (Part 436.1(a)(21) (44 FR 49970-71).

3. **Adaptation:** If the UFOC is registered or used in one state, but will be used in another without a franchise registration law, answers to state-specific questions must be changed to refer to the law of the state in which the UFOC is used.

4. **Updating:** If the UFOC is registered in a state, it must be updated as required by the state's franchise law. If the same UFOC is also adapted for use in a nonregistration state, updating must occur as required by the law of the state where the UFOC is registered. If the UFOC is not registered in a state with a franchise registration law, it must be revised annually and updated quarterly as required by the Rule.

5. **Presumption:** The Commission will presume the sufficiency, adequacy and accuracy of a UFOC that is registered by a state, when it is used in that state.

D. **UFOC vs. Rule:** Many franchisors have adopted the UFOC disclosure format because roughly half of the thirteen states with franchise registration requirements will not accept the Rule document for filing. When a format is chosen, all disclosure must conform to its requirements. Franchisors may not pick and choose provisions from each format when making disclosures (44 FR 49970).

E. **Rule Primacy:** If the UFOC is used, several key Rule provisions will still apply:

1. **Scope:** Disclosure will be required in all cases required by the Rule, regardless of whether it would be required by state law.

2. **Coverage:** The Rule will determine who is obligated to comply, regardless of whether they would be required to make disclosures under state law.

3. **Disclosure Timing:** When disclosures must be made will be governed by the Rule, unless state law requires even earlier disclosure.

4. **Other Material:** No information may appear in a disclosure document not required by the Rule or by non-preempted state law, regardless of the format used, and no representations may be made that contradict a disclosure.

5. **Contracts:** Failure to provide potential franchisees with final agreements at least 5 days before signing will be a Rule violation regardless of the disclosure format used.

6. **Refunds:** Failure to make promised refunds also will be a Rule violation regardless of which document is used.

V. Potential Liability for Violations

A. **FTC Action:** Rule violations may subject franchisors, franchise brokers, their officers and agents to significant liabilities in FTC enforcement actions.

1. **Remedies:** The FTC Act provides the Commission with a broad range of remedies for Rule violations:

a. **Injunctions:** Section 13(b) of the Act authorizes preliminary and permanent injunctions against Rule violations (15 U.S.C. § 53(b)). Rule cases routinely have sought and obtained injunctions against Rule violations and misrepresentations in the offer or sale of any business venture, whether or not covered by the Rule.

b. **Asset Freezes:** Acting under their inherent equity powers, the courts have routinely granted preliminary asset freezes in appropriate Rule cases. The assets frozen have included both corporate assets and the personal assets, including real and personal property, of key officers and directors.

c. **Civil Penalties:** Section 5(m)(1)(A) of the Act authorizes civil penalties of up to $11,000 for each violation of the Rule (15 U.S.C. § 45(m)(1)(A)). The courts have granted civil penalties of as much as $870,000 in a Rule case to date.

d. **Monetary Redress:** Section 19(b) of the Act authorizes the Commission to seek monetary redress on behalf of investors injured economically by a Rule violation

(15 U.S.C. § 57b). The courts have granted consumer redress of as much as $4.9 million in a Rule case to date.

  e. **Other Redress:** Section 19(b) of the Act also authorizes such other forms of redress as the court finds necessary to redress injury to consumers from a Rule violation, including rescission or reformation of contracts, the return of property and public notice of the Rule violation. Courts may also grant similar relief under their inherent equity powers.

 2. **Personal Liability:** Individuals who formulate, direct and control the franchisor's activities can expect to be named individually for violations committed in the franchisor's name, together with the franchisor entity, and held personally liable for civil penalties and consumer redress.

 3. **Liability for Others:** Franchisors and their key officers and executives are responsible for violations by persons acting in their behalf, including independent franchise brokers, subfranchisors, and the franchisor's own sales personnel.

B. **Private Actions:** The courts have held that the FTC Act generally may not be enforced by private lawsuits.

 1. **Rule Claims:** The Commission expressed its view when the Rule was issued that private actions should be permitted by the courts for Rule violations (43 FR 59723; 44 FR 49971). To date, no federal court has permitted a private action for Rule violations.

 2. **State Disclosure Law Claims:** Each of the franchise laws in the fifteen states with franchise registration and/or disclosure requirements authorizes private actions for state franchise law violations.

 3. **State FTC Act Claims:** The courts in some states have interpreted state deceptive practices laws ("little FTC Acts") as permitting private actions for Rule violations.

VI. **Legal Resources**

A. **Text of Rule:** 16 C.F.R. Part 436.

B. **Statement of Basis and Purpose:** 43 FR 59614_59733 (Dec. 21, 1978) (Discusses the evidentiary basis for promulgation of the Rule, and shows Commission intent and interpretation of its provisions, particularly helpful in resolving coverage questions).

C. **Final Interpretive Guides:** 44 FR 49966_49992 (Aug. 24, 1979) (Final statement of policy and interpretation of each of the Rule's requirements—important discussions of coverage issues, use of the UFOC, and requirements for basic and earnings claims disclosures in the Rule's disclosure format

D. **Staff Advisory Opinions:** Business Franchise Guide (CCH) 6380 et seq. (Interpretive opinions issued in response to requests for interpretation of coverage questions and disclosure requirements pursuant to 16 C.F.R. §§ 1.2_1.4).

Last updated: Thursday, February 08, 2001

FINANCING YOUR FRANCHISED BUSINESS

In studying this chapter, you will:

- **Understand the financing requirements of a franchisee.**

- **Learn about possible funding sources for a franchisee.**

- **Understand the franchisor's role in providing funding for franchisees.**

- **Be able to distinguish among available financing methods, including franchisor, family, banks, and outside funding agencies.**

- **Develop an understanding of how to prepare a financial package for a loan application.**

INCIDENT

Mary wants to open her own executive placement service. For the past ten years, she has been working for an executive placement agency and is competent at matching employees with employers and vice versa. She believes there is a local need for a placement service for employers and discontented executives. To begin such a business, Mary needs a large network of employees and employers. She has decided that the best and quickest way to accomplish this is to become a franchisee of a large, national employment service franchise.

Mary's chief concern is how she will finance the venture. Although she has some savings, she is realistic about how much capital is necessary to start a business. She must consider start-up costs and business expenses, as well as all fees that must be paid to a franchisor. She is confused about the many alternatives. Which type of financing would she be most likely to qualify for? What would be the most attractive payment plan in the short and long run? Would it be possible to finance the venture with several types of loans?

16-1 INTRODUCTION

The primary goal of any company is to make a profit. In a franchise system, if franchisees are unable to make a profit, the company will not survive, and the franchisees will be forced out of business. A primary goal of the franchisee is likewise to generate a profit and thus increase personal wealth. One of the main ways for owners to increase their wealth is to increase the value of the business.

Profitability is very important, as are growth, sound investment, financial stability, and good management.

16-2 FINANCIAL OBLIGATIONS OF FRANCHISEES

Before franchisees can seriously think about making a profit, they obviously must choose a franchise system and open a franchised unit. The opening involves several important financial considerations, particularly start-up costs. Start-up costs include building expenses (land, building, equipment, fixtures, decorating, remodeling); one to three months' salaries and wages, inventory, and advertising costs; business expenses (including telephone and utilities, insurance, legal, and other professional fees, vehicles, supplies, and licenses); and living expenses (moving expenses, salary for owner or manager). These costs are crucial considerations for the franchisee.

In addition to the start-up or turnkey costs associated with beginning a business, the franchisee is also required to pay the franchisor several fees, including:

1. Franchising fees

2. Royalty fees

3. Advertising fees

4. Training fees

5. Other fees

The franchisee's major financial obligation is to the franchisor. This obligation includes an upfront franchising fee which usually ranges from $5,000 to $50,000. In addition to paying the franchising fee, the franchisee is expected to pay royalty fees (3 to 7 percent of gross revenues) on a weekly, biweekly, or monthly basis; advertising fees (0.5 to 4 percent of gross revenues); and sometimes leasing or rental fees, either a fixed monthly payment or from 1 to 8 percent of gross revenues. Besides these basic expenditures, the franchisee may incur the costs of initial training—travel, lodging, and meals. Also, the franchisee should be alert to the possibility of additional costs relating to on-site visitations, computer rental fees, equipment leasing fees, or travel expenses to regional or national franchisor meetings.

All fees required for the franchisee to pay the franchisor are listed in items 5, 6 and 7 of the Uniform Franchise Offering Circular (UFOC). Item five requires the franchisor to disclose to the franchisee the amount of the one-time **initial franchise fee**. This may simply be stated as the following: "All franchisees pay a $25,000 lump sum, nonrefundable franchise fee when they sign the franchise agreement. If Logan Farms grants you a second subsequent franchise during the term of an effective Franchise Agreement, the franchise fee for each subsequent franchise granted you will be $10,000. The franchisee fee is deemed to be fully earned by Logan Farms upon execution and delivery of the Franchise Agreement."[1]

16-3 OTHER FRANCHISEE REQUIREMENTS OR OBLIGATIONS

The franchisee is generally required to purchase specific items of equipment or inventory often carrying the logo of the franchisor. The equipment used by the franchisee must meet the specifications set by the franchisor. Most franchisors do not require the franchisee to purchase directly from the franchisor, rather, the franchisee has latitude to purchase supplies from various sources. Thus, it is generally held that the franchisee, although obligated to acquire the equipment and items of inventory listed in the franchising agreement, is not required to purchase these items from the

FRANCHISE CAPTIAL REQUIREMENTS - AN EXAMPLE

	Lower Cost	Moderate Cost	Higher Cost	When Due
Initial Franchise Fee	$ 15,000	$ 15,000	$ 15,000	Upon Signing Fanchise Agreement
Real Estate (Estimated Deposit of 2 Months Rent	2,000	5,000	12,000	Upon Signing Intent To Sublease
Leasehold Improvements	42,000	79,000	105,000	Prorated During Construction
Equipment Security Deposit	3,500	5,500	8,000	Before Equipment Is Ordered
Security System	1,000	2,500	6,000	When Ordered
Freight Charges	2,750	4,000	4,000	On Delivery
Outside Signage	2,000	4,000	8,000	When Ordered
Opening Inventory	4,000	5,000	5,500	Within One Week Of Opening
Insurance	800	1,500	2,500	Before Opening
Supplies	500	1,000	1,300	Before Opening
Training Expenses Including Travel and Lodging	1,500	2,500	3,500	During Training
Legal and Accounting Services	500	2,000	3,500	Before Opening
Opening Advertising	2,500	3,250	4,000	When Opening
Miscellaneous Expenses (Business Licenses, Utility Deposits, Small Equipment and Surplus Capital	4,000	6,000	8,000	As Needed
3 Months Additional Funds	12,000	26,000	42,000	As Needed
Estimated Total Investment	$ 94,050	$ 162,250	$ 228,300	

Adapted from SUBWAY® Franchising Capital Requirements, April. 2007

franchisor. The franchisee may purchase all such items from any reputable approved supplier. The franchisee is not required, but may have the option, of acquiring all or any of these items from the franchisor. To the best understanding of the franchisor, there are numerous sources of supply of most such items. The franchisee is initially advised to purchase a few items bearing the franchisor's trademarks and logos from the supplier approved by the franchisor.

The franchisor is required to specify in writing, in both the disclosure document and the contract, any obligations a franchisee has which may result in profit to the franchisor. Although the franchisor may not require a franchisee to make purchases from the parent corporation, the franchisor may require that the franchisee obtain equipment, furniture, and fixtures from an approved list of suppliers who meet or exceed the prescribed standards as established by the franchisor.

The franchisor is also required in the Uniform Franchise Offering Circular to state the franchisee's initial investment. Often, though, the franchisor will strive to provide some low, middle, and high estimates for the prospective franchisee. (See the example in Figure 16-1.)

Franchisors work rather hard to establish estimates of total start-up expenses. They want the franchisee to realize the total amount to be expended before the business start-up. It is important for the franchisor to be honest with the franchisee. The franchisee must recognize that the figures are only estimates that will vary from one location to another. Franchisees need to know the basis of the estimates made by the franchisor and perform their own business and financial analyses before making any final decisions. The total cost of any franchise operation will depend on a number of factors, including the location of the franchise and the local market and economic conditions. The franchisee may use any estimates provided by the franchisor, but should seek additional information from other franchisees, suppliers, and builders in order to arrive at more accurate final cost figures.

INITIAL INVESTMENTS

	Estimated Amounts (1,500 sq. ft. Shop)	Method of Payment	When Due	To Whom Payment Is Made
Initial Franchise Fee	$25,000	Lump Sum	Execution of Franchise Agreement	Logan Farms
Real Estate and Improvements—Leased Premises	2,000 to 3,000 per month	Monthly	As Incurred	Lessor
Real Estate—Build-out Costs	80,000 to 130,000	Lump Sum	As Incurred	Lessor; Contractor
Security Deposits; Rent Prepayment	3,000 to 4,000	Lump Sum	As Incurred; At Lease Signing	Utilities:Leassor
Opening Inventory	25,000	As Incurred	Prior to Opening	Vendors
Training Expenses Including Lodging and Travel	Varies	As Incurred	Prior to Opening	Vendors
Opening Advertising	25,000	As Incurred	Prior to Opening	Vendors
Insurance	1,500 to 2,000	Lump Sum (possibly installments)	Prior to Opening	Insurance Company
Advertising Costs—3 Months	N/A	N/A	N/A	N/A
6 Months Additional Funds	50,000	As Incurred	As Incurred	Vendors, utilities, employees
ESTIMATED TOTAL INVESTMENT	$266,500 to $354,000			

FIGURE 16-1

Logan Farms Honey Glazed Hams

Adapted from Logan Farms Glazed Hams, UFCO, pp. 7-8, 1995

16-4   FRANCHISOR FINANCING ARRANGEMENTS

Almost every franchisee must utilize outside financial sources; and franchising, like any business opportunity, is a risk. Because of its use of established business formats, proven products, and effective advertising techniques, however, franchising reduces the chance of failure of small business entrepreneurs. The franchisee has basically four major financial resources: (1) the franchisor; (2) family, friends, and relatives; (3) the bank; and (4) venture capitalists or outside funding agencies.

Ideally, business start-up or expansion would always be financed by self-generated capital. In the real world, however, most franchisees and franchisors are unable to start a franchising program on existing capital resources. Even established franchisees who wish to expand into multiunit franchises find it difficult to generate sufficient internal capital.

FINANCING YOUR FRANCHISED BUSINESS **399**

16-4a   Some Arrangements by Franchisors

Most franchisors will not become involved with the financing of new franchises, although a few of the well-established franchisors, including McDonald's and Kwik Kopy Corporation, will help finance franchisees. One of the main reasons for franchising is that it enables the franchisor to use the capital of franchisees to expand and develop franchised units. Therefore, most franchisors require the franchisee to have sufficient capital to pay the initial franchising fee as well as to start and develop the franchised unit. In disclosure documents, many franchisors state that "neither the franchisor, nor any of its related agents, offer either directly or indirectly any financing arrangements or opportunities to any prospective franchisees."

The two opposing schools of thought regarding financing by the franchisor are (1) that lending is not a primary business and should not be engaged in, and (2) that financing should be offered to prospective franchisees to encourage buildups and the development of multiunit franchisees. Almost all franchisors, however, prefer that franchisees have at least part of their own capital committed to the franchised unit. Virtually no franchisors provide 100 percent backing without some financial commitment on the part of the franchisee to develop the franchising business. Most franchisors also prefer the franchisee to pay all initial franchising fees out of pocket. For instance, the $40,000 franchising fee for Dunkin' Donuts of America, Inc., must be paid entirely out of pocket. Dunkin' Donuts will help finance all of the equipment needed, with the franchisee having the option of either a straight loan or a leasing package. None of the big four rental car businesses—Hertz Corporation (New York), Avis Rent-A-Car, Inc. (Garden City, NY), National Car Rental System, Inc. (Minneapolis), and Budget Rent-A-Car (Chicago)—offer financing for franchisees. They require that the entire franchising fee be financed up front by the franchisee, but will help develop lines of credit from the major automotive companies or third-party lenders.

Some franchisors, including the Memphis, Tennessee–based Merry Maids housekeeping franchise, will finance up to 60 percent of the initial investment capital requirement because they want to help franchisees get started. They know that the franchise system's growth comes from franchisees and from the royalties franchisees will pay to the franchisor. The 7-ELEVEN franchise division of Southland Corporation will provide financing for a portion of the costs. This lessens the burden of financing on franchisees and encourages a strong relationship between the franchisor and the franchisee. Both the cleaning service Jani-King International, Inc. (Dallas, Texas) and the business services UPS Stores Inc. (Carlsbad, California) will provide financial assistance for the franchisee.

It is important to mention, however, that franchising fees may differ even within the same franchise system, depending on the number of franchises to be opened. For instance, one system may reduce the base franchising fee of $20,000 per store to $16,000 per store if five or more stores are to be opened, and to $11,000 per store if ten stores are to be opened. Another franchise system might reduce the initial royalty fee of 4.5 percent of gross revenues for a single store to 3.3 percent if three or more stores are opened.

When a multiunit program is started, the franchisee should work with the franchisor to develop a payment schedule. For example, if the franchisee agrees to open ten units over a five-year period, the franchising fee payments may be arranged to include one-half of the total fees payable when the original agreement is signed. This one-time, upfront fee is generally nonrefundable. The balance of each of the ten franchising fees would then be payable as each unit opens.

Once they are fully developed and staffed, some franchisors will have sufficient resources to help finance the start-up costs of their franchisees. New franchisors rarely become involved with the financing of either franchising fees or start-up costs simply because these franchisors do not have sufficient capital available.

One franchisor that provides financial backing to new franchisees is Kwik Kopy Corporation, which makes ten-year financing available to start-up franchisees in need of assistance (see Figure 16-2).

KWIK KOPY CORPORATION: SUMMARY OF FINANCING OFFERED

Item Financed (Source)	Amount Financed	Down Payment	Term (Yrs)	APR %	Security Required	Liability upon Default	Loss of Legal Right on Default
Initial Franchise Fee	$20,000	$5,000	Up to 120 months	0	Personal Guarantee	Loss of Franchise— Unpaid loan plus maximum legal rate of interest	Entire unpaid balance of loan is immediately due and payable
Equipment	$110,000	NA	60 to 84 months	Varies with Prime Rate	Business Assets	Loss of Franchise— Unpaid loan plus maximum legal rate of interest	Equipment is repossessed and sold
Start-up Costs	$69,500	$59,000	60 to 84 months	Varies with Prime Rate	Business and Personal Assets	Loss of Franchise— Unpaid loan plus maximum legal rate of interest	Assets are repossessed and sold
Prepaid Expenses	$10,000	$5,000	60 to 84 months	Varies with Prime Rate	Business and Personal Assets	Loss of Franchise— Unpaid loan plus maximum legal rate of interest	Assets are repossessed and sold

FIGURE **16-2**

Kwik Kopy Corporation

16-4b   Other Financing Arrangements Provided by the Franchisor

Some franchisors may make arrangements with a commercial lender to provide financing of certain franchising fees, start-up costs, fixtures, equipment, and furniture to prospective franchisees who meet the lender's financial requirements. The terms and conditions are established by the lending institution for the franchisee and may be changed without the knowledge or consent of the franchisor. These loans are usually secured by a combination of real and personal property, and a portion of this financing may be guaranteed by or through the franchisor.

Certain franchisors may provide discounts on the initial franchising fee to franchisees making full cash payments prior to their attending training programs. This kind of discount is more likely to be offered by small franchisors than by large franchise systems. It is important to understand the total initial investment required to start a franchise. This is explained in item 7 of the Critter Care UFOC (see Figure 16-3).

16-5   FINANCIAL RESOURCES OF FRANCHISEES

Financing may be properly defined as the acquisition of funds to cover expenses and to allow the purchasing of assets which provide revenue for a new business. The franchise's capital structure is the makeup of its business finances—that is, how much is debt (borrowed money) and how much is equity (owner's share).

CRITTER CARE: INITIAL INVESTMENT

	Amount	Method of Payment	When Due	To Whom Payment Is Made
Initial Franchise Fee	$6,500	Lump Sum	When Franchise Agreement Is Signed	Critter Care
Training Expenses Including Travel and Lodging	$800 - $1,300	As Arranged	As Arranged	Suppliers, Lodging, Transportation, and Meals
Real Estate	Varies	As Arranged	As Arranged	Seller
Equipment	$500 - $900	As Arranged	As Arranged	Suppliers
Miscellaneous Opening Costs	$200 - $500	As Arranged	As Arranged	Advertising Agencies and Suppliers
Opening Inventory and Start-up Supplies	$50 - $100	As Arranged	As Arranged	Suppliers and Employees
Working Capital	$500 - $2,900	As Needed	As Arranged	Vendors and Employees
Insurance	$450 - $600	Lump Sum, In Advance or Installments	Annually, Semiannually, or Quarterly	Insurer
Other Prepaid Expenses	$700 - $1,450	As Arranged	Monthly	Utility Companies
Additional Funds - 3 months royalty and advertising fees	$195	Lump Sum	Monthly	Critter Care
TOTAL	$9,900 - $14,450			

FIGURE **16-3**

Critter Care

16-5a   Debt Financing and Equity Financing

Every franchisee needs to understand the two primary forms of long-term financing available to a franchise: debt financing and equity financing (see Figure 16-4). **Equity financing** is selling the ownership of the company to other investors. This includes dividing the business and its managerial responsibilities among the different partners, owners, or investors. The original owner does not have to repay these other investors in cash, but instead gives them a share of the business profits and managerial responsibilities. The investors receive money from the business through the division of profits in the form of dividends. The primary sources of equity capital include oneself, one's friends and relatives, and venture capital companies.

Debt financing may be divided into two categories—financing for working capital and financing for capital expenditures. The advantage of debt financing is that it enables one to borrow money and pay it back to the lender over time, on an appropriate, affordable repayment schedule. The major sources of debt financing include banks and other financial institutions, friends, and relatives.

Debt financing for working capital (current assets - current liabilities) ordinarily involves short-term debt incurred to help purchase inventories or cover accounts payable. This is often necessary when inventories and payrolls must be increased in order to generate higher sales or profits for the

EQUITY CAPITAL	DEBT CAPITAL
(1) Money Invested,	(1) Money borrowed,
(2) Ownership	(2) Debt
(3) Dividends and Profits	(3) Repayment required
Private Investors	**Private Lenders**
Personal Savings	Banks
Friends and Relatives	Asset-based Lenders
Angels	Trade Credit
Partners	Commercial Finance Companies
Corporations	Savings and Loan
Venture Capital Companies	Equipment Suppliers
"Going Public" - Stock Sale	Insurance Companies
Private Placements - Regulation D	Credit Unions
Foreign Stock Markets	Stock Brokerage Houses
Government Investors	**Government Lenders**
State	Small Business Administration (SBA)
Local	SBICs
	SBLCs
	State and Local Loan and Development Programs

FIGURE **16-4**

Money Needed

HOW MUCH DOES A SMOOTHIE KING FRANCHISE COST?

Financial Investment Dynamics

Initial Investment	LOW	HIGH
Franchise Fee	$20,000	$20,000
First Month's Rental & Deposit	$5,000	$8,000
Equipment	$23,000	$28,000
Fixtures/Signage	$14,000	$18,000
Leasehold Improvements	$35,000	$75,000
Start-up Supplies, Inventory	$13,000	$15,000
Opening Advertising	$3,000	$5,000
Training	$1,300	$2,000
Insurance	$1,200	$2,500
Other Prepaid Expenses*	$1,500	$2,500
Legal, Accounting, and Organizational Costs	$1,000	$2,000
Miscellaneous Costs	$2,000	$3,000
Additional Funds	$15,000	$30,000
Additional Development Costs (multiunit franchisees)	$0	$10,000
TOTAL	$135,000	$221,000

The difference between low or high investment levels exists because of varying store sizes and real estate costs.
*Prepaid expenses include grand opening expenses, travel/training, legal/accounting, insurance, permits, and deposits.

FIVE Cs of CREDIT

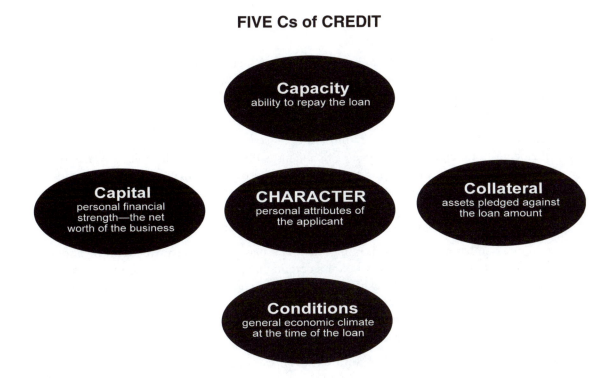

franchise. Working capital debt is usually financed through short-term bank loans, trade credits, or credit unions, whereas financing for working capital is normally short-term financing for capital expenditures (land, building, equipment, and fixtures) and is almost always obtained through long-term debt agreements. Capital expenditure financing is most often required for start-up expansion or for remodeling of the franchise. The major sources of capital expenditure financing include commercial banks, the Small Business Administration, venture capitalists, vendors, life insurance companies, and other commercial lenders.

When borrowing money, it is important that the franchisee understand the "five Cs" of debt financing, as the lender will be examining these same elements.

The franchisee should be aware that borrowing is both an art and a science. The owner's ability to obtain the money is going to be based on personal history, credit history, business track record, and ability to effectively (and legally, of course) influence the lender.

Debt Financing

The capital structure of the franchise may include short-term, intermediate-term, and long-term financing.

Short-Term Financing—generally involves the use of money for less than one year. These funds are often sought for needs such as the purchase of inventory or specialty sales items. Short-term financing is frequently used to handle the lag period between the time when expenses are incurred (cash outlay) and the time when sales revenues are received (cash input). The franchisee may usually secure this type of financing through trade credit, commercial paper, unsecured bank loans, or inventory financing.

Trade credit, the most common form of short-term financing, is a means by which the franchisee can receive credit from suppliers and/or service companies. The supplier (seller) generally allows the franchisee (buyer) a certain number of days before the bill must be paid. The trade period may be from 30 to 120 days, usually with little or no interest charged for this period. Franchisees' ability to obtain trade credit is determined almost solely by their reputation and credit history.

Commercial paper is a short-term promissory note which the franchisee signs and sells to an investor. It is normally sold for short periods, from 30 to 270 days. Because it is very difficult for most franchisees to afford, this practice is ordinarily reserved for large corporations with strong financial backing.

Intermediate-Term Financing—is most often used to meet a firm's one- to three-year financing requirements. This type of financing is normally quite flexible and is frequently used by franchisees undergoing rapid growth. The company may initially seek short-term financing, which the bank may extend for a one- or two-year period; but the bank is usually unwilling to give additional extensions. Many franchisees look to intermediate-term financing as a way to obtain funds for starting up or for limited expansion.

If the franchisee has a strong credit rating, the bank may provide an **unsecured or signature loan**. This type of bank loan may be for a certain line of credit, a revolving credit agreement, or a transaction loan. Or, a franchisee may be able to obtain an **inventory loan** based on the inventory on hand. Most banks in this case require the franchisee to actually present the purchase orders and an audited account of inventory on hand. These types of loans are generally not available to franchisees, although they may be in certain cases.

Long-Term Financing—is most often used to provide funds for the purchase of permanent assets, which may include land, buildings, and certain types of equipment. Long-term financing ordinarily involves a period of five to twenty years. These arrangements are typically handled not by banks, but by such institutions as insurance companies, pension funds, or the Small Business Administration, or by the issuance of bonds or stocks.

There are also new companies developing in the United States which will provide sale-lease back financing for land, buildings, and equipment specifically for franchisees. Franchise Finance Corporation of America (FFCA) is a financial institution which offers private financing to franchisees primarily in the restaurant industry for the purchase of land, buildings, and equipment. FFCA provides franchisees with a financing package of fixed and affordable rates and sufficiently long lease terms for development of franchise locations. The financing offered by FFCA provides 100 percent financing for land, building, and equipment from a single source.

RULES OF BORROWING CAPITAL

Rule 1: Obtain an introduction from a friend or professional before meeting the investor to add credibility.

Rule 2: Ensure that the stated sources and uses of capital are equal in amount— no hidden variations.

Rule 3: Do not negotiate in the business plan—that plan should be real.

Rule 4: Know your business plan—know every aspect of what you are going to do.

Rule 5: Be ready to rethink your business plan—you may receive positive and thoughtful suggestions to improve your business.

Types of Debt Financing

Franchisees can utilize several types of debt financing when they are in need of capital to improve or expand their businesses.

Bank Term Loans. A term loan is a formal agreement between a bank and the franchisee for the use of a specific sum of money (principal) at a given interest rate for a specific period of time (term). These loans normally require that portions of both the interest and the principal be repaid on a monthly basis. Occasionally a balloon payment may be allowed, by which only a portion of the principal is repaid during the term of the loan and a large "balloon" payment is due at maturity. These loans often require collateral—land, buildings, fixtures, equipment, or other fixed assets— that is promised to the bank if the franchisee is unable to meet the repayment requirements.

Equipment Lease Financing. An important financial program which has become more widely available in recent years is the lease financing arrangement. This arrangement enables the franchisee to obtain equipment at a lower cost, eliminate risk of ownership, and obtain service and maintenance agreements from the lessor. Many franchises which use unique equipment often seek to arrange lease arrangements for their franchisees through third parties (see Figure 16-5).

Equipment Financing. Certain franchisors will arrange to finance the necessary start-up equipment through a leasing company. The terms and conditions of the lease financing are determined by the leasing company and the franchisee, and they may be easily changed without the knowledge or consent of the franchisor. An initial payment equal to the first and last monthly installments may be required. These types of financial arrangements are often made outside the control of the franchisor. Under certain conditions, however, the franchisor may be the lessor, in which case the franchisee is liable and responsible to the franchisor. At the end of the leasing agreement, the franchisee typically has the option to purchase the equipment outright (at its fair market value). If the franchise is terminated for any reason, the lease becomes immediately due and payable in full.

A franchisee who has decided to purchase equipment may be able to obtain a loan using the equipment as collateral. Banks, finance companies, and equipment manufacturers often engage in this type of lending. The franchisee may decide to use a manufacturer or finance company to obtain this type of loan, leaving bank loans to be used for other asset accounts.

Federal Financing. In 1953, Congress passed the Small Business Act, by which it established the Small Business Administration (SBA) to help small businesses (including franchisees) obtain loans for start-ups and other activities. The SBA helps franchisees obtain capital through (1) the SBA loan guarantee program, (2) the Federal Registry, (3) the 502 program, or (4) small business investment companies (SBICs).

The SBA-guaranteed loan program was established to help small businesses in the acquisition, construction, or improvement of a building; the purchase of inventory and equipment; start-up costs; and working capital. Effective December 22, 2000, a maximum loan amount of $2 million has been established for 7(a) loans; however, the maximum dollar amount the SBA can guaranty is generally $1 million. Small loans carry a maximum guaranty of 85 percent. Loans are considered small if the gross loan amount is $150,000 or less. For loans greater than $150,000, the maximum guaranty is 75 percent, with interest rates usually 2 to 3 percent above prime. Most working capital

Equipment Cost	$33,800
Estimated Freight	1,700
Total Estimated Cost (without sales tax)	$35,500

Lease Payments: 8 years @ $370 per month plus any applicable sales tax. Purchase option at the end of lease term.
Franchise owner has an option to purchase the leased equipment at the end of the eight-year period for the then fair market value.

FIGURE 16-5

Equipment Package—Lease Program of a Printing Franchise System

loans are to be repaid within seven years, equipment loans within ten years, and real estate purchases within twenty-five years. Most SBA-guaranteed loans require personal guarantees of the officers, directors, or stockholders.

SMALL BUSINESS ADMINISTRATION'S FRANCHISE REGISTRY

SBA's new Franchise Registry is a good example of helping small business owners through cooperation between government and industry. The dedicated efforts of SBA employees, franchisees, franchisors, and lenders have led to streamlined eligibility guidelines and operating procedures that will reduce costs and processing time and help SBA serve its customers better.

The Registry lists names of franchise companies whose franchisees enjoy the benefits of a streamlined review process for SBA loan applications. Loan applications for registered franchisors can be reviewed and processed quickly and efficiently. Small business owners get better service and quicker loans.

Listing on this registry means that the franchise agreement does not impose unacceptable control provisions on a franchisee (which could result in affiliation with a franchisor). The lender and/or SBA must still consider and evaluate, with respect to each application for SBA financing, factors such as general eligibility, creditworthiness, conflicts of interest, character, use of proceeds, and discrimination.

Additionally, Minority Enterprise Small Business Investment Companies (MESBICs) provide limited investment capital. MESBICs have been established to help "disadvantaged Americans" obtain funds for business activities. MESBICs are officially SBICs. Those qualifying for MESBIC loans normally fall into three categories: ethnic minorities, U.S. military personnel, and U.S. citizens who have been hampered by social, economic, or other personal difficulties.

Equity Financing

There are several means by which a franchisee can obtain equity financing in order to improve or expand a business.

Stock Sales. A franchisee may obtain long-term financing by selling stock to family and friends or to the public through public offerings. The stockholders become the actual owners of the corporation or franchise, and they bear the risk of the business. If the business fails, the stockholders lose their investment. If the business succeeds, they earn a return on their investment in the form of dividends paid by the business or through the appreciation of the stock's price.

One advantage of common stock financing is that the franchisee is not obligated to pay dividends, as long as the stockholders agree to this when the stock is issued. Many franchisees who are able to sell stock do not anticipate paying dividends for ten years or more. A second advantage of common stock financing is that there is no set maturity date by which repayment has to be made.

The issuance of common stock often enables the franchisee to obtain the funds necessary to start the franchise. The franchisee needs to be careful, however, to maintain managerial control of the franchise. Owners of common stock have a right to a voice in management. As long as the franchisee is able to maintain 51 percent ownership of the business, the franchisee will be able to run the business according to plan.

Partnership. A rather common method of financing any business is to include partners in the business. **Partnerships** may be developed based on the desire of individuals to work together and the agreement to contribute certain initial capital for anticipated outlays. All general partners may act as agents or representatives of the franchise. In a general partnership, all partners are fully liable for all the debts of the business and may be actively involved in its management. Each partner is taxed individually on a share of the profits.

CAPITAL INVESTMENTS

DEBT

1. **Term loans**—debt instruments providing a fixed sum of money, with interest and principle repaid over a defined period of time.
2. **Line of credit**—usually tied into working capital. This agreement allows the borrower to obtain money and maintain a fluctuating debt balance—usually for inventory purposes.
3. **Convertible bond**—debt instruments issued by a corporation to creditors called bondholders. The convertible option allows the bondholder to convert the bond into a predetermined number of shares of stock (usually common shares) within a given period of time.
4. **Bond with stock warrant**—a bond sold with a warrant which allows the bondholder to purchase a defined number of stock shares at a designated price during a defined period of time.
5. **Preferred stock**—an equity instrument yielding dividend rights over common stock and collects a steady dividend, fixed as a percentage of the market price.
6. **Convertible preferred stock**—now the preferred stock may be converted into common stock at the stockholder's option.
7. **Common stock**—the basic equity instrument used to secure capital in return for a share of the business. There are two types of common stock: Voting stock allows holders to maintain the right to have a say in the company management; nonvoting stock does not allow holders to have a say in company operations.

A second form of partnership involves limited partners. The **limited partnership** must include at least one general partner, usually the franchisee. The limited partners' liability is limited to the amount of capital contributed or the amount of risk they agree to bear. Limited partners are not allowed to help run or manage the franchise. When a partner does participate in management, that person automatically becomes a general partner, and so will incur the same risk and liability as that of any other general partner.

Many franchisees use limited partnerships in order to raise capital to start a franchise. Limited partners may be able to invest $10,000 to $20,000 for a 5 to 10 percent interest in the business. This means that a general partner may be able to raise $100,000 while only giving up 50 percent of the business and retaining all of the managerial responsibilities. Limited partners reduce their financial risk and liability, because their maximum losses are "limited" to the amount invested and the loans which they agree to guarantee. The main advantages for the limited partner are the opportunities to share in a profitable venture and to receive personal tax benefits.

Venture Capital Companies. Venture capital companies have been formulated to provide profits for their owners by helping businesses grow and, to a limited extent, by assisting business start-ups. Venture capitalists are seeking entrepreneurs who are achievers and who have a positive and aggressive approach to life and business. A franchisee should have complete understanding of the franchise situation before approaching a venture capitalist.

Venture capitalists review and analyze a business based on a number of factors: the entrepreneur's personal investment, upside or profit potential, downside risk, additional funding available, and exit opportunities. Individuals who are unwilling to invest their own money usually find it difficult to attract venture capital. Most venture capitalists seek a profit target of five times the initial investment to be returned over a five-year period. If the initial investment were to double over the five-year period, this would compute to a rate of return of only 15 percent per annum. Multiplying the initial investment by three over a five-year period would yield a compounded annual return on investment of only 25 percent. The "five times" figure yields a compounded annual return of 38 percent; the venture capitalist will be very interested in this investment. What we have given are only general guidelines, however, for each investment has a particular profit target based on the risk and profitability potential of the firm.

The final agreement which the franchisee makes with a venture capitalist firm is usually broken down into five major sections, as follows:[2]

1. Terms of investment

2. Collateral and/or security

3. Conditions of the investment

4. Presentations

5. Conditions of commitment

The terms of the investment depend on whether the venture capitalist is providing a loan or intends to purchase shares. For example, the venture capitalist company may make a loan of $300,000 for ten years at an annual interest rate of 12 percent, or it may purchase 100,000 shares of common stock in the company at $3 per share. The collateral and security of the loan or investment is often secured with second mortgages, second deeds of trust, and/or a life insurance policy on the life of the franchisee for the amount of the loan.

Conditions of the investment are requirements which must be fulfilled. Generally included are financial statements issued at weekly, biweekly, monthly, and yearly intervals. Additionally, written reports of the firm's activities are often sent out monthly. Conditions are also established and contracted so that no change in control or ownership of the company can occur without the consent of the venture capitalist firm. The conditions of the investment include how the money will be used, debt or equity position of the venture capital firm, and assurance that no lawsuits against the company are currently outstanding and that no taxes are past due. The conditions of the commitment simply state how the funds will be paid and what the closing situation will be—whether it will be a buy-back or a sale by the venture capitalist firm back to the franchisee.

FRANCHISEES GO PUBLIC BY ISSUING IPOS

Team Rental Group Inc., from Daytona Beach, Florida, is the largest Budget Rent-A-Car franchisee in the United States, going public in August 1994. The beginning price was $9.50 for its initial public offering (IPO). Two years later, the NASDAQ traded stock was priced at $17.50. Team Rental saw the revenues grow from $24 million in 1994 to $400 million within two years. The company also branched out into truck rentals, airport parking concessions, and sales facilities for used rental vehicles. The company now has over 162 Budget franchises and additional sales locations for used vehicles in thirteen states. The firm has also been acquiring Budget locations in Southern California and Arizona.

Supertel Hospitality Inc., from Norfolk, Nebraska, develops Super 8 motels. In May 1994, this firm did an IPO at $10 a share and brought in $18.5 million. The company had thirty-seven properties at the time of the IPO, and now operates fifty-two Super 8 motels and is building its first Wingate franchise in Irving, Texas. The company's stock has risen to $11.25 a share and the partners' equity has grown from $12 million to $24 million.

16-6 LOCATION

Choosing the right location is never easy. Among the many considerations are the important financial concerns. One important financial ratio for retail franchising is the location selection ratio or first year sales/start-up costs. This ratio is best when it equals one (1) or better.

$$\text{Location Selection Ratio} = \frac{\text{First Year Sales}}{\text{Start-up Costs}} = 1.0 \text{ or higher}$$

Simply explained—if it costs $650,000 to open (turnkey costs including land, building, equipment, fixtures, and furniture) a quick service restaurant (QSR) then you should have sales of $650,000 for that start-up year. One QSR franchisee's ideal ratio is 1.2 (with 24.8 percent food costs, or COGS, and 18.5 percent labor costs)—then they make some good profit. One time they were looking for a new quick service restaurant location, but they could not come close to a 1.0 ratio so they were forced to pull out. This ratio will vary from one franchise system to another, but the guideline is important for both franchisors and franchisees.

16-7 PREPARING A FINANCIAL PACKAGE

The franchisee needs to realize the importance of preparing and properly documenting a financial package which may be shown to prospective investors. This package should include all information required by the lending office. It is designed simply to explain the needs for the loan, the amount requested, and the specific purposes or uses of the loan amount. When properly completed, a financial package should enable the bank, loan office, or investor to understand the operations, functions, and potential profitability of the franchise.

A properly prepared financial package would include the following:

1. **Executive Summary**

   a. Company name and address

   b. Contact person

   c. Type of business franchise

   d. Objective of the franchise

   e. Management

   f. History of the franchisor

   g. Amount requested (including collateral)

   h. Use of funds (including financial history and financial projections for three to five years)

   i. Exit

2. **Marketing**

   a. Product description

   b. Target market

   c. Location (property and facilities)

   d. Price determination

   e. Marketing strategy including promotion and advertising

    f. Industry

    g. Competition

3. **Management**

    a. Directors and officers (names and history of individuals)

    b. Key employees

    c. Organizational structure

    d. Management strategy

    e. Labor force and employees

    f. Policies about management

    g. Risk factors

    h. Remuneration (wage and salary administration)

    i. Stock option plans

    j. Inventory control methods

4. **Accounting, Finance, and Taxes**

    a. Start-up or turnkey costs

    b. Equity and credit references

    c. Proposed financing (loans or equity: amounts, types, and conditions)

    d. Collateral

    e. Return on investment

    f. Projected income statement

    g. Projected balance sheet

    h. Projected cash flow (first year)

    i. Working capital

    j. Breakeven analysis

    k. Provisions for taxation

    l. Sale/buy-back of equity

5. **Legal Aspects**

    a. Financial agreements (conditions, guarantees)

    b. Franchise agreements, licenses, and other legal documents

    c. Business structure

    d. Insurance: types and costs

6. **Appendix**

    a. Product literature, brochures, pictures, articles, graphs, charts, layouts, diagrams, resumes, other

    b. Brochures

    c. Pictures, etc.

16-7a   Executive Summary

The executive summary is the most crucial part of the financial presentation because it explains the business and sparks the interest of the investor. It spells out what is intended to happen. In addition, the executive summary should include the amount requested and how it will be used, that is, for land, buildings, fixtures, furnishings, and equipment.

    The franchisee needs to state clearly and precisely what is going to be done and how it is going to be done. The summary should be short, no longer than three pages. The business proposal which follows is generally attached, but most bank officers or investors will not be interested in plowing through a detailed proposal until they understand the business from a summary position. The summary is designed to entice the bank officer or investor into an interest in the business proposal and the franchise. Therefore, the executive summary is, in effect, an advertising document, a sales pitch for the franchisee and the franchise.

16-7b   Marketing

The marketing section should indicate to the financial officer how the business is going to generate its profit. Here the franchisee must accurately and in great detail describe the product or service which will be offered by the franchise. It is also important to identify the target market or customers. Facts about the location, promotion, advertising, competition, industry, supplies, and any information regarding the marketing strategy should also be included. It is important to remember that the lending officer ordinarily has a limited knowledge of the franchise or business that is planned.

16-7c   Management

In the management section, the franchisee lists the names and histories of all principal directors, officers, and owners of the franchise. This may include only the principal franchisee, or it may involve several people, including spouses. The organizational structure should also be outlined. All management policies, remunerations, wage and salary guidelines, key employees, and any management strategies should be discussed in this section. Again, the loan officer will have a limited knowledge of the specific management requirements of the franchise. It is important that this section of the financial package accurately and thoroughly explain the management functions and operations which will occur in the franchise.

16-7d   Accounting, Finance, and Taxes

One of the most important items in any financial package is the start-up or turnkey analysis. The section containing this information should enumerate all expenses which are necessary before the first customer sets foot in the franchise outlet. Information about the proposed financing and its use must be presented. If the franchisee will be establishing a fast-food restaurant, then costs might include building and land; utilities and telephone; insurance, legal, and advertising expenses; fixtures, equipment, cash registers, window display fixtures, tables, chairs, lighting, outside and inside signs, and delivery equipment; inventory; permits; installation of equipment, counters, cabinets, shelves, and even plumbing and restroom facilities. All of these costs need to be itemized and a total projected.

It would also be appropriate for the franchisee to develop pro forma income statements and balance sheets. As we know from earlier discussions, these are projected income statements for the first three years of operation as well as balance sheets generally for the three years of operation. An investor or loan officer may also request to see pro forma cash flow statements projected for the first three years of operation (see Figure 16-6). Other information about working capital, breakeven volume, output, sales, and provisions for taxation should even be included in this section.

16-7e   Legal Requirements

The franchisee should include in the financial package the franchising agreement between the franchisor and the franchisee. This will enable the loan officer to understand all contracts, licenses, and other legal requirements of the business. Additionally, the loan officer will often want to know the business structure—proprietorship, partnership, or corporation—which the principle owner will use. It is also appropriate in this section to include information about the types and costs of insurance which the new franchise will use.

16-7f   Appendix

The appendix includes any additional product literature, pictures, articles, brochures, diagrams, or layouts which may be appropriate for the business. It may also include financial accounting or marketing diagrams or charts which may relate to discussions in the rest of the package.

16-8   LEASING

A problem which can bedevil any franchisee is the numerous minute details often found in the lease agreements. Often the franchisees get so tied up in the details of starting a new business, obtaining financing, surviving the training experiences, and hiring new employees that the leasing provisions are often overlooked. There are certain steps that the franchisee must take to ensure a correct and profitable lease. These steps include:

1. Study the franchise agreement's statements on leasing. In many cases the franchisor will be responsible for the lease negotiations and sign the actual lease agreement. The franchisor may select the location, sign the lease, and then sublease the space back to the franchisee. This way the franchisor controls the location. If the franchisee is terminated, then the franchisor gets the premises and the franchisee is left out in the cold. Often the franchisor can negotiate better leasing terms from the landlord than the franchisee. Even when the franchisee is granted the right to choose the site, and negotiate the lease, it is generally required that the lease be submitted to the franchisor for final approval.

2. Understand who pays what expenses. A general rule of thumb is that the landlord or mall owners pay for nothing. This means that the franchisee will often have to pay for additional insurance, mall security, upkeep and maintenance of common areas, mall advertising, and the mandatory store owners association. It is important to know not only what the costs are, but how the costs are figured.

3. Signage and trademarks. Will the franchisee be able to use the franchisor's logo and signage inside and outside the store? Will the lease allow the franchisee to remodel the premises to the franchisor's specifications? What happens to the signage, fixtures, and equipment if the lease is terminated?

4. The franchisee should also try to obtain a promise from the landlord or mall developers that they will not rent space to a competing business.

FRANCHISEE	Month 1	Month 2	Month 3	Month 4	Month 5	Month 6	Month 7	Month 8	Month 9	Month 10	Month 11	Month 12	Year Total
CASH FLOW:													
Revenue	40,000	35,000	38,000	43,000	48,000	53,000	58,000	63,000	68,000	73,000	78,000	83,000	680,000
TOTAL CASH AVAILABLE	40,000	35,000	36,000	43,000	48,000	53,000	58,000	63,000	68,000	73,000	78,000	83,000	680,000
DISBURSMENTS:													
Food	13,200	11,550	12,540	14,190	15,840	17,490	19,140	20,790	22,440	24,090	25,740	27,390	224,400
Paper/Other	800	700	760	860	960	1,060	1,160	1,260	1,360	1,460	1,560	1,660	13,600
Direct Labor	4,800	4,200	4,560	5,160	5,760	6,360	6,960	7,560	8,160	8,760	9,380	9,960	81,600
Salaries													
Manager	2,083	2,083	2,063	2,083	2,083	2,083	2,083	2,083	2,083	2,083	2,083	2,083	24,996
Asst. Managers	1,334	1,334	1,334	1,334	1,334	1,334	1,334	1,334	1,334	1,334	1,334	1,334	16,008
Payroll Taxes													
FICA	629	583	610	656	702	748	794	840	886	932	977	1,023	9,379
Unemployment	123	114	120	129	138	147	156	165	174	183	192	201	1,839
Rent	1,800	1,600	1,600	1,600	1,600	1,800	1,600	1,600	1,600	1,600	1,600	1,600	19,200
Advertising	1,200	1,050	1,140	1,290	1,440	1,590	1,740	1,890	2,040	2,190	2,340	2,490	20,400
Royalty Fee	2,000	1,750	1,900	2,150	2,400	2,650	2,900	3,150	3,400	3,650	3,900	4,150	34,000
Travel	200	200	200	200	200	200	200	200	200	200	200	200	2,400
Accounting	150	150	150	150	150	150	150	150	150	150	150	150	1,800
Loan Repayment	2,000	2,000	2,000	2,000	2,000	2,000	2,000	2,000	2,000	2,000	2,000	2,000	24,000
Insurance	120	120	120	120	120	120	120	120	120	120	120	120	1,440
Other Cash Outflows													
Utilities	1,200	1,200	1,200	1,200	1,200	1,200	1,200	1,200	1,200	1,200	1,200	1,200	14,400
Gas	80	80	80	80	80	80	80	80	80	80	80	80	960
Water	70	70	70	70	70	70	70	70	70	70	70	70	840
Sewerage	100	100	100	100	100	100	100	100	100	100	100	100	1,200
Phone	160	160	160	160	160	180	160	160	160	160	160	160	1,920
Miscellaneous	200	200	200	200	200	200	200	200	200	200	200	200	2,400
Federal Income Taxes	0	0	2,903	0	0	5,522	0	0	16,133	0	0	28,264	52,823
TOTAL DISBURSMENTS	32,049	29,244	33,830	33,732	36,537	44,864	42,148	44,951	63,890	50,561	53,366	84,435	549,605
NET CASH FLOW	7,951	5,756	4,170	9,268	11,463	8,136	15,854	18,049	4,110	22,439	24,634	(1,435)	
CUMULATIVE CASH FLOW	7,951	13,707	17,678	27,146	38,609	46,745	62,599	80,647	84,758	107,197	131,831	130,395	

FIGURE 16-6

Hypothetical Monthly Cash Flow Statement—Franchisee First Year

FRANCHISEE	Month 1	Month 2	Month 3	Month 4	Month 5	Month 6	Month 7	Month 8	Month 9	Month 10	Month 11	Month 12	Year Total
CASH FLOW:													
Revenue	41,500	36,500	39,500	44,500	49,500	54,500	59,500	64,500	69,500	74,500	79,500	84,500	698,000
TOTAL CASH AVAILABLE	41,500	36,500	39,500	44,500	49,500	54,500	59,500	64,500	69,500	74,500	79,500	84,500	698,000
DISBURSMENTS:													
Food	13,695	12,045	13,035	14,685	16,335	17,985	19,635	21,285	22,935	24,585	26,235	27,885	230,340
Paper/Other	830	730	790	890	990	1,090	1,190	1,290	1,390	1,490	1,590	1,690	13,960
Direct Labor	4,980	4,380	4,740	5,340	5,940	6,540	7,140	7,740	8,340	8,940	9,540	10,140	83,760
Salaries													
Manager	2,333	2,333	2,333	2,333	2,333	2,333	2,333	2,333	2,333	2,333	2,333	2,333	27,996
Asst. Managers	3,000	3,000	3,000	3,000	3,000	3,000	3,000	3,000	3,000	3,000	3,000	3,000	36,000
Payroll Taxes													
FICA	789	743	771	816	862	908	954	1,000	1,046	1,092	1,138	1,184	11,303
Unemployment	155	146	151	160	169	178	187	196	205	214	223	232	2,216
Rent	1,800	1,800	1,800	1,800	1,800	1,800	1,800	1,800	1,800	1,800	1,800	1,800	21,600
Advertising	1,245	1,095	1,185	1,335	1,485	1,635	1,785	1,935	2,085	2,235	2,385	2,535	20,940
Royalty Fee	2,075	1,825	1,975	2,225	2,475	2,725	2,975	3,225	3,475	3,725	3,975	4,225	34,900
Travel	300	300	300	300	300	300	300	300	300	300	300	300	3,600
Accounting	200	200	200	200	200	200	200	200	200	200	200	200	2,400
Loan Repayment	2,000	2,000	2,000	2,000	2,000	2,000	2,000	2,000	2,000	2,000	2,000	2,000	24,000
Insurance	160	160	160	160	160	160	160	160	160	160	160	160	1,920
Other Cash Outflows													
Utilities	1,400	1,400	1,400	1,400	1,400	1,400	1,400	1,400	1,400	1,400	1,400	1,400	16,800
Gas	90	90	90	90	90	90	90	90	90	90	90	90	1,080
Water	80	80	80	80	80	80	80	80	80	80	80	80	960
Sewerage	110	110	110	110	110	110	110	110	110	110	110	110	1,320
Phone	165	165	165	165	165	165	165	165	165	165	165	165	1,980
Miscellaneous	200	200	200	200	200	200	200	200	200	200	200	200	2,400
Federal Income Taxes	0	0	1,609	0	0	3,651	0	0	9,905	0	0	23,860	39,025
TOTAL DISBURSMENTS	35,807	32,802	36,094	37,290	40,094	46,550	45,704	48,509	61,219	54,119	56,924	83,589	578,500
NET CASH FLOW	5,893	3,698	3,406	7,210	9,406	7,950	13,796	15,991	8,281	20,381	22,576	911	
CUMULATIVE CASH FLOW	136,289	139,987	143,393	150,603	160,009	167,959	181,754	197,745	206,026	226,407	248,983	249,895	

FIGURE **16-6 (continued)**

Hypothetical Monthly Cash Flow Statement—Franchisee Second Year

FRANCHISEE	Month 1	Month 2	Month 3	Month 4	Month 5	Month 6	Month 7	Month 8	Month 9	Month 10	Month 11	Month 12	Year Total
CASH FLOW:													
Revenue	44,000	39,000	42,000	47,000	52,000	57,000	62,000	67,000	72,000	77,000	82,000	87,000	728,000
TOTAL CASH AVAILABLE	44,000	39,000	42,000	47,000	52,000	57,000	62,000	67,000	72,000	77,000	82,000	87,000	728,000
DISBURSMENTS:													
Food	14,520	12,870	13,860	15,510	17,160	18,810	20,460	22,110	23,780	25,410	27,060	28,710	240,240
Paper/Other	880	780	840	940	1,040	1,140	1,240	1,340	1,440	1,540	1,640	1,740	14,560
Direct Labor	5,280	4,680	5,040	5,640	6,240	6,840	7,440	8,040	8,640	9,240	9,840	10,440	87,360
Salaries													
Manager	2,583	2,583	2,583	2,583	2,583	2,583	2,583	2,583	2,583	2,583	2,583	2,583	30,996
Asst. Managers	3,250	3,250	3,250	3,250	3,250	3,250	3,250	3,250	3,250	3,250	3,250	3,250	39,000
Payroll Taxes													
FICA	850	804	832	878	924	969	1,015	1,061	1,107	1,153	1,199	1,245	12,038
Unemployment	187	158	163	172	181	190	199	208	217	226	235	244	2,360
Rent	2,000	2,000	2,000	2,000	2,000	2,000	2,000	2,000	2,000	2,000	2,000	2,000	24,000
Advertising	1,320	1,170	1,260	1,410	1,560	1,710	1,860	2,010	2,160	2,310	2,460	2,610	21,840
Royalty Fee	2,200	1,950	2,100	2,350	2,600	2,850	3,100	3,350	3,600	3,850	4,100	4,350	36,400
Travel	400	400	400	400	400	400	400	400	400	400	400	400	4,800
Accounting	250	250	250	250	250	250	250	250	250	250	250	250	3,000
Loan Repayment	2,000	2,000	2,000	2,000	2,000	2,000	2,000	2,000	2,000	2,000	2,000	2,000	24,000
Insurance	180	180	180	180	180	180	180	180	180	180	180	180	2,160
Other Cash Outflows													
Utilities	1,600	1,600	1,800	1,600	1,600	1,600	1,600	1,600	1,600	1,600	1,600	1,600	19,200
Gas	100	100	100	100	100	100	100	100	100	100	100	100	1,200
Water	90	90	90	90	90	90	90	90	90	90	90	90	1,060
Sewerage	120	120	120	120	120	120	120	120	120	120	120	120	1,440
Phone	170	170	170	170	170	170	170	170	170	170	170	170	2,040
Miscellaneous	200	200	200	200	200	200	200	200	200	200	200	200	2,400
Federal Income Taxes	0	0	1,323	0	0	3,364	0	0	8,671	0	0	22,297	35,656
TOTAL DISBURSMENTS	38,160	35,355	38,361	39,843	42,648	48,817	48,257	51,062	62,539	56,672	59,477	84,579	605,771
NET CASH FLOW	5,840	3,645	3,639	7,157	9,352	8,183	13,743	15,938	9,461	20,328	22,523	2,421	
CUMULATIVE CASH FLOW	255,735	259,380	263,019	270,176	279,529	287,712	301,454	317,392	326,853	347,181	369,704	372,124	

FIGURE **16-6 (continued)**
Hypothetical Monthly Cash Flow Statement—Franchisee Third Year

5. Obtain provision for an adequate "cure period" to allow the franchisee to maintain the property in case of temporary cash flow or other problems.

6. Obtain a leasing term to coincide with the franchise agreement. The lease should contain a right-to-renew clause—one that allows a sufficient number of renewals to cover the number of years in the franchise agreement. The lease should also contain provisions for emergencies as well as what happens if the franchisor goes out of business or the franchisee is terminated.

Remember that everything in a lease is negotiable—if the landlord really wants the franchisee.

16-8a   When It's Time to Sell

Owning and operating as a franchisee can be great. At some point, the franchisee will want to retire or find that the amount of work is too great, or perhaps realize the franchise has failed to perform up to expectations. Regardless of the reason, what happens when the franchisee wants out?

Joanna Ossinger's article "Closing Time," in *The Wall Street Journal* (March 19, 2007) gives a concise view of the factors a franchisee should consider at that time. First, inform the parent company (franchise system headquarters) of your intentions. Selling a franchise is not the same as selling just another store. The parent company usually has the legal right of first refusal and must approve the new owner also. Most often the parent company will be willing to help in order to make sure the franchise system has strong operators. Yet, some franchise systems are not helpful. Most franchise systems do not have an exit strategy built into their franchise agreement.

Most franchisors will cooperate with franchisees' intent to exit the business, but are usually not interested in helping the franchisee find a buyer for the business. From the franchisor's perspective, the amount of help may depend on whether the brand is saturated in the area in question. If the franchisor is not interested in adding stores in the area, a prospective buyer's only option is to buy an existing franchisee store. If the area in question is not saturated, then the franchisor is likely to be more interested in selling new units than in transferring (through sale) existing ones. Some big franchise chains such as McDonald's and Subway tend to be more heavily involved in resale of franchisee stores because they are often responsible on the lease at the store site. Subway is on the lease at most of its locations, and its real estate arm is extensively involved in resale as a result.

If the parent company is not providing much assistance, then the franchisee may want to seek assistance from a professional. For example, FranchiseResales helps owners by using an outside valuation firm to help franchisees estimate the worth of their franchise, helps broker the deal between buyer and seller, and coordinates the sales process with the franchisor to make sure potential buyers meet with the parent company's approval. The price of this type of assistance can be hefty, averaging perhaps 10 percent of the sales with a minimum of $12,500. Other real estate companies help sell businesses as well, with varying services offered.

Often the best potential buyer of an existing franchise store is another franchisee of the same franchise chain within the area. They can be easily located in the area and already know the business.

When closing the deal on purchase of an existing franchise business, the franchisor usually has the right to match the terms offered to a potential buyer. One needs to remember, if the franchisor does not repurchase the franchisee business, it has the legal right to approve or reject the potential purchaser. Potential buyers should be aware that they must sign the current franchise agreement, which could be far different from the one the seller signed perhaps years ago. The franchisor has a duty to project the franchise system and to make sure a prospective franchisee (the potential buyer of an existing franchise store) is fully informed.

NING YOUR FRANCHISED BUSINESS

Craig Cormack

Cormack Restaurant Management, Inc.

In the summer of 1975, Craig Cormack faced a tough decision: cut his hair or lose the second job he needed for college tuition. Money was tight and "Dad felt I needed this job" to cover his prelaw studies at Creighton University. So he applied with the new Burger King franchisee in Sioux Falls, South Dakota. The haircut was a necessity—he had no idea it would change his life.

"I had to cut my hair three times before they'd give me a job," Craig says, but he finally passed muster and signed on with the crew of 100. After just four weeks, Cormack was offered the position of assistant manager. Throughout the summer Cormack had "every intention of going back to school, but when it came time to return, I was enjoying the challenge too much."

By then, the franchisee had taken Cormack under his wing and was expanding into a second restaurant in Sioux Falls. Cormack accepted the job as restaurant manager working his way up to director of operations inside of four years. He attributes his interest and drive to being part of "something that was growing." He was already weighing in his own mind the possibilities of wanting to create something on his own.

In 1980, Burger King Corporation had taken back two restaurants in Lincoln, Nebraska, and they were ready to sell. "I was eager to be an entrepreneur on my own ... so eager," Craig laughs, " that the restaurant could have been in Antarctica and I would have gone for it." By August, he had taken the leap and became a franchisee. He had just turned twenty-four.

But there was a downside. Cormack's father had helped fund his son's venture with his retirement money, and Cormack felt duty-bound to work day and night to pay back his father. When a Burger King came up for sale in

nearby Hastings, Cormack immediately become interested.

He purchased the restaurant, bought out his partner, paid back his father a year later, and never looked back, explaining, "basically, we just kept building." In 1988, he took advantage of an opportunity to buy restaurants in Salina, Manhattan, and Junction City, Kansas, and added them to his growing Lincoln operations. Today he owns thirty-three Burger King restaurants in Nebraska, Kansas, and South Dakota.

Cormack states his philosophy of running a profitable business as follows: "Our success is based upon obtaining a strong commitment from our employees to be the best. Hopefully no one feels that he/she works for me, but we work together. As long as we can keep good people, we will continue to grow." Many of Cormack's key management people have been with him since his start in 1980. In 1997, the passion for Cormack was getting weak. He felt the need to ensure the company would be in good hands. Top management began to buy into the business and will eventually have controlling interest in the company which they helped build.

Cormack was instrumental in forming an association of Burger King franchisees in 1988. The Mid-America Franchisee Association represents over 300 restaurants in the upper Midwest and is part of the National Burger King Association. In addition, he served as an original board of director of Restaurant Services Inc., which became the national purchasing co-op for Burger King in 1992. He was chairman of the distribution committee, which created a national contract for distributors and franchisees. He serves on various civic organizations and feels strongly about the importance of community involvement.

When he isn't working, Cormack has a passion for car racing in the summer and skiing in Colorado in the winter.

Summary

One of the essential ingredients of the proper operation of a franchised business is the sufficient financial planning and support of that business. It is important for all involved parties to recognize the financial obligations associated with purchasing and developing a franchise operation, including franchising fees, royalty fees, advertising fees, training fees, and other associated costs. Some franchisors, typically those who have been in existence for a long time, will provide financial support to potential franchisees; however, most franchisors are unable to offer such assistance, and franchisees must seek financing on their own. A prospective franchisee must determine if financial support is available from the franchisor.

The franchisee needs to research sources of potential financial support—family, friends, relatives, and financial organizations, including banks, credit unions, and other lending institutions. The franchisee must determine if he or she will accept debt financing (generally from banks or financial institutions) or equity financing (generally from family, friends, or relatives). The franchisee must also prepare a business plan or feasibility study showing the cost and projected income from the franchising operation. This may be used to show prospective contributors the financial strength and investment potential of the franchised business. When it becomes time to sell or retire, a franchisee should cooperate as best as possible with the parent company. The ultimate sale or closure of the business will, by necessity, involve the franchise parent—whose prime interest is to protect the interests and strengths of the system itself.

Key Terms

Bank term loans: a formal agreement between a bank and the franchisee for the use of a specific sum of money (principal) at a given interest rate for a specific time (term); normally require that portions of both the interest and the principal be repaid on a monthly basis.

Commercial paper: a short-term promissory note which the franchisee signs and sells to an investor, normally for short periods, from 30 to 270 days; because it is difficult for most franchisees to afford, this practice is ordinarily reserved for large corporations with strong financial backing.

Debt financing: borrowing money from banks, other financial institutions, friends, and relatives and paying it back to the lender over time, on an appropriate, affordable repayment schedule.

Equipment lease financing: an arrangement enabling the franchisee to obtain equipment at a lower cost, eliminate risk of ownership, and obtain service and maintenance agreements from the leaser.

Equity financing: selling the ownership of a company to other investors, including yourself, friends, and relatives, and venture capital companies, who receive a share of profits and managerial responsibilities.

Initial franchise fee: an initial lump sum, nonrefundable franchise fee paid by franchisees upon singing the franchise agreement.

Intermediate-term financing: most often used to meet a firm's one- to three-year financing requirements and is frequently used by franchisees undergoing rapid growth.

Inventory loan: a bank loan secured by the company's inventory on hand, generally not available to franchisees.

Limited partnership: a form of partnership including at least one general partner, usually the franchisee, and limited partners whose liability is limited to the amount of capital contributed or the amount of risk they agree to bear; prevents the running or managing of the franchise.

Long-term financing: used to provide funds for the purchase of permanent assets, which may include land, buildings, and certain types of equipment, ordinarily for a period of five to twenty years, and usually by such institutions as insurance companies, pension funds, or the Small Business Administration, or by the issuance of bonds or stocks.

Partnership: a common method of financing in which ownership is shared by one or more partners who may act as agents or representatives of the franchise; in a general partnership, all partners are fully liable for all the debts of the business and may be actively involved in its management.

Short-term financing: borrowing through trade credit, commercial paper, unsecured bank loans, or inventory financing for needs such as the purchase of inventory or specialty sales items to be repaid in less than one year

Trade credit: the most common form of short-term financing; a means by which the franchisee can receive credit from suppliers and/or service companies; the supplier (seller) generally allows the franchisee (buyer) a certain number of days before the bill must be paid.

Unsecured or signature loan: a bank loan for a certain line of credit, a revolving credit agreement, or a transaction loan.

REVIEW QUESTIONS

1. What are the possible financial obligations of a franchisee relative to becoming a franchisee?

2. What general financial arrangements will most franchisors provide new franchisees in their franchised business? Why?

3. What type of financing, debt or equity, is appropriate for a franchisee?

4. Why is a business plan or feasibility study important in developing the financial package of a franchisee?

5. What are the major components of a feasibility study?

6. What are the factors associated with an exit strategy for existing franchisees?

CASE STUDY

A Franchised Dry Cleaning Business

Dry cleaning is a $5 billion industry primarily because the natural fabrics popular today, such as wool and linen, require professional cleaning. For more than five decades, customers have known and trusted franchised dry cleaners for service and quality in cleaning their nonwashable clothing.

Guy and Ardis recently purchased and opened their franchise dry cleaning business. To help select a suitable location, the franchisor used a computerized market evaluation system that included in-depth mapping and demographic studies as well as customer profile reports. This system provided information on the age, gender, family income, occupation, lifestyle, and education of the consumers in the target area. The franchisor also customized the store design and plant layout to ensure efficient workflow and provided a comprehensive training program. The advertising guidelines and programs provided by the franchisor have given Guy and Ardis a strong edge in opening their store and in developing their clientele. They are looking forward to additional promotional and advertising materials that have been designed to generate immediate traffic and build a strong image of the store in the community. They are interested in opening another store as soon as this one becomes successful and they are able to realize a profit.

The total capital required to start the franchise was approximately $300,000. This included the initial franchising fee of $25,000, the cleaning equipment cost of $175,000, and other necessities of opening the business, such as lease improvements, working capital, and miscellaneous expenditures. In addition, the franchisor's regional manager served as liaison between the franchisee and the home office, providing consultation on business plans and operations and updates on services and materials available from the franchisor.

Guy and Ardis are excited about their franchise, but are uncertain about their legal obligations, especially with respect to the franchisor. Can they provide additional services besides those required by the franchisor? Will they have the opportunity to modify their franchising agreement? The term of their franchising agreement was a period of five years, but Guy and Ardis are concerned that the franchisor may be able to terminate the agreement after the franchise has become successful. They are also not sure what they will do with the franchise when they retire. Could they sell the franchise to their children? Additionally, they have leased the land and the building for a ten-year period. They want to find out if this would create a conflict with their five-year franchising agreement.

Source: a compilation of costs and initial agreement from various franchise systems, 2007.

CASE QUESTIONS

1. What are the legal rights of a franchisee?

2. Should Guy and Ardis have their own legal counsel?

3. What legal action should Guy and Ardis take to ensure the continuation of the franchise?

4. How should a franchisee respond to a franchisor with regard to legal matters?

REFERENCES

Bracker, Jeffrey S. and John N. Pearson, "The Impact of Franchising on the Financial Performance of Small Firms," *Journal of the Academy of Marketing Science* 14(4) (Winter 1986): 10–17.

Business Loans and the SBA (Washington, DC: U.S. Small Business Administration, July 1994), FI-0006.

Carey, T. W., "Bean Counting Made Easy," *PC World* 13(9) (September 1995): 164–176.

Carney, M. and E. Gedajlovic, "Vertical Integration in Franchise Systems: Agency Theory and Resource Explanations," *Strategic Management Journal* 12 (1991): 607–629.

Fratrik, Mark R., Ronald N. Lafferty, and Roger D. Blair, "Unanswered Questions about Franchising," *Southern Economic Journal* 51 (January 1985): 927.

Garsson, Robert, "Franchise Program Will Turn a Profit in 1986, First Interstate Chief Says: Acknowledges that Mandatory Name Change Is a Stumbling Block," *American Banker* 149 (28 February 1984): 3.

Gladstone, David J., *Venture Capital Handbook* (Reston, VA: Reston Publishing Company, Inc., 1983).

Horngreen, C. and T. Harrison, *Principles of Accounting*, 2nd ed. (Englewood Cliffs, NJ: Prentice Hall , 1995).

Jones, Constance and The Philip Lief Group, *The 220 Best Franchises to Buy: The Source Book for Evaluating the Best Franchising Opportunities* (New York: Bantam Books, Inc., 1996).

Kaufmann, P. P. and F. Lafontaine, "Costs of Control: The Source of Economic Rents for McDonald's Franchisees," *The Journal of Law and Economics* 37(2) (1994): 417–453.

Lafontaine, F. and P. Kaufmann, "The Evolution of Ownership Patterns in Franchise Systems," *Journal of Retailing* 70(2) (1994): 97–113.

Ossinger, Joanna L., "Closing Time: If You're Ready to Sell Your Franchise, Here's a Look at What You Need to Know," *The Wall Street Journal* (R919 March 2007): R9.

Pollock, Andy, "Sell the Business Format and Grow Bigger," *Accountancy* 98 (October 1986): 90.

"Small Fast-Growth Firms Feel Chill of Shareholder Suits," *The Wall Street Journal* (5 April 1994): B2.

Vassallo, J. J., "Tapping Capital for Small Companies," *Journal of Accountancy* (August 1993): 44–46.

NOTES

1. Logan Farms Honey Glazed Hams (UFOC, 1995), 5.
2. David J. Gladstone, *Venture Capital Handbook* (Reston, VA: Reston Publishing Co., Inc., 1983).

APPENDIX

Finances for Franchisees

Franchise Capital Services, A Division of Federated Capital, is committed to servicing the equipment and leasehold improvement financing needs of established franchise operators. FCS recognizes that brand awareness and franchisor strength are critical to the success of the franchisee.

Heller Financial is still here for C&G, Quick Service Restaurant operators as well as Hotel Financing. With a tight financial market, the demise of securitization lending, and flat same-store sales, many operators today may be without the financing they need for growth—or even to survive.

Brava Capital offers non-SBA financing for start-up franchisees, multiunit operators, and franchise company stores; advances up to 95 percent of project cost, terms to ten years. Each applicant is reviewed on its own merits. The most important criteria is satisfactory personal and business credit and good actual or projected cash flow and reserves.

GMAC Commercial Mortgage specializes in franchise finance, with expertise in the hospitality, restaurant, leisure, and health care industries. They also offer equipment financing for commercial/industrial projects. They offer 100 percent FF&E financing with competitive rates and terms, superior customer service, and the flexibility to structure finance packages to meet the needs of clients. Their experience allows them to consider projections for future cash flow in our underwriting, leading to a higher approval rate, and more money, for qualified borrowers.

AMRESCO's Business Lending Group has a wide range of financing products suitable for franchise business owners. Focusing on small- to medium-sized business, it offers competitive cash flow–based loans that include attractive long-term, fixed, and floating rates and terms up to twenty years. AMRESCO is committed to finding financing solutions to borrower needs such as capital improvements, acquisitions, ownership recapitalization, and cash flow enhancement. Since 1993, AMRESCO has loaned nearly $2 billion to franchises. Borrower requirements include franchisee must be within an AMRESCO Approved Concept; the franchisee must have at least two years of applicable experience with a respectable credit history; and landlords who own property that is used to operate an AMRESCO Approved Concept franchised business are also eligible.

MARKETING THE FRANCHISEE BUSINESS

In studying this chapter, you will:

- **Understand the concepts of marketing.**

- **Know about the history and value of marketing.**

- **Know how to develop a marketing strategy.**

- **Understand the importance of marketing segments.**

- **Learn about the marketing mix and its importance to the franchisee.**

- **Understand the advertising budgeting approaches.**

- **Learn about the use and role of promotion in advertising.**

INCIDENT

Jon and Elisabeth were married recently and have decided to start their own business. Jon is a recent graduate of the university, majoring in computer science. Both Jon and Elisabeth love animals. They have always been desirous of working with animals and developing a special breed of dog.

They have researched different business opportunities extensively and have worked with the local university to determine different opportunities available to them. Both of them have decided that they would like to try to work with a pet care service business. Upon looking around, they have investigated different existing business opportunities and they believe that they would like to become Critter Care franchisees. Elisabeth enjoys the extensive training program which they have described and also has talked to several of the different franchisees who speak highly of the franchisor and their opportunities which they have found in their businesses. Upon further investigation, Jon enjoys the computer system they are developing as well as their recordkeeping and routing systems.

After meeting with the franchisor and reading the appropriate advertising brochures, UFOC, and franchise agreement, they have decided to join the Critter Care family.

The uncertainties of Jon and Elisabeth concern the marketing aspects in their own local community. They live in the South in a fairly large city and would like to develop a strong market in their area. They have seen the wonderful advertisements of the franchisor, and public relations materials developed by a professional firm from Chicago for the franchise. Jon and Elisabeth also realize, however, that they are going to have to work within their own system. They need to know how much they should advertise, how to determine their market segment, and how to grow their market.

17-1 INTRODUCTION

Franchisees are people who desire to go into business for themselves. Thousands of people each year will start their own businesses, but only a few will succeed. While many organizations and individuals spend time investigating the opportunity and the requirements of starting a new business, the entrepreneur is actually opening and developing a new business. The entrepreneur provides the desire, insight, and strong gut feeling, and will place savings and career on the line to start a business.

The franchisee is technically an entrepreneur. The franchisee is the one who will make the final decision whether to start a franchised business. Entrepreneurs will need a cadre of individuals to help them develop, run, and manage the business. They will need to hire people to operate the store and ensure its success. However, the franchisee will take the greatest risk by investing personal savings, leaving a secure job, mortgaging a home, and often locating in a new community to start an operation which, while often highly successful, may be undercapitalized and simply might not succeed.

The franchisee has no new, unique characteristics or traits which will ensure success. There is no stereotypical successful franchisee. Franchisees come with all sorts of personalities, characteristics, and abilities. The entrepreneur is generally hardworking, often technically competent in the endeavor chosen, innovative, creative, a controller, and a doer.

The personality characteristics often associated with successful franchisees as well as other entrepreneurs and small business owners would include ambition, strong self-motivation, ability to think on one's feet, willingness to accept personal responsibility, ability to see the big picture, responsiveness, and stick-to-itiveness. Most franchisees are the independent, self-reliant type rather than the "company-man" type. They prefer innovative rather than routine work patterns and are willing to take moderate risks rather than needing security. Contrary to what some might believe, franchisees are not gamblers. They make a point of minimizing risk before ever starting a business.

Successful franchisees are of all ages and both sexes. Ray Kroc started McDonald's Corporation at age fifty-two and Colonel Harlan Sanders began Kentucky Fried Chicken at the retirement age of sixty-five, whereas J. Willard Marriott began the Marriott empire in his early twenties and Sybil Ferguson was in her early forties when she started the Diet Center franchise system. In fact, as women become a more prevalent force in the business world, they are also taking on and starting more and more successful franchised businesses.

17-2 MARKETING

Marketing affects the franchisor, the franchisee, and consumers. The franchisor, who faces challenges in deciding how to place and sell products, must also examine a number of critical issues. The franchisee wants to offer the right mix to optimize sales, and the consumer wants, of course, a reliable product.

17-2a An Example of Marketing

The effects of marketing may be illustrated through the following example.

The Franchisor

Jim Herzberg is a franchisor who specializes in computer hardware and software. To be effective in his job, he must look at the following major critical issues.

- What is the target market for computer hardware and software?
- What computer hardware do consumers want?
- What should be the pricing structure for different computers?
- What guarantees, warranties, or services should be provided to the consumer?
- What kinds of advertising, personal selling displays, and giveaways should be provided to move the products?
- What kind of design and packaging should be used?

As a franchisor, Jim faces numerous challenges as he tries to decide how to place and sell his product in the market. The computer market can be tricky and often demanding. The franchisor must utilize up-to-the-minute marketing skills and talents to be successful with the consumer and with the franchisee.

The Franchisee

Charlene Babcock, a computer store franchisee, is interested in offering the right mix of computer hardware and software to optimize her store's sales. Charlene sees many computer components and watches closely the products being developed and introduced into the market. She has the following questions to answer.

- Is there a good mix of computers available to sell to the consumer?
- Are the right brand names fairly represented?
- Are the prices competitive and fair?
- Is the sales staff helpful, courteous, and honest?
- Are there sufficient guarantees and warranties on the products?
- Is there sufficient advertising and promotion of the store and its products?
- Does the franchisor provide sufficient marketing assistance for the franchised unit?
- Are there many customers with loyalty to Charlene's franchised outlet?

The Consumer

Ken Spero works in a downtown business and wants to purchase a new personal computer from Charlene's store for his home. Both he and his spouse are interested in using it for personal and business activities. They are looking for word processing and financial software. Ken is specifically interested in finding answers to the following questions.

- Is this a reliable franchised outlet?
- Will this franchisee provide sufficient service and guarantees after I purchase this product?
- Are the brand names reputable?
- Is the hardware exactly what I want, at the right price?
- Are the manufacturers making a high-quality product that I would feel secure in buying?
- Were the salespeople and service people fair and honest in dealing with me?
- Is the advertising fair and honest in its approach?

Ken is concerned about purchasing the right product at an affordable price. He also knows he will need some initial training and help in using the computer system. He hopes that he can take some instructional courses either through the franchise or at the community college. Marketing is an important aspect of the franchisee's business. Most progressive and committed franchisees will address at least four major areas of marketing, either by themselves or with the assistance of the franchisors, which include marketing services, advertising services, field marketing, and marketing research.

17-2b   Marketing Services

The franchisor generally provides marketing services to the franchisee which include essential target market analysis, sales analysis, new product development, and product improvement. Before new products and promotions are developed and introduced to consumers, they must be thoroughly researched and analyzed. Most major franchisors will provide these services to their franchisees because they encourage sales and increase profitability for the franchisees.

The marketing services area should help develop the market and sales forecasting required by the franchise. In addition, a measurement of market demand and a marketing information system will generally be developed. Market plans and market controls will be established for the franchisee. An analysis of the demographic, economic, ecological, technological, political, and cultural environments will often be performed and provided to the franchisee. Market segments will also be developed and analyzed.

17-2c   Advertising Services

Advertising, one of the major activities of a franchised business, is a form of communication which often provides legitimacy to a product or service and frequently encourages buyers to purchase a product. Advertising is often persuasive, expressive, and personal as it attempts to create wants or needs in consumers (see Figure 17-1) and show how these needs may be satisfied through the use of a particular product or service. The three key words most often used in advertising are *free, now,* and *new,* the latter of which may be used to describe a product up to six months after its introduction.

In making an advertising decision, a franchisor or franchisee will focus on five major areas: (1) development of objectives, (2) budget considerations, (3) message development, (4) choice of media, and (5) evaluation of feedback. The primary objectives of advertising are often either to inform, persuade, or remind. Advertising to inform encourages customers to come into the store to purchase some product or service and is generally used during the introductory or growth stages of a business product. Advertising to persuade is often utilized during the maturity stage of a product, and advertising to remind is not used until the declining stages of product sales. To deliver their message effectively, most franchisors will utilize every available advertising method and media, including television, radio, print, billboards, and point-of-purchase displays.

The franchisee should rely heavily on the franchisor's advertising materials. Often a franchisor has already developed materials and advertisements for all the different media. The franchisee needs to work with the franchisor to develop the proper advertising mix and present it to the local consumer markets.

17-2d   Field Marketing

Possibly one of the greatest advantages a franchising organization provides a franchisee is an in-depth field marketing program. Franchisors may divide the country into regions to help provide on-the-spot marketing services for each franchisee. A field marketing representative will often assist the franchisee in analyzing local market situations and conditions. The representative will also recommend advertising and marketing procedures to maximize business opportunities and profits.

Better health.
Greater strength, vigor, endurance; possibility of longer life.

More money.
For spending, saving, or giving to others.

Greater popularity.
Through a more attractive personality or through personal accomplishments.

Improved appearance.
Beauty, style, better physical build, cleanliness.

Security in old age.
Independence; provision for age or adversity.

Praise from others.
For one's intelligence, knowledge, appearance, or other evidence of superiority.

More comfort.
Ease; luxury; self-indulgence; convenience.

More leisure.
For travel, hobbies, rest, play, self-development.

Pride of accomplishment.
Overcoming obstacles and competition; desire to "do things well."

Business advancement.
Better job; success; reward for merit; be your own boss.

Social advancement.
Moving in better circles; social acceptance; "keeping up with the Joneses."

Increased enjoyment.
From entertainment, food, drink, and other physical contacts.

Source: Charles Piper, University of Nebraska, Advertising Department, 1996.

FIGURE **17-1**
Twelve Basic Advertising Appeals

The field marketing representative brings to the franchisee the complete advertising and marketing resources of the franchisor. The franchisor may provide many promotional items which the franchisee can readily use in local media as well as give away or sell to customers. Corporate marketing specialists work with public relations, promotion, and advertising agencies at both national and local levels to help create and implement highly successful marketing programs. The combined power of franchisor and franchisee advertising dollars ensures greater coverage than can be achieved by independent stores.

17-2e   Marketing Research

Almost every franchisee at some time will need marketing research. Marketing research is beneficial to a franchisee, for it helps to determine target markets, advertising successes, promotional activities, repeat customer business, market position of franchise, sales forecasting, sales potential, and product acceptance.

Marketing research can easily be performed by the franchisee alone or in cooperation with the franchisor. Franchisees may develop their own marketing research questionnaires to attempt to determine consumers' preferences and buying behaviors.

A basic marketing research outline might include questionnaire development, market sample design, data collection, and analysis and forecasting. The marketing research questionnaire may be categorized into different themes, which might include:

- Where do consumers go to make purchases?

- Why do they go there?

- Is the pricing fair?

- Are the services and products valuable?

Once several major themes have been developed, three or four questions may be constructed for each theme, including:

- Which convenience food store do you patronize most often?

- What do you consider to be your primary fast-food restaurant—the one from which you buy mostly lunches or the one from which you buy mostly dinners?

- Why do you go to that particular restaurant?

- How does home cleaning business A compare with home cleaning businesses B and C?

- How would you compare a McDonald's advertisement with a Burger King advertisement?

- Have you ever read, seen, or heard any advertisements for restaurant A?

- Can you recall the slogan for restaurant A?

Once the questionnaire has been developed, the franchisee may collect the information in one of three ways—by mail, telephone, or personal interview. Once the information has been collected, the franchisee may simply add the figures and analyze their relevance to the business.

17-2f Franchisor Support

Most franchising agreements require that the franchisee pay a percentage of gross revenues to a national advertising budget. This percentage is often approximately 1 to 5 percent of gross sales, which is placed in a headquarters marketing fund. The advertising fees are divided between national network television buys and local marketing efforts. The local funds are often spent in the local area of dominant influence (ADI) through the combined efforts of local franchisees. (An ADI is a specific television viewing audience.) In many franchising agreements, the franchise headquarters has little discretion over the funds, but most franchising organizations have established marketing franchisee councils which provide input from franchisees on marketing decisions. These councils often determine how advertising funds which have been received by the franchisor will be allocated.

Most franchisor marketing plans are developed annually (see Figure 17-2). Specific programs for regional or local areas are usually developed on a quarterly or monthly basis. In some markets where a franchisee controls the entire franchising population, the franchisee will also oversee local marketing programs. If these programs would deviate from the national campaign, the approval of corporate headquarters is generally required. Many franchisees budget additional funds for local advertising and promotions.

Fiscal 2008
First, Second, Third, Fourth Quarters

Program	JAN 1234	FEB 1234	MAR 12345	APR 1234	MAY 12345	JUNE 12345	JULY 1234	AUG 12345	SEPT 1234	OCT 1234	NOV 12345	DEC 1234
National Program	CHICKEN		BREAKFAST			BIG HAMBURGER			BREAKFAST			TOY
National Program		HAMBURGER		CHICKEN	CHICKEN			99¢ SALE		BIG HAMBURGER	PROM	
National Program			BIG HAMBURGER	BIG HAMBURGER								
Regional Program				BIG HAMBURGER		BREAKFAST		FRIES			CHEESEBURGER	
Regional Program	KIDS' FOOD				CHEESEBURGER				BREAKFAST			
Local Options	KIDS' FOOD	FRIES	KITES	COMBO ORDER	CAMERA PROM			CHICKEN	BIG HAM-BURGER	KIDS PROM	CHEESE-BURGER	
Local Options		BREAK-FAST	CHEESE-BURGER				BACON BURGER					TOY PROM

FIGURE **17-2**

Marketing Calendar

NEW IN FAST-FOOD DELIVERY

A Pittsburg firm, Hyperactive Technologies, has developed a system based on computer vision and artificial intelligence systems to help manage the kitchens at quick service restaurants. The system, known as Hyperactive Bob, scans the parking lot for incoming cars; cross-references traffic patterns against data about the bell curve of orders, time of day, cooking times, and current amount of food in the restaurant's warming bins; and then issues cooking orders to employees manning the grill or deep fryer. Hyperactive Bob combines machine intelligence with human activity. By tightly linking cooking time with incoming traffic, food will get cooked when it is needed, which can increase customer satisfaction. Recent installations of Hyperactive Bob include 115 Zaxby's in the southeastern United States and in pilot systems of Popeye's and Jack in the Box outlets. Carl's Jr. is likely to initiate a pilot program soon.

Based on Michael Kanellos, "For Fast-Food, Call in the Robots," 2 April 2007, httpo:// news.com.com/2102-11394_3-6170097.html?tag-st.lutil.print.

17-2g   Focus Groups

Another marketing practice important to franchisees is the development and use of a focus group, or a target market consumer group, which meets to discuss the advantages and disadvantages of the franchise's marketing and advertising ideas. The focus group consists of individuals who use or purchase the product. The group is generally eight to sixteen people is size and when they meet they ask certain questions about the use and development of advertising relative to the product. The focus group is usually led by a moderator from the franchise who directs the discussion of the group.

The focus group often investigates the major marketing aspects of the business, including the product and its uses, the design or modification of the product, promotion and selling of the product, the advertising timetable, the advertising platform, and the preparation of advertising or ideas concerning advertising. The members of the focus group are asked to express their honest opinions and attitudes about these areas. The outline presented in Figure 17-3 may be used in guiding their discussion.

The advertising platform consists of primary and secondary objectives of the business. The members of the focus group discuss what they believe should be the primary uses of the product and how the product will interest the consumer (see Figure 17-3). In addition, the advertising platform also develops and describes the target audiences, including the primary audience (heavy users) and secondary audiences, and describes the media/selling mix which might be utilized to help promote the product. Major benefits of using the product should also be identified and discussed by the focus group. Secondary and supporting benefits should be enumerated, and the positioning of the business in the marketplace should be discussed as well as how it might be improved to sell more product or service. The focus group should also discuss how to measure the effectiveness of advertisements.

Throughout the discussion of the focus group, ideas are often developed and may even be used as the headline or body of advertising copy or as the slogan line, which is often the tail of the advertising copy. Most of the focus group discussions are recorded so that the ideas generated may be reviewed and used at a later time.

One franchisee asked a group of customers if they would meet one afternoon every three months to discuss the products and services provided by the franchise. The franchisee generally

?		?	*WHO*	1.	Define users.
	?		**WHAT**	2.	Determine what users want.
?	?	?		3.	Discuss design or modification of product.
	?	?	**HOW**	4.	Decide how to promote and sell product.
?	?	?	WHEN	5.	Develop advertising and marketing timetables.
?		?	**HOW MUCH**	6.	Measure effects of advertising and modify as needed.
	?	?		7.	Seek outside help.
?			*WHAT*	8.	Prepare the advertising platform.
?	?		WHAT	9.	Prepare the advertising.

ADVERTISING PLATFORM

Objectives
Target Audiences
Primary Audience (Heavy User)
   Secondary Audience
Media/Selling Mix
Major Benefits
   12 Basic Appeals
   Secondary/Supporting Benefits
Positioning
Measurability

Source: Charles Piper, University of Nebraska, Advertising Department, 1996.

FIGURE 17-3

Focus Groups: Advertising/Promotion

provided food and also a token gift for all participants. This franchisee also met for about an hour each week with the franchisor's staff to discuss promotion and advertising opportunities. The staff got heavily involved in the advertising program and created many of their own advertisements, and they reviewed advertisements from other franchisees, used those that were the best, and discarded the others. The franchise system made a twofold increase in profits during the first year that focus groups were used.

17-3 MARKETING STRATEGY

The process of managing the marketing side of the franchise business is generally referred to as marketing strategy. This generally begins with a complete analysis of the company situation and is basically divided into four parts: analysis, marketing planning, implementation, and control. The total development of the marketing strategy will therefore develop into a useful marketing plan which can be implemented and controlled throughout the operation of the franchise.

MARKETING STRATEGY

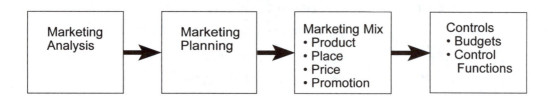

17-3a   Marketing Analysis

It is first best to develop an analysis of the business. This would consist of analyzing the current market situation and would review all relevant background data concerning the market, product, competition, and distribution systems. In addition, an analysis should be undertaken, identifying the firm's strengths, weaknesses, opportunities, and threats (SWOT analysis). Here the main strengths of the businesses will be listed along with the weaknesses. In addition, the threats and opportunities surrounding the business should also be analyzed. The marketing analysis will gather the information which needs to be used as inputs for each of the other planning, implementation, and control functions.

FEDEX KINK'S TESTING EXPANSION OF OFFICE SUPPLY CONCEPT

In Missouri and Florida, FedEx Kinko's is testing a retail format that converts its normal 6,000-square-foot stores into places where a customer can make copies, get signs made, send a package, and shop for a wide array of office supplies. Dallas-based FedEx Kinko's has overhauled twenty stores in the Orlando and St. Louis markets. At test stores, customers will find a Wi-Fi Bar, purple shopping carts, and retail sales personnel across the sales floor. There are upgraded shipping counters as well. The office supply retail business has been dominated by giants such as Staples, which has 1,800 big box stores, and Office Depot, which has over 1,000 locations in the United States alone. Now, FexEx Kinkos' is positioning itself to become a significant retail player as well.

Based on Sandra Zaragoza, "FedEx Kinko's Takes Aim at Big-box Suppliers," Dallas Business Journal *(2 October 2006).*

17-3b   Marketing Planning

It is now that the franchisee needs to decide what to do with the business. The plan will detail those activities and events that will help the company obtain the overall strategic choices of the franchisee. The marketing plan will generally contain the following sections: (1) executive summary; (2) mission, goals, and objectives; (3) products and/or services; (4) location/place; (5) price and pricing strategy; (6) promotion, advertising, personal selling, sales promotion, and publicity; (7) budgets; and (8) controls.

The executive summary will be a short summary of the main goals and recommendations of the plan. This will help the management understand the major points and objectives of the business and will focus management on the specifics of developing the franchising organization.

The mission statement will contain the overall vision of the business followed by the goals and objectives of the business. The operational objectives of the business need to contain three specific parts: definition of objective, quantity, and time frame. For instance, the objective may be to have

Product	Place	Price	Promotion
Quality	Site location	List prices	Sales promotion
Features	Access/egress	Credit terms	Advertising
Services	Zoning	Costs	Personal selling
Assortment	Lighting	Margins	Publicity
Brand	Suppliers	Discounts	Media
Packaging	Storage	Returns	Training
Warranties	Transportation	Markups	Costs
Guarantees	Logistics	Skimming/penetration	Layout

FIGURE **17-4**

Franchisee Marketing Mix Variables

$42,000 in sales for each of the first and second months that the store is open. The definable objective is sales, the quantity measured is $42,000, and the time frame is each of the first and second months after the store is opened.

The products and/or services discussion needs to include the quality, variety, features, packaging, sizes and services, returns, and warranties that are being offered (see Figure 17-4). These aspects need to be well defined and developed before the business is opened.

The place or location is important because of the local customers and the nearby transportation, distribution channels, maintaining inventory levels, and coverage of the target market. The pricing decision is important because a price list needs to be developed and, in addition, the franchisee needs to understand any discounts, credit terms, payment periods, or allowances which will be granted. The franchisee also needs to know the cost of the products and/or services which will be provided.

The promotion aspects the franchisee needs to be aware of include the advertising, personal selling, sales promotion, and publicity used to enhance its sales and invite customers into the store. It should be remembered that advertising generally works well to draw the customer into the store, but it is the quality of product and service which generally draws the customer back.

The budgets need to be developed by the franchisee to determine the cash flow needs of the business as well as forecast the profit and loss for the store. The franchisee needs to be well aware of all the financial commitments involved in promoting the products and choosing the right location, and in making the proper pricing decisions.

The control function describes how the progress of the plan is going to be monitored. This generally includes measuring results of sales as well as the cost of goods sold and labor costs. The results need to be tabulated and any corrective action needs to be able to be performed. The control system should identify to the franchisee any need for change in the current operation.

17-4   MARKET SEGMENTS

Even if the demand for the product or service looks good, there is a need to determine which groups of customers or which segments of the community might be the best purchasers of the franchise's goods or services. We can group customers in different ways based on the following:

GEOGRAPHIC FACTORS	cities, counties, regions, neighborhoods
DEMOGRAPHIC FACTORS	age, sex, education, income
PSYCHOGRAPHIC FACTORS	social classes or lifestyles
BEHAVIORAL FACTORS	including usage rates, frequencies, purchasing occasions, and benefits desired

As defined in Chapter 6, a *market segment* is a grouping of customers who will respond similarly to a given set of marketing promotions. For instance, some customers care mainly about price and therefore would have a desire to purchase the hamburger from McDonald's rather than from Chili's. (See also "Franchisee's Market Segment/Service Area" in section 17-6.)

THE "I'M LOVING IT" NEXT-GENERATION PROGRAM

Mary Dillon, executive vice president and global head of marketing for McDonald's, has introduced McDonald's to YouTube, Webisodes (short Web-based episodes), cell phone text messaging in Japan, and podcasts—all places where the "young adult" and those who consider themselves "forever young" now can be found. She is tweaking how McDonald's gets its message to customers by crafting campaigns for the Internet, mobile phones, and other alternative outlets. She has shifted the focus of the "I'm Loving It" slogan to "I'm at the Beginning of It" at the end of the slogan to bring attention to McDonald's increasingly healthful menu items.

Based on John Schmeltzer, "McDonald's Next Generation Marketing Chief Mary Dillon Has Introduced the Once-conventional Fast-food Giant to YouTube, Podcasts," Chicago Tribune, 25 March 2007, www.chicagotribune.com/business/chi-0703230619.

17-5   TARGET MARKETS

The target market is involved with evaluating each market segment and selecting one or more segments for entry. For example, McDonald's has chosen as their primary target market children ages three to eleven years. A large part of the McDonald's promotional budget is spent on inviting children to come and eat at their restaurant. Most all parents with young children understand the success of this advertising when they ask their kids where they would like to go out to eat dinner that evening. Often the loud cry resounds throughout the home in a single word: "McDonald's!"

Casual dining places such as Applebee's, Chili's, or Jason's Deli have evolved primarily with adults as their main target market. These companies, rather than seeking families as their main clients, are trying to entice the businesspeople and other adults as they seat their evening meals.

LONG ISLAND, NEW YORK, TARGETED BY NATIONAL FRANCHISES

Familiar franchise system names are ramping up their numbers in Long Island, and new chains plan to open first locations there in the spring of 2007. Newcomers include Fantastic Sams hair salons and Saladworks, with hope to open about a dozen locations. Fatburger opens its first Long Island location in late spring 2007. According to FranNet information, Long Island is probably one of the biggest markets where franchise systems are looking.

Based on Carrie Mason-Draffen, "National Franchises Targeting Long Island," 2 April 2007, www.newswday.com/business/ny-bzfran0328,0,307891.

17-6 FRANCHISOR MARKETING SUPPORT SYSTEMS

Most franchisors have developed through the ages a system of providing marketing services for the franchisees. These services generally include: grand opening packages, continuous advertising support, and other marketing and promotional items.

Many franchisors have developed a system of grand opening procedures for their franchisees. This often includes prepared articles for distribution to the local newspapers and local business magazines. In addition, there is often a set grand opening tradition which includes ribbon cutting as well as providing samples to early customers. In addition, banners, flyers, brochures, and newspaper advertisements are also included. Often, a yellow page advertisement is provided in different sizes for different localities.

The franchisor may often supply additional advertising which may be used by the franchisee at their discretion. (See Figure 17-5.) The largest franchisors will generally provide a yearly advertising package which includes national, regional, and even local television advertisements. They will send out suggestions for local advertising based on their national or regional advertising programs. This will also include specials that are associated with movies, sporting events, or special holiday seasons. McDonald's has a long-term contract with Disney to provide distribution through the McDonald's restaurants for figurines and products related to Disney movies. Prior to McDonald's, Burger King had a three-year contract with Disney to provide the same materials. Most franchisees strongly prefer this type of endorsement procedure because they have learned that many customers bring their families to purchase these knick-knacks for their children and, at the same time, purchase food for themselves.

The advertising for smaller franchisors often includes suggestions for direct marketing, newspaper advertisements, yellow page advertisements, and on some occasions, billboard advertisements. Most newer franchisors will not spend the time or the money to develop television advertising because of the excessive costs associated with such development.

Other marketing techniques that some franchisors will provide include the development of clothing items, t-shirts, caps, and jackets which bear the logo and name of the franchisor. Many franchisors also invite local franchisees to support sporting events in the area, including sponsoring youth football, soccer, and baseball teams.

To Inform	To Persuade	To Remind
Tell the market about a new product/service	Build brand loyalty	Remind customers that the product may be desired in future
Describe available products/services	Encourage buyers to purchase now	Keep the product in the mind of the customers
Explain how the product works	Change buyers perceptions	Maintain top-of-the-mind awareness
Suggest new uses of the product	Encourage buyers to switch to our brand	Remind buyers that the product will soon be discontinued
Build the image of the company	Show need satisfaction	Remind buyers that the sale will soon be over

FIGURE **17-5**

Advertising Objectives

Franchisees should learn from their franchisors all the marketing and advertising tools which are available to them. These are generally provided to the franchisees at cost and the franchisee can use these for the development of their local businesses.

17-6a   Marketing by the Franchisee

As a franchisee, one does not have to be artsy or a creative type. The franchisor is responsible for most, if not all, of the new and developmental approaches to marketing the franchise brand and products/services. The franchisor will initiate and implement regional and/or national marketing campaigns for the franchise network and provide a wealth of marketing materials for franchisees' use at the local level.

Basically, marketing of franchised products and services can be divided into the national or regional level and the local level. As mentioned, the franchisor charges an advertising fee, often based on sales revenues, from each franchisee to assist in the development and implementation of regional and national marketing advertising themes. Some franchise systems charge the franchisee a set dollar amount based on the sales transaction—without regard to the dollar amount of the sale. Others may have a sliding percentage scale based on revenue levels by month, quarter, or year. For example, a professional business services franchise system charges its franchisees 1.5 percent of gross sales with a minimum of $500 per month regardless of how low the sales volume may be, but also has a maximum of $2,750 regardless of the monthly sales volume.

A survey of the membership of the International Franchise Association was conducted to determine franchise systems' approach to advertising. From the 570 respondents to the survey, the following results were tabulated,[1]

- Of the responding franchise systems, 27 percent require no advertising fee.

- Almost 17 percent of the respondents require a regional or local advertising fee.

- Nearly one-half (49 percent) require a national advertising fund, supported by fees from franchisees.

- About 70 percent (405 respondents) charge a fee ranging from 0.10 percent to 2 percent.

- About 3 percent have an advertising fee in excess of 5 percent.

Ideally, franchisees should have input into the decision-making process that determines the regional and/or national marketing campaigns. Sometimes it is the Franchisee Advisory Council (FAC) of a franchise system that serves this purpose. Some franchise systems have developed a separate committee or council to provide advice and counsel for the national or regional marketing campaigns while others seek no input from franchisees.

Be cautious. Look for assurance from the franchisor that the franchisees are getting value for their advertising fees paid. A franchise system should use the advertising fees collected only for the purpose of funding the advertising/marketing functions of the franchise system. Typically, the advertising fund can be used to not only market the brand, trademarks, products/services to the general public, but also to market the franchise system to potential franchisees. Often franchisor's charge the administrative costs of franchisee recruitment to the advertising fund. Franchisees should become knowledgeable of the amount and kinds of charges made by the franchisor to the advertising fund. Also, franchisees should find out if company-owned franchise locations contribute to the advertising fund, and whether corporate locations contribute on the same basis that the franchisees contribute to the fund. Some franchise systems have a different approach to the advertising fee for corporate locations than for franchisee locations. Read your franchise agreement.

Franchisees may want to develop a checklist with regard to the regional-to-national advertising fund that may contain questions such as the following:

- Do franchisee-owned and corporate-owned locations contribute equally (on the exact same basis) to the advertising fund?

- How much are franchisees required to spend on advertising? Do I understand the formula?

- How much is a franchisee required to spend on advertising locally in addition to the national advertising fund?

- What proportion of the advertising fund is allocated to getting new customers? To getting new franchisees? Does the franchisor contribute to the fund? On what basis? What results (transactions and/or sales revenues) at the local level can be attributed to the advertising fund?

- Can the franchisor unilaterally change the contribution requirements to the fund?

- Is there separate accounting of the advertising fund? Does the franchisor provide a statement of sources and uses of funds? Is the fund audited? Is the audited statement available to franchisees?

- How often do new marketing (or advertising) campaigns appear? Have the campaigns proven to be effective for increasing sales revenues at the local level?

- Does the franchisor provide marketing materials to franchisees that logically and reasonably "tie in" local advertising efforts with national campaigns?

- Must the franchisor approve a franchisee's local advertising plans and materials?

- Does the franchisor expect the individual franchisees to create all advertising materials and conduct marketing campaigns?

- What are the plans for future marketing campaigns by the franchise system? When are franchisees informed? Do franchisees have the right of advice and consent for future campaigns?

Keep in mind, the advertising fund and the approach to determine the fee structure are set up primarily to help the franchise system. An individual franchisee location may or may not benefit to the same degree that other franchisees may benefit or that the franchise system itself benefits from its advertising and marketing campaigns. As indicated in the IFA survey, one of four franchise systems (actually 27 percent) does not require an advertising fee. As a result, the primary, perhaps sole, responsibility for marketing the franchise brand of products or services is in the hands of the individual franchisees at the local level.

Local Marketing

Many franchise chains are of insufficient size or revenue base to run national, or even regional, marketing campaigns. They may not have enough units. The units may be too thinly spread to achieve economy of scope through mass media advertising and promotions. Or, they may be too new to afford to fund regional or national advertising campaigns. If a franchise system is too small, too new, or too thinly spread geographically to effectively utilize regional or national advertising, an individual franchisees still can utilize those media on a local basis. Additionally, in the future, the franchise system may have sufficient growth and development to implement regional or nationally scoped media buys.

Typical to franchise systems as described previously, the franchisor may require, or at minimum recommend, that each franchisee provide a certain level of advertising expenditure. Some franchise systems provide for advertising cooperatives at local levels for the pooling of resources of several, or more, franchisees in order to afford TV, radio, print, and other means of local advertising on a cost-effective basis.

If the franchisor does not provide for brand recognition, why should the individual franchisee do it? Consider, if four independent franchisees within the same city of 80,000 population "do their own thing" when advertising in different media with different types of promotions in different ways, the overall effect can be not only confusing to the target customer group but also not cost effective. The wise franchisor will help the local franchisees to cooperate locally so that the targeted customer group gets the same message in a consistent manner. Franchisors that help out at the local level realize that the independent franchisees know their community and their particular customer base better than the franchisor does.

The Franchisee's Market Segment/Service Area

Perhaps the most important decision that a franchise company makes is choosing the customer category it wishes to target to provide its products and services. Successful franchise systems have carefully developed a composite profile of the targeted customer group. A franchise system that has not developed a vision of what it wants to be and who is the desired customer is not likely to have control over the competitive forces that shape its business activity. In other words, if a franchise system tries to be all things to all people, it is not a business in the true sense of the word, because that franchise system has failed to define itself and its product/market scope and approach.

RING UP THE PROFITS AT THE GYM

There are at least twenty-four different fitness concepts available as franchises amoung the IFA's membership. Since 2000, interest in health and fitness has exploded; the number of health and fitness clubs has reached an all-time high of 27,000 in 2007.

Based on Darrell Smith, "Ringing Up Gym Profit," Sacramento Bee, *27 March 2007,* www.sacbee.com/103/v-p0rint/story/142532.html.

A franchise system will have a rationale provided to its franchisees to support why local franchisees should mass market the product and service or market to a segment of the overall market. **Market segmentation** is a process by which a franchise system divides a large market into smaller groupings or clusters of customers who have similar characteristics. Most franchise systems are apt to use a market segmentation approach, because not all people in the market may qualify or be interested in buying the product or service offered, nor can the franchise system satisfy every kind of customer want or need. Therefore, most franchise systems target those segments, or a single segment of the market, which they can serve most successfully. If the franchise company does not have a clear, comprehensive profile of the firm's primary customer group or groups, the franchisee is not likely to attract a sufficient customer base to have the franchised unit survive. There are five steps that must take place sometime in order to complete a market segmentation process (see Figure 17-6).

Step	Activity
1.	Define and analyze the market.
2.	Identify and describe potential segment(s).
3.	Choose the segment(s) the firm can serve most successfully.
4.	Determine the product/service positioning strategy.
5.	Develop and implement the marketing program.

FIGURE **17-6**

Market Segmentation Process

Before a market can be analyzed, its constraints or parameters must be determined and linked directly to the franchise system's overall mission and business definition. Markets can be defined either by type of *customers, product and service, geography,* or *location*. Once the boundaries are determined, the market size and growth rate, extent of competition in the environment and other factors such as government regulation, overall economic condition, power of suppliers, and so forth, should be determined. The firm should define the market in sufficiently narrow terms to create a focused market strategy for the market segment targeted, or for each of the market segments the firm intends to target.

MARKET SEGMENTATION: HISPANICS/BLACKS

In 2007, the buying power of Hispanics is expected to reach $863 billion, surpassing Black buying power of $847 billion in the United States.

Based on Marc Diener, "Deal Power," Entrepreneur (December 2006): 98.

Customer types should be aggregated into homogeneous groupings and a profile developed for each type of customer group to be targeted. The attractiveness of each customer segment should be evaluated and potential market segments ranked in terms of their desirability and likelihood of the firm's success to meet the wants and needs of each specific segment under analysis. Often, secondary data, interviews, observation, customer surveys, and/or focus groups may be needed in order to acquire sufficient relevant information about each potential market segment to make a wise business decision.

"BIG MOVES"

In Dayton, Ohio, Tom Peebles has build his local storage franchise into quite the successful operation. He recently opened a new warehouse for his Portable on Demand Storage (PODS) units in nearby West Carrollton. As more and more consumers use PODS for short-term storage or for moving, PODS is increasing its number of franchisees nationwide to keep up with rising demand. Peebles's company is projected to over $20 million in sales just from the franchises it owns in Chicago and in Ft. Lauderdale and Tampa, Florida. The service industry is ripe for franchising, as such franchises can offer low start-up costs and a speedy return on initial investment.

Adapted from M. Fowler, "Big Moves," Dayton Business Journal, 5 May 2003, www.dayton.bcentral.com.

Since products or services and markets are so closely linked, it is crucial for the franchise organization to define what constitutes the best "fit" 'between the products and services and the wants and needs of the specific market segment targeted. What product and service features are most desired by customers in the market segment? How important is price? Is price the dominating factor in making choice, or secondary? How important is convenience? How important is speed and service in delivery? Is a warranty or guarantee important? To what degree? The answers to these questions will help determine how the franchise should position its product or service with regard to competitor offerings in the market segment.

Once positioning factors are known, the tactical marketing plan can be developed and objectives determined for the marketing program. The marketing mix should be carefully examined so that a consistent positioning strategy can be implemented (see Figure 17-7). Once implemented,

Position by Product Attribute (e.g., a lighter or lower calorie beer)

Position on Quality (e.g., "at Ford, Quality is Job One.")

Position by Product User (e.g., "This is a family place.")

Position by Use or Application (e.g., "best" hair designs for men)

Position vs. Competitors (e.g., "As no. two, we try harder.")

Position by Price (e.g., Rolls Royce automobile, or movie rentals: two for $1 with kids' movies rented free)

Position by Benefit, Identity, or Needs (e.g., a franchised bank system positioning to attract Korean Americans)

FIGURE **17-7**

Key Factors for Product and Service Positioning

- **Wear your nametag** wherever you go. Let your nametag be a free advertisement for you and your business.

- **Always ask your customers how they heard of your business.** Keep a tally sheet or categorized "scorecard" next to the register and by the telephone. This helps the franchisee learn which advertisements and promotions are working for you.

- **Accept competitor coupons.** Don't tell your customers they entered the *wrong* store or reached the *wrong* service supplier; instead let them know they came to the *right* store for the product or service. Also, you are positioning yourself to introduce your service to a new customer while *not* giving them a reason to visit your competitors.

- **Conduct frequent informal marketing surveys.** Ask regular, as well as irregular, customers how they heard of your business. Use tally sheets with day and date. Notice purchase patterns of regulars and *irregular* customers. Noting such data by date and time of day is vital market information.

FIGURE **17-8**

Free (Almost) to Promote Your Franchised Business
Source: Adapted from Barbara Janszen, "FREE Ways to Promote Your Business," *Centercourt* (San Diego: IFX International Inc., January 2003), 2.

---

the marketing strategy should be monitored, controlled, and evaluated to see if the strategy achieves the planned objectives (see Figure 17-8).

Local Marketing

In the development of a local marketing campaign, the most important factor is the determination of what communication goals the individual franchisee is trying to achieve. In franchising, the core ingredient or value is the brand, trademark, and logo. The key is to communicate the value of the product or service through a single or varied means of communication to influence the attitudes and behavior of the targeted customer group. To assess the effectiveness of a local marketing campaign, the individual franchisees must determine the method that will be used to manage the demand that results from the marketing effort and monitor the sales transactions and total volume. Ultimately, the purpose of a **marketing communication** is to differentiate the franchisee's products and services from those of the competition and to enhance the brand's position in the local marketplace (see Figure 17-9).

When a franchisee starts to implement a local marketing campaign, start with the franchisor. Often, franchisors will help franchisees by providing demographic profiles of known market segment customer groups and promotional materials or approaches that have proven to work well at other franchisee locations. In fact, many franchisors prepare promotional and advertising materials specifically for franchisee use, such as point-of-sale materials, print media advertising

Influence customer attitudes and behavior by

  I. Providing information that will

  II. Build franchise brand equity/quality/value that

  III. Communicates product/service differences/characteristics, in ways that will satisfy customer wants and needs, and

  IV. Enhance brand and franchisee unit position in contrast to the competition while Effectively managing the product/service demand and sales volume.

FIGURE **17-9**

Franchisee Marketing Communication Goals

layouts, model direct mail pieces, public relations kits, and coupons that can be modified to fit the conditions or customer grouping at the local level. Today, many of these materials are sent to the franchisee by CD-ROM, the Internet, or the franchise system's intranet.

Not always will the advertising or promotional materials fit the local franchisee's needs with precision. For example, suppose the product featured in a specific national promotion lacks local demand, or the approach (e.g., television and radio) has failed to work well with a particular franchisee's customer base. In these types of situations, sometimes the franchise system will allow the franchisee to put his own creative juices to work, concocting whatever it is that the franchisee believes will effectively attract customers within the primary targeted customer groups. The crucial factor for determining what approach to use in reaching the customer is *knowing the customer*. For example, a master franchisee (nine units) located in a midwestern city with a sales marketing area of 220,000 population has determined that direct mail and on-the-counter coupons have proven to be more effective in increasing demand for a specific sandwich than radio or TV advertising. At the national level, the franchise system has found that TV advertising has been most effective for the majority of its franchisees and company stores; but, sometimes local conditions or specific customer demographics and needs can vary significantly enough that, a franchisee may be allowed to utilize a different approach to attract customers to the specific promotion product or service.

17-6b   Evaluation of a Specific Sales Promotion

Often, promotions are run and specific sales weekends or days take place, but the franchisee may be clueless as to the impact the promotion has on total revenue or toward increasing number of sales transactions. Is there a simple way to measure the impact of a specific promotion's communication costs with regard to the sales generated? Yes. Following is a simple and understandable means for franchisees to measure the impact or effect of a specific promotion. The concept is known as **communications elasticity**. The Specific Promotional Communication (SPC) is measured by *the change in sales volume for each 1 percent change in total marketing communications effort applied to the specific promotion.*

Sales Change ($ and/or # of transactions)   =   **Current volume of sales ($ and/or #s)**

                                                  X

                                                  Percent change in the marketing communications effort for the specific promotion being evaluated

                                                  X

                                                  Product (or Service) price

Suppose that a 1 percent change in the marketing communications effort produces a 12 percent change in volume, as determined by the forgoing formula. It is likely that the franchisee would be willing to run that specific promotion or one similar to it in the future.

Let's take another example. A franchised home cleaning service that steam-cleans carpeting, rugs, and padded furniture has a standard price for cleaning three rooms of carpeting at $139. Assume the average total sales for the past twelve months for this specific service was $8,757 in sales revenue per month. This amount of revenue and number of clients served (sixty-three) on this type of cleaning project is normal for a month. A special direct mail promotion is made to all households that had purchased this service in the last six months to four years to remind them of this service and to urge them to call for an appointment to have their carpets cleaned. The direct mail promotion cost is $350, and 3,750 households were contacted. What would be the cost per household? Can the impact of the promotion be measured?

Over the next two months, the number of transactions for this specific type of service was tabulated and compared to the average number of three-room cleaning services performed in a typical month. The two monthly sales levels reached seventy-eight transactions in month 1 and sixty-nine transactions in month 2. Assuming there was no prior sales promotion for this service, the communications elasticity can be measured using the following formula.

$$\text{Sales change} = 78 + 69 = 147 \text{ transactions} \times \$139.00 = \$20,433.00 \text{ total sales}$$
$$\text{Standard sales} = 63 + 63 = 126 \text{ transactions} \times \$139.00 = \$17,514.00 \text{ total sales}$$

Because this measurement period was two months, the totals for sales change and standard sales would be divided in half to get an average monthly figure, as follows:

Sales change level = 147/2 = 73.5 transactions/month × $139.00 = $10,216.50

Standard sales level = 63 transactions with total revenues of   8,757.00

Total increase in revenue for each month evaluated   = $1,459.50

The price of the promotion ($350) / $ 1,459.50 = 24 percent

Thus, for each $1 spent on the promotion, the franchisee got a net increase of just over $3. Was the cost of the promotion worth the cost? Yes, it appears to be so.

Let's consider a different marketing communications problem. Perhaps the most often asked question is, "How effective is my advertising dollar in bringing customers in to purchase my products/services?" Franchise systems of national scope often develop what is often called a **consumer response index (CRI)**, which represents the changes in customer awareness of advertisements, their comprehension of advertising copy content, and interest or conviction that can measure overall customer response. The formula is calculated as follows:

CRI = % aware × % comprehending × % showing interest × % intending to buy × % purchasing

Let's assume that a hardware store franchisee contracted for a thirty-second radio spot that would run five times per day on a random rotation basis for thirty days on a local radio station. The awareness of the advertisement was calculated to be 60 percent; comprehension of the ad was calculated at 51 percent; interest in the specific product promotion (a set of wrenches and screw drivers at 20 percent off) was found to be 75 percent; the intention to purchase was determined to be 65 percent; and the actual purchase of the promoted wrench and screwdriver set was at 80 percent. The CRI would be calculated as follows:

CRI = 0.60 × 0.51 × 0.75 × 0.65 × 0.80 = 0.119 or 11.9 percent

The impact of the advertisement is likely to have had a specific customer response rate of almost 12 percent. Let's assume that the rate of purchase response for the price of the advertisement is deemed inadequate by the franchisee. The franchisee indicates little or no interest in advertisements that do not generate, say, at least a 20 percent increase over the normal level of purchases for the product or service. The media firm (whether radio, television, newspaper, direct mailer, or website) could review the message, form of delivery, and results and come back to the franchisee with a counteroffer. Let's suggest that the media firm believes it can increase comprehension by modifying the advertisement with a mix of reasons why the wrench/screwdriver set is an excellent buy. Assume that the radio station believes it can increase comprehension to 66 percent instead of 51 percent Would that change be sufficient for the franchisee to buy another round of advertisement? Let's see.

$$CRI = 0.60 \times 0.66 \times 0.75 \times 0.65 \times 0.80 = 0.193 \text{ or } 19.3 \text{ percent}$$

Perhaps the increase would be sufficient to entice the franchisee to buy another month's advertisement, or perhaps not. The percentage increase to 19.3 percent is near but does not equal or exceed the minimum expectation (20 percent) set by the franchisee. Both of the formulae provided are used extensively within the franchise industry and advertising agencies to determine communications elasticity and advertisement effectiveness.

17-6c   Buying Local Media Advertisement

Obviously, media companies will promote their own media as the best form of advertising. But which one is the best? The best is the one that works. A franchised hand tools firm found that they could make their point to potential customers best by using outdoor billboards and radio rather than by television and newsprint. Some restaurant franchise systems believe television is the most effective. Others say newsprint with a coupon is best. Yet, others swear by direct mail. Some see the Internet as the best media, particularly for attracting potential franchisees.

Basically, a franchisee should ask the question: "What am I trying to accomplish with the advertisement?" If the franchisee wants to maximize the number of exposures to the brand or a specific product, use multiple media. This approach gives the franchisee and franchise system the possibility of more "points of influence" on the potential customer, provides variety in exposure to avoid the losing customer interest, and reinforces the central theme of the message.

> The ultimate objective of a marketing campaign aimed at the consumer is to create brand loyalty. A franchise system wants customers to remain loyal to the franchise system—and even at a specific franchised location—no matter what price your competitors offer them, nor what product substitutes they offer, and no matter what services they offer.

More than radio, television, and newspapers work to get the message out to consumers. For example, franchise systems have been known to effectively use aircraft (Goodyear, Budweiser), t-shirts (Coke), calendars (most auto franchises), transit buses (Hardees), ball hats (Miller beer), flags (Re/Max), and other approaches to communicate a brand, trademark, logo, or product or service.

Television

The central question for a franchisee is: What programs provide the best audience for your advertisement or promotion? Should the franchisee advertise on a local independent or a network station? On cable? Should the ad by run during prime time, late night, afternoons, evenings, or all the time? Often the franchisor can help by providing demographic information that has been learned about the customer on a district, regional, or national basis. These demographics are a big help for the local franchisee in determining which time slots to use. The local TV stations will gladly provide advice, given their experience with your industry and products or services, as to how the franchisee should use the advertising dollar to most effectively reach customers.

What about the message style? Should it be factual, or emotional, or humorous? Should it be youthful? Should it be shown in a real-life setting, as a hard-nosed brand comparison, or be authoritative? There is no one or best answer, but studies by media consultants and marketers have found that the following styles seem to work well.

- Humor will sell.

- Celebrity spokespersons make good endorsements.

- Direct brand comparisons work by product feature and/or price.

- Commercials with children and perhaps their parents show success.

- Real-life, believable situations create a truthful sales pitch.

Radio

When choosing radio to send the message, the franchisee has three things to utilize: music, sound effects, and words. From these three sources, the mental image that the franchisee wants to portray to the listener must be developed. Radio is a favorite for many retailers. It has proven to have good "pull" because of its broad reach. Tips to remember include:

- Stick with one idea.

- Get to your target listener at the start of your ad (e.g., "Do you need a haircut?")

- Engage the listener's imagination. A mental picture is a must.

- Mention your brand and/or product name early and often. For some franchisees, particularly business services, the telephone number could be important also.

- Use background sound effects carefully. Don't confuse the listener.

Outdoor Advertising

Banners, flags, signs, posters, bumper stickers, transit bus flats, t-shirts, ball hats, and billboards fit the category of outdoor advertising. These examples can serve as powerful media when designed appropriately and provide the information desired to be delivered. This kind of advertising can do the following:

- Build brand or product image.

- Provide helpful information.

- Direct potential customers to the franchisee/location.

- Be a reminder of a good product/service delivered.

Newsprint

Most franchise systems budget a sizable amount, if not the largest amount, for print advertising. The exception is the major franchise systems and corporate chains of national and international scope that primarily use television. For most local, area-wide, and regional marketing exposures, print advertising is often considered the most affordable, flexible, and effective advertising medium. Direct response advertisements seem to be particularly effective. A direct response ad is one that asks the reader to take an action or make a response to the ad (e.g., come in with coupon, call for information, give contact information for a contest entry form).

Public Relations/Publicity/Special Events

A special event is anything that draws attention to the franchisee and the branded products and services, by drawing attention to the franchise first. For example, a franchisee of United Van Lines contracted to bring Peter, Paul and Mary in for a free concert held at the public park in a midwestern city of 100,000 people. The newspaper, radio stations, and TV channels carried information about this special event prior to, during, and following the concert. The franchisee got considerably more "advertising" for his moving services firm by sponsoring this popular singing team than could have ever been purchased across the three major media in his town for the price he paid.

Public relations is meant to seek publicity for marketing purposes. To get publicity, the story you have to tell, generally, will need to answer either of these two broad questions: Is the business story entertaining? (Most are not.) Or, is the story truly newsworthy? Events that are not considered "news" are those stories that seem to be *old* stories (that journalists have covered before), that provide *your version* of why your products or services are so good, that identify a new product and how it differs from the competition, or that are self-serving, boring, or inconsequential to the general public.

When looking to get publicity for the local franchisee firm and products/services, the key to remember is *product quality*. The two primary reasons why a journalist or radio or TV commentator would create a news story is your product or service is (1) sufficiently unique to warrant a story for the general public, and (2) is better or worse than expected. The best way to get publicity for your business is to truly provide a superior product and service. The best way to get a negative story is to have something bad happen. That will be covered immediately, perhaps intensively.

Word of Mouth

When customers talk, potential customers listen. Remember, word of mouth is the most credible form of advertising you can get. The personal experience of one customer talking about your product or service to another person has a huge impact on attraction of new customers. A franchisee cannot control what a customer will say about the franchised product or service; however, there are some ways that a franchisee can seek to influence the word-of-mouth communications that will take place. First, use exciting on-site displays and creative media advertisements. For example, sweepstakes, premiums, and contests often draw special attention and can create positive word-of-mouth exposure. Second, be sure to make your product or service truly special. Make it clearly the "best in class." Unexpected high quality is worth talking about. Third, do something good for the local community, that is, socially responsible acts that are out of the ordinary, not expected, and will draw attention to your firm. The United Van Lines event is a classic example of this. Buying a swingset for the public park's playground, sponsoring an amateur production performed by local actors and actresses, providing alcohol-free refreshments at the after-prom event, and other such promotions, can draw significant and positive word-of-mouth advertising for the franchised business.

MARKETING TRENDS TO WATCH FOR IN 2008–2010

- For college grads: move your marketing dollars into online media.

- Affluence of working women: increasing in size. The best way to reach them may be online. Working women with family income of $75,000 or more are growing in number and 94 percent access the Internet with about one-half being heavy users of the Internet.

- Asian population: represent a prospect group with higher than average household incomes and education levels.

- Simultaneous media usage. There is no such thing as a captive media audience—many are participating in more than one form of media at any one time. For example, nearly 66 percent watch television while reading and over 50 percent listen to the radio while reading.

- Online research is having a profound impact on sales. Whether a firm is e-business or brick and mortar, a website is a must.

17-6d   Budgeting for Franchisee Marketing Promotions

One of the more challenging decisions for a franchisee is to determine what size marketing budget (dollar amount) is necessary to be effective in the local marketplace for the franchisee. At what level is the franchisee spending too little? Too much? Often the resulting initial budget is based on advice from the franchisor and the franchisee's expectations about the competitive conditions in the local market. There are a variety of approaches that a franchisee can employ to develop and effectively utilize a marketing budget, as shown in Figure 17-10.

There are other, more elaborate approaches to budgeting for marketing and advertising expenditures. The abovementioned approaches appear to be the most common due to their ease of understanding and application. The budget decision is difficult, because it is not easy to financially record a direct correlation or determine a precise measure between marketing/advertising and sales.

---

1. **Available Funds Approach.** Franchisee limits budget to funds available on hand. This method, though often used, has proven to be the least effective approach to budget for marketing/advertising because a minimum threshold spending level exists depending on local competitive conditions. That minimum threshold level is essential in order to have any meaningful effect.

2. **Competitive Parity Approach.** Franchisee spends as much as competitors to maintain parity in marketplace. Often used in retail.

3. **Percentage of Sales Approach.** Easiest to implement. Franchisee allocates a fixed percentage of sales to marketing/advertising. Often used by some ethical drug store franchise systems.

4. **Fixed Sum Approach.** Franchisee budgets a fixed amount for marketing/advertising based on number of transactions or units sold. The appropriation is not affected by change in product/service

FIGURE **17-10**

Budget Approaches for Marketing/Advertising

17-6e   Multiunit Franchisees

A current phenomenon spreading throughout the franchising field is that of franchisees with multiple units. When franchisees purchase their first unit, many are already looking to add more units as soon as the first one is operating successfully. Second, third, and fourth stores are often developed as rapidly as possible, utilizing the profits and revenues from previous franchises to help build these units.

The key to franchisees becoming multiunit operators quickly and successfully is for them to get the right people to staff and oversee the units. Usually the franchisee has staked almost all resources in the start-up and development of the first franchised business. It is difficult to find people willing to make similar commitments. The key to proper expansion is never to lower one's standards or expectations of people but to find those with the proper strengths and expertise.

Some franchisors may offer franchises only to franchisees who agree to establish a specific number of units during a certain period, for example, five new units in four years. The number of units to be developed under a multiunit agreement and the time period for development will vary according to market potential and available capital. The initial agreement is often referred to as an *area development agreement*. A separate *franchise agreement* is executed for each successive unit developed.

Multiunit franchisees generally are located in urban areas with high population densities. This allows the franchisees greater ease in the management of locations and closer liaison with management and employees. Multiunit franchisees, while wearing many hats, need to work very closely with the people hired to manage operations at each unit, for these are the people who will become the supervisors and directors of operations throughout the subsystem.

"FRANCHISES GRAVITATE TO AMERICAN MARKET"

Nontraditional Mexican franchises are bidding to nab a share of the U.S. restaurant market. While such American giants as McDonald's and Starbucks have had great success throughout Latin America, only a handful of Mexican-owned chains have made strides in the United States until recently. Now, such chains as CoCo Express, El Fogoncito, and Taco Inn are readying plans for an expansion north of the border. The real challenge for several chains is to secure a solid American partner who understands the rules of the U.S. franchising market.

Adapted from Jenalia Moreno, "Franchises Gravitate to American Market," Houston Chronicle *(8 May 2003): 1, www.chron.com.*

Concerning the management of the franchise subsystem, Craig Cormack, owner of twenty-four Burger King franchises in Nebraska, Kansas, and South Dakota, suggests that "the franchisee multiunit corporate structure will vary greatly depending on the size of the company. The operation supervisor needs to be in place for each four to six restaurants (for a franchisee developing quickly, an operation supervisor should be in place at the second restaurant). After three operation supervisors are in place, a position needs to be created to oversee the operation personnel. This individual should oversee between three and six operation supervisors"[2] (See Figure 17-11)

Cormack further states that "because of the capabilities of personal computers, accounting now can be done in-house with as few as two or three stores. About the time the franchisee develops ten to [twelve] restaurants, they should begin to look at having an individual to administer and coordinate marketing programs. Unless a franchisor has very aggressive expansion plans, most franchisees will be involved in their own development."[3]

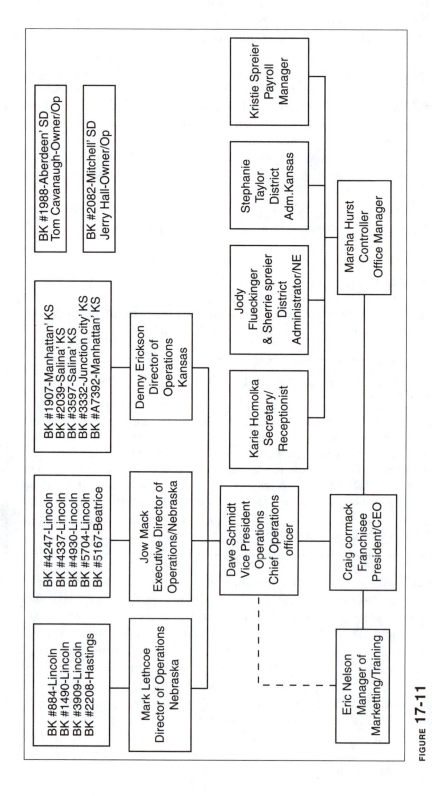

FIGURE **17-11**

Cormack Enterprises, Inc. Organization Chart

Administrative costs for most multiunit franchisees are typically 3 to 6 percent of total sales. These costs will pay salaries of both professional and clerical staff made necessary by the multiunit corporate structure. This corporate staff becomes the liaison between the franchisor and the franchisee-managed stores.

Charles L. Valluzzo

McDonald's

Charlie Valluzzo epitomizes franchising in America. Born in Ohio and raised in Michigan, Charlie graduated from Western Michigan University in 1962, with a bachelor of arts degree in business administration. That same year, he started in his own business as a franchisee by opening a McDonald's in Joplin, Missouri.

In 1964, a larger market opened that would enable more than one location to be developed. That market was Baton Rouge, Louisiana. That two-store market has grown to a thirty-five-store market today. When asked about his success in the fast-food industry, Charlie replies, "This business just didn't take off. We had a period there, and it was quite a long period of time, when all I hoped I could do was to meet my payroll and to pay my note every month at the bank." However, hard work and dedication have paid off in the long run as he now employs well over 2,000 people. Charlie has been recognized by countless organizations for his excellence in business. In 1984, he received the Golden Arch Award, the highest recognition given in the McDonald's system, and only four are awarded every two years. In 1991, Charlie received Restaurateur of the Year award, presented by the Louisiana Restaurant Association. This was the first time that the award was presented to an individual in the fast-food industry. Charlie was also presented with the Business Person of the Year award in 1995 by the Baton Rouge Business Report.

Even though managing thirty-five restaurants takes a tremendous amount of time, Charlie still manages to work in the restaurants daily, alongside the crew members, doing whatever needs to be done to serve the customers. Many times, Charlie can be found in the drive-thru, handing food to customers and wishing them a "great day." *He can also be found cooking, cashiering, and cleaning as the need arises.*

Charlie also believes in supporting the community that has allowed him to be so successful. He serves on numerous boards throughout the community, and is well known for his donations of both food and money to many organizations in the community. He supports all the local elementary schools through "honor roll cards," which reward the children with food from McDonald's for making the honor roll. Charlie's theory is: "Supporting the community and actively improving your surroundings, not only makes Baton Rouge, Louisiana, a better place, but serves as the building blocks for the improvement of the entire United States," In 1995, *Charlie was awarded the Golden Deeds Award, which recognizes the individual who has contributed the most time, energy, and resources to the Baton Rouge community.*

Charlie believes strongly in supporting and rewarding the employees who work alongside him. He rewards high school students for their grades with a "good grades, great pay" program, where they earn raises for excelling in school. He also provides a scholarship program for employees attending any one of three local colleges. In 1968, Charlie started a profit sharing plan. Employees who meet certain criteria, such as age and length of employment, receive a contribution out of company profits into a retirement account each year. Charlie firmly believes that people who work together and support each other result in a more successful, productive restaurant. From 1964 to the present, Charlie has put in countless hours of hard work, worrying, and caring for the people around him. In the long run, it seems to have paid off. He is well known not only for his success as a McDonald's franchisee, but also for his caring and support of his employees and community.

SUMMARY

The franchisee is an entrepreneur who has decided to utilize the operating format of an existing organization to start a new business. Franchisees are generally independent people who enjoy the excitement of a new business opportunity.

Franchisees learn quickly that they must wear several different hats. One of the most important hats is that of a marketer as promoter and advertiser. The franchisee will be responsible for all local advertising and will work with the franchisor to develop major advertising programs. Because advertising is important to the success of the franchisee's plan and program, the franchisee needs to make sure that the field marketing research and franchisor support are all appropriately developed and used. The franchisee should also learn how to use focus groups to explore why consumers prefer or dislike the products or services being offered. Focus groups are an important marketing tool for the franchisee.

Multiunit franchisees are becoming increasingly more common in franchising. These owners of two or more stores generally located in heavily populated urban areas have become a major influence in many franchising organizations and may often be found with ten to twenty different franchised stores.

KEY TERMS

Communication elasticity: The change is sales volume for each one percent change in total marketing communications effort applied to a specific franchise system (or local) promotion.

Consumer response index (CRI): Represents the changes in customer awareness of advertisements, their comprehension of advertising copy content and interest or conviction that can measure overall customer response.

Marketing communication: the purpose of which is to differentiate the franchise system's products and services from those of the competition and to enhance the brand's position in the marketplace.

Market segmentation: Means an approach used to determine target markets by geographic, demographic, psychographic and/or behavior factors associated with a targeted customer group. The approach is often used to divide a large market into smaller groupings or clusters of customers who have similar characteristics.

REVIEW QUESTIONS

1. What is a marketing calendar?

2. Why and when is it advisable to use focus groups?

3. What is the role of marketing for the franchisee?

4. Discuss how a franchisee uses the franchisor's marketing program.

5. Describe and compose the approaches to local marketing available to most franchisees.

6. Discuss multiunit franchisees and their role in franchising today.

7. Discuss the various approaches to marketing/advertising, identifying strengths and weaknesses of each.

CASE STUDY

Ben and Jerry's

In 1978, two gentlemen from Vermont desired to produce a premium ice cream that they decided to name after themselves—Ben Cohen and Jerry Greenfield—or Ben and Jerry's Homemade. Sales have skyrocketed in the last twenty years, and Ben and Jerry now own four company-owned stores and eighty-six franchise stores. They currently have a franchise fee of $25,000, royalty fee of 4 percent, and a monthly fee used for advertising. Their total investment runs between $175,000 and $200,000.

Since opening their shop in Burlington, Vermont, sales have climbed to over $200 million with over 600 employees. What has been their marketing success? Ben and Jerry are both creative in developing innovative flavors such as Cherry Garcia, Chocolate Chip Cookie Dough, and Rain Forest Crunch. Their customers also know that 7.5 percent of Ben and Jerry's pretax profits are donated to environmental and social causes. They had a company policy in which the highest paid employee may not make more than seven times the lowest paid worker.

In 1993, they faced stiff competition in the super premium ice cream category and following their first loss since going public in 1984, they started to search for a new CEO to lead the company to success. Ben and Jerry conducted their own CEO search in their own formidable style. They developed an essay contest entitled, "Yo, I Am Your CEO." This contest drew over 20,000 CEO hopefuls, but these energetic owners finally made a conventional choice—they hired corporate turn-around consultant Robert Holland, Jr.

CASE QUESTIONS

1. Develop a list of methods that you would use as a franchisee of Ben and Jerry's Homemade for your local market.

2. Who is the target market for Ben and Jerry's Homemade?

3. Develop a marketing strategy which you would use as the local franchisee to market Ben and Jerry's Homemade.

4. What are some of the best methods of advertising that Ben and Jerry's could use to recruit additional end consumers?

REFERENCES

Advertising Age, 740 N. Rush St., Chicago, IL 60611.

Anderson, Carol H. and Julian W. Vincze, *Strategic Marketing Management* (New York: Houghton Mifflin Company, 2000).

Bangs, D. H., *The Market Planning Guide*, 4th ed. (Dover, NH: Upstart Publishing, Inc., 1995).

Cooper, Robin and Robert S. Kaplan, "Profit Priorities from Activity-based Costing," *Harvard Business Review* (May-June 1991).

Diener, Marc, "Deal Power," *Entrepreneur* (December 2006):98.

Janszen, Barbara, "Five FREE (or Almost Free) Ways to Promote Your Business," *Centercourt* (San Diego: IFX International, January 2003), 2.

Kanellos, Michael, "For Fast-Food, Call in the Robots," 2 April 2007, http:/anews/com.com/2102-11394_3-6170097.html?tag-st.lutil.print.

Kaufmann, P., "Master Franchising: At What Price Growth?" *Franchise Update* (second quarter 1993): 25–27.

Kaufmann, P. and R. Dant, "Multi-Unit Franchising: Growth and Management Issues," *Journal of Business Venturing* (1997).

Kaufmann, P. and S. Kim, "Master Franchising and System Growth Rates," *Journal of Marketing Channels* 4(1/2) 49–64.

Kotler, Philip, *Marketing Management: Analysis, Planning, Implementation, and Control*, 9th ed. (Englewood Cliffs, NJ: Prentice Hall, 1997).

Kotler, Philip, and Alan R. Andreasen, *Strategic Management for Nonprofit Organizations*, 5th ed. (Englewood Cliffs, NJ: Prentice Hall, 1996).

Lamb, Charles W., Jr., Joseph F. Hair, Jr., and Carl McDaniel, *Principles of Marketing*, 2nd ed. (Cincinnati: South-Western Publishing Co., 1994).

Levinson, J.C., *Guerrilla Marketing* (Boston: Houghton Mifflin, 1993).

Levinson, J.C., *Guerrilla Marketing Excellence* (Boston: Houghton Mifflin, 1993).

Mason-Draffen, Carrie, "National Franchises Targeting Long Island," *Newsday.com*, 2 April 2007, www.newsday.com/business/ny-bzfran0328,0,307891.story.

McCarthy, E. Jerome,*Basic Marketing: A Managerial Approach* (Homewood, IL: Irwin, 1996).

Schmeltzer, John, "McDonald's Next Generation Marketing Chief Mary Dillon Has Introduced the Once-conventional Fast-food Giant to YouTube," *Chicago Tribune* (27 March 2007).

Smith, Darrell, "Ringing Up Gym Profit," *Sacramento Bee* (23 March 2007).

Thomas, Dave and Michael Seid, *Franchising for Dummies* (New York: IDG Books, 2000).

Zaragoza, Sandra, "FedEx Kinko's Takes Aim at Big-bix Suppliers," *Dallas Business Journal* (2 October 2006).

NOTES

1. D. Thomas and M. Seid, *Franchising for Dummies* (New York: IDG Books, 2000), 174.
2. Craig Cormack, president, Cormack Enterprises. Material presented in Visiting Executive Lecturer Series at the University of Nebraska-Lincoln, April 7, 1987.
3. Ibid.

MANAGING THE FRANCHISEE BUSINESS*

In studying this chapter, you will:

- **Learn about contractual duties and responsibilities of a franchisee.**
- **Learn about characteristics of family-owned businesses.**
- **Identify and understand essentials of the management process in a franchised business.**
- **Learn techniques for managing human resources.**
- **Learn about opportunities for women and minorities in franchising.**

INCIDENT

Andrea's Interiors and Accents is a small but growing franchise system in the Midwest. The firm specializes in providing unique design and construction of high-quality draperies, other window coverings, carpeting, furniture, accent pieces, and unique silk floral arrangements. There are six franchised locations. In a given location, sales associates are responsible for providing customer service, ensuring customer satisfaction, and making sales. Observations, informal information, industry sales estimates, and a review of company records generated by each location suggest that one franchised location is underperforming the others and the industry in general.

Laura Moral, owner of the franchise that is underperforming the others, is concerned about the situation. She finds that local market conditions are stable. Advertising, pricing, and other marketing factors are being applied in the same manner as the other franchised locations. However, the sales results are weak. Discussion between Laura and Andrea brings agreement that sales associate performance, not marketing, is the issue.

Laura pays her sales associates an above-average base compensation. An individual-based commission plan was attempted by the franchise system nine months ago. The sales associates at each franchised location asked that management, the individual franchisees, and the franchise system drop the program when they had determined it caused dysfunctional competition among the sales associates and across locations. The sales associates recognized the need for a more fluid team approach to sales, sales support, and customer satisfaction.

---

* This chapter is prepared in conjunction with Dyanne Ferk, Associate Professor of Business Administration, University of Illinois-Springfield.

Laura asked Andrea for help; she contacted other franchisees to learn how they were dealing with this issue and received corporate support and assistance to help turn around the negative situation. A survey was developed involving all franchised locations. Laura's sales associates collected observational measures, which were carefully recorded and used to classify sales associate behaviors. Sales associates were involved in the study by self-reporting and collection of observational data. Measures were made across all days and locations to determine a representative sales month. Behavior was classified; direct measures of customer satisfaction were collected immediately following a sale and from a telephone follow-up survey two weeks after a sale. The results helped the franchise system address and correct a problem that could have had serious negative consequences to any of the franchised locations and to the franchise system itself. Laura and her sales associates received recognition and an award for quality improvement by cooperating with each other and handily meeting sales objectives. Laura and her sales associates are happy. Andrea is happy too.

18-1 INTRODUCTION

Franchisees are entrepreneurs. They own and operate their own businesses. They are not gamblers or high-risk takers. Franchising enables individuals to become independent business owners, reducing the risk of failure because of the franchisor's past experience and expertise. A strong franchisor is able to provide ongoing support in marketing, finance, research, product development, and even management problems (as shown in the chapter opening incident).

A franchisee is in a legal contract for a period of time with a franchise system. The franchisor and franchisee have duties to perform and responsibilities to honor. When something goes wrong, or a problem arises between the franchisor and the franchisee, what are the legal implications for the franchisee? For the franchisor? The ideal franchisor–franchisee relationship is built on mutual trust, consideration, and cooperation. Through effective management operations and maximum market effort, both franchisor and franchisee can reap substantial product sales and enhance profitability for one another.

In this chapter, we address two major topic areas. First, as independent business owners operating a franchise unit, franchisees should understand the legal rights they have as members of a franchise system. These rights are addressed in five major categories: (1) franchisor–franchisee relationship, (2) franchising agreement, (3) defense manual, (4) a layman's discussion of the laws regulating franchising, and (5) the most common legal problems of franchisees. This information is important, for it shapes what a franchisee can and cannot do not only as a franchisee but also as an entrepreneur who is responsible for effective planning, organizing, leading, and controlling a business venture. The second part of the chapter addresses major areas that a franchisee, as an entrepreneur, must understand in order to effectively manage the business in a competitive environment. Topics covered include management philosophy, planning, organization, human resource needs, leadership, coordination, and decision making.

18-2 FRANCHISOR–FRANCHISEE RELATIONSHIP

While the franchisor and the franchisee need to rely on each other for success, it is the franchisor that generally retains absolute power in contractual relationships with franchisees. Franchisors traditionally wish to be able to keep franchisees under their thumb. This is one reason why it is vital for franchisees to be aware of the power and authority franchisors derive from the contractual relationship. The franchisee should understand the nature of the power and authority that franchisors generally possess, as well as the limits of that power. The franchisee should save any information which might be used later as a defense against actions brought by the franchisor in case of coercion or termination. This information would be stored in the franchisee's defense manual, which will be discussed later in this chapter.

Most franchisees have committed their entire life savings and all their available time to the development of their franchise. Too often they do not anticipate the business problems that can arise, but foresee only great success and profits. Some of these problems can result from a lack of understanding about the power of the franchisor. Other problems are simply the result of being in business.

18-2a Termination

Possibly the major business problem associated with a franchised business is termination of the franchising agreement by the franchisor. Most franchising agreements make termination an easy and relatively inexpensive action for the franchisor to take against the franchisee. It may often be done without cause or justifiable reason, so the franchisee should be aware of this possibility.

A bitter legal feud is taking place between the family of a baseball legend, Roger Maris, and Anheuser-Busch Cos. Inc., the largest beer franchise system in the world. The Marises and the brewery have gone to court several times since Anheuser-Busch terminated the family's beer distributorship in 1997. Round one went to the brewery. In 1999, a federal jury found the brewery was not liable for anti-trust violations alleged by the Marises. The Maris family has indicated that this time things may be different.[1]

Since post-Prohibition times, the brewer has made efforts to streamline its far-flung network of distributors (franchisees), and in doing so have sometimes clashed with people such as the Marises, who have prospered through their lucrative wholesale contracts. The number of wholesale distributors has steadily declined over the years to 2,347 in 2000 from 3,492 in 1987 according to the National Beer Wholesalers Association.[2]

Experts say the firms such as Busch, Miller, and Coors are trying to reduce their number of distributors as large retailers seek to bypass the wholesaler (franchisee) and deal directly with the brewer (franchisor). The beer industry is based on a three-tier system of brewers, distributors, and retailers, a system dating to the years just after the end of Prohibition in the 1930s. The system has worked well for Anheuser-Busch, which controls nearly half of the U.S. beer market.[3]

In today's beer industry, however, having a commanding market share may not be enough. Beer sales have not been growing in recent years, making it more difficult for breweries to turn market share into profits. Apparently, Anheuser-Busch has been pursuing a two-pronged strategy to cut costs and improve profitability. One strategy has been to revamp its bulky supply chain (company-owned and franchisee-owned distribution network). Anheuser-Busch set up a series of regional distribution centers to speed shipments to wholesalers. The strategy helped the brewery reduce shipping lanes and direct the bulk of its products toward selected distributors. Also, this approach allowed the company to gain greater control over its transportation network, which the wholesalers have, historically, operated. The second piece of the strategy has been to reduce the number of wholesalers by folding what Anheuser-Busch considered to be underperforming distributors into stronger wholesale territories. This process is known as realignment.[4]

It is suggested that Anheuser-Busch, as well as other major breweries, may need to downsize their distribution system to make more deals with fewer dealers. Under this context, the best wholesalers will take over the weaker ones. Apparently, a 1996 confidential report prepared by a midlevel brewery manager spells out this strategy with some detail. Accordingly, Busch would seek to set up wholesale territories where total annual market volume would be ideally about 6 million cases—or about $90 million in sales, but a wholesale territory would be more than 2 million cases. Also, it is reported that Anheuser-Busch identified major areas where the highest need and greatest opportunities would exist for realignment. The overall goal would be to increase the geographic size and scope of a wholesale (franchisee's or company-owned location's) territory. Under this plan, about 150 distributors were identified as underperforming, based on such criteria as exclusivity, the brewery's relationship with the particular wholesaler, and willingness to invest time and money into the business and employees. The brewery had developed a plan to identify underperforming wholesalers and developed a strategy to acquire them. The brewery could later turn those businesses and lucrative territories over to other distributors. The plan ranks each wholesaler/distributor on a one to five system on how likely it would be that a distributor would sell its business. The plan apparently suggested that Anheuser-Busch needed to "create incentive and motivation or heavy crew pressure" to convince wholesale distributors to sell. The brewery apparently exerts tremendous influence over distributors through very detailed contracts, and frequently sends market evaluation teams (field personnel) known as crews to monitor performance and compliance of the distributors with their contract.[5]

The Marises argue that the brewery sent a team to their warehouse in Florida to lay the groundwork for a brewery takeover of their wholesale beer business. Whether the 1996 confidential report helps the Marises in their legal contest with the brewery is of question. Apparently, the business strategy by Anheuser-Busch is sound. The question is: In implementing a sound business strategy, did Anheuser-Busch step over the line?[6]

The inequality of bargaining power which exists between most franchisors and franchisees is sizable. Fast-food franchisees are especially dependent on the trademarks and distinctive designs of their franchises. If their agreements are not renewed, they ordinarily will not be able to retain the facilities, goodwill, or specialized equipment of the franchise system.

The federal government has left it up to the states to legislate the right of termination or nonrenewal of franchises. Many state legislatures are in the process of developing laws concerning termination and nonrenewal. In most cases, the franchisor must show "good cause" or justification for either action. Both the laws and the court decisions have shown a preference for the franchisee if good cause for termination or nonrenewal has not been demonstrated by the franchisor.

Many contracts will provide for automatic renewal as long as the franchisee is not in violation of any of the conditions or provisions of the agreement. In other cases, the franchisee may be given an option to renew as long as he or she agrees to renew under current conditions and obligations, that is, signing a new agreement which may contain different conditions and stipulations, completing a remodeling or renovation program, paying a renewal fee, and agreeing to any new royalty, advertising, or other fees under the new franchising contract. The franchisor may also reserve the right of automatic termination in case of bankruptcy, insolvency, criminal conviction, refusal to do business, abandonment, or loss of the lease. If a default occurs, the franchisee is often given a period of time to solve the problem.

18-3   THE FRANCHISING AGREEMENT

When properly constructed, the franchising agreement takes into account the interests of both parties. However, franchising agreements are generally prepared and written by attorneys who seek to maximize the franchisor's position. Almost without exception, the written agreement will place the franchisor in the dominant economic and legal position.

The problems which arise in any franchising agreements may result from the franchisor's right to terminate the arrangement without cause and the short-term nature of the agreement, in which the right to renew is controlled solely by the franchisor. The written agreement generally maximizes the franchisor's rights while minimizing the franchisees' rights which may exist under state contract law and/or the Uniform Commercial Code. An important point to make here is that all franchising documents need not be the same. Many franchisees wield the economic and personal power to negotiate favorable franchising agreements for themselves and their franchises.

To ensure a favorable franchising agreement, the franchisee should develop a negotiating team. This team should consist of the franchisee, plus at least two other members, an attorney, and an accountant. An attorney who is knowledgeable about franchising and the needs of a small business can provide great assistance in the negotiating process. An accountant experienced in franchising can point out financial obligations the franchisee will be taking on by signing the agreement. Negotiable areas would include the territory granted for operation of the franchise; right of first refusal for additional franchises near the original territory; financing for the land, building, and/or equipment; rights of termination and renewal; and method of payment for financial obligations to the franchisor. The accountant should also be able to make a basic determination of whether the prospective franchisee could live up to the financial obligations of the franchising agreement.

18-3a   Contract Rights

The franchisee should realize that a number of rights are granted in the written franchising agreement. These rights include but are not exclusive to the following:

Treatment by the franchisor in a fair and equitable manner

Long-term or automatically renewable agreement

Termination only upon proof of good cause

Fair and equitable performance standards

Fair and equitable quotas and/or allocations

Written and complete statements of all alleged discrepancies or deficiencies

Right to require franchisor to prove all matters of discrepancy or deficiency

Right of transfer to franchisee's heirs

Right to transfer or sell business

Right to relocate within designated sales area

Exclusive or territorial rights (when applicable)

Warranty reimbursement for services rendered

Creation of an independent appeals board

Right to develop independent franchisee trade association and advisory counsel

Termination—typically, ninety days' notice, right to sell franchise, subject to franchisor's agreement

Adequate compensation for damages and losses on property and future profits

Right of appeal to appeals board

The franchising agreement is often lengthy, technical, and complicated. Steps should be taken by both franchisor and franchisee to ensure that the length and complexity are minimized. Overly technical documents do not benefit either party.

18-3b   Other Rights

Some other rights need to be protected in the franchising agreement. For example, franchisees in some businesses may be required to carry large inventories of parts for last year's models, potentially resulting in considerable loss due to obsolescence. Franchisors should be required to provide the right to the franchisee to return slow-moving or obsolete parts.

In addition, for protection of their franchise system, some franchisors also require that franchisees and their families not engage in similar businesses for a specified period after the franchising agreement expires. For example, this "covenant not to compete" may prohibit the franchisee from starting a similar business within twenty miles of the franchise and for two years after the termination of the agreement. Covenants not to compete are generally considered valid if their terms are reasonable with respect to time, area, and activity.

A long-term contract often helps develop goodwill between the franchisor and the franchisee. A renewal clause in the agreement also helps foster positive attitudes and a constructive relationship between the two parties.

The franchisor does not need unlimited power to terminate as protection against poor franchisee performance. Performance may be controlled through enforced quality standards and sales quotas. Competition among franchisees is beneficial and a requirement to meet expected levels is common. Most franchisees are quick to encourage fellow franchisees to improve poor performance.

18-4   THE FRANCHISE DEFENSE MANUAL

To avoid termination or nonrenewal of the franchising agreement, the franchisee must follow proper practices and procedures of the business. As a kind of leverage against the inherent business advantages held by the franchisor, a franchisee should keep track of all the suggestions and correspondence from the franchisor's organization. This information is collectively referred to as the **franchise defense manual**. The defense manual should contain the following items.

Documents stating legal rights, including copy of franchising agreement and current law relative to franchising

Information and dated records

Accounting requirements

Pricing policies

Quotas and/or allocation requirements purchasing or buying requirements for all products

Purchasing or buying requirements for all products

Purchasing requirements for any accessories, supplies, or parts

Advertising fee requirements

Any coercion, threats, or pressure tactics employed by franchisor

Favored franchisees

Sales policies and positions

Copies of all documents received from the franchisor

Transcripts of conversations with attorney, accountant, and business consultant

Written explanations of any unfair sales quotas or new requirements

Names of staff members present at meetings with the franchisor and appropriate records of these meetings.

Records of trade association and franchisee group meetings

Record of refusal to sign documents concerning unfair quotas, regulations, or any deficiencies

Written records of all promises made by the franchisor

It is important that every franchisee maintain a thorough, chronological file of all interactions with the franchisor. This file will become very important if at any future time differences arise between the franchisor and the franchisee. It is also important that the franchisee have documented proof of any allegation of wrongdoing or misconduct made by the franchisor. Generally, franchisors with proper legal consultants will not make mistakes in their relationships with the franchisee. However, their field representatives may make statements which could be helpful to a franchisee in proving wrongful acts by the franchisor.

The three main points in keeping a defense manual may be summarized as follows: (1) consult an attorney or accountant if ever anything goes amiss in the franchising relationship; (2) keep written documents of all transactions with the franchisor; and (3) make sure two or more officers of the franchisee are present at all important meetings with the franchisor. It is important for the franchisee to work constructively with the franchisor's organization. It is also important that the franchisee work well with other franchisees within the franchise system. These relationships can provide psychological and practical support in improving business practices and in bolstering the franchisee should any problems with the franchisor occur.

18-4a   The Family-Owned Business

Family-owned and/or controlled firms account for approximately 80 to 90 percent of all incorporated firms in the United States. Approximately 33 percent of the *Fortune 500* firms are family-owned and/or controlled and over 50 percent of publicly traded firms are under family control or family influence. On the negative side, approximately 80 percent of family businesses fail within five years. Of surviving firms, only about 30 percent are successfully transferred to the second generation; however, not all family businesses that are not passed on to the next generation go out of business, but many do. The odds are worse in the transition between the second and third generation of family ownership, when only about 12 percent of such businesses remain in the same family.[7] A brief statistical summary of family businesses in the United States is presented in Figure 18-1.

Building a family business so that it can last across two or more generations is often the dream of many franchisees as well as franchisors. Family businesses that are built to last have the recognizable tension between preserving and protecting the "core" of what has made the business

---

Family Businesses:

- Constitute between 80 and 98 percent of all businesses in the world's free economies.

- Generate 49 percent of the GDP in the United States.

- Employ about 85 percent of the U.S. workforce.

- Employ more than 85 percent of the working people around the world.

- Created 70 to 80 percent of all new jobs in the United States in the past ten years.

- Reports annual revenues greater than $25 million: 35,000.

- Total number of family firms in the United States is between 17 million and 23 million.

FIGURE **18-1**

Statistical Summary of Family Businesses in the United States

Sources: Beehr, T., J. Drexler, and S. Faulkner, "Working in Small Family Businesses: Empirical Comparisons to Non-family Business," *Journal of Organizational behavior* 18 (1997); J. Astrachan and M. Carey, *Family Businesses in the U.S. Economy*, (Washington, DC: Center for the Study of Taxation, 1994); S. Oster, *Competitive Analysis* (New York: Oxford University Press, 1999); Ernesto J. Posa, *Family Business* (Cincinnati: Thompson-Southwestern, 2004).

successful while promoting growth and being willing to adapt to changing competitive dynamics. In franchising, at the core of this tension is the franchisor–franchisee contract as well as individual motivation and mutuality of trust between franchisor and franchisee.

Today, across most all categories of business and industry, franchise systems are considered by many to be on the cutting edge of system and unit-level performance, job creation, quality of product and service, return on investment, capability, and speed to market for new products and services. Truly, it is the unique business relationship between franchisor and franchisee that—for many families—provides the opportunity for successful initiation, growth, maintenance, and transition to the next generation of profitable business enterprises. It appears that there are particular strengths identifiable in family businesses as franchise systems and franchised units. These strengths include the following:

- Concentrated ownership structure and control leads to higher overall business-level productivity.

- Desire to foster recognition as well as protection of the family name and reputation often translates into higher product/service quality for the customer as well as higher than average returns on investment.

- Family agreement and focus upon the specific customer segments targeted and niches to be penetrated and preserved often result in higher return on investment.

- The nature of the family interaction—ownership, management, family unity, support for capital continuity, skills and knowledge transfer and flexibility to adjust to changing market and supply conditions—can be great assets in franchised family businesses.

Therefore, the family business is in a uniquely strong position when operating in a franchised context. Family needs and expectations can be effectively balanced through optimizing ownership, management and family strengths and characteristics, along with greater opportunity for controlling costs as well as capabilities of utilizing the unique advantages that families can provide to achieve competitive advantage in the marketplace. In many franchise systems, the family business is one of the primary "secrets" of success as systems as well as individual franchised units.

18-5 LAWS REGULATING FRANCHISING

Laws have been established in the United States to help those who may be injured by certain business practices. Franchising as a method of doing business continues to be significantly regulated by the laws and rules of the federal government. Franchising is regulated at the federal level throughout all states because of the disclosure requirements of the Federal Trade Commission Rule. The laws regulating franchising that are important for franchisees may be put into the following four categories: (1) what the franchisor can do, (2) what the franchisor cannot do, (3) what the franchisee can do, and (4) what the franchisee cannot do.

18-5a   What the Franchisor Can Do

The franchisor legally establishes a relationship with a franchisee through the franchising agreement. The franchising agreement is a legally enforceable contract. It normally contains many provisions with respect to the day-to-day operations of the franchise and it also calls upon the franchisee to live up to the quality standards of the business by adhering to the operations manual. The operations manual is the rule book and encyclopedia of activities for the business.

There are several areas in which the franchisor may choose to have significant control over or establish specific requirements for franchisees: establishing a territory; determining royalty, advertising, and other fees and how they shall be paid; requiring direct participation by franchisees in the actual operations of the franchise; and placing any restrictions on goods and services offered by the franchisee.

In the franchising agreement, the franchisor usually reserves the right to specify territorial restrictions and arrangements. Under the contract, the franchisee is ordinarily granted a specific, exclusive geographic area in which to operate the franchise. The location is considered exclusive in that the franchisor will not place another outlet, franchised or company owned, within that territory. Some franchise contracts have virtually no territorial restrictions, while others may contain a county, market area, regional area, or state-sized territory.

The franchisor may specifically ban the franchisee from operating outside the agreed-upon territory. This territorial clause may require, then, that the franchisee sell products andservices only from a given location.

Laws governing territorial restrictions have become complex and are now often judged under the "rule of reason." The Supreme Court has favored the rule of reason rather than stating that all territorial restrictions are per se illegal. A territorial restriction simply defines a geographical area outside which the franchisee is not permitted to sell products. The rule of reason allows the court to investigate all circumstances surrounding the imposition of such restrictions. Thus, franchisors offer commercial justifications for allocating territorial rights. These justifications may include quality control, as well as the encouragement of promotional activities, private investment, or growth opportunities for specific dealers. Certain territorial restrictions, therefore, may be found to be legal because they are beneficial to both the franchisor and the franchisee.

The franchisor may also legally require the payment of fees in a franchising relationship. Franchisees will usually pay a one-time license fee or franchising fee which allows them to use the trademark and/or "system" of the franchisor. This fee also includes all costs of the franchisor for training and other services and for maintaining standards throughout the system.

The royalty fee is generally a fixed percentage of gross sales which is remitted to the headquarters organization. There is usually little or no room for negotiation of the royalty fee. The franchisor also may require the franchisee to use a standard recordkeeping system which allows for an easy method of auditing and reporting gross sales and activities of the franchisee. Royalty fees which enable franchisees to earn a respectable profit and an attractive return on investment and also provide the franchisor with income sufficient to cover expenses and profits will generally be acceptable to both parties.

The franchisor may also require an advertising fee payment. This contribution, like the royalty fee, is often a percentage of gross sales, though it may be a flat sum based on an assessment for items sold. The franchisee may also be required to make minimal payments for local advertising in addition to contributions for regional or national advertising. Franchisees should be aware of all fee payments that will be required by the franchise system.

Franchisors may also specify hours of operation and develop quality control mechanisms to protect standards of operation. Quality controls are used to ensure that the products and services offered throughout the franchise system consistently meet the standards established by the franchisor.

Through the quality control mechanism, the franchisor may also control the appearance of the store, as well as its interior layout and design. The franchisor may stipulate what the store may or may not carry and display, and may require that the franchisee buy only from the franchisor or authorized suppliers.

18-5b   What the Franchisor Cannot Do

The franchisor is required to conduct business in a reasonable and fair manner. Franchisors may not engage in unfair business practices or violate the contract or franchising agreement, nor may they engage in price fixing, require tying arrangements, or make any representations about actual or potential sales except in the manner set forth by the Federal Trade Commission.

Price fixing occurs when the independence of the pricing decision by those who resell another's goods is hindered or diminished through coercion. The franchisor has the right to charge whatever price it wishes for the products it sells to the franchisees. However, the franchisor does not have the right to influence or determine the price at which the franchisees must sell the product to their customers. This is price fixing and the practice is illegal.

The practical, real-life experiences of many franchisees demonstrate that these rules, laws, and regulations are not always adequate. For example, although price fixing is illegal, if McDonald's runs a national campaign advertising breakfast for ninety-nine cents, then any franchisee who does not participate may incur the ill feelings of customers. Although laws exist to protect franchisees, the franchisees may still feel intense pressure to participate in sales promotions, purchase unwanted items, or take part in other advertised activities.

Another illegal practice is the *tying arrangement*. As discussed in Chapter 14, this occurs when the franchisor offers a product the franchisee wants to buy such as an automobile (tying product) and requires the franchisee to buy an additional product—tires, batteries, accessories (tied product)—the franchisee does not want or would not otherwise buy. If the franchisor tells the franchisee that he or she will not be able to purchase the automobile without also purchasing tires, batteries, and accessories, then this is a tying arrangement, and it is illegal under antitrust laws.

The franchisor must follow the Federal Trade Commission's trade regulation rule regarding the sale of franchises to prospective franchisees. The rule states that the franchisor may not make any actual or potential sales representations except in compliance with this rule. The rule further requires disclosure, but not registration, of offerings or sales of any franchises throughout the United States. If any earnings claims or sales claims are made in an oral, written, or visual representation to a prospective franchisee, the franchisor is required under the rule to present to the franchisee a formal earnings claim document. Further, any earnings claims made in the media that suggest a specific level or range of potential or actual sales, income, growth, or profits also require a formal earnings claim document.

An earnings claim document must contain materials sufficient to substantiate the accuracy of the claim that a franchise in a specific geographic area will be able to reach a certain level of sales. In addition, any document claiming earnings or profits must also report the percentage of franchisees earning more than and/or less than what is claimed. A statement must also be presented explaining the basis and assumptions upon which the earnings claim was made.

18-5c What the Franchisee Can Do

The franchisee is often limited by the franchising agreement which is to be signed. The terms of the agreement have often already been approved by other franchisees, and it is important that it remains generally intact and not be modified to any great extent if at all. Most franchise salespersons are not permitted by the franchisor to negotiate any of the terms of the agreement. However, franchisees do have certain rights and opportunities to negotiate the terms of their specific agreement, and they of course have the final option of whether to purchase the franchise.

Within the structure of the franchising agreement, the prospective franchisee may often negotiate the territory granted for the operation of the franchise. The franchisee has the right to discuss territorial boundaries and limitations and to suggest possible locations. The franchisee also has the right to negotiate a right of first refusal for additional franchises that may later be opened within the territory in which the franchise has been established. This right of first refusal is important to the franchisee and should be negotiated into the contract.

Also, the franchisee may find it important to discuss and negotiate the financing of the franchise purchase price. The franchisor may propose different methods of financing the franchising fee or the purchase of equipment, land, or building associated with the franchise operation. The method of financing may be through either the franchisor, independent banks, or venture capitalist firms. All of this is subject to negotiation.

In addition, the franchisee has the right to set the price structure for all sales at the business. Price fixing is illegal and the franchisee has the final say in determining all prices on goods and services.

Franchisees may also negotiate for themselves and their employees the amount of training to be received at the national or regional headquarters and at the franchised business outlet. They may also negotiate the amount of grand opening support and any additional service support to be provided by the franchisor.

18-5d   What the Franchisee Cannot Do

The franchisee must adhere to the signed franchising agreement as well as to the operations manual of the franchise organization. The franchisee is restricted from involvement in group boycotts or horizontal territorial restrictions.

Group boycotts occur when two or more franchisees join to exclude a third or prospective franchisee. Such action is prohibited as an intrinsic violation of the Sherman Antitrust Act. Let's say a franchisor asks a group of franchisees in the state of Ohio if a prospective franchisee should be allowed to operate in the Ohio region; the group says no, whereupon the franchise is denied. A group boycott would be in effect, and the franchisor would thus be in violation of the Sherman Act.

Note that by statute, these kinds of business practices (price fixing, tying arrangements, etc.) are automatically presumed to be unreasonable restraints of trade. Under legal standards guided by a "rule of reason," however, the court considers the circumstances or the franchisor's motives before making a final determination.

Cases in which franchisees seek to exclude other franchisees from specified territories or activity are referred to as horizontal territorial restrictions and are still per se illegal. The term *horizontal* simply means it is operators or competitors selling similar products who unite to exclude a third party from competing. It is illegal for franchisees to band together to exclude a prospective franchisee from any fair business opportunity.

18-6   COMMON LEGAL PROBLEMS OF FRANCHISEES

Franchising relationships are not always harmonious. Porter and Renforth have identified the ten most common legal problems encountered by franchisees, as listed in Table 18-1. The most frequent problems concern the sharing of advertising costs by franchisees, particularly when they believe they have not received their fair share of advertising expenditures. This usually occurs when local franchisees feel their areas have been neglected or have not received sufficient attention. Franchisees often wish to write into the contract the specific amount of advertising to be utilized in local areas. Other frequent difficulties involve evaluation of the minimum performance requirements established by franchisors. Many times franchisees see these requirements as problem areas created by the franchisor, or they feel the franchisor does not require all franchisees to adhere to the same standards. Franchisees sometimes disagree with the inspection evaluations and request further elaboration by the franchisor but the franchisor may be reluctant to offer additional clarification of the evaluations, often creating serious problems between franchisors and franchisees.

Occasional problems also exist because of the royalty and fee payments owed to the franchisor. These payments must be clearly understood and outlined in the contract. Special attention should be paid to the definition of gross revenues upon which almost all royalty and fee payments are

TABLE
18-1   TEN MOST COMMON LEGAL PROBLEMS OF FRANCHISEES

Frequent Problems	Rank*
Sharing Advertising Costs	1
Inspection/Evaluation by Franchisor	2
Minimum Performance Requirements	3
Occasional Problems	
Royalty Payments	4
Fees for Support Services	5
Territorial Limits	6
Rare Problems	
Penalties for Violation of Contract	7
Restrictions on Products or Prices	8
Employee Conduct/Training Requirements	9
Limits on Competitive Businesses	10

*The ranks were determined by summing the weights assigned (on a point scale of 1 to 5) to each factor by the survey respondents.
Source: Porter, James L. and William Renforth, "Franchise Agreements: Spotting the Important Legal Issues," *Journal of Small Business Management* 16(4) (October 1978): 27–31.

based. Also, if fees are to be charged for support services, these should be spelled out at the beginning of the relationship.

Territorial limits are also an occasional source of problems between franchisors and franchisees. These kinds of difficulties are often precluded by an understanding of the definite boundaries and the conditions of first refusal for additional franchises in the territory. Other problems which have been reported but have occurred only rarely include penalties for violation of contract, restrictions on products or prices, employee conduct/training requirements, and limits on competitive businesses. One such problem occurred when a franchisee of a large, nationally known fast-food franchise began to offer Jell-O as a regular menu item. He was quickly told by the franchisor that this was inappropriate and not within the franchising agreement and was requested to stop serving Jell-O at the restaurant.

Most franchisees will never have legal difficulties with their franchisor. There are some major differences between franchisees who often have legal troubles and those who rarely have such problems. Most franchisees who avoid or experience few legal difficulties are usually successful, profitable, and willing to follow the format of the franchisor. Franchisees with legal problems are often less successful, discontented in their franchising relationship, and generally heedless of the uniform procedures and standards of the franchise.

Some identifying characteristics of franchisees with and without legal problems have been identified by Porter and Renforth. Franchisees who are able to avoid legal problems have usually had previous business experience, know their rights in the franchising agreement, conduct independent market research, and are able to negotiate the terms of their franchising agreements. These are some of the areas identified in Table 18-2.

It has been noted that franchisees with legal problems are often involved in their first business undertaking, do not receive professional legal advice, typically accept franchisor's projections without independent research, and have problems in other areas of the business. Often the success of franchisees who can avoid legal problems results from a positive attitude. The prior experience of these franchisees enables them to conduct negotiations with diplomacy and professionalism. They

TABLE 18-2 CHARACTERISTICS OF FRANCHISEES WITH AND WITHOUT LEGAL PROBLEMS	
Franchisees with Problems	**Franchisees without Problems**
Are involved in their first business undertaking	Have previous business experience
Do not have the agreement reviewed by their own lawyer	Obtain legal counsel to review the franchising agreement
Accept standard contracts without modification to accommodate individual or local conditions	Request modification of standard agreement formats
Generally have problems in other operational areas of the business	Have generally successful, profitable businesses
Accept franchisors' estimates without verification	Conduct an independent market survey
View business as a zero-sum game	Expect to resolve occasional, routine legal disagreements in the normal course of business

often utilize private attorneys, market research firms, and independent advertising agencies. Successful franchisees have a cooperative, win-win relationship with the franchisor. They anticipate difficulties but expect to resolve occasional disagreements that arise during normal business activities. To minimize potential problems it is advisable for the franchisees to negotiate the original franchising agreement to accommodate local or special conditions. It is also advisable for franchisees to work to maintain a strong, productive relationship with the franchisor.

18-7   MANAGEMENT: A SYSTEM OF THOUGHT AND ACTION

In the most fundamental view, a franchisee is an entrepreneur concerned with the basic management functions of planning, organizing, directing and leading, and controlling. However, the franchisee also works cooperatively with the franchisor or headquarters organization.

A franchisee is granted the opportunity to use a proven trademark, service mark, products, services, and operating procedures of the franchise system. The product or service should provide quality and dependability, which should encourage customers to return for additional purchases. Comprehensive training in the management approach, marketing activities, financial reporting, and the franchisor's operational methods help ensure friendly, courteous, and efficient on-site management and operations for the business owner/entrepreneur (franchisee) and employees.

Usually each franchise system contains elements unique to that organization. Over time, ownership values and experience as well as environmental influences shape the view of the franchise system's top management on what constitutes a good approach to management. Economic, political, social, and technological influences in the general business environment and within the specific industry that the franchise systems operate shape the overall management philosophy. Such influence is identifiable by the franchise system in terms of resource availability and distribution; degree and type of government regulation on the firm and industry; approach to citizenship the franchise system expresses as based upon the needs, social values, and standards of the communities where the franchise system operates; and the nature of technology, its advances, and refinements. These shape operational characteristics, as well as the franchisor's planning, control, and feedback methods.

18-7a   Management Philosophy

Each franchise system owner/management is responsible for developing the theoretical framework from which good management practice can be identified, learned, and applied effectively. Most franchise systems have utilized a blend of five perspectives on management: classical, behavioral, quantitative, systems, and contingency approaches to management. Each perspective is based on different assumptions about objectives to be sought and human behavior at the worksite experienced within the franchise system over time.

The **classical management perspective** is rooted in management experience in manufacturing firms such as Ford Motor, General Motors, and Singer Sewing Machine Company, that typified U.S. industrialization in the early part of the twentieth century. The classical perspective includes a scientific impersonal approach to management that focuses on productivity of the individual worker. This approach suggests there is a "one best way" to perform each separate work task. For every task required to be done to produce the product, the firm should develop optimal procedures. Thus, with each task being performed in the best or ideal way, maximum productivity will take place. To accomplish this objective, management must incorporate several basic expectations, which include:

Development of work standards. Standard methods would need to be developed for each job to be performed within the organization. Selected workers must have the appropriate skill and ability for each job. Workers should be trained by management in the standard methods being required on each job. Workers are to implement work as planned for and scheduled by management. A good wage would be the best wage to motivate workers to their fullest capabilities. In addition, there should be standard work days, scheduled lunch breaks and rest periods, and removal of unsafe working conditions.

By using this approach, there would be a significant improvement in an organization's output without having substantial increase in costs, which would result in increased profitability. The focus of this approach is at the operations or functional level within a firm.

Work was viewed from a top-down approach. To be a successful manager, one must understand basic management functions of planning, organizing, directing (commanding or leading), and controlling.

The management focus on the overall business system is based on rules, policies and procedures, a fixed hierarchy of authority, and a clear division of labor.

Division of labor. Duties are divided into simple, specialized tasks so that the firm can use its workers and other resources more efficiently. A pyramid-shaped hierarchical structure ranks job positions by the amount of power and authority each has. Power and authority should increase at successively higher levels; each lower-level position is to be under direct control of one higher-level position. A complete set of rules and procedures provide guidelines and policies for performing all required duties. Rules should be clearly stated and workers should strictly adhere to the rules. Individualism is to be shunned. Personal favoritism should be avoided. Specific duties of workers should dictate behavior. The rules and procedures should be uniformly and impersonally applied to all workers. All workers are to be selected on the basis of technical competence and promotions should be based strictly upon job-related performance.

In general, the classical perspectives emphasizes (1) a scientific approach to task specialization and standardization at the functional and operating levels of the firm; (2) management functions of planning, organizing, directing, and controlling that emanated from the top to the bottom of the firm; and (3) a rational and impersonal organizational design based on rules and procedures to provide for operational efficiency, managerial effectiveness, and enhanced profitability.

The **behavioral management perspective** is a result of managers becoming more aware that human behavior has a significant impact on the performance of workers. The decline in hours required for an average work week, rise of unionism, ability of subordinates to influence a manager's decisions, improved working conditions, and increased educational levels of workers were changes that influenced how managers implemented the planning, direction, and controlling processes. Significant contribution came from Mary Parker Follett, an early management scholar. She concluded that coordination was the key to effective management and developed four principles to promote effective work groups.[8]

Coordination requires that people be in direct contact with one another.

Coordination is a continuous, ongoing process.

Coordination is essential in the initial stages of any endeavor.

Coordination must address all factors within any phase of any endeavor.

Elton Mayo[9] and the team from the Harvard Research Group recognized that the human element could play a significant role in determining worker behavior and output. Douglas McGregor[10] developed the Theory X and Theory Y propositions. Theory X managers would perceive their subordinates having an inherent dislike of work and that they will avoid work if at all possible. Further, subordinates will need to be coerced, threatened, or directed to get them to work toward achieving the organization's goals. Also, subordinates have little ambition, will avoid responsibility, and prefer to be directed. This theory would suggest management to exercise an authoritarian style, telling workers what to do and how to do it. Theory Y suggests that subordinates enjoy work, get satisfaction from performing a job well done, are self-motivated, display ambition, and receive satisfaction from achieving organizational goals. A manager who views subordinates in this manner would likely utilize a participative style, elicit their opinions, and encourage their involvement in decision making.

The **quantitative management perspective** was developed during World War II and the extremely complex problems associated with the war effort as waged on two fronts. The quantitative perspective focuses on decision making in which an alternative course of action is selected as a solution to some problem. The four basic characteristics are as follows:

Decision-making focus

Measurable criteria

Quantitative modeling to assess impact of each alternative

Usefulness and necessity of computers

This approach requires establishing measurable criteria so that alternatives can be compared before a choice is made. Quantitative models assess the impact of each alternative on the criteria. Often, computer usage is helpful in the problem-solving process, particularly for complex quantitative formulations. A host of quantitative tools have evolved such as linear programming, network and queuing models, game theory, inventory models, and statistical decision theory.

The **systems management perspective** developed as operations research teams confronted exceedingly complex problems which required breaking down the overall problem into component parts, identifying the nature of the parts and their interrelationships in order to simplify the model-building process. A system can be viewed as comprising three ingredients:

Inputs, such as material—workers, capital and equipment

Transformation process—the mechanism by which inputs are converted to outputs

Outputs—the good, service, or information desired by the system user; and the interaction of these ingredients and information flows

The interaction and information flow is often about the status and performance of the system. An open system is one that must interact with its external environment to survive, like any franchise system or other business organization. A closed system does not interact with the environment.

The **contingency management perspective** proposes there is no one best approach to management. It recognizes that any one, combination, or all preceding four perspectives can be used for different situations.[11] Which managerial perspective is best to use would be the one believed to be most effective in a given situation. Thus, managers should identify the key contingencies, or variables, in a given organizational situation. Type of technology being used—small batch, mass production, or continuous process—can have significant effect on the level of human interaction and involvement. Other important variables include organizational size, culture, and degree of change in the environment. For example, large organizations in stable environments and markets tend to utilize a bureaucratic form of organization. Formal organization, strong policies, and intricate operational procedures have been used by Ford, General Motors, Chrysler, and other automotive franchise systems very effectively. In contrast, some small franchise systems appear to rely more on functional skill available within different franchised units, use informality in problem solving, and provide for more autonomy at the franchisee level to achieve desired results. Therefore, the proper management style is dependent upon the key variables within a given situation. Thus, there is no "one best way" to design and manage a franchise system.

18-7b Planning

Planning can help the franchisee feel confident that the firm can respond to changing business demands, market conditions, and customer expectations. Planning is a process where the franchisee builds a business plan as well as a strategic plan that includes all the activities that lead to determining the firm's mission, goals, objectives, and actions. Planning identifies the appropriate courses of action necessary to achieve the objectives. From another perspective, quality planning means that decisions made today will produce desired results in the future. Usually, planning that achieves results is systematic and continuous. Leading franchise systems involve people at all levels of the system to ensure an effective planning process.

A business plan is a document developed by the franchisee for use as an overall guide for the business and may be useful to attract investors to the firm. (See also Chapter 3.) A financial plan is a subsection of the business plan and has strong linkage with data from the marketing subsection. Often, it has brief narrative statements and relies heavily on numbers. The financial plan requires financial analysis and projections. It should identify market demand, rate of growth in the market as well as for the firm's sales in that market, the amount of time before sales will make a profit, what can be expected as a rate of return on investment, and how likely the expected rate of return can continue.

Numerous benefits can be realized by the franchisee developing a business plan. First, it requires the franchisee to establishing a planning horizon some distance into the future about which it is logical to plan. High growth markets and markets with continual technological advances may require a three-, five- or seven-year planning horizon. Slow growth markets may require no more than a one- to two-year planning horizon. Second, the franchisee must analyze the external environment, particularly to identify the competitive conditions the new venture is likely to confront. The franchisee will want to study the economic trends of the community, population growth, demographic trends, customer baseand any other market-related factors that can impact the new franchised venture. Third, the initial plan should identify the distinctive strengths the new firm will have in relation to the competition. Fourth, the plan shows how resources are distributed across functional areas of the firm, and may show how resources are directly related to specific objectives to be pursued in accordance with the overall objectives and sales projections. Fifth, the plan must be useful as both a communication and motivation channel for the franchisee, appealing to employees and external stakeholders such as the investors and lending institutions, and the franchisor. Sixth, the plan should be useful as a reasonable basis for comparison with later plans in order to track firm progress toward achieving goals and objectives.

The strategic planning process may be the most important task for the franchisee, whether as a new franchise entrepreneur or an experienced franchisee. All activities of entry and running the business venture—financing, hiring, operations, marketing, distribution, and other functions—link directly to the overall strategy chosen by the franchisee. The strategic planning process has four stages as follows:

1. Determining the nature of the venture

2. Analyzing market opportunitiesand venture capabilities and identifying distinct competencies

3. Developing the overall venture strategy and supporting tactical strategies

4. Implementing the actual operations including acquiring needed resources determining controls, and acquiring the means for monitoring work and product and service quality

A critical feature of planning for both franchisee and for the franchise system is identification of a distinctive competence. The distinctive competence for the franchise system often relates directly to the product or service process quality or value. Distinctive competence for the franchisee, however, may be price, convenience, times of availability, service after sale, and so on. Though the distinctive competencies of the franchisor and franchisee can differ, they should be consistent and supportive of each other. Questions such as the following will help a franchisee identify distinctive competence.

Does the franchise system offer a unique product?

What is/are the unique feature(s)?

Is the product protected by patents?

Is there anything unique about distribution, for example, direct to customer? Is there anything unique about customer service, for example, speed or quality? Is there anything unique or specialized about repair or service after sale? Is there a product warranty? Is the warranty above the norm for the competition? Is there something special about your employment package, for example, factors that may encourage loyalty, longevity, and growth within the business? If you have a sales force, is there anything distinctive about them as a group, for example, extent of experience, friendliness?

Providing honest answers to such questions can help uncover competencies as well as opportunities for improvement. Several other points should be considered also. Not all franchise systems truly have a distinct competence. For those that do, not always is that franchise system successful. For example, one may develop a technologically superior mousetrap, but if the price is too high or the customer doesn't know about it or demand the product, then the business venture is likely to be lackluster or fail. Further, seldom is a distinctive competence sustainable over time. If you enjoy a competitive advantage in the marketplace based on a distinct competence and you are profitable, eventually competition will try to copy your approach, product features, or service. At some point, the wise franchisee realizes that sooner or later any particular advantage held in the marketplace will be met or exceeded by the competition. Thus, the task for the franchise system and franchisee is to maximize the return from your distinctive competence while such competence exists and adjust your strategy appropriately when competitors make inroads. Perhaps a change in hours available, additional locations, or new product/service feature or warranty can increase customer interest while decreasing competitor impact on your sales and market share.

A current example can serve to highlight the importance of planning, core competence, and competitive advantage. McDonald's is long noted for sticking closely with their core products. Recently, they are testing to see how far they can stretch their famous name and brands. In the winter of 2001, McDonald's opened a McCafe gourmet coffee shop and a Denny's-style restaurant called McDonald's with the Diner Inside. Other possible changes to come may include rolling out more dessert kiosks under a new brand called McTreat, and a concept called McSnack, which would offer a limited menu in airports and malls.

At select New York City, Chicago, and California McDonald restaurants, a partnership with Intel will allow purchasers of an Extra Value Meal to receive an added benefit—60 minutes of high-speed wireless Internet access. McDonald's touts it as a great way for customers to "unwire, unwind, enjoy an Extra Value Meal and catch up on email." This is one more example of McDonald's exploiting its convenience and customer service competencies at a new level.[12]

Franchisees of McDonald's look to the parent company to provide the planning, research, and development of new products and delivery mechanisms. The franchisees must plan and implement at their own locations, but central planning by McDonald's at Oak Brook, Illinois, can impact products and even availability of brands at the franchisee/retail level. It is incumbent upon franchisees not only to plan for the future but also to be flexible and adaptable enough to modify their plans and methods of implementation in order to keep up with long-term interests of the franchise system and the customers' ever-changing wants and needs.

18-7c   Organization

There are many ways to organize and operate a franchise business. For some, the initial organizational design will be simple. In fact, the franchisee may be the only person in the business, performing all the functions of the organization. Many franchise systems are geared toward a franchisee who wants part-time to full-time responsibility that does not grow beyond the level of the "one man band" size. Some franchise systems look for an entrepreneurial franchisee who wants to start small but seeks growth and expanding market share. For these franchisees, as the workload increases the organizational structure will need to expand to include additional employees with defined duties. Other franchise systems will recommend an organizational design including all the major activities required to operate it efficiently and effectively.

A franchisee's organization structure is a framework of jobs and departments that directs individual and group behavior toward achieving the firm's objectives. One of the most significant decisions about organization is to determine how specialized jobs will be. By dividing work tasks into narrow specialties, the franchisee/business owner gains the advantage of division of labor. Job specialization has been a hallmark of America's work culture, as exemplified particularly through manufacturing and then applied toward other industries and service businesses.

To what extent should the franchisee employ job specialization? That is, to what extent should the workflow of the franchised operations be set up based on job scope (breadth) in contrast to job specialization (depth)? The advantages of high job specialization with a narrow range of tasks include high productivity, generally lower cost of labor per unit of output, higher wages when efficiency is high, utilization of unskilled labor, predictable work (performance) schedules, and control of workflow—both quantity and quality—by management. Disadvantages of job specialization include boredom due to high routinization of work, poor morale over time, lack of pride in work being performed, and low job interest.

In contrast, providing for greater breadth within specific jobs provides the advantages of acquiring and maintaining high skill among the workers, having high-quality output, and having workers who take pride in their work and who generally demonstrate high interest in their respective jobs. The weaknesses of designing an organization with broad job scope include typically lower productivity per unit of output when compared to output for organizations utilizing high job specialization, higher cost per unit of output, poor managerial control over quantity and quality, and less predictable output scheduling.

Given the highly competitive nature of most franchised businesses, the strengths of job specialization are often considered more advantageous than its weaknesses. Thus, most franchise systems tend to use job specialization to the extent possible in production and sale of franchised product/service. However, more recently, movement is taking place toward greater job breadth in industries with significant market growth by franchise systems in professional services, business services, financial services, recreation, and health care.

The second question for the franchisee is, To what extent should authority be delegated or distributed in the organization? Authority can be centralized or decentralized. Decentralization is the process of delegating to an employee the right to make a decision without obtaining approval from the immediate supervisor. True decentralization also includes the right to identify issues, define problems, and recommend solution strategies. Decentralization is the spreading downward and outward of authority in order to provide decision-making opportunity and responsibility for employees at each level in the franchise business. At the other extreme, centralization is the process of retaining or holding authority in the hands of the franchisee. It may also be holding on to the power to make decisions by the franchisee and other select, high-level managers. Other employees in the franchised business have very limited, if any, decision-making authority, yet are held accountable for implementing the decisions made by the franchisee and/or other top managers. There is a general trend in franchising to decentralize authority and decision making as much as possible. Successful franchise systems have found that central office managers and independent franchisee-owners who develop their own decision-making skills, are more motivated to perform, exercise more autonomy, and feel a stronger link between their individual performance and the firm's profitability.

The third organizational question is, How does one group the jobs in accordance with some logical arrangement? As a franchise system grows in size, and as job specialization increases, jobs should be grouped to achieve both efficiency and effectiveness. In the small franchisee-owned unit, the franchisee may perform all the functions or can often supervise everyone employed. In contrast, in many auto-related franchises, retail, health care, and food franchises, managerial positions are developed for departments and for shifts, with added supervisory positions created according to some plan so that the operations can run smoothly.

There are a number of ways a franchise business can be departmentalized. The four most common means for departmentalizing a franchised business include departmentation by function, product, customer, and geography. Grouping jobs according to the functions of the organization, that is, by operations, marketing, finance/accounting, and personnel/human resources, is called functional departmentation. This approach establishes departments or group operations based on commonality of skills and similarity of tasks, taking advantage of both job and task specialization. Functional departmentation (see Figure 18-2) tends to work best when the franchise business is small to midsize, provides a single product or a primary product with closely associated complimentary products/services (e.g., hamburger, fries and drink), and the competitive conditions are fairly stable. There are other structural forms, but the functional form of organization is used predominantly by small and growing franchise systems. It is the most commonly used form of departmentation within most franchise systems.

The franchise system and the franchisee must develop a formal, explicit organizational design so that all members of the franchise unit know their responsibilities and expectations concerning their performance. There are six typical areas covered within a franchise organization and operations scheme. These materials should be covered within the operations and administrative manuals provided by the franchisor. Table 18-3 identifies the seminal elements of a franchise organizational design.

Training required by the franchisee, either on or off the job, must be specified in terms of skills to be acquired, knowledge to be learned, formal education to be attained, or experience to be gained.

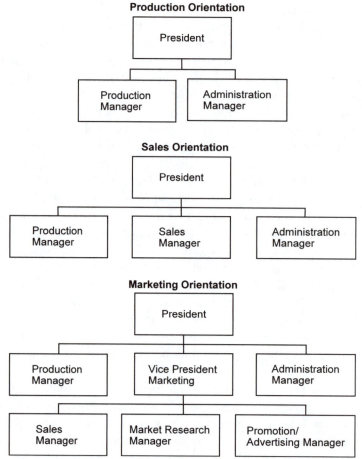

FIGURE **18-2**

Functional Departmentation by Orientation

AREAS COVERED IN A FRANCHISE ORGANIZATIONAL DESIGN

The method or means of organizational structure should define the duties for each job and relationships to other jobs within the firm. These relationships are usually shown in an organizational chart.

The planning approach and evaluation scheme should link all activities to the goals and objectives sought by the franchise. It is the responsibility of the franchisee, as entrepreneur, to spell out the goals, identify specific objectives, identify how the objectives will be achieved, and how employee performance will be measured and evaluated. Sales projections, daily sales logs, expenditure reports, and profitability will indicate progress toward objectives. The franchisor's field representative may prove to be a valuable asset to guide and counsel the franchisee in these deliberations.

The franchisee and the key managerial staff are responsible for providing the rewards for work such as wage scale for each job and classification of similar jobs, opportunities for promotion, bonuses, transfers, and so on.

The franchisee is responsible for determining the guidelines to be used for selection of employees. Often, the franchise system provides job titles, job descriptions, sample personnel policies, and performance expectations for each position. This information, policies, and job titles can be of great value to the new franchisee.

The operations process must be identified. A flowchart can depict the physical process of materials/supplies movement through a production operation, the decision process, alternatives and criteria about a certain activity, or a combination of the two. The franchise system operations manual should be extremely helpful to the franchisee for delineating the sequences and decision content required within the franchise's operations. The workflow, or sequence, for each franchise product or service and descriptions of what is to be done by whom and with what equipment is an invaluable asset to the franchisee, particularly in the first several years of operation as a franchisee unit.

BLENDED LEARNING: THE CONVERGENCE OF E-LEARNING AND MEETINGS

Blended learning—learning events that combine elements of Internet and in-person instruction—is a rapidly growing trend in e-learning. The most productive online learning experiences allow students to interact with each other or the instructor. In addition, resources and references are often involved, and online students must do assignments. Blended learning initially received acceptance at colleges and universities, where online-delivered readings and discussions increasingly supported classroom instruction. A similar effort provides the opportunity of broadening and improving the instructional experience for franchisors and their customers. Blended learning appears to be most effective for learning that is concentrated on one subject. This type of learning is also better oriented to the manner in which adults learn.

Adapted from Jeff Ward and Gary A. LaBranche, "Blended Learning: The Convergence of E-learning and Meetings," Franchising World 35(4) (June 2003): 22.

Among the legal forms of organization are proprietorship, partnership, and the corporation. The typical corporate form is the **C corporation**, but the S corporation has grown in popularity because of its simplicity and advantages associated with the typical proprietorship. Each legal form of ownership is identified by distinguishing characteristics. Choosing which legal form is best for a particular franchisee is truly an entrepreneurial decision because the factors involved can vary in importance to the franchisor, the customer, and even suppliers to the business.

The franchisor may prefer that a franchisee be organized as a sole proprietorship so that the franchisee has unlimited liability back to the franchisor. On the other hand, the franchisor may recommend the franchisee to incorporate, or set up a limited or general partnership. It is likely that the franchise system will recommend to the prospective franchisee what legal form of organization has worked best for the franchisor–franchisee relationship. There is no one "best" legal form. The most appropriate legal form is the one that meets both the franchisor's and the franchisee's common needs and interests as partners for profitability. A new franchisee should consult with a CPA or attorney to have the current legal requirements and tax code information available so the franchisee can make the optimal decision about legal organizational form.

The **sole proprietorship** is the most common form of franchisee business ownership. The franchisee, as an individual business owner, is liable for all the business' liabilities and has a right to all the profits excluding royalty or other franchisor fees. Most beginning franchisees prefer to start their entrepreneurial venture as a sole proprietor because proprietorship is simple to enter, operate, and terminate. Also, it provides for relative freedom of action and control. The proprietorship is taxed at the owner's personal income tax rate. There are some negative factors to operating the franchised business as a proprietorship. The business and its owner are one in the same. The business must terminate (close, stop business) with the owner's death. If the business cannot pay its bills, the franchisee—as owner—must use personal assets to pay them. The capital that can be put together to start and continue to fund the business is limited by the amount of capital the owner alone can put together Sole proprietorships also tend to have difficulty obtaining credit and may pay higher rates for credit granted until the firm is well established as a successful business.

A partnership is a voluntary association of two or more persons who agree to co-own a business for profit. The partnership is similar to the proprietorship in that it has limited life, unlimited liability of the partner/owners for debt incurred, and the partners are taxed on profits and loss as individuals. The partnership has distinct advantages not available in a proprietorship. The partnership has a larger pool of talent available to make decisions, perform the work, and share the risk.

However, it may be difficult to transfer ownership. The problem of unlimited liability in the partnership organization can be avoided by forming a limited partnership. Limited partners invest money; they cannot take an active role in the operations of the franchise business or be held liable for debts undertaken by the active partner. If the business fails, limited partners are liable only to the extent of their investment.

The regular *corporation* is the legal form found to be most used as business firms survive and grow. Although only about 20 percent of all the total number of U.S. businesses are legally formed as corporations, they account for 90 percent of all sales revenues. This is why most people equate corporations with big business. The corporation is a legal entity. It can sue and be sued; buy, hold, and sell property; make and sell products or services to customers; and can even be tried and punished under criminal law. The primary advantages of the general corporate form include liability limited to the extent of investment by each stockholder; life of the corporation is continuous and independent of the individual owners/investors' lives; ownership can be easily transferred through sale of stock; and the corporation may have an easier time raising money. This last advantage stems from the corporation's ability to sell shares of stock to investors which increases the amount of equity in the business. Further, the franchisee, or primary owner, can sell the business to another party without dissolving the corporation, if such action is allowable by the franchisor–franchisee contract.

The corporation is closely regulated. It must have a corporate charter filed with the state of incorporation. States will vary as to taxes, business fees, liability for debts, minimum sum contributed by the founder, rules for issuance of stock, and the minimum number of persons needed to constitute a legal board of directors for the business. The corporation typically requires more extensive recordkeeping and other documentation of its business dealings.

The **S corporation** is an alternative to the regular corporate form which began in 1958. It quickly became popular because it avoids double taxation. The franchisee and other shareholders are taxed as partners; they do not have to pay taxes on dividends twice. The S corporation retains all other corporate advantages such as limited liability for shareholders. There are some restrictions on the S corporation. The S corporation must be domestic; that is, it cannot be part of another corporation. It must be independently owned and operated. Only individuals and estates of individuals can be shareholders. (This keeps other corporations from buying shares of its stock to seek control and then have the corporation operate as a "puppet" of the larger, controlling interest corporation.) The S corporation can have no more than thirty-five shareholders, and nonresident aliens cannot be shareholders. One can argue that the S corporation differs little from the regular corporation, because it may be no more than a corporation with limited size and capital structure. Table 18-4 provides a summary of the central points of sole proprietorship, partnership, and corporate forms of organization.

IFA'S VETFRAN INITIATIVE

Prospective franchisees who are veterans may want to consider companies that have signed up with Veterans Transition Franchise Initiative (VetFran), IFA's program promoting access to franchise ownership to former military personnel. These franchising companies have agreed to offer U.S. veterans special incentives to ease the way for those who want to achieve the dream of small business ownership. A list of franchise companies participating in VetFran can be found at www.franchise.org.

TABLE 18-4 SUMMARY OF LEGAL ORGANIZATIONAL FORMS

Forms of Ownership	Advantages	Disadvantages
Sole proprietorship	1. Ease of formation 2. Sole ownership of profits 3. Decision making and control invested in one owner 4. Flexibility 5. Relative freedom from governmental control 6. Freedom from corporate business taxes	1. Unlimited liability 2. Lack of continuity 3. Less available capital 4. Relative difficulty in obtaining long-term financing 5. Relatively limited viewpoint and experience
Partnership	1. Ease of formation 2. Direct rewards 3. Growth and performance facilitated 4. Flexibility 5. Relative freedom from governmental control and regulation 6. Possible tax advantage	1. Unlimited liability of at least one partner 2. Lack of continuity 3. Relative difficulty in obtaining large sums of capital 4. Being bound by the action of just one partner 5. Difficulty of disposing of partnership interest
Corporation	1. Limited liability 2. Easy transfer of ownership 3. Unlimited life 4. Relative ease of securing capital in large amounts 5. Increased ability and expertise	1. Activity restrictions 2. Lack of representation 3. Regulation 4. Organizing expenses

18-8   HUMAN RESOURCE MANAGEMENT

Many franchise systems have a personnel manual to help guide franchisee human resources policies and procedures that they strongly suggest franchisees adopt. Some franchisers merely recommend that the franchisee follow the human resource guidelines that the franchiser utilizes for the corporate entity, whereas other franchise systems leave the franchisees to their own devices, not offering help in this arena of management. However, most of the franchise systems with minimal human resource guidance involve contracts with franchisees that will rarely grow beyond the size of a few employees.

When a franchise system does not provide personnel policies or guidelines that franchisees can utilize, the franchisee should take necessary steps to develop appropriate personnel policies and processes including hiring methods.

If you are to succeed as the franchisee of a growing business, you must have a highly performing workforce to efficiently and effectively provide your product or service. In reality, you must persuade the best qualified people to come to work in your franchise operation; maintain their interest, motivation, and knowledge so they are willing and able to perform successfully; and then retain them as productive employees.

Attracting the best and the brightest employees begins with creating an organization where good employees want to work. Such an organization offers well-designed jobs, good compensation, and opportunities for personal development through training and perhaps even career advancement.

18-8a   Step One: Understand the Applicable Employment Laws and Regulations

It is important that the franchisee understand the legal context in which the business must operate. Whether one chooses to outsource personnel activities such as the hiring processes or conduct these activities in-house, the franchisee is still responsible for compliance with applicable federal and state requirements. The franchisee should begin by becoming familiar with the employment laws of the particular state in which the franchise units reside as well as the federal statutes that apply to all firms in all states. Table 18-5 provides a list and brief synopsis of major federal statutes and their coverage of employers.

18-8b   Step Two: Define the Job Duties and Responsibilities

It is important to define the duties and responsibilities, as well as the job specifications, required for successful job performance. This step refers to identifying the primary tasks, duties, and responsibilities that are a regular and essential part of a job. Of course, not every duty to be performed will be identified in advance; however, this planning process provides an opportunity for the franchisee to visualize the successful operation of the business and determine how a particular position and incumbent can add value to business operations.

The next step is to determine the job specifications required for a qualified incumbent to successfully perform the job. Job specifications, also called job qualifications, are the skills, knowledge, abilities, and physical and personality requirements (SKAPPs) an incumbent must possess to successfully perform the job duties and responsibilities. Job specifications are usually stated in terms of minimum and preferred education and experience requirements. See Table 18-6 for the components of a job description. It is important that job specifications be related to job and performance to eliminate conflicts with ADA requirements.

If the franchise system has provided job descriptions to be used by the franchisee, there may be a requirement to adhere precisely to these job descriptions as well as an active discouragement of any creative changes or modifications to the job descriptions and thereby the operational processes on the part of the franchisee. This should be recognized as a means of control on the part of the franchisor. Making changes may be seen as intent to change one or more functional characteristics or qualities of the franchised operations process. Such action may be a violation of the franchise contract. Check the operations manual and contract carefully before making modifications to jobs or creating new job titles and descriptions on one's own.

18-8c   Step Three: Recruit to Fill the Vacancy

The nature of the vacancy to be filled will determine to some extent the best recruiting sources to be used. In general, however, employee referrals or recommendations have been found to be one of the best sources for high-quality employees.[13] The referring employees can acquaint the prospective employee with the company, the organizational culture and values, and even aspects of the job to be filled, thereby providing the applicant with an accurate company and job preview.

Newspapers continue to be a popular source for employees seeking information about employment opportunities according to a 1998 study. Most newspaper classified advertisements eventually end up posted on the Internet through the electronic version of the newspaper, which can provide an added bonus.[14]

Although the Internet is increasingly used for recruiting and job searches, it is not necessarily the best alternative for a company that is seeking local candidates. Rarely do postings on a national job search site such as Monster.com or Americas Job Bank generate a high percentage of usable resumes. Resumes from these types of sources tend to be forwarded for a multitude of jobs without

TABLE 18-5

Applicable Federal Employment Laws and Regulations	Number of Employees
1938 Fair Labor Standards Act (FLSA) Establishes a minimum wage. Establishes exempt and nonexempt classifications under FLSA and overtime pay requirements. The child-labor provisions of FLSA set the minimum age for employment with unlimited hours at sixteen years of age. For hazardous occupations, the age is eighteen years. Those aged fourteen to fifteen may work with limitations.	Two or four more and engaged in Interstate Commerce
1963 Equal Pay Act Prohibits paying different wages based on gender. Similar pay must be given for jobs requiring equal skills, effort, or responsibility or jobs performed under similar working conditions.	Two or four more and engaged in Interstate Commerce
1964 Title VII, Civil Rights Act Prohibits employment discrimination based on race, color, religion, gender, or national origin. Includes equal opportunity in training programs. Illegal to discriminate because of pregnancy, childbirth, or related conditions. Prohibits sexual harassments.	Fifteen
1967 Age Discrimination in Employment Act (ADEA) Prohibits discrimination in employment based on age for persons age forty and over. Generally forbids mandatory retirement based on age.	Twenty
1986 Immigration Reform and Control Act (Amended 1990) It is illegal for an employer to hire a person who is not authorized to work in the United States. Employers must verify that a new employee is eligible to work in the United States and record eligibility on Form I-9. The 1990 amendment prohibits discrimination against foreign-looking job applicants and establishes penalties for hiring illegal aliens.	All sized employers
1978 Pregnancy Discrimination Act Employers must provide access to medical benefits and sick leave on the same basis as such benefits are provided to other employees or for other medical conditions.	Fifteen
1988 Employee Polygraph Protection Act Provides broad prohibitions on the use of lie detector tests in employment. With a few narrowly defined exceptions for "security-sensitive" positions, it is unlawful for employers to use lie detectors in employment decisions.	All sized employers
1990 Americans with Disabilities Act (ADA) Protects qualified individuals with disabilities from discrimination in the workplace, including access to training and career development. A qualified individual is one who can perform the essential function of the job with or without reasonable accommodation. Preemployment physicals may only be required after an offer of employment has been extended.	Fifteen
1993 Family and Medical Leave Act (FMLA) Employees are entitled to take up to twelve weeks of unpaid leave during any twelve-month period to care for a family member or because of a serious health condition of the employee. An employee must have worked at least twelve months for the employer and 1,250 hours in the past year to be eligible. Employees are entitled to take leave in the following cases: serious health condition of a spouse, child, or parent; serious health condition of the employee; birth of a child or adoption or foster-care placement of a child.	Fifty (FT or PT) within seventy-five miles

the applicant even knowing which specific jobs they are applying for. As a result, these applicants may not meet the minimum qualifications of the job or even be interested in the geographic area for the job. If your franchise has a website, include an option on the site for applicants to learn about career and employment opportunities. Once you've prepared the online ad for your own site, look into posting it at other locally oriented sites such as the chamber of commerce, local educational institutions (e.g., community colleges, universities, technical colleges), and state employment

TABLE 18-6   **COMPONENTS OF A JOB DESCRIPTION**

Job Title: A succinct short descriptive name for the job.

General Summary Description: A one- or two-sentence general description of the job responsibilities.

Essential Duties and Responsibilities: A list of six to ten primary tasks, duties, and responsibilities that are a regular and essential part of the job. These statements should begin with active verbs to communicate the nature of the work activities. Sample action verbs are *directs, coordinates, researches, performs, ensures, develops, inputs, evaluates, approves, creates, mixes, prepares, searches, schedules, sorts, drives, loads, writes,* and *procures.*

Required Skills, Knowledge, Abilities, and Physical and Personality Characteristics (SKAPPs): State specific knowledge requirements, such as familiarity, awareness, or understanding gained about a body of information through experience or education. State required skills. A skill is an observable competence to perform a learned psychomotor act. List abilities. Abilities constitute a present competence to perform an observable behavior that results in an observable product. Indicate personality requirements. One should include only those related to successful performance of the job. Indicate physical requirements which should highlight any unusual physical requirements necessary such as standing, walking, climbing, stooping, kneeling, lifting, pulling, pushing, and other working conditions (i.e., outdoors in extreme weather).

Minimum desired education and/or experience requirements required.

offices. The challenge is to narrow advertising to the types of recruitment sources that have in the past or that you anticipate will yield highly qualified applicants.[15]

Another source of talent is student interns or cooperative education students. These students typically combine school and work that includes developmental assignments where they learn about an industry, company, and occupation. The work-study period provides the employer an opportunity to review the work of the intern. Upon completion of their educational program, interns who performed successfully can then be hired full time.

Temporary workers are increasingly being used as a primary source of workers for a variety of employers, including franchised firms. Employers see the temporary assignments as a risk-free probationary period during which they may end the temporary assignment without providing any rationale if they are not completely satisfied. If they are satisfied with the employee's work, the employer may offer the temporary worker employment with the company. As a result of this practice of employers contracting for temporary employees, Manpower was the largest private employer in the year 2000. In 2007, Manpower remains as one of the world's largest employers, serving over 400,000 client firms worldwide through 4,400 offices in 23 countries.

Regardless of the recruitment source, hiring is about selecting the applicant who is best qualified to perform the particular job. In order to decide who is best qualified, the franchisee needs to gather information about those who apply for the job. Information about applicants can be obtained from resumes, employment applications, background investigations, or directly from the applicant during the employment interview.

Resumes are probably the most commonly used source of information about applicants, but also problematic if used in isolation. From a franchisee's perspective, the problem with a resume is that the applicant controls the content of the resume. Applicants are likely to provide different information in their resumes, perhaps even illegal or inappropriate information (e.g., marital status, height, weight, race, religion). Even though the franchisee would not request this information, it is part of the applicant's file. An applicant may allege the information was used in a discriminatory manner and later allege discrimination.

Furthermore, because of the different formats for resumes, there is no guarantee that a resume will contain the information a franchisee needs to make an employment decision. In addition, because there are no specific requirements for information, an applicant can simply chose to omit or exaggerate information that does not reflect favorably upon them. Studies indicate that as many as 33 to 40 percent of resumes contain fraudulent information.

18-8d Franchisee's Own Employment Application Form

All applicants interested in employment should be asked to complete the franchisee's employment application form. The application form should request a record of basic information about the candidate who is applying for a job. All questions asked should be related to the job for which the applicant is applying. Unlike the resume, the information requested is chosen by the franchisee and the same information is obtained from all candidates for the position available. The application form should include a statement whereby the applicant verifies that the information provided on the application is truthful and a space where the applicant signs and dates the form. If hired, falsification of information on the application may be grounds for dismissal. Once hired, the application form should become a part of the employee's personnel record. All applications of those not hired should be treated the same—either destroyed, returned, or retained for a specified period of time, but usually not longer than one year. If a franchisor does not provide a recommended application form, then the franchisee can get a generalized form from an office supply store. See Figure 18-3 for a sample statementwhich the franchisee may want to include with the application form.

Franchisee Firm Name Address	APPLICATION FOR EMPLOYMENT (SAMPLE)	An Equal Opportunity Employer

I understand and agree to the following terms that:

1. Any material misrepresentation or deliberate omission of act in my application justifies refusal of employment, or if employed, termination from employment.

2. I understand that (Franchisee Firm) can make a thorough investigation of my entire work history from data given in this application, related papers or oral interviews and obtain additional information about my background. I agree to release (Franchisee Firm) from all liability that may arise from the results of any investigation.

3. I agree that if I am employed, I may be terminated by (Franchisee Firm) at any time without liability for wage or salary except such as may have been earned at the date of termination. Further, I agree to submit to search of my person, any locker assigned to me, any coat, handbag or packages, and waive all claims for damages as result of such examination.

4. If a contingent offer of employment is made to me, I authorize any physician or hospital to release any information which may be needed to determine my ability to perform essential duties of a job I am considered for prior to employment or in the future(if state laws permit). Further, I agree to submit to alcohol and/or drug screening tests if requested at any time prior to or during my employment.

5. Business needs may make the following conditions mandatory: overtime, shift work, a rotating work schedule, or schedule other than Monday through Friday. I accept these conditions for continuing employment.

6. I understand that this is an application for employment, that no employment contract is being offered, and that if I am employed, such employment is for no definite period of time. And, if or when a significant decrease in work occurs, it may result in the layoff of employees. Employees retained will be those who have excelled in their assigned positions regardless of length of service.

7. I understand that (Franchisee Firm) can change wages, benefits, work schedules, job responsibilities, or other conditions of work at any time without my prior consent.

I have read and understand the above statement.

DATE: _____   SIGNATURE _____

FIGURE 18-3

Sample Statement to Accompany Application Form

TABLE **18-7**	**WHEN TO LOOK CLOSER—EMPLOYMENT APPLICATION RED FLAGS**

- Is there a logical sequence to the applicant's job changes? Do the reasons given for changing jobs make sense?

- Look for conflicting details or overlapping dates of employment.

- Look for gaps in employment dates. Is there the potential for the omission of unfavorable employment work? Has the applicant changed employers after only a short time on the job without advancing to a better job? Do job titles and the job duties described match?

- Ask for written permission to contact previous employers and references and to verify education. (A dishonest applicant may drop out at this point.)

Any paperwork the franchisee receives from an employment applicant is worth careful review to assess its validity and to help the franchisee determine who among the applicants should advance further in the hiring process. Table 18-7 identifies areas of the employment application that should be reviewed carefully. The franchisee must be careful not to "pry" too deeply to the point where the franchisee may be stepping into discriminatory areas. For example, if a man was off work on disability leave, he is not obliged to tell the franchisee the nature of the disability.

18-8e   Step Four: The Selection Interview

The selection interview is an opportunity to interact personally with candidates for employment. The selection interview should be planned in advance and approached as one would any other important meeting. Preparing for a successful selection interview brings together what the franchisee knows about the vacant job and the applicant for that job. The structured interview consistently yields more reliable and valid interview outcomes than other types of interviews.[16] It consists of a set of preplanned questions without deviation from these questions. The semistructured interview uses a set of planned, standardized questions asked of all job applicants, but also allows the interviewer to deviate from those questions to ask other related questions. The interviewer is able to pursue job-related questions with each candidate based on the nature of each individual interview. The advantage of using the semistructured interview approach is that similar types of job-related information is obtained from all candidates and also there is less likelihood of problems if a candidate files a discrimination complaint.

In generating interview questions, the two types of questions that are most effective in eliciting job-related responses are behavioral description questions and hypothetical questions. Each is discussed in this section, and illustrations are provided that may be tailored by franchisees for their individual use.

18-8f   Behavioral Description Questions

Behavioral description questions are based on the belief that past behavior is the best predictor of future behavior. Applicants are asked to give specific examples of how they have responded in past situations. Answers may be related to past work, academic, or personal settings. Questions might begin with the following phrases.

Tell me about a time when you...

How did you...

How have you...

How have you handled...

Recall a time when you...

Describe a situation when you...

18-8g Hypothetical Questions

Hypothetical questions encourage applicants to think about how they might respond if put into a particular situation. The emphasis is on how interviewees think they would respond and their thought processes. Questions might begin with the following phrases.

What if...

How would you react if...

What would you do if...

How would you respond if...

Once the franchisee has developed the set of open-ended questions and structured them into the interview plan, the next question involves who should be involved in conducting the job interview. Careful consideration should be given to determine who would be the most appropriate person(s) to conduct the interview. Should it be the franchisee? Should it be a day or night supervisor? Should it be a crew chief of a work group? It may be appropriate that the interview be conducted by the franchisee and one or more persons from the firm with direct oversight of the position to be filled. The reasons may seem obvious. An interview involving the franchisee and additional staff can ensure that the following occurs.

- No questions are missed in the interview.

- Integrity remains throughout the interview process.

- Documentation of the responses during the interview is accurate.

- Additional company eyes and ears are available in the event there is an unfounded allegation of discrimination made by the interviewee.

Interviewers should make notes of the responses from each candidate during the interviews. It is not necessary to take detailed notes, but enough should be recorded so that the candidates can be differentiated from one another and be remembered individually at the end of all of the interviews. Care should be taken that only job-related information is documented, as these data may be available in the event any type of complaint is filed. Figure 18-4 provides a model sequence to follow during the interview process.

18-8h Step Five: Conduct a Background Investigation

Applicants who appear to be finalists are usually subjected to some level of a background investigation, which includes verification of the information on their application such as education and employment experience. At this point, prior employers and references should be contacted, and education and eligibility to work in the United States verified. These tasks may be performed by the franchisee or contracted out. If performed by the franchisee, the applicant should be asked to provide a written authorization for the franchisee or a designee to make these inquiries. Almost half of the states have laws that protect employers from potential legal actions when they provide "good-faith references."[17]

Greet the Candidate

- Thank the person for coming in today at the appointed time.

- Introduce oneself and any other interviewers

Establish Rapport and Set the Tone for the Interview

- Make the candidate feel welcome.

- Get the candidate to talk about something of personal interest.

Give an Overview of the Purpose of the Interview

- Get the interview on track. "We are here to interview for the position of..."

- "We will be taking some notes."

Elicit Information about the Candidate

- Consult the prepared behavioral and/or hypothetical questions.

- Listen, Listen, Listen.

- Allow a few moments of silence between questions and before answers to allow time for the candidate to think, relax, and respond.

Briefly Describe the Job and the Franchise Business

- Give a realistic job interview.

- Tell the truth about the job, the firm, and the working conditions.

Ask the Candidate for Questions and Allow Time for Responses

Close the Interview

- Signal that the interview is complete (e.g., put pen down, move note pad forward, lean back in chair, or other appropriate behavioral movements that would indicate intent to close).

- "We hope to make a decision about this job (soon) (in the next two weeks) etc."

- "Thank you for coming in for the interview." Close with meaningful handshake, if that seems appropriate.

- Stand up and walk the candidate out of the interview area.

FIGURE **18-4**

A Model Sequence for a Successful Candidate Selection Interview Process

---

18-8i   Step Six: Make a Conditional Job Offer

Based on the full range of information obtained during the selection process, a conditional job offer may be made to a candidate. The job offer is usually conditional based on successfully passing certain medical tests such as a physical exam or substance abuse test. For those employers covered under the Americans with Disabilities Act, a physical examination may only be required once a conditional job offer has been extended.

In essence there are six primary steps that a franchisee should take when approaching the hiring of a new employee. The steps are as follows:

- **Step One.** *Understand the applicable employment laws and regulations.*

- **Step Two.** *Define the job duties and responsibilities and the job specifications required for successful performance.*

- **Step Three.** *Recruit to fill the vacancy.*

- **Step Four.** *Host the selection interview.*

- **Step Five.** *Conduct a background investigation.*

- **Step Six.** *Make a conditional job offer.*

The money, time, and effort spent to recruit and hire a new employee is only the beginning of the investment you make in your company's human capital. A new hire requires information, resources, and motivation to perform satisfactorily. Once hired, this person must be introduced to your organization and trained to effectively perform the duties of the new position. Employee training has been shown to impact employee satisfaction, particularly among younger employees. For those employees who received no training, 70 percent were satisfied with their jobs; when employees received at least six days of training within the previous year, job satisfaction increased to 84 percent.[18]

Chick-fil-A restaurants provide another example of investing in human capital for results in their program for high-achieving high school employees. These part-time employees are offered $1,000 to $2,000 in college scholarship money while employed for Chick-fil-A and are eligible to compete for up to $18,000 in scholarships to attend Berry College in Rome, Georgia. The company not only creates employee satisfaction and loyalty but also creates "... a pipeline of talent for its full-time recruiting needs; more than half of the new restaurant operators have worked previously at a Chick-fil-A stores as a part-timer." In an industry where the average turnover among store operators is 35 percent, it is less than 5 percent a year at Chick-fil-A.[19]

Motivation is the desire within people that causes them to act. Variables related to the job, the work context, and the quality of supervision may influence employee motivation. How a job is designed refers to how job tasks, duties, and responsibilities are combined to create a specific job that an individual will perform. Job design can influence performance, job satisfaction, and physical and mental health. An understanding of the nature of job design and its potential impact on employees will allow the franchise manager to better understand and manage human resources. Person/job fit is an important concept that involves matching people with jobs that have appropriate characteristics. The job characteristics model developed by Hackman and Oldham identifies five important design characteristics of jobs.

- Skill variety—extent to which work requires multiple different activities

- Task identity—extent to which the job includes a "whole" identifiable unit of work from start to finish that is a definable product

- Task significance—amount of impact the job has on others

- Autonomy—extent of individual freedom and discretion in the work and scheduling

- Feedback—amount of information received about performance

Appropriate adjustments to these job characteristics based on the person/job fit have resulted in improved performance, productivity, and quality.[20] Employee satisfaction and health are also positively impacted by the appropriate job-person fit based on research indications.

While on the job, employees need to continue receiving feedback that they are doing a good job. More than 40 percent of the employers who participated in a 2002 survey indicated they are finding recognition programs to be helpful in motivating and retaining employees. One example is Avis, the car rental company, which has had a program to recognize outstanding performers since 1999.[21]

Satisfied employees are less likely to be absent from work or turn over their position—two costly personnel problems.[22] Having to fill in for absent or resigned employees, overtime, temporaries, and the manager's or owner's time are obvious costs and inconveniences. More subtle are the opportunities lost because an employee with a given knowledge or skill is missing at any given time.

Some absenteeism and turnover is inevitable. The franchisee, working with the franchiser, should work to improve those factors that can be controlled in order to minimize and manage absenteeism and turnover. For example, would a flexible work schedule reduce absences due to employee personal business?

With an eye toward retention, the franchisee should evaluate the total compensation package offered to employees to ensure it is competitive with similar types of employers. A fair and equitable system can help minimize turnover—particularly if the company offers a unique package of benefits not offered by others. When evaluating job benefits, think broadly in terms of factors such as the flexibility you offer as an employer, the flexibility offered by the job, the opportunities for growth and advancement on the job and with the organization, the training and development offered, as well as the traditional compensation and benefits package.

The single largest resource expense for most businesses is human resources. At the end of every business day, these human resources walk out the door without any guarantee that they will return the next day. The successful franchisee must effectively deal with the acquisition, maintenance, and retention of productive human resources. This will be a dynamic issue for the franchisee. The challenge will be to balance attention to the tasks related to the functional aspects of the business with management of the human components of the business.

18-8j Leadership

Leadership can be defined as the ability to stimulate and guide individuals or groups toward accomplishing the tasks required to achieve a business goal or objective. A comparison of characteristics of traditional managers and the franchisee entrepreneur shows decided differences between the typical corporate culture as contrasted with the culture of the typical franchised business.

Traditional managers are motivated by reward systems that offer promotions, staff, perks, and power. Such managers, as nonowners, tend to be risk averse in trying to avoid mistakes and creating surprises for the ownership. These managers tend to delegate authority instead of having direct involvement and usually agree with those in senior management positions. They will devote their time to meeting quotas, monitoring budgets, and planning on a weekly, monthly, quarterly, or annual basis.

In the role as leader, the franchisee's behavior toward employees and others reflects personal style. Discussions with franchisees of Dunkin' Donuts, Taco Bell, Jani-King, Precision Tune, Merry Maids, and Petland indicate that there is no one best leadership style; rather, the best style is the one appropriate to meet the needs of the people (e.g., employees) and the situation. Effective leadership is based on the leader being accepted by the followers or employees. The franchisee's leadership is accepted when the followers freely and willingly accept the direction given. Successful franchisees are self-confident and seem to make decisions easily; and, their subordinates easily accept the direction and willingly carry out requests.

The effective leader will encourage employees to make suggestions and then follow up with as many of them as possible. Discussion with employees of a local Sir Speedy Printing, Inc. franchise affirms the age-old belief that good leaders provide employees opportunity for self-expression, ownership of their work, and recognition for work well done. When the franchisee and employees are excited about their work, motivation is likely to be high. Though high motivation does not guarantee high performance, high performance is seldom found without it.

Franchisees, as small business owners, are often highly self-motivated. As such, they may make the mistake of assuming that all their employees should be as self-motivated and committed to the business as they are. This can be a critical mistake and result in the franchisee failing to develop the leadership skills needed to achieve and maintain a highly motivated employee group.

Now that you own your own business, you are its leader. Being a leader requires a new mindset. You need to actively mentor others—your employees. Exude a positive outlook and a genuine interest in the work that you and each of your employees are doing—together. Care about each person's progress. Give them feedback—not just year-end or quarterly assessments. Make every significant event a teaching moment. Indicate what you like about what they are doing and ways they can improve. Use total candor with employees, which is an underlying factor in great leaders.

18-8k Coordination

Coordination is the arrangement of individual and group efforts to provide a unified action in pursuit of a common purpose. In essence, coordination is a means for the franchised unit to achieve any or all of the franchise's objectives (e.g., customer satisfaction, speedy delivery, efficient service, quality care). Coordination involves encouraging the completion of individual or group efforts in a systematic or organized way that is appropriate for the overall task. The order of synchronization of tasks for creation of a meal, construction of a sandwich, completion of a home cleaning, and providing a preschool lesson to children are examples of coordination.

Establishing and maintaining coordination can require close supervision of employees or may allow for significant employee discretion. In any event, the franchisee should not leave coordination to chance. It requires purposeful managerial action. It is a continuing process. It is essential that the communication process is clear and understandable.

In the simplest view, coordination is a set of mechanisms used to link the functions of a franchised business action together. In a small franchise, the managerial hierarchy instilled by the franchisee provides for the necessary consistency. When the franchisee provides general supervision over all functions of the business, the impersonal means of coordination are also "personalized" by the franchisee's personality and style of decision making.

18-8l Decision Making

As the franchise business adds additional units or expands operations, the franchisee may find it wholly impractical to be involved within and make decisions in each area of the enterprise. When franchisees realize they are overworked or overstressed, they begin to look for more efficient or effective ways of linking work units to one another. For a franchisor, growth may mean rethinking how to reorganize an entire franchise system. In either case, a mix of impersonal and personal methods of coordination are possible. The impersonal methods of coordination are modifications or extensions of the organization structure and the pattern of established job groupings. Generally, as a franchise system grows, the firm relies on impersonal control methods such as the rules, policies, and procedures so critical to assure consistency and standardization in service and product delivery. These impersonal rules or methods are necessary and must be understood and implemented, across the franchise system, regardless of location, amount of prior experience, or amount of time an employee has been retained or a franchisee has been in business within the franchise system. Formal rules, policies, and clearly stated objectives help unify effort at any given location and across locations of the franchise system. However, impersonal methods alone are insufficient. Personal methods of coordination provide for the flexibility so often necessary to achieve high performance and quality service. Personal methods include use of the grapevine, informal groups, committees or work teams, and common values. See Table 18-8.

| TABLE 18-8 | INTERPERSONAL AND PERSONAL METHODS OF COORDINATION |

Impersonal Methods

Written rules, policies, and procedures. These may include work schedules rotational assignments, budget allocations, and short-term plans.

Specialize Staff Units. When deemed needed, specialized units such as personnel office, bidding office, contracting office, etc., may be necessary to assure consistency.

Information systems. This may include computerized recordkeeping systems, budget and sales forecasts, suggestion systems, newsletters, or e-mail.

Personal Methods

Grapevine or informal group communications. Though often such communications are the fastest, they are also liable to be inaccurate. Such methods should be followed up by a formal method of coordination.

Committee or Work Teams. These allow for individual participation, communication across functions or hierarchy levels, and are good for communicating complex, qualitative information especially when problem identification or problem solving is necessary across departments or units of operation.

Common Values. The franchise system's overall mission, the franchisee's management philosophy, and code of ethics are examples. These values can be built into the franchised system and each franchised unit by careful selection, training, socialization, enforcement, or reinforcement.

18-9   OPPORTUNITIES FOR WOMEN AND MINORITIES IN FRANCHISING

The scope of franchising today is a far cry from the days when franchising almost exclusively meant auto, gas, beverages, food, or lodging. The typical image of a franchisee was that of a white family man running a franchised business. The scope of franchising and the typical image of who is a franchisee has changed considerably. Today, women and minorities represent the fastest growing segment of franchisee business ownership. More and more women are entering franchising, not only as franchisees but also as franchisors and owners of other businesses. The National Foundation of Women Business Owners (NFWBO) reports that there are 9.1 million women-owned businesses in the United States, representing about 38 percent of all businesses, employing more than 27 million people, and generating more than $3.6 trillion in sales.[23]

"WOMEN, MINORITY FRANCHISEES INCREASE AT MCDONALDS"

McDonald's reports that 44 percent of new franchisees who joined the system in 2002 were women and minorities. These two groups own over 1,500 McDonalds units posting sales of more than $2 billion. Also, McDonald's is using minority and women suppliers for around 40 percent of its food and paper product purchases.

Adapted from Alexander Delroy, "Women, Minority Franchisees Increase at McDonalds," Chicago Tribune Online *(2 May 2003).*

The word on the street in franchising is that women make such great franchise leaders because franchising is all about building lasting relationships, a forte of women. Women are known for trying to work things out, like to get consensus,and are good listeners. Each quality is a necessary skill that franchise leaders must develop. Women have come into franchising in different ways, but common to most is the desire to help other women succeed. The International Franchise Association recognized the significant role of women in franchising and formed the Women's Franchise Committee in the early 1990s which "promotes women's participation in franchising by providing opportunities for the exchange of ideas, resources and experiences." This committee has been a boon for women to network with each other regarding business solutions pertinent to their careers in franchising.

Since 1990, in the United States, major changes have occurred in the composition of the workforce, the competitive marketplace, and the customer base. The United States, as a whole, has become more diverse in its population, age patterns and characteristics, work life, and styles of family living. In response to these and other changes, many franchisors have been developing diversity strategies and programs to respond to a more diverse business environment, marketplace, and population demographics. Some of the shifts are identified in Figure 18-5.

Franchising provides a good living for hundreds of thousands of people. It is important that minority persons realize that they have the opportunity to be in franchising also. Ethnic and racial diversity has become an imperative in much of American business. The growth of Black, Asian, Hispanic, and other populations has made minorities an attractive consumer class with ever-increasing buying power. Not only do minority groups have buying power, but they also are acquiring their own franchises.

For example, Adolphus Crenshaw acquired his first McDonald's franchise at the time it was losing $30,000 annually, but that didn't stop him from turning the business around to realize a six-

---

Race:

281.4 million people were counted, a 13.2 percent increase from 1990.

- 26.9 million were "White," an increase of 5.9 to 8.6 percent

- 35.3 million were "Hispanic," an increase of 57.9 percent

- 34.7 million were "Black," an increase of 15.6 to 21.5 percent

- 10.2 million were "Asian," an increase of 48 to 72 percent

Gender:

- Females outnumber males by 6 million.

- One in every two women was married, living with a spouse; one in four was a college graduate, and one in seven worked in an executive, administrative, or managerial capacity.

- Between 1989 and 1995, women accounted for 85 percent of the total increase in the number of workers with more than one job.

Disabilities and Age:

- People with disabilities make up 20 percent of the 2000 population.

- Two-thirds of Americans who live to age sixty-five are alive today; and they outnumber those age twenty-five and younger.

- The average fifty-five-year-old is expected to live to age eighty-three.

- People born after 1964 will spend more on caring for aging parents than for their children.

Other Trends:

- By 2005, 85 percent of those entering the workforce will be women, people of color, and immigrants.

- By 2013, the Hispanic population will surpass the African American population.

- The number of elderly will double in the space of one generation.

FIGURE **18-5**

2000 U.S. Census Highlights
Sources: U.S. Census. Percentage ranges under Race are due to a change in the 2000 Census that recorded, for example, "Asian" and "Asian and other race."

figure profit within his first year in business as a franchisee. In that first year, Crenshaw worked sixteen hours a day for 363 days to turn his franchised small business around. Raised in a disadvantaged neighborhood in Baltimore, and being the first in his family to attend college, Crenshaw was accustomed to succeeding against the odds. So, when McDonald's offered him the chance to open three restaurants at Denver International Airport, Crenshaw jumped at the idea. In his first year as the franchisee at the Denver Airport, Crenshaw became a member of McDonald's Million Dollar Sales Club and was awarded the Outstanding Store Award. Today, Crenshaw's stores exceed $6 million in sales each year and he is planning for retirement.[24]

U.S. POPULATION TO BECOME "MAJORITY MINORITY"

A report published in 2003 by the Brookings Institution's Center on Urban and Metropolitan Policy outlines dramatic shifts that are reshaping the complexion and racial composition of the 100 largest cities in America over the past ten years. The analysis highlights patterns that reflect the increasing diversity of the U.S. urban populations. For example, almost one-half of the largest cities no longer have majority white populations. The nation's largest cities lost large numbers of white residents. White population loss was widespread. Of the 100 largest cities in 1990, 71 lost at least 2 percent of their population by 2000. In 20 cities, white population loss exceeded 20 percent.

Adapted from http://www.franchise.org/news/usatoday/feb2003.asp

---

McDonald's is but one of many franchise companies seeking success-oriented minorities to join their team. Also, the shift toward a service-oriented economy has led to the development of a number of franchise concepts that require little overhead or can be run from a home office, reducing the amount of capital needed to "buy in" with many franchise systems. Having sufficient capital to get started has been a significant barrier keeping many minorities and others from entering franchising and other business ventures. But, today nearly one-half of the franchise companies in the United States have initial investment requirements below $10,000. Willing lenders, committed franchisors, and an encouraging business climate are coming together, which enhances opportunities for women and minority ownership in franchised businesses.[25]

PURCHASING POWER OF MINORITIES: 2000–2045

In September 2000, the Minority Business Development Agency (MBDA) of the Department of Commerce issued a report on projected purchasing power of minorities for the period 2000 to 2045. MBDA pointed out that the minority population over the age of fifteen had increased its purchasing power by 47 percent from 1990 to 1998. During the same period, non-Hispanic whites increased their purchasing power by only 18 percent. By 2045, minority purchasing power will be between $4 trillion and $6.1 trillion. Thus, minority populations may count for between 44 and 70 percent in the total increase in U.S. purchasing power from 2000 to 2045.

Given the rapidly growing numbers and increasing purchasing power, ethnic and racial minorities are quickly becoming the most sought after consumer segment by business and industry. Many franchise systems are moving to position themselves to embrace these emerging market consumers. This means that franchise systems are recruiting more minorities as franchisees, employees, vendors, and suppliers. For many franchise companies, diversity efforts have gone beyond being "forward thinking" to embracing minority populations as an imperative for business growth and survival.

18-9a   Women in Franchising

Women are starting their own businesses at twice the rate of men and a franchise would seem to be an ideal way for women to have their own business.[26] Yet Samuel Crawford, a Women in Franchising senior consultant reports, "There's not so much of a glass ceiling keeping women from purchasing a franchise as there is a 'green ceiling'—money."[27] While women own 38 percent of all U.S. companies, they receive less than 2 percent of venture capital. A recent report by the National Foundation of Women Business Owners (NFWBO) found that although women's access to capital is increasing, the amount of credit granted to women still trails that of men.[28] Franchises typically require an infusion of capital to begin the business, whereas women business owners tend to start will little or no money and use earnings to grow their business.

What can franchisers and women interested in becoming franchisees do to increase the number of women in franchised businesses?

In 2006, women-owned businesses are expected to generate $1.1 trillion in revenue.

Adapted from "Best Practices" Entrepreneur *(December 2006): 22.*

Women have become a major force in America's workforce. Women are rapidly seeking opportunities to balance work with home and family obligations. Thus, the largest group of prospective franchisees, as an interest group, is the adult female.

Franchise systems are developing approaches to work effectively with women who are interested in becoming or are already franchised business owners. For act6ions being taken, see Figure 18-9 below.

18-9b   Actions for Franchisors

- Develop a formal mentoring program for women franchisees. Church's Chicken has such a program called the Professional Mentoring Program, which is designed to pair women who want to become franchisee partners with women who are currently successful partners in the Church's franchise system. The results for participants have been positive.[29]

- Explore alternatives to assist women with understanding and tackling financing issues. Purchasing a franchise often requires a sizable investment upfront. Women have a tendency to start a business with little or no money and use their earnings to grow the business.

- Feature high-profile, successful women associated with the franchising system as spokespersons for the franchise system.

- Ensure your communications and promotional materials are gender neutral.

18-9c   Prospective Franchisees

- Perform a skills inventory/assessment. Women are sometimes reluctant to give themselves credit for past accomplishments.

- Keep options open. Explore nontraditional opportunities if they match your skill set. "A lot of women don't believe they have it or they're afraid to prove they have it," says Dina Dwyer Owens, CEO and president of the Dwyer Group, a corporation focused on such traditional male operations as plumbing and electrical work.[30]

- Seek out role models. Talk to franchisees and franchisers. The International Franchise Association has a Women's Franchise Community Profiles in Success page that identifies women in franchising who are willing to be mentors.

- "Just do it!" says Hala Moddelmog, president of Church's Chicken. Women need to step up to the plate to explore franchising alternatives and then take action to make a franchise business opportunity a reality.[31]

Florine Mark

The WW Group

Florine Mark is president and CEO of The WW Group, the largest franchise of Weight Watchers International, which includes Detroit, Boston, Cleveland, Pittsburgh, Cincinnati, St. Louis, Ontario, and Mexico. This multifaceted entrepreneur and marketing expert comes from meek beginnings, having built her internationally recognized weight loss enterprise from the ground up.

In addition to running a successful business, Florine is associated with some of the country's most prestigious affiliations. In 1996, Florine was appointed chair of the Detroit Branch of the Federal Reserve Board of Chicago, where she remained an active participant until the end of her term in December 1999. She was also appointed by John Engler to he Governor's Council on Physical Fitness for the state of Michigan, she serves as a national board mMember for the Boy Scouts of America, and she serves on the American Heart Association Advisory Board. Florine also serves on the board of directors for the Meadowbrook Insurance Company, which is publicly traded on the NYSE and English Gardens, a privately held company.

Florine is a popular motivational speaker, speaking regularly to diverse groups across the country including business, health, and women's organizations. As a leader in preventative medicine, Florine has partnered Weight Watchers with many national health organizations, including Blue Cross/Blue Shield and Phalon.

Prior to finally losing fifty pounds and keeping it off on the Weight Watchers program, Florine tried every fad diet around, including a near-fatal bout with diet pills. She often tells

members that she previously lost the same fifty pounds at least ten times— which adds up to a whopping 500 pounds.

Desperate to take off the pounds for good, Florine joined the fledgling Weight Watchers program in New York in 1966. In four months, she lost forty pounds. Empowered by her success and eager to share it with others desiring to lose weight, Florine decided to bring the only program that had ever worked for her back to Detroit.

Florine's illustrious career is filled with numerous national and local awards. She's been included in Crain's Detroit Business' list of the 100 Most Influential Women in Detroit, and her awards include The National Association of Women Business Owners Award; The Greater Detroit Chamber of Commerce Lifetime Achievement Award; and The Distinguished Entrepreneur Award. She's also been honored by the Detroit Free Press, the City of Detroit, and the state of Michigan for outstanding community service and achievement.

In 1990, Florine was recognized as the Michigan Entrepreneur of the Year by Inc. Magazine and Merrill Lynch, and she was named 1997 Laureate in the southeast Michigan Business Hall of Fame by Junior Achievement. Florine has also been honored in the past for her work by such reputable community organizations as the March of Dimes, the National Kidney Foundation, and the American Lung Association.

The year 1999 was especially memorable for Florine, as she was honored in Monaco as one the thirty Leading Entrepreneurs in the World. That same year, Florine was also named Oakland County's Executive of the Year; and she was the recipient of Northwood University's "Most Distinguished Woman" award for 1999.

Being fortunate enough to have had such a positive, long-lasting experience change her life, Florine makes it a point to give back to the community by volunteering everywhere she can.

By continuing to reach out and share her story with others, Florine Mark hopes to inspire, educate, and motivate people to make a lifelong commitment to happiness, health, fitness, and nutrition and most of all, to be the very best they can be.

SUMMARY

It is important for both the franchisor and franchisee to understand the rights and responsibilities they have in their respective businesses. Some laws and regulations favor the franchisor; others serve to support the position of the franchisee. Most important is that both parties realize the value of a fair and equitable franchising agreement, the need for a franchisee to maintain a defense manual, an awareness of the laws governing franchising, and an understanding of the common legal problems of franchisees.

An understanding of these rights and responsibilities as they relate to franchising laws can help the franchisee to have a long and successful franchising operation. When the laws are followed, the participants in a franchise relationship are more likely to enjoy profitable business ventures.

A franchise system, at corporate or franchisee level, begins with people. The franchise mission and goals shape the overall purpose and guide the methods chosen for division of labor, hierarchy of authority, departmentation, and even the approach toward describing the various jobs necessary to accomplish franchise goals and objectives. The franchisee is responsible for developing the business plan, setting performance objectives, and identifying the actions needed to accomplish them. The legal form of organization must be determined and the amount of resources necessary to operate acquired. Once initial planning is completed, the franchisee must break the work to be done into tasks that can be performed by individuals or groups. This is called division of labor. Division of labor and a pattern of departmentation for both corporate and the individual franchise unit serves to mobilize the work of many people to achieve the common purpose.

When an organization divides labor into small components, specific job duties and responsibilities must be identified. When complete, an approach must be determined to coordinate the work efforts to ensure that the work performed accomplishes or helps reach the objectives. The hierarchy of authority, wherein jobs with increasing authority are ranked higher in the organizational structure, facilitates coordination across the franchised unit as well as the franchise system itself. For example, hierarchy of authority is well defined in many franchised food systems such as McDonald's, Wendy's, Pizza Hut, and Taco Bell. Shift supervisors wear different color uniforms, ties, or hats, and may have special name tags. Such designations also help when a problem arises. A supervisor can be clearly identified from other employees. Effective leadership and coordination of work are critical ingredients of a franchisee's "job" as owner-entrepreneur of a franchise.

KEY TERMS

Behavioral management perspective: a management philosophy based on an awareness that human behavior has a significant impact on the performance of workers, emphasizing a participative management style in which workers' opinions are elicited and involved in decision making.

C corporation: a business organization that is a legal entity with liability limited to the extent of investment by each stockholder; life of the corporation is continuous and independent of the individual owners/investors lives; ownership can be easily transferred through sale of stock; and the corporation may have an easier time raising money.

Classical management perspective: a management philosophy emphasizing a scientific approach to task specialization and standardization, planning, organizing, directing, and controlling that emanated from the top down and a rational and impersonal organizational design based on rules and procedures to provide for operational efficiency, managerial effectiveness, and enhanced profitability.

Contingency management perspective: a management philosophy that assumes there is no one best approach and that managers should identify the key contingencies, or variables, in a given organization and use an approach believed to be most effective in a given situation.

Franchise defense manual: a record of all the suggestions and correspondence from the franchisor's organization kept in the event differences arise between the franchisor and the franchisee.

Management philosophy: the theoretical framework from which good management practice can be identified, learned, and applied effectively.

Quantitative management perspective: a management philosophy focusing on decision making in which an alternative course of action is selected as a solution to some problem based on measurable criteria, quantitative modeling to assess impact of each alternative, often using computers.

S corporation: alternative to the regular corporate in which the franchisee and other shareholders are taxed as partners and do not pay taxes on dividends twice; retains all other corporate advantages such as limited liability for shareholders, but has other restrictions including that it must be "domestic," and independently owned and operated.

Sole proprietorship: the most common form of franchisee business ownership in which the franchisee is the business owner, liable for all the business's liabilities, with the right to all the profits excluding royalty or other franchisor fees.

Systems management perspective: a managerial approach which focuses on the nature and inter-relationships of the component systems in a business in order to simplify their control and direction.

REVIEW QUESTIONS

1. Identify the legal rights of a franchisee in a franchising relationship.

2. Discuss the franchisee's rights in negotiating a franchising agreement.

3. Identify the advantages of keeping a franchise defense manual.

4. Briefly describe the laws regulating franchise activities. Which laws are favorable to franchises?

5. What territorial rights and restrictions are attached to a franchising agreement?

6. What are the most common legal problems of franchisees?

7. Discuss each of the essentials of the management process as applied in a franchise business.

8. Identify each type of organization structure and discuss their differences.

9. Discuss each major factor in the hiring process.

10. Discuss opportunities available for women and minorities in franchising.

CASE STUDY

Key Traits for Success as Franchisees

Perhaps the most troubling, yet important question facing a franchise company concerns selecting the "right" person as the next franchisee. Franchise companies want to sign up franchisees who are likely to succeed as owners of their own businesses as well as develop and maintain a strong loyalty to the franchise company. But, what personality traits and behavioral patterns does it take to succeed as a franchisee? And what leads toward failure?

Interviews from within franchise companies, reading opinion editorial pieces in franchise trade publications, and relevant academic research studies suggest that there is no one best answer to the question. Clearly, the available studies and opinions are inconclusive. Yet, by combining the available information, the following characteristics may typify those potential franchisees who are likely to succeed, and those who may be likely to fail.

The "ideal" potential franchisee, who would likely succeed, may display a substantial number of the following traits or behavior preferences.

- The person is motivated and has a strong internal need to succeed, to be successful.

- This person would want to lead others rather than be led.

- This person will stand up and take charge in the absence of a leader.

- When taking the lead is not possible or appropriate, this person will align with the leader; this person will not create conflict by trying to subvert or directly oppose the formal leader when leadership is apparent and being demonstrated.

- The person has tolerance for conflict and strain; this person has sufficient determination to see things clearly and act calmly, even in the face of adversity.

- The person has low tolerance for confusion and disorder. This person leads an orderly life without being a "control freak." This person can plan the day and work the plan without becoming compulsive or fussy about details.

- The person is more than confident, with a proper self-knowledge and self-esteem.

- This person can define goals and outline actions necessary to achieve those goals.

- This person not only looks toward success, but also can see the success already.

- The person demonstrates self-reliance. This person is introspective, having the ability to analyze problems, identifying own strengths and weaknesses without externalizing or "dumping" the problem on to others.

- This person can own up to faults and mistakes, then move on healthfully, without self-incrimination.

There appears to also be personality traits and/or behavioral factors that can lead toward, and may even predict, failure as a franchise. These traits and factors are as follows:

- The person exhibits an unrealistic view of what it takes to run a business.

- This person expects to become rich in the short term, having no real understanding that it takes hard work and long hours to establish a business.

- This person underestimates the real capitalization required for the business. This person may have misrepresented to the franchisor actual capitalization.

- The person does not truly follow the franchise program. This person is not very introspective, is ready to blame the franchisor, customers, or others for "bad luck" or failure.

- This person has had an unrealistic view of *this* business, no longer liking the current business.

- After experiencing real work and long hours, this person decides that being in business—or being in *this* business—is not desirable.

- This person is not a leader nor has a plan. The person hasn't established and subsequently achieved significant life goals.

- The person may want to be a leader, but in reality exhibits the traits of a spoiler.

CASE QUESTIONS

1. What steps can a franchisor take to learn about such personality traits and behavior patterns?

2. Are some of these traits more/less important if the franchisee is required to operate from a storefront instead of being a home-based franchisee?

3. Which of the "ideal" traits and behavior patterns do you think are descriptive exclusively of a franchisee business owner in contrast to an independent business owner?

4. Would the "ideal" traits fit all franchise business sectors equally? Would the "failure" traits fit all franchise business sectors equally?

5. Which "ideal" traits and which "failure" traits would you suggest are most important? Least important?

REFERENCES

Astrachan, J. and M. Carey, *Family Businesses in the U.S. Economy* (Washington, DC: Center for the Study of Taxation, 1994).

Axelrad, Normal D. and Lewis G. Rudnick, "Overviews in Laws Affecting Franchising," *Franchising: A Planning and Sales Compliance Guide* (Chicago: Commerce Clearinghouse, Inc., 1987).

Bachler, Christopher J., "Resume Fraud: Lies, Omissions and Exaggerations," *Personnel Journal* (June 1995): 51–60.

Beehr, T., J. Drexler, and S. Faulkner, "Working in Small Family Businesses: Empirical Comparisons to Non-Family Businesses," *Journal of Organizational Behavior* 18 (1997).

Bernard, Chester I., *The Functions of the Executive* (Cambridge, MA: Harvard University Press, 1938).

Boulding, Kenneth E., "General Systems Theory—The Skeleton of Science," *Management Science* 2(3) (April 1956): 197–208.

Braun, Ernest A., "Policy Issues and Franchising," *Franchise Law Review* 1(1) (Winter 1986).

Bureau of National Affairs, *Bulletin to Management* (BNA Policy and Practice Series) 49(26) (2 July 1998): 205.

Campion, Michael A., David K. Palmer, and James E. Campion, "A Review of Structure in the Selection Interview," *Personnel Psychology* 50 (1997): 655.

Fayol, Henri, *Industrial and General Administration*, Coubrough, J. A., trans. (Geneva: International Management Institute, 1930).

Hammand, Alexander, *Franchise Rights—A Self Defense Manual* (Grenvale, NY: Panel Publishers, 1979).

Herzberg, Frederick, Bernard Mausner, and Barbara Synderman, *The Motivation to Work* (New York: Wiley, 1959); and Herzberg, Frederick, *Work and the Nature of Man* (New York: World Publishing, 1966) and "One More Time: How Do You Motivate Employees?" *Harvard Business Review* 46(1) (January-February 1968): 53–62. See also Caudron, Shari, "Keys to Starting a TQM Program," *Personnel Journal* (February 1993): 35.

Hofstede, Geert, "Motivation, Leadership and Organization: Do American Theories Apply Abroad?" *Organizational Dynamics* (Summer 1980): 54–56.

Kast, Fremont E. and James E. Rosenzweig, "General Systems Theory: Applications for Organization and Management," *Academy of Management Journal* 15(4) (December 1972): 447–465.

Knight, Russell M., "The Independence of the Franchisee Entrepreneur," *Journal of Small Business Management* 22 (April 1984): 53.

LaGrassa, Kara, "Franchise Companies Seek Out Minority Entrepreneurs," *USA TODAY* (7 March 2001): B13.

Lee, Thomas, "Another Round in Brewer, Maris Fight Begins Today," *St. Louis Post-Dispatch* (1 May 2001): A1, A5.

March, James G. and Herbert A. Simon, *Organizations* (New York: Wiley, 1959).

Maslow, Abraham H., *Motivation and Personality*, 2nd ed. (New York: Harper and Row, 1970), 35–58.

Mayo, Elton, *The Human Problems of an Industrial Civilization* (NewYork: McMillan, 1953); and Roethlesberger, F. J. and W. J. Dickson, *Management and the Worker* (Cambridge, MA: Harvard University Press, 1939).

McClelland, David,*The Achieving Society* (Princeton, NJ: Van Nostrand Reinhold, 1961).

Moad, Jeff, "Strength in Numbers," *Datamation* 32 (June 1985): 44.

Oster, S., *Competitive Analysis* (New York: Oxford University Press, 1999).

Parker, L. D., "Control in Organizational Life: The Contribution of Mary Parker Follett," *Academy of Management Review* 9(4) (October 1984): 736–745.

Porter, James L. and William Renforth, "Franchise Agreements: Spotting the Important Legal Issues," *Journal of Small Business Management* 16(4) (October 1978): 27–31.

Posa, Ernesto J., *Family Business* (Cincinnati, OH: Thompson-Southwestern, 2004).

Sachdev, Ameet, "McDonald's Auditions Several New Acts," *Chicago Tribune* (16 May 2001): sec 3, 1.

Selz, David D., "Legal Considerations," *Complete Handbook of Franchising* (Reading, MA: Addison-Wesley Publishing Co., 1982).

Sheffet, Mary Jane and Deborah L. Scammon, "Legal Issues in Dual Distribution Systems," *Proceedings of the Society of Franchising* (1986).

"Survey of All-Time Champs Reveals Ups and Downs," *Inc. 500, Inc. Magazine* (2000): 38–40.

Ward, Jeff, "Blended Learning: The Convergence of E-learning and Meetings," *Franchising World* 35(4) (June 2003): 22.

"Women Increasingly Turning to Franchising for Opportunities," *USA TODAY* (7 February 2001): B11.

Zeidman, Philip F. and H. Brett Lowell, *Franchising* (New York: Federal Publications, Inc., 1986).

NOTES

1. Adapted from Thomas Lee, "Another Round in Brewer, Maris Fight Begins Today," *St. Louis Post-Dispatch* (1 May 2001): A1.
2. Ibid.

3. Ibid.

4. Ibid, A5.

5. Ibid.

6. Ibid.

7. Frank Wadsworth and Kathryn B. Morgan, "Second Generation Franchisee Study," *17th Annual International Society of Franchising Conference Proceedings* (San Antonio, TX, February 2003).

8. L. D. Parker, "Control in Organizational Life: The Contribution of Mary Parker Follett," *Academy of Management Review* 9(4) (October 1984): 736–745.

9. Elton Mayo, *The Human Problems of an Industrial Civilization* (New York: McMillan, 1953); and F. J. Roethlesberger and W. J. Dickson, *Management and the Worker* (Cambridge, MA: Harvard University Press, 1939).

10. Geert Hofstede, "Motivation, Leadership and Organizations: Do American Theories Apply Abroad?" *Organizational Dynamics* (Summer 1980): 54–56.

11. Frederick Herzberg, Bernard Mausner, and Barbara Synderman, *The Motivation to Work* (New York: Wiley, 1959); and Frederick Herzberg, *Work and the Nature of Man* (New York: World Publishing, 1966) and *One More Time: How Do You Motivate Employees? Harvard Business Review* 46(1) (January–February 1968): 53–62. See also Shari Caudron, "Keys to Starting a TQM Program," *Personnel Journal* (February 1993): 35.

12. McDonald's Press Release, 11 March 2003, http://mcdonalds.com/countries/usa/whatsnew/pressrelease/2003/03112003/index.html.

13. Raymond H. Hinchcliffe, *LIMRA's Market Facts Ouarterly* 20(1) (Spring 2001): 30–83; Elaine McShulskis, *HR Magazine* 41(3) (March 1996): 16–18.

14. *Bulletin to Management* (Bureau of National Affairs [BNA] Policy and Practice Series) 49(26) (2 July 1998): 210.

15. Lin Grensing-Pophal, "Catch a Candidate," *Credit Union Management* 24(2) (February 2001): 32–36.

16. Michael A. Campion, David K. Palmer, and James E. Campion, "A Review of Structure in the Selection Interview," *Personnel Psychology* 50 (1997): 655.

17. Frances A. McMorris, "Ex-Bosses Face Less Peril Giving Honest Job References," *Wall Street Journal* (8 July 1996): B1.

18. "Industry Report 1998," *Training Magazine* (October 1998).

19. Nancy L. Breuer, "Employee Loyalty and Retention Make Chick-fil-A a Success," Workforce.com.

20. Joan Rentsch and Robert Stell, "Testing and Durability of Job Characteristics and Predictors of Absenteeism over a Six-Year Period," *Personnel Psychology* 51 (1998): 165.

21. Kemba J. Kunham, "Amid Sinking Workplace Morale, Employers Turn to Recognition," *Wall Street Journal* (19 November 2002).

22. W. Griffeth Rodger, Peter W. Hom, and S. Lawrence, "Comparative Tests of Multivariate Models of Recruiting Sources Effects," *Journal of Management* 32(1) (1997): 19-36.

23. "Women Increasingly Turning to Franchising for Opportunities," *USA TODAY* (7 February 2001): 11B.

24. Kara LaGrassa, "Franchise Companies Seek out Minority Entrepreneurs," *USA TODAY* (7 March 2001): 13B.

25. Ibid.

26. Devlin Smith, "A Woman's Place," *Entrepreneur*, 21 October 2002, Entrepreneur.com, http://www.entrepreneur.com/franzone/article/0,5847,303923,00.html.

27. Cynthia Griffin, "Mixing It up," (November 2001).

28. Ibid.

29. Smith, "A Woman's Place."

30. Griffin, "Mixing It up."

31. Smith, "A Woman's Place," 2.

The Franchising Relationship

In studying this chapter, you will:

- Learn about the four phases of the franchisor–franchisee relationship.
- Understand the advantages and disadvantages of franchise advisory councils (FACs).
- Realize the importance of communication, awareness, rapport, and expertise in a franchising relationship.
- Understand some of the principal areas of concern to franchisees in the franchising program.
- Understand the importance of advertising, pricing, and profits for the franchisee.

INCIDENT

Yvonne is a successful decorative rug franchisor. Her daughter Colleen wants to start one of Yvonne's decorative rug franchises. Colleen has had relatively little business experience but has graduated from a local college with a business degree in accounting.

Yvonne wants to help her daughter get started in business, but she has reservations about involving her as a franchisee. Yvonne believes she must consider the other franchisees and how they would feel about the franchisor's relative becoming a franchisee.

Is Yvonne right to be concerned? Would prospective franchisees that Yvonne had turned down have any legal right to take action against her if they think Colleen is no more qualified than they are to operate a decorative rug business? How should Yvonne handle this situation?

19-1 Franchisor or Franchisee

Which one is more important? Steering power or pedal power?

STEERING POWER   PEDAL POWER

Both types of power are equally important. It takes steering and pedal power to properly ride and direct a bicycle. Lance Armstrong took a lot of steering power, pedal power, and willpower to win consecutive Tours de France.

Now let's ask the question, Which one is more important—the franchisor or the franchisee?

FRANCHISOR   FRANCHISEE

Both the franchisor and the franchisee are equally important. It takes the franchisor and the franchisee to properly guide and direct a franchise system. They need to learn to work together to bring about the optimal success for each other and for themselves. This is not a superior to subordinate relationship. This is a partnership—like a good marriage.

19-2 PHASES OF THE FRANCHISING RELATIONSHIP

The most critical facet of the franchised business is the relationship between the franchisor and the franchisee. This relationship often follows the basic steps of a new business or a product life cycle; that is, it goes through the following stages: (1) introduction, (2) growth, (3) maturity, and (4) decline/development (see Figure 19-1).

19-2a Introduction

The introduction of the relationship between the franchisor and the franchisee should be one of trust, mutual interdependence, and a shared desire for success and profitability. On the part of the franchisee, the relationship starts out as one of extreme optimism, often blind faith, and expectation

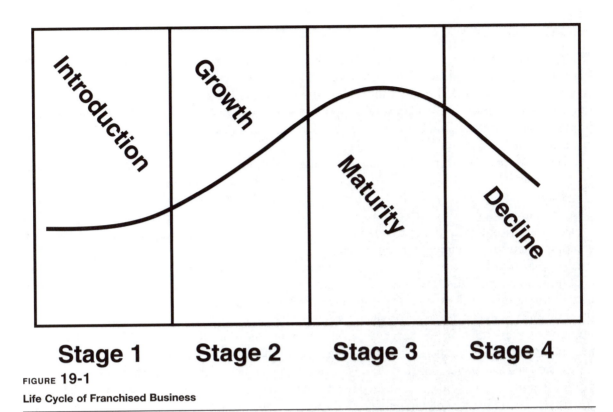

FIGURE 19-1

Life Cycle of Franchised Business

of great success. The franchisor also puts forth its best face, because it is interested in making a positive and friendly approach to the franchisee, but the franchisor will also be measuring the qualifications and selling to the franchisee during the initial encounters. It is during this initial stage that the rapport, understanding, and confidence between the franchisor's organization and the franchisee develop.

19-2b   Growth Stage

When the franchisee has the grand opening and the business then commences operations, the growth stage begins. From the time the franchisee has signed the franchising agreement and begins the training program to become a qualified operator, the franchisor–franchisee relationship begins to develop. A thorough training program will build a strong and close relationship between the franchisor and the franchisee. Assistance with the grand opening, layout, and initial advertising and promotion will strengthen the relationship and help to cement a positive bond between the franchisor and the franchisee.

The support system provided by the franchisor to the franchisee for the ensuing months and years will help solidify the relationship. This relationship may be cultivated through Internet and intranet exchanges, e-mail, bimonthly or quarterly magazines or newsletters, telephone calls, plus local, regional, or national franchisee clubs and even birthday calls from the franchisor expressing personal regards for the franchisee. The franchisor's field representative should provide support materials, accounting aids, marketing suggestions, and promotional and advertising support on a regular basis to maintain an active franchising relationship.

If the support systems are not properly set up, however, and if the franchisor offers only a second-rate training program or fails to provide ongoing support services, the relationship will likely become strained and unproductive. When communication with the home office breaks down, the franchisor–franchisee relationship is severely threatened.

19-2c Maturity

The third phase of the franchisor–franchisee relationship is referred to as the maturity stage. In this stage, the franchisor and franchisee know what to expect from each other. If the relationship has gone well, they have developed a mutual friendship and understanding. The franchisee is able to rely on the franchisor to provide useful support services, advertisements, marketing aids, and new products. In return, the franchisor can expect good sales volumes, clean stores, and quality services from the franchisee.

The maturity stage of the franchisor–franchisee relationship revolves around the communication and interaction between the two principals. Franchisees attend the annual franchisor–franchisee meeting and participate in local or regional franchisee meetings, and they carefully read company newsletters and/or magazines and participate in other local or regional activities. They utilize the new products or services being provided, implement new programs, and use the new computer software developed for the system.

The hazard of the maturity stage exists when franchisees feels they are no longer receiving continued value from the franchisor. Franchisees expect ongoing support and direction as well as new products and services from the franchisor. For some franchisees, just the opportunity to use the franchisor's name, logo, or products is often sufficient continuing value. Other franchisees require extra attention in the form of frequent communication, assistance with advertising and marketing, and other additional support services from the franchisor.

It is during the maturation stage that franchisees get an idea of the franchisor's competence and expertise and begin either to question or to value the franchisor's contributions. Many new franchisees find this a difficult period, because the franchisor is continuing to try to sell new franchises to prospective franchisees and so may often ignore the needs of existing franchisees. This can cause a strain in communication and in the relationship, and may bring the franchisee to question the worth of the franchisor in the operation of the franchise. The franchisor needs to make an effort to provide communication and support to all its franchisees.

19-2d Decline/Development

The final phase of a franchisor–franchisee relationship often involves the decline of the business and may lead to the franchisee seeking termination of any contractual obligations. Alternatively, in the final phase, the franchisee may develop a stronger relationship and seal the bond with the franchisor as the business continues to grow and prosper. This generally occurs when the franchisor follows the guidelines in Table 19-1. If a franchisor is only interested in selling more and more franchises without providing support services to existing franchisees, then most of the relationships with these franchisees will decline, business will begin to fall off, and lawsuits will commence.

During the decline stage, many franchisees start to relax their compliance with the rules, regulations, and standards of the franchisor. Those who become disenchanted with the franchisor may seek to terminate the franchise. If a franchisor allows this decline to occur in relationships with many franchisees, the franchise system will eventually collapse. It is critical that the franchisor who seeks to remain a strong business entity provide continuing support services for all franchisees. Inevitably, there will be some who become disenchanted, but the franchisor must work with these franchisees to restore a positive relationship which will bring strength and prosperity to the franchising organization.

During the decline/development stage, the franchisee has to face many new problems and concerns. If solutions are not found, then the franchisee may blame and find fault with the franchisor. The franchisee may often question the royalty, advertising, and other fee requirements. The franchisor, on the other hand, may question the gratitude and loyalty of the franchisee. If

TABLE 19-1   GUIDELINES OF THE FRANCHISOR–FRANCHISEE RELATIONSHIP

Franchisor	Franchisee
1. Develops strong training program	Participates in all training opportunities
2. Holds national and regional meetings	Attends all national and regional meetings
3. Develops franchise advisory council (FAC)	Participates in all FAC activities
4. Supports and maintains advertising committee	Gets involved in advertising and promotional committee activities
5. Develops newsletters, memos, and other means of information exchange	Provides information about franchise for newsletters and memos
6. Develops 24-hour toll-free hotline	Utilizes hotline when appropriate
7. Develops incentives for performance and sales	Participates in incentive programs
8. Develops award structure for achievers	Seeks and achieves awards
9. Develops promotional advertising packages and fliers	Obtains information and develops promotions for other franchisees
10. Provides financial and managerial reports	Uses the information in these reports to improve the franchised business

franchisors fail to provide for effective communication or offer incentives and rewards, then franchisees may go elsewhere to find contentment and success. (See Table 19-2.)

Problems may occur between the franchisor and the franchisee as they build their relationship. Franchisors must realize they need to extend themselves in their communication and development of the franchise system. It is important for the franchisor to meet and listen to the franchisees. In fact, many franchisors seek all of their information about new products and services from franchisees rather than through R&D departments at the corporate headquarters, as franchisees often

TABLE 19-2   FRANCHISOR–FRANCHISEE PROBLEMS AND THEIR RESOLUTIONS

PROBLEMS	RESOLUTIONS
1. Poor advertising and promotional materials	Use franchisees on advertising and promotional committee
2. Incomplete operating manuals	Use franchisees to help update and revise manuals
3. Poor training	Revamp training program and use suggestions of franchisees for how to improve training
4. Lack of proper disclosure of information	Improve newsletters, memos, and communication materials
5. Inadequate availability for advice	Set up hotlines and increase number of field representatives
6. Inadequate marketing research	Establish franchisee marketing research committees and improve headquarters marketing research programs
7. Insufficient follow-up training and information	Offer refresher courses, and publish bulletins and updates on operating procedures
8. Inadequate equipment package	Form franchisee advisory council to evaluate and improve equipment and procedures
9. Inappropriate or poor site selections	Evaluate and improve site selection criteria for both franchisor and franchisees

have the best insight into the products or services customers want. Franchisors are wise to listen to and support franchisees in the development of their businesses.

19-3 FRANCHISOR RELATIONSHIP MARKETING

Franchisors today face their toughest competition in decades and need to develop a solid foundation with the franchisees and their end consumers to succeed. There is every indication that things are not only difficult but things can get worse in the near future. The franchisor needs to develop a customer and marketing philosophy which focuses on the success and satisfaction of both the franchisee and the end consumer. The marketing concept focuses on doing a better job of fulfilling and satisfying customer needs.

Today, in our buyers' markets, customers have a wide range of products and services from which to choose. If the franchisor fails to deliver an acceptable product to the franchisee, then the franchisee will quickly lose confidence and soon lose customers. The franchisees are becoming more educated and demand higher quality and value. The decline of the U.S. automotive industry, camera industry, and even consumer electronics provides widespread evidence that average quality will lose customer confidence and sales.

To succeed today the franchisor needs a new philosophy. To become a winner the franchisor must become franchisee centered and customer centered. The franchisor must deliver superior value and quality to their dual target customers. They must learn to build franchisees, build customers, and not just provide products or services. They must develop their skills in people development rather than just product development.

One of the best examples of relationship marketing or the effort to improve franchisee and customer satisfaction is the McDonald's Corporation. The 31,500 McDonald's restaurants do not attract customers because of their love for the hamburgers but because these customers flock to the

---

SUCCESS MAGAZINE—FRANCHISEE SATISFACTION RANKING

In the spring of 2001, *SUCCESS* magazine published its Franchisee Satisfaction Ranking, which allowed franchisees to grade their franchisor. Unit owners were chosen at random and asked to respond to questions relating to their satisfaction overall and in the areas of finances, training, and field support. Their responses were based on a scale of 1 to 5 (dissatisfied to most satisfied). Overall satisfaction was given a weight in the rankings of 40 percent. The other three categories (financial, training, and field support) accounted for 20 percent each of the total score. These companies received the highest marks in the ranking.

1. McDonald's
2. Color-Glo
3. American Leak Detection
4. Weed Man
5. Wireless Zone
6. Home Cleaning Centers of America
7. Sports Clips/Command Performance
8. Primrose Schools
9. Tumbleweed Southwest Mesquite Grill & Bar
10. Planet Beach Tanning Salons

Source: "Franchising: Gold 200 Franchisee Satisfaction Ranking," SUCCESS (Feb-March 2001): 74–92.

McDonald's system. Many other restaurants are noted for better tasting hamburgers; however, McDonald's has finely tuned its system that develops customer satisfaction through what the company calls QSCV—quality, service, cleanliness, and value. This system contains valuable components of both internal and external operations. It has been able to successfully develop partnerships with its franchisees, employees, suppliers, and producers throughout the world to jointly develop exceptionally high franchisee and customer value.

The key to developing a strong franchisor–franchisee relationship focuses on sound **relationship/management marketing**. This unique relationship involves the creation, maintenance, and enhancement of strong relationships between the franchisor and the franchisee and customers. Increasingly, the franchisors are moving away from focus on individual transactions and are moving toward a necessary focus on building value-added relationships with the franchisee and end consumers. The development of relationship management/marketing is oriented toward establishing strong relationships in the long term. The final goal is to be able to deliver long-term value to franchisees as well as to customers and to measure this success in terms of franchisee and customer satisfaction. This requires all of the franchisor's people and departments to work together as a team to serve the franchisee and the customer. It requires the development of relationships at all levels including financial, social, technical, and legal. The end result of this development will be high franchisee and customer loyalty.

It is easy to distinguish between the five levels or relationships that are formed with franchisees (and even customers) who now own or are using the franchise business. These levels include:

1. **Elementary** The franchisor has sold the franchise to the franchisee but does not actively follow up with the franchisee.

2. **Reactive** The franchisor now sells another franchise and encourages the franchisee to call with questions or concerns.

3. **Accountable** The franchisor contacts the franchisee shortly after the sale of the franchise to determine if the franchisee is satisfied. The franchisor would also solicit and encourage the franchisee to make suggestions for any specific improvement or to correct any faults. This information would help the franchisor improve the system and operations.

4. **Proactive** The franchisor phones the franchisee from time to time with suggestions about operations and inquiring about ways to help.

5. **Partnership** The franchisor recognizes the partnership with new the franchisee. Both will work continuously to develop new ways to deliver better value to each other. A company that has been able to move through this series of relationships and has developed an outstanding franchisor–franchisee relationship program is Kwik Kopy Inc. This firm's "sweathogs" call each franchisee every month to inquire how they may be of service and what needs the franchisee has. They continuously look for ways to provide value to each other and to help each other improve the system and operations of the company. This has led even to the establishment and development of Copy Club Inc., which is a new franchise business geared more toward personal copying needs than small business copying.

19-3a   Franchise Advisory Councils

Franchise advisory councils (FACs) are generally set up by the franchisor to encourage communication, creativity, ingenuity, and responsiveness from its franchisees. At the same time, FACs are a formalized method of coordinating a relationship between the individual units and the corporate headquarters. Most FACs are started at the initiative of the parent company, although some have arisen out of a need to discuss the concerns and problems of franchised unit owners.

Costs of group meetings are covered by some corporations while the costs of meetings in other systems are independently met through franchisee membership dues. Franchise advisory councils have proven very beneficial to many franchised organizations. Sometimes franchisees will use FACs to solve problems or present suggestions to the franchisor.

Merry Maids, Inc., the leader in the domestic cleaning industry, has a FAC of eleven geographic regions. A coordinator is appointed by the headquarters office for each region. These coordinators call for semiannual regional meetings to offer marketing and service ideas. For the franchisees, as well as for the franchisor, this council provides an opportunity to have many questions answered.

Franchisors can also benefit from **franchisee organizations**. They can gain valuable insights from franchisee reactions to new products and services as well as receive practical advice and marketing suggestions. Additionally, many new products developed at the franchisee level are first presented to the franchise organization before being submitted to the headquarters organization, allowing other franchisees a chance to express their opinions or offer suggestions about the product before it is brought to the attention of the franchisor.

Merry Maids also provides a system of rewarding its franchisees for different levels of sales performance. This has proven to be a huge incentive to the franchisees. The awards range from the Statesman Circle (which almost all franchisees will receive) to the exclusive President's Circle, given to only the top 1 percent in sales volume. Other honors include the Monarch Circle, Diplomat Circle, Regency Circle, and Chancellor Circle awards. The names and pictures of the recipients are included in the monthly newsletter.

Midas International Corporation's franchise advisory council came into being when franchisees joined to represent their specific interests to the corporate headquarters. Midas subsequently started its own advisory committee and paid all franchisee expenses for travel and lodging. Later the membership decided to support the FAC entirely by franchisee dues. Midas today has an outstanding record of franchisee relations, with a strong franchise advisory council and a supportive headquarters operation. Franchise advisory councils are important means of providing strategic plans and pointing the way for future success and growth of the franchise system.

The development of a franchise advisory council must be carefully undertaken with the cooperation of all franchisees and the corporate headquarters. Major areas of concern which need to be investigated before the council is developed include creation, membership, functions/committees, meetings, role of the franchisor, expenses, officers, and legal and administrative functions. (See Figure 19-2.) It is important that all franchisees be included within the advisory council or at least have representatives on the council. The advisory council enables franchisees to discuss new products and services and promotional/advertising programs, as well as the success and failure of different operations. Franchisees must not become involved in discussing pricing or the acceptance or nonacceptance of prospective franchisees, because these two activities are illegal under antitrust legislation.

One of the major advantages in developing a franchise advisory council is to promote and improve communication between the franchisor and the franchisee. Many franchisors use a vast variety of methods to reach franchisees including the Internet, newsletters, bulletins, manuals, and the telephone to strengthen the communications with franchisees. However, even the best of communications systems still make it difficult for the franchisor to understand all the serious concerns which franchisees may have concerning the company's operations. The advantage of developing the franchise advisory council is to move away from one-way communication systems to an interactive or two-way system which the FAC develops. This "preventive medicine" allows the franchisor to avoid conflict, learn about the concerns of the franchisees, and saves tens of thousands of dollars in lost revenues through litigation, bad publicity, and attorney fees.

1. **CREATION**
   a. *By franchisor*
   b. *By franchisees*
   c. *Jointly*

2. **MEMBERSHIP**
   a. *Appointed by franchisor*
   b. *Open to all franchisees*
   c. *Elected by franchisees*

3. **FUNCTIONS/COMMITTEES**
   a. *Advertising/marketing*
   b. *Operations*
   c. *Services*
   d. *Research and development*
   e. *Finance*

4. **MEETINGS**
   a. *National (once a year)*
   b. *Regional (one to four times a year)*
   c. *Committees (two or more times per year)*

5. **FRANCHISOR ROLE**
   a. *Top management*
   b. *Limited/advisory*

6. **EXPENSES**
   a. *Shared (most common)*
   b. *Franchisees pay all*
   c. *Franchisor pays all*

7. **OFFICERS**
   a. *President or chairman*
   b. *Secretary/Treasurer*
   c. *Vice-presidents*

8. **LEGAL AND ADMINISTRATIVE**
   a. *Do not discuss pricing*
   b. *Do not discuss who can or cannot be a franchisee*
   c. *Do not exclude anyone from FAC without good cause*
   d. *Do have a written set of bylaws*
   e. *Do use agendas and minutes*
   f. *Do follow-ups*

FIGURE **19-2**
Franchise Advisory Council

Probably the most common permanent group with a FAC is the advertising council. Because most franchise companies charge advertising fees in addition to their royalties, the franchisees want a say in determining how those fees are used. By the development of an advertising council, the franchisees have an effective way to input and manage the franchisor advertising funds.

19-4 C.A.R.E.

Probably the main ingredient in the franchisor–franchisee relationship is the feeling that the franchisor cares about the success and activities of the franchisee. **C.A.R.E.** refers to vital ingredients of the relationship—communication, awareness, rapport, and expertise.

19-4a Communication

One of the major concerns of a strong franchisor is that the franchisee always be able to communicate and feel a part of the franchisor's organization. Effective communication is a key to any successful business activities. Most franchising organizations create newsletters to help enhance communication throughout the system.

In addition, many franchisors use franchisees to form advertising committees, new product and development committees, grievance committees, and operations committees. Franchisors will often provide regional seminars, training programs, and field representatives to ensure that communications are kept strong.

19-4b Awareness

Awareness is an important ingredient of a successful franchise system. The franchisor should make its franchisees aware that they are appreciated and are a vital component in the success of the organization. Most franchisors provide awards to show their awareness of franchisee performance levels. Some franchisors offer performance incentives, such as cash or trips, for successful franchisees. These kinds of things enhance the awareness between the franchisor and the franchisee. Franchisors should also take periodic surveys of their franchisees to learn their feelings and concerns. Also, franchisors can encourage local or regional clubs to help franchisees support each other as well as develop common advertising and marketing systems.

19-4c Rapport

The franchisor should try to develop a strong personal rapport with each franchisee. Some franchisors do this by providing birthday gifts, flowers on special days, and remembrances for services performed or goals reached. Additionally, recognition is often given at annual meetings or through the newsletters for promotional service, publicity service, performance levels, and even community service. Developing rapport will help keep the franchise system strong and unified.

19-4d Expertise

The franchisor needs to provide expertise to the franchisees. Most of the initial meetings are concerned with the nuts and bolts of the operation, but as the relationship matures, meetings should concentrate on specific areas such as finance, management, personal growth, marketing, and even special promotions. A toll-free hotline is often set up to allow the franchisee immediate access to the expertise in the central office. The headquarters may provide computer expertise and marketing and promotional expertise, as well as product or service research and development.

The franchisor–franchisee relationship will amount to nothing if the franchisor fails to demonstrate genuine care. The franchisor must deal openly and honestly, with integrity and mutual respect for the franchisee. The Golden Rule is directly applicable to the franchising relationship. When it is followed, success, prosperity, and growth will more likely occur. When it is not followed, franchisees will become disenchanted, legal problems will arise, and the franchise will generally fail.

ICED (parent company to Kwik Kopy Printing, the Copy Club, American Wholesale Thermographers, the Ink Well, Franklin's, and Cypress Publishing) has developed a unique program for helping children of franchisees grow to become the new owners of the business. The program is entitled "Rising Star." A rising star is typically a family member, identified by the owner to succeed in the ownership of the business at the desire of the franchisee. This program as developed by ICED assists the preparation of the next generation to succeed as the owners of the franchising center. The Rising Star program consists of inviting members to seminars, a directory of rising stars, different focus groups, separate newsletters, monthly magazine articles, and special sessions at national conventions. This program is in conjunction with the franchisor's desire to continue the operation of the franchise with qualified franchisees. The children of the owner's will be taught all the operations of the franchise and will be able to help their parents as they turn the ownership over to their own children.

Steve Hammerstein

President and CEO of International Center for Entrepreneurial Development, Inc. and Past Chairman of IFA

When I was president of Kwik Kopy Corporation, we always urged our printing center owners to take full advantage of the tools and programs offered. Most are opportunities to share what has been learned by each member of our franchise family. Our records show that the most active center owners are the ones who participated—sought full benefit from the franchise—were the most successful. Well, you have to practice what you preach. At least that is what we concluded when we were considering whether or not to renew our membership in the International Franchise Association (IFA). We agreed with its purpose to safeguard franchising but questioned its high price tag. So, we got involved—committee assignments, a seat on the board of directors, officer positions, and ultimately I had the honor of chairing the association.

When we got involved, there was no longer any mystic surrounding the organization or the persons directing it. Whatever we thought it was or was not was replaced with what it is. The IFA like so many other organizations becomes what its members want it to be.

When I served on the executive committee, significant ongoing change in the IFA included the addition of franchisee members, election of a franchisee to the board of directors, election of a woman to the executive committee, and increased dues funding to protect franchising in legislative arenas. It is ironic that we participated in increasing the "high" membership dues which had caused our involvement in the first place!

For this change to happen it had to be embraced by the membership, but that doesn't mean everyone gave it a full body hug. Some resisted, some were willing just to go along, but others gave it a high level of commitment. The reaction to change within the IFA is not unlike that encountered within any franchise system.

Through franchising one becomes part of something bigger, and becomes better as a result. Kwik Kopy Corporation became part of something bigger in 1992 with the formation of the International Center for Entrepreneurial Development, Inc. (ICED). This venture established alliances with others in franchising and added other compatible franchise systems to our own. In response to the needs of many smaller franchises, ICED started its own business venture to assist start-up and smaller franchise systems. Northwest Forest, the 117-acre campus of ICED, was expanded to offer facilities and expertise to those systems and helps support seven franchise systems.

Yet, there is always more to learn from a variety of sources. At one IFA CEO roundtable, I described in vivid detail and with concern the challenges we faced within the printing industry with all the new and emerging digital technology. Printing center owners were seeking direction on which equipment to obtain and what services to offer. Reaction came quickly from CEOs of fast-food franchises. To them I was describing opportunities they wished they could have—new revenue-producing services for the center owners and more of a need for help from the franchisor. As one of them put it, "There are only so many ways you can dress up a hamburger." We got no pity from those guys. Instead, because someone offered a different perspective, we gained a valuable insight.

ICED does not question the value of its membership in the IFA. In fact, we search for new ways to participate and to share with others in franchising. We also preach with renewed vigor the value of participation to the franchisees of our various systems. Full benefit results from full participation whether you are a franchisee or a franchisor. Why should you settle for less from or for yourself?

Summary

The relationship between the franchisor and the franchisee is critical to the success of both parties. The relationship can be examined in the context of a business life cycle, since it goes through four phases as follows: first, the *introduction*—the development of understanding between the parties, building hope for success and relying upon each other to perform their respective functions; second, *growth*—from the grand opening onward, regular and effective support and service between the parties to achieve results for the franchised business; third, *maturity*—mutual respect and understanding demonstrated by continued interaction between franchisor and franchisees to maintain the franchise system, making modifications as they become necessary; and fourth, *decline/development*—decline or termination of the relationship, often as a result of a decrease in the level of business activity, which may be due to failure by the franchisor and/or franchisees to maintain high standards, discontinuity of services by the franchisor, or disenchantment by the franchisee. These conditions may foster a rejuvenation and further development of the franchise system if the partners are able to revive respect and trust for each other.

Franchise advisory councils are a popular and proven means of addressing the differences that can develop in the franchising relationship. These councils may be established either by direct action of the franchisor or by voluntary participation of the franchisees.

Generally, a franchise advisory council, whether formally or informally established, serves as a communication vehicle for both franchisor and franchisee. A council can be used to present suggestions, solve problems, and provide information through conferences, newsletters, and sponsored training sessions. The topics addressed can be as varied as changes under consideration in the franchising agreement, promotions for the coming year, new product development efforts, new equipment, equipment modifications, performance standards, and financial reporting methods. Even sensitive matters such as store renovations, franchise termination, and fairness and compliance are often addressed by advisory councils to the satisfaction of franchisor and franchisees.

For the franchisee, the advisory council can serve as a "big brother" in dealings with the usually more powerful franchisor. For the franchisor, the council is often a vehicle for receiving new ideas for the front lines of the business, revealing problem areas that need attention, and disseminating and legitimating important information of which all franchisees should be aware.

Key Terms

C.A.R.E: Vital ingredients in the franchisor-franchisee relationship as: communication, awareness, rapport, and expertise.

Franchise advisory councils (FACs): set up by the franchisor to encourage communication, creativity, ingenuity, and responsiveness from its franchisees; a formalized method of coordinating a relationship between the individual units and the corporate headquarters.

Franchise organizations: help franchisors gain valuable insights from franchisee reactions to new products and services as well as receive practical advice and marketing suggestions; provide an opportunity for the presentation of many new products developed at the franchisee level before they are submitted to the headquarters organization; allow franchisees a chance to express their opinions or offer suggestions about a new product before it is presented to the franchisor.

Relationship/management marketing: the creation, maintenance, and enhancement of strong relationships between the franchisor and the franchisee/customers; oriented toward establishing strong relationships in the long term, delivering value to franchisees/customers, and measuring this success in terms of franchisee/customer satisfaction.

REVIEW QUESTIONS

1. Of what importance is it that the franchisor–franchisee relationship goes through different stages of development?

2. Are franchise advisory councils of value to either the franchisor or the franchisee? Discuss.

3. Is it important that the franchisor and the franchisee be aware of each other and develop a rapport in their interactions?

CASE STUDY

Smoothie King®

Smoothie King® is a tremendous franchise that is growing by leaps and bounds, because it offers two concepts in one. First are the Smoothie King Smoothies—delicious blends of real fruits, pure juices, and nutritional supplements available in over forty flavors. Second is the wide selection of branded nutritional products such as vitamins, minerals, low-fat snacks, sports nutrition supplements, and more. The company has found that combining these two concepts into one creates a unique business opportunity that helps to broaden customer appeal; and it may be just what everyone is looking for.

Currently, there are over 225 store units operating in twenty-two states with excess of $65 million in total systemwide sales. *Entrepreneur* has rated Smoothie King as the number-one franchise in its category for the past six years. For single-unit franchisees, the owner can develop one store and the franchise fee is $20,000. For multiple-unit franchisees, the owner can develop

START-UP COSTS

Financial Investment Dynamics		
Initial Investment	LOW	HIGH
Franchise Fee	$20,000	$20,000
First Month's Rental and Deposit	$5,000	$8,000
Equipment	$23,000	$28,000
Fixtures/Signage	$14,000	$18,000
Leasehold Improvements	$35,000	$75,000
Start-up Supplies, Inventory	$13,000	$15,000
Opening Advertising	$3,000	$5,000
Training	$1,300	$2,000
Insurance	$1,200	$2,500
Other Prepaid Expenses*	$1,500	$2,500
Legal, Accounting, and Organizational Costs	$1,000	$2,000
Miscellaneous Costs	$2,000	$3,000
Additional Funds	$15,000	$30,000
Additional Development Costs (multiunit franchisees)	$0	$10,000
TOTAL	$135,000	$221,000

The difference between low or high investment levels exists because of varying store sizes and real estate costs.
*Prepaid expenses include grand opening expenses, travel/training, legal/accounting, insurance, permits, and deposits.

There is an ongoing royalty fee of 5 percent of weekly gross sales. Advertising expenses include reserving 2 percent of your weekly gross sales to be spent by you on local marketing. An additional advertising expense of up to 2 percnet, currently 1 percent, of weekly gross sales may be required to be paid into the Smoothie King Advertising Fund.
Source: Information provided courtesy of Smoothie King® (April 2001).

multiple stores in a predefined territory. The franchise fees are $20,000 for the first unit, $17,000 each for units 2 through 4, and $15,000 for units 5 and beyond. There is also a $5,000 development fee for each unit beyond the first.

Smoothie King franchises are generally 800 to 1,200 square feet; however, smaller or larger stores are an option. They are usually located in neighborhood and community strip centers, power centers, shopping malls, and downtown business district locations. The optimal area is typically densely populated, has significant traffic count, is highly visible, and is located near numerous traffic generators.

CASE QUESTIONS

1. What are the advantages and disadvantages of a Smoothie King® franchise?

2. What additional information would you request from a franchisor before signing a franchising agreement?

3. Would Smoothie King® be a good franchise to invest in? Why or why not?

4. What else would you need to know before entering into a franchising agreement with Smoothie King®?

REFERENCES

Axelrad, Norman D., and Lewis G. Rudnick, "The Franchisee and the Franchise Relationship," *Franchising: A Planning and Sales Plans Guide* (Chicago: Commerce Clearinghouse, Inc., 1987), 39–50.

Bergen, M., S. Dutta, and O. C. Walker, Jr., "Agency Relationships in Marketing: A Review of the Implications and Applications of Agency and Related Theories," *Journal of Marketing* 56 (July 1992): 1–24.

Heide, J. B., "Interorganizational Governance in Marketing Channels," *Journal of Marketing* 58 (January 1994): 71–85.

Justis, Robert T. and Richard J. Judd, "Master Franchising: A New Look," *Journal of Small Business Management* 24 (July 1986): 16.

Knight, Russell M., "Franchising from the Franchisor and Franchisee Points of View," *Journal of Small Business Management* 24 (July 1986): 8.

Kostecka, Andrew, "What Is Franchising?" *Franchise Opportunities Handbook* (Washington, DC: U.S. Department of Commerce, International Trade Administration, November 1987), xxix–xxxiii.

Luxenberg, Stan, "Growing Plains," *Roadside Empires, How the Chains Franchised America* (New York: Penguin Books , 1986), 220–251.

Michie, Donald A. and Stanley D. Sibley, "Channel Member Satisfaction: Controversy Resolved," *Journal of the Academy of Marketing Science* 13 (Winter 1985): 188–205.

Nedell, Harold, "Marriage and Divorce—Franchise Style," *The Franchise Game* (New York: Olemco Publishing , 1980), 35–39.

Seltz, David D., "Providing Supportive Backup to Franchisees," *The Complete Book of Franchising* (Reading, MA: Addison-Wesley Publishing Co., 1982), 171–196.

FRANCHISOR SUPPORT SERVICES

In studying this chapter, you will:

- **Understand the services provided by a franchisor to a franchisee.**

- **Be able to recognize success programs provided by franchisors.**

- **Realize the importance of an effective communication system to the franchisor–franchisee relationship.**

- **Understand the importance of the field representatives or middlemen.**

- **Recognize the value of franchisor training and what it generally entails.**

- **Understand the contents of a training manual or training program necessary for the development of the franchisee.**

INCIDENT

Jon has been a franchisee for four years. He has been successful in selling sports apparel in the shopping mall in his community. In the first three years of his operation, Jon became one of the top 100 sellers of the entire franchising system. In this past year, however, Jon has started to run into problems with two of his employees and has not had the sales volume of the prior three years. He is wondering how he might be able to improve relationships with these two employees or if he should simply discharge them and get two new employees. He is quite concerned about replacing these two people because of their extensive training background and sales ability. However, the other seven employees are beginning to look at their behavior and to wonder if they can get away with some of the same activities.

Jon is interested in contacting his franchisor but he does not know for sure what he wants to ask. He knows he wants help from the franchisor in either providing additional training for the two problem employees or firing them. Jon has an additional problem in that he has never asked the franchisor for anything before in his career. He seldom talks to the franchise headquarters except every six months when they make a mandatory call to his office and he asks them to call back at a later time when he does not have a customer. The franchisor never calls. Jon is wondering what he should ask and what he should expect from the franchisor to help him with this problem. Jon also wants to review his inventory with the franchisor to see if part of his stock may be too old and may also be a cause of his falling sales. What should Jon do? What should Jon expect?

20-1   FRANCHISEE SUPPORT

Constructive support of franchisees is essential for efficient operation and ultimate success of a franchise system. The franchisor is responsible for developing and maintaining a support organization which satisfies the needs of each franchisee. Through training, the franchisor attempts to instill confidence in franchisees so they can be more productive and profitable in their implementation of the franchisor's methods. Also, the franchisee should leave the training program with a thorough knowledge of the operational requirements and processes of the franchise system. Franchisees-in-training should be made to feel that, if they adhere to the franchisor's proven approach, success will follow.

The franchisor's support organization and training are presented together in this chapter because these are the primary methods of support a franchisee receives. The major responsibility of the support organization or office of the franchisor is to develop and maintain sufficient and accurate communication between the franchisee and the parent organization. A prospective franchisor should be aware of the primary motivations one generally has in seeking a franchise opportunity: profitability, chance for self-employment, ability to run one's own business and be very successful at it, and opportunity to enjoy growth through the franchising arrangement. The franchisor's support structure should be designed to help franchisees realize these goals. Figure 20-1 details elements of a franchisor's support service checklist. Figure 20-2 illustrates the initial franchisor support services for a new franchise store.

20-1a   Profitability

The most compelling reason for a person to enter business of any type is the opportunity to make a profit. Capitalism is founded on the notions of free markets and profitability. A franchisor must assist the franchisee in making a healthy profit, for if the franchisee is successful, the franchisor will also succeed. Franchisees are usually happiest when sales are strong and there is a good margin of profit over costs. They become discouraged when sales slide or profits shrink. The franchisor's support staff serves as the intermediary between the franchisor and the franchisee, providing training, insights, and helpful suggestions to maintain strong sales and improve profitability for the franchisee.

20-1b   Self-Employment

One of the most exciting features of being in business is the opportunity of being one's own boss. Many new entrepreneurs have left their jobs because of conflicts with superiors or subordinates, reluctance to follow someone else's policies and procedures, or the feeling of not being able to make a positive contribution to the organization. Franchising provides such people the opportunity to be self-employed without having to learn on their own how to be successful through trial and error. The franchisee has the advantage of being able to look to the franchisor's proven approach and methods, which can be seen as a form of trust by the franchisee in the franchisor. Maintaining the bond of trust is not easy, as it must be nurtured and proven repeatedly. It is the franchisor's support staff that provides the methods, programs, and suggestions for improvement and assists in solving problems, if necessary, to help the independent business owner, as a franchisee, to achieve success in business. The support staff needs to realize that, while franchisees continually rely on the franchisor to assist in the development of the business, they value their independence as well. Support staff should not demean or take away from the franchisee's independence as a business owner but should offer assistance and elicit cooperation along the lines beneficial to the franchisee and the franchising organization.

HOME INSTEAD SENIOR CARE "RECOGNIZES" FRANCHISEES

Award Trip: Home Instead Senior Care provides a free trip to Mexico to its top 20 percent of franchisees in recognition of their outstanding sales efforts. In the year 2008, the franchisee had to reach an average sales of $100,000 for each of four months (May, June, July, and August), or total sales of $400,000 for three free nights, $500,000 for four free nights, and $600,000 for five free nights. The following year it will go up to $450,000, $550,000, and $650,000 respectively.

National Convention: The firm's annual national convention is designed to inform, educate, and entertain. The convention starts on Thursday afternoon at 2:00 discussing recruiting and retention, with a giant general session that evening; Friday morning at 8:00 they start with another general session followed by workshops, regional rallies, reception/dinner, and the big Xpotential Games (or Survivor Jam— the franchisees like to have competition between areas); Saturday is filled with the general session, workshops, and the evening gala awards banquet coupled with celebration and dancing.

Award Levels: Every quarter, Home Instead Senior Care publishes a newsletter which contains a picture and a paragraph about each franchisee who has reached a new sales level during the previous quarter. Franchisees like all of the recognition. Each time the company publishes its newsletter it is worth the 5 percent royalty franchisees pay, because they show it to their staff and everyone buys into the goals of growth and more sales. The firm's award levels are based on obtaining monthly sales of:

Cornerstone Awards Level I	($20,000) to Level V ($100,000);
Presidential Awards Level I	($125,000) to Level III ($175,000);
Hallmark Awards Level I	($200,000) to Level III ($300,000);
Legacy Award	$400,000, and their new one
Founders Award	$500,000 (at least one franchisee has sales over $500,000 a month)

20-1c   Striving to Be Successful

All of us desire to be successful. In our personal lives we seek affiliation, acceptance, recognition, and status within our peer groups. In business, we want to lead or be part of a successful organization. Franchisees are like most other businesspeople. They want their businesses to succeed and grow in size and profitability.

Franchisors need to recognize that the franchisee's strong motivation to succeed is probably similar to their own motivation to become successful. A franchisor should provide whatever services, supplies, products, or support will enable the franchisee to improve the business. Success breeds success and the greatest support for a franchisee is the opportunity for success. A franchisor's support staff should offer instruction, praise, encouragement, and other positive communication to the franchisee. A franchisee will not be successful if negative attitudes develop about the business, its future, the relationship with the franchisor, or the franchisee's abilities as a capable business owner.

20-1d   Opportunity for Growth

Countless franchisees, facing the drudgery and daily trials of running a business, lose hope about expanding the business. Their energies are consumed with day-to-day operational concerns and the desire to keep up with the routines of business. Many franchisees would love to expand, but they

RATING: 5=Excellent; 4=High; 3=Average; 2=Low; 1-Poor					
FRANCHISOR TRAINING	5	4	3	2	1
Preopening Training					
Opening Training					
Postopening Training					
Training from other Franchisees					
Ongoing Support Training					
Employee Training Materials					
Conventions/Seminar Training					
Field Training					
COMMUNICATIONS					
Telephone Calls					
Field Visits					
Internet Web Site					
Intranet Web Site					
Extranet Web Site					
E-mail					
Field Visits					
Newsletters					
Letters					
Other Publications					
Annual Conventions					
Seminars/Workshops					
Headquarters Visits					
Other Methods					
CONVENTIONS/MEETINGS					
Training					
Social Events					
Vendor Exhibits					
Interaction with Franchisor Staff					
Interaction with other Franchisees					

FIGURE **20-1**

Franchisor Support Service Checklist

feel they lack the energy, that they would be taking too great a financial risk, or that they would not get enough support from the franchisor.

At some point in the development and operation of a business, the owner will want the business to grow. The success of a franchise system depends on growth, and for this reason the franchisor

ADMINISTRATIVE	5	4	3	2	1
Reception/Switchboard Personnel					
Purchasing					
Mailroom					
Site Selection/Development Support					
Technical Support					
Equipment Support					
Site Evaluations					
Franchisee Advisory Councils					
MARKETING ASSISTANCE					
Advertising Support					
Franchisee Advertising Council					
Co-op Advertising					
Advertising "Slicks"					
TV/Commercial Videos					
Radio Ads					
Yellow Page Ads					
Advertising Flyers/Brochures					
Advertising Support					
Door Hangers					
OVERALL EVALUATIONS					
Training					
Communications					
Marketing					
Advertising					
Conventions/Seminars					
Administration					
Interaction with Other Franchisees					

FIGURE **20-1**
Continued

should be aware of the growth intentions of its franchisees. Being provided those services, new products or applications, marketing techniques, and carefully planned and franchisor-supported promotional campaigns will help franchisees keep a positive outlook on the business and continue to look for ways to expand the business and increase its profitability.

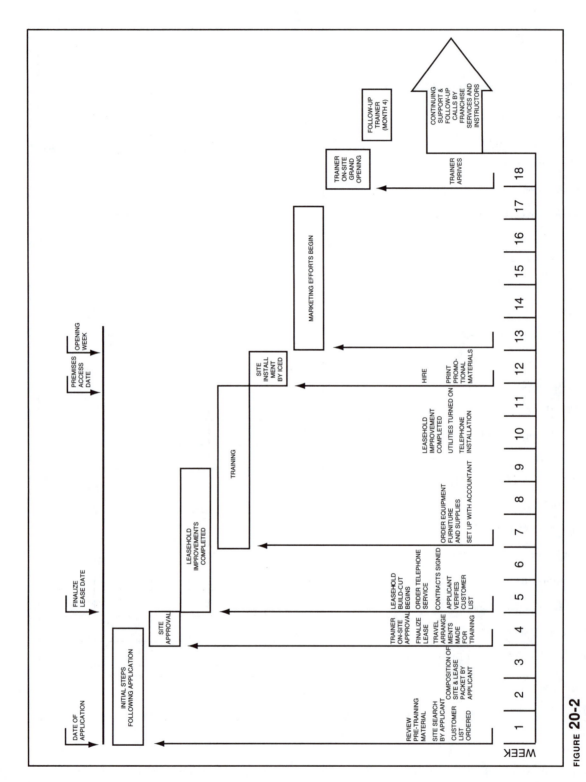

FIGURE **20-2**

Starting the Store: Initial Support Services for the New Franchise Store

20-1e   A Success Story

A field representative for a large franchised restaurant system entered one of the system's units. To her delight, the restaurant was busy and had a friendly ambience. The franchisees of this particular restaurant, Tom and Alice, are husband and wife who have been franchisees for four years. They are pleased with their franchise and with their franchisor. Tom and Alice are a hard-working couple, and during the first eighteen months of operation, they often spent ten to fourteen hours every day working at the store. Their two teenage children help out after school and on weekends. Tom handles all food operations, including preparation and sales, and he is responsible for maintaining the general appearance of the building and grounds. Alice supervises the staff, oversees customer relations, and maintains the recordkeeping system.

The restaurant is bright, clean, and nicely decorated. The counter clerks wear neatly pressed uniforms and hats that display the logo of the franchise. Work and service counters are kept spotless, food-storage areas are clean, and food processing is performed according to the standards of the franchise system.

The clientele is primarily families and downtown workers. The restaurant is often used for business lunches and in the evening is frequently filled with students from a local university as well as with families coming into the downtown area.

The owners appear to be contented. They follow the directions of the franchisor and use the operations manual as their "bible." They abide by the sales manual and serve the full range of menu items provided by the franchisor. Tom and Alice realize that extra effort is needed to keep the restaurant clean and tidy, but they know the profits and success that result from the quality service they provide and are committed to doing whatever is necessary to maintain the high standards of the franchise system.

20-1f   A Failure Story

In the southwestern section of the same city, the field representative enters another franchisee's restaurant, located along a major traffic-way leading to the city's shopping mall three blocks away. At this location, she notices a number of problems right away. The restrooms appear neglected, perhaps not cleaned for the past several days. In the dining area, papers, straws, and plates litter three of the nine tables. Only two of seven employees are wearing a uniform; one wears a cap with the franchise logo, and the rest are wearing blue jeans and t-shirts. The storefront could use a coat of paint. A small plot of grass in front of the restaurant is overrun with weeds. Windows look filmy and dirty. The kitchen and food processing areas are cluttered with spilled food and empty cups and storage containers.

The franchisee does not seem interested in taking time to mingle with the customers or serve them a second cup of coffee. A waitress approaches the field representative, asking her how to handle a customer complaining about cold food. Discussion with the franchisee leaves the field representative feeling that he is sour and full of complaints. He blames many of his problems on inferior equipment and lack of proper training. And although he has not followed suggested pricing guidelines, nor did he purchase the recommended equipment for the restaurant when he opened for business, he complains that sales are unsteady and the equipment is insufficient to handle the orders during peak periods. He complains about sunlight coming through the windows and creating uncomfortable temperatures in the restaurant; however, he did not follow the recommended architectural design supplied by the franchisor. This franchisee has stated that he wants to get out of the business, having had four profitable months, three breakeven months, and five "loss" months in the past year. He believes that the major problems are insufficient sales, poor communication with employees, and a lack of understanding and the "right kind" of support from the franchisor. Yet his location is in a strong business area and the field representative has devoted more of her time and energy and more company resources to helping this franchisee over the past two years than she has provided to Tom and Alice in the past four years.

20-2 COMMUNICATION

Constructive, positive communication is one of the requirements of a successful business. Areas of accountability need to be delineated between franchisor and franchisee, as well as between franchisee and employees. This means that objectives, performance standards, and duties must be clearly understood and accepted. Information systems used in the franchise system, which form the links between performance, managerial accounting, and decision making, must also be understood. Information usage—who gets what information, from whom, and how often—forms the basis of an effective feedback system. The feedback system of the franchise organization should make everyone aware of the importance of two-way communication—of listening, offering constructive criticism, motivating employees, and using incentives and rewards.

The support and the training provided by the franchisor to the franchisee will foster the development and maintenance of a communication system for the franchise. The effectiveness (or ineffectiveness) of the communication system will dramatically affect the success of the system. It is important for the franchisor to be accurately informed about the various activities and changes taking place within the franchise system as the company seeks to improve performance and profitability. Effective communication through carefully planned systems of information, recognition, and reporting is critical for continued growth and development of the franchised business. Communication is also integral to the superior–subordinate relationships within the franchisor's and the franchisee's organizations. The more effective the communication, the more effective will be the supervision. Of the various approaches to developing effective communications between franchisor and franchisee, the following methods have been most successfully used by franchise systems: telephone contacts, Internet websites, e-mail, mail contacts, personal visits by the franchisor's field representative to the franchisee, franchisee subgroup meetings, and corporate meetings.

20-2a Telephone Contacts

One-to-one verbal communication is a highly effective mode of communication. Frequent contact helps to ensure closeness and continuity within a relationship. As contact tapers off, the closeness diminishes, and questions can even arise about the reasons for developing and continuing the relationship. In a franchise system, telephone contacts are important to keep the franchisee informed about plans or current activities of the parent company, to evaluate franchisee performance or records, and to let the franchisee know what assistance to expect from the franchisor. Phone contacts can be set up in various ways. Strongly service-oriented franchisors encourage their field representatives to make contact not only on a planned, routine basis, but also spontaneously, or even by using a different approach such as a conference call involving several franchisees.

Planned telephone calls to the franchisee on a particular day each week or month are very useful. Such calls are typically franchisor initiated and are meant to discuss sales levels, product and service support, and advertising and promotional plans, as well as to respond to questions or issues raised by the franchisee during the previous call. These calls help develop the interrelationship between franchisor and franchisee and can be a mainstay of support between them. The calls should be friendly, helpful, and positive. They are not intended for faultfinding or for enhancing the power of the franchisor over the franchisee.

Spontaneous telephone calls tend to boost the morale and feelings of interdependence of the franchisee and the franchisor. It can be exciting for a franchisee to receive a call from the home office "just to find out how things are going." Such calls help the franchisor understand the immediate concerns of the franchisee, get a feel for the franchisee's general attitude over time, and determine if there is anything the parent company could or should be doing over and above the regular services it is providing. These calls are often cordial, designed to help improve communication between franchisor and franchisee. However, the spontaneous call can instill fear. The franchisee may wonder, "Why am I getting a call from the home office? What have I done now?" The franchisor should try to dispel any feelings of fear, keeping the tone of the conversation amicable and showing genuine interest in the franchisee's progress.

Conference calls provide an effective means of contacting several franchisees at the same time. These calls are generally prearranged by letter or earlier phone contact to help ensure "attendance" of franchisees within a district, area, or region. Such calls are generally used to inform franchisees of new product or service activities by the franchisor, new advertisements or upcoming promotions, or new contests or customer relations projects. The conference call is an effective way to instill in franchisees their importance both as individuals and as members of the franchise team. Franchisors generally consider the expenses of conference calls to be low when they consider the goodwill fostered and the results often obtained with these calls.

20-2b   Internet Websites

The Internet is a worldwide telecommunications network that permits people from around the world to use their computers to access and exchange information, data, pictures, sound, articles, and files without regard to location or the kind of computer they are using. The Internet has rapidly become one of the best methods of communicating throughout the world. Most all franchising companies have developed their own websites—even The Rug Place had a website before selling the first franchise. McDonald's website is simply www.mcdonalds.com.

Today, on the Internet, we can advertise, communicate with our franchisees, build brand awareness, offer coupons, develop focus groups, obtain lead generations, process sales, and even conduct marketing surveys. In addition, we can expand the Internet into an **intranet** and allow our franchisees private access to confidential information provided by the franchisor only by using a secret password. The intranet permits the franchisees to read reports from the franchisor and even review the operations manual and updated corrections. The franchisees may even discuss with other franchisees their feelings and activities by use of a chat room.

An additional password would further allow the franchisees, and franchisor, to work with their suppliers on an **extranet**. Here orders may be placed after reviewing the products provided by the supplier.

20-2c   E-Mail

E-mail has become the preferred method of communication for many people. Instead of phoning or sending regular mail, many individuals and companies send e-mail messages back and forth to staff, different companies, franchisors, franchisees, and family members. As franchising continues to grow, so too will the use of e-mail. Words of encouragement, support, and instruction can be easily delivered at a fraction of the cost and in less time than other communication methods.

20-2d   Mail Contacts

Use of the mail is the primary method of providing and explaining instructions, supplying advertising and promotional materials, and discussing any legal matters that arise. Mail contact also is the principal means of reporting district sales levels and personnel changes within the company, distributing newsletters, and providing evaluative reports to franchisees. Mail is often used to provide follow-up information after spontaneous or conference calls, giving suggestions for advertising, promotions, or general marketing, or perhaps responding to a question or issue raised by a franchisee.

BUILDING BLOCKS FOR CUSTOMER SERVICE

Listen to customers!

Plan your work, work your plan!

Underpromise/overproduce!

Smile!

Goal—100 percent customer satisfaction!

Give customers more than they expect!

Provide "wow" for the customer!

Solicit the customers' opinion!

Be willing to change!

Sell benefits!

Provide friendly services!

Be sincere—fakes are easily spotted!

Follow up and follow through!

Be persistent, not a pest!

Love your neighbor as yourself!

Letters are often sent on a regular basis from the sales manager and/or the president of the franchise system to franchisees to assure them of continued support and service from the home office. Personal letters from the franchisor to a franchisee suggest the acceptance and importance of the individual franchisee in the franchise system.

House organs or **newsletters** can be effective in explaining various activities within the franchised company, recognizing top salespeople or locations, expressing the opinions of the president, announcing new territories or new franchisees, and presenting other information of a positive and helpful nature. A good newsletter will contain the following information.

Cover Story (what is currently going on or coming up in the near future)

Letter from the President

Honor Franchisee Staff Members

Salutations of Franchisee Sales Achievement Award Recipients

Headquarters Information

Success Stories

Other Information

Information about Each New Franchisee

Activity reports are required by almost all franchised firms on a weekly or biweekly basis. These reports typically address such information as sales volume, number of sales, expenses, callbacks, and sales to individuals, community groups, and institutions. The central thrust is to provide a picture of the type of sale made, by client category (if important in that business) and by expenses incurred for each category of sales. Each week the home office may send out the report forms for the franchisee to complete, detailing the sales activities, expenses, personnel costs and/or changes, and other activities important for tracking performance. Each month the franchisee manager at the home office may develop a franchisee profile which illustrates the strengths and weaknesses of each unit within a district, area, or region. Activity reports are helpful for the franchisor to make constructive suggestions to individual franchisees for improving operations and/or congratulating franchisees for work well done.

20-2e Visits

Personal visits by a representative of the franchise home office are important to the franchisee. These visits are usually made by field representatives of the franchisor, but are occasionally made by the franchising company's president, vice president, franchising director, sales manager, or regional or district supervisor. The personal visit is a good public relations tool the franchising company can use to encourage and uplift the spirits of the franchisees and their employees. Personal visits are also effective for addressing problems raised by the franchisee or the franchising company, showing genuine commitment to resolve any such problems.

Initially, the most important reason for field visits is to get to know franchisees on their own turf. By the time the business is open and operating, the franchisee has probably met the president and support staff from the home office. However, personal meetings on the turf of the franchisee are different from meetings at the home office. Usually, "get-acquainted" visits to the new unit in the early months of operation are brief and supportive, and are beneficial to both franchisor and franchisee.

Support-service visits to the franchisee should not be confused with get-acquainted visits. The primary purpose of the franchisor's support staff is to provide service to the franchisee. Their visits should aim toward helping resolve problems that arise in the franchisee's operations and providing advice and assistance in meeting reporting requirements of the franchisor, as well as giving helpful hints in dealing with changing competitive conditions. Support service is of little value when advice consists of knee-jerk or off-the-cuff opinions. Careful consideration of the specific problems raised by the franchisee should be made by the home office prior to the support-service visit. In this way, advice, assistance, and specific recommendations will carry the weight of thorough consideration before they are presented. A franchisee will readily see the difference between blue-sky suggestions and thoughtful counsel.

Training visits are usually made by members of the home office staff. Often the staff members who make these visits are involved in the preopening and grand opening training of the respective franchisees. The franchisee must be able to see the value of the royalty fees being returned to the business, and one important way of accomplishing this is to provide service through training visits. These visits usually address either (1) problems in business operation that can be overcome by additional on-site training of the franchisee and staff, or (2) changes in operating procedures or personnel, financial, or marketing approaches recommended by the franchisor. Training is perhaps the greatest intangible benefit or service provided by the franchisor to the franchisees.

20-2f Franchisee Subgroup Meetings

Meetings between franchisees can be beneficial to the franchisees as well as to the parent company. Many franchisors have learned through experience that one of the greatest forms of support for weaker franchised units is the sharing of experience, techniques, and advice by stronger, more successful franchisees. Some franchisees tend to reject recommendations or suggestions from the home office, yet readily accept criticism and suggestions from their franchisee peers. Because peer group influence is always a strong determinant of people's attitudes and behavior, it can serve to benefit the franchisees as well as the franchisor through franchisee meetings.

One approach used to encourage franchisee meetings is for the franchisor to assist in the development of area, district, or regional franchisee organizations. These groups may meet on a quarterly, semiannual, or yearly basis to discuss problems and strengths of their respective businesses. In these meetings, one or more franchisees may come forth to assist other, typically newer, franchisees with training and support. The meetings usually follow a seminar format, with workshops, training sessions, or panel discussions devoted to topics of specific interest to attending franchisees. Sometimes franchisee councils call meetings to draw franchisees from adjoining territories for training and sharing of information. These regional meetings are usually under the direction of the more successful franchisees of the district or region and have franchisor representation available to assist in training and participate in informal interchanges about common problems, conditions, or approaches used within the franchise system.

20-2g   Corporate Meetings

Corporate meetings are often utilized by franchisors to bring together franchisees on an annual or other regular basis to share information and provide training. At these meetings, an informal atmosphere is encouraged through dinners or social gatherings. The training sessions or seminars are designed to refresh and improve managerial skills and provide a forum for presentations about company performance, new products and services or marketing techniques, and any changes in operational procedures or reporting requirements. Often, open dialogue is encouraged through formal discussions, question-and-answer periods, and informal gatherings.

20-3   THE FIELD REPRESENTATIVE

An effective means of communication between franchisor and franchisee is the franchisor's field representative. The field representative helps ensure a smooth, continuing relationship between franchisee and franchisor. Small franchise organizations without a staff of field representatives often depend on the legal, contractual agreement to maintain the franchisor–franchisee relationship, which can lead to the relationship being "controlled" through use of the written contract. Large, successful franchise systems have found the field representative almost indispensable to developing and maintaining a positive, cooperative relationship with the franchisees.

Field representatives (or middlemen) hold numerous titles (see Table 20-1), but the functions and operations generally remain the same. Field representatives are under the direction of the franchisor to be the eyes, ears, and mouth of the company. They are assigned territories or a group of franchisees, and they have the task of overseeing, supervising, evaluating, servicing, and motivating their franchisees.

TABLE 20-1   TYPICAL "MIDDLEMAN" TITLES USED IN FRANCHISING

Field Representative	Business Management Representative
Field Consultant	Regional (Area) Marketing Manager
Area Manager	Services Representative
Field Coordinator	Sales Representative

Typically, the larger the franchise chain, the more complex is the field representation network. For example, several large national chains use regional managers to coordinate and provide franchisor services to franchisees. Each regional manager might supervise three or four area managers, each of whom supervises perhaps five to seven district managers. Each district manager in turn would be responsible for and supervise approximately ten individual franchised units. Such an authority structure seems complex, but it can provide for steady contact downward and upward through the reporting and service lines of communication. A structured, responsible approach to reporting and servicing units in the field suggests that a franchisee should be visited at least every two weeks by the representative.

The middleman function is to help support the franchisee's business. The field representative may wear a variety of hats—that of handholder, tyrant, wise parent, or sympathizer. The effective field representative learns to be sensitive to the needs of the franchisee, demonstrating an interest in helping the franchisee to increase profits. The field representative, as a middleman, can be said to perform five distinct functions for the franchising firm: (1) to represent the franchisor in the franchisor–franchisee relationship; (2) to act as a consultant to the franchisee, providing problem-solving skills and professional advice that will help the franchisee become even more successful; (3) to provide training at the franchisee's site for employees as well as for the franchisees themselves; (4) to serve essentially as a management guide for the franchisee, helping the franchisee/entrepreneur develop managerial competence in decision making, delegation, recordkeeping, and operations control; and (5) to be a motivator for the franchisee. The overall goal of the field representative is to help franchisees reach their potential and to nurture a positive attitude and maintain high morale among franchisees and their employees.

20-4 FRANCHISEE TRAINING

Training is at the heart of any successful franchising business, and is an important part of a franchisor's program for growth and development. In one sense, the franchising process can be viewed as an attempt to reproduce in other locations the successful model or prototype operation. This depends heavily on effective transfer of knowledge and skills from one location to another. Training will develop the attitudes, opinions, skills, and knowledge the franchisee needs to be successful.

Many persons interested in becoming franchisees lack specific experience in the business they seek to enter. A formal training process is often the primary, if not the only, approach used to teach the necessary business operations that will enable one to succeed in the business. The investment in a good training program will be repaid many times over by a strong revenue stream and a happy owner. Most of the operational problems which occur with a franchisee could have been overcome with proper training.

20-4a Developing a Training Operation

The training component of a franchise system involves three major actions by a franchisor: designing and implementing a training unit or function, establishing a training location, and developing the training program, including the philosophy, learning, and skills to be achieved and the methods to be used in providing the training. Almost every franchisor has a training unit or training function formally established within the franchise organization. The person in charge of training typically has experience in each major function of the franchisor's business. This person may have originally been a trainee, an assistant manager, a franchisee, an original partner, a manager at a competitive company, or even someone from outside the industry; there appears to be no specific career development pattern for one performing this important function. However, there are two critical requirements that must be met by anyone put in charge of a franchisee training program: The person must be knowledgeable about effective training

UNIVERSITY NET FRANCHISEES TRAINING: "UNIVERSITIES" AND HIGH TECHNOLOGY

Franchisee training is going hands on, and using high technology to make it work. Hamburger University (McDonald's) and Dunkin' Donuts University have long been the mainstays in franchisee training. Many franchisors today provide weeks of training at their own "universities" and then arrange for hands-on training with an existing franchisee for another week or two. Next franchisor support personnel are sent to help the new owner through their first few weeks of business. Ongoing training may include annual conventions, regional meetings, and high-tech programs such as videos, daily electronic messages, intranet, interactive CD-ROMS, and satellite broadcasts.

Miracle Ear uses the first two weeks of training to cover all the facets of business and nothing about looking into people's ears. They cover managing a business, financial planning, hiring, developing a staff, and even ordering product. Likewise, there are no burger cookers or milkshake machines at Sonic University in Oklahoma City. The first week for a Sonic franchisee is spent on leadership training, personnel, team building, and customer service. They then work with other Sonic franchisees for a thirty-day training program in their restaurants. Sylvan Learning Center franchisees receive a two-hour live satellite TV program from the Columbia, Maryland, franchisor every other month via the Sylvan work.

processes and must have both depth and breadth of understanding of the operational needs and characteristics that will ensure success in the particular franchised business. The reason such depth and breadth is necessary is that this person needs to be able to incorporate into the training program (1) production/operations methods of the franchised business, (2) accounting, marketing, and personnel practices, and (3) effective methods of developing and maintaining constructive franchisor–franchisee relationships. Usually, because the training function is critically important to the continuity and growth of the franchise system, the head of training is part of the upper management of the organization.

The training center for a franchisor can be located almost anywhere. Typically, the center is the original location of the franchisor, or the prototype (if the original location is not used as the prototype). Training centers may also be located regionally. Some franchisors, such as McDonald's (Chicago, Illinois) or Dunkin' Donuts of America (Braintree, Massachusetts), choose to centralize training to enhance their control of the training process and ensure continuity of subject matter to be presented. Holiday Inns, Inc. offers course work for new franchisees at its Holiday Inn University in Memphis, Tennessee, and Long John Silver's provides training at the Jerrico Center in Lexington, Kentucky.

Training programs vary considerably from one franchise system to another. Most franchisee training programs are at least five days long and may last for up to two months. Alternative training programs are often provided that vary in length, complexity, and subject matter. Training enables the franchisor to teach the franchisees and other employees the skills necessary for them to be successful within the franchise system.

Development of the training program is usually grounded in a philosophy of learning, by which the training objectives, the skills to be learned, and the training methods to be utilized are carefully put together. The franchisee needs to learn the business rather than be taught or simply given training about the franchise through books or manuals. The business is best learned through a blend of lectures, group discussions, situational problem analysis, and independent, hands-on performance under the guidance of experienced trainers. The focus is often on self-application through actual performance of operations required within the franchise system, whether the training takes place in a training center or on the job at the franchisee's own franchised business.

Franchisee training is generally divided into three major components: (1) preopening training, (2) grand opening training, and (3) continuing (postopening) training.

20-4b   Preopening Training

Probably the most intensive training occurs during the preopening period. Most franchise systems require at least one week, with some systems offering as much as 300 hours of preopening training. This training typically consists of classroom as well as hands-on experience. Subjects often addressed include planning the franchised business, hiring, purchasing, merchandising, advertising, business management, cash and inventory control, and production/operational methods.

Many franchisors have found that working with a limited number of franchisees, say between three and twelve, works best, providing sufficient peer interaction while allowing sufficient individuality to enable participants to get the most out of the learning experiences. Franchisees have the opportunity to meet and discuss their expectations, desires, strengths, and worries with other franchisees as they individually and collectively anticipate running their own operation. When franchisees meet for training, their interaction is helpful in developing loyalty to the franchise system, creating individual identity within the franchise organization, and learning or improving skills of operation for the franchise.

A franchisee training program usually includes a training manual, which may be the operations manual as well (see Table 20-2). This manual covers topics pertinent to the franchised business, including the system utilized by the franchisor, finance, marketing, operations, service/production, and management/personnel. The training manual, which may also include audio or videotapes, typically provides descriptions of all franchise operations and usually includes operating procedures suggested or required by the franchisor. As such, the manual is important to both franchisor and franchisee. For the franchisor, the manual not only offers a training approach, but also affords protection in case any dispute or question arises regarding appropriateness of methods used in training franchisees. For franchisees, the manual provides an organized approach to the information they need to know in order to function effectively within the business environment of the franchisor. Thus, the manual provides a ready reference to refresh the memory or to solve a specific problem that arises during a workday.

20-4c   Grand Opening Training

Most franchisors send either the training manager or a member of the training unit to work with the new franchisee for the grand opening of a franchised business. Such service may or may not be available for smaller, service-oriented franchised businesses. Grand opening training consists of one to two weeks of in-depth work experience in which the trainer assists the franchisee with the grand opening of the business. The trainer, alone or with the new franchisee (which is preferable), trains the staff in operating procedures associated with service/production, finance, marketing, and operations. The franchisor's representative often stays with the franchisee until the newly opened unit is running smoothly, which may take from several days to several weeks. The length of time can vary considerably as a result of the normal difficulties of any grand opening or because of unexpected problems or complexities. Some service-oriented franchisors provide between two and seven weeks from the time the training begins to the actual grand opening of the franchised business. This period includes one to three weeks of intensive training at headquarters as well as one to three weeks of on-site training to prepare for the forthcoming grand opening. At the time of the grand opening, the franchisor representative stays with the new franchisee for the first full week of operation. Most franchisors are convinced that the same trainer should follow through with the

TABLE 20-2   SAMPLE CONTENTS OF A FRANCHISEE TRAINING MANUAL

INTRODUCTION

Executive Summary

Industry Information

Franchisor Information

Required Activities with Franchisor

Contracts, Licenses, Permits

FINANCE

Balance Sheet

Income Statement

Source and Use of Funds Statement

Cash Budget

Recordkeeping Procedures

Cash Register Procedures

Credit Sales Procedures

Check Sales Procedures

Petty Cash

Reconciliations: Bank, Cash, Sales

Night Deposits

Payroll

Social Security

Withholding Taxes

Leases

Insurance

MARKETING

Target Market

Customer Groups

Advertising

Promotion

Preopening Activities

Grand Opening

Postopening Activities

Merchandising

Customer Relations

Product/Service Definitions and Descriptions

OPERATIONS

(See Operating Manual)

Personnel

Store Operations

Housekeeping

Maintenance Management

Sales Operations

    Inventory

Unit Operations

SERVICE/PRODUCTION

Equipment Ordering and Specifications

    Inventory Control

    Ordering Control from Suppliers and Franchisors,

    and Cost Schedule

    Serving

        Service/Product Preparation Methods

    Warehouse Store Methods

Sanitary Control

    Kitchen Operation

Portion Operation and Control

MANAGEMENT/PERSONNEL

Job Specifications

Recruitment

    Selection

Training

    Development and Maintaining Work Logs

    Motivation of Employees

    Personnel Development

    Labor Laws and Regulations

franchisee from headquarters training through the grand opening of the business. This closeness helps build the business relationship between the franchisor and the franchisee, giving evidence of the franchisor's commitment to serving the franchisee and hopefully earning loyalty, enthusiasm, and team spirit from the franchisee in return.

20-4d   Continuing Training Programs

As a group, franchisors do not follow a consistent approach to continuing education or training of their franchisees. Some franchisors provide no training beyond the formal preopening training. Some franchisors provide training at quarterly, semiannual, or annual meetings between the franchisor and the franchisees. Others hold seminars on specific topics of current interest to franchisees as the need arises. Some of the large, national or international franchise systems provide a regular schedule of training at their headquarters or at the site of the franchisee requesting the training. Considered in its broadest context, most franchisor-provided training is more or less informal and takes place through a one-to-one relationship, addressing specific problems or needs of the franchisee. The training is given during the regular weekly or monthly visit by the field representative to the franchise site and addresses such areas as quality control, financial or accounting methods, advertising or marketing developments, or new methods, equipment, or products and services being introduced by the franchisor. In addition, some franchisors provide specialized training and advice to some franchisees but not to others. For example, a franchisee who has a territory that appears ripe for expansion may receive training or assistance in location analysis, market analysis, lease negotiations, or building design and construction services. Also, specific marketing plans may be developed area by area within a franchise system to help franchisees capitalize on differing demographics and consumer attitudes toward the system's product or service. Such marketing programs are usually developed at franchisee-funded marketing departments located at the system headquarters.

Many franchising firms provide ongoing training to their franchisees and the employees of the franchisees. Ongoing training varies widely from franchisor to franchisor and from industry to industry. Regional and national meetings for franchisees are often loaded with training opportunities such as marketing updates, industry trends, new product and service developments, franchisor policy and procedure changes, or informal exchanges of ideas among franchisees themselves or between franchisors and franchisees. Many franchised companies utilize their home office training facility for these conference-type training programs as well as for focused, hands-on training of franchisees or their employees in new operations or financial and accounting procedures.

Field representatives play an important role in the delivery of continued training. They often work directly with the franchisee at the business site, providing expert counsel, giving on-the-spot management and operational suggestions, providing instructional video or audio materials for the franchisee and employees, and serving as a conduit for sharing new ideas that are developing across the franchise system.

Ongoing training is the primary method for most franchisors to initiate new products or services into the franchise system. The franchisor has responsibility to provide continuing improvement in operational procedures that reflect the latest and best techniques for providing product and service to the customer. The franchisor also is usually responsible for developing any new products and services or modifying existing products to meet the changing needs of the customer. The ongoing training format is the ideal vehicle for transferring the knowledge and skills required to keep the franchise system lean, current, and efficient.

Success Story

Pete and Laura Wakeman
Great Harvest Bread Co.

The aroma of freshly baked honey whole wheat bread wafts from an old worn-down fair booth as a window is cracked to let in some cool air. The year is 1972, and inside are two young ambitious kids mixing dough by hand, kneading bread, and dancing to some funky music. After all the bread is baked, they load it up and go and sell it from a card table along the roadside in Durham, Connecticut, to passersby, using the money to put themselves through Cornell University. Meet Pete and Laura Wakeman, founders of Great Harvest Franchising.

Pete and Laura's lifelong dream was to own a dairy farm in Wisconsin, but they took a slight change of course after making a trip out west to Montana in 1975, after graduating from college. On an epic hike from Yellowstone to Glacier Park, they fell in love with the beautiful landscape and the sense of freedom from city life. Shortly after their trip, they decided that Great Falls, Montana, was where they wanted to make their home. Initially, Pete labored on various wheat farms in the area while Laura worked as a nutritionist for the Great Falls schools.

In January 1976, they opened the first Great Harvest Bread Company, in Great Falls, after taking over a defunct bakery for the princely sum of $200. The idea of a whole wheat bakery specializing in just bread was unheard of at that time, especially in a small rural town. During the first few weeks of the bakery's operation, lines formed outside the doors before they would even open. The entire day's baking—all done by hand from scratch—usually sold out in less than an hour.

As the business grew and prospered, more and more people became interested in learning to make great bread and especially in how they could start their own Great Harvest Bread Companies. In 1978, Pete and Laura met this demand and the first Great Harvest franchisee opened, in Kalispell, Montana.

Two years later, Pete and Laura formed a corporation and began to expand their system of baking handmade moist, delicious whole wheat bread nationwide. For a while, Pete ran the franchise part of the business and Laura continued to run the bakery. By 1982, the franchise end of things was just too big and time consuming for one person

to handle, so the couple chose to sell the bakery in Great Falls, and concentrate on franchising.

Pete and Laura had decided that they wanted to live in a smaller community, one that offered all the outdoor recreational opportunities they loved so much. They made a systematic search for the perfect town, looking throughout the upper Rockies region and even into Canada. In the spring of 1983, the southwest Montana ranching town of Dillon (pop. 5,000) became Great Harvest's corporate headquarters.

As far as the business went, all Pete and Laura felt they needed were phones, a post office, and a place to buy office supplies. Dillon turned out to be ideal for them and for the company. By 1987, they had seventeen franchised bakeries and even opened a small bakery to provide bread for their new community. In 1996, the Wakemans reached a personal milestone with their one hundredth Great Harvest Bakery. In November 2000, they made the front cover of Inc. magazine with an article about their innovative methods of franchising. A second article appeared in the Inc. February 2001 issue explaining their philosophies for balancing work with personal loves. Great Harvest was recognized in the October 2000 issue of Success magazine as being the seventieth best franchise of the top 2,500 in the United States. Now with more than 135 bakeries open in over thirty states, steady growth, and more than twenty-five employees in Dillon, Laura says they still try to have a good life, have fun, and enjoy themselves. We do that with our business as well. We love selling bread.

SUMMARY

Constructive support of franchisees is essential for effective operation and overall success of a franchise system. A franchisor is responsible for developing a support organization that ensures sufficient and accurate communication between the franchisor and the franchisee. The support organization should address the needs of both parties, ensuring that their expectations concerning profitability and adequate planning and control are met, and that any problems are handled promptly and with a shared concern for their resolution. Obviously, appropriate and accurate communication is of critical importance. Phone and mail contacts, as well as personal visits, are made by most franchising organizations to their franchisees. The purpose of these visits may be to address a local problem, to provide training, to fulfill the requirements of a field review, or simply to maintain a personal, one-to-one contact.

Franchisees may call meetings among themselves as well. Many of them have learned that one of the best forms of support is the sharing of experiences and techniques among fellow franchisees, the result of which often is to help weaker franchisees become stronger. Most franchisees are aware that a weak link affects all others in the system, so they are usually interested in strengthening that weak link.

From one perspective, the franchising process can be viewed as an attempt to reproduce in other locations the successful model or prototype operation of the franchisor. Reproducing the model heavily depends on effective transfer of knowledge and skills from one location to the other. This is evidence of the critical importance of an effective training program for franchising.

The development of a training function of a franchisor has three major components: design and implementation of the training unit, establishment of a training location or locations, and development of the precise content of the training to be imparted. The actual training typically includes instruction emphasizing the philosophy of the franchising organization and the required information and critical skills that will enable one to operate effectively as a franchisee, through the use of effective formal and informal training techniques that ensure the franchisee-in-training is adequately exposed and provided the realistic opportunity to learn everything necessary to begin operation as a licensed franchisee of the franchising system. Usually the production or service methods are carefully reviewed; the accounting, marketing, and personnel practices are worked out; and the ways to maintain the franchisor–franchisee relationship on both a personal and a professional level are discussed. Franchisee training is often divided into three areas—preopening (formal), grand opening (on-site), and continuing (postopening) training. Many franchisors have found that preopening training tends to be more effective when a limited number of franchisees are involved, say between three and twelve persons. The smaller group provides sufficient peer interaction while allowing sufficient individuality, in order to maximize the learning experience necessary before one is ready to operate a franchised unit.

KEY TERMS

Activity reports: required by almost all franchised firms on a weekly or biweekly basis; typically address such information as sales volume, number of sales, expenses, call-backs, and sales to individuals, community groups, and institutions; very helpful for the franchisor to make constructive suggestions to individual franchisees for improving operations and/or congratulating franchisees for work well done.

Conference calls: provide an effective means of contacting several franchisees at the same time; generally prearranged by letter or earlier phone contact to help ensure "attendance" of franchisees within a district, area, or region; used to inform franchisees of new product/service activities by the franchisor, new advertisements or upcoming promotions, or new contests or customer relations projects.

Extranet: like intranet, but with an additional password which allows the franchisees, and franchisor, to work with their suppliers, review products, and place orders.

House organs or newsletters: effective in explaining various activities within the franchised company, recognizing top salespeople or locations, expressing the opinions of the president, announcing new territories or new franchisees, and presenting other information of a positive and helpful nature.

Intranet: an expansion of the Internet which allows a franchisor's franchisees private access to confidential information provided by the franchisor only by using a secret password; permits the franchisees to read reports from the franchisor and even review the operations manual and updated corrections.

Personal visits: usually made by a field representative from the franchise home office to the franchisee, occasionally made by the franchising company's president, vice president, franchising director, sales manager, or regional or district supervisor; a good public relations tool the franchising company can use to encourage and uplift the spirits of the franchisees and their employees; also effective for addressing problems raised by the franchisee or the franchising company, showing genuine commitment to resolve any such problems.

Planned telephone calls: typically franchisor initiated and are meant to discuss sales levels, product/service support, and advertising and promotional plans, as well as to respond to questions or issues raised by the franchisee; should be friendly, helpful, and positive and are not intended for faultfinding or for enhancing the power of the franchisor over the franchisee.

Spontaneous telephone calls: boost the morale and feelings of interdependence of the franchisee and the franchisor; help the franchisor understand the immediate concerns of the franchisee, get a feel for the franchisee's general attitude over time, and determine if there is anything the parent company could or should be doing over and above the regular services it is providing.

Training visits: usually made by members of the home office staff; help the franchisee see the value of the royalty fees being returned to the business by addressing things such as problems in business operation that can be overcome by additional on-site training of the franchisee and staff, or changes in operating procedures or personnel, financial, or marketing approaches recommended by the franchisor.

REVIEW QUESTIONS

1. Why should a franchisor have a support organization? What function does it serve for the franchisor? For the franchisee?

2. Identify the different types of visits that a franchising organization makes to a franchisee's business. Explain the purpose of each type.

3. Effective support is ensured by effective communication between the franchisor and the franchisee. Explain what is meant by this statement.

4. Why do many franchisors consider training of franchisees to be critical to the development and growth of a franchise system?

5. Identify and briefly describe the three major types of training a franchisee might expect from the franchisor.

CASE STUDY

7-Eleven: A Way of Life

7-ELEVEN Inc. of Dallas, Texas, operates the 7-ELEVEN convenience -store chain in twenty-six states, the District of Columbia, and five provinces of Canada. 7-ELEVEN Inc.is the largest operator and franchiser of convenience stores in the world. There are over 7,200 7-ELEVEN stores in operation throughout the United States, serving over 8 million customers every day. A typical 7-ELEVEN store carries over 3,000 items, including soft drinks, groceries, beer, tobacco, magazines, housewares, and health and beauty aids. Other items, particularly fast foods, are regularly being added to the product offerings.

7-ELEVEN Inc., then known as Southland pioneered the convenience store concept in 1927, when it opened as an ice company that also sold milk, bread, and eggs as a convenience to its customers. The name "7-ELEVEN" originated in 1946, when the stores operated between the hours of 7 A.M. and 11 P.M. Today the vast majority of 7-ELEVEN stores are open twenty-four hours.

There are basically two operational types of 7-ELEVEN stores. The neighborhood type is operated as an updated version of the mom-and-pop store. Forty percent of the stores are operated by franchisees, with the remainder being managed by the corporation. Of the franchised locations, many are owned and operated by couples whose families also work in the store. The typical 7-ELEVEN store is in a suburban location with easy access. However, 7-ELEVEN also operates "city stores" in some densely populated urban areas. The store's competition is broad-based, including fast-food restaurants, other convenience stores, supermarkets, and "g-stores" (gasoline stations with a small convenience store on the premises).

On the marketing side, the 7-ELEVEN management team works to develop programs to attract additional customers and bring in existing customers more often. Recently, two segments of the population were being targeted: older people, who historically have not been convenience-store customers, and working women.

Franchisees have played a significant role in the success of 7-ELEVEN stores. In fact, many franchisees have been with the company for more than thirty years. Not only do they understand the business, but they also do an excellent job of tailoring their stores to the needs of the neighborhoods they serve. Many of the successful market programs provided by 7-ELEVEN stores were first introduced by various franchisees and are more an integral part of the entire 7-ELEVEN system in the United States.

The 7-ELEVEN real estate representatives research and select potential sites based on population, traffic flow, convenience to homes, and competition. The company buys or leases a site, builds the unit, and leases to the franchisee. Typically, all equipment in the store, including heating and air conditioning units, shelving, cash registers, refrigerators, and vaults, is leased to the franchisee. Once control has been taken, the franchisee is responsible for maintaining the equipment. The company arranges for the initial inventory, and the franchisee is responsible thereafter for ordering and stocking merchandise. 7-ELEVEN provides lists of recommended merchandise and retail prices, as well as names of vendors that offer high-quality merchandise at a competitive price; some recommended vendors may be affiliated with 7-ELEVEN, and some merchandise may be produced by divisions of the parent company. However, franchisees are free to purchase merchandise from any vendor and establish their store's retail prices.

Before being accepted by 7-ELEVEN as a franchisee, the applicant is required to complete the Store Operations Training Program, which includes (1) actual two-week, in-store experience at a 7-ELEVEN training store in order to learn the basic operations; and (2) a one-week formal training program at one of the regional training centers. The prospective franchisee learns a variety of management skills, techniques, and procedures essential to the successful operation of a 7-ELEVEN store. The cost of the training is included in the initial franchising fee paid by the applicant. After completion of these two training periods, the applicant has about one week prior to opening the store. The purpose of this is to allow the new franchisee time to clear up any personal business, hire staff for the new store, and prepare for the grand opening. During this time, as well as during the grand opening period, 7-ELEVEN provides support staff to assist and advise the new franchisee.

About 250 to 300 prospective franchisees enter the 7-ELEVEN training cycle each year. Applicants entering the training programs are evaluated at each stage, from the initial meeting to the actual changeovers just prior to the grand opening of the store. There is no single set of criteria used to evaluate a franchise applicant. However, personality traits, entrepreneurial in-terests, and financial capacity, as well as the evaluation of the field representatives, are significant in selection of applicants for entry into the training program. The training staff also makes recommendations concerning each applicant/trainee. Training staff can also recommend that trainees be disqualified, a form of quality control so that 7-ELEVEN can avoid having poorly prepared and unmotivated franchisees representing the franchise system.

The new franchisee has 120 days after becoming a franchisee to terminate and not continue as a franchisee. If the franchisee chooses to leave during this period, the company will refund the franchising fee, less any training expenses, a practice not common to many other franchising companies in this field. What this policy does is to allow some breathing and thinking room for the new franchisee to determine if the arrangement is satisfactory.

Source: http://www.7-eleven.com/franchising/moreaboutfranchising.asp

CASE QUESTIONS

1. Why would 7-ELEVEN want to maintain a policy allowing the franchisee to completely back out after being selected, trained, and assisted into operation as a full-fledged franchisee?

2. Do you think the policy of refunding the franchising fee should be more common in franchising? Why or why not?

3. What costs and benefits accrue to 7-ELEVEN by having such a refund policy?

4. How might this policy affect the selection of representatives and training staffs of 7-ELEVEN stores?

REFERENCES

Atkinson, John W., "Motivational Determinants of Risk Taking Behavior," *Psychology Review* 64(6) (1957): 359–372.

Dunnigan, J. A., "Keeping It Altogether—Franchisors Reveal How They Maintain 'Family Ties,'" *Entrepreneurs Franchise Yearbook* 2 (1987/88): 294–304.

Frazier, Gary L., "On the Measurement of Interfirm Power in Channels of Distribution," *Journal of Marketing Research* 20 (May 1983): 58–66.

Hotsh, Ripley, "Dear Diary: I'm Now a Franchisee," *Nation's Business* (November 1985): 53–60.

Justis, Robert, "Franchisors: Have You Hugged Your Franchisee Today?" *Nation's Business* (February 1985): 46–49.

Justis, Robert T., *Managing Your Small Business* (Englewood Cliffs, NJ: Prentice-Hall, Inc., 1981).

Kushell, Robert, "Is Being Z for Thee?" *Entrepreneurs Franchise Yearbook* 1 (1987): 27–31.

Lambert, Douglas M. and Christine Lewis, "The Methodology for Assessing Franchisee Expectations and Perceptions of Franchisor Role Performance," *Proceedings of the Society of Franchising* (Lincoln: University of Nebraska-Lincoln, September 1986).

Luxenberg, Stan, "The Ideal Operator," *Roadside Empires* (New York: Penguin Books, 1986).

Mayo, Ken, "Retailer, Train Thyself," *Business Computer Systems* 3(9) (September 1984): 66–74.

Ruekert, Robert and Gilbert Churchill, Jr., "Reliability and Validity of Alternative Measures of Channel Members Satisfaction," *Journal of Marketing Research* 21 (May 1984): 226–233.

Sato, Gayle, "Who Is the Ideal Franchisee?" *Entrepreneurs Franchise Yearbook* 2 (1987/1988): 14–21.

Stanworth, John and James Curran, "How Franchising Brings a New Perspective to Us and Them," *Personnel Management* 15(9) (September 1983): 34–37.

SOCIAL RESPONSIBILITY AND BUSINESS ETHICS*

In studying this chapter, you will:

- **Define business ethics and be able to describe the three levels of ethical standards.**

- **Define social responsibility and describe the three primary views of social responsibility.**

- **Understand the nature of business's responsibility to its task and societal environments.**

- **Discuss arguments for and against social responsibility.**

- **Identify ethical factors in a decision situation.**

- **Identify social responsibility topics and issues in franchising.**

- **Identify and discuss the key terms in the language of ethics.**

- **Identify and describe the philosophic bases for ethical decision making.**

- **Understand and describe ways in which franchising is at the forefront of social responsibility programs of action in business.**

INCIDENT

Rich and Caroline are owners-operators of a small fast-food franchise that specializes in short orders and exotic coffees and teas. They run their business with the assistance of their daughter, Olivia, and four part-time employees. Caroline is a vegetarian who believes that consumption of meat or dairy products is undesirable for her. One of the meat options at their business is the traditional hamburger.

Caroline does some experimentation by mixing soy bean flour into the hamburger patties for home consumption. She realizes that Rich and Olivia cannot tell the difference when soy bean content in the hamburger mix does not exceed 35 percent of total volume.

Caroline has the responsibility of preparing the hamburger patties, assuring a sufficient amount is in storage and available to meet daily customer demand. Alone, Caroline begins to create a mix

---

° Prepared in conjunction with Mark Pucklik, Associate Professor of Business Administration, University of Illinois-Springfield.

that does not exceed 25 percent soy with 75 percent meat to serve as "hamburger." She is aware that the business is not required to identify fat grams per sandwich and the franchisor does not have a hard-and-fast 100 percent all-beef requirement for such sandwiches. She believes mixing soy with beef is perfectly okay, because people who purchase a hamburger at their franchise will be consuming less saturated fat, and that using a 25 percent to 75 percent soy-to-beef ratio for the hamburger will help their customers become more healthy, even though the customer does not know it.

Is this right for Caroline to do? Is it legal? Is her action socially responsible? Is her conduct ethical?

Rachele is a successful franchisee of educational products and learning technologies for children. She has always been a student herself, taking classes for self-enrichment as well as skill development on an as-desired basis for the past fifteen years. Recently, Rachele completed a course in the history of entrepreneurship from a nearby university. During the course she became intrigued by a book published by Andrew Carnegie, the founder of U.S. Steel Corporation, entitled *The Gospel of Wealth* which was published in 1899.

Carnegie's book set forth the classical statement of corporate social responsibility which was based on two principles. First, the charity principle challenges the more fortunate members of a society to assist the less fortunate members in direct ways or indirectly, as through churches, settlement houses, and so on. It is from this concept that the Community Chest movement began in the 1920s, which would today be likely known as the United Fund. Second, the stewardship principle, based on biblical concepts, suggests business and wealthy individuals should view themselves as stewards or caretakers, to hold and maintain their property "in trust" for the benefit of the whole society. U.S. Steel, acting on Carnegie's ideas, established the Carnegie Foundation which embarked on an active program of philanthropy. One of the early programs of action was to assist communities in building libraries. As a result of that program, there are Carnegie Libraries in numerous towns and communities across the United States which might have never been able to develop and afford a local library.

Rachele believes she has come to learn the true meaning of social responsibility. She has taken the two Carnegie principles as the philosophic underpinning to assess any requests for cash contribution, volunteerism, and any product or service "giveaways." At this point, Rachele is content by providing her "fair share" through the United Fund program and politely refuses all other requests.

Is Rachele's position on social responsibility reasonable in today's world? Should her firm do more? Are there any drawbacks to the two principles that Carnegie cited 100 years ago?

21-1   INTRODUCTION

What does society expect from business? Does business have a social obligation? What does it mean to be socially responsible? Prior to the 1960s, when activist movements began questioning the economic objectives of business, the concept of social responsibility drew little attention. At that time, were large corporations irresponsible to minorities and females due to the obvious absence of female and minority managers at the time? Was Dow Corning Company socially irresponsible by marketing breast implants when data were available suggesting that leaking silicone could be a health hazard? Was the rapidly developing fast-food industry insensitive to environmental concerns as many independent and franchise systems packaged their food products in plastic containers?

There is no worldwide standard for ethical behavior, no global standard of conduct for businesspeople. Ethics is a sensitive and complex issue. Developing and maintaining an ethical perspective is crucial to the creation and protection of the firm's reputation. Succumbing to ethical temptations will ultimately destroy a business's reputation. Reputation is one of the firm's most precious and fragile assets.

21-1a   Social Responsibility

Before the 1960s few people would even ask questions about social responsibility. Even today, logical and well-reasoned arguments can be made for both sides of the social responsibility issue (see Figures 21-1 and 21-2). The times have changed. Large and small businesses, independent and

---

Public Opinion. The public expects that business should pursue social as well as economic goals.

Public Image. Because the public considers social goals as important, businesses can create a positive public image by pursuing social goals.

Balance of Power and Responsibility. Business has power in society. It should carry an equal amount of responsibility to balance with the power. When businesses' power is greater than responsibility, that imbalance can work against the well-being of society.

Expertise to Solve Problems. Getting business involved can help solve some difficult social problems which may create a higher quality of life and make our communities more desirable and able to attract and hold skilled employees and their families.

Discouragement of Any Further Government Regulation. Government regulation adds to the economic costs of goods and services produced by business and may restrict the owner/manager decision flexibility. If business becomes more socially responsible, perhaps then, business could expect less government regulation.

Stockholder Interests. Social responsibility will improve the price of a business's stock in the long run. Stock markets will view the socially responsible firm as less risky and open to public attack. Thus, the markets will reward the responsible firm with a higher price-earnings ratio.

Ethical Obligation. A business can—and should—have a conscience. Business should be socially responsible because responsible action is right, not only for their sake, but also for the sake of stockholders and society.

FIGURE **21-1**

Arguments for Social Responsibility of Business

Profit maximization is violated. This is the classical economic perspective. Business is most socially responsible by attending strictly to its economic interests, leaving other activities to other institutions. In this way, society will have available the most competitive price for the products and services it needs.

The purpose of business is diluted. Pursuing social goals dilutes business's primary purpose: to produce the best product or service at the least cost. Society may suffer when both social and economic goals are combined and poorly accomplished.

Business is granted too much power. Business is already powerful. If business pursues social goals, it will have even greater power.

Costs are to be born by consumer. Costs will be incurred. Someone has to pay for the socially responsible program or activity. Business must absorb these costs or pass them on to consumers in higher prices.

Accountability must be maintained. Our system of government provides for political representatives of the people. Political representatives pursue social goals and are held accountable for their actions through the voting booth. This is not the case for business, which has no direct line of accountability to the general public. The business is responsible to its particular consumers through its products and services.

Business lacks appropriate social skill. The outlook, attitudes, and abilities found in business are oriented primarily toward economic factors. Businesspeople are not oriented toward nor have developed skill through training, to deal with social issues.

Broad public support is lacking. Evidence of a broad mandate from society for business to address social issues is lacking. The general public is divided on this often heated topic of debate. Actions taken where there is such divided support are likely to fail.

FIGURE **21-2**

Arguments against Social Responsibility of Business

franchised, durable product and service companies are regularly confronted with decisions that have added a dimension of social responsibility along with pricing, employee relations, product quality and resource conservation on a regular basis.

21-1b   The Environment of Business

Business firms do not exist in a vacuum. They exist because society or some segment of it needs a particular product or service. As long as the firm provides the product at an acceptable level of quality, convenience, and price, and that product continues to meet the need of society, the firm can exist over time. Ownership and senior management must be aware of the variables and forces in its environment. A firm's environment contains factors and influences that have direct interest within and can impact the firm positively and negatively. The principle responsibility of the franchise system and its independent franchisees is an economic one: at a minimum, earn sufficient profits to stay in business, serve customers products and/or services that meet their needs, and create jobs. However, society has extended its demands on business, requiring business also to meet an evolving set of ethic, legal, and social responsibilities. In the United States, business operates in an environment that has diverse interests and responsibilities tightly entwined. In an overall perspective, the franchise system and each franchisee has a set of external **stakeholders**, or groups or individuals who affect and are affected by the business firm (see Figure 21-3). The groups internal to the firm may include employees, investors, boards of directors, management, and possibly a union or two for both franchisor and franchisee organizations. From an external perspective, groups likely to be affected by the firm, and those likely to seek to influence the firm, include customers, creditors, suppliers, governmental bodies at all levels, the general public, and possibly one or more special interest groups.

The concept that business should be socially responsible is rationally appealing, until one asks the question: "responsible to whom?" The task environment is that group of parties or interests that have a definite stake in the continued well-being of the firm. These groups are called stakeholders because they are affected by—and they directly affect—achievement of the businesses' goals and

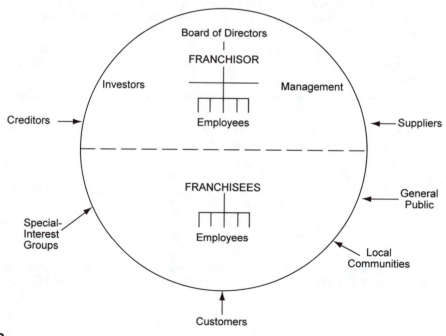

FIGURE **21-3**

Typical Firm Stakeholders

objectives. Typical are the owners/stockholders, employees, suppliers, customers, the community, special interest groups, and government that depicts typical stakeholders and their relationships. Should a business be responsible or responsive to only one or two of these stakeholders? Should there be a priority ranking among the stakeholders? Or should the business have an equal responsibility to all of its stakeholders?

At a societal level the questions asked address the institutions of society, not the specific actors, events, and factors of a particular business in its competitive environment. Questions such as the following would arise and need to be addressed. What role should government—local, state, federal— play in regulating the marketplace? Should gross inequalities in wealth, social status, and power be tolerated? For example, the salary for Michael Jordan of the Chicago Bulls basketball team was set at $38 million for the 1997-1998 season. This does not count for any endorsement fees or royalties that bring to him added millions of dollars a year. In 2007, a talented baseball player signed a contract for $138 million for a five-year period. Should such a salary for playing games "be tolerated" when a person performing domestic work at a Chicago hotel/motel may make $14,000 a year? This inequity may be an issue for some people. For others, the following example may be more important. In the United States during the 1980s, while worker pay increased on average 53 percent, corporate profits rose 78% percent, and CEO compensation rose a whopping 212 percent. In 1980, average compensation for a CEO was 42 times the pay of a factory worker. In 1990, average CEO total compensation was 157 times what factory workers earned. This trend has not changed as we entered the twenty-first century.

Societal-level questions usually are an ongoing debate among major institutions in society. For example, as the federal government increasingly shifts the burden of social welfare policies to the states, what is the role of the states to provide for the less fortunate in society? Also, how much can society expect that nonprofit organizations will provide? How much will be provided by religious institutions? What should be the responsibility of public education? Of the communities in which we live? What should the family be responsible for providing? As franchisors, franchisees, and as individuals, each of us try to shape these debates. Certainly, we will not, on an individual basis, provide the "one-and-only" or the "best" answer to these social issues and questions. What about business? What should be businesses' role toward resolving social issues?

Social responsibility, in its most simple definition, consists of the obligations a business has to society. These obligations extend into many areas. Because of such diversity in the expectations that can be created, the door is opened to ask one more question: "To what extent should business be socially responsible?" Social action by business firms can be classified into three categories: social obligation, social responsibility, and social responsiveness. **Social obligation** takes place when a business meets legal and regulatory requirements, discloses information about itself only when required, and contributes only when direct benefit to the business can be clearly shown. *Social responsibility* takes place when the business firm seeks to ensure that its current practices meet social norms, will admit deficiencies and seek to correct or improve a situation, provides information about itself more freely, and contributes to noncontroversial and established social causes. **Social responsiveness** is an apparent business practice when the firm makes information about itself freely available to the public, accepts formal and informal input from outside interests in its decision making, is willing to be publicly evaluated on its activities, and will support and contribute to not only the established social causes but also the new controversial interests or groups whose needs are unfulfilled and becoming increasingly important. Figure 21-4 provides another perspective for depicting levels of social responsibility on a scale of one to ten, with ten describing the highest level of commitment.

21-1c   An Ethical Perspective

Ethics can be described as fundamental moral values and standards that form the foundation for organizational decision making and set the tone for interaction with stakeholders. There are three levels of ethical standards:[1]

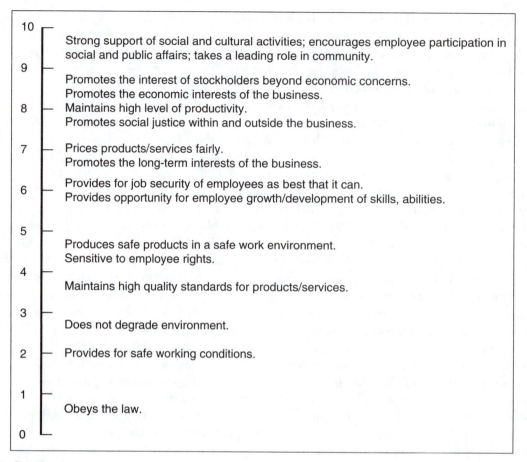

FIGURE **21-4**

Social Responsibility Scale

Adapted from Kimberly Boal and Newman Perry, "The Cognitive Structure of Corporate Social Responsibility," *Journal of Management* (Fall/Winter 1985): 71–82.

1. *The law* identifies for society as a whole what actions are permitted and which are not. The law sets a minimum standard for behavior. It does not determine morality or ethics. Ethical standards for conduct can reach beyond the limits of law. Simply obeying the law is insufficient as a guide for ethical behavior because so few, if any, ethical issues are so clear and unidimensional that the law can serve as the "acid test" for making ethical choice.

2. *The businesses' policies and procedures* provide the guidelines and precedence for management and employees in making daily decisions. Many franchise systems have developed written codes of ethics covering everything from customer service through sexual harassment, to hiring, promotion, and discharge. It is said that more than 90 percent of firms listed on the Fortune 500 have written codes of ethics.

3. *The moral stance that individuals will take* when faced with a decision that is not covered by a formal policy, procedure, or rule reflects personal character. The values learned in childhood from parents, other siblings, religious organizations, and schools are key ingredients at this level. Clearly, prior training is a significant determinant of ethical behavior in adulthood. A company's culture can either support or undermine an employee's beliefs about what constitutes ethical behavior.

Principles of Personal Ethics:

- Do we (franchise system) have a rule or policy for a case like this?

- Does this decision meet my standards of how people should interact?

- Is the decision consistent with my own religious beliefs and sense of personal responsibility?

- How will I feel about myself tomorrow if I do this?

- Does the decision involve deceiving others in any way?

Rights and Social Justice:

- Would I feel the decision, and resulting action, would be fair or just if I was on the other side of the decision?

- Would this decision and resulting action distribute benefits justly?

- Would this decision distribute hardships or burdens justly?

- Would this action allow others freedom of choice in this matter?

- How would I feel if this action would be done to me or someone close to me?

Consequences, Outcomes, and Public Knowledge:

- What are the short-term and long-term consequences of this decision and action?

- Will anyone be hurt by this action?

- Will this action create good?

- Will this action prevent harm?

- Who will benefit from this decision and action?

- How will I feel if this action becomes public knowledge?

- Will I be able to adequately explain why I took this action?

- Would others see my decision to be morally right and ethically just?

Rational and Intuitive Harmony:

- Have I considered all points of view?

- Have I searched for all feasible alternatives?

- Are there other ways I could look at this situation?

- Does my inner sense tell me that the decision, as I have made it, is right?

- Have I listened to my inner self?

- Even if the decision is rationally sound for the situation at hand and I can publicly defend my choice, does my inner sense tell me this is right?

FIGURE **21-5**

Franchise Checklist of Questions to Assist in Identifying Ethical Factors in a Decision Situation

Source: Personal interviews and discussions with franchise systems management and individual franchisees from various franchise companies, including Mail Boxes Etc., 7-Eleven, Dunkin' Donuts, Ziebart-Tidy Car, Spring-Green Lawn Care, Long John Silver's, Duraclean, Bixby's Bagels, Shakey's Pizza and Buffet, American Speedy, Hardees, Medicine Shoppe, Kentucky Fried Chicken, Days Inn, and Maaco.

To successfully address the myriad decisions faced on a daily basis, franchisors and franchisees need to develop for themselves a workable ethical framework to guide them in their decision making. For discussion with a number of franchise businesses, both newer and long-established franchisors and franchisees seem to agree on the following common points. First, realize when a decision has an ethical issue or component within it. Second, when an ethical matter is clearly at stake, identify the particular stakeholder(s) that can be affected by the decision. Third, generate alternative courses of action that consider the ethical dimension of the problem or issue confronted (see Figure 21-5). Fourth, choose the appropriate ethical course of action from the alternatives available that is also consistent with the firm's objectives, overall goals, and values. Though these four points are simple and reasonable, putting these points into action may not be easy; however, to do so will be rewarding.

Another reason why business should take social responsibility and ethics seriously is because the customer is watching, keeping tabs on everyone's behavior. To illustrate, the Walker Group found that nearly 90 percent of consumers they surveyed indicated that if quality, service, and price are equal among competitors, the firm with the best reputation for social responsibility will likely get their business. About 70 percent indicated that they avoided doing business with a particular firm. Of this "boycotting" group of consumers, nearly 48 percent indicated that their unwillingness to purchase from a particular firm was attributed to unethical business practices.[2]

The pressure to take a shortcut or to ignore an ethical standard is always present. Without a supportive code of ethics it can become difficult for business owners and their employees to make the "right" choice. According to one franchise system president, "A bad cup of coffee served in Syracuse affects the sale of future cups of coffee in Albany, Newark, Manhattan and Queens." The implications are broader than lost sales of cups of coffee. An unethical or irresponsible decision resulting in a negative experience by a customer or employee at one franchised location can seriously damage the reputation of other franchise locations almost instantly.

21-1d   Complexities of Responsible and Ethical Management

A franchise system, at the corporate and franchisee levels, can take clear, identifiable actions of a socially responsible nature. Many of these actions can be quantified and highlighted for internal and external notice or attention to demonstrate the social responsiveness of the firm. Ethics is another matter. The ethics factor is intangible and almost impossible to quantify; but, ethical decision making and the resulting actions are clearly recognizable by employees and customers. A franchise system's ethical stance will affect employees' perceptions of the workplace and customers' perception of the company and the value and quality of products and services.

The breadth or scope of social responsibility for many franchise systems is considerable. Most franchise systems will address issues that concern their product or service, internal human resource management, fair business practices, and perhaps community involvement. Other franchise systems have these concerns and environmental and energy conservation issues as well. See Table 21-1 for a listing of probable areas where social responsible action is required by law, desired by community interests, or deemed morally right or socially appropriate.

Business ethics involves behavioral standards and expectations as well as moral values that franchise system ownership and management, as well as the franchisee organization's ownership and management, face in financing, operating, and marketing their products and services. Business ethics can have a different meaning to different people. What do you think when you hear the word *ethics*?

Many people will think in terms of behavior rules or standards. Others will immediately think in terms of right and wrong. The common denominator across these ideas is decision making. To study ethics, in its simplest form, is to study decision making. The franchisor and individual franchisees can face literally thousands of decision each day. If the franchisee was to consciously consider each decision possibility that may arise, the franchisee would never have the time to act upon those decisions promptly and effectively. How does a manager, owner, or employee get through the day? All people have an ethical system internal to their cognitive and subconscious. Mental stimuli based on preexisting decision rules guide the great majority of the decisions people make on a daily basis. In a sense, then, the study of a person's conscious and subconscious decision rules can be seen as the study of ethics.

Each person has developed an extensive set of decision rules to guide their everyday decision making. These rules, or guidelines, constitute a person's value system. Values are the fundamental principles that are used to shape behavior. Many forces are involved in the creation of each person's

TABLE 21-1 SOCIAL RESPONSIBILITY TOPICS/ISSUES FOR FRANCHISE SYSTEMS

Products:

— Product safety

— Pollution potential of our products/services

— Nutritional value of our products

— Packaging and labeling of our products

Human Resource Management:

— Employee health and safety

— Employee training and development

— Physical fitness and stress management program

— Child care/day-care support or facilities for parents

— Remedial education for disadvantaged employees

— Alcohol and drug counseling programs

— Career counseling

Fair Business Practices:

— Employment opportunity and advancement for women and minorities

— Employment opportunity and advancement for disadvantaged persons

— Support for minority- and women-owned franchises

Community Citizenship:

— Support of local arts and/or children programs

— Support of community recreation programs

— Cooperation in community projects (e.g., United Fund, service projects)

— Sponsorship of public health/awareness projects

— Donations of employee time, products, services or cash

Energy and Environment:

— Conversation of energy in production and marketing of products/services

— Recycling of packages, product waste, etc.

— Pollution control

— Conservation of natural resources

Adapted from Donald Kuratko and Richard Hodgetts, "What Is the Nature of Social Responsibility," *Entrepreneurship: A Contemporary Approach* (New York: Dryden Press, 1998), 165.

values. The family is, perhaps, the most significant influence on the creation of a person's values. It is no mistake that children often hold values similar to that of their parents. Society has also exerted a great influence upon our values. Factors such as religion, education, community expectations, and the law are involved in the process of identifying and transmitting values to the next generation of citizens. In like fashion, the decision principles and practices of past and current businesses tend to shape the business decisions of the future.

Sometimes a person's values can act as a "shortcut" through a reasoned decision-making process, quickly bringing closure to an apparently complex decision simply and decisively. At other times, a person's values can override a seemingly easy decision by bringing forth additional rules or criteria creating a complex, conflict-ridden decision context.

When a person is faced with a decision-making opportunity or problem, the subconscious consults the value system stored in the intellect to determine if a decision rule exists to process the situation confronted. If so, the stimuli are routed through an attitude, that is, a predisposition to a certain action, which is likely to result in a behavior consistent with the values held. This process is instantaneous, which allows a person to quickly process the thousands of decisions one is faced with each day.

There is a common misconception held by some people about business that juxtaposes ethics and profits, that is, that profitability and ethical decision making are not possible. The myth is that, if the firm is profitable and has had sustained growth, then it is not likely that the firm utilizes ethical standards in its business decision making. In reality, firms can, and do, make substantial profits without compromising the integrity of the firm or the individual.

21-1e   Ethical Dilemmas

A franchisee, like any other business entrepreneur, is faced with ethical dilemmas on a daily basis. Figure 21-6 depicts the four main facts associated with ethical dilemmas that can rise due to the complexity and, at times, the speed with which business decisions must be made. One can see why a code of conduct or code of ethics can be helpful to businesspeople such as franchisors and franchisees.

Many firms have learned that moral principles and ethical standards not only enhance profitability but that such behavior brings other benefits as well. First, an ethical framework for decision making guides owners, managers, and employees as they cope with increasingly complex demands placed on a firm by the network of stakeholders (recall Figure 21-3). Dealing with diverse, and at times conflicting, demands is much simpler and potentially easier if the franchisee and franchise system have a solid ethical foundation on which to base the multiplicity of business decisions. Second, the franchise system and the franchisee can avoid the damaging effects associated with a reputation of being an unethical business. Unethical business practices may prove to be profitable in the very short run; however, over time, improper behavior and unethical decisions will take a toll on profitability, customer confidence in the firm and its products and services, employee morale and loyalty, and stockholder assessment of the long-term investment value of the firm.

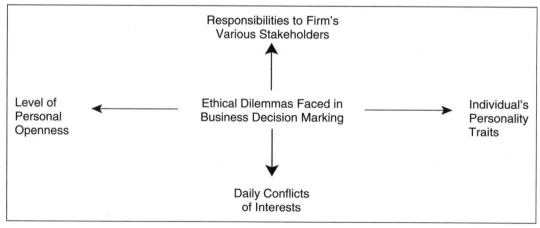

FIGURE **21-6**

Main Factors Shaping Ethical Dilemmas in Business

21-1f   Key Terms in the Language of Ethics

Whether consciously or unconsciously, each of us as a business owner or an employee engage in some kind of ethical reasoning—if not decision making—every day. As one seeks to improve ethical reasoning, or at least understand it more fully, one should consider the key terms involved: *values, rules, rights, duties,* and *relationships.*

- *Values.* When one values something, you want it or you want it to happen. There is some permanence about a value; it is good unto itself, like peace, serenity, and goodwill toward mankind. The values one seeks often constitute the answer to the "why" questions of one's life. Why do you want to be a franchisee? Why are you reading this book? Why do you need more money? Why do you want to advance in an organization or your career?

- *Rules.* Moral rules serve as guides for people in situations when competing interests are in conflict. Moral rules include the Golden Rule, or treat men and women with equal respect and consideration. A further example is, "I can cut material costs 10 percent by reducing the meat portion by 0.5 ounce and increasing the sauce by 0.5 ounce. This will improve contributions to profit margins by 8 percent. Should I do it?" The moral rules often become tie breakers, or guidelines that resolve internal disagreements such as my own greed in contrast to providing the appropriate meat portion for the customer. Moral rules, which serve as decision-making guides for behavior, become, over time, internalized values.

- *Rights.* A right is an area of freedom, flexibility, or autonomy. Typically, rights are limited, not absolute. That is, my rights are often limited by the rights of others. For example, a franchisee has the right to an opinion regarding business matters and to make that opinion known to the franchisor. However, a franchisee does not have the right to slander or libel the franchisor.

- *Duties.* Duties are correlated with rights. In accordance with the franchise contract, where the franchisor has a right, the franchisee often has a duty. The converse is true also. Where the franchisee has a right, the franchisor has a duty. For example, if the franchise agreement calls for payment of fees on a weekly basis, the franchisee has the duty to comply. Similarly, the franchisor has the duty to provide a sufficient amount of product, supply, and so forth, to the franchisee that would allow the franchisee to meet customer demands of the local marketplace and be profitable.

- *Relationships.* We are connected to one another by a web of relationships. We need one another for mutual support and to help us achieve short- and long-term goals and aspirations. Relationships pervade moral life, from childhood through adult life. It is often said that effective management is about relationships. In doing so, we are stating that management has a large moral and ethical component.

These moral concepts, which in combination can be called common rules or principles for living, also apply directly in the daily practice of business. First, common morality requires that a person respects other people, whose desires are important and whose interests are legitimate. Second, just as people "own" their own body and we respect that ownership, we must also respect their property. Respect for the ownership of property is an important ideal, playing a prominent role at the foundation of capitalism. Third, moral as well as legal rights and duties provide the ways for preventing and solving conflicts. If we had to constantly worry about our safety, offering no trust or belief that others will respect us and we do not respect them in turn, very little would ever be bought or sold. Fourth, most people want to believe that other people will do what they say. Without the general rule or belief that people will keep their word (keep their promise), social interaction as well as business would come to a complete stop. Anarchy would reign supreme. Finally, business organizations, like human communities, are sustained by the recognition that people depend on each other and, at times, may need the assistance or help of others.

21-1g   Philosophic Bases for Ethical Decision Making

Philosophers have developed theories to describe the behavior of individuals who share common value systems. These moral philosophies can be useful in identifying the values that guide, or may even drive, individual behavior in the marketplace. Most moral philosophies can be classed into three distinct contexts: consequentialism, ethical formalism, and justice. Each is addressed in this section.

Consequentialism is a philosophy that considers a decision to be correct, right, and/or acceptable if the decision and its resulting behavior accomplish the intended results such as pleasure, knowledge, profit, customer satisfaction, or career growth. Internal to this philosophy are two separate, distinct theoretic positions known as *egoism* and *utilitarianism*. Both of these philosophic constructs are said to guide decision making in business.

- **Egoism** defines right, correct, or acceptable conduct in terms of positive consequences for the individual. Egoists believe one should make decisions that will maximize self-interest. For example, individuals using this philosophic base for decision making would look into the future to identify what action(s) to take that would maximize the greatest or best possible outcome for oneself. Whatever course of action that produces the greatest good for the individual of any alternatives is the right or correct decision to make. Many people believe that egoists are inherently unethical because they focus on their own welfare to the exclusion of others and the firm, believing they will take advantage of any opportunity to exploit consumers, employees, or other stakeholders in order to maximize personal benefit or gain.

- **Utilitarianism** concerns decision consequences. Utilitarian rule followers seek the greatest good for the greatest number of people. A utilitarian decision maker would calculate the utility of the criterion that measures each of the possible alternative decisions and their consequences, then choose the option that achieves the greatest good for the largest number of people (stakeholders, constituents). Through the use of decision tools such as cost-benefit analysis, it is possible to develop a uniform decision-making algorithm to assess each option. This process removes emotion and self-interest from the decision.

Ethical formalism is a moral philosophy that focuses on the rights of individuals and on the intentions associated with a particular behavior rather than the outcome or consequence of the intended behavior. Ethical formalists regard certain behaviors as inherently right. Their determination of "rightness" is directly related to individual needs, interests, or desires, not to those of society. Ethical formalism is sometimes referred to as nonconsequentialism, because of the primacy of respect for the rights of the person, or persons, not for large groups or society in general. Unlike utilitarians, ethical formalists contend that there are some things that people should not do under any circumstances. For example, an ethical formalist would consider it unethical for a restaurant that has found salmonella in its food processing to continue to serve meals without informing the customers or acknowledging the condition to the general public. In contrast, a utilitarian-oriented decision maker might weigh the short-term cost of a few sick customers to the overall level of business that could be done without interruption while the salmonella situation is cleared up. A utilitarian view would hold that, as long as it would not be illegal, a few customers getting sick (the cost), while the great majority of customers can dine happily (the benefit), it is worth keeping the restaurant open during the thorough cleansing of the kitchen and dining areas.

Justice theory directly relates to the concept of fairness. Justice demands fair treatment and due reward in accordance with ethical or legal standards. In a business, this requires that the rules used to determine justice be based on the perceived rights of individuals and on the intentions associated with the intended business action or interaction. Therefore, justice is more likely to be based on nonconsequentialist philosophies than on the opposite. Justice primarily addresses the issue of what individuals believe they are due based on their rights and performance at the workplace. In terms of economic justice, five possible principles guide the decision.

- Each person should receive an equal share;

- To each according to one's individual need;

- To each according to individual effort;

- To each according to one's contributions; or

- To each according to merit, that is, based on assessment of performance.

Of course, the choice of a principle of economic justice need not be limited to one of these principles. Individually and collectively, society, the courts, mediators, owners, managers, supervisors, and others can apply different principles in different circumstances. Sometimes multiple principles can be utilized in a single situation. For example, most franchise systems carefully determine means to assess work and output using a combination of these theoretical bases when determining compensation for employees. Factors that are often used include work performance by number of units or orders completed, longevity in the position, cooperative attitude, customer attention, promptness to work, promptness to assist a customer need, and awareness of detail.

21-2   ETHICS PROGRAMS GETTING HIGH PRIORITY

Ethics officers now exist in over half of all multinational companies recently surveyed by the Conference Board. The Ethics and Compliance Officers Association, a U.S.-based, nonprofit organization for Ethics and Compliance Officers, has more than 1,300 members who have some kind of ethics responsibility in their organizations. When the Ethics and Compliance Officers Association (ECOA) began in 1991, it had fewer than thirty members.

The International Franchise Association (IFA), the largest and premier representative association for franchise systems, has a detailed code of ethics for its membership. The IFA's Code of Ethics appears in its entirety at the end of this chapter.

It is important to realize that there is no single correct or "best" moral philosophy that can be applied toward resolving all ethical and/or legal issues at the workplace. Each philosophy discussed herein presents a distinct, ideal perspective. Most people—owners, managers, employees, customers, and others—seem to adapt to and use various moral philosophies as they interpret the context of different decision-making situations. Moreover, research studies suggest that individuals may apply different moral principles or philosophies in different decision situations over time. Thus, a decision rule or criterion will not always be held constant in an individual's intellect and lower consciousness. As people mature, they may even change their value structure, placing higher priority on certain criteria that at an earlier time would have been rejected out of hand.

This discussion of business ethics brings forth the extreme importance for a franchise system to develop and utilize a credo or code of ethics for the entire franchise system. A franchise system should develop a personnel (or human resources) manual that provides guidance for decision making based on a set of principles that the ownership and top management believe to be appropriate and effective toward developing and maintaining a franchise system of integrity as well as profitability. Figure 21-7 provides a set of questions that can be used to examine ethical factors that shape business decisions. Questions such as these can help the franchisor and franchisees develop a meaningful code of ethics for decision making throughout the franchise system.

The list in Figure 21-7 is not conclusive, but it does provide a frame of reference for decision makers in franchised businesses as they wrestle with the routine, complex, and uncertain issues that confront their businesses daily. Surely, ethical considerations can be difficult to define, set into

The Individual

- What feelings and beliefs are coming into conflict in this situation?

- What value is most critical in this situation that will help me enhance my understanding of what is taking place and what is right?

- Of the conflicting values in this situation, which values are most deeply rooted in me?

- What is my intention in making this decision, personally and for the firm?

- Can my decision and/or action be harmful or hurt anyone?

- How do my personal intentions compare with the probable results of the decision?

- Can I disclose this decision and its basis for action to others? To my family?

The Franchise Firm

- Have I defined the problem accurately?

- What point of view is most likely to be accepted inside the firm and influence the thinking of others?

- What are other strong and persuasive interpretations of the ethics of this situation?

- Does the process for resolution manifest the values I care about for the firm?

- Can I discuss the problem with affected persons before making/announcing the choice?

FIGURE **21-7**

Questions Pertinent toward Creating an Ethical Frame of Reference or Code of Ethics for Business Decision Making

policy statements, implement, and evaluate. Continually, personal values and subjective moral beliefs are constantly surfacing that can influence the decision-making process.

A number of franchise systems have created a code of ethics to guide decision making at both the franchisor and the franchisee levels. Though a code of ethics or code of conduct cannot be forced upon an independent franchisee by the franchisor, the franchise system can strongly recommended the code of ethics to the franchisees and provide training in accordance with the ethical guidelines and policies. Some franchise systems have not promulgated a code of ethics. Discussions within the industry with directors of franchising, vice presidents of operations, field personnel, and franchisees strongly suggest that franchise systems that have a code of conduct or ethical guidelines seem to operate more smoothly, equitably, and successfully than those that do not.

21-2a   The Franchise Industry and Social Responsibility

Franchising is a specific type of business that stands out in terms of its economic performance as well as its social responsibility practices. As an "industry," franchising is imbued with a body of regulations to provide equity and fair play for both the franchisor and the franchisee. The UFOC document is much like a charter or constitution, demonstrating how franchisors and franchisees will work with one another for their self-interests and the needs of the consumer. No other industry or business arena can claim such a strong document to guide and regulate its business practices.

The initiation and development of advisory councils in franchising is a hallmark to the rest of business about what can be accomplished through cooperation. Some franchise systems have had franchisee advisory councils operating smoothly for twenty years or more. Most nationally recognized franchise systems have developed advisory councils. Some franchisee advisory councils have been independently developed. When that is the case, often the franchisor plays a significant role in ensuring cooperative efforts for an open forum for franchisee interests and issues to be heard and be responded to by the franchise system. Further, most newer franchise systems consider the development of a franchise advisory council (or at least an advertising council/board) as an anticipated and necessary step along the path of growth and development of the franchise system. Advisory councils are a clear signal to franchisees, prospective franchises, legislators, and government regulators that franchisors and franchisees can work together to resolve their issues while enhancing their economic and social contributions to the betterment of society.

Franchise systems, particularly in restaurants, fast-food restaurants, and convenience stores, have taken the lead in recycling paper and minimizing the use of nonrecyclable plastics. Food franchise systems are at the forefront by returning to paper wrapping of sandwiches and the enhanced use of paper cups and paper bags for the carrying of food. Franchised systems in the lawn and garden industry are often cited as leaders in the careful and appropriate use of chemicals for lawns and gardens. Franchised staffing services and employment agencies have increased opportunities for skill development and employment for women and minorities on an unprecedented scale in the past fifteen to twenty years.

Franchise systems tend to operate in the most competitive markets available in the United States and worldwide. Therefore, it is incumbent that the franchise systems and franchisees be technically competent and current in technical applications appropriate to their business endeavors. Maintaining the technological edge provides opportunities for franchise systems to develop jobs that require enhanced skills in a variety of business settings. Many franchise systems are undergoing structural and process changes to improve performance and afford opportunity for employee growth and development. In the long-term, these efforts should enhance the economic well-being of the firms, employees, and franchisees.

21-2b Ethical Issues in Marketing

Ethics in marketing includes the principles and standards that guide the behavior of individuals and groups in making marketing decisions. Standards of conduct that support ethical decision making in marketing require that a franchise system's management and independent franchisee unit owners accept responsibility for their actions. A company (franchise system) may fail to balance the desire for profits against the wishes and needs of society. Maintaining this balance often demands compromises and trade-offs, and may even require changes in a planned marketing strategy. If a balance is not maintained, society may require that government create more regulation in a given industry to require responsible behavior of firms within a given industry and across industries. Thus, many long-standing, successful franchise systems have policies and marketing practices to ensure ethical conduct that avoids the inflexibility and expense of regulation. Figure 21-8 lists potential ethical marketing issues.

As mentioned, the International Franchise Association has a membership of over 800 successful franchise systems, which represent over 70 percent of the registered franchise companies in the United States. The IFA has a code of ethics that is intended to guide and assist franchise systems to establish best practices through firm policies and implementation standards at the system and individual franchisee levels. This code of ethics is a framework to establish and maintain ethical behavior in all franchise relationships. Figure 21-9 cites the code for your review.

21-2c Social Responsiveness of Franchise Systems in Action

Franchise firms are often cited by magazines such as *Black Enterprise* in "The Franchise 50," *Women's Enterprise* in "100 Best Franchises for Women," the *OTC Review* in "100 Best Managed Companies on NASDAQ," and other independent publishing companies that have recognized the social responsiveness of franchising toward improving management practices and enhancing opportunities for minorities and women.

Product Issues:

Misrepresentation of goods or services

Misleading warranties

Reducing package contents, but not package size

Misrepresenting the franchise system's capabilities

Distribution Issues:

Tying contracts

Withholding product or promotional support from franchisees

Withholding product availability to franchisees or to customers

Promotional Issues:

False or misleading advertising at franchise system or franchisee unit level

High-pressure selling

Lying about product or service quality, price, features, availability, etc.

Bait and switch advertising

Pricing Issues:

Price discrimination

Price fixing

Fraudulent refund policies

Price deception

FIGURE **21-8**

Possible Ethical Issues in Marketing

International Franchise Association's CODE OF ETHICS

PREFACE:

The International Franchise Association Code of Ethics is intended to establish a framework for the implementation of best practices in the franchise relationships of IFA members. The Code represents the ideals to which all IFA members agree to subscribe in their franchise relationships. The Code is one component of the IFA's self-regulation program, which also includes the IFA Ombudsman and revisions to the IFA bylaws that will streamline the enforcement mechanism for the Code. The Code is not intended to anticipate the solution to every challenge that may arise in a franchise relationship, but rather to provide a set of core values that are the basis for the resolution of the challenges that may arise in franchise relationships. Also the Code is not intended to establish standards to be applied by third parties, such as the courts, but to create a framework under which IFA and its members will govern themselves. The IFA's members believe that adherence to the values expressed in the IFA Code will result in healthy, productive and mutually beneficial franchise relationships. The Code, like franchising, is dynamic and may be revised to reflect the most current developments in structuring and maintaining franchise relationships.

TRUST, TRUTH, AND HONESTY:

Foundations of Franchising

Every franchise relationship is founded on the mutual commitment of both parties to fulfill their obligations under the franchise agreement. Each party will fulfill its obligations, will act consistent with the interests of the brand and will not act so as to harm the brand and system. This willing interdependence between franchisors and franchisees, and the trust and honesty upon which it is founded, has made franchising a worldwide success as a strategy for business growth.

Honesty embodies openness, candor and truthfulness. Franchisees and franchisors commit to sharing ideas and information and to face challenges in clear, direct terms. IFA members will be sincere in word, act and character—reputable and without deception.

FIGURE **21-9**

International Franchise Association's CODE OF ETHICS

The public image and reputation of the franchise system is one of its most valuable and enduring assets. A positive image and reputation will create value for franchisors and franchisees, attract investment in existing and new outlets from franchisees and from new franchise operators, help capture additional market share and enhance consumer loyalty and satisfaction. The can only be achieved with trust, truth and honesty between franchisors and franchisees.

MUTUAL RESPECT AND REWARD:

Winning Together, As a Team

The success of franchise systems depends upon both franchisors and franchisees attaining their goals. The IFA's members believe that franchisors cannot be successful unless their franchisees are also successful, and conversely, that franchisees will not succeed unless their franchisor is also successful. IFA members believe that a franchise system should be committed to help its franchisees succeed, and that such efforts are likely to create value for the system and attract new investment in the system.

IFA's members are committed to showing respect and consideration for each other and to those with whom they do business. Mutual respect includes recognizing and honoring extraordinary achievement and exemplary commitment to the system. IFA members believe that franchisors and franchisees share the responsibility for improving their franchise system in a manner that rewards both franchisors and franchisees.

OPEN AND FREQUENT COMMUNICATION:

Successful franchise systems thrive on it

IFA's members believe that franchising is a unique form of business. Nowhere else in the world does there exist a business relationship that embodies such a significant degree of mutual interdependence. IFA members believe that to be successful, this unique relationship requires continual and effective communication between franchisees and franchisors.

IFA's members recognize that misunderstanding and loss of trust and consensus on the direction of a franchise system can develop when franchisors and franchisees fail to communicate effectively. Effective communication requires openness, candor and trust and is an integral component of a successful franchise system. Effective communication is an essential predicate for consensus and collaboration, the resolution of differences, progress and innovation.

To foster franchising as a unique and enormously successful relationship, IFA's members commit to establishing and maintaining programs that promote effective communication within franchise systems. These programs should be widely publicized within systems, available to all members of the franchise system and should facilitate frequent dialogue within franchise systems. IFA members are encouraged to also utilize the IFA Ombudsman to assist in enhancing communication and collaboration about issues affecting the franchise system.

OBEY THE LAW:

A responsibility to preserve the promise of franchising

IFA's members enthusiastically support full compliance with, and vigorous enforcement of, all applicable federal and state franchise regulations. This commitment is fundamental to enhancing and safeguarding the business environment for franchising. IFA's members believe that the information provided during the presale disclosure process is the cornerstone of a positive business climate for franchising, and is the basis for successful and mutually beneficial franchise relationships.

CONFLICT RESOLUTION:

IFA's members are realistic about franchise relationships, and recognize that from time to time disputes will arise in those relationships. IFA's members are committed to the amicable and prompt resolution of these disputes. IFA members believe that franchise systems should establish a method for internal dispute resolution and should publicize and encourage use of such dispute resolution mechanisms. For these reasons, the IFA has created the IFA Ombudsman program, an independent third-part who can assist franchisors and franchisees by facilitating dialogue to avoid disputes and to work together to resolve disputes. The IFA also strongly recommends the use of the National Franchise Mediation Program (NFMP) when a more structured mediation service is needed to help resolve differences.

Support of IFA and the Member Code of Ethics

Franchisees and franchisors have a responsibility to voice their concerns and offer suggestions on how the Code and the International Franchise Association can best meet the needs of its members. Franchisors and franchisees commit to supporting and promoting the initiatives of the IFA and advocating adherence to the letter and spirit of the Member Code of Ethics. Members who feel that another member has violated the Code in their U.S. operations may file a formal written complaint with the President of the IFA.

FIGURE 21-9

Continued

Franchise systems that have entered the global marketplace have gained from their experience in addressing social responsibility opportunities in the domestic (U.S.) markets. Typical social responsibility issues may include immigration, disabilities, glass ceilings, civil rights, and work-life balance issues such as dependent care, family leaves, and workforce flexibility. Arguably, it can be demonstrated that the United States is the most socially responsible country in the world.

The social responsibility programs utilized by franchised and other business firms in the United States have become strengths that underlie attempts to capitalize on diversity challenges in the international marketplace. A number of franchise firms are seeking ways to enhance business effectiveness through diversity and social responsibility issues in various foreign markets. Building social responsiveness and diversity strategies for the spread of franchising throughout the world is not an easy task. Learning to understand the economics of a particular foreign country is one thing; understanding its culture, language, and societal issues is another. Global franchise systems have not made the mistake to assume that "what works in the United States will work elsewhere," but they are finding that more applies than what might have been originally thought. The core concepts of culture, ethics, and moral principles, though differences are found to exist, have remarkable similarities across cultures and continents.

A new kind of franchise company has emerged since the 1950s. Today's franchise systems not only fulfill their economic and legal responsibilities, but also their ethical and social responsibilities. The most compelling reason for social responsible action by franchise systems, as well as any other business, is known to most businesspeople as the "iron law of responsibility," the meaning of which is, in the long-run, those who do not use their power in a manner society considers responsible will tend to lose it. In other words, if a firm does not meet the needs of society (which may be broader than economic transactions), then society will take the charter away (not support the business).

Lawrence "Doc" Cohen

Doc & Associates

Doc Cohen first started with the Original Great American Chocolate Chip Cookie Company in 1978. He was living in California when his sister in Atlanta told him about a Great American Cookie Co. franchise in her local mall. He was skeptical at first. Doc thought a person would have to sell a lot of cookies to make profits in a mall atmosphere. Doc started to research the cookie industry, the competition, and the company itself. He believed this to be a good investment. In early 1978, he met with the representatives of the company intending to become a franchisee in California. The store was going to be in a mall a few minutes from his house. At the meeting, Great American Cookie Co. told him that he could not open a franchise in California due to a state franchise disclosure law (which would later become a federal law). The company would, however, offer

him one of eight other possible locations and let him own that franchise. He researched the locations and found that the best prospect was in Lafayette, Louisiana. At that time, Lafayette had the highest per capita rate of spending on food, outside the home, in the country. When he signed the agreement for Lafayette, he had not gone there yet, and he had not read the agreement.

He was quite surprised to find out that there were no flights to Lafayette and even more surprised when he realized he had to drive through the swamp to get there. He trained with the Great American Cookie Co. in Atlanta to become a franchisee in February 1979. At the time he had no money. Doc had borrowed money from his sister and brother-in-law who had to get the money on loans from a bank. As a way to save $500 a week, Doc became the construction superintendent of his store and another store in the mall. This job required him to go back and forth *getting specialists to work on his projects. The mall itself was supposed to open with one hundred thirty stores, including four department stores. Instead, it opened with only thirty-two stores, and two department stores. The franchise store opened with the highest opening in the history of the Great American Cookie Co.*

In November 1979, Doc opened his second store in Cortana Mall, Baton Rouge, Louisiana. For this store, he went to the Louisiana National Bank with a bag of cookies as his business card. They helped him get started by giving him a loan for $50,000. His third store was in Panama City, Florida. This store was in a mall, but at the end of a corridor with no department store on the end. The store ended up being an anchor store in the mall. In the beginning, payroll often exceeded profits. It was three years before a department store finally was built. Luckily, the bank stood by Doc Cohen because he followed the philosophy, "If the bank is going to hear bad news, make sure they hear it from you."

His other huge success was in Corpus Christi, Texas, in another mall. The store had so much traffic in the first week that a two-shift staff had to work twenty-four hours a day to bake enough cookies to fill demand. The second week after opening was Valentine's Day week, and during that time staff sold over $30,000 worth of cookies. The traffic was so heavy that the finish on the tiles was rubbed off of the floor in front of the store.

For the first seven stores, Doc ran them from the kitchen table. He did not hire a bookkeeper until 1982. For ten years, the daily cash control (balance that shows everyday bills and checks that have gone out) was in the negative six figures, because Doc used the next week's sales to pay last week's bills.

The amazing part was that he was paying off the debt faster than he was incurring it, and he never had a year when there was an overall loss.

Doc continued to expand further and further. He had stores in seven states at one point and his unit in Houston was the top performer for Great American Cookie Co. His Baton Rouge store was second, and the original Lafayette store was in the top five. Overall, Doc has owned thirty-five units in the past nineteen years. In 1998, Mrs. Fields bought out Great American Cookie Co., and the Doc sold out to the franchisor. After that Doc bought three new stores from Mrs. Fields: a Great American Cookie Co. in Katy, Texas; a Pretzel Time in Panama City, Florida with a partner; and a Great American Cookie Co. in Vero Beach, Florida, with a partner. He still works in the office doing financial statements for his three stores and managing construction of the stores. He is considering opening additional units with Mrs. Fields' who owns Great American Cookie Co., Pretzel Time, Pretzel Maker, and TCBY. He likes the company's concepts and brands.

When you ask Doc Cohen how he became so successful, he will tell you people make the difference. In 1998, when he sold the twenty-three units he had at the time, half of the store managers had been with him for over fifteen years and one-fourth of the managers had been with him for over ten years. At his home office, some of the staff had been there for almost twenty years. This loyalty of employees shows their support for the company. He gives credit to the people in the real estate business and the workers in his company. To Doc, he is not the success story; the people who supported him are the real story.

SUMMARY

Social responsibility has emerged as a major challenge for business firms, both in the United States and abroad. Social responsibility consists of obligations a business has to society. The socially motivated actions can be classified into three categories: social obligation, social responsibility, and social responsiveness. Over time, the concept of social responsibility has changed. It appears that more involvement by business is being desired by the general public toward resolution of social ills and weaknesses than at any time before in our history.

Ethics is a set of principles for a behavioral code that explains right and wrong. It may also outline moral duty, obligation, and rules with resulting impact on relationships of both a personal and business nature. Businesses establish codes of ethics, or codes of conduct, to help their employees make decisions. A code of conduct is a statement of ethical practices or guidelines that the business firm follows. Ethical codes are becoming more widespread among U.S. business and are proving to be more meaningful in their implementation.

In spite of the lack of clarity surrounding social responsibility, cultural diversity, and morality, ethics will continue to be a major issue for business into the twenty-first century. In this regard, the franchise industry is not asleep at the wheel.

The law of franchising has established the basic groundwork for building social responsiveness within franchise systems. To persons who watch franchising as an industry, it is clear that franchising is in the forefront on a number of social responsibility and responsiveness issues. It would be difficult for any other industry to show the same or a similar level of development in terms of social responsibility dimensions to the extent shown by franchising. The franchise industry is taking a mature, reasoned, and responsive approach to the law, its franchisees, employees, customers, and the general public.

Increasingly, business is seeing a need to go beyond "doing well" and reach for "doing good" for its stakeholders—employees, customers, communities, government, and stockholders. Franchising has been at the forefront on a number of key social responsibility issues. As the world becomes more of a common marketplace, the franchise industry can be expected to continue as a leading force in demonstrating social responsibility and ethical business practices in the United States and throughout the world.

KEY TERMS

Consequentialism: a philosophy that considers a decision to be correct or right if the decision and its resulting behavior accomplish the intended results of the int4ended behavior.

Egoism: right or acceptable conduct in terms of positive consequences for the individual; that is, make decisions that will maximize self-interest.

Ethical formalism: a moral philosophy that focuses on the rights of individuals and on the intentions associated with a particular behavior rather than the outcome or consequences of the intended behavior.

Justice theory: directly relates to concept of fairness. Justice demands fair treatment and due reward in accordance with ethical or legal standards.

Social obligation: when a business meets legal and regulatory requirements, discloses information about itself when required and contributes when direct benefit to the business can be clearly shown.

Social responsibility: the obligations a business has to its society.

Social responsiveness: where a firm makes information about itself freely available to the public, accepts formal and informal input from outside interests in its decision making, is willing to be publicly evaluated, and will support and contribute to established social causes but also new interests or groups whose needs are unfulfilled and becoming increasingly important.

Stakeholders: groups or individuals who affect and are affected by the business firm, which may include the board of directors, employees, investors, community members, management, possibly a union, creditors, suppliers, government bodies and the general public.

Utilitarianism: concern is about decision consequences. Utilitarian rule followers seek the greatest good for the greatest number of people.

REVIEW QUESTIONS

1. Describe business ethics and discuss the three levels of ethical standards.

2. Describe social responsibility and discuss the three primary views of social responsibility.

3. Describe the nature of business's responsibility to the task and societal environments.

4. List and discuss the arguments for social responsibility.

5. List and discuss the arguments against social responsibility.

6. Identify the ethical categories associated with a decision situation, providing example questions within each category.

7. Demonstrate your understanding about the social responsibility topics and issues for franchise firms.

8. Identify and describe the key terms in the language of ethics.

9. Identify and discuss how the franchising industry has demonstrated its commitment to social responsibility and social responsiveness.

FRANCHISING QUIZ: FACT OR FICTION?

1. T F McDonald's restaurants in India do not serve beef—including Big Macs—but you can purchase an all-lamb version of the sandwich, called a Maharaja Mac.

2. T F More people are eating specialized pizzas with a wide array of toppings varying from the traditional cheese, pepperoni, and sausage, to the exotic and bizarre alligator and banana.

3. T F According to a 1996 survey conducted for *Franchise Times*, 76 percent of franchisees consider themselves either "very satisfied" or "somewhat satisfied" with franchising.

4. T F In the same *Franchise Times* survey, 73 percent said they would recommend franchise ownership to others.

5. T F Although nonfranchise small businesses are still having difficulties in acquiring sufficient financing, banks and nonbank lenders are more willing to loan money to franchises, particularly high-quality franchises with national reputations

6. T F The more money franchisees earn, the more they are willing to look for additional units or franchises.

7. T F According to the Small Business Administration (SBA), since the 1970s small businesses have created two of every three net new jobs.

8. T F Franchisees are typical small businesses, according to the National Federation of Independent Business (NFIB), in that they primarily fund their start-up businesses with personal savings (51 percent).

9. T F In the United States, one of every twelve business establishments is a franchised business.

10. T F A new franchised business opens every eight minutes of every business day.

(If you answered "True" to all questions, you are correct.)

REFERENCES

Baker, Sherry, "Ethical Judgement," *Executive Excellence* (March 1992): 7–8.

Boal, Kimberly and Perry Newman, "The Cognitive Structure of Corporate Responsibility," *Journal of Management* (Fall/Winter 1985): 71–82.

McGarvey, J, "Do the Right Thing," *Entrepreneur* (October 1992): 66–67.

Laczniak, Gene, "Business Ethics: A Manager's Primer," *Business* (Jan/Feb/Mar 1983): 23–29.

Murphy, Patrick, "Implementing Business Ethics," *Journal of Business Ethics* 7 (1988): 907–915.

Davidson, Jacqueline, "Responsibility Reaps Rewards," *Small Business Requests* (February 1993): 56.

Hisrich, Robert D. and Michael P. Peters, *Entrepreneurship*, 4th ed. (New York: Irwin McGraw-Hall, 1998).

Kuratko, Donald and Richard Hodgetts, "What Is the Nature of Social Responsibility?" *Entrepreneurship a Contemporary Approach*, 4th ed. (New York: Dryden Press, 1998), 165.

Pierce, Jon L. and John W. Newstrom, *The Manager's Bookshelf: A Mosaic of Contemporary View*, 5th ed. (Upper Saddle River, NJ: Prentice-Hall, Inc., 2000).

Richardson, John E., ed., *Business Ethics 2000/2001* (Guilford, CT: Sluice Dock, 2000).

Scarborough, Norman and Thomas Zimmer, *Effective Small Business Management*, 5th ed. (Upper Saddle River, NJ: Prentice Hall, Inc., 1996), 49–60.

Robbins, Stephen P. and David A. De Cenzo, *Fundamentals of Management*, 2nd ed. (Upper Saddle River, NJ: Prentice Hall, Inc., 1998), 39–44.

Wheelen, Thomas and David J. Hunger, *Strategic Management and Business Policy*, 5th ed. (New York: Addison-Wesley Publishing Company, 1995), 57–78.

Wheelen, Thomas and David J. Hunger, *Strategic Management and Business Policy* (Upper Saddle River, NJ: Prentice-Hall, Inc., 2000).

Zimmerer, Thomas W. and Norman M. Scarborough, *Essentials of Entrepreneurship and Small Business Management*, 2nd ed. (Upper Saddle River, NJ: Prentice-Hall, Inc., 1998).

NOTES

1. Thomas G. Labrecque, "Good Ethics Is Good Business," *USA Today Magazine* (May 1990): 20–21.
2. Ibid.

INTERNATIONAL FRANCHISING

In studying this chapter, you will:

- Learn about how to start franchising internationally.

- Understand why you should franchise internationally.

- Know about the different levels of growth of franchising in foreign countries.

- Be able to understand those steps and considerations necessary to engage in international franchising and the different ways of accomplishing them.

- Understand the hindrances associated with franchising in international marketplaces.

- Get an idea of what the future will hold for international franchising.

INCIDENT

Kunio Morita is interested in becoming a franchisee of a U.S.-based franchise company in Japan. Kunio spent two years studying at the University of Southern California before returning to his homeland. During his time in the United States, Kunio became aware of the large role franchising plays in the U.S. economy. He wrote to several U.S. franchisors who he believed had product and services that would be appropriate and successful in his native country. Through the correspondence and literature supplied, he has learned that most U.S. franchisors that operate on an international basis do so by utilizing a master franchisee or conglomerate organizational structure within the host country. Thus, Kunio believes his best approach would be to contact a local corporation handling the franchise that he desires to open.

Kunio is interested primarily in becoming a fast-food restauranteur in Japan. There are many fast-food restaurants in Japan and Kunio knows they are expensive to start. Through friends and relatives, however, he would be able to raise approximately $112,000. This would enable him to open a small restaurant or food-service business because in Japan such businesses are generally only half the size of those in the United States.

Some of the most attractive points of owning and operating a franchise in Japan are the advertising, marketing, and promotional packages that have been developed by the franchisors. The franchisor would also help him in the selection of the site and the layout of the store. In addition, two to six weeks' training would be provided. Quality control and proper franchisee performance are closely monitored in the Japanese firms. Kunio believes he would be a big success if he could just get the store open and operating properly.

22-1   INTRODUCTION

American franchisors generally consider their market to be consumers living in the United States. The domestic market is so big that most franchisors see little if any reason to export or go elsewhere to improve their profits or business. It is both simpler and safer to develop the U.S. market and advertise to the American consumer. This eliminates the need to learn a foreign language, become accustomed to foreign laws and regulations, handle foreign currency, experience legal and political uncertainties, or even adapt the product to local cultures and conditions.

Franchising is becoming an increasing international activity with many U.S. franchisors going abroad and many foreign franchisors entering the United States. From 1971 to 1985, U.S. franchisors developed foreign outlets at a rate of 17 percent per year. This is almost twice as fast as they added domestic outlets. Today, because of this steady increase in foreign expansion, more than 1,000 U.S. companies have more than 250,000 franchised outlets overseas. It is expected that by the year 2010, at least 60 percent of all franchisors in the United States will have foreign outlets.

Franchising in Japan represents sales of $114 million with more than 750 active franchisors and 177,000 franchise stores in operation. The largest U.S.-based franchisors operating in Japan include 7-Eleven with 11,100 units, followed by McDonald's 2,400 units, and Kentucky Fried Chicken's 1,000 stores. McDonald's has even met the demands of the local culture by adding the Teriyaki McBurger, a sausage patty on a bun with teriyaki sauce. KFC Corporation's foreign sales ($4.6 billion with 5,600 stores) exceed their domestic sales ($4.3 billion with 5,231 stores). Brazilian franchises generated approximately $7.2 billion in sales in 1999 and Chile accounts for $200 million in sales.

KFC now has over 1,600 outlets in China, part of the current 2,300 different franchise systems there. Yum Brands, which owns KFC, Pizza Hut, and Chinese-style East Dawning restaurants in China, have over 2,000 restaurants and generate nearly a third of Yum's global operating profits, with more than 100,000 Chinese workers. McDonald's has more than 50,000 employees on mainland China and they plan on opening 100 restaurants a year to the more than 800 restaurants in the country.

There are, however, two good reasons why a franchisor may initially become involved with international marketing. First, franchisors may be pushed into foreign markets because of the lack of expansion opportunities in the United States; they may have already exhausted all the available territories and major marketing areas. Second, the franchisor may be pulled into the foreign market by growing opportunities and demand for the product abroad. Coca-Cola and Chrysler, both major franchising companies, earn more than half their profits in foreign markets. Other companies find that foreign operations may grow faster than domestic fields.

Coca-Cola has been able to overcome the difficulties of foreign laws, trademark infringements, foreign exchange, different languages, and different cultures to become one of the largest international franchisors in the world. The company has had its share of difficulties, however. After it had entered the Chinese market in 1982, it found that one translation of its trademark, "Coca-Cola," was "backbite the wax tadpole." After some professional advice, the Chinese characters which Coca-Cola currently uses translate as "permit the mouth to rejoice."

Most international expansion of American franchise businesses occurs through the sale of franchises to foreign nationals, companies, or conglomerates. From the years 1975 through 2000, between 73 and 94 percent of all foreign outlets of U.S. franchise businesses were established through foreign franchisees. This show of strength for foreign businesspeople has been one of the mainstays in U.S. franchisors' success abroad. The big secret, then, is to find the right foreign individual, company, or conglomerate business.

22-2   THE INTERNATIONAL MARKETPLACE

The decision to sell in foreign markets requires that a franchisor learn many new aspects of business. The company needs to develop a thorough understanding of international commerce, trade laws, economic considerations, political environments, and markets. International sales have also increased from 25 percent to 250 percent over the last five years.

As stated, China, with a population of more than 1.3 billion people, currently has over 2,300 chains using franchising. Today, Yum Brands (KFC, Pizza Hut, and Taco Bell) opens company-owned stores and operates each store for about twelve months before training and delegating the store to a new franchisee. It is expected that by the year 2010 nearly one-third of China's total retail sales will be through franchised systems.

The international trade environment has changed significantly during the past decade. Japan remains as a leading economic power in world markets. The international financial system has developed a strong currency exchange and has improved currency convertibility. The United States has fallen into an unfavorable balance of trade and has seen its dominant position in world markets erode. Major oil-producing countries have emerged as economic powers and as important investors in international trade. New markets have rapidly grown in the Pacific Rim countries, gradually opened in China, the oil-rich Arab countries, and to a limited extent Western and Eastern Europe.

Canada, Japan, Australia, and the United Kingdom are today the most popular countries for U.S. international franchise expansion. These are closely followed by France, West Germany, Singapore, and Malaysia as markets most often targeted by franchise developers.

The increase of franchising in international markets is due to several important economic and demographic trends in foreign countries.

1. Increased disposable income

2. Rising educational levels

3. Universal cultural trends, increasing number of women in the working force

4. Shorter work weeks

5. Younger generations willing to try new products

6. Demographic concentrations of people in urban areas

7. Smaller families with two or more incomes

Kentucky Fried Chicken anticipates increased growth in international markets especially because of the growing numbers of working women and the increase in available disposable income. It seeks to expand into countries with these characteristics.

McDonald's continues to grow. In the near future, McDonald's anticipates opening about 1,700 to 1,900 new McDonald's restaurants, including 650 stores in Asia/Pacific, 550 in Europe, 350 in Latin America, 200 in the United States, and the remainder in the Middle East, Africa, and Canada. Surprisingly, more than 85 percent of these new stores will be built outside of the United States. Their growth is primarily in the international field and most of their profits now come from their international businesses. They have established a model for businesses everywhere, not just franchising. McDonald's logo, training, standards, service, and legendary consistency are things that have changed the way U.S. companies do business and the way that U.S. companies are perceived in foreign countries. They have a unique business success that continues to grow, expand, and be a positive influence and force for the United States.

22-3   INTERNATIONAL FRANCHISE EVOLUTION

There is a distinct pattern in the evolution of franchising growth in foreign countries. While franchising continues to grow around the world it is interesting to look at the distinct patterns of that expansion. This growth pattern may be summarized in the following five steps.

1. Foreign hospitality franchises

2. Domestic hospitality franchises

3. Foreign retail, business services, and other franchises

4. Domestic franchises

5. Exporting domestic franchises

22-3a   Foreign Hospitality Franchises

The first sources of franchising in a foreign country are generally found in the hospitality industry, including hotels and convenience or fast-food restaurants. Many countries have welcomed international franchised hotels such as Hyatt, Marriott, Hilton, and Renaissance hotels. The hotel industry is generally invited to prepare the way for foreign visitors and economic development. These same countries also invite McDonald's, Burger King, Wendy's, Kentucky Fried Chicken, and Church's Fried Chicken. China is rapidly expanding with foreign franchisors and their **hospitality franchises**.

22-3b   Domestic Hospitality Franchises

Following the invasion of foreign franchises, the local business community or government often understands the potential profits in these new businesses and they develop their own businesses following these foreign franchise successes. The Chinese built an almost identical five-star hotel two blocks down from the five-star Sheraton Great Wall Hotel in Beijing. Bob's Hamburgers is the largest fast-food hamburger business in Brazil—even larger than McDonald's. These businesses are often preferred by the local nationals because of their local tastes, adoptions, and ambience. Local franchise systems are generally encouraged, and are rapidly developed following the technology introduced by the foreign companies.

22-3c   Foreign Retail, Business Services, and Other Franchises

Once franchising has been introduced into a country, many local businesspeople will seek out other profitable franchises to bring into their country. In addition to fast-food restaurants, other retail and service franchises will be added to the local community. Businesses such as Kwik Kopy and UPS Store have found success in foreign countries.

22-3d   Domestic Franchises

This is the time for widespread expansion of franchising throughout the country as local businesspeople develop their own **domestic franchise** businesses and expand their systems across their country. Now the local business community will compete with the foreign systems and the country will generally choose the best of the systems—often local businesses will emerge as strong systems that offer some local specialties. This is an exciting time for business expansion and growth. The Wendy's Ice Cream Parlor's of Australia have been very successful and they are now located across the country.

22-3e Exporting Domestic Franchises

Fast Frame Inc. and The Body Shoppe are highly successful franchise systems that been brought to the United States from England. The exportation of franchise systems from other countries into the United States is the last step in the development of franchising in foreign countries. Many countries have business ideas and products that would sell well within the United States. Once they have successfully expanded their businesses in their own countries then they will be able to think of expanding into other countries.

22-3f Legal and Trade Restrictions

A franchisor seeking to develop markets in foreign countries needs to be aware of the various restrictions of world trade. **Tariffs**—taxes levied by a government against specific imported products—are the most common restrictions in international trade. Tariffs may be based on a product's value, weight, or volume. They are generally designed to raise taxes for government (revenue tariff) or to protect domestic products or firms (protective tariff). An additional trade restriction facing exporters is the **quota**—a limit on the amount of goods that the importing country will allow into that country in specific business classifications. Quotas are also designed to protect domestic industry, prices, and employment, as well as to maintain a favorable trade balance. Another trade restriction, the **embargo**, simply bans all products in a prescribed classification.

A major problem that many franchisors will also face is an **exchange control**, which regulates the currency exchange between countries. An exchange control limits the amount of foreign exchange available and regulates its exchange rate against other currencies. A franchisor may find it difficult, if not impossible, to return profits to the home country. In addition, U.S. franchisors may face nontariff barriers such as discrimination against American products or prices. Some governments even establish quality standards or standards of operation which discriminate specifically against U.S. products.

22-4 INFLUENCES ON INTERNATIONAL BUSINESS

As shown in Figure 22-1, the success of a franchise if a foreign setting is influenced by both external and internal factors and their interaction. Economic and cultural conditions need to be carefully considered.

22-4a Economic Considerations

The three major characteristics which a franchisor must analyze before investing in a business in a foreign country are the country's distribution of income, its industrial structure, and its political and legal environment. The distribution of income may be categorized into six different types.

1. Variable family incomes

2. Mostly low family incomes

3. Very low or very high family incomes

4. Low, medium, and high family incomes

5. Mostly medium family incomes

6. Mostly high family incomes

It would be difficult for General Motors or Ford Motor to sell Cadillacs, Continentals, or other luxury cars in countries within income distribution type 1 or 2. Most restaurant franchisors would primarily be interested in the income distribution types 3 through 6.

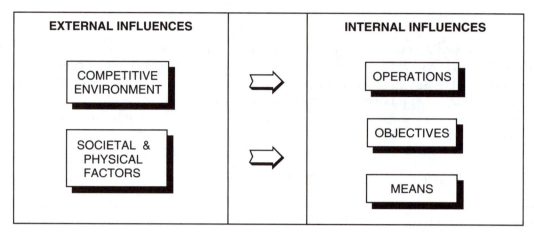

FIGURE **22-1**

Influences on International Business

The country's industrial structure is a vital indicator of its economic strength and growth potential. The industrial structure may be broken down into three common classifications.

1. Developed, industrialized nations

2. Developing, emerging, industrializing nations

3. Nondeveloped, nonindustrialized nations

In the nondeveloped, **nonindustrialized nations**, most of the population is engaged in simple agricultural production. The people consume a great deal of their own output and exchange or barter the rest for other services or goods. These nations provide little real opportunity for franchised operations. On the other hand, both the developed, industrialized nations and the developing, emerging nations provide strong opportunities for franchised outlets. Many franchisors including Coca-Cola, Kentucky Fried Chicken, and Hertz have all sold franchises in European, South American, and Pacific Rim countries.

22-4b   Political and Legal Environment

The franchisor, before beginning to invest in foreign operations, should investigate many aspects of foreign markets, among which would be political stability, monetary controls, and government regulations.

It is vimportant for a franchisor to gauge the political stability in the prospective host country. Many governments change hands every four to ten years. One regime that allows a franchisor access to the country's market may be replaced by a government that is opposed to the franchisor's business or methods. The franchisor should also be aware of the monetary controls a country places on its currency. A fluctuating exchange rate offers monetary instability. Some countries may have very restrictive exchange controls that make it difficult for the franchisee to remit payment to the franchisor or to send profits from the foreign country back to the home office.

Government regulations and bureaucracy are also prevalent in foreign markets. Although unacceptable by U.S. business standards, many foreign officials expect a suitable payment (consulting fee) to be made by franchisors expanding into their countries. One common method to circumvent government restrictions for at least a limited time is to use members of the ruling party as franchisees in a particular country.

Additionally, it is important to understand how generally receptive foreign countries are to having franchised businesses operate within their countries. Many countries, Mexico included, provide investment incentives, site location services, and favorable currency exchanges to attract foreign businesses to their country. Other countries establish import quotas, currency controls, and requirements that a high percentage of the management team be citizens. These kinds of restrictions often cause franchisors to leave countries even after they have already become established.

MCDONALD'S GOES INTERNATIONAL

McDonald's is the world's largest restaurant chain and it continues to grow at an astonishing rate. McDonald's has almost half of the globally branded quick service restaurants outside the United States, and they generate almost two-thirds of the sales. With approximately 14,000 units in the United States and over 17,000 elsewhere around the world, this giant continues to grow. International operations now account for 52 percent of operating profits and 54 percent of revenues, whereas domestic operations account for only 48 percent and 46 percent, respectively. An investor who purchased 100 shares of McDonald's stock for $2,250 when it went public in 1965 today has 37,180 shares worth $1.7 million.

22-5   INTERNATIONAL MARKETING DECISION

Before the final decision is made to enter foreign markets, it is important that an analysis of different countries and markets be completed. The franchisor must determine if marketing opportunities in other countries are strong enough to allow entry into the international franchising field. The decision to start international franchising should include five major steps. We discuss the steps in this section.

22-5a   Appraising and Deciding to Franchise Internationally

A growing number of franchisors are making the decision to take advantage of the opportunities of expanding their systems outside the United States. Although the expansion into international markets demands extra preparation and effort by the franchisor, the rewards are often substantial, especially when the franchisor is able to gain a dominant position in the foreign market. The franchisor must consider the practical financial and profit issues before entering the foreign market. It must analyze and appraise the profitability and longevity of a foreign market. The distance required to deliver product and services may be prohibitive, or the language and cultural differences may adversely affect operations. The franchisor should seek advice about the receptivity of the foreign market to the product or service. It is best that the product or service be test-marketed in the foreign country before formal development of a franchising system in that market. Many foreign countries also have legal limitations on the form of investment and technology transfer allowable in those countries.

Before entering any foreign market, the franchisor needs to appraise the opportunity of securing trademark registration and of dealing with reputable and competent companies or individuals, and it should review and be able to understand all applicable foreign laws. The franchisor may determine that it would be impossible to enter a particular foreign market simply because the host country is unwilling to comply with international trademark laws or because competent and reliable franchisees would be too difficult to find.

22-5b   Which Countries to Enter

The franchisor must determine the suitability and compatibility of any country or market into which the franchisor would expand. The country should be analyzed for economic stability, political and legal environment, stage of economic development, and target market demand. In addition, it would be appropriate to analyze and estimate (1) current market potential, (2) sales potential, (3) future market, (4) expense and cost estimates, (5) profit potential, and (6) potential return on investment.

Each country should be analyzed in terms of its economic and market potential. It may be easiest to begin with English-speaking countries, most of which have common cultures, language, and somewhat similar consumer preferences. However, it is also important to realize that even countries that share a language have unique cultures and may have different market demands for specific products. It would be appropriate to perform marketing research in the preferred countries to determine possible market demand and sales potential. The countries should be ranked according to their market potential, market growth, potential profit, cost of doing business, risk level, and cooperative attitude.

22-5c   How to Start

Once the franchisor has decided which country to enter (and it should only enter one at a time), it must decide the best mode of starting a business in that country. There are five major starting strategies, as shown in Figure 22-2 and Figure 22-3: (1) establishing a master franchisee, (2) joint venture (doing business with foreign companies or individuals), (3) licensing, (4) direct investment, and (5) **exporting** (producing at home and selling abroad). Each of these strategies has different costs, risks, commitments, and profits associated with it.

Master Franchisee

The **master franchisee** may be an individual, small business, large corporation, or conglomerate which assumes the rights and obligations of establishing franchises throughout the country. The franchisee is taught all the operations and developments in the business by the franchisor. Normally the franchisee starts one or two stores during the first year and expands to approximately thirty

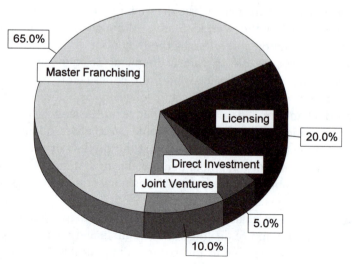

FIGURE 22-2

International Franchising: Method of Franchising

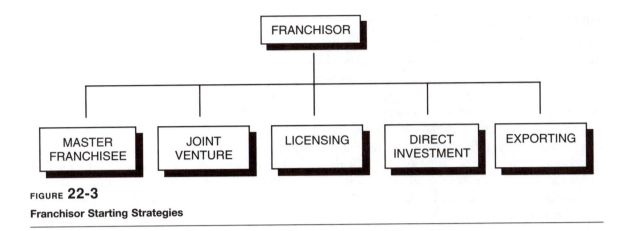

FIGURE **22-3**

FIGURE **22-3**

Franchisor Starting Strategies

stores within five to ten years. Master franchisees may choose either to engage subfranchisees or to open all stores themselves.

The master franchisee in a foreign country assumes the role of franchisor. Royalty fees are generally paid by each subfranchisee through the master franchisees; the master franchisees keep up to 50 percent of these royalty payments and submit the other 50 percent back to the headquarters operation. Almost all advertising fees are also paid directly to the master franchisee, who then uses them for local (or national) advertising.

The **U.S. Commercial Service (USCS)** is the international arm of the U.S. Department of Commerce, and can be easily contacted through any U.S embassy. The USCS exists primarily to help U.S. companies sell products and services to other countries, and bring the proceeds back to the United States. They have special programs which help U.S. franchise systems find effective and successful master franchisees in their specific countries.

Regarding the use of master franchisees, the IFA survey reports: "Master franchising is the method used by 57 percent of responding members franchising internationally ... Individual contracts (licenses) are used by 19 percent of respondents to the new survey, joint ventures by 12 percent and foreign subsidiaries (direct investment) by 6 percent. Of those responding, 66 percent have an international division in their corporate structure to oversee foreign franchise development."

Figure 22-4 outlines international franchise opportunities and the factors involved in deciding the best method of entry.

Identify International Opportunities	Identify Resources and SWOT	Methods of Entry	DECISION— GO/NO GO	Franchising Outcomes
Extend Markets	Legal/Trade restrictions	Master Franchisee	PROS	Product Utilization
Improve Profits	Economic Considerations	Joint Venture	☒ Just Do It	Product Adaptation
Location Opportunities	Political/Legal Environment	Licensing	☐ Don't Do It	Product Invention
Market Demand	Strengths/Weaknesses/ Opportunities/Threats	Direct Investment	CONS	
Strong Franchisee		Exporting		

FIGURE **22-4**

International Franchise Opportunities

Joint Venturing

An often-used form of franchise investment in foreign countries is the **joint venture**. With this method, the franchisor joins with local citizens in setting up production and/or market locations. The advantage of joint ventures is that they lead to investment by both the franchisor and the franchisee in the foreign business operations. Joint ventures are generally established through (1) joint ownership ventures, (2) management contracting, and (3) contract manufacturing.

Many foreign countries require that the franchisor invest or buy interest in the local franchised unit before starting the business. This joint ownership venture pairs local investors with the franchisor in the creation of local businesses with shared ownership and control. McDonald's Corporation opened a joint venture restaurant in the popular Piazza di Spagna in Rome. Italy is a major large European market McDonald's has entered and the Rome location is a joint venture between Food Italia Spa and McDonald's. In 1985, McDonald's also entered Mexico. In compliance with Mexican law, McDonald's owns 49 percent and a Mexican partner owns the remaining 51 percent. At the end of April 2000 there are 175 McDonald's restaurants with more than 8,000 employees throughout the country. The partner also received twelve months of training at Hamburger University at the McDonald's headquarters in suburban Chicago, Illinois.

A second method of joint venturing is through management contracts by which the franchisor provides management know-how to the foreign company, which furnishes the necessary capital and obtains the necessary licenses and permits to start the business. The Hilton Hotel system uses management contracts to manage its hotels throughout the world. This method allows the franchisor a low-risk entry into foreign markets. An additional way of entering foreign markets is to contract manufacturing in the foreign countries. Most major automotive manufacturers have agreements with foreign countries and governments to allow the manufacturing and selling of their products in foreign markets.

Licensing

One of the most common methods of international franchising is for the franchisor (licensor) to enter into an agreement with a licensee (franchisee) and offer the right to use a product, good, service, trademark, trade secret, patent, or other valuable item in return for a royalty fee. The licensee gains the extra knowledge and capability of the franchisor and enables the franchisor to enter the market at little or no risk. Coca-Cola has entered most of its international markets by licensing bottlers (technically, franchising bottlers) throughout the world and providing the syrup necessary to produce the soft drink.

Direct Investment

The fourth method of entering foreign markets is direct investment, by which the franchisor simply invests in company-owned stores in foreign countries. This is a high-risk way of entering foreign markets, however, and franchisors are well advised to avoid this method. But after several franchises have already been established, it may be appropriate for a franchisor to begin direct investment and establish company-owned stores. Direct ownership does show the country and its people the desire of the franchisor to invest in the country's growth and development. The franchisor maintains full control over the operation and management of the franchise. The major problem with this type of investment is the exposure of a large investor to many business and political risks. Currency controls, market changes, or even expropriation may cause the demise of these franchises in foreign countries.

Exporting

Many franchisors, including General Motors and Goodyear Tire and Rubber, enter foreign markets through exporting. They manufacture their products here in the United States and sell them

FRANCHISOR PROVIDES	FRANCHISEE PROVIDES
Exclusive Territory—rights to develop the franchise in a given country or territory.	**Country Know-how**—ability to work within the rules and laws of the home country.
Products/Services—exclusive products, specs, recipes, guidelines, supplies.	**Capital**—provides funds necessary to set up and operate the business in a foreign country.
Training—initial, ongoing, support training for staff.	**Experience**—ability to build the franchising system in the home country.
Systems—accounting, operating, control, financial, promotional.	**Management**—provides the skills necessary to operate and manage several franchising units.
Support—site selection, grand opening, bulk purchasing, marketing, advertising.	**Effort**—commits labor and energy to build an expanding business successfully.
Rights—intellectual property rights regarding trade name, logos, trademarks, patents, operating manuals, and style.	**Commitment to follow franchising system**—a strong effort to follow the exact prescribed methods and procedures of the system.
Experience—tested operations and business practices, track record, demand for products.	**Desire**—vision and burning desire to build and expand an established business system.
Equipment—items for making the product or delivering the service; uniforms, computers.	**Family**—sometimes involved in the setup and building of the business.

FIGURE **22-5**
International Franchising Provisions

through franchisees to customers in foreign countries. The foreign franchisee becomes the dealer or operator for the franchisor. The products may or may not be specially modified for the foreign market. This method of entering foreign markets is generally the least costly and requires the minimum change in the operation of the franchisor's company.

22-5d Franchise Program

Franchising organizations which operate in foreign countries must decide how much to change their franchising program, if at all, to adapt to conditions abroad. It is important when deciding how to franchise in foreign countries that the franchisor examine the product, promotion, price, and distribution system. The marketing plan must be carefully developed and adapted to local conditions.

Three major strategies may be used to sell products in a foreign market. The first strategy is **straight product utilization,** by which the franchisor offers the same product in the foreign market as in the domestic country. Before this is done, it is important that marketing research be performed to ascertain the attitudes of consumers toward the product. Generally, the Coca-Cola Company has been very successful in using this method to introduce its soft drink throughout the world; however, straight product utilization has failed for other companies because many cultures simply do not use the same products as used in the United States.

The second product strategy is called **product adaptation** and involves changing the product to meet local conditions and consumer demands. Many companies find it necessary to adapt their product to customer preference to ensure greater marketability and profitability for the franchising organization.

Harris Cooper, former president, chairman, and CEO of International Dairy Queen, Inc., recalls starting a Dairy Queen franchise in Japan with a big grand opening and favorable press coverage. Many Japanese came into the store and bought ice cream, but they were not returning to make repeat purchases. Market research indicated that nearly everyone enjoyed the ice cream but it failed to reveal why customers were not coming back. Finally, after many visits, investigations, and transoceanic phone calls, Cooper suggested the employees look in the garbage cans, and there was the answer: The Japanese were not finishing the portions being offered. Nearly every dish had some ice cream left in it. The lesson: The Japanese eat smaller portions. The franchisee reduced the size of the serving and also cut the price proportionally. Dairy Queen is now quite successful in Japan. Many other franchised restaurants are also doing well internationally.

Product invention is the third strategy, and as one might assume, it requires the creation of a new product. Many fast-food companies that enter foreign markets may add to their basic menu to include local food favorites. These foods may even become major items on the basic menu. For example, McDonald's in Hawaii serves a cup of saimin (noodle soup) as part of the menu. Product invention is the most costly of all the basic strategies, but it may also provide the greatest appeal for the customers. Product invention is also generally adopted after a product has been used and it has been determined that the new product has increased sales and profits.

Promotion

Franchisors may continue to use their same promotional advertisements abroad or adapt them to the local market. What may be appropriate in the home country may be offensive in the foreign country. Sometimes the advertisement can simply be translated into the foreign language, with new photographs depicting local citizens rather than Americans. Often, however, it may be best just to develop a different advertising or promotional program from the beginning in order to be sure to reach the target audience in that country.

Price

Franchisors find it is often necessary to change pricing structure for foreign operations. The population may have lower incomes and lowering the price is necessary in order to sell the goods or services. The low price may also be required to build market share or simply to promote the product. Charging a lower price in a foreign country than that in the home country is referred to as "dumping." Some countries levy fines on companies that are dumping products (getting rid of excess production) into their country. Pricing decisions should be left with the local franchisee in accordance with the costs and profit motives of the company.

Channels of Distribution

Distribution begins at the organization headquarters, then moves to the channel between nations, and finally to the channel within a nation. All three channels are very important to ensure the successful distribution and availability of product in the foreign country. The headquarters organization is responsible for ensuring that a domestically manufactured or developed product makes it to the exporting dock in the franchisor's country. Those people involved with the channel between nations ensure that the products are shipped to overseas markets. The third link, or channel within a nation, sees to it that the product arrives at the retail outlet in a condition to be sold to consumers.

For many franchisors, the final channel, the one within a country, may be the only channel for the franchise system. This channel is activated when the product arrives in the foreign country and is distributed within that country. At this time, it is important and necessary that all people involved in delivering the product to the store are properly managed and supervised. In less developed countries, distributors and importers are very important and must be carefully sought out and enlisted. Many franchisors will be required to offer exclusive distribution rights to a local "product" distributor and the organization's ability to provide the product to the store will depend on how well the local distributor has been chosen.

Franchise Organization

Almost every franchise system handles international franchising activities in its own peculiar way. The organizational arrangements for international franchising often depend on the company's method of operation within those foreign countries. The franchising organization generally establishes either an export department or an international division. An export department is responsible primarily for shipments of goods or products. As activities continue to grow, this department will often become an international division. The international division will eventually become involved in a number of different international markets and business ventures. The franchisor will have to determine how it will interact with each particular country and develop its franchises within that country. Most of these activities will be done in one of the methods by which master franchisees are provided joint ownership of the franchise organizations.

INTERNATIONAL NEGOTIATING COMPANY

One franchisor, the International Center for Entrepreneurial Development (ICED), brings representatives from their franchisees together once a year with their supplier representatives to determine pricing, services, and other supplier benefits for the franchisees. The results of these meetings are adopted by the franchisor and passed directly on the franchise owners throughout the system. One year, the representatives were Gary Atwood, Kwik Kopy Printing owner from Richmond, Virginia; Kim Barrett, Franklin's owner from Nashville, Tennessee; Sheila Schaefer, Kwik Kopy Printing owner from Palm Bay, Florida; Alan Kinstler, The Ink Well owner from Fairfield, Ohio; Richard Harrison, an AWT and Copy Club owner from Houston, Texas; and Jim Broyles, Kwik Kopy Printing owner from Collinsville, Illinois.

22-6 HINDRANCES TO INTERNATIONAL FRANCHISING

Many U.S. franchisors have voiced their reluctance to expand into foreign countries because of government red tape, high costs, and import restrictions.

Originally, Kentucky Fried Chicken moved into Korea with four franchised stores. It entered the Korean market cautiously, because of concern about the quality and availability of chicken in Korea. This is in sharp contrast to its experience in Japan, where 305 franchised and 168 company-owned KFCs had already been established. The major difference appears to be that the government controls regarding chicken production in Korea are much more stringent than those in Japan.

Hoteliers are also interested in foreign markets, and they too have run into government red tape and have found it necessary to proceed slowly. The rule of thumb is one hotel at a time and one property at a time. They wait to see how the government will respond to that hotel and if restrictions will be lessened.

Cookie franchisors often find it difficult to get through existing channels of distribution in foreign marketplaces. They tend to look for partners with power or "oomph" in the local marketplace. The local partner could be either a master franchisee or a joint venture partner. Standard royalty fees would be approximately 4 to 5 percent, while some governments estimate the value of the franchise trademark from 6 to 8 percent, payable to the host country.

22-7 INTERNATIONAL FRANCHISING IN THE FUTURE

Franchising will be an even more prevalent method of doing business in the future. Today, over 40 percent of all retail sales in the United States are through franchised outlets. Franchising is growing throughout the world. Many franchise companies today see that most of their sales and profits come from foreign operations.

Prior to World War II, *franchising* was a little-used word in the U.S. business vocabulary. Today, it is an integral part of our economy and refers to an entire method of doing business rather than a simple distribution system relating to a single product. Franchising today refers to an ability to standardize and replicate business practices and formats which provide quality products and services to the consumer.

Franchising will continue to grow because of the benefits it provides both franchisors and franchisees. Through franchising, new businesses are able to start up without extensive capital outlays by the headquarters organization. Even though the market demand and profit potential may exist, it is still difficult for franchisors to readily raise capital for expansion. The franchising method provides this capital through the franchisees.

The franchisees are able to act as entrepreneurs and start in proven and profitable businesses by investing their money in a complete business format. For franchisees, this means being able to adopt a proven product or service and offer it through their own private businesses. The franchising method provides franchisees with the opportunity to realize the American dream of financial independence and success through owning their own business.

As franchising continues to grow, franchisors will continue to utilize their technical skills and knowledge to help franchisees learn daily operations, choose the best locations, establish proper marketing and promotional activities, develop appropriate procedures and policies for personnel, and improve all aspects of the marketing format. Franchising will continue to grow in the service sector, especially in professional and computerized services.

Franchising markets will grow as manufacturers and distributors of high-tech equipment utilize franchised outlets to sell their products. Computers, telecommunication services, and information processing will all be expanded through franchised stores. Franchisors of food products will continue to expand, especially in specialty and/or ethnic food areas. Nonfood retailing will continue to expand to accommodate demands for new products.

We will also see growth in the number of multiunit franchisees and in the adoption and utilization of franchise advisory councils and associations. The advisory councils have shown to be strong and supportive groups for franchisors. They have often been the source for new products and innovation for companies.

Name recognition and product quality are two reasons why franchising will continue to grow into the twenty-first century. More companies will utilize the franchising method for the sale of their products and services. Franchisors will realize the importance of private ownership by the franchisees as one of the great motivating forces in a marketing system and so will use the franchising concept to expand into almost all industries in which individuals can establish private stores to sell products or services. Franchising will probably be the main method of doing business in this new century.

Russell J. Frith, Lawn Doctor

Russell J. Frith, president and CEO of Lawn Doctor, Inc. for the past twenty-three years, joined the $60 million lawn care company as a customer. Russell said, "I had a small house on a quarter-acre lot in the suburbs of Philadelphia. I tried to plant a yard and after spending a lot of money, I couldn't get it to work." Russell employed the services of his

local Lawn Doctor dealer and became friendly with the technician who serviced the lawns in the area. The technician suggested Russell call the president and cofounder of Lawn Doctor, Inc., Tony Giordano, to discuss marketing ideas.

Tony hired Russell as a franchise sales manager, a position Russell held for three years, until he was promoted to vice president and chief operating officer. Shortly after, he was elected to Lawn Doctor's board of directors. Tony died unexpectedly in 1983 and Russell was appointed CEO of Lawn Doctor. When asked about the transition, Russell said, "The biggest challenge was to see that the key elements were put into place so that business would go on. While I was second in command, I did think about getting assigned to president or CEO some day. Certainly, it's very hard to prepare yourself when it happens suddenly." Since Russell has joined Lawn Doctor, the number of franchises has grown from under 40 to over 400.

Russell was born and raised in Philadelphia. He graduated from LaSalle University with degrees in marketing and accounting, attending school at night while working as a manager at the local Acme Supermarket during the day. Russell said, "As Acme's store manager, I was able to gain the practical business skills that would later help me at Lawn Doctor." It worked. A quarter of a century of franchising experience and an unmatched understanding of the lawn care industry have helped Russell turn Lawn Doctor into the largest and most respected lawn care franchise in the United States.

With Russell as president, Lawn Doctor has been awarded a wealth of recognition, including being ranked as one of the country's best franchises by Success magazine and the prestigious accounting firm of Ernst and Young. Both the Wall Street Journal and USA Today have turned to Russell as an expert source of information, and he was the focus of Lawn and Landscape magazine's cover story, "Franchise the Entrepreneurial Spirit." He was also an industry representative on the Environmental Protection Agency's Federal Pesticide Advisory Council. Russell has been a lecturer at the Wharton School of Business's Entrepreneurial Studies Program and his current title is Second Vice-Chairman on the Board of Directors and Chairman of the Budget, Finance and Audit Committee of the International Franchise Association. Russell is treasurer of IFA's Education Foundation. He was also the president of the Professional Lawn Care Association of America (PLCAA), as well as founding president of its Education Foundation. In 1993, Russell was honored as Landscape Management's "Man of the Year."

Russell knows what it takes to get a national franchise company to the top, and recognizes the CEO's responsibility to keep it there. Russell said, "The integrity of the CEO of the company and how important trust is in the whole organization is something that you have to think about all the time. People have a level of expectation as to how you should conduct yourself, and if you don't conduct yourself in that way, it will have a negative and rippling effect throughout the organization."

SUMMARY

International franchising is important in world commerce, and it provides mutually beneficial returns for both the home and host countries. International franchising by U.S. franchisors continues to increase and allows U.S. businesses to gain international recognition and promote their trade names, trademarks, products, and services abroad. The U.S. form of franchising is one of the most competitive forms of business in the world today. Successful franchised businesses are often sought by foreign countries and they provide local entrepreneurs and businesspeople the opportunity to develop new businesses and operations.

Canada is the largest foreign market for U.S. franchisors. Japan is the second largest market, with rapid growth in categories such as restaurants, convenience food stores, donut shops, and ice cream shops. Other countries are growing in their use of U.S. franchised businesses as well. Opportunities for growth continue to be available for franchisors in foreign markets.

Auto and truck rental services and restaurants are the businesses most frequently franchised internationally. Other major franchised businesses operating outside the United States include educational products and services, equipment rental services, convenience stores, retailing (nonfood), automotive products and services, and business aids and services.

International franchising is the wave of the future as more and more franchisors in the United States seek foreign markets. Many companies from Japan and Europe are currently looking to enter into the U.S. marketplace through franchised units, including automotive manufacturers, electronics manufacturers, and computer hardware and software stores. International franchising is another step in making the world smaller and more livable.

KEY TERMS

U.S. Commercial Service (USCS): the international arm of the US Department of Commerce dealing with international business development.

Hospitality franchises: includes hotels and convenience or fast-food restaurants.

Domestic franchises: local businesspeople develop their own franchise businesses and expand their systems across their own country.

Tariffs: taxes levied by a government against specific imported products; the most common restrictions in international trade.

Quota: a limit on the amount of goods that the importing country will allow into that country in specific business classifications.

Embargo: simply bans all products in a prescribed classification.

Exchange control: regulates the currency exchange between countries.

Nonindustrialized nations: most of the population is engaged in simple agricultural production.

Master franchisee: may be an individual, small business, large corporation, or conglomerate which assumes the rights and obligations of establishing franchises throughout a country.

Joint venture: often-used form of franchising in which the franchisor joins with local citizens in setting up production and/or market locations.

Licensing: where the franchisor (licensor) enters into an agreement with a licensee (franchisee) and offers the right to use a product, good, service, trademark, trade secret, patent, or other valuable item in return for a royalty fee.

Direct investment: franchisor simply invests in company-owned stores in foreign countries.

Exporting: franchisor manufactures products in the United States and sells them through franchisees to customers in foreign countries.

Straight product utilization: franchisor offers the same product in the foreign markets in the domestic country.

Product adaptation: involves changing the product to meet local conditions and consumer demands.

Product invention: requires the creation of a new product.

REVIEW QUESTIONS

1. Discuss the importance of analyzing the international marketplace before entering a country with a foreign franchise.

2. Define the economic considerations which are important in analyzing foreign markets for franchising.

3. Discuss the international marketing decision and analyze what steps need to be taken before starting a foreign operation.

4. Review the five different methods of starting a franchise in a foreign country.

5. Discuss the advantages and disadvantages of international franchising.

CASE STUDY

Home Instead Senior Care

Home Instead Senior Care is clearly the international leader in the nonmedical, at-home senior care field. No other company has experienced the growth and acceptance that Home Instead has enjoyed since starting in 1994. They are a network with annual sales of $720 million, with more than 550 franchises operating in forty-nine states and eleven foreign countries.

No segment of the population has as great an impact on society than those people sixty-five years of age and older. Few companies—and particularly those in franchising—have capitalized on these opportunities. Home Instead has! Just look at the facts: Today, about 13 percent of all Americans are age sixty-five and older. By the year 2030, this figure will increase to 20 percent. Only 5 percent of the elderly population live in a nursing home. The remaining 95 percent live alone, with a spouse, or they move in with a family member. Eldercare is expected to replace childcare as the top concern among U.S. employees by the year 2010.

Home Instead Senior Care provides a meaningful solution for the elderly, who prefer to remain at home. Their quality of life is enhanced without the stress and hardships of interrupted routines and changes in their daily habits. Our part-time, full-time, and around-the-clock services are designed for people who are capable of managing their physical needs, but require assistance, supervision, light housework, errands, and/or companionship to remain in their homes.

The initial franchising fee is $18,500, plus a royalty fee equal to 5 percent of the gross sales. The start-up costs for a Home Instead Senior Care franchise range from $24,300 to $31,300. The franchisor provides no financial assistance to the franchisee.

Start-up Costs

Personal start-up cash required: $5,800 to $12,800. Total investment required: $24,300 to $31,300. Total investment required includes $18,500 franchise fee.

Initial Franchising Fee	$ 18,500
Total	$ 24,300 - $ 31,300

Lori wants to buy a Home Instead Senior Care franchise for Singapore. She is excited about the opportunities available, but does not currently have sufficient financing to start. She has $15,000 of personal savings and would really like to start within the next six months.

CASE QUESTIONS

1. How much money must Lori have to start the franchise?

2. Where should Lori go for additional financing?

3. What should Lori know about Singapore before franchising? Why?

4. How important is it for Lori to be a native of Singapore before starting to franchise?

REFERENCES

Ashman, Richard T., "Born in the U.S.A.," "Although Uniquely American in Method and Style, Franchising is Making a Hit Internationally," *Nation's Business* 74 (November 1986): 41.

Bartlett, Christopher A. and Sumantra Ghoshal, Sumantra, *Managing Across Borders* (Cambridge, MA: Harvard Business School Press, 1989).

Brennan, Denise M., "International," *Restaurant Business Magazine* 86 (20 March 1987): 172.

Cherkasky, William B., "Foreign Markets Open for Franchisors," *Nation's Restaurant News* 19 (12 August 1985): 11.

Clark, Terry, "National Boundaries, Border Zones, and Market Strategy: A Conceptual Framework and Theoretical Model of Secondary Boundary Effects," *Journal of Marketing* (July 1994): 67–80.

Coulombe, Charles A., "Global Expansion: The Unstoppable Crusade," *Success* (September 1994): 18–20.

Dunnigan, J. A., "Franchising in Maple Leaf Country," *Entrepreneurs Franchise Yearbook* 2 (1987/88): 308–312.

Gilmour, John, "Business Expansion through Franchising," *Accountant's Magazine* 90 (August 1986): 26.

International Franchise Association, *The Future of Franchising: Looking Twenty-Five Years Ahead to the Year 2010* (Washington, DC: The Naisbitt Group for IFA, 1986), 1.

Justis, Robert T. and Cheryl Babcock, "Franchising: Strategies in East Asia," *Proceedings of the Pan Pacific Conference*, May 1987, 588–590.

Justis, Robert T. and Eiji Kuriyama, "Franchising: A Growing Phenomena in Japan," *Proceedings of the Pan Pacific Conference*, May 1987, 571–587.

Kandemir, Destan, and G. Tomas Hult, "A Conceptualization of an Organizational Learning Culture in International Joint Ventures," *Industrial Marketing Management* 34(5) (July 2005): 98.

Karel, Willem, Jan, "Brand Strategy Positions Products World-Wide," *Journal of Business Strategy* 3 (May-June 1991): 16–19.

Keegan, Warren J., *Multinational Marketing Management*, 5th ed. (Englewood Cliffs, NJ: Prentice Hall, 1995).

Schmitt, Bernard H. and Yigang Pan, "In Asia, the Supermarket Means Sales," *The New York Times* (19 February 1995), 3, sec. 11:2.

Wooldridge, J. "Fast Food Universe," *Miami Herald* (28 November 2004): J1.

Zeidman, Philip F., "Franchising 'Down Under': New Legislation Poses a Challenge to Australian Food Service Operators," *Nation's Restaurant News* 20 (6 October 1986), F51.

IN-DEPTH CASE STUDY: THE HARLEY-DAVIDSON MOTORCYCLE COMPANY*

23-1   HISTORY

Harley Davidson has become a leader in the motorcycle industry. The company has become an icon with many riders and nonriders alike. Harley-Davidson was started by William Harley and friend Arthur R. Davidson in 1903. In that year, Mr. Harley and Mr. Davidson made their first motorcycle available to the public under the Harley-Davidson name. The company started in a ten by fifteen foot shed in the backyard of the Davidson's family home in Milwaukee, Wisconsin.

In 1907, the company moved to Juneau Avenue, where the company has its present offices. Also in that year, the company was incorporated into Harley-Davidson and the stock was split between the founders. By 1911, the Harley-Davidson logo with the bar and shield was trademarked at the U.S. Patent Office. In 1918, "almost half of all Harley-Davidson motorcycles produced [were] sold for use by the U.S. military in World War I. At War's end, it is estimated that the Army used some 20,000 motorcycles in their efforts, most of which were Harley-Davidsons."[1]

Through the next fifty years, Harley-Davidson would grow and create new products in the motorcycling industry. In 1969, Harley-Davidson made the strategic decision to merge with American Machine and Foundry Company (AMF), a longtime producer of leisure products. Harley-Davidson under the management of AMF started producing more motorcycles. By the mid-1970s, production of Harley-Davidson motorcycles had almost tripled. During this time, the Japanese motorcycle makers gained ground on Harley-Davidson because of AMF's continuance of ignoring key competition. Harleys became know as the "mechanics bikes," because of their reduced reliability. In 1975, Honda Motor Company introduced the Gold Wing, which directly competed with Harley-Davidson's premier motorcycle. Because the Gold Wing was cheaper, the market share held by Harley-Davidson dwindled.

The AMF years for the company saw weak profits due to (1) increased competition in the market from strong overseas competitors, and (2) decreased quality in the overall product line in comparison to the competition. In 1981, thirteen Harley-Davidson senior executives signed a letter of intent to purchase Harley-Davidson Motor Company from AMF. By mid-June, the buyback was official, and the phrase "The Eagle Soars Alone" becomes a rallying cry. The $65 million buyout signaled a changing time for Harley-Davidson. Once privatization of Harley-Davidson was complete, a materials as needed (MAN) application became part of the production process. In this

---

* This case was prepared by Douglas Cluney, MBA candidate at University of Illinois at Springfield, under the direction of Richard Judd. Sources are from public documentation of Harley-Davidson Company and a personal interview with an HD franchisee. All rights are reserved by the authors.

system, motorcycle parts and raw materials are purchased and built only as required. This approach dramatically lowered production costs and improved quality, which Harley-Davidson desperately needed at the time. The buyer power of Harley-Davidson became evident again by way of supply vendors' increased quality of production parts and strict standards initiated in the motorcycle assembly process.

Ensuing years saw Harley Davidson continuing to struggle in the face of strong foreign competition. In 1985, the company found itself on the doorstep of closure. HD made a deal with Heller Financial to continue the funding of its operations. In 1986, the company listed on the American Stock Exchange (ASE), the first time since the merger with AMF. In 1987, Harley-Davidson was listed on the New York Stock Exchange (NYSE).

During the private years of HD, research and development of products became a big issue. Company managers utilized a computer-aided design (CAD) system to make changes to the production line in order to increase efficiency. The system had a direct payoff with efficiency of operations almost doubling.

In 1992, the Harley Davidson Company acquired a minority interest in the Buell Motorcycle Company, a manufacturer of sport and performance motorcycles. Minor ownership in Buell was based on an opportunity for Harley-Davidson to compete in other small market niches. In 1998, Harley Davidson bought an additional 49 percent interest in Buell. Erik Buell was named chairman of Buell operations. In 1998, Harley-Davidson established its first international presence in Manaus, Brazil.

Harley-Davidson improved supply chain management by calling on the help of former John Deere and Honda employee Garry Berryman. Because of the intense bureaucratic structure, Berryman had to transform the supply chain management system in the right direction. With the help of the Web and new technology, Berryman formed alliances with suppliers to help bring an end to faulty supply chain systems. The new system helped Harley-Davidson increase efficiency of operations and the satisfaction of customers.

Since the late 1990s, Harley-Davidson has introduced many new ideas and concepts into the motorcycle industry. The company has several factories, including those located in Wauwatosa, Wisconsin; York, Pennsylvania; and Kansas City, Missouri. With the invention of the V-Rod, Harley-Davidson intends to gain market share in the younger-age market segments. The V-Rod is Harley-Davidson's first motorcycle to combine fuel injection, overhead cams, and liquid cooling; and it delivers 115 horsepower.

23-2   CORPORATE GOVERNANCE

The Harley-Davidson Board of Directors and management believe that the company, in the interests of its stakeholders, should embrace corporate governance practices in keeping with the leadership position in business and current legislation and rules.[2] Harley-Davidson management believes in independence and structures of its committees to ensure fair and equitable running of the organization. Since the company went public, the board has improved the profitability and efficiency of operations. President and CEO, James L. Ziemer, states that "excellent corporate governance has been a long standing practice at harley-Davidson, because it makes good business sense". The HD Board is composed of accomplished leaders from a range of industries who meet regularly to plan for future growth and review Company objectives."[3] See Figure 23-1 lists the 2007 members of the board.

> Directors who are employees of the Company do not receive any special compensation for their services as directors. Directors who are not employees of the Company ('Non-employee Directors') receive an annual retainer fee of $100,000, an additional annual retainer of $10,000 for serving as the chair of the Audit Committee and an additional annual retainer fee of $5,000

BARRY K. ALLEN, has been a director of the company since 1992.

RICHARD I. BEATTIE, has been a director of the company since 1996.

GEORGE H. CONRADES, has been a director of the company since May 2002.

SARA L. LEVINSON,, has been a director of the company since 1996.

GEORGE L. MILES, JR., has been a director of the company since August 2002.

JEFFREY L. BLEUSTEIN, has served as Chairman of the Board and is the former CEO. He has been a director of the company since 1996.

DONALD A. JAMES, has been a director of the company since 1991. He is the Chairman and CEO of a large independent franchise HD dealership network.

JAMES A. NORLING, has been a director of the company since 1993.

JOCHEN ZEITS, The newly elected member of the Board of Directors, is Chief Executive Officer and Chairman of Puma AG. Jochen brings a wealth of international consumer products experience as well as financial management, market and brand management expertise to the Board.

FIGURE **23-1**

Harley-Davidson Board of Directors Directors (2007)

Source: Harley-Davidson, Inc. *website.* August 16, 2007.

for serving as chair of the Human Resources Committee or Nominating Committee. Members of the Audit Committee, other than the Chair, receive an additional $5,000 annual retainer fee for serving as a member of the Audit Committee. A Non-employee Director may elect to receive 50% or 100% of the annual fee to be paid in each calendar year in the form of Common Stock based upon the fair market value of the Common Stock at the time of the annual meeting of shareholders. Directors must receive a minimum of one-half (1/2) of their annual retainer in Company Common Stock until the Director reaches the stock ownership goals established in the Director and Senior Executive Stock Ownership Guidelines for Harley-Davidson, Inc.

In addition, a clothing allowance of $1,500 to purchase Harley-Davidson® MotorClothes® apparel and accessories is also provided to Non-employee Directors, along with a discount on Company products that is the same discount available to all employees of the Company.[4]

In 2005, the directors of Harley-Davidson and executive officers owned 4,625,205 shares of stock collectively. The biggest shareholder of them all was Bleustein with 2,061,255 shares. The largest shareholder, AXA Assurance I.A.R.D. Mutuelle, owned 19,222,080 shares.

23-3   CODE OF ETHICS

Harley-Davidson's code of ethics is appropriately titled, "Everyday Values: A Harley-Davidson Code of Business Conduct."

On January 20, 2003, the Board approved a revised Code of Business Conduct that applies to all employees of the Company as well as the directors. The Code of Business Conduct is a comprehensive document that is based on the Company's corporate values: *Tell the Truth, Be Fair, Keep Your Promises, Respect the Individual* and *Encourage Intellectual Curiosity.* The Code of Business Conduct updates the 1992 version and is intended to promote honest and ethical conduct and to provide guidance for the appropriate handling of various business situations. The Code of Business Conduct discusses the following issues: communications (e.g., e-mail, internet, voicemail, media contact), compliance with laws, confidential information and intellectual property, conflict of interest, environmental responsibilities, fair dealing (e.g., accurate advertising, antitrust laws, gifts, selecting suppliers), fair employment, fraud and misrepresentation, government, insider trading, privacy, work environment, and reporting procedures. The Code of Business Conduct provides that employees and directors have a responsibility to report possible violations of the Code of Business Conduct by calling a toll free number set forth in the Code of Business Conduct. The General Counsel of the Company regularly reports to the Nominating Committee on matters related to the Code of Business Conduct.[5]

In the code of ethics, the CEO addresses the entire organization in a letter stating that the Harley-Davidson company is a family. Also, the employees feel a "strong sense of pride knowing that you have been entrusted with preserving the Harley-Davidson legacy."[6]

Harley-Davidson also has a financial code of ethics. The document reiterates the general code by stating the employees' and executives' responsibility to be ethical. The code regarding finances helps to "ensure full, fair, accurate, timely, and understandable disclosure of financial and other information regarding the Company."[7] The financial code states twelve guiding principles that employees should follow. Some of them include avoiding conflicts of interest, acting honestly and ethically, complying with all rules and regulations, maintaining skills for the company's needs, and promoting ethical behavior in the workplace. If any of the principles are violated, the company can discipline or even terminate employment of the individual.

23-4   HARLEY OWNERS GROUP AND MARKETING

The Harley Owners Group, or HOG for short, had 840,000 members in 1,370 chapters worldwide in 2003. Today there are nearly 1 million members. The group has changed the way that Harley riders feel and changed the image of Harley-Davidson. In August 2003, HOG celebrated its twenty-year anniversary. The mission of the Harley Owners Group is "To Ride and Have Fun." HOG is a way that Harley-Davidson makes their motorcycles one big family. As the largest motorcycle club in the world, Harley-Davidson does what no other company can do, which is to "Be a member of a Family." The group even has its own magazine called *Hog Tales*, the official publication of the Harley Owners Group®. Harley-Davidson also publishes a magazine called the *Enthusiast*. HOG hosts many rallies and events around the world, with riding and meeting new people its top priorities. Like HOG, the Buell Riders Adventure Group (BRAG) was created to act as a family support for owners of Buell motorcycles. Both groups give a sense of companionship that no other motorcycle group has achieved. These groups also promote Harley-Davidson's favorable visibility and strengthen the relationships among the Harley-Davidson family.

Harley-Davidson markets in a variety of ways, including dealer promotions, customer events, and advertising through television, print, and direct mailings. In one promotion, Harley teamed with Ford to create the Harley-Davidson Ford truck. "Ford built 8,200 F-150 extended-cab Harley-Davidsons with exclusive Harley-Davidson badging, 20-inch chrome wheels and a distinct grille."[8] The business-to-business relationship helped both companies. Harley also sponsors major racing events and rallies. "The Company website (www.harley-davidson.com) is also utilized to market its products and services and features an online catalog which allows customers to create and share product wish lists, utilize a dealer locator and place catalog orders. Internet catalog orders are fulfilled by participating authorized Harley-Davidson dealers as selected by the customer." [9]

23-5   DISTRIBUTION [10]

23-5a   Distribution in the United States

Harley-Davidson's basic channel of distribution in the United States for its motorcycles and related products consists of approximately 648 independently owned full service Harley-Davidson dealerships to whom the company sells directly. This includes 439 combined Harley-Davidson and Buell dealerships. There are no Buell-only dealerships. With respect to sales of new motorcycles, approximately 81 percent of the U.S. dealerships sell the company's motorcycles exclusively. All dealerships stock and sell the company's genuine replacement parts, accessories, and MotorClothes™ apparel and collectibles, and perform service for the company's motorcycles. The company also sells a smaller portion of its parts and accessories and general merchandise through *nontraditional* retail outlets. The nontraditional outlets, which are extensions of the main dealership, consist of secondary retail locations (SRLs), alternate retail outlets (AROs), and seasonal retail outlets (SROs). SRLs, also known as Harley Shops, are satellites of the main dealership and are developed to meet the service needs of the company's riding customers. Harley Shops also provide replacement parts and accessories, MotorClothes apparel, and collectibles, and are authorized to sell new motorcycles. AROs are located primarily in high-traffic areas such as malls, airports, or popular vacation destinations and focus on selling the company's MotorClothes apparel and collectibles and licensed products. SROs are located in similar high-traffic areas, but operate on a seasonal basis out of temporary locations such as vendor kiosks. AROs and SROs are not authorized to sell new motorcycles. There are approximately eighty-five SRLs, fifty-five AROs, and ten SROs located in the United States.

23-5b   Distribution in Europe

Harley-Davidson's European management team is based out of a subsidiary located in the United Kingdom and is responsible for all sales, marketing, and distribution activities in the European region (Europe/Middle East/Africa). The United Kingdom operation is further supported by six subsidiaries in France, Germany, Italy, the Netherlands, Spain, Switzerland, and eight independent distributors throughout the region. In the European region, there are approximately 383 independent Harley-Davidson dealerships serving thirty-two country markets. This includes 247 combined Harley-Davidson and Buell dealerships. Buell is further represented by ten dealerships that do not sell Harley-Davidson motorcycles. In addition, the company's dealer network includes thirty-one AROs across the thirty-two European country markets.

23-5c   Distribution in Asia/Pacific

The Asia/Pacific region is currently served by 221 independent HD dealers serving nine country markets. Of these dealers, ninety sell both Harley-Davidson and Buell products, whereas three are Buell-only dealerships. Japan, which is the largest market in this region, is managed directly from the company's subsidiary in Tokyo. Operations of this subsidiary include sales, marketing, and distribution of product to the country's network of 159 independent dealers. Independent distributors manage distribution for the region's second largest market, Australia/New Zealand, with fifty-three dealerships currently in operation. Of these, twenty-four sell both Harley-Davidson and Buell products. The company ships product directly from its U.S. operations to the remaining Asia/Pacific dealerships which are located in East and Southeast Asia.

23-5d   Distribution in Latin America

In Latin America, fifteen country markets are served by thirty dealerships and six AROs/SROs. Mexico is currently the largest Harley-Davidson market in Latin America. Mexico's ten independent dealers are served by an independent distributor who distributes product through a warehouse in Laredo, Texas. In Brazil, the region's second largest market, motorcycles and related products are distributed by an independent distributor. Some models sold in Brazil are assembled locally at the company's subsidiary in Manaus. The remaining dealerships in Latin America receive product that is shipped directly from the company's U.S. operation.

23-5e Distribution in Canada

In Canada, there are approximately seventy-five independent Harley-Davidson dealerships, one independent stand-alone Buell dealership, and six AROs, all served by a single independent distributor, Fred Deeley Imports Ltd. This network includes forty-two combined Harley-Davidson and Buell dealerships resulting in a total of forty-three Buell dealerships in Canada.

23-6 COMPETITION

Competition in the motorcycle industry is just like in any other market. Some companies have most of the market share and others have the rest. Fortunately, Harley-Davidson has most of the market share in the United States. Competition for Harley-Davidson is based on the highly competitive 651+cc market.("cc" means cubic inch motor displacement size).. Harley-Davidson's major competitors are based outside the United States and generally have financial and marketing resources that are substantially greater than those of Harley. "They also have larger worldwide revenue and are more diversified than the Company. In addition to these larger, established competitors, the Company has competitors headquartered in the U.S. The U.S. competitors generally offer heavyweight motorcycles with traditional styling that compete directly with many of the Company's products. These competitors currently have production and sales volumes that are lower than the Company's and does not hold a significant market share."[11]

Competition in the heavyweight market is based on such factors as price, quality, reliability, styling, product features, customer preference, and warranties. "The Company emphasizes quality, reliability, and styling in its products and offers a [two-] year warranty for its motorcycles. The Company regards its support of the motorcycling lifestyle in the form of events, rides, rallies, H.O.G.® and its financing through HDFS as a competitive advantage. In general, resale prices for used Harley-Davidson motorcycles, as a percentage of prices when new, are significantly higher than resale prices for used motorcycles of the Company's competitors."[12]

23-7 MARKET SHARE

In the United States, Harley-Davidson competes primarily in the touring and custom segments of the heavyweight motorcycle division. These segments accounted for 82 percent of total heavyweight retail unit sales in 2003 in the United States. The most profitable motorcycles for Harley-Davidson are the custom and touring motorcycles which represent one-half the total U.S. motorcycle market. "For the last 16 years, the Company has led the industry in domestic (United States) retail unit sales of heavyweight motorcycles. The Company's share of the heavyweight market was 50.3% in 2003 compared to 48.2% in 2002. This share is significantly greater than the Company's largest competitor in the domestic market which ended 2003 with an 18.4% market share."[13] Figure 23-2 shows the U.S. market share from 1999 to 2003.

Note in Figure 23-2 that the Harley-Davidson brand has increased over the past three years, whereas the Buell brand has become stagnate.

International markets have been a problem for Harley-Davidson. (See Figure 23-3.) The company has a majority of share in the Asia/Pacific market at 25.8 percent, but has a minority share behind five other manufacturers in Europe. The market share in Europe is 8.1 percent behind Honda's 16.7 percent, Yamaha's 16 percent, Suzuki's 15.5 percent, BMW's 15.3 percent, and Kawasaki's 10 percent.[14]

	Year Ended December 31,				
	2003	**2002**	**2001**	**2000**	**1999**
New U.S. Registrations (thousands of units):					
Total market new registrations	461.2	442.3	394.3	340.0	275.6
Harley-Davidson new registrations	228.4	209.3	177.4	155.1	134.5
Buell new registrations	3.5	2.9	2.6	4.2	3.9
Total company new registrations	231.9	212.2	180.0	159.3	138.4
Percentage Market Share:					
Harley-Davidson® motorcycles	49.5%	47.5%	45.0%	45.6%	48.8%
Buell® motorcycles	0.8	0.7	0.7	1.2	1.4
Total Company	50.3	48.2	45.7	46.8	50.2
Honda	18.4	19.8	20.5	18.5	16.4
Suzuki	9.8	9.6	10.8	9.3	9.4
Kawasaki	6.7	6.9	8.0	9.0	10.3
Yamaha	8.5	8.9	7.9	8.4	7.0
Other	6.3	6.6	7.1	8.0	6.7
Total	100.0%	100.0%	100.0%	100.0%	100.0%

*Motorcycle registration and market share information has been derived from data published by the Motorcycle Industry Council (MIC).

FIGURE 23-2

Market Share of U.S. Heavyweight Motorcycles* (Engine Displacement of 651+cc)

Source: Harley-Davidson, Inc., *2003 Form 10-K, 9.*

23-8 DEMOGRAPHICS

Harley-Davison has increased interest among women riders. A big component is the new designs of the stores and the family atmosphere of the Harley Clubs. Figure 23-4 shows the slight increase of female Harley owners over the past few years. Figures 23-5 and 23-6 profile likely buyers and the increase of median age of a rider. In 2003, the average age is approximately forty-seven, which could be contributed to the aging population of the United States. Median income also raised, indicating Harley-Davidson's strong reputation for desirability among the wealthy (see Figure 23-6). Harley has tried to appeal to the younger generation as well by creating the Sportster. The company also made it attractive to buy: "Harley used a no money down promotion to move its smallest bike, the Sportster."[15] With Harley apparel and better stores, the company brings more women into the stores than ever before. "Harley's new riders are women, and most buyers are in their mid- to upper 40s."[16]

23-9 PRODUCT AND PRICING

As stated, Harley-Davidson has many styles of motorcycles. The V-Rod and the Sportster have been great additions to the Harley-Davidson line. The manufacturing of the motorcycles involves many operations, including purchasing from suppliers with long-term mutually beneficial agreements.

	2003		2002		2001	
	Units	% Share	Units	% Share	Units	% Share
North America[1]						
Harley-Davidson new registrations	238.3	48.1%	220.1	46.4%	185.6	43.9%
Buell new registrations	3.7	0.8	3.0	0.6	2.7	0.6
Company registrations	242.0	48.9%	223.1	47.0%	188.3	44.5%
Market new registrations	495.5		475.0		422.8	
Europe[2]						
Harley-Davidson new registrations	26.3	8.1%	23.5	7.1%	22.8	7.1%
Buell new registrations	4.0	1.2	1.9	0.6	2.3	0.7
Company registrations	30.3	9.3%	25.5	7.7%	25.1	7.8%
Market new registrations	323.1		331.8		319.9	
Japan/Australia[3]						
Harley-Davidson new registrations	15.2	25.8%	13.6	21.3%	12.7	20.4%
Buell new registrations	1.0	1.7	0.7	1.2	0.7	1.2
Company registrations	16.2	27.5%	14.3	22.5%	13.4	21.6%
Market new registrations	58.9		63.9		2.1	
Total[4]						
Harley-Davidson new registrations	279.8	31.9%	257.2	29.6%	221.1	27.5%
Buell new registrations	8.7	1.0	5.6	0.7	5.7	0.7
Company registrations	288.5	32.9%	262.8	30.3%	226.8	28.2%
Market new registrations	877.5		870.7		804.8	

[1] Includes the United States and Canada. Data provided by the Motorcycle Industry Council (MIC).
[2] Europe data, provided by Giral S.A., includes retail sales in Austria, Belgium, France, Germany, Italy, The Netherlands, Spain, Switzerland, United Kingdom, Denmark, Finland, Greece, Norway, Portugal, and Sweden.
[3] Data provided by ERG International and industry sources.
[4] Includes the North American, European, and Japan/Australia markets as defined above.

FIGURE 23-3

Worldwide Heavyweight Motorcycle Registration Data (Engine Displacement of 651+cc) (Units in thousands)
Source: Harley-Davidson, Inc., *2003 Form 10-K.*

GENDER	1999	2000	2001	2002	2003
Male	91%	91%	91%	91%	90%
Female	9%	9%	9%	9%	10%

FIGURE 23-4

Demographic Profile (1999–2003)
Source: Harley-Davidson, Demographics.com, accessed August 2004.

44%	Owned Harley-Davidson® motorcycle previously
28%	Coming off of competitive motorcycle
28%	New to motorcycling or haven't owned a motorcycle for at least the past five years

FIGURE **23-5**

2003 Purchasers
Source: Harley-Davidson, Demographics.com, accessed August 2004.

FIGURE **23-6**

Median Age and Income
Source: Harley-Davidson, Demographics.com, accessed August 2004.

Through the relationships of the suppliers, Harley gains access to "technical and commercial resources for application directly to product design, development and manufacturing initiatives and gains commitment from suppliers to advance Company interests efficiently and effectively"[17]. Harley-Davidson also has a strategy for its manufacturing. It is designed to increase capacity, improve product quality, reduce costs, and increase flexibility to respond to changes in the marketplace. "The Motor Company incorporates manufacturing techniques focused on continuous improvement. These techniques, which include employee involvement, just-in-time inventory principles, partnering agreements with the local unions, high performance work organizations and statistical process control, are designed to improve product quality, productivity and asset utilization in the production of Harley-Davidson® motorcycles."[18]

The future products of the company will likely have the same style that made Harley-Davidson a popular name. In an interview with *Money* magazine, Bleustein said the new products will display much innovation: "There's a lot of life left in our classical line concept, so we're planning a lot of innovation around that. We're also developing a whole line around the V-Rod motorcycle—a new line of high-performance motorcycles, our first with liquid-cooled engines."[19]

Another hot product of Harley-Davidson is the MotorClothes apparel and collectibles. General merchandise grew from 2002 to 2003 by 13 percent, not including the spike in sales for the hundredth year anniversary merchandise. The gross sales for general merchandise were $211.4 million in 2003. Sales in general merchandise has risen every year for the past five years.

Pricing of the motorcycles depends on style and options. Most of Harley-Davidson motorcycles are custom, so they are built to order. Suggested retail prices can range from the lower $20,000 for an Ultra Classic Electra Glide-FLHTCUI down to about $7,000 for a Sportster. The higher end motorcycles are equipped for long-distance trips with windshields, saddlebags, fairings, and luggage carriers. The highest volume in the Harley-Davidson product line is the custom motorcycles. Like the Toyota of the car industry, the customs command a premium price because of the options and high resale value.

As stated, Harley-Davidson has major manufacturing plants in Kansas City, Missouri; York, Pennsylvania; and Wauwatosa, Wisconsin. In 2007, HD offices and other manufacturing facilities are located around the world. The newest facility in York reached full production capability in early 2004. The Softail motorcycles are built in the York facility. This "flexible" manufacturing facility can modify its operations processes to other manufacturing needs of HD. "From 1996 to 2003, Harley-Davidson added more than 2 million square feet of production and design space and capital expenditures on facilities and production capabilities have been 1.5 billion in the last 5 years."[20] Capacity management is the key to success of the manufacturing operations of Harley-Davidson.

23-10 GOVERNMENTAL REGULATIONS

As a manufacturer of motorcycles, HD has similar regulations to those of the auto industry. The EPA watches for waste and emissions output of not only the manufacturing plant, but also the finished product—a Harley-Davidson motorcycle. "The Company is involved with government agencies and groups of potentially responsible parties in various environmental matters, including a matter involving the clean up of soil and groundwater contamination at its York, Pennsylvania facility. The Company estimates that its share of the future Response Costs at the York facility will be approximately $7.3 million."[21]OSHA watches over the safety of the employees in the manufacturing plants. In 2002, however, a major governmental regulation hit Harley hard in the form of steel tariffs imposed by the U.S. government on the European Union. U.S. tariffs threatened Harley-Davidson's sales in Europe. "Domestic steel buyers eager to circumvent the three-year tariffs will have lobbyists and sympathetic lawmakers vociferously making their case to the Administration. Combine that with threats from Europe to retaliate against American steel and other goods—from Florida oranges to Harley-Davidson motorcycles—and the result could be loopholes big enough to drive a flatbed of cold-rolled sheet metal through."[22]

China's restrictions on foreign imports are hurting potential profits for Harley-Davidson. The Chinese market produces about half (14 million) of the world's total motorcycles. The stronger Chinese economy means that people are finding new ways to get travel. "Harley's straight talkers said out load what few groveling multinational bigwigs dare to utter in public about China—that its barriers are hurting foreign business even after the country's entry into the World Trade Organization. Clearly, foreign suppliers of motorcycles aren't benefiting from China's prosperity—imports actually fell to 296 motorcycles last year, worth $1 million, compared with 1,833 bikes in 2001, worth $1.3 million."[23]

23-11 DEALERSHIP FRANCHISE

Harley-Davidson has a vast network of dealers in the company. Every dealership is independently owned and operated. The Harley-Davidson company does not run any of the stores that sell motorcycles or apparel. There are approximately 650 independently owned full service Harley-Davidson franchised dealerships to which the company sells directly. Refer to section 23-5a for additional data regarding distribution.

Consider one independent dealer, Stan Hall, of Hall's Harley-Davidson. Hall had just moved into a bigger and better facility. "Since 1999, nearly 500 U.S. Harley-Davidson dealerships have expanded, relocated, or undergone renovation."[24] Harley-Davidson assigns potential markets by population. "They assign a number to a market. The number of bikes is governed by size and square feet of the facility."[25] The core products such as motorcycles and parts are sold at traditional stores. Stan also went on to say that Harley-Davidson gives special marketing rights to the independent dealerships if they have adequate facilities.

Another aspect of Harley-Davidson is the dealership network of apparel. "Apparel is attracting more women customers into the store. Cash flow at Christmas time has increased because of the apparel."[26] Hall also went on to say that it seems like women are encouraging men to stop at the stores now because of the selection of apparel and jewelry offered at the dealerships.

When it comes to quality control over the dealership system, Harley-Davidson has a system. "Harley-Davidson has a Bar and Shield criteria for standards at the dealerships. It is a point system in which advertising, service, computer system, and other criteria are measured. If you score high, the dealership will get extra motorcycles to sell."[27] The dealerships also get measured by how other dealerships are selling. For a fee, Harley-Davidson will send the dealership sales from comparable sized dealerships in a report called the "Dealer Dashboard." The report is a good way for the franchisee to gauge the potential profitability of the dealership. Also, it helps determine if changes are needed to the dealership to help increase sales and profits.

Harley-Davison and its dealership network seem to work good together. Because of the demand for the Harley-Davidson products, the motorcycles almost sell themselves. There may be a concern with one aspect of Harley-Davidson moving forward. With the new facility in York, the capacity to build more motorcycles has increased. So, the concern of overproduction and over-crowding of the market has increased. The future will determine if the market can sustain an increase in production.

23-12   FINANCIAL SERVICES[28]

Harley-Davidson Financial Services (HDFS) serves the customers of Harley-Davidson and Buell motorcycles. HDFS is engaged in the business of financing and servicing wholesale inventory receivables and consumer retail loans (primarily for the purchase of motorcycles). Additionally, HDFS is an agency for certain unaffiliated insurance carriers providing property and casualty insurance and extended service contracts to motorcycle owners. HDFS conducts business in the United States, Canada, and Europe.

HDFS, operating under the trade name Harley-Davidson Credit and Insurance, provides whole-sale financial services to Harley-Davidson and Buell dealers and retail financing to consumers. Wholesale financial services include floor plan and open account financing of motorcycles and motorcycle parts and accessories, real estate loans, computer loans, showroom remodeling loans, and the brokerage of a range of commercial insurance products. HDFS offers wholesale financial services to Harley-Davidson dealers in the United States and Canada, and during 2003, approximately 95 percent of such dealers utilized those services. Prior to August 2002, HDFS offered wholesale financing to some of the company's European motorcycle dealers through a joint venture with Transamerica Distribution Finance. In August 2002, HDFS terminated this joint venture relationship and began directly serving the wholesale financing needs of some European dealers. The wholesale finance operations of HDFS are located in Plano, Texas, and Oxford, England.

Retail financial services include installment lending for new and used Harley-Davidson and Buell motorcycles and the brokerage of a range of motorcycle insurance policies and extended service warranty agreements. HDFS acts as an insurance agent and does not assume underwriting risk with regard to insurance policies and extended service warranty agreements.

23-13 FINANCIALS

Harley-Davidson has been strong in the motorcycle field for a long time. The company has continually sold every motorcycle it manufactures. "Harley is, indeed, burning tread. Over the past five years, sales have grown 18% per year compounded, while earnings shot up 26% annually."[29] Harley has also been able to sustain double-digit revenues for eighteen years. The CEO of Harley was asked about sustaining the growth: "New products, exciting new services are a very important part of our business model. We spend well over $1 billion expanding capacity over the last decade, the idea being to grow our production capacity steadily, while also growing demand for our products. You always need something exciting coming along that will sustain your growth in the future."[30]

The income statement, balance sheet, and cash flows statement are given for inspection of the company's overall assessment, as shown in Figures 23-7, 23-8, and 23-9. The figures were all year ending December 31, 2003. The income and cash flows statements have three years' worth of data and the balance sheet has two years' worth. At the end of 2003, Harley-Davidson's earnings per share were $2.52, up from $1.92 one year earlier. Net income rose by almost 31.1 percent from 2002 to 2003, and consolidated revenue was $4.62 billion, a 13 percent increase over 2002. The rise could be attributed to the hundred-year anniversary of Harley-Davidson. "The Company shipped 291,147 Harley-Davidson motorcycles in 2003, a 10.4% increase over 2002 and nearly double the 150,818 motorcycles produced just five years ago. Retail sales of Harley-Davidson motorcycles for 2003 grow 8.8% in the United States, 11.8% in Europe, and 8.3% in Japan, outpacing the

---

HARLEY-DAVIDSON, INC.
CONSOLIDATED STATEMENTS OF INCOME
YEARS ENDED DECEMBER 31, 2003, 2002, AND 2001
(IN THOUSANDS, EXCEPT PER SHARE AMOUNTS)

	2003	2002	2001
Net revenue	$ 4,624,274	$ 4,090,970	$ 3,406,786
Cost of goods sold	2,958,708	2,673,129	2,253,815
Gross profit	1,665,566	1,417,841	1,152,971
Financial services income	279,459	211,500	181,545
Financial services expense	111,586	107,273	120,272
Operating income from financial services	167,873	104,227	61,273
Selling, administrative and engineering expense	684,175	639,366	551,743
Income from operations	1,149,264	882,702	662,501
Interest income, net	23,088	16,541	17,478
Other, net	(6,317)	(13,416)	(6,524)
Income before provision for income taxes	1,166,035	885,827	673,455
Provision for income taxes	405,107	305,610	235,709
Net income	$760,928	$580,217	$437,746
Basic earnings per common share	$ 2.52	$1.92	$1.45
Diluted earnings per common share	$ 2.50	$1.90	$1.43
Cash dividends per common share	$ 0.195	$0.135	$0.115

FIGURE **23-7**

Income

HARLEY-DAVIDSON, INC.
CONSOLIDATED BALANCE SHEETS
DECEMBER 31, 2003 AND 2002
(IN THOUSANDS, EXCEPT SHARE AMOUNTS)

	2003	2002
ASSETS		
Current assets:		
Cash and cash equivalents	$812,449	$280,928
Marketable securities	510,211	514,800
Accounts receivable, net	112,406	108,694
Current portion of finance receivables, net	1,001,990	855,771
Inventories	207,726	218,156
Deferred income taxes	51,156	41,430
Prepaid expenses & other current assets	33,189	46,807
Total current assets	2,729,127	2,066,586
Finance receivables, net	735,859	589,809
Property, plant, and equipment, net	1,046,310	1,032,596
Goodwill	53,678	49,930
Other assets	358,114	122,296
	$4,923,088	$3,861,217
LIABILITIES AND SHAREHOLDERS' EQUITY		
Current liabilities:		
Accounts payable	$223,902	$226,977
Accrued expenses and other liabilities	407,566	380,496
Current portion of finance debt	324,305	382,579
Total current liabilities	955,773	990,052
Finance debt	670,000	380,000
Other long-term liabilities	86,337	123,353
Postretirement health care benefits	127,444	105,419
Deferred income taxes	125,842	29,478
Commitments and contingencies (Note 5) (delete)		
Shareholders' equity:		
Series A Junior participating preferred stock, none issued	—	—
Common stock, 326,489,291 and 325,298,404 shares issued in 2003 and 2002, respectively	3,266	3,254
Additional paid-in capital	419,455	386,284
Retained earnings	3,074,037	2,372,095
Accumulated other comprehensive income (loss)	47,174	(46,266)
	3,543,932	2,715,367
Less:		
Treasury stock (24,978,798 and 22,636,295 shares in 2003 and 2002, respectively), at cost	(586,240)	(482,360)
Unearned compensation	—	(92)
Total shareholders' equity	2,957,692	2,232,915
	$4,923,088	$3,861,217

FIGURE 23-8

Balance Sheets

HARLEY-DAVIDSON, INC.
CONSOLIDATED STATEMENTS OF CASH FLOWS
YEARS ENDED DECEMBER 31, 2003, 2002, AND 2001
(IN THOUSANDS)

	2003	2002	2001
Cash flows from operating activities:			
Net income	$760,928	$580,217	$437,746
Adjustments to reconcile net income to net cash provided by operating activities:			
Depreciation and amortization	196,918	175,778	153,061
Provision for long-term employee benefits	76,422	57,124	40,882
Provision for finance credit losses	4,076	6,167	22,178
Current year gain on securitizations	(82,221)	(56,139)	(45,037)
Collection of retained securitization interests	118,113	89,970	58,421
Contributions to pension plans	(192,000)	(153,636)	(19,294)
Tax benefit from the exercise of stock options	13,805	14,452	44,968
Deferred income taxes	42,105	38,560	(3,539)
Other	16,051	7,057	3,045
Net changes in current assets and current liabilities	(18,644)	16,089	57,773
Total adjustments	174,625	195,422	312,458
Net cash provided by operating activities	935,553	775,639	750,204
Cash flows from investing activities:			
Capital expenditures	(227,230)	(323,866)	(290,381)
Finance receivables acquired or originated	(6,528,945)	(5,574,248)	(4,349,940)
Finance receivables collected	4,536,661	3,933,125	3,123,941
Proceeds from securitizations	1,724,060	1,246,262	956,849
Purchase of marketable securities	(1,143,898)	(1,508,285)	(247,989)
Sales and redemptions of marketable securities	1,145,000	1,190,114	51,978
Other, net	9,690	22,813	(9,361)
Net cash used in investing activities	(484,662)	(1,014,085)	(764,903)
Cash flows from financing activities:			
Proceeds from issuance of medium term notes	399,953	—	—
Net (decrease) increase other finance debt	(175,835)	165,528	152,542
Dividends paid	(58,986)	(41,457)	(35,428)
Purchase of common stock for treasury	(103,880)	(56,814)	(111,552)
Issuance of common stock under employee stock option plans	19,378	12,679	28,839
Net cash provided by financing activities	80,630	79,936	34,401
Net increase (decrease) in cash and cash equivalents	531,521	(158,510)	19,702
Cash and cash equivalents:			
At beginning of year	280,928	439,438	419,736
At end of year	$812,449	$280,928	$439,438

FIGURE **23-9**

Cash Flows

Source: Harley-Davidson, Inc., *2003 Form 10K.*

YEAR-END MARKET VALUE OF $100 INVESTED ON 12/31/86

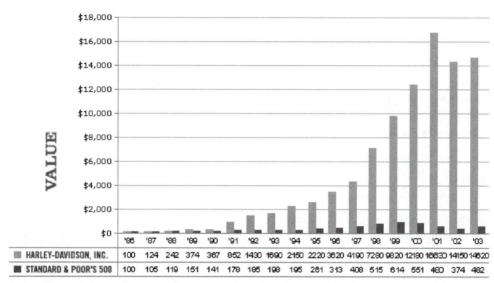

	'86	'87	'88	'89	'90	'91	'92	'93	'94	'95	'96	'97	'98	'99	'00	'01	'02	'03
HARLEY-DAVIDSON, INC.	100	124	242	374	367	852	1430	1690	2150	2220	3620	4190	7280	9820	12180	16630	14150	14620
STANDARD & POOR'S 500	100	105	119	151	141	178	185	198	195	261	313	408	515	614	551	480	374	482

If you had invested $100 in Harley-Davidson, Inc. common stock at the end of 1986, the year of our IPO, and reinvested all dividends, the value of your investment on December 31, 2003, would have been approximately $14,620.

FIGURE 23-10

Year-end Market Value of $100 Invested on December 31, 1986

Source: www.harley-davidson.com, accessed August 2004.

---

heavyweight motorcycle industry in those markets. Parts and Accessories revenue increased 13.3% to $712.8 million in 2003. Revenue for General Merchandise, which consists of MotorCloths™ apparel and collectibles, totaled $211.4 million."[31] Total liabilities fell from the current portion of financed debt, but increased in accrued expenses and other liabilities. Net cash flows had a substantial increase from 2002. Most of the cash flows came from the proceeds from insurance of medium term notes. The income tax rate is 34.7 percent for the year 2003. The current ratio for the year 2003 is 2.9 percent.

Harley-Davidson is listed on the NYSE under the symbol HDI. Harley-Davidson stock has performed extremely well over the past few years. The stock has gained more capital for Harley to use. Many have wondered how long Harley-Davidson can keep up the pace. The stock price has increased even during the recession period of 2002. The demand for Harley-Davidson motorcycles and the management's eye on expenses keep the price at a steady upward pace. In the initial public offering, no one would have imagined the price of the stock today. Figure 23-10 shows that $100 invested in Harley-Davison stock in 1986 is worth about $16,000 today (2007).

OPERATING HIGHLIGHTS OF HARLEY-DAVIDSON, INC. 2007:

Harley Davidson is a brand admired by young and old alike and recognized around the world. During the most recent ten year period (1996-2006) compound annual growth rates for revenues and earnings have been better than 14 percent and 23 percent, respectively. In 2006, motorcycles comprise 80 percent of sales, while parts and accessories comprise 15 percent and apparel and collectibles contribute 5 percent to overall sales. Operating highlights for 2006 are given below:

- $5.8 billion total revenue (up 8.6 percent from 2005)

- $1.04 billion net incomes (up 8.7 percent from 2005

- Repurchased 19.3 million shares of stock

- Return on average equity > 35 percent
- 349,196 H-D units shipped (up 6.1 percent from 2005)
- $3.93 annual EPS (up 15.2 percent from 2005)

Source: Harley-Davidson Fact sheet. www.Harley-Davidson.com access August 15-17, 2007.

The leadership of Harley Davidson appear to be firmly focused on the long-term by growing value and further strengthening the brand. The worldwide market for motorcycles is robust. The seasoned management team is supported by an empowered workforce and dealer network look forward to a bright future for Harley Davidson Motorcycle Company.

SUMMARY

Harley-Davidson Inc. has a long heritage of freedom on the road. Started in 1903, incorporated in 1981, and publicly traded in 1986, Harley has become an American icon. The continued growth in the company and family-oriented groups can reward Harley for years to come. "With a solid balance sheet, a return on equity of greater than 20% for the last 18 years, demonstrated cash-generating ability, state-of-the-art factories, a steady stream of new products and services, strong brands and the prospects of sustainable mid-teen annual earnings growth, Harley-Davidson is a great investment now and for the future."[32] With the dealership network of 1,300 stores, a clear mission, and strong leadership, Harley Davidson is likely to be a strong performer for both the company itself and its franchise dealer network for years to come.

Some questions remain to ponder. Should the franchise dealer network be expanded or should HD expand through corporate locations primarily or exclusively? What is the future of motorcycles as a means of travel as gas and oil costs continue to rise? What implications might there be for the company in the future? Should HD consider entering the motorbike or motor scooter markets? The baby boomer and the mid-to-upper-income buyers are the centerpiece of the customer base. What changes might there be in the future? Are there other customer segments that HD should consider? Can HD get stronger market penetration abroad? To do so, what countries, what kinds of cycles, and at what prices could HD produce and serve effectively? These are some of the questions that HD may be considering at this time.

NOTES

1. www.harley-davidson.com/history.
2. Harley-Davidson, Inc., *Corporate Governance Policy*, adopted 11 *December, 2002*.
3. Ibid., *2003 Annual Report*, 7.
4. Ibid., *2003 Proxy Statement*, 18. and HD Factsheet at www.HarleyDavison.com, *August 17, 2007*.
5. Ibid., 17.
6. Ibid., *Code of Business Conduct*, 4.
7. Ibid., *Financial Code of Ethics*, 1.
8. Jason Stein, "Marketing Matches Made in Heaven," *Automotive News* 78(6064) (27 October 2003).
9. Harley-Davidson, Inc., *2003 Form 10-K*, 6.
10. Ibid., 6–7.
11. Ibid., 8.
12. Ibid.
13. Ibid., 9.
14. Ibid., 2003 Annual Report, 41.
15. Jonathon Fahey, "Speed Bump," *Forbes* 171(13) (*23 June 2003*).
16. Joseph Weber, "Hurdles on the Road to Hog Heaven," *Business Week* (3857) (*10 November 2003*).
17. Harley-Davidson, Inc., *2003 Form 10-K*, 11.

18. Ibid.
19. Ellen McGirt, "Harley's Easy Rider," *Money* 32(9) (*September 2003*).
20. Harley-Davidson, Inc., *2003 Annual Report*, 14.
21. Ibid., *10-Q* (6 August 2004), 25–26.
22. Richard S. Dunham, "Those Steel Tariffs Look Anything but Ironclad," *Business Week* (3781) (*6 May 2002*).
23. Russell Flannery and Patricia Huang, "No HOGs Here," *Forbes Global* 6(17) (*15 September 2003*).
24. Harley-Davidson, Inc., *2003 Annual Report*, 20.
25. Stan Hall, owner Hall's Harley-Davidson, Springfield, IL, interview Summer *2004*.
26. Ibid.
27. Ibid.
28. Harley-Davidson, Inc., *2003 Form 10-K*, 13.
29. Anne Kates Smith, "Best of the Best: A Legendary Favorite," *Kiplinger's Personal Finance* 57(9) (*September 2003*).
30. Ellen McGirt, "Harley's Easy Rider," *Money* 32(9) (*September 2003*).
31. Harley-Davidson, Inc., *2003 Annual Report*, 6.
32. Ibid., 8.

FRANCHISE INFORMATION ON THE INTERNET

FAVORITE FRANCHISING ADDRESSES

Franchise Handbook: http://www.franchisehandbook.com
> This site is a comprehensive and up-to-date database of information for and about the franchisee industry with exhaustive directories, lists of consultants, news, and articles.

Franchise Times: http://www.franchisetimes.com
> The site provides vital information on how to manage your franchise as well as how to buy, or purchase, a new franchise. This information is fundamental for both the franchisor and franchisee. You can also find a treasure trove of information about the countries top franchisors. You can subscribe to **Franchise Times** magazine directly from this site.

International Franchise Association: http://www.franchise.org
> Learn about franchising from the largest franchising association in the world.

Franchise Help: http://www.franchisehelp.com/
> This is a one-stop site for many things in franchising in operation since 1996. It is a great source for information for both the franchisee and franchisor.

Business Owner's Toolkit: http://www.toolkit.cch.com/tools/tools.asp
> This is where you'll find ready-to-use business tools to help you get the job done faster and easier. The site offers problem-solving help with more than 5,000 pages of free tips, checklists, case studies, and business templates tfor small business owners and entrepreneurs.

Women's Franchise Network: http://www.franchise.org.wfn
> The Women's Franchise Network can help you meet successful women entrepreneurs and launch your own career in franchising. The Women's Franchise Network is a division of the International Franchise Association.

Bison: http://www.bison1.com
> This is one of the finest resources for exploring the world of franchise opportunities. Lists are available for over 250 franchises and other opportunities. This is strictly business, and Bison provides access to some of the most current information about franchising available today, with a goal of matching qualified entrepreneurs with successful businesses.

Centercourt: http://www.centercourt.com
> Visit hundreds of franchise and business opportunities. Receive tips on buying a franchise. Learn about new business financing. Study the selection of commercial sites. Provides manuals online.

Be The Boss: http://www.betheboss.com
> Investigate different franchises and find the one that's right for you—then apply instantly on-line. Learn more about today's to franchisors and read franchising articles, worksheets and find the latest links to related websites.

The Sales Marketing Network: http://www.info-now.com
> This is a how-to and reference center for sales and marketing information. Here you can find answers to your sales questions and hook up with research, seminars, trade shows, books and more. Great articles and links are updated regularly, and the service is free thanks to on-line advertising support.

FAVORITE NEWSPAPER/MAGAZINE ADDRESSES

Entrepreneur Magazine: http://www.entrepreneur.com
> Travel through the "Franchise Zone." Then take a tour through the amazing "Franchise 500" and learn about the top franchises in the world. Now talk with the experts and leave a message on the "Message Board." Read articles about what is happening in Franchising.

"SUCCESS:" http://www.successmagazine.com
> Read timely articles about successful people and businesses. Read articles from recent issues, order books, get subscription information, and even write a letter to the editor.

Franchise UPDATE: http://www.franchise-update.com
> This magazine is a management resource for franchisors and focuses on providing useful information in the form of magazines, annual publications, survey reports and research.

Franchise Times: http://www.franchisetimes.com
> This magazine delivers news and information for franchisees, franchisors, and investors in timely articles about all aspects of franchising.

USA Today: www.usatoday.com
> Read the current news now. Find out what is happenings now from one of the leading newspapers in the world.

Wall Street Journal: www.wsj.com

Dun & Bradstreet Information Services: www.dnb.com

The Forbes Group: www.forbesgroup.com

FAVORITE BUSINESS ADDRESSES

U.S. Economic Census: http://www.census.gov/epcd/www/econ97.html
> Every five years the U.S. government publishes their Economic Census—it can now be found on the Web.

Lifestyle Market Analyst: http://www.srds.com/portal/main?action=LinkHit&frameset=yes&link=ips
> The Lifestyle Market Analyst is fully integrated so you can find market, demographic, and lifestyle data several ways! A neat and necessary marketing information source.

RMA Annual Statement Studies: http://www.rmahq.org/
> The Risk Management Association (RMA) is a professional association focused on identifying, assess, and managing credit, operational, and market risk. RMA's Annual Statement Studies is

the only source of comparative financial data derived directly from more than 150,000 statements of commercial bank borrowers and prospects.

Visa—Small Business: http://www.visa.com/fb/smbiz/main.htm
Advice on starting and running your own enterprise includes links for women and minorities in business.

OTHER ADDRESSES

AT&T Business Network: www.bnet.att.com

Hoover's Online: www.hoovers.com

Sales and Marketing Executives International: www.smel.org

Sales and Marketing Network: www.info-now.com

Standard & Poor's Marketplace at Quote.Com: www.quote.com/info/mscope.html

The Exhibitor Network: www.exhibitor.com

National Association for Female Executives (NAFE): www.nafe.com

The Internet 800/888 Directory: inter800.com/search.htm

World Wide Yellow Pages: www.yellow.com

4Airlines: www.4airlines.com

American Business Information: www.lookupUSA.com

Speakers Online: speakers.com

Expertise Center: www.expertcenter.com

Greater Talent Network: greatertalent.com

CIA World Factbook: www.odci.gov/cia/publications/nsolo/wfb-all.htm

FRANCHISE ORGANIZATIONS

INTERNATIONAL FRANCHISE ASSOCIATION

1350 New York Ave. NW Ste. 900
Washington, D.C. 20005-4709
USA
Phone: 202-628-8000
Fax: 202-628-0812
Email Address: ifa@franchise.org
Web Site: http:www.franchise.org

This national trade association (IFA) is for both franchisors and franchisees. The International Franchise Association was formed in 1960 by a group of franchise company executives who saw a need for an organization that would: (1) speak on behalf of franchising before government bodies and the general public; (2) provide services to member companies and those interested in franchising and licensed distribution; (3) set standards of franchising business practice; (4) serve as a central point for franchising data and information; (5) provide a forum for the exchange of experiences among member companies; and (6) offer educational programs for top executive and managers. They are the largest representative of franchisors and franchisees in the world. They are an active trade association representing both the franchisors and franchisees to the general public and to legislative groups.

AMERICAN FRANCHISEE ASSOCIATION

53 West Jackson Boulevard, Suite 1157
Chicago, Illinois 60604
Phone: 312-431-0545
Fax: 312-431-1469
Web Site: http://www.franchisee.org/

The American Franchisee Association (AFA) is a national trade association of franchisees and dealers, founded in 1993. The mission of the AFA is to improve the industry of franchising and to protect its members' economic investments in their businesses. The AFA works to change the rules and laws that govern franchising on both the state and federal level. In 1995 the AFA organized its franchisee and dealer membership nationwide, attaining the election of 137 delegates from 27 different chains to attend the White House Conference on Small Business in Washington,

DC where franchisee legal issues were among the final 60 recommendations presented to the President and Congress for immediate action. In 1996 franchisees from 30 different chains worked to develop the AFA's Model Responsible Franchise Practices Act ("Model Act"). The purpose of the Model Act is to promote the growth of franchising through a uniform set of standards.

AMERICAN ASSOCIATION OF FRANCHISEES & DEALERS

PO Box 81887
San Diego, CA 92138-1887
USA
Phone: 800-733-9858
Fax: 619-209-3777
Email Address: Benefits@AAFD.org
Web Site: http://www.aafd.org

The AAFD, a 6,000 member organization, is a national non-profit trade association representing the rights and interests of franchisees and independent dealers throughout the United States. The AADD works toward establishing self-regulating systems assuring fairness in franchise relationships. They have developed the AAFD's Fair Franchising Standards to be helpful to accredit franchisors as a guide for prospective purchasers of franchises. The mission of the AAFD is "To define, identify and to use marketplace solutions to promote Total Quality Franchising."

GLOSSARY

Acid test also called the "quick ratio"; another type of liquidity ratio; developed by subtracting current inventory from total current assets and dividing that figure by current liabilities

Accounting the process of measuring and reporting the financial information of the franchise; the measurement and record of money, assets, and resources and their flow through the company

Accounting system an approach to recordkeeping developed by the franchisor and explained to the franchisee; includes aspects of both financial reporting and financial analysis

Accounts receivable management addresses the firm's policies and activities associated with the selling of product or service on credit

Activity or efficiency ratios measure the franchise's ability to use capital and assets to maximum efficiency; generally consist of three calculations: inventory turnover, collection period ratio, and the fixed asset turnover

Activity reports required by almost all franchised firms on a weekly or biweekly basis; typically address such information as sales volume, number of sales, expenses, call-backs, and sales to individuals, community groups, and institutions; very helpful for the franchisor to make constructive suggestions to individual franchisees for improving operations and/or congratulating franchisees for work well done

Advertising manual a guide to effective communication and promotion of the franchised product to the targeted audience covering at least four topics: advertising, promotion, graphics and signage, and public relations

Advertising, promotion, and sales programs address the amount and type of advertising and sales promotion a particular franchise plans to pursue

Application Service Provider (ASP) a new type of service provider which promises to make information systems investment more economical and affordable to the franchise community by delivering and managing applications and computer services from remote data centers for multiple users via the Internet or a private network

Arbitrary mark a dictionary word that has been used arbitrarily to identify particular products and services, such as CAMEL® for cigarettes, APPLE® for computers, and CREST® for toothpaste; also considered strong trademarks

Area development agreement a variation on the basic single-unit franchise relationship; allows a developer to build a number of franchised businesses in a particular market area; each franchise will be governed by the terms of a franchise agreement granted by the franchisor

Area representative usually an employee of the franchisor with the right to solicit for prospective franchisees but does not have the right to contract with franchisees Also, often the area representative has responsibility for training franchisees, providing periodic inspections on franchised units, sets marketing and advertising schedules and may provide consulting to franchisees

Augmentation expanding the working knowledge profiles by offering new services to current customers with the goal of increasing the value-added services to the customers

Balance sheet also called "a statement of financial position or condition"; an accounting statement which illustrates the value of the assets, liabilities, and equity (net worth) of a franchise at a specific time

Bank term loans a formal agreement between a bank and the franchisee for the use of a specific sum of money (principal) at a given interest rate for a specific time (term); normally require that portions of both the interest and the principal be repaid on a monthly basis

Behavioral management perspective a management philosophy based on an awareness that human behavior has a significant impact on the performance of workers, emphasizing a participative management style in which workers' opinions are elicited and involved in decision making

Brand identifies the franchise system, can be a trademark, name, logo, or symbol representing the franchise

Brand equity the uniqueness of a franchise system which is necessary for its competitive advantage in the marketplace, consists of four dimensions: brand loyalty, brand awareness, perceived quality of brand, and brand association

Business-format franchising involves a specific format or approach required by the franchisor of the franchisee to following when providing the products and/or services to the customer

Business image the image the franchise system "packages" about itself for public consumption

Business-opportunity approach an informal generic description about the franchisor-franchisee relationship, wherein an owner of a product or service grants rights to an individual for local distribution and/or sales of the goods or services who, in return, provides a fee or royalty back to the owner

Business plan a document developed by the franchisee for use as a strategic guide for managing a business requiring the franchisee to establish a planning horizon, analyze the external environment, study economic trends, identify the business's strengths in relation to the competition, and determine how resources are distributed

Buying power index (BPI) statistics found for each of the geographic subunits of a particular DMA which suggest the consumer buying power available in a particular area; can be compared to the buying power judged necessary for a single unit to operate profitably within a proposed geographic area; determined using three basic elements: population, effective buying income, and retail sales

CARE an acronym for the key to the franchisor–franchisee relationship: the feeling that the franchisor cares about the success and activities of the franchisee; refers to the elements of communication, awareness, rapport, and expertise

Cash flow statement allows separate business owners to understand the cash position and to monitor seasonal periods and broader cyclic trends, as well as identify the business's strengths and weaknesses

C corporation a business organization that is a legal entity with liability limited to the extent of investment by each stockholder; life of the corporation is continuous and independent of the individual owner's/investor's lives; ownership can be easily transferred through sale of stock; and the corporation may have an easier time raising money

Classical management perspective a management philosophy emphasizing a scientific approach to task specialization and standardization, planning, organizing, directing, and controlling that emanated from the top down and a rational and impersonal organizational design based on rules and procedures to provide for operational efficiency, managerial effectiveness, and enhanced profitability

Clayton Act a supplemental law to the Sherman Act of 1914; prohibits certain practices between sellers and buyers; its provisions are particularly relevant to the business practices of franchisors and franchisees

Co-branding when two brands are combined in a business offering, also called "dual branding," "multibranding," "cross-system franchising," and "strategic alliance"; now considered a standard business practice for franchises

Commercial paper a short-term promissory note which the franchisee signs and sells to an investor, normally for short periods, from 30 to 270 days; because it is difficult for most franchisees to afford, this practice is ordinarily reserved for large corporations with strong financial backing

Communication elasticity the change is sales volume for each one percent change in total marketing communications effort applied to a specific franchise system (or local) promotion

Communication system helps the franchisor communicate efficiently and effectively with business units, prospective franchisees, suppliers, and the government

Company units business units which the company owns and wants to use as role models for franchisees

Comparative franchised business should normally be located near competitors so that potential customers can compare products

Competitive franchised business offers the same or similar kinds of products or services that other franchised or independent businesses provide within the community; convenience is a major factor in determining site location

Conference calls provide an effective means of contacting several franchisees at the same time; generally prearranged by letter or earlier phone contact to help ensure "attendance" of franchisees within a district, area, or region; used to inform franchisees of new product/service activities by the franchisor, new advertisements or upcoming promotions, or new contests or customer relations projects

Consequentialism a philosophy that considers a decision to be correct or right if the decision and its resulting behavior accomplish the intended results of the intended behavior

Consumer response index (CRI) represents the changes in customer awareness of advertisements, their comprehension of advertising copy content and interest or conviction that can measure overall customer response

Contingency management perspective a management philosophy that assumes there is no one best approach and that managers should identify the key contingencies, or variables, in a given organization and use an approach believed to be most effective in a given situation

Contract a legally enforceable agreement such as the franchise agreement, which represents the binding understanding between the franchisor and the franchisee

Convenience goods or services goods frequently purchased that are usually low-to-competitively prices, are staples, emergency or impulse buys

Conversion taking a proven working knowledge profile as a service for other franchise companies with the goal of converting the working profile into a salable service

Copyright a property right provided by the government in an original work of authorship that is fixed in a tangible form; protects an author's exclusive right to use and exploit literary, dramatic, musical, artistic, and certain other intellectual works; protects the original *expression* of an idea, not the idea itself

Current assets a business's cash, accounts receivable, and inventory that can be changed into cash within a brief period of time, usually twelve months from the date of the balance sheet or one cycle of the business's operations

Current liabilities debts or obligations payable by the franchised firm within a normal cycle of the business, or twelve months

Current ratio one type of liquidity ratio; current assets divided by current liabilities, with both figures coming from the balance sheet

Customer profiles help franchises stay customer centered by finding the right customers, that is, 20 percent of customers generating 80 percent of total sales

Debt financing borrowing money from banks, other financial institutions, friends, and relatives and paying it back to the lender over time, on an appropriate, affordable repayment schedule

Descriptive mark weak trademark which describes a good or service; receives little or no protection from the courts unless it has become recognized in the marketplace and thus has acquired "secondary meaning"

Designated marketing areas (DMAs) units on the AC Nielsen ratings map, which divides the United States into franchise market/ geographic areas based on dominant television market areas; help determine the number of potential franchised units the franchisor would like to have within a specified geographic area; may be made up of counties in one, two, or more contiguous states

Direct investment franchisor simply invests in company-owned stores in foreign countries

Disclosure document also called an "offering circular"; the FTC rule requires the delivery of this document to a prospective franchisee for a franchise purchase anywhere in the United States; must contain information that responds to the list of disclosures contained in the twenty-three topic sections

Distribution the costs of services expected by a franchisee from a franchisor, such as providing inventory, supplies, or products through the franchise distribution system

Diversification creating new markets to provide new products or services with the goal of creating new working knowledge to support new products or services in current or new markets

Domestic franchises local businesspeople develop their own franchise businesses and expand their systems across their own country

Egoism right or acceptable conduct in terms of positive consequences for the individual; that is, make decisions that will maximize self-interest

Embargo simply bans all products in a prescribed classification

Equipment lease financing an arrangement enabling the franchisee to obtain equipment at a lower cost, eliminate risk of ownership, and obtain service and maintenance agreements from the leaser

Equity also called "net worth"; the owner's claim on the assets of the business

Equity financing selling the ownership of a company to other investors, including yourself, friends, and relatives, and venture capital companies, who receive a share of profits and managerial responsibilities

Established franchisees business units which the franchisor headquarters needs to provide with incentives to encourage their expansion

Ethical formalism a moral philosophy that focuses on the rights of individuals and on the intentions associated with a particular behavior rather than the outcome or consequences of the intended behavior

Exchange control regulates the currency exchange between countries

Exporting franchisor manufactures products in the United States and sells them through franchisees to customers in foreign countries

Extension using proven working knowledge to enter new markets with the goal of extending current successful knowledge to serve new customers in the new market

Extranet like intranet, but with an additional password which allows the franchisees, and franchisor, to work with their suppliers, review products, and place orders

Fanciful or coined mark strong trademark which the courts will provide with the greatest protection; term that has no meaning apart from its trademark usage, and through advertising and frequent displays has come to be associated with a particular product and service

Feasibility study determines the likelihood of success that would result from developing an existing business into a franchise operation; should contain sufficient information to enable either a franchisor or a franchisee to make a final decision

Field support manual identifies the services provided by the franchisor to each franchisee, including such services as training, inspection, recordkeeping, financial planning, and quality-control standards and procedures, as well as recommend forms and procedures for use in evaluating the performance of the franchised business

Financial flow a written documentation or recording of business transactions shown through financial statements, which provide a franchisor and franchisees the basic format to report the financial activities of a franchise network or franchised unit

Financial planning refers to the franchisor's and franchisees' abilities to plan and forecast the appropriate use of funds for the franchise system and any particular franchised unit

Fixed assets also called "plant and equipment"; the resources the firm owns or acquires for use in running the business, generally not intended for resale but can be leased

Follow-up contact information form provides basic information about the first contact; including the type of information provided and activities completed that comprise a step-by-step sequence leading to an agreement between the prospect and the franchisor

Formal training program a structured program for the franchisor to help new franchisees develop specific knowledge about the franchise system and the business factors important to running a successful franchised unit

Format the approach to be used by a franchisee in providing the franchisor's product or service line to the customer

Four (4) Ps of selling different types of benefits: power, profit, pleasure, and prestige

Franchise advisory councils (FACs) set up by the franchisor to encourage communication, creativity, ingenuity, and responsiveness from its franchisees; a formalized method of coordinating a relationship between the individual units and the corporate headquarters

Franchise broker an independent third party who solicits prospective franchisees for the franchisor

Franchise defense manual a record of all the suggestions and correspondence from the franchisor's organization kept in the event differences arise between the franchisor and the franchisee

Franchise development system helps the franchisor contact and build relationships with prospective franchisees using applications software for tasks such as marketing, contact management, and real estate management

Franchisee the individual or business granted the right by the franchisor to operate in accordance with the chosen method to produce or sell the product or service

Franchisee organizations help franchisors gain valuable insights from franchisee reactions to new products and services as well as receive practical advice and marketing suggestions; provide an opportunity for the presentation of many new products developed at the franchisee level before they are submitted to the headquarters organization; allow franchisees a chance to express their opinions or offer suggestions about a new product before it is presented to the franchisor

Franchise support system supports business units using applications software for tasks such as help desk, performance tracking, marketing, and auditing

Franchising a business opportunity by which the owner (producer or distributor) of a service or a trademarked product grants exclusive rights to an individual for the local distribution and/or sale of the service or product, and in return receives a payment or royalty and conformance to quality standards

Franchisor the individual or business granting the business rights to a franchisee

Franchisor headquarters office management system helps the franchisor deal with office issues using applications software for tasks such as human resource management, accounting, and financing

Franchisor support package measures taken by franchisors to maintain wholesome franchisor–franchisee relationships

Frequent customers the customers a store should do its best to keep

FTC rule a trade regulation rule adopted by the Federal Trade Commission in 1979 to regulate all franchise sales in the United States; built on a single idea: that investors armed with key information will be able to make well-informed and wise investment decisions for themselves; requires the delivery of a detailed and rather extensive disclosure document to a prospective franchisee but does not otherwise control the franchisor's business practices

Generally accepted accounting principles(GAAP) widely agreed-upon definitions, procedures, conventions, and forms which are used to develop financial statements which may be used and understood by anyone

Generic term dictionary word or other common expression that describes in common fashion a product or service and can never become a trademark or service mark, although the combination of two otherwise generic terms can form a protectable trademark

Halo effect when a strong, well-known franchise system links with a lesser known one and the second gets lost in the "halo" of the first

Heterogeneous shopping goods or services the focus is on product or service qualities or characteristics with price being a second-level or lower-order concern to the purchaser

Homogenous shopping goods or services goods purchased less frequently than convenience goods; the customer typically shops around for the best bargain among highly similar goods or services

Hospitality franchises includes hotels and convenience or fast-food restaurants

House organs or newsletters effective in explaining various activities within the franchised company, recognizing top salespeople or locations, expressing the opinions of the president, announcing new territories or new franchisees, and presenting other information of a positive and helpful nature

Income sales, fees, or revenues flowing into the franchised business

Income statement also called "profit and loss," or "statement of earnings"; a record of revenues versus expenses for a stated period, such as a day, week, month, quarter, or year; shows the accounting profits or losses of a business through accounting of receipts/revenues minus expenses

Infrequent customers the customers a store needs to provide with incentives in order to encourage them to buy more

Initial franchise fee an initial lump sum, nonrefundable franchise fee paid by franchisees upon singing the franchise agreement

Innovation applying successful working knowledge to provide different products or services with the goal of applying existing proven knowledge to new products or services

Inseparability the simultaneous production and consumption of a service; for example, franchised dental service

Intangibility the lack of tangibility of a product or service such as what can be seen, smelled, tasted or heard prior to purchase

Intellectual property a collection of intangible rights including trademarks, copyrights, patents, trade secrets; intangible assets that can be protected by the law like other forms of private property

Intensification improving the working knowledge profiles to serve the current customers better

Intermediate-term financing most often used to meet a firm's one- to three-year financing requirements and is frequently used by franchisees undergoing rapid growth

Intranet an expansion of the Internet which allows a franchisor's franchisees private access to confidential information provided by the franchisor only by using a secret password; permits the franchisees to read reports from the franchisor and even review the operations manual and updated corrections

Introductory folder part of the sales package given to the prospective franchisee by the franchisor; a two-sided information sheet about the franchising opportunity, including an introductory statement and an invitation to prospective franchisees to join the franchise

Inventory loan a bank loan secured by the company's inventory on hand, generally not available to franchisees

Joint venture often-used form of franchising in which the franchisor joins with local citizens in setting up production and/or market locations

Justice theory directly relates to concept of fairness; justice demands fair treatment and due reward in accordance with ethical or legal standards

Lanham Act the federal Trademark Act of 1946, which provides a national system of registration and public notice of trademark rights, prohibits deceptive practices in the marketing of goods and services, and provides for a registration process by which the trademark owner may secure these rights for its mark

Leverage ratios measure long-term debt and the franchisor's ability to take care of the obligations associated with this type of debt; use balance sheet information

Licensing where the franchisor (licensor) enters into an agreement with a licensee (franchisee) and offers the right to use a product, good, service, trademark, trade secret, patent, or other valuable item in return for a royalty fee

Limited partnership a form of partnership including at least one general partner, usually the franchisee, and limited partners whose liability is limited to the amount of capital contributed or the amount of risk they agree to bear; prevents the running or managing of the franchise

Liquidity ratios indicate how well the franchise meets its short-term debts or financial obligations

Location model a three-step approach which helps franchisors take steps to develop expansion plans for their franchise system and determine specific sites within a chosen area: (1) designated marketing areas, (2) buying power index, and (3) individual site analysis

Lockbox means the franchise business has a post office box for receiving payments from franchisees (and others) that is managed by a commercial bank

Long-term assets also called "long-term investments"; holdings the franchised firm intends to keep for at least one year; typically yield an interest accrued or dividend paid back to the firm

Long-term financing used to provide funds for the purchase of permanent assets, which may include land, buildings, and certain types of equipment, ordinarily for a period of five to twenty years, and usually by such institutions as insurance companies, pension funds, or the Small Business Administration, or by the issuance of bonds or stocks

Long-term liabilities debts normally used to finance capital assets such as buildings, machinery, or fixed assets; contractual obligations which must be paid when due, generally after a period that exceeds twelve months or one cycle of business

Management philosophy the theoretical framework from which good management practice can be identified, learned, and applied effectively

Marketing involves everything it takes to get a product or service into the buyer's hands

Marketing communication the purpose of which is to differentiate the franchise system's products and services from those of the competition and to enhance the brand's position in the marketplace

Marketing manual describes the franchisor's marketing philosophy; discusses in detail the features and characteristics used to market the franchised business's offering, including information about packaging, labeling, and consumer services that franchisees should make available

Marketing mix controllable factors to be considered in combination to satisfy the needs or wants of customers in the target market

Market segmentation means an approach used to determine target markets by geographic, demographic, psychographic and/or behavior factors associated with a targeted customer group The approach is often used to divide a large market into smaller groupings or clusters of customers who have similar characteristics

Marketing strategy consists of identifying one or more target markets and creation of a marketing mix to reach the targeted customer group

Market ratios useful in assessing the performance of the common stock of the franchised firm, if it is a corporation

Market segment a grouping of customers who will respond similarly to a given set of marketing promotions

Market share refers to the portion of total market volume a business would likely have under normal operating conditions

Master franchisee may be an individual, small business, large corporation, or conglomerate which assumes the rights and obligations of establishing franchises throughout a country

Mission statement an introduction to the buyer in forty words or less, should cover the following: (1) name and company name, (2) business objective, (3) the type of problem to be solved for the customer, and (4) benefits of the business

Multiunit franchisee one who owns and operates more than one franchised unit and has often be granted geographic areas within or near urban areas

Net profit also called "final profit" or the "bottom line"; the sum of all revenues minus the sum of all expenses; the profit figure which a franchise reports; the amount of earnings available which may be used to reinvest in the business, pay dividends to shareholders, provide bonuses, or provide additional product/service research and development for the franchise system

Net working capital refers to current assets minus current liabilities

Nonindustrialized nations most of the population is engaged in simple agricultural production

Ongoing training on-site training provided by field staff of the franchisor after the franchisee has entered business

Opening benefit begins the actual sale and moves toward the close, based on the prospective buyer's problem or need; provides an opportunity for them to improve themselves and their situation; divided into four classifications known as the 4 Ps of selling

Operating expenses all the expenses incurred in the operations of the business; may be summarized by adding the general/administrative expenses, selling expenses, and depreciation expenses

Operating franchise an owner-operator run franchise business usually with an exclusive territory who usually does not have the right to establish sub-franchisees or licensees

Operating manual the bible of the franchise system that is a ready and regular reference to address the vagaries and uncertainties of day-to-day operations of the franchised business

Operations package the second part of a franchise package, usually fairly extensive and often put in the form of manuals; assists the

franchisee to properly conduct the operations of the franchise

Overhead the costs of doing business, such as sources of supply, distribution and inventory scheduling, warehousing, and the cost of acquiring and maintaining the name, design, and copyrights of the franchise

Partnership a common method of financing in which ownership is shared by one or more partners who may act as agents or representatives of the franchise; in a general partnership, all partners are fully liable for all the debts of the business and may be actively involved in its management

Patent a protectable property right granted by the government that protects an invention, new device, or innovation

Patent and Trademark Office (PTO) administers the national system of registration and public notice of trademark rights as provided by the Lanham Act; registration gives a trademark owner the benefit of nationwide protection, access to federal courts to protect those rights, and "constructive notice" to everyone that the mark is protected

Perishability means that a particular good, component or service cannot be inventoried or stored over a period of time

Personal contact information sheet form for recording preliminary information about a prospective franchisee, including the prospect's name, address, and phone number, how the contact was made, and an impression of that initial contact, recorded by the person contacted

Personality profiles working knowledge to help franchisors recruit potentially successful franchisees with personality traits such as a strong work ethic, self-esteem, and a commitment to service; identified through comprehensive analyses of sales and performance reports with respect to these traits

Personal visits usually made by a field representative from the franchise home office to the franchisee, occasionally made by the franchising company's president, vice president, franchising director, sales manager, or regional or district supervisor; a good public relations tool the franchising company can use to encourage and uplift the spirits of the franchisees and their employees; also effective for addressing problems raised by the franchisee or the franchising company, showing genuine commitment to resolve any such problems

PERT (project evaluation review technique) chart a simple, clearly delineated set of related events presented in sequence; outlines the "critical path" necessary to complete a project, such as the establishing of additional franchised units

Planned telephone calls typically franchisor initiated and are meant to discuss sales levels, product/service support, and advertising and promotional plans, as well as to respond to questions or issues raised by the franchisee; should be friendly, helpful, and positive and are not intended for faultfinding or for enhancing the power of the franchisor over the franchisee

Policies guidelines for employee actions

Potential customers the customers a store wants to start buying

Pre-opening manual includes checklists of activities and steps that must be completed before a grand opening can take place

Price fixing an illegal attempt by the franchisor to influence or determine the price at which the franchisees must sell a product to customers

Primary service area (PSA) an area from which a retail goods or service provider can expect to attract two-thirds or more of its business activity for the proposed business; needs to be large enough to sustain business activity and turn a profit; helps evaluate possible locations for a prospective business, identifying locations with convenient customer access and no heavy competition; determined using a drive or walk time

analysis to determine zones of probable coverage

Procedures the steps or elements within a process that are considered appropriate for performing assigned tasks

Product a unique set of physical and psychological characteristics or attributes designed to satisfy the wants or needs of a targeted customer group

Product adaptation involves changing the product to meet local conditions and consumer demands

Product and trade name franchising a franchising relationship in which the dealer acquires the trade name, trademark, and/or product from the franchisor/supplier

Product invention requires the creation of a new product

Product profiles help franchises stay market-led by focusing on the right products, that is, the 20 percent of the total products that generate 80 percent of product sales

Profitability ratios developed from the income statement and measure the ability of the franchise organization to turn sales into profits and to generate profit from assets

Pro forma balance sheet is a budget or plan about the assets and liabilities of the business It is a natural extension of the cash flow and income statement

Pro forma statements are estimated financial statements for future periods

Promotional package the carefully prepared information developed and given by the franchisor to prospective franchisees in order to (1) solicit franchisee applicants to the franchise system, (2) provide basic information about the franchise, and (3) illustrate the follow-up forms used to sign franchisees

Quantitative management perspective a management philosophy focusing on decision making in which an alternative course of action is selected as a solution to some problem based on measurable criteria, quantitative modeling to assess impact of each alternative, often using computers

Quota a limit on the amount of goods that the importing country will allow into that country in specific business classifications

Recordkeeping manual describes a standardized accounting and recordkeeping system that will provide a means of obtaining accurate financial information with a minimum of time and effort

Recruitment package consists of a recruitment brochure, a disclosure document, and other information about the benefits and opportunities of becoming a franchisee with the franchise system; used as part of the franchisor's response to initial inquiries by a prospective franchisee

Reinvested earnings also called "retained earnings"; funds which the franchisor pumps back into the business which are often subject to significant IRS regulations

Relationship/management marketing the creation, maintenance, and enhancement of strong relationships between the franchisor and the franchisee/customers; oriented toward establishing strong relationships in the long term, delivering value to franchisees/customers, and measuring this success in terms of franchisee/customer satisfaction

Robinson-Patman Act of 1936 prohibits price discrimination by sellers in the prices they charge to similarly situation buyers

Sales brochure also part of the sales package, an in-depth explanation of the franchise, which may include a letter from the franchisor, an invitation to become involved in the franchising business, testimonials from existing franchisees, or pictures illustrating a typical franchise operation, as well as financing and background information; also includes an application to become a franchisee

Sales forecast means to project sales in the next period or year It is simply an extrapolation of past sales set in terms of the

general economic conditions for the local economy. Four different approaches are commonly utilized by franchise systems

Sales playbook a flexible document developed by salespeople to help them reach out to the customer; generally includes sections for a mission statement, inquiries, opening benefits, listening, and close

Satellites additional vending sites which generally have no production facilities; need to be within a three- or four-mile radius of the main store so the franchisee can easily manage and visit the satellite units regularly

Service mark like a trademark, but identifies an intangible service instead of a product

S corporation alternative to the regular corporate in which the franchisee and other shareholders are taxed as partners and do not pay taxes on dividends twice; retains all other corporate advantages such as limited liability for shareholders, but has other restrictions including that it must be "domestic," and independently owned and operated

Sherman Act the Antitrust Act of 1890, introduced by Senator John Sherman of Ohio; aimed to eliminate the economic and political problems caused by monopoly power and prohibited monopolization and combinations and conspiracies to monopolize; addressed and prohibited pernicious activity on a smaller business scale by targeting all concerted action that might injure competition

Short-term financing borrowing through trade credit, commercial paper, unsecured bank loans, or inventory financing for needs such as the purchase of inventory or specialty sales items to be repaid in less than one year

Site inspection manual describes each item that is included in an inspection, along with the criteria used and procedures to be followed by the franchisee including a daily or weekly log for the franchisee to complete

Site profiles working knowledge to help prospective franchisees select good business sites; enlist vital elements of value and risk for sites identified based on experience

Situation audit an attempt to determine the firm's current operating situation in the context of its external (environmental) and internal factors and conditions that affect its operations

Social obligation when a business meets legal and regulatory requirements, discloses information about itself when required and contributes when direct benefit to the business can be clearly shown

Social responsibility the obligations a business has to its society

Social responsiveness where a firm makes information about itself freely available to the public, accepts formal and informal input from outside interests in its decision making, is willing to be publicly evaluated, and will support and contribute to established social causes but also new interests or groups whose needs are unfulfilled and becoming increasingly important

Sole proprietorship the most common form of franchisee business ownership in which the franchisee is the business owner, liable for all the business's liabilities, with the right to all the profits excluding royalty or other franchisor fees

Specialty products or services include a wide array of possibilities; generally providers are fewer in number than shopping goods providers and usually offer unique features to the customer and charge higher prices

Spontaneous telephone calls boost the morale and feelings of interdependence of the franchisee and the franchisor; help the franchisor understand the immediate concerns of the franchisee, get a feel for the franchisee's general attitude over time, and determine if there is anything the parent company could or should be doing over and above the regular services it is providing

Stakeholders groups or individuals who affect and are affected by the business firm, which may include the board of directors, employees, investors, community members, management, possibly a union, creditors, suppliers, government bodies and the general public

Start-up franchisees new business units which the franchisor headquarters should do its best to support

Straight product utilization franchisor offers the same product in the foreign market s in the domestic country

Strategic planning the process of formulating and maintaining organizational objectives and operational capacities to allow the franchise organization to function effectively within its ever-changing environment

Subfranchising contract an expansion program in which a subfranchisor is granted the right to locate and sell individual franchises to individual investors in a defined region

Suggestive mark trademark that does not describe a product or service but rather a feature or quality of the product or service; requires some imagination for the consumer to make the connection between the mark and the aspect of the product or service being sold

Suppliers/government contact management system helps the franchisor contact and build relationships with suppliers and the government using applications software for tasks such as scheduling and reminders

Supporting objectives quantifiable targets or "hoped-for" results in each of the major functions of the business in terms of planning, organizing, and controlling the management activities of the franchise organization

Systems management perspective a managerial approach which focuses on the nature and interrelationships of the component systems in a business in order to simplify their control and direction

Target franchisee a prospective franchisee with high chances of success; one who shares certain characteristics with existing successful franchisees and whose past experience has given them the drive necessary to overcome difficulties and succeed

Target trade areas likely areas in which to open new franchised outlets, where competitive advantage is most favorable; can include specific cities, counties, or sections within cities

Tariffs taxes levied by a government against specific imported products; the most common restrictions in international trade

Trade credit the most common form of short-term financing; a means by which the franchisee can receive credit from suppliers and/or service companies; the supplier (seller) generally allows the franchisee (buyer) a certain number of days before the bill must be paid

Trademark a word, name, phrase, symbol, or a design that is used by a manufacturer or merchant to identify and distinguish its goods from those sold by others and to indicate the source of a product or the quality of a product

Trade secrets confidential business information that is treated in a confidential or secret manner and that would have independent economic value if it were in the hands of a competitor

Training manual a guide for teaching operating procedures and personnel management used in formal and ongoing training programs; ideally fills in the gaps between the knowledge of a prospective franchisee or future employee and the level of performance expected by the franchisor

Training visits usually made by members of the home office staff; help the franchisee see the value of the royalty fees being returned to the business by addressing things such as problems in business operation that can be overcome by additional on-site training of the franchisee and staff, or changes in operating procedures or personnel, financial, or marketing approaches recommended by the franchisor

Turnkey cost also called start-up cost, any expense incurred by the franchisor when readying a new franchise for its first customers, such as land, building, furniture, fixtures, equipment, and personnel costs

Tying arrangements prohibited by the Clayton Act; when a seller conditions the sale of one product on the purchase of another product and thus "ties" the products together

Uniform Franchise Offering Circular (UFOC) a disclosure document outlining business activities which the Federal Trade Commission (FTC) requires from all franchisors

Unique franchised business typically has a craft or high-quality image associated with the product or delivery of the service; the uniqueness of the product or service and the limited number of competitors draws customers from a wider geographic area than other business types

Unsecured or signature loan a bank loan for a certain line of credit, a revolving credit agreement, or a transaction loan

Utilitarianism concern is about decision consequences. Utilitarian rule followers seek the greatest good for the greatest number of people

US Commercial Service(USCS) the international arm of the US Department of Commerce dealing with international business development

Value-cost-risk (VCR) procedures used to simplify the process of comparing the alternative sites for a potential franchised unit when building a site profile

Variability the random, or unwanted, levels of quality that the customer can receive as they purchase, receive and consume the product or service

Work made for hire a work created by an employee in the scope of the job and to which

the employer owns the copyright; an
exception to copyright laws which say that
only the author or coauthor of a work, or a
person to whom the author has assigned legal
rights, is protected by the copyright

INDEX